HISTORICAL
OF THE BUFF

Capt. Maurice Henry Woods
3-rd Royal West Kent
Reg.
Serving France 1st Buffs.
1915
and especially at the second
Battle of Hooge Aug. 1915

Shepherd's Close
Leatherhead
1924

By Lady Butler

A MAN OF KENT

From the Original in the possession of Major-General
Sir E. G. T. Bainbridge, K.C.B.

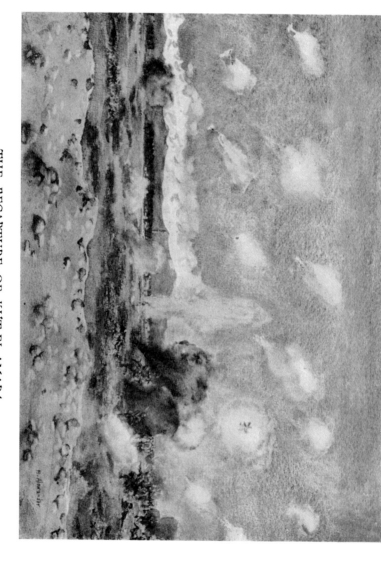

THE RECAPTURE OF KUT-EL-AMARA

On the right a company of the Buffs is seen advancing on the Turkish position, which rests on the right bank of the river, roughly indicated by the bursting shrapnel. Kut, with its tall minaret, is seen in the dark palm-grove across the river. Beyond are the Pushtikuh Hills and the snow-capped Persian mountains. The tall yellow column (centre) is spray from lyddite bursting in the river.

From a sketch made from the parapet in foreground by Herbert Alexander, A.R.W.S.

HISTORICAL RECORDS OF
THE BUFFS

EAST KENT REGIMENT
(3RD FOOT) FORMERLY DESIGNATED
THE HOLLAND REGIMENT
AND PRINCE GEORGE OF
DENMARK'S REGIMENT

1914-1919

BY

COLONEL R. S. H. MOODY, C.B., p.s.c.

LATE THE BUFFS

LONDON

THE MEDICI SOCIETY, LIMITED

MCMXXII

Printed and bound by Antony Rowe Ltd, Eastbourne

PREFACE

IT has been said that a preface to a book is merely to give an opportunity to the author to make excuses for his shortcomings, and this is to a certain extent correct.

The chief point that seems to call for explanation in the case of this work is the condensation of a very long story into a very brief space. Economy demands that the book containing the history of the Buffs during the momentous years from 1914 to 1919 shall not stretch its length beyond a certain limit, and it is difficult to pack the stories of eight fighting battalions for four years into the required space; yet it is feared that the unavoidable price of a more lengthy volume or volumes might perhaps be prohibitive in the cases of many individuals deeply interested in the regiment.

Thus it is clear that if all battles and engagements are to be described, what may perhaps be considered as a bald record of events is not altogether avoidable.

The intervals between the great fights were fairly well filled with minor enterprises and with individual acts of gallantry, all of which ought to be recorded, but it is a misfortune that many brave deeds done by single men or very small parties can find no record in these pages. Several were performed that were not reported at the time, as is so often the case in war, when everyone of rank is so occupied with his urgent duties that it is more or less a chance whether or no he notices the heroism of individuals about him.

PREFACE

Where possible, the names of the officers who became casualties in any fight are given in the text after the record of the battle, but only the number in the case of other ranks. It is unfortunate, but quite unavoidable, that the names of private soldiers should not appear with those of their officers, as they all took equal share and risk; there are, however, roughly thirty-three soldiers in the army without commissions to every one who bears one, and if all individual casualties were recorded the pages would be mostly long lists of names. Wherever possible the recipients of honours have been named in the account as the news of their decorations reached their battalion. This, however, is not a very reliable series of records, as it is feared that many names may be omitted, though this should not be so in the full lists given in the Appendices. Errors or omissions may, however, have crept in even here, as the names of Buff soldiers honoured have had to be picked out of long gazettes giving thousands of awards at a time. Miss Tomlinson very kindly devoted months of monotonous and very careful labour to this work.

The groundwork or skeleton of this history has been found in the battalion, brigade or divisional war diaries, access to which has been afforded by the staff at No. 2 Cavendish Square, where the Historical Section of the Committee of Imperial Defence works. One member of this staff is Major F. W. Tomlinson, of the Buffs, and it is natural that he should give his able assistance to the author, but, in addition, everyone at the office referred to has been most patiently kind and obliging and has spared no trouble in turning up required maps and documents, and it is meet that their uniform goodness should be here recorded.

PREFACE

But the framework put together at Cavendish Square had to be filled in and furnished. In times of war and stress a commanding officer has very often not much time in which to write, and some perhaps were readier with the sword than with the pen. The diaries are consequently often meagre as regards description, and what they lacked had to be made good with the aid of personal narratives and diaries furnished by men who had fought and survived. The appeal made by the author for this kind of assistance, and for information on certain points not clear to him, has been most courteously and punctually responded to by so many past and present officers that to name them all would be to insert here a considerable list, but, amongst others, he takes this opportunity to thank especially Colonels J. Body, W. A. Eaton, A. O'B. ffrench Blake (R.E.K.M.R.), L. I. B. Hulke, P. Kingsland, R. McDouall, J. Munn Mace, R. Pellatt (Q.O. Rifles of Canada), R. E. Power and A. L. Ransome (Dorsetshire Regiment) ; Majors F. W. Foster, G. Kingsford, G. P. Layborn, and R. T. Monier-Williams ; and Captains Campbell Page and W. Peake.

Thanks are also due to Lt.-Colonel Ponsonby for information gleaned from his book, *West Kent (Q.O.) Yeomanry and* 10th *(Yeomanry) Battalion The Buffs,* and also to Captain Coley-Bromfield, a Military Knight of Windsor, who has drawn the neater of those little maps which will be found between the pages.

R. S. H. Moody.

The list of subscribers, without whose help this book could not have been produced, is printed on pages 549–554.

CONTENTS

CONTENTS

CONTENTS

CONTENTS

CHAPTER XI

THE WESTERN FRONT
CONTINUATION TILL MARCH, 1918

CHAPTER XII

THE QUEEN'S OWN RIFLES OF CANADA

CHAPTER XIII

THE END OF THE SALONICA AND MESOPO-
TAMIA CAMPAIGNS

CONTENTS

CHAPTER XIV

HOLDING ON

CHAPTER XV

THE GRAND RESULT

CHAPTER XVI

LIST OF APPENDICES

LIST OF APPENDICES

ILLUSTRATIONS

PLATES IN COLOUR

A MAN OF KENT

    (After the painting by Lady Butler)   *Frontispiece*

THE RECAPTURE OF KUT EL AMARA

    (After the painting by Herbert Alexander, A.R.W.S.,
    Lieut. 5th Bn. The Buffs)

PLATES IN MONOCHROME

LIST OF MAPS

FOREWORD

TO read this record of the part played by the Buffs in the desperate fighting of the early months of the war, in turning the tide of the enemy's success and in the crowning victories, fills me with pride.

No pen can adequately convey the true measure of the constancy and valour of those men who endured and fought through the daily hardships, the hourly perils, the nerve strain during darkness—and this under the conditions of modern warfare, in battles which lasted not hours but weeks, with the added horrors of high explosives, gas poisoning, flame throwers, tanks and machine guns, delay-action mines and other mechanical and inhuman devices. Through all these trials the spirit of the regiment—of the Men of Kent— never faltered, its certain hope of victory never wavered.

For over three hundred and fifty years the historic name and high traditions of the Buffs have been in the keeping of the generations of men who followed each other in one or other of the so-called Regular battalions; during the Great War eight battalions, including two Territorial, took the field, and six others served at home. No less than thirty-two thousand men passed through the ranks of the regiment, of whom over five thousand gave their lives for their King and Country. But in spite of the great increase of numbers, and in spite of all the new dangers and perils, there was no change in the spirit, no weakening in the sense of duty which have always animated the Buffs; new and old battalions alike maintained, and more than maintained, the glory of the name handed down to them.

The recital of those deeds, and a description of the character of the war and conditions in which they achieved them, cannot therefore but inspire those who come after them in the battalions of the Buffs; so that should they too in their generation be called on to pass through the fiery ordeal, they also may, in the faith of their fathers, pass through unshaken to final victory.

Arthur Paget
Colonel The Buffs.

CHAPTER I

THE FIRST BATTALION GOES TO WAR

I. Introductory

IN the early hours of Tuesday morning the 5th August, 1914, the British Foreign Office issued this statement: "Owing to the summary rejection by " the German Government of the request made by " His Majesty's Government for assurances that the " neutrality of Belgium will be respected, His Majesty's " Ambassador at Berlin has received his passports and " His Majesty's Government have declared to the " German Government that a state of war exists " between Great Britain and Germany as from 11 p.m. " on the 4th August." Thus was the British Empire officially informed that the Great War had, at last, come upon Europe. Actually the Government had given orders for the mobilization of the Army some eight hours earlier, at 4 p.m. on the 4th; so that at that hour on that day this history properly begins.

The war took Great Britain by surprise. This does not mean that England was totally unprepared for such an eventuality; though comparatively small our land forces were in a condition of readiness and efficiency never before equalled. Nor does it mean that the idea of a war with Germany was new; through many years its likelihood had been canvassed and openly speculated upon both by soldiers, headed by the veteran Earl Roberts, and politicians. But it does mean that the man in the street did not think it would come in our time, and certainly no one could see any possible connection between the assassination of the Archduke Franz Ferdinand and his Consort at

THE 1st BATTALION GOES TO WAR

Serajevo on 28th June and an international war on a vast scale. The British temperament is not in its nature warlike ; Englishmen do not soldier, like some, from a sheer love of soldiering. That is why the mass of the nation has always been steadily averse to conscription. In spite of warnings it was willing to take the risk, preferring quality to quantity where its army was concerned.

It is perhaps well to give here, in this introductory, in order to link up the story that is to follow with the past history of the regiment, a brief outline of the changes which went to the making of the British Army as it was at the beginning of hostilities, and the situation which led to the war.

The South African War had brought it home to the Government that the system initiated in 1871 failed to meet modern needs in certain fundamental respects. It was realized that drastic reforms were overdue ; that new methods were essential. The work of reorganization was undertaken by Mr. (now Lord) Haldane, then Secretary of State for War; it was made all the more imperative by the aggressive and openly ambitious imperialism of Germany. Whilst still relying in the first instance on her naval supremacy, England could no longer think in terms of small forces fighting in far-flung corners of her mighty Empire. The danger loomed nearer home, and the possibility of a British force at grips with a foe across the narrow seas had to be faced ; nay more, it had to be provided for and planned against. An agreement was made with France, our ancient enemy on many a bloody field, and the General Staffs of the two countries explored the measures necessary for the defence of the frontiers from the sea to the Vosges.

This *entente* was little more than a friendly understanding, and so little was England under any obligation to go to the aid of France that the actual position

2

INTRODUCTORY

of the British Expeditionary Force was not settled until after the outbreak of war. Whether Great Britain would have remained neutral had Germany not forced her hand by invading Belgium, cannot now be stated. What is known is that Germany believed she would remain neutral; that, harassed by the threat of civil war in Ireland and other domestic difficulties, she would content herself as a looker-on. Therein Germany made her first big mistake. She made her second when she assumed that the British Army was too negligible to be seriously considered, and that if it came into the field at all it would arrive too late to affect the issue. Germany counted on a swift and fatal thrust across Flanders at the heart of France. She underestimated British feeling upon the treaty rights guaranteeing the integrity of Belgium, and she also forgot that Britain would look upon her advent, entrenched on the Belgian coast, as an intolerable menace. Thus, as events shaped, Belgium was the tinder on which the spark was struck that lighted the war-torch in Britain.

As regards the reconstruction undertaken by Haldane great progress had been made. The Army Council had taken the place of a commander-in-chief; the Imperial General Staff had been set up; the Militia, which had been converted into the Special Reserve, was ready to train and despatch recruits as required by the regular battalions; and the Territorials were organized on the same principle as the First Line, and, although they were under strength and only partially trained, it was thought that many old Territorials would rejoin in case of war and that complete units would be able to take the field after a few months' training. In addition, the universities and public schools had responded to the invitation to turn their units into Officers' Training Corps and a reserve of men capable of leadership in a time of crisis had thus been created. Above all, the

Expeditionary Force, consisting of six divisions and a cavalry division, was ready to move at a moment's notice. This finely tempered weapon, this wonderful fusion of skill and discipline with British courage, this " contemptible little army " was ready to thrust or parry, wherever it might be sent and against whatever odds.

II. Events Following the Outbreak of War

Before trying to follow the history of any particular unit it is, of course, necessary to bear in mind the military proceedings as a whole. Most people have a general idea of what took place in the different theatres of war, but events are apt to be forgotten, and it may be as well before describing any particular operations to remind the reader how it came about that such operations became necessary.

On the 4th August, 1914, war was declared with Germany, and in compliance with prearranged and carefully drawn up plans that Power, having already declared war on France on the 3rd, proceeded at once to violate the neutrality of Belgium whose roads supplied the easiest way to the heart of France, and the idea was to strike that country prostrate before Russia was ready to move. It was well understood that the Russians must be slower than any of the other immediate combatants to mobilize their forces.

Thus, on the 5th August, the Germans, who thoroughly recognized the advantage of getting in the first blow, were opposite Liége and occupied that city five days afterwards, although the last fort did not fall until the 17th. On the 14th August the French, too, were in Belgium, and between the 12th and 17th the British Expeditionary Force had landed on the coast and the army was moved into position extending from Condé through Mons and Binche.

During the few days prior to the British landing the

4

Belgians had been driven steadily backward by over-whelming forces, as also had the French ; and as the British Expeditionary Force only consisted of four divisions (the 1st, 2nd, 3rd and 5th) and a cavalry division its numbers were far too small to make any very perceptible alteration in the situation. The result was a steady general retreat of all the Allies commencing on the 24th August and lasting to the 5th September, by which time the armies were behind the River Marne and in the immediate neighbourhood of Paris, and the British base had necessarily been shifted from the Channel ports to the mouth of the Loire.

A cold statement that the Great War opened with a rapid retreat conveys the truth perhaps, but not all of it. Never in its long history of adventure and heroism had the British Army covered itself with such glory. There are retreats and retreats in war. When an army runs away that disaster is described under this term, and there seems to be no other correct military expression for what happened in Flanders and France in August, 1914, though, as a matter of fact, the little army sent from these shores was fighting one long continuous battle against overwhelming odds; its artillery completely outnumbered; its infantry facing death and wounds in the most soldierlike spirit possible to any troops, quite unable to understand why the movement was backward and not forward, but resolved to a man to get some of their own back when their time came.

On the 5th September the retreat had ceased, and by this date the German Colonies of Togoland and Samoa had been wrested from them and their fleet had learnt what the British sailor was capable of, notably in the Bight of Heligoland on the 28th August.

On the 6th September the tide of war had turned on land: a general offensive by French and British troops had commenced, the Battle of the Marne begun and Paris saved.

Strictly speaking, there was no Battle of the Marne, the fighting between the 6th and 10th of September being desultory and chiefly in the nature of independent and to a great extent disconnected engagements, but the struggle or series of struggles, however described, proved, indeed, a turning point—the British crossed the river on the 9th and the Germans were in full retreat.

On the 13th the Allies recovered the important town of Soissons and forced the passage of the Aisne, on which river the enemy stood to fight, and there the combatants were still engaged on the 20th, for now the German retreat was over; on this day the British Expeditionary Force was reinforced by the British 6th Division (16th, 17th and 18th Infantry Brigades) which had landed on the 10th September, and the Buffs once more in their long history came into the presence of England's foes.

All this time the Territorial Force was working hard to fit itself to help, and in a short time the bulk of it was sent to India to release our forces there which were promptly sent to France.

Meanwhile the new armies, whose numbers under the voluntary system were such as to fill every Englishman with pride, were straining every nerve to prepare themselves for war, and they were drafted off to the different fighting theatres as fast as they could be armed and equipped. The most wonderful fact of the early days of the war was the way that Kitchener's appeal for recruits was answered. Thousands and thousands of quiet, peaceable citizens, who had never dreamed of anything to do with soldiering, much less of getting into uniform and themselves going off to fight, men from every rank of life, now thronged and jostled each other at the recruiting offices. They took

6

long railway journeys at their own expense, or walked miles if they had no money, for the pleasure of standing, often for days, in queues waiting their turn to enlist. They faced the doctor with fear, hiding their disabilities, and passed the test with a sigh of relief.

What was true of England was true to an equal extent of the Colonies and oversea possessions, and the total number of soldiers raised, equipped and put into the firing line astonished ourselves almost as much as it dismayed the Germans, whose reckonings in this respect, as in all others, were completely at fault. The Queen's Own Rifles of Canada, the Allied Regiment of Canadian Militia, was represented in several of those gallant battalions which sailed in such numbers from their shores and which did such glorious service in France and Flanders.

The story of the struggle is so long, and the Buffs fought in so many theatres and places, that the clearest and best way of describing the deeds of the regiment appears to be the division of the eventful years of 1914 to 1918 into sections, so that the story of each battalion of the regiment may appear as clearly as possible between certain approximate dates. Of course, this system must be to a certain extent elastic, for, if a fixed date happened to be one during which a particular unit was in the midst of a very particular job, it would obviously be better to finish the description of that operation before drifting off to the doings of its brother Buffs somewhere else. The doings of the ten battalions, then, which together formed the regiment of Buffs, are what the reader is invited to consider in the following pages.

III. Move to France and the Battle of the Aisne

The 1st Battalion on the 4th August, 1914, was quartered at Fermoy in Ireland and the 2nd was in

7

India. It is obvious, therefore, that as the 2nd Battalion had to come home, the 4th and 5th to complete their training, and all others to be not only trained, but raised before they could add their splendid quota to the glory of the Buffs, the story of the first period of the war up to the 17th November, 1914, must mainly concern the senior battalion of the regiment. This date is taken because it was then that the desperate attempt of the Germans to hack their way through to Calais and the Channel ports finally proved a failure, and in France and Belgium heavy, murderous and continuous fighting merged into stonewall tactics, if tactics they could be called: when each of the opposing sides dug themselves in and when the long, dull, trying period of trench warfare set in on the Western Front. Up to this date no attempt had been made to force the Dardanelles. In fact, Turkey had only become a declared enemy a very few days and Italy was still at peace.

The 1st Buffs were, as has been said, at Fermoy. Their brigade was the 16th and the Brigadier-General was E. C. Ingouville-Williams, C.B., D.S.O., himself a very well-known old Buff who, after being adjutant of the 2nd Battalion, distinguished himself as commander of a column in the Boer War and was promoted out of the regiment, as is sometimes the fate of soldiers who serve in a "slow-promotion" corps. The other battalions of the 16th Brigade were the 1st Leicestershire Regiment, 1st King's Shropshire Light Infantry (K.S.L.I.) and the 2nd York and Lancaster Regiment; it will be useful to remember the names of these battalions as they must naturally be frequently referred to in the following narrative, and they were the close and very good comrades of our men.

The history of the 1st Battalion had, up to this time and since the commencement of the war, been briefly as follows: as early as the 29th July directions had

8

been received that certain precautionary measures were to be taken at once, and on the 4th August the order for mobilization reached the battalion at Fermoy. Almost immediately the strength was augmented by 554 reservists, many of whom were wearing the Indian Frontier and South African Medals. Thus a very fine battalion resulted. The commanding officer, Lt.-Colonel H. C. de la M. Hill, was a well-known musketry expert, and he had with him Brevet-Colonel Julian Hasler, who had distinguished himself in both the campaigns alluded to, Major E. H. Finch Hatton, who won his D.S.O. in South Africa, Major R. McDouall, who also gained a D.S.O. in the same war, and many another good officer. The sergeants were very highly trained, so much so, indeed, that nearly all the survivors were made commissioned officers within a few months of the battalion reaching the shores of France. The privates, after the great influx of reservists, were composed of brisk and energetic youngsters, keen and bold, and steady old soldiers— invaluable as a stiffening.

It proved afterwards that " the dash was all on the side of the youngsters, but the old reservists were a great backbone in holding off the German advance— in trench warfare they were excellent—in fact, they liked it."[1]

On the 12th August the battalion left Fermoy, and after a troublous journey reached Cambridge on the 19th. As everybody knows that the song of " Tipperary" was most popular at this time in the Army, it may be interesting to note that it was first played by this battalion. It was arranged by Bandmaster Elvin for the band a year before and the score was lent to many other units. The stay at Cambridge, which lasted up to the 8th September, was beneficial in so far that it remade soldiers of the reservists whose

[1] A letter from Lt.-Colonel R. McDouall.

physical condition had somewhat deteriorated during a long spell of civil life. The battalion was hospitably entertained by Christ's College; the officers were entertained at the High Table and frequent presents of fruit, chiefly mulberries, from Milton's Mulberry Tree, were sent to the men.[1]

On the 8th September at noon the 1st Battalion The Buffs, together with the 2nd York and Lancaster Regiment, sailed for the mouth of the Loire to which Sir John French had now transferred his base. The journey was made by rail and march after the port of St. Nazaire was reached, the train starting at dim dawn on the 11th and taking the route: Nantes, Angers, Tours, Verdun, Paris to Mortcerf, a twenty-six-hour journey. The ensuing eight days' march was not without incident and not without discomfort, but there was excitement, too. Heavy firing was heard all day on the 12th. The first taste of outpost duty in war time came the following night. Billets were used each night, but these were not always of the best and the weather was generally execrable. The billets, which one night consisted of a cowshed, were sometimes shared with Belgian refugees, and altogether it was with a sort of relief that the real fighting line was reached at last at 2.30 a.m. on the 21st September. Vailly on the Aisne was entered and the Fifth and Royal Fusiliers relieved in the trenches at that place, A, C and D Companies being in the front line with B in reserve.

It will be remembered that the Germans, after their retreat from the Marne, were now standing fast, and that in its turn the Allied pursuit was checked upon the Aisne. The enemy knew somehow that fresh troops were now in front of them and, hoping to find an inferior article to that they had been sampling for the

[1] To commemorate the connection of the Buffs with Christ's College, a gold beaker has recently been presented to the 1st Battalion by Sir A. E. Shipley, G.B.E., Master of Christ's College.

last month, determined to attack and try what they were made of.

The Buffs were on the left of the brigade line, on the crest of a small plateau beyond the river, and the enemy's trenches were on the far slope, from two hundred to seven hundred yards away, with all the best of the situation because, owing to the shape of the ground, our artillery had great difficulty in aiding this particular part of the line, whereas the Germans were very closely supported by their guns. On the right was an improvised sub-section of defence consisting of the Norfolk Regiment and King's Shropshire Light Infantry, under Colonel Hasler of the Buffs.

The attack commenced at 8 p.m., lasted for two and a half hours, and was a failure. The firing was heavy and the attempt was resolute enough, but as the locality was difficult for our guns the Buffs employed prolonged rapid fire as a substitute and succeeded in repulsing the onslaught. Major E. H. Finch Hatton, D.S.O., and Captain F. C. R. Studd were wounded in the action, two men were killed and five wounded.

The battalion remained in these trenches till the 13th October and suffered several casualties. In fact, each day added a few to the killed and wounded, and each day brought to light some good quality in the men. The first name in the regiment to be brought to notice for gallantry was No. 9967 Corpl. Randall who, himself wounded, on the 2nd October showed great courage in attending to Pte. Hamilton under fire. Hamilton, however, did not survive. The stretcher bearers, too, were proved to be a most gallant set of men—stretcher bearers always are somehow. The sight of the pain and mutilation of others seems to bring out a sort of ferocious tenderness on the part of those who protect and assist the maimed. Pte. Medway was conspicuous even amongst these devoted fellows.

Particularly heavy firing along the whole line and

including reserves occurred on the 9th October. The church at Vailly was struck and ten horses belonging to the regimental transport were killed close to it. The hospital also suffered.

Early in October it appeared to Sir John French that it was advisable to withdraw the army from the Aisne and strongly reinforce the forces in the north with a view to outflanking the enemy and so making him withdraw from his position. In fact, each army at this time was trying to outflank the other, because frontal fighting, owing to the complete system of entrenchments in vogue on both sides, was found to bring no practical results. This accounted for the fact that in a very short time flanks ceased to exist, for one soon rested on the sea and the other on neutral Switzerland. French's first attempt at outflanking was rendered abortive by the German capture of Antwerp, and so the war developed into a fierce struggle for the coast, which may be said to have commenced on the 11th October and continued till the 17th November; the enemy's idea being to seize Calais and the Channel ports and so make up for their failure to capture Paris.

This struggle is sometimes called the Battle of Flanders, but it in reality included several fights, the chief of these being collectively described as the Battles of Ypres, 1914. Of course, the great move from the Aisne to the neighbourhood of St. Omer and Hazebrouck took time, and it was not till the 19th October that the move was completed. General Foch, whose headquarters were at Doullens, at this time commanded all French troops north of Noyon and our Commander-in-Chief had arranged with him a general wheel of troops to the right, in order to menace the German flank; this arrangement was made before the fall of Antwerp. It brought the English 7th Division to Ypres; caused heavy fighting for the 3rd Division about Givenchy, which lasted for three weeks; moved the 4th Division to the north and 6th to south of the town of Armentieres, and was the immediate cause of the flight which followed at Radinghem.

Antwerp fell on the 9th October, and this event released 90,000 enemy troops, and the Germans also at this time brought four fresh Army Corps from their Eastern or Russian front, and so the English Army and that part of the French one which was in its neighbourhood were facing greatly superior numbers. As far as the Buffs were concerned they were relieved in their trenches on the Aisne by French troops on the 12th of the month, marched to Bazoches with the rest of the 16th Brigade and there entrained for Cassel, which they reached on the 13th. The relief of the trenches at Vailly was carried out successfully, but not altogether without difficulty. The enemy seemed to have an idea of what was going on and fired a number of flares, and a searchlight was also seen. The wheels of the transport were, however, covered with straw, as was the floor of the pontoon bridge over the river, in order to deaden noise. The French took up their position very quietly and very quickly, and the battalion re-crossed the Aisne at 2.15 a.m., the last of the brigade marching by Rouge Croix and Oultersteene.

The 16th Brigade was directed to Bois Grenier on the 17th as reserve to the division. The 17th was also sent here and the 18th to Armentieres, about four miles to the north. During the morning, however, as hostile firing was heard and observed, certain alterations were made by the 6th Division by order of superior authority, and it took up and constructed a defensive position along a new line: the 17th Brigade on the left, 18th in the centre and 16th on the right from Croix Marechal to Rouge de Bout—French cavalry being on the right again.

On the 18th October the 17th and 18th Brigades advanced to ascertain what the enemy was doing about

Perenchies, le Paradis and La Vallée, and to discover his strength, and in connection with this movement the 16th Brigade was ordered to send one battalion towards La Vallée and Bacquart. The Buffs were selected and the York and Lancasters were sent to Bridoux to cover their right flank. At 10.30 on this Sunday morning the Buffs debouched from Grand Flamengrie Farm with orders to seize the line of the Hameau de Bas–La Vallée road, but not to get seriously involved. B, C and D Companies deployed, with A in reserve.

IV. Battle of Armentieres: Action at Radinghem

Before reaching the above line the battalion got orders to take the village of Radinghem.

Just beyond this village is a fairly high ridge or plateau on which stands the Chateau de Flandres, and there is a wood on the edge of the plateau screening the house from the village, the distance between this wood and the south edge of the village being about three hundred yards.

Brevet Colonel Julian Hasler was in command of the forward or firing line which advanced through Radinghem, seized the ridge and, pushing on, took the Chateau where severe hand-to-hand fighting occurred. But soon considerable German reinforcements coming up, the Buffs had to abandon the Chateau itself, though they still clung to the edge of the wood.

During the attack Company Sergeant-Major Brady, with nineteen men of C Company, on surmounting a piece of rising ground, suddenly found himself about two hundred yards from a German battalion in close order. Each Buff had three hundred rounds of ammunition, and one of the most beautiful displays of rapid firing ever made was the result: that particular German battalion was very quickly " put out of action," as they say on field days. The successful attack on the Chateau de Flandres was immensely helped by Major Bayley's company of the York and Lancaster Regiment, which had worked its way round to take the enemy in flank; so that when these men approached, the enemy had hastily to withdraw. Without a doubt the Buffs owe very much to this gallant company.

At 6.10 p.m. the situation was looking serious, but after a German counter-attack had been repulsed things became better. Then orders came to hand over Radinghem to some French cavalry and to withdraw. When the Frenchmen arrived, however, they were found to be only 130 strong, so the Buffs and York and Lancaster consolidated themselves on the south edge of the village and settled in for the night. The artillery, a mixed brigade under Lt.-Colonel Humphrey, had most nobly supported the infantry during the day. Later on, when the regiment had more experience, they found that the devotion to duty shown by the Gunners at Radinghem was quite a normal state of things with that arm, and was so looked for as a matter of course that notice was hardly taken of their excellent work, but in this, almost their first battle of the war, praise of the Gunners was in every man's mouth.

On the 19th touch was obtained with the 18th Brigade at the railway crossing east of Bas Champs. At 3 p.m. the 16th Brigade was ordered to withdraw to Bois Grenier and to leave one battalion only at Radinghem. The consequence of this was of course that, the York and Lancaster being withdrawn, the Buffs were left alone to occupy the lines which last night had been constructed for both regiments.

The morning of the 20th opened with very heavy artillery fire from the enemy's guns of large calibre, and then the German infantry pressed very heavily. About 2 p.m. Colonel Hasler was badly wounded,[1] and com-

---

[1] Julian Hasler recovered from his wounds, rejoined the battalion in December and was given command of the 11th Brigade in February, 1915. He was unhappily killed on the 26th April, 1915. His fine fight-

mand of the front line devolved on Major McDouall. At 3 p.m. the artillery reported that the Germans were advancing along the two roads from Le Maisnil leading to Radinghem. This meant that the Buffs would probably be surrounded, as touch with the 18th Brigade and French cavalry had failed, and indeed it was ultimately found that these troops had been driven back. At 3.35 and again at 4 o'clock McDouall reported that the situation was very serious, but that he was holding on ; that the machine guns were knocked out, the trench on his left hitherto held by C Company had been captured and that he was "in a tight corner." He received orders to retire company by company, and replied that it was very difficult, but that " We will do the best we can." At 4.50 came a message from the brigade to hold on at all costs and promising the support of two companies of the York and Lancaster. The Headquarter party of the battalion manned a barricade in the village and McDouall retired, the work being carried out in a most soldierly manner, and at 7 p.m. the promised help arrived, followed half an hour later by the brigadier himself, who ordered the front of the village to be held, unaware that both flanks were exposed. A staff officer of the division, however, shortly arrived who was acquainted with the situation, and he directed the retirement of the Buffs, which was carried out without trouble, as the enemy was not enterprising and appeared to have had enough of the battalion. At 1 a.m. on the

ing qualities ensured his success as a soldier, whilst his great personal charm secured him many more firm friends than most of us can claim ; his death was deeply mourned not only by the regiment, but throughout the army.

Born on the 16th October, 1868, he joined the Buffs in 1888. He saw service in Chitral (1895), N.W. Frontier (Malakand, etc., 1897-8), South African War (1899-1902 ; brevet major), N. Nigeria (1903, Kano-Sokoto campaign), N. Nigeria (1906 ; in command ; brevet lieutenant-colonel). He was promoted brevet-colonel 11th January, 1910.

21st the rear guard cleared the village, and that morning Grand Flamengrie Farm was reached again and billets resumed.

In this action the Buffs lost Lieuts. J. D. Phillips, R. McDougall, M. Noott and R. S. Glyn killed, and Colonel J. Hasler and Lieuts. G. F. Hamilton, C. C. Stanfield and Orwan wounded. Of the rank and file 17 were reported killed and 62 missing, but these were undoubtedly all or nearly all killed ; 57 were wounded. The regiment earned great praise for the stand it made at Radinghem, and, though it will be impossible in this history accurately to chronicle each honour and reward as conferred, it is interesting to note that on the 28th November No. 8922 Sgt. J. McNeir was awarded the D.C.M. for the gallant manner in which he brought up his platoon to the support of B Company at Chateau de Flandres, near Radinghem, on the 20th October, 1914, and that :—

"On the 20th October, 1914, at Chateau de Flandres, " near Radinghem, Sergeant Forwood continued to " serve his machine guns, after the officer in charge had " been killed, until all the team and both the guns had " been knocked out by heavy artillery, himself being " wounded in five places. He crawled in and reported " the situation." Sergeant Forwood was awarded the D.C.M., and the incident is described by a General Officer, who later on commanded the 6th Division, as being typical of the fierce fighting at this time.

On the 23rd October a heavy attack developed at dawn against the Shropshire and York and Lancaster battalions and part of the line, which consisted of isolated trenches only, was rendered untenable by machine guns which the shape of the ground enabled the enemy to bring up. This attack was a very bold one and Germans were actually bayoneted in the trenches, and two hundred dead were counted opposite one of the Shropshire defences.

c   17

THE 1st BATTALION GOES TO WAR

At one time there was a gap just east of Bridoux, caused by some of the trenches being lost and others still held, and matters were in rather a confused state, so, to clear up the situation, Lieut. G. R. Thornhill's platoon of the Buffs, under the direction and guidance of Major Clemson of the York and Lancaster Regiment, was pushed forward from the Touquet–La Boutillerie road by some dongas running south. There appeared to be no enemy in the gap, and on approaching one of the trenches Thornhill and his men rushed forward to secure it, when he and several of his followers were shot down by a concealed machine gun. Indeed, only ten returned, bringing with them seven wounded men, but they were obliged to leave Thornhill, who was actually in the trench, and several others. Pte. Pearce made a manly effort at rescue and managed to drag Pte. Bull in, but could not reach his officer. Both A and C Companies employed the bayonet on this day, counter-attacking in front of the Shropshire and the Leicester-shire trenches.

It is not so very long ago that many thoughtful army officers were of opinion that the days of the bayonet were over for ever; but then, of course, no one at all dreamed in the summer of 1914 that soldiers would again fight in iron helmets or throw grenades, and there have been many similar surprises during this war.

There seems to be no doubt that from the 23rd to the 25th of October the situation of the 16th Brigade was very critical, and indeed Br.-General Ingouville-Williams twice reported that this was the case. The reason was that the line held was not continuous and it was impossible to make it so, on account of the great number of Germans who were attacking. It was therefore resolved to construct a proper line of trenches 100 yards or so south of the Touquet–La Boutillerie road and to withdraw into it; but as, during the whole of the 23rd, the Leicestershire right flank was being en-

18

veloped, new dispositions were made by Brigadiers Williams and Congreve in consultation ; they resolved that the Leicestershire should hold their trenches east of the railway and then bend back along it—a most prominent salient and with a poor field of fire, but the best that could be done till the new trenches were ready for occupation.

On the 24th October loud cheering was heard in this direction, and it was feared that the Leicestershire had been rushed, and a company of the Buffs and another of the York and Lancaster were immediately deployed to take the supposedly successful enemy in flank. Verbal reports came in during the morning to Brigade H.Q. at La Touquet that the Leicestershire battalion had been forced to retire, that some posts had been surrounded and that no officers were left. This account, however, fortunately proved to have been exaggerated. The enemy had, in fact, made a small gap in the line, occupying the railway, but the good old battalion from Leicestershire had quickly closed it and, though it had suffered severely, it still held its own and was moreover in touch with the King's Shropshire Light Infantry.

On the 25th the withdrawal of the whole brigade to the newly made trenches which had been carefully prepared was carried out without a hitch, but in most unpleasantly wet weather.

The student, interested in the tactical movements of military forces, rarely thinks of weather and other little details, but to the poor suffering soldier weather, punctual or fairly punctual delivery of rations (not forgetting the rum), baths, clean clothes, nature of shelter by day and night, and even the phases of the moon seem almost of more importance than the chance of a few casualties.

C.S.M. Stone and Sgt. Stock had been highly complimented during these last few days, as was Corpl.

19

Marsh for his good reconnoitring work; but this occurred to the N.C.O.'s and men of the Buffs so frequently from 1914 to 1918 that it is impossible to refer to all acts of devotion and gallantry. It may well be noted, however, that on the 25th October C Company was resolutely attacked, the enemy getting within seventy yards of their trench, and that Captain E. B. Chichester showed all the gallantry of his English ancestry, cheering on his men and showing a noble example till he fell mortally wounded. D Company gallantly repulsed German attacks at 8 and at 9 o'clock and then retired to a prepared position in rear. The Buffs' casualties this day were Captain Chichester and Lieut. Stock killed, Lieuts. R. W. Homan and Child wounded, five other ranks killed, twenty wounded and two missing.

About this time the discovery seems to have been made that officers could be supplied not only from civilians in England, but from highly trained, very gallant and thoroughly reliable non-commissioned officers, who were daily adding to their war experience; so Company Sergeant-Majors (C.S.M.) Nesbit and Stone, Sgts. Corrall, Stock and Orwin, and a little later on Company Quarter-Master Sergeant (C.Q.M.S.) Sayer, C.S.M. Kesby, C.S.M. Price, and Sgts. King, Hallan and Harris were promoted to be 2nd Lieutenants. Most of them, alas, were sent out of the regiment, which was a great blow, but of course the needs of the Army as a whole must always be the first consideration.

On the 5th November the death took place of Major-General R. G. Kekewich,[1] C.B., Colonel of the Buffs;

[1] Robert George Kekewich, second son of Trehawke Kekewich, of Peamore, Devon, was born on the 17th June, 1854, and joined the Buffs on the 2nd December, 1874. He fought in the Perak expedition of 1875-6, and in the Soudan, 1884-5, where he gained a brevet majority. He was employed as D.A.A.G. in the Soudan campaign of 1888, and afterwards as military secretary to the C.-in-C., Madras, and was engaged in the operations in Burma 1892-3. He was promoted

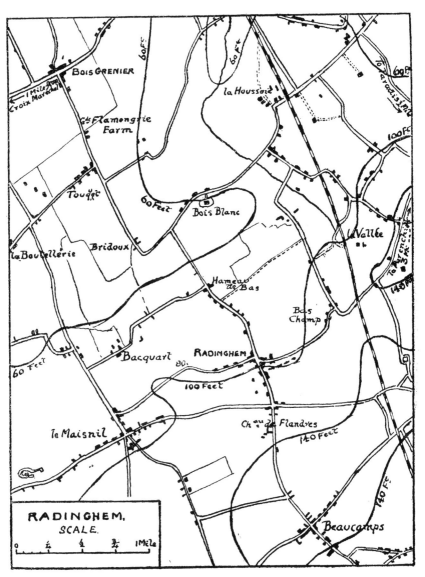

RADINGHEM

NOVEMBER, 1914

General the Right Honourable Sir Arthur Paget,[1] P.C., G.C.B., K.C.V.O., was appointed to succeed him. On the 15th November Colonel H. C. de la M. Hill, the commanding officer, was invalided home and Major McDouall temporarily took over the battalion. This was the first of a long series of changes in the command, which was the common fate of all units.

After the very strenuous attack by the Germans had died away the 1st Battalion had a longish spell of comparative quiet. Casualties, which in one of our frequent minor wars would have made a stir, were of regular occurrence and almost taken for granted; the records show almost every day something like two killed and five wounded, and drafts to replace these good fellows

into the Loyal Regiment (North Lancashire) and commanded the 1st Battalion of that regiment in the South African War. He commanded the garrison during the siege of Kimberley ; received the rank of brevet-colonel and the C.B., and in August, 1902, was specially promoted major-general. He was appointed colonel of the Buffs on the 5th October, 1909.

[1] Arthur Henry Fitzroy Paget, eldest son of General Lord Alfred Paget, was born on the 1st March, 1851, and entered the Scots Guards in 1869. He served in the Ashanti War, 1873 ; in the Soudan, 1885 ; in Burma, 1887–8, and again in the Soudan in 1888–9. He commanded the 1st Scots Guards in the South African War and later the 20th Brigade, being specially promoted major-general. He commanded the 1st Division from 1902-6, during which time he received the C.B. and the K.C.V.O. and was promoted lieutenant-general. He was made a K.C.B. in 1907, and the following year was appointed G.O.C. Eastern Command. He was an Aide-de-camp General to His Majesty from 1910-14. In 1912 he was appointed General Officer Commanding-in-Chief the Forces in Ireland and advanced to the dignity of Privy Councillor, and the following year was promoted general and received the G.C.B. In January, 1915, General Paget was sent on a Special Mission to Russia and the Balkan States and was received by the Tzar of Russia and the Kings of Roumania, Bulgaria, Servia and Greece. The following year he was sent by His Majesty King George V to convey the Field-Marshal's baton to the Tzar of Russia. In 1917 he visited Verdun, representing His Majesty, to confer on that town the Military Cross.

were fairly often arriving from England. Later on the relief of units actually in the trenches by others in rear occurred at short intervals, but it may be noted here that on the 24th November the Buffs, when relieved by the Shropshire Light Infantry, had been no less than four weeks and six days in the front line, east of Bois Grenier.

During the winter the wet weather, followed by frosts, caused the sides of the trenches to fall in, and the low-lying nature of the country made it impossible to drain them properly; so it was decided, as a temporary measure, to abandon the ditches themselves and build and man breastworks in lieu. These were generally placed just in rear of the old works so that the latter could be reoccupied when the weather improved.

Of course, the long, dull and dreary trench warfare was not entirely without incident. A poem by Captain C. W. Blackall[1] describes in graphic verse how one of the ration carriers being a little late in slipping into the safety of the trench was bowled over by the enemy and was at first supposed to be dead, but he managed after a while to crawl in somehow and in spite of his agony he brought in his sack of bacon with him. That is the sort of spirit which, when it animates everyone in an army, renders that force absolutely unconquerable. It has often been the same. On the Indian frontier once a Buff soldier was apparently killed. Someone bent over him to take any possible last message. The man was in agony and shot in the stomach, but he could just speak. " Where's my bloody rifle? " was all he said.

On St. George's Day, 1915, the enemy had the audacity to stick out a flag at their sap head and on it was inscribed the words " Gott strafe England." 2nd Lieut. Corrall, Sergt. Vigors and Pte. Russell

---

[1] Captain Blackall, an old Militia and Special Reserve officer, was killed on the 24th March, 1918, whilst attached to the 4th South Staffordshire Regiment.

disapproved of this, as showing an improperly defiant attitude, so they crept out and triumphantly brought it in with them.

The Army Commander, Sir Horace Smith-Dorrien, inspected the battalion in the spring and was much struck with the smart turn-out. Such is custom and the result of training and education. The Buffs must be smartly turned-out, and conditions and circumstances have nothing to do with the matter.

It was on the 3rd May that the 1st Battalion and the rest of the 16th Brigade first heard of the German gas attacks, which occurred north-east of Ypres and to which reference will be made in the next chapter. Precautionary measures were taken, but the second battle of Ypres did not greatly affect the troops so far south of the town as was the 6th Division, but about 1,500 shells fell into Armentieres on the 6th May. On the last day of this month a move was made to the neighbourhood of Bailleul and Poperinghe—the village of Wittenhoek, four miles south of the latter town, being the Buffs' billet.

On the 2nd June it so happened that the 2nd Battalion, whose adventures are now to be related, were in Poperinghe, and so, in the nature of things, a meeting, which will be referred to later, had to be arranged.

It must be remembered in reading the foregoing pages, and indeed in studying the next chapter also, that the enemy was, during the last quarter of 1914 and early in the next year, making a well-organized and very determined attempt to gain Calais and the coast of the English Channel, and that enormous masses of men were devoted to this effort, as well as artillery vastly superior in weight of metal to that which our side could then by any possibility bring to bear. The English lines of communication ran across the Channel, and it is a maxim of war that if such lines are lost the army that relies on them must either win an overwhelming victory or surrender. If Calais had been won by the Germans the connection between England and her armies would have been to a great extent severed, for how could reinforcements, munitions and necessaries daily cross the Channel under heavy and continuous fire, and repeated and constant attacks from submarine bases?

At Radinghem and at Ypres then, our regiment was helping to defend England from a dreadful and unprecedented disaster, and Men of Kent must further consider that to a certain extent, at any rate, the Buffs were, more than any other regiment, defending their own homeland, for if hostile batteries of modern long-range guns could have been planted on Cape Gris Nez, not only would Dover harbour and dockyard have been destroyed, but, knowing the Germans as we do now, we may be pretty certain that Hythe, Folkestone, Sandgate and perhaps Deal would soon have been in as ruinous a condition as were, a little later, Rheims, Arras and Ypres.

Leaving the 1st Battalion for a while doing its duty in the neighbourhood of Poperinghe, we will now turn our attention to the story of the 2nd Battalion from India.

CHAPTER II

THE 2ND BATTALION TAKES ITS SHARE

I. Returns to England

THE opening of hostilities found the head-quarters of the 2nd Battalion at Wellington in India. It was, like most units which have been some time abroad, a very fine body of men, in spite of the fact that Wellington is not exactly a training centre and that three detachments were provided by the battalion. Very early in the war it was called upon to send home, to the assistance of the new armies in course of formation, some of the most useful members of the battalion staff and many of the very best sergeants. Training was, however, continued, and in November orders arrived to sail for England on being relieved by Territorial troops, who had quite forgotten apparently that they were home service soldiers only, directly England wanted them abroad.

On leaving the East the Buffs had to leave behind a depot which consisted of a few men passed unfit, all the women and children, and the property of the messes, regimental institutes, Army Temperance Association and rifle ranges ; this was under the command of Captain Howard Smith. The only things that went home with the fighting men were the Colours and the mess silver.

The battalion embarked at Bombay on the 16th November on the Cunard ship *Ultonia*, which was old, slow and dirty, and fearfully overcrowded owing to the 2nd Battalion East Yorkshire regiment being also on board. The ship was under convoy together with thirty-three others, and the whole made Plymouth instead of Southampton on the 23rd December, after making a wide detour in the Atlantic to avoid submarines. The Buffs were bundled off their ship in great haste and without their kits; they got off somehow to Winchester, where they found themselves on a cold, bleak down, in pouring rain and with but very meagre equipment—cooking-pots being one of the very many items that were deficient. An Army Service wagon or two ultimately came along and threw some blankets upon the wet ground, and some bread and meat on top of them, and went away; but of course their drivers were not responsible for cooking-pots. Christmas, 1914, may have been a merry one in many places, even in the trenches to a certain extent, but it is doubtful if the 2nd Battalion of the Buffs ever spent a more miserable one. Certainly Captain Tomlinson's company got plum puddings, but that was the one bright spot.

The battalion, together with the 3rd Royal Fusiliers, 2nd East Surrey and the 3rd Middlesex, all from India, found itself in the 85th Infantry Brigade under Br.-General A. J. Chapman, C.B., who had Captain C. J. Deverell for brigade major. The brigade was part of the 28th Division—Major-General Bulfin, C.V.O., C.B. Captain L. Fort, and afterwards Lieut. the Hon. P. G. Scarlett, was appointed staff captain to the 85th Brigade.

Military exercises of an intensive kind were, of course, the daily lot of the men while at Winchester, particularly so because the latest pattern rifle (not used in India) had just been issued to them. A furlough of three clear days to 25 per cent of the soldiers at a time was, however, granted, so that those just returned from India, after a foreign tour of nearly ten years, might get a glimpse of their friends before starting for a new and sterner foreign service. A few drafts of new men arrived, but it must be understood that these reinforcements for each and all of the battalions during the four years under consideration were of such frequent occurrence as to render constant reference to them both tiresome and superfluous. It may easily be understood that the strength of a unit must constantly be varying. A hard-fought action would reduce the numbers enormously, as well as did the regular drain by death, wounds and disease during the weary trench work.

The only events worthy of record during the stay at Winchester were a violent squall which did great damage to the tents on the 28th December, and a grand inspection of the division by His Majesty the King accompanied by Lord Kitchener on the 12th January, 1915. The battalion moved into billets in the city on the 6th January, the officers being accommodated in Winchester College.[1]

It is only fair to note here that the newly issued boots were not of proper quality: the heels came off and the nails went through. Later on, in France, the men experienced a good deal of quite unnecessary hardship on account of their boots, which to an infantry soldier are only of second importance to his weapons. Some one was to blame, of course, presumably the contractor, and it seems that in every war these men must make their fortunes at the expense of the soldier.

Most judges agree that English soldiers are seldom seen to such perfection of training and physique as in India, and the infantry of the 28th Division was entirely composed of units from that country, so that all who saw these troops prior to embarkation for France agreed that no finer body of infantry had ever taken the field.

---

1 " Other chambers in College were occupied by officers of the " Buffs, and these officers had their ante-room in VIIth Chamber and " their mess in College Hall. Hence the small oak shield, carved with " the Buffs' Dragon, which may now be seen on the north side of the " Hall. This was a parting gift from Captain F. W. Tomlinson."— *The Wykehamist*, No. 538, February, 1915.

The start was made on the 16th January, on which day the division marched to Southampton, and a trying march it was; though well timed and arranged by the staff, sufficient consideration was not given to the length of the journey by foot, the state of the weather nor the weight each soldier had to carry.

II. ARRIVES ON WESTERN FRONT

Next day the Buffs embarked for Havre, for the Channel ports were safe enough by this time. On the 21st they detrained at Hazebrouck and marched to Rouge Croix (4½ miles N.E.), after one of those terrible French railway journeys, during which sanitary arrangements are non-existent. The battalion now became a fighting unit in the great struggle that was raging round Ypres.

It is good in winter time to have plenty of warm clothing and protection from the weather, but the kits at this period were terribly heavy to carry. Later on regular parties were told off to take what was required from the billets to the trenches and so on, but at first the soldier, in addition to his regular sixty-two pounds' weight of kit, was burdened with a fur coat, gum boots and spare sandbags, all very excellent things to have with one, but a bit of a job to get over the ground with.

On the 28th January the brigade was inspected by the Commander-in-Chief, accompanied by the Prince of Wales. During the month of February the Germans made several more or less determined attempts to pierce the British line near Ypres, and sometimes with partial success. On the 4th of the month the 85th Brigade, being at Ouderdom, received news that their comrades of the 83rd were being attacked south-west of the city, so two battalions started at once to the rescue, and these were followed two hours later by the Buffs and Middlesex, who entered the place and remained in readiness in the cavalry barracks.

The 5th February brought some counter-marching. At 4.30 a.m. the battalion started to march back again to Ouderdom as being not wanted and was then told to stand by in readiness to move again, as the 84th Brigade was now in trouble to the south of Ypres. This march, however, was not performed till the following day, by the evening of which both the Buffs and East Surreys were back in the cavalry barracks, and from there they went into the trenches, the Buffs' Headquarters being at Ferme Chapelle.

The experience of the next few days was a terrible one; the trenches, which had just been taken over from the French, were in very bad condition indeed: they were knee-deep in water, and with parapets so rotten as not to be bullet proof. Very soon this state of things had its effect and numbers of the men were suffering from swollen feet and frost-bite.

III. "O" TRENCH

The brigade front at this time was intersected at right angles by the Ypres-Comines Canal, which divided it into what were known as the Right and Left Sections of Defence. Immediately north of the canal the Left Section of Defence was entrusted to the Buffs and 3rd Royal Fusiliers, these battalions relieving each other as ordered; and the south or the Right Section of Defence to the 2nd East Surrey and the 3rd Middlesex. Each section had its own battalion headquarters. A small part of the southern section was also held by one company of the Buffs (Captain Worthington). The other battalions of the brigade were in somewhat similar conditions to the Buffs, and were daily and rapidly being reduced in fighting strength and efficiency, chiefly through frost-bite and sickness. So serious had things become owing to this reduction in fighting strength that, by the 13th February, it was decided to relieve the brigade, and to withdraw it to recoup and

29

refit as soon as other troops were available to replace it in the line.

It had already been decided by the higher command that a part of the line then being held by the 3rd Middlesex and the 2nd East Surrey, south of the canal, was to be shortened by the construction of new trenches a little in rear of trenches " O " and " P." This work had already been started, and was, on the night of the 14th February, being continued by the 3rd Middlesex, which temporarily withdrew the garrisons from " O " and " P " trenches for the purpose of digging, leaving those trenches in charge of small covering parties only.

The Germans, who up till then had been showing very little local activity, unexpectedly raided and captured " O " trench and prevented its reoccupation by the Middlesex ; without delay they reversed the parapet, wired the front on our side and took all necessary steps for resisting any attempts at recapture.

During the night 14th/15th February the Buffs were relieved by the 3rd Royal Fusiliers from their unenviable position in the trenches as recorded above, and were withdrawn a short distance to Chateau Rosenthal (Bedford House), on the Ypres–St. Eloi road, to rest. By the time the reliefs had been completed and the battalion had settled down to rest the night was far spent.

Shortly before dawn alarming rumours reached Battalion H.Q. that the enemy had broken through the Middlesex and were advancing on Ypres. Colonel Geddes reported accordingly to Brigade H.Q., and the battalion was at once turned out in readiness for any eventuality. Soon after daybreak orders were received to move out and hold the canal bank south-east of Langhof. Although fairly heavily shelled *en route*, the battalion crossed the canal without loss and assembled on the north side, under cover of the canal embankment. Here it was subsequently joined by the brigadier

30

and some of the brigade staff and remained awaiting developments throughout the rest of the morning.

About 2.30 p.m. the 2nd East Surrey, assisted by as many of the Middlesex as it had been possible to collect, were ordered to recapture " O " trench. No arrangements had apparently been made for artillery support, and moreover this attack had to be made over ground deep in mud, devoid of any cover and without any previous reconnaissance or guides. From the Buffs' rendezvous nothing could be seen of what was taking place on the far side of the embankment, where the attack had been launched. About 4.30 p.m. the Buffs (less one company which remained with the brigadier in reserve) were ordered to reinforce the East Surrey, who, owing to extremely heavy losses, were reported to be held up and unable to make further progress. As the leading company of the Buffs broke cover it came under artillery fire which caused many casualties, including its commander, Major F. S. Reeves, wounded, and Lieut. R. M. Heywood, killed. Neither the whereabouts of the East Surreys nor the direction of the objective were known, and by this time darkness was fast approaching. However, the three companies continued the advance in the dusk and by good fortune came up with some of the East Surreys, who, having reached a point some five hundred yards from the objective, were unable to advance any further. The Buffs passed through them and continued to advance until they reached a point about three hundred yards from the objective, which by this time, however, was completely hidden in the darkness which had by now intervened. At this point a subaltern of the East Surrey Regiment, who had lost his platoon, was met, and he volunteered to act as guide. The leading company again pushed on, but, owing to the difficulty of keeping touch and maintaining direction in the dark, a part of the battalion found itself held up by wire and suffering

31

heavy losses from fire from more than one direction. At this juncture Colonel Geddes wisely determined to withdraw the battalion, which was only done with the greatest difficulty.

Whilst the above operations were in progress, half a battalion of the 2nd Northumberland Fusiliers, sent from the 84th Brigade, had arrived in the dark at the rendezvous on the canal bank, where the brigadier and the reserve company of the Buffs (Major R. E. Power) were waiting. As nothing was known of the military situation, nor of the whereabouts of the Buffs nor of the East Surrey Regiment, from whom no reports had been received since dark, the brigadier ordered the reserve company of the Buffs to go out and find the rest of the battalion. He himself started with them. After going a short distance they came across a building full of wounded which was found to be the Battalion H.Q. of the Right Section of Defence, then occupied by the headquarters of the 3rd Middlesex Regiment. Here a guide was procured, and the company proceeded in the direction in which the remainder of the battalion and the 2nd East Surrey had gone. Before it had gone far, however, it luckily met Colonel Geddes returning. The battalion (less half Major Power's company, detached to occupy a front-line trench) reached the canal about 10.30 p.m., and was sent back at 1 a.m. to Chateau Rosenthal to get a meal and rest.

During the morning of the 15th February, 1915, a conference was held at Brigade H.Q., and it was decided to renew the attack on the lost trench " O " on that night. The brigadier at first decided to carry out this operation with the Buffs and East Surrey Regiment only, but these two battalions had together only about three hundred men available, owing to the casualties of the previous day and the losses sustained during the recent tour in the trenches. Two companies of the 2nd

Northumberland Fusiliers (84th Brigade) were, therefore, added to this small force, which was placed under
command of Colonel Geddes. In the written orders
issued to units it was stated that "O" trench was to be
retaken at all costs and held until reliefs arrived. The
G.O.C. 28th Division stated that the 85th Brigade,
which, owing to the severe losses from fire and sickness
already incurred, was to have been at once withdrawn
from the line and sent back to recoup and refit, would
not be relieved until the lost trench "O" had been
recaptured.

At 7 p.m. the Buffs (less half D Company)[1] and 2nd
East Surrey Regiment (less one and a half companies)
assembled at the place ordered, that is, on the road
junction on the Ypres–St. Eloi road, 620 yards south
of the canal. From this point the column, led by the
Buffs, marched via the road leading east towards Oost-
hoek, as far as the Battalion H.Q. of the Right Sections
of Defence, where the 2nd Northumberland Fusiliers
(less two companies) joined and followed in reserve.
Leaving here at 7.40 p.m. and moving in file, closed up,
the column was skilfully guided some two thousand
yards across country by Lieut. J. A. H. Wood, 2nd East
Surrey, to the position of deployment (the north-east
end of a spinney about 150 yards north of "O" trench),
which was reached without opposition or casualties at
about 8.40 p.m. On reaching the position of deployment
the Buffs, under Major L. I. B. Hulke, having previously
fixed bayonets, silently deployed into line to the left,
in single rank, without extending, and lay down in the
deep mud. The East Surreys, acting in a similar
manner, formed a second line twenty yards in rear with
the 2nd Northumberland Fusiliers some fifty yards be-

---

[1] This half-company, under Major R. E. Power, had not rejoined
the battalion the previous night, having been detailed to occupy an
unfinished trench in the front line. Lieut. J. W. Butts Archer was
killed whilst superintending a working party.

hind them. Selected scouts of the Buffs were sent out
to reconnoitre and cut the enemy's wire and to report
on the intervening ground, which was quite unknown
to all those about to take part in this attack. Such
complete silence had been maintained during the advance and deployment that the presence of the column
was unknown to the enemy until a prearranged artillery bombardment of his trenches commenced at 8.55
p.m. The shells all appeared to take effect against the
main German position, and consequently well beyond
the immediate objective. They unfortunately had the
undesired effect of putting the defenders on the *qui
vive*, for they at once manned the trench " O," sent
up flares, which revealed the position of the attacking
force, and opened on it a withering fire from rifles,
machine guns and trench mortars.

The time ordered for the assault was 9 p.m., and the
right of the Buffs was detailed to direct. Immediately
the enemy opened fire it was apparent from the shells
which, following one another in quick succession, burst
immediately behind and close to the Buffs, that the
enemy had the exact range. Realizing this, Major
Hulke at once gave the order to advance. Just in front
of the Buffs the ground sloped somewhat steeply downwards towards the objective for about fifty yards.
Nothing could have been finer than the dash and the
steady determination with which the whole line, like
one man, arose and went forward down this slope. The
configuration of the ground, and the unhesitating
manner in which the order to advance was carried out,
undoubtedly saved the battalion from serious losses at
this stage, as the more quickly the advance down the
slope was made the higher above the men's heads rained
the storm of shells and bullets on to, and beyond, the
position which the battalion had just vacated.

From the bottom of the slope the advance had to be
made across heavy ground, ankle deep in mud and

devoid of cover, for a distance of about 120 yards, the last part of which was up a steep incline. Except for the enemy's flares it was pitch dark. Against the heavy frontal fire from the trench, and enfilade machine-gun fire from the left flank, the battalion forged ahead with magnificent determination, and in spite of serious casualties, most of which were sustained when the level ground at the foot of the first slope was reached, fought its way through the wire and finally assaulted and gained a footing in the trench. The enemy, who had kept up a heavy fire until the Buffs were within ten yards of the trench, disappeared in the dark, apparently down a communication trench and also towards the western end of "O" trench.

Major C. L. Porter was wounded and many other ranks killed and wounded during the attack, but ten officers and about sixty other ranks succeeded in entering the trench. Major Hulke immediately reorganized and distributed these along the trench, starting from the extreme left, and arranged for the protection of the right flank by the construction of a sandbag traverse, which was built, under fire from rifle and bombs, under Captain Morgan's supervision, assisted by Lieut. Laing. A considerable number had already been wounded; parties had to be employed in repairing and strengthening the parapet, whilst others had to be told off to assist those detailed to man the parapet, in clearing the jammed rifles and supplying them with cleaned ammunition. When all these deductions from the sixty odd other ranks who had succeeded in gaining a footing in the trench had been made, it was found that only sufficient men remained to hold about fifty out of a probable two hundred yards of trench. Whilst the above arrangements were in progress the enemy started sniping and throwing bombs, apparently from a communication trench and from the western end of "O" trench, which was still in their hands. Bombs at that time were weapons of warfare of which the 28th Division had had no previous experience whatever, and owing to the darkness, the non-provision of maps and lack of previous information about, or knowledge of, the trench, it was very difficult to locate the places from which the enemy were throwing them and sniping. However, Captain F. W. Tomlinson, Captain L. Fort and 2nd Lieut. E. F. D. Strettell discovered the whereabouts of a party of the enemy's bombers and rushed it; demolished the sandbag wall, from under cover of which bombs were being thrown, and cleared the enemy out of the trench. Captain Tomlinson seized the bayonet of one of the enemy, who turned tail. Captain L. Fort, who a few days previously had shown the greatest courage and resource whilst in charge of an officers' reconnoitring patrol, was killed, and 2nd Lieut. E. F. D. Strettell was severely wounded in this gallant enterprise, which undoubtedly saved many lives and further casualties in the battalion, as the enemy afterwards ceased bombing and apparently withdrew.

Owing to the mud, with which everybody and everything was smothered, a large number of the rifles became jammed and unserviceable. After holding on for three hours, as the promised support had not arrived the position of the Buffs was by now (midnight) somewhat critical. Major Hulke therefore sent 2nd Lieut. J. A. Wood (2nd East Surrey), accompanied by No. 9522 Pte. W. J. White, to report the situation to Colonel Geddes, and eventually the former returned, guiding a company of the 2nd Suffolk Regiment. He reported that both the 2nd Northumberland Fusiliers and 2nd East Surrey had lost their way in the dark, and that the former had been now ordered to follow the 2nd Suffolk Regiment. They did not, however, arrive at " O " trench before the Buffs were relieved.

As soon as the company of the Suffolks had taken

36

over the portion of the trench the Buffs were holding, they had to work their surplus men along the trench beyond the sandbag traverse which the battalion had built, and extend them further to the right. In trying to do this they met with considerable opposition from parties of the enemy, who were in the western part of the trench. As the officer in command of this company appeared to meet with some difficulty in overcoming this opposition, Major Hulke offered to remain with his handful of men until it got sufficiently light to see what the real situation was. This offer, however, was refused, and, in accordance with the orders issued, Major Hulke therefore withdrew the Buffs, leaving in charge of the Suffolks any wounded who were unable to be removed without stretchers—of which there were none available. Great difficulty was experienced in carrying out the withdrawal over the fire-swept morass which had to be crossed, lit up, as it was, by almost incessant star-shell and flares. By crawling through the mud between the flares, a few yards at a time, and by lying down as flat as possible whilst any light remained, was the only way of proceeding, but many lives, including Sgt. Rosam, were lost during the first part of the withdrawal: although the distance was not more than 150 yards, it took half an hour to reach the original place of deployment.

After a few hours' rest in the cavalry barracks in Ypres the battalion marched into scattered billets in and around Reninghelst. On the same afternoon the services of 2nd Lieut. C. W. Laing were asked for to act as guide to another brigade detailed on that night to recapture " O " trench, which the enemy had again taken possession of very shortly after the Buffs had been relieved. In spite of his arduous experiences of the previous night's fighting and want of rest, 2nd Lieut. C. W. Laing undertook this hazardous enterprise, and carried it out successfully.

IV. Trench Warfare near Ypres

On the 19th February the battalion was attached to the 3rd Division and went into billets at Locre, marching to Westoutre for baths and clean clothes. There was a regular system in working this necessary ablution arrangement. Men cast off their filthy underclothing, which was taken from them, and after a bath, clean underclothes, which had once belonged to other people, were provided and the old ones were never seen again by the original owners. At first this caused a certain amount of grumbling amongst careful men, who were liable to become possessed of somewhat more ragged articles than they handed in, but it was soon found that things generally came right in the long run.

A new line of trenches were occupied on the 22nd, and these were found to be much preferable and more desirable in every way than those last occupied. There is no doubt that the French were more careless as regards the cleanliness as well as the general efficiency of their trenches than were our own people, and it seems that the 2nd Buffs were rather unfortunate in very frequently relieving our Allies instead of other British troops. These new and better works were at Kemmel, and the battalion alternated between this place and Locre till the 23rd March, when it was billeted at Dickebusch. Captain A. S. Cresswell was killed by a sniper on the 12th March.

On the 10th April, after a trying turn at St. Eloi, the battalion marched to Zonnebeke and relieved the 153rd French Regiment, the 85th Brigade having three battalions in the front line, with the Buffs in the centre, three companies in the fire trenches and one in support. About the middle of the line was the Broodseinde cross-roads, where the enemy's trenches approached very close to our own, at one point to within five feet. This portion of the field is upon a plateau which commands the Ypres road, and was of great tactical importance. Forward of a trench which lay to the south-west of the cross-roads, the enemy had that morning rushed a parallel in which the French had laid a mine that was to have been fired before they handed over. After blocking this mine up, the enemy had retained possession of that part of the work in which it had been laid. Of this fact the French were either ignorant or, at any rate, they made no report of it. Two attempts were made to dislodge them, in which Captain Hood, Lieut. Whitaker (both of whom were wounded) and 2nd Lieut. Chapman did good work.

In the meantime the Germans had established a heavy trench mortar in a position, secure from our artillery, from which they brought a merciless fire to bear on our lines, especially on B Company which was on the cross-roads. This was the 2nd Battalion's first experience of this weapon. Serious damage was done to the parapets and many casualties resulted. During this four days' tour 1 officer and 22 other ranks were killed and 4 officers and 62 other ranks wounded. The battalion was relieved by the 3rd Royal Fusiliers on the morning of the 14th and marched back to billets at St. Jean, about one mile east of Ypres. A and D Companies were sent into the reserve dug-outs west of Zonnebeke, but rejoined at St. Jean the next day. After another short turn in the trenches the battalion on the 21st found itself bivouacked in open fields near St. Jean, where shelters and dug-outs were arranged for, because the town of Ypres was now being too heavily shelled for troops to make use of billeting accommodation there, or, in fact, to pass through the town at all.

V. Second Battle of Ypres

The second battle of Ypres has brought more obloquy and ill-fame on the German nation than even Marathon brought glory to the Athenians. It appears to have been well understood by scientific men that a noisome and poisonous gas could be so carried down wind that no man could breathe its suffocating fumes and live for long, and further that he must die in agony. At the ineffectual conference at the Hague it had been arranged between the representatives of the several nations, including Germany, that the use of such a disgusting and brutal weapon should be barred between civilized enemies, and nobody thought any more about it, but the German beast is not a gentleman and he ruled that the brave old days when foeman fought with a chivalrous regard for his opponent were to cease, at any rate as far as the much-vaunted Fatherland was concerned, and so this battle which we are now to consider goes down in history as the first great combat in which unfair and blackguardly methods were adopted.

The commencement of this tremendous battle is best described in Sir John French's own words, which are here quoted from his despatches : " It was at the " commencement of the Second Battle of Ypres on the " evening of the 22nd April that the enemy first made " use of asphyxiating gas.

" Some days previously I had complied with General " Joffre's request to take over the trenches occupied by " the French, and on the evening of the 22nd the " troops holding the lines east of Ypres were posted as " follows :—

" From Steenstraate to the east of Langemarck, as " far as the Poelcappelle road, a French division.

" Thence, in a south-easterly direction towards the " Passchendaele-Becelaere road, the Canadian division.

40

YPRES FROM NEAR MENIN GATE

" Thence, a division took up the line in a southerly
" direction east of Zonnebeke to a point west of
" Becelaere, whence another division continued the
" line south-east to the northern limit of the corps on
" its right.

" Of the 5th Corps there were four battalions in
" Divisional Reserve about Ypres; the Canadian
" Division had one battalion in Divisional Reserve and
" the 1st Canadian Brigade in Army Reserve. An
" infantry brigade, which had just been withdrawn
" after suffering heavy losses on Hill 60, was resting
" about Vlamertinghe.

" Following a heavy bombardment, the enemy
" attacked the French division at about 5 p.m., using
" asphyxiating gases for the first time. Aircraft re-
" ported that at about 5 p.m. thick yellow smoke had
" been seen issuing from the German trenches between
" Langemarck and Bixschoote. The French reported
" that two simultaneous attacks had been made east of
" the Ypres-Staden railway, in which these asphyxiating
" gases had been employed.

" What follows almost defies description. The effect
" of these poisonous gases was so virulent as to render
" the whole of the line held by the French division
" mentioned above practically incapable of any action
" at all. It was at first impossible for anyone to
" realize what had actually happened. The smoke and
" fumes hid everything from sight, and hundreds of
" men were thrown into a comatose or dying con-
" dition, and within an hour the whole position had to
" be abandoned, together with about 50 guns.

" I wish particularly to repudiate any idea of
" attaching the least blame to the French division for
" this unfortunate incident.

" After all the examples our gallant Allies have
" shown of dogged and tenacious courage in the many
" trying situations in which they have been placed

41

" throughout the course of this campaign, it is quite
" superfluous for me to dwell on this aspect of the
" incident, and I would only express my firm con-
" viction that, if any troops in the world had been able
" to hold their trenches in the face of such a treacher-
" ous and altogether unexpected onslaught, the French
" division would have stood firm.

" The left flank of the Canadian division was thus
" left dangerously exposed to serious attack in flank,
" and there appeared to be a prospect of their being
" overwhelmed and of a successful attempt by the
" Germans to cut off the British troops occupying the
" salient to the east.

" In spite of the danger to which they were exposed
" the Canadians held their ground with a magnificent
" display of tenacity and courage, and it is not too
" much to say that the bearing and conduct of these
" splendid troops averted a disaster which might have
" been attended with the most serious consequences.

" They were supported with great promptitude by
" the reserves of the divisions holding the salient and
" by a brigade which had been resting in billets."

Now, of course, the commander-in-chief of a large
army cannot possibly in his reports home go into
details concerning brigades and battalions, but as the
reader will see later this " brigade resting in billets "
comprised amongst others the 2nd Battalion of the
Buffs. The story as far as the Buffs are concerned is as
follows :—

The 1st Battalion was still twelve miles or so south
of Ypres, but the 2nd was, as has been seen, on the
afternoon of the 22nd of April, bivouacked in fields
at St. Jean, which village was about four miles back
from the front British line of trenches. The Middlesex
and Buffs were that night to relieve the rest of the
brigade in the trenches about Zonnebeke. Considerable

Canadian forces were in the immediate vicinity of the Buffs.

About 5 o'clock on the evening of the 22nd April there was a sudden very sharp outburst of the enemy's artillery, and a cloud of greenish vapour was noticed away on the left of the line. Heavy machine-gun firing was heard, evidently coming from the enemy, a very long way inside what was the British line, and bullets came spattering into St. Jean, which place ought to have been safe enough from this kind of fire. Half an hour after the commencement of the bombardment many French soldiers were observed retiring rapidly and in a disordered manner. These men were mostly Turcos and Zouaves and, poor fellows, had been taken entirely by surprise by the new and horrible methods of the enemy. They had, of course, no protection against gas at that time, and they simply fled as if the Devil were after them. It was thought by the English at first that the gas attack was nothing, and preparations were at first continued for carrying out the relief alluded to above, but it soon became evident that something very serious indeed had occurred and, at 8.30 p.m., Colonel Geddes was placed in command of all troops in St. Jean, Major Power taking over the Buff battalion.

Geddes soon received another battalion from Ypres, and at first he had his old adjutant, Lieut. Hon. P. G. Scarlett, with him as staff officer, but the latter was relieved the same night and rejoined the details of the 85th Brigade, of which he was staff captain, and which were soon fighting hard at Zonnebeke. Geddes was later joined by detachments of two other battalions, and his force during the next few days was destined to play an extraordinarily fine rôle. These troops were all there was between the Canadians left near Wieltje and the Canal, and it became theirs to guard an otherwise open road to Ypres.

43

The Canadians with whom Geddes' Detachment, as it was officially nominated, was soon ordered to act, immediately stood to, as did the Buffs and Middlesex, as well as the 4th King's Own Royal Lancasters, the battalion which had come from Ypres.

Meanwhile, the French troops were streaming down the road towards Ypres, while the Englishmen were standing nonchalantly in the streets of St. Jean, and the Canadians calmly marching north and north-east in the direction from which the foreign troops were retiring. The Buffs took up a position covering St. Jean, facing north and north-east, with the Middlesex on their left and the King's Own in reserve.

At night it was found that the Canadian left flank was turned and the 3rd Canadian Brigade requesting that a company should be sent up to St. Julien to help and support them, Captain Tomlinson with B Company was sent, though the Englishmen were themselves hardly pressed. At 2 a.m. on the 23rd, Geddes received instructions that he was to act under orders of the Canadian Division, and was told by that unit to co-operate on the Canadian left. At 3.30 the Buffs, less B Company, was ordered to Wieltje and thence in a northerly direction to get touch with the 3rd Canadian Brigade. The men took some time to collect for the counter-attack, and it was after 4 o'clock and broad daylight when the battalion moved off, preceded by an advance guard under Captain Barnard.

About eight hundred yards north of Wieltje some dug-outs and trenches were reached, which were occupied by Canadians. These trenches were screened by a hedge, under cover of which the Buffs closed up. Beyond was open country, so the battalion at once deployed and was immediately subjected to furious machine-gun and rifle fire from the enemy, who were entrenched in two parallel lines about 1,200 and

44

BATTLEFIELD NEAR ST. JULIEN

900 yards distant on rising ground sloping to the north. Moving at the double, platoon followed platoon in quick succession in the open, many casualties occurring. Two companies soon reached a farm four hundred yards on, while the remaining company took advantage of the frail cover afforded by a fence, 150 yards behind the farm, around which were a few Canadians, from whom Major Power ascertained that there was a space of about a quarter of a mile to the east, only lightly held by the French. On it were three parallel lines of trenches facing north with their right resting on the G.H.Q. wire. Major Power, seeing the danger of this, ordered the battalion to advance half-right and occupy the forward of the three trenches. In it were found a few men of the 1st Zouaves. The Buffs therefore advanced by rushes across the open and lost heavily: Captain J. McB. Ronald being killed, Lieut. D. A. Wilkins severely wounded and some eighty casualties of other ranks occurring. Two companies occupied the front line, while the third (D) was in a trench facing east along the G.H.Q. wire, which is the last fortified line back from the enemy, and the fact that our troops were now practically defending that meant, of course, that the enemy had penetrated all defences but one on this northern flank of the Ypres salient. The rest of the day the battalion was subjected to heavy shelling and rifle fire. The remainder of the Zouaves withdrew, and the Buffs then completely occupied the gap between the Canadian companies.

The 24th April proved an unfortunate day. D Company was moved at the urgent request of the 3rd Canadian Brigade to a position across the Wieltje–St. Julien road, but at 7 a.m. Captain Tomlinson's B Company, which had been detached late on the 22nd to the succour of the Canadians, was completely surrounded by the enemy, and after losing very heavily, practically all the survivors were made prisoners.

Among the killed were Lieut. W. G. Jackson and 2nd Lieut. C. W. Laing. The Canadians and others who saw this company attack stated that this little force was entirely responsible for the saving of the Canadian left, and also that practically the whole company was killed, wounded or taken prisoner, including Tomlinson, who had again shown great gallantry. On this 24th of April, as well as the two following days, the shelling was most severe, and the men suffered much from the poisonous fumes given off on the bursting of the shells. D Company was relieved by the Canadians on the morning of the 25th and resumed its old place, thrown back at an angle from A's right flank.

The battalion being relieved by the 4th Battalion Rifle Brigade, got back to dug-outs at St. Jean on the 27th, but the constant and persistent shelling continued there all day and, on the 28th, the Buffs received orders to rejoin the 85th Brigade at Verlorenhoek, Geddes' detachment having been broken up.

Colonel Geddes had thus again shown his worth; he combined experience and valour with a strong understanding and much intellectual power, and had, it would seem, a fine future before him. His brilliant handling of the critical situation so suddenly forced on him undoubtedly prevented the Germans from pressing home the attack so successfully begun on the 22nd. To the great loss of his regiment and his country, a shell entered the room in which he was sitting on the morning of the 28th and killed him instantly.[1]

Although the 29th and 30th of April proved quiet days for the regiment at Verlorenhoek this was but a lull in the awful and pitiless storm. The most marked

---

[1] Augustus David Geddes was born on the 6th June, 1866, and joined the Buffs on the 5th February, 1887; he was adjutant of the 2nd Battalion from 1898 until 1900, when he was severely wounded, in the South African War. After being some years on the staff, he was promoted to command the 2nd Battalion in 1911.

46

feature of the next few days was the failure of the artillery to support the overdriven foot soldiers. This, of course, was in no possible way the fault of the glorious gunners, but gun fire cannot be kept up without an adequate supply of material. Throughout the whole period since the first break in the line on the night of the 22nd April all the troops in this area had been constantly subjected to violent artillery bombardment from a large mass of guns with an unlimited supply of ammunition. It proved impossible, whilst under such a vastly superior fire of artillery and gas, to dig efficient trenches or properly reorganize the line after the confusion and demoralization caused by the first great gas surprise; consequently a withdrawal to a new line some little way further back became imperative, and this was carried out successfully during the first four days of May.

Meantime, they were doing their duty in England; drafts were coming out to replace those who had fallen, and the hard-tried battalion was pulling itself together for the further upholding of the great cause and for the honour of the corps.

On the 1st May a fresh draft of men had arrived from England. There was no time to allot them to companies, so, for the time being, they were kept together and put entire into a new support trench in front of a wood, and the very next day they came under really extraordinarily heavy shell fire, to which our gunners were unable to reply. It was the most trying initiation into warfare that young soldiers ever had to undergo, and the shelling was renewed at dawn on the 3rd of the month, so that Captain Archer Houblon, who commanded, reported many casualties, his parapet blown in and the situation critical. During the whole of this day the shelling was quite abnormal in intensity and our gunners could make hardly any reply. In the afternoon the bombard-

47

ment is described as sounding like machine-gun fire, being, as it was, so rapid and incessant. The enemy meanwhile rushed a trench called D.5, there being few, if any, Buffs to resist them. It had been occupied by Captain Howard Smith, Lieut. G. R. Howe and some eighty men of C Company. The whole party was reported missing, and it was believed nearly all were killed or wounded. There were during these days no communication trenches and the firing was too hot to permit of men moving from one work to another, so that parties were completely isolated.

The following is an extract from the official diary, a document which deals only with the plainest facts, related in the simplest language. There is never any exaggeration in the official diaries : " The Germans " now occupied the woods behind D.5, a movement " which made D.4 quite untenable; they were held up, " however, by a small party of Buffs under 2nd Lieut. " Backhouse and a company of Royal Fusiliers under " Captain Ford, who gallantly held on to the new sup- " port trench despite fearsome enfilade fire from heavy " howitzers and other artillery. Captain Houblon and " Lieut. Sharp and remainder of D Company who " were still holding D.4, were now being enfiladed by " Germans from D.5 and taken in reverse from the " wood. Captain Houblon, therefore, was compelled " to retire along the trench line, a movement which was " carried out steadily. The Germans were still pressing " forward and soon occupied a portion of the new " support trench where it joined D.4. Our men and " the enemy were now only a few yards apart, un- " fortunately the enemy were in greater numbers and " a far stronger situation. Many of the enemy were " shot, especially when they filed out of the wood " in front of D.5. In the retirement we also lost " heavily.

" The two last men in D.4 were Company Sergt.-

48

" Major Port and No. 7852 Pte. F. Campbell, both of
" C Company. These two bravely kept the enemy off
" while the others got away, and were able eventually
" both to follow under very heavy fire.

" Lieut. Sharp was wounded, but was able, with the
" survivors of Captain Houblon's party, to reach D.3
" and later D.1, held by Captain Barnard with A
" Company. When the musketry and machine-gun
" fire opened in the wood, Major Power instantly
" decided to send up the support company to the
" ridge south-west of the wood with the object of
" checking the enemy's advance and of reinforcing
" Captain Ford's company of Fusiliers in the new
" support trench. The exact situation at the time was
" unknown. On the way up Major Power was wounded
" in the chest."

From about 3.45 p.m. to 6 p.m. the enemy plastered,
bombarded and searched the ridge with a storm of
artillery fire, but the Royal Fusiliers and a few of the
2nd East Yorkshire stood their ground and the enemy
showed no inclination to advance from the wood. Any
moment our people hoped to hear our artillery open,
but hoped in vain. If only our guns could have got on
to the wood, the enemy must have suffered heavily. As
it was the contest was an unequal one. It was our
infantry alone against the enemy's infantry in force
and a most powerful combination of the enemy's
artillery. Fortunately for us the attack of the enemy's
infantry lacked push and determination. Things
quieted down towards dusk, the enemy contenting
himself with remaining where he was, enabling our
retirement, which was ordered for the night 3rd/4th
May, to be carried out quite steadily with a minimum
of loss, all wounded men, spare ammunition and tools
being brought away. The remnants of the battalion
moved back to bivouacs in a wood near Poperinghe on

E   49 the 4th of the month, where it was congratulated by General Plumer on the excellent work it had done and where it remained till the 8th. There is no doubt that the Buffs had been fortunate in having in Major Power a worthy successor to their late colonel. That officer was, however, now on the sick list from a severe wound in the chest, and the command had fallen to Captain Jackson, who held it for a few days until the arrival of a very senior captain, Worthington, who was given the temporary rank of lieut-colonel.

The total casualties from 22nd April to 4th May were :—

Officers killed 6:

Colonel A. D. Geddes, Captain J. McB. Ronald, Lieuts. E. H. U. Buttanshaw and W. G. Jackson, 2nd Lieuts. C. W. Laing and P. T. Featherstonhaugh-Frampton.

Officers wounded 9:

Major R. E. Power, Lieuts. A. D. Wilkins, J. B. Sharp and D. V. Thomas, 2nd Lieuts. L. M. S. Essell, E. B. Backhouse, R. M. Watson, G. Seath and S. Rivers.

Wounded and Missing 2:

Captain F. W. Tomlinson and Lieut. G. R. Howe.

Missing 2:

Captain L. Howard Smith and Lieut. A. L. D. Ryder.

The other rank casualties are most difficult to account for, particularly in respect of the 150 men of the two drafts that arrived on the 30th April and the 1st May respectively. These men's names were not known. Also many men were buried in the trenches and it was impossible to obtain identity discs. The following figures are approximate; it is certain, however, that many others were killed, including the majority of the above-mentioned drafts:—

Killed	67
Wounded	259
Wounded and missing . . .	13
Missing	363

A total of 17 officers and 702 other ranks.

It may be conceived and understood from this list of losses that the old " Contemptible " army had by now disappeared. A few officers, including promoted N.C.O.'s, and some veteran soldiers, still existed; many of them, having partially recovered from wounds and sickness, were now in military employment in England, but, roughly speaking, the soldiers fighting in France were new men, who, a year before, never thought it possible that they would be fighting the battles of their Country; but still the drafts arrived and still the men composing them were called upon to die or be maimed. It was a sad thing in the case above recorded for the poor lads of the drafts who had just left Kent full of life, zeal and enthusiasm to be obliterated immediately on reaching their long-desired goal, their regiment, and even before they had been allotted to companies.

At daylight on the 8th May very heavy bombardment was heard, and at 8.30 a.m. the Buffs, still under the command of Captain Jackson, were ordered to a camp west of Ypres on the Zonnebeke road. Here were found very poor and dilapidated trenches with demolished parapets, but these were ordered to be held at all costs, and here the battalion was shelled all day. B Company set to work to dig itself into a new support trench about two hundred yards behind the main fire one. Towards midnight on the 12th, after almost continuous shelling during the preceding days, the battalion was relieved by the Life Guards and moved back to Poperinghe.

The next night the Buffs, with the Northumberland Fusiliers, Cheshire Regiment and 1st Battalion York and Lancasters were formed into a temporary composite brigade under Br.-General Bols, and told to be in readiness to move at a moment's notice, but on the 19th the 85th Brigade took over this duty from Bols' men, the Buffs having in the interval received a large draft of 5 officers and 350 men.

On the 20th the Commander-in-Chief, Sir John French, made a speech to the 85th Brigade, as well as to others, of which the following is an extract:—

" I came over to say a few words to you and to tell
" you how much I, as Commander-in-Chief of this
" Army, appreciate the splendid work that you have all
" done during the recent fighting. You have fought
" the Second Battle of Ypres, which will rank amongst
" the most desperate and hardest fights of the war.
" You may have thought because you were not
" attacking the enemy that you were not helping to
" shorten the war. On the contrary, by your splendid
" endurance and bravery, you have done a great deal
" to shorten it. In this, the Second Battle of Ypres,
" the Germans tried by every means in their power to
" get possession of that unfortunate town. They con-
" centrated large forces of troops and artillery, and
" further than that they had recourse to that mean and
" dastardly practice, hitherto unheard of in civilized
" warfare, namely, the use of asphyxiating gases. You
" have performed the most difficult, arduous and
" terrific task of withstanding a stupendous bombard-
" ment by heavy artillery, probably the fiercest
" artillery fire ever directed against troops, and warded
" off the enemy's attacks with magnificent bravery.
" By your steadiness and devotion, both the German
" plans were frustrated. He was unable to get posses-

52

" sion of Ypres—if he had done this he would probably
" have succeeded in preventing neutral Powers from
" intervening—and he was also unable to distract us
" from delivering our attack in conjunction with the
" French in the Arras–Armentieres district. Had you
" failed to repulse his attacks, and made it necessary
" for more troops to be sent to your assistance, our
" operations in the south might not have been able to
" take place, and would certainly not have been so
" successful as they have been. Your Colours have
" many famous names emblazoned on them, but none
" will be more famous or more well-deserved than that
" of the Second Battle of Ypres. I want you one and
" all to understand how thoroughly I realize and
" appreciate what you have done. I wish to thank you,
" each officer, non-commissioned officer and man, for
" the services you have rendered by doing your duty
" so magnificently, and I am sure that your Country
" will thank you too."

At 2.45 a.m. on the 24th May the Germans attacked
as a final effort the whole front from Wieltje to the
Menin road. This began with gas for four and a half
hours and a very heavy bombardment with gas shells,
combined with " Flammenwerfen," a terrible imple-
ment for ejecting liquid fire, new at this time. Then
the enemy advanced in very heavy masses and gained
the snipers' line, but was repulsed in each attempt to
get further. Two companies of the 8th Middlesex and
one company East Surrey immediately north of the
railway gave way in consequence of the gas. There
was cavalry on the right of the 85th Brigade and these
were at the same time heavily attacked, so that the
O.C. Buffs, which was the right battalion of the G.H.Q.
line, was asked for help. The message came at 4.30
a.m. and was from Captain Court, 9th Lancers, who
said that his men were " on their knees," but holding

out. Captain Barnard with A Company followed by half of C, under Lieut. Swayne, at once started for the rescue to reinforce the trenches north and south of the Menin road, and thus on this day the Buffs fought in two separate parties. At 6.30 orders came to reinforce the 3rd Royal Fusiliers, who meant to retake their lost trench, and B Company, with the remaining half of C, went up, leaving for the present D Company in the G.H.Q. line. Directly it left the reserve line this party came under very heavy shell fire and lost badly. Major Johnstone of the Fusiliers, however, organized his counter-stroke, but it was beaten off, he himself being wounded, Lieut. D. W. Hammond of the Buffs killed and many men of both regiments lost.

The enemy appeared to be in great strength, so the remainder of the Buffs was ordered up to assist the Royal Fusiliers at a level crossing on the railway, but all this time the enemy's shell fire was terrific and the crossing became merely a death-trap. However, about 1 p.m. D Company issued from the G.H.Q. lines and tried to come on, though it was almost an impossibility. It was a terrible undertaking and only about thirty men, under 2nd Lieut. Mantle, managed the journey. The situation was most critical as the enemy were working round the right. About 5 p.m. a counter-attack by the 84th Brigade, though held up, relieved matters somewhat. At nightfall the attack was continued by 84th and 80th Brigades, but was not successful owing to the terrific rifle and machine-gun fire directed upon it by the enemy. There were many casualties. Numbers of Cheshire, Welsh, K.S.L.I. and other regiments retired into the road cutting held by the Buffs and 3rd Royal Fusiliers.

Referring to the other party of the battalion which, under Captain Barnard, had been sent to assist the cavalry who were holding their own so well, the

54

following extract from the official diary describes its
adventures:—

" Captain Barnard having received orders to rein-
" force the 9th Lancers, moved east along the Menin
" road under shrapnel fire, meeting on the way scores
" of gassed and wounded men retiring from trenches
" north of the Menin–Ypres road. Eventually about
" 150 men of A Company filed into the Hooge
" trenches, the occupants of which were suffering
" badly from the gas—especially the officers. Besides
" the 9th Lancers, there were portions of the 18th
" Hussars, 4th Yorkshires, York and Lancasters and
" 5th D.L.I. Captain Grenfell, V.C., 9th Lancers, was
" in command. A Company spread all along the five
" hundred yards of trenches. The enemy were found
" to be enveloping our left or north flank and had
" pushed on one thousand yards west of it. A Com-
" pany then swung round and formed a new firing
" line facing north to meet the new menace."

For three days, until the night of the 26th to 27th,
the company maintained its position and accounted for
several of the enemy. The men were subjected to
continuous fire from the enemy's artillery, snipers and
large trench mortars. It was a case of digging in all
day and night. Some of the trenches were knee deep
in water. No rations were received for two days and
the company was in great difficulties, and a trying
situation for the whole period up to the night of 26th/
27th, when it was relieved and moved back to G.H.Q.
line. The 25th of the month was devoted to the collection and reorganization of what was left of B, C and
D Companies under difficulties owing to the many
stragglers from other corps. The enemy fortunately
slackened his fierce attacks and at nightfall many
wounded were collected, and after a couple of com-

paratively quiet days in the trenches the battalion marched back to billets east of Poperinghe.

After the narration of such terrible scenes as have been described it is pleasant to record a happy social event which, though a civilian reader may possibly regard it as of trivial importance, bears a very different aspect in the eyes of the English soldier. In all or nearly all foreign armies the battalions of a regiment are parts of the same tactical unit, but this does not obtain in our Army. The nature of our military duties causes the necessity of one battalion being abroad while the other remains at home, and it is almost unheard of that two battalions should serve together. There are old and retired Buffs who remember the meeting of the 1st and 2nd Battalions at Singapore about the year 1885. The occasion was celebrated then in what might now be considered almost too jovial a manner, but its rare occurrence made it very memorable. Again, after the Boer War when the 2nd Battalion, recently home from South Africa, was quartered in Dover, the 1st, back from Aden, was sent there also. These meetings are still remembered by the survivors of those who served in 1885 and 1904. On the 2nd June, then, in the midst of a tremendous war, it so happening that both the old units were resting at the same time and near the same place, the 2nd Battalion made a route march to Wittenhoek to visit its sister battalion which was in bivouac there. It was an historical event as far as the old regiment was concerned, though, alas, the two portions of it were not the same men that wore the Dragon on their collars a year before. Still, there were certain old friendships to renew and the Buffs were still the Buffs after all.

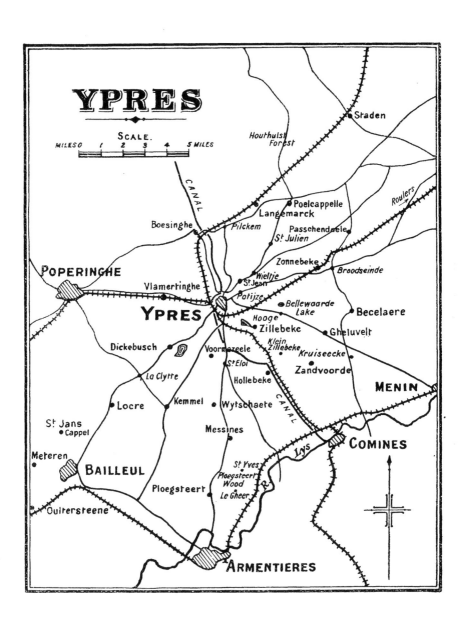

CHAPTER III

THE PREPARATION AND THE START OF MORE BATTALIONS

I. Summary of Events

WHEN the crash came in August, 1914, the only British forces ready to assist were, of course, the units composing the regular army, and it was soon seen that these were numerically far too few for a struggle of the present magnitude; and though we were only bound by treaty to furnish a certain number of soldiers, that number would only serve to show our goodwill, but could not possibly do much towards the decision of the result. As far as it went the old regular army proved itself to be the finest and most highly trained in Europe, but it was a lamentably small force even when reinforced by the good and seasoned Indian and other oversea regiments, battalions and batteries. England had engaged herself in an enormous task and she recognized, if but very slowly, that it was so. When the awakening began everybody, or nearly everybody, male or female, was anxious to do his or her share, and so it came to pass that, while the first fierce fighting was going on in Flanders and in France, Englishmen left in our island were enlisting, drilling, training and working with tremendous energy to equip and place in the field new and larger armies wherewith to fight out the quarrel on more even terms. The regular army, it was recognized, was but an advance guard, and it was for it to hold the field until the others had prepared themselves.

In addition to those engaged there were trained or partially trained troops, but many more than these

57

were required. These partially trained men were the recruits at the depot, the 3rd (Special Reserve) Battalion, and the Territorials. No better material could be found anywhere than these latter, but the annual fortnight's training, together with periodical musketry work and other drills and exercises, which the soldier might attend or not as he pleased, did not suffice to enable the units to take the field at once in a great European war. In this chapter will be found a short account of how the required soldiers were provided as far as East Kent was concerned, and some of the methods by which it was arranged that the Old Buffs who hail from there should be expanded into a far larger regiment, and the ranks of all its battalions kept up to strength; for it was quite clear that draft after draft of fresh men would continually have to cross the seas to supply the waste of war.

But first it may be as well to record very briefly the progress of and changes in the general situation of the world from September, 1914, when the 1st Battalion landed in France, up to the middle of the following year. On the 29th October, 1914, Turkey entered the war as an ally of Germany. On the 2nd November the Russians, who were of course on our side, but who were slower to mobilize than other countries, entered East Prussia and great hopes were entertained that their having taken the field in force would do wonders to bring the enemy to ruin. Even the most pessimistic saw that the presence of their armies in Germany itself ought to ease the pressure on the Western Front. On the 3rd November, Turkey being now an enemy, the forts on the Dardanelles were first bombarded by an English and French fleet, and this bombardment was repeated on the 19th February, 1915, and several times during the month of March.

The 14th November saw a check to the Russians and a powerful German invasion of Poland. On the 17th

SUMMARY OF EVENTS

November a British force landed on the shore of the Persian Gulf. The 20th November saw the commencement of a series of small fights and skirmishes in Egypt. This country was nominally part of the Turkish Empire, and the suzerain power made more than one attempt to enforce the claim and to cross the Suez Canal, without, however, any more success than the establishment of yet another theatre of war and the consequent holding up of British troops. The Australians and New Zealanders, however, arrived in Cairo two days before Christmas and the province was safe enough after that, although before that date the Indian soldiers, together with the Egyptians themselves, had gallantly kept the foe in check.

On the 22nd March, 1915, Przemysl capitulated to the Russians, who took 120,000 prisoners and 700 big guns. On the 25th April Anglo-French troops landed on both shores of the Dardanelles and soon established themselves across the Gallipoli Peninsula. On the 28th a very powerful Austro-German offensive developed in Galicia. The 3rd May was the date on which Italy denounced the Triple Alliance, to which she had been an adherent for so many years. There was much fighting in Gallipoli on the 6th, and on the 7th the world was startled by the cold-blooded cruelty of the enemy in torpedoing the *Lusitania* off the coast of Ireland, and it was demonstrated to all that the taking of innocent and non-combatant lives was a recognized part of the German programme.

Italy declared war on Austria on the 23rd May.

An important article appeared in *The Times* on the 14th May on the shortage of munitions.

In France, of course, war went on furiously all the time. Ypres was attacked on the 29th November and the 10th and 14th December, 1914. There was fierce fighting about St. Eloi in the middle of February, and in March came the battles of Neuve Chapelle and St. Eloi.

Nor was the war confined to the land: the battle of Coronel in the Pacific on the 1st November, 1914, saw the loss of the British cruisers *Good Hope* and *Monmouth*, and the battle of the Dogger Bank took place on the 24th January, 1915.

There was another event which happened during this period which was of the greatest interest to a very deserving section of the army. In previous wars, with the exception of the all-glorious and much-longed-for V.C., there was no military decoration, if we except the D.S.O., that was to be earned by junior officers or warrant officers. The C.B. and C.M.G. were reserved for generals and officers of field rank. His Majesty the King, recognizing that many most deserving juniors amongst his faithful soldiers could hope for nothing beyond the universal War Medal, instituted on the 28th December, 1914, the Military Cross, limited to officers below the rank of major, and certain warrant officers, and many a gallant young fellow can now vie with his senior in the legitimate and proper display of trophies.

This idea was further developed, in March, 1916, by the grant of a Military Medal (M.M.) to those non-commissioned officers and privates who had performed acts of gallantry which, in this war, at any rate, were not considered quite sufficiently important to earn the V.C.

II. DUTIES AT THE DEPOT

The depot of the Buffs is at Canterbury, which is also the headquarters of the 4th (Territorial) Battalion. During peace the headquarters and the permanent elements of the 3rd or Special Reserve Battalion occupied the depot. As Special Reserve officers only gave a small portion of their time to the profession of soldiering they were reinforced, so to speak, by a few regular officers and other ranks who administered the depot.

THE DEPOT

When war broke out, Lt.-Colonel H. D. Hirst commanded the 3rd Battalion, but as he, like all Special Reserve officers and as the Militia before them, lived at his home, the depot was commanded by Major W. A. Eaton, an experienced regular major of the regiment.

Directly mobilization was ordered, it was the duty of the depot and 3rd Battalion staff to call up, clothe and equip all Army Reservists and to despatch all who were passed fit for general service to join the 1st Battalion at Fermoy. This work began early on the morning of the 5th August and was completed during the night of the 6th, having been carried through without a moment's break. In all about 850 Army Reservists were called up, and of these some 700 were sent, in three trains, to Ireland.

On Saturday, 8th August, the 3rd Special Reserve Battalion was mobilized, about 500 strong; and the men gave good proof of their fitness by marching that same night from the barracks at Canterbury to the Citadel Barracks at Dover, a good eighteen miles.

Although very few of the people in authority seemed to expect a great war, still minute preparations had been made beforehand for a sudden mobilization, and amongst these it had been arranged that the officers on the Reserve of Officers list (not to be confused with Special Reserve) should each be told off in peace time to the job they would have to do in war. These officers were, practically speaking, all those who had retired and were still under the age of fifty-seven. Of them, some had been detailed to join at Canterbury on mobilization to take over the depot, Colonel G. V. Dauglish, a late commanding officer of the 1st Battalion, being appointed to command. On the departure of the 3rd Battalion for Dover, the depot, with its staff of reserve officers and a few details, proceeded to deal with the recruits who were already coming in fast.

Recruits for the New Army were at first trained at

61

the depot, though in practice they were trained by regular officers, lent for the purpose. As the strength of a company was raised, it was sent with the officers as a complete unit to its battalion; but this system did not last, recruits being afterwards sent direct to their battalions. Other training and the preparation of drafts for the front was carried out by the 3rd Battalion and, later, by the 9th as well.

The Officer Commanding the depot was also in charge of the East Kent Recruiting Area. The barracks were very soon crowded by the number of recruits, and, as new recruiting conditions developed, a large staff of men and women were employed in the recruiting offices, making it necessary for extra accommodation to be provided in the town. The Territorial battalions had their separate recruiting arrangements. It is interesting to recall the helpfulness of the recruits in the early days in making the best of a difficult and only partially organized job, and of old Buffs, non-commissioned officers and men, who re-enlisted for the depot and active service. It may be noted that while special efforts were made to get stout fellows for the Buffs, these efforts had to be co-ordinated with the duty of the Recruiting Area to obtain recruits for the Army generally.

The depot gradually acquired many and varied duties both towards the regiment and the Service generally. To mention a few: the storage and cataloguing of the heavy baggage of the regular battalions and of innumerable kits; the supply of clothing and necessaries during the early months by direct purchase from dealers; the charge of the 2nd Battalion band boys; and—a difficult task for the adjutant—the responsibility for all invalids of the regiment from overseas. These, taken on the strength of the depot, had to be traced in the various hospitals and touch kept with them till passed to the 3rd or 9th Battalion on discharge from hospital. Convalescents were for a long period sent to the depot for hardening before rejoining for service. A novel feature was the Agricultural Company, under a special officer, comprising men of different regiments from overseas or on home service. These men were employed in large numbers on farms, the depot being responsible for their general supervision and for arrangements with the farmers as to employment, pay, board and lodging.

Among old Buffs and others serving at different times during the war at the depot and in the Recruiting Area were: Majors F. Bradley Dyne, R. G. A. Marriott, D.S.O., G. A. Porter, A. H. Tylden-Pattenson, D.S.O. (Adjutant), and Captain H. H. C. Baird, D.S.O.; Major W. Tufnell, M.B.E., and Captain V. T. Dampier Palmer, O.B.E. (Recruiting Officer), late 3rd Battalion The Buffs ; Captain S. Kelsey Burge (Agricultural Officer), late 4th Battalion ; Major H. Paine, late Cheshire Regiment ; Major G. Croft (Quartermaster), late Royal Sussex Regiment ; R.S.M. J. W. Harris, C.S.M. G. Holmes, Col.-Sgts. F. H. Wright and F. H. Sheppard, Orderly Room Clerk F. Freeman.

III. THE 3RD (S.R.) BATTALION

As regards details of the various battalions which in 1914 were either home units or being raised in England, the 3rd had, when Militia, served with distinction in South Africa. It was now, as has been said, under the command of Lt.-Colonel Hirst, but its duties, as well as its name, had undergone marked change. Fifteen years before it had volunteered as a unit for active service, had been accepted and had proved its value. Now a much more weary and thankless task was required of the Special Reserve. It must accept thousands and thousands of recruits, equip them, train them and then, as soon as the men showed promise of doing the battalion real credit, draft them off to the other Buffs at the seat of war, never to see them again unless, returning maimed or worn out, a few should drift back to Dover marked for " home service only." Truly a heart-breaking job for the colonel and his staff.

The station of the battalion was the Citadel at Dover, and its strength at times exceeded a hundred officers and two thousand other ranks. Drafts for service were constantly being despatched and the gaps thus left as constantly being filled up, mostly by fresh recruits, both officers and men; either those joining late because they at first had failed to understand the urgent need there was for their services, or because they were so many months older than when war commenced and now could pass muster as men, often by the help of a little forgetfulness as to the exact date of their birth. It was quite remarkable not only in Kent, but throughout the country, how many young lads, thorough men in everything except years, struggled to get accepted as officers or soldiers. Many people in 1914 entertained the idea that the British race had deteriorated in manly qualities from the old stock, but the spirit shown at home, as well as the work done abroad, very conclusively proved the contrary.

The history of the 3rd Battalion during the momentous years was a monotonous one. It could be nothing else. It took men, trained men and sent men out, but how it trained them and what sort of men it sent out is well exemplified by the following official report written by Lieut. A. Howard Reed (4th Battalion) to Colonel Hirst relative to a draft despatched by him for the 10th Battalion late in the year 1917 : " I have the " honour to report on the conduct of the men of the " draft from your Battalion on the occasion of the tor- " pedoing of H.M.S. . . . as follows:—

" The whole draft paraded at their station with the " utmost calmness. L.-Sgt. Canfor (who had been

" blown up by the explosion, and who was severely
" shaken) called the roll . . . whilst the men detailed
" cut loose the rafts, the remainder sang until the rafts
" were launched. L.-Corpl. Baker volunteered to jump
" from the rails to secure a raft which had no painter.
" This he did, and succeeded in bringing it alongside,
" thereby assuring the safety of about twenty men.
" Owing to their splendid discipline, I was able to get
" every man safely into the water, and clinging to rafts.
" After about two and a half hours in the water we
" were rescued, with the exception of one man (Pte.
" Howlett) of whom I can find no trace. Whilst on the
" rafts the men sang continuously, and cheered the
" work of rescue, and generally behaved in a most gal-
" lant manner. I am unable, of course, to give you any
" details of the terrible affair, which was enough to try
" the courage of the bravest men, but I wish to say, Sir,
" that the behaviour of these men was above reproach.
" I am proud to have been in command of such a draft,
" and, in my opinion, their conduct nobly upheld the
" honour of our Regiment, and deserves a place in the
" history of the deeds accomplished by it. Recommen-
" dations have been asked for, and I have submitted the
" names of Sgt. Canfor, L.-Corpl. Baker and one
" Private."

Commenting privately on this adventure, Howard
Reed stated: " I had planned out in advance exactly
" what to do if we got hit, as it was up to me to do the
" best for them when the emergency arose. I was for-
" tunate in having men who unhesitatingly obeyed my
" orders, showed absolute trust in myself and behaved
" like heroes." The name of the vessel was the *Aragon*,
and the date of the disaster the 30th December, 1917.

IVA. 4TH BATTALION

The 4th and 5th Battalions of the Buffs were Territorials, and when war was declared they were both out

for their annual training at Longmore with their division—" The Home Counties." Every Territorial unit had what was called special service sections—that is, a few selected men were always held in readiness to guard, in case of sudden emergencies, important strategic points throughout the country. These special sections of the 4th Battalion were mobilized as early as 28th July—a week before war broke out—and were consequently amongst the very first to be put on a war footing, at a time, indeed, when very few of their countrymen had begun to think that England was on the verge of this tremendous epoch of her history. These men were despatched to safeguard the wireless stations in Thanet and the cable at Dumpton Gap. On the 5th August the battalion was completely mobilized at Dover and was in the new Connaught Barracks there to guard the nearest point to the Continent till their place could be taken by the 3rd or Special Reserve Battalion. A few days later the Kent Infantry Brigade retired to Canterbury and was billeted there.

Here Lt.-Colonel G. Gosling, commanding, called for volunteers to serve in France or elsewhere abroad, and in response to his appeal enough stout fellows volunteered to serve anywhere to ensure that the 4th Buffs could be reckoned on as an overseas unit. Those who failed to volunteer formed the nucleus of a new battalion for home service only and were denominated the 2/4th Battalion.

The following extract from the *Kentish Gazette* describes the situation after the battalion became an overseas unit:—

" Towards the end of August, 1914, when the Ger-
" mans were devastating Belgium and there were grave
" probabilities of a raid on the coast, the 4th Battalion
" was suddenly ordered to Thanet. Recruits flocked in
" from East Kent until the battalion was nearly 1,300
" strong. The training was carried on under difficult

" conditions and a great deal of discomfort, but the
" cheerful willingness to learn made things easy, so that
" by the middle of October a very fine battalion was
" ready to be sent wherever required. Just before the
" end of October, 1914, the 4th Battalion and part of
" the Home Counties Division was ordered to India, to
" enable the Regulars to be moved from India to
" France."

It is noteworthy that of this rush of patriotic young
men to swell the ranks of the 4th Battalion, which is
referred to in the extract I have quoted, forty-four
students from Wye College joined in one day.

It was on the 29th October that the battalion left
Thanet, as did all the rest of the Home Counties Division, with the exception of the 4th Royal West Surrey,
detached for other important services. At Suez and
Aden the convoy was delayed three and four days respectively owing to the activity of the Turks, who had
already attacked Perim and were now threatening the
Canal. In fact, the battalion disembarked at Suez and
marched through the town as a demonstration.

IVB. 5TH BATTALION

The early war history of the 5th Battalion, which it
will be remembered was also a Territorial one, re-
sembles that of its twin the 4th. Indeed, the two were
together in the Kentish Brigade of the Home Counties
Division. On mobilization it was sent to Dover, afterwards to Canterbury and then to Sandwich, where it
relieved the Kent Cyclists, and late in October it too
sailed for India in the *Corsican,* under command of
Lt.-Colonel Munn-Mace, T.D. It was quartered at
Kamptee and formed part of the Jubbulpore Brigade,
for on the arrival of the Territorial divisions from
England in relief of the white part of the Indian garrison, their original home organization in brigades and

divisions fell through, and each unit had to join the brigades and divisions already existing in India.

Whatever could be made of the existing British forces, however, could never suffice to meet the great emergency. Huge new armies must be formed, trained and, what was still more difficult, equipped to go direct to the seat of war ; and so our island became for the first time in its history one vast training camp, and every man that was a man and young enough turned his hand to war. Times were almost as critical during certain periods of the Napoleonic Wars a hundred years before, but, of course, in those days campaigns, however important, were fought with very small armies because there was nothing to transport, feed and supply the same but a few sailing ships by sea and horse-drawn carts by land. But now times had changed in this respect and each nation put in the field the largest force it could muster and equip. So steps were at once taken in England.

V. THE 6TH BATTALION

On the 22nd August, 1914, Major W. A. Eaton, who had been in command of the depot until the mobilization of the 3rd Battalion, which he accompanied to Dover, received a telegram ordering him to proceed to Colchester to take over command of a 6th Battalion of his regiment about to be raised there. On arrival with his servant[1] he found nothing but some empty barracks which had been vacated in haste. That evening, however, a draft consisting of Captain B. E. Furley, Lieut. (adjutant) T. Wheler, 2nd Lieut. E. H. Allen and about one hundred men arrived—the nucleus of the first Service Battalion of the Buffs to be raised, a

---

[1] No. L/8907 Pte. David Alexander served in France continuously throughout the war until he was killed a few weeks before the Armistice, having won the Military Medal and attained the rank of company sergeant major.

battalion consisting of men who had without hesitation responded to Lord Kitchener's call to arms.

Drafts arrived almost daily, as did officers, old and new: Major C. P. Lloyd as second in command, Lieut. D. K. Anderson, who happened to be home on leave from India, and, as Regimental Sergeant-Major and Quartermaster-Sergeant respectively, N. Linwood and A. Scragg, both of whom came to join the battalion without a moment's delay at the urgent request of the commanding officer. 2nd Lieut. Hugh Brodie, well known at Canterbury as an " Old Stager," was the first New Army officer to report, and he was soon followed by others. Practically the last two drafts were composed of men, in all about 250, from the firm of William Cory and Son, Ltd.,[1] who went to form D Company under Captain G. B. T. Friend. This company was always known as Cory's, and 2nd Lieut. Hamilton Greig, son of the managing director, was afterwards posted to it on transfer. Soon the battalion was over strength, but more men kept on arriving, turning up without warning from all sorts of directions.

Anyone who served with one of Kitchener's battalions during the latter part of 1914 and the beginning of the following year will remember what it was like. Genuine hard work and honest efforts on the part of all to make bricks with so very little straw. It is easier to collect heroes for the defence of their country than to arm, clothe and equip them; and the number of men got very far in advance of the amount of necessaries for them. A new battalion at this period was not a pretty sight. A very ugly and shoddy suit of blue was doled

---

[1] In those days many firms promised extravagant terms to those of their employees who enlisted, but in many cases such undertakings were not fulfilled. Messrs. Cory and Son, let it be said to their undying credit, played the game throughout by their men and their dependents, and were moreover the most liberal supporters of any fund that was for the benefit of the battalion.

out to the soldier, with a civilian greatcoat and generally a dummy rifle, and with this turn-out he did real strenuous drill and training. Old service rifles, for drill purposes only, began to come in later on, and the men gradually obtained sufficient blankets and clothing. Nothing daunted the spirit of the troops, however, and life was cheery enough.

In November the 6th Battalion moved into hutments at Sandling Camp, near Shorncliffe. Owing to the rain and lack of any drainage system, the camp quickly became a sea of mud, the huts uninhabitable, even with tents inside ; and so, just before Christmas, the battalion went into billets about the villages of Elham and Lyminge, and very good billets they were. The householders one and all seemed to vie with each other as to who could do their men the best. Nor will the officers ever forget all the kindness which was shown to them.

The following is an extract from a letter written by the commanding officer, after clothing and rifles had at last been issued :—

" It was on one Sunday while we were in these billets
" that the battalion, accompanied by the band of the
" 3rd Battalion, generously lent to us for the occasion,
" went to Canterbury and attended a special service
" most kindly arranged for us by the Dean[1] at the
" Cathedral, and at which we were privileged to hand
" in the Colours of the 2nd Battalion recently returned
" from India and gone to the front. With reference to
" this occasion I cannot refrain from quoting the fol-
" lowing extract from a letter received by me from an
" old Buff officer temporarily doing duty at the depot:

[1] The Dean, the Very Rev. Henry Wace, D.D., in arranging the service wrote as follows : " I assure you we regard it as one of our first and most honourable duties in the Cathedral to welcome the County Regiment."

" ' I cannot say how delighted I was at the appear-
" ance of your regiment. It was simply magnificent.
" Candidly I do not think I ever saw a finer body of
" men in any battalion since I joined the 1st in Cawn-
" pore in 1878. They were a fine lot averaging thir-
" teen years' service, but I think your lot even topped
" them.' "

The ceremony above referred to took place on the
31st January, 1915, and more advanced training at
Aldershot lasted from about then till the 1st June, when
yet another warlike body of Buffs made the great move
and sailed for France to show of what stuff the old
regiment was made. This battalion belonged to the
37th Infantry Brigade of the 12th Division, the Brigadier being G. A. Fowler, and the Divisional Commander Major-General James Spens, C.B. (brother to
a well-known and much beloved old Buff), but he was
succeeded by Major-General F. D. V. Wing, C.B.,
when the division went to France. The other battalions of the 37th Brigade were: 6th Queens, 7th East
Surrey, 6th Royal West Kent.

The officers embarking for France were:—

Commanding Officer.	Lt.-Colonel W. A. Eaton.
2nd in Command.	Major C. P. Lloyd.
Adjutant.	Captain T. Wheler.
Quartermaster.	Lieut. N. Linwood.

A Company.	*B Company.*
Major B. E. Furley.	Captain R. P. Wedd.
Lieut. H. W. Brodie.	,, Lord Teynham.
,, T. H. Crowther.	Lieut. C. D. Gullick.
2nd Lieut. J. C. Page.	2nd Lieut. J. C. T. Leigh.
,, C. W. B. Marsh.	,, S. A. Erle-
,, D. Lambert.	bach.

C Company.	*D Company.*
Captain C. E. G. David-	Captain G. B. T. Friend.
son.	Major A. Soames, D.S.O.
Lieut. P. A. C. Kelsey.	(acting).
,,　R. O. C. Ward.	Lieut. R. Hodgson.
2nd Lieut. C. E. H. Druitt.	,,　A. L. Gullick.
,,　C. Bainbridge.	2nd Lieut. G. H. Greig.
	,,　R. H. Williams.

Transport Officer.

Lieut. A. D. R. Terry.

Medical Officer.

Lieut. J. R. Driberg.

R.S.M. W. Jeffries.　　　R.Q.M.S. A. J. Scragg.

After a day at Boulogne the battalion went by train to St. Omer and from there marched to Remilly-Werquin. Here it had two or three days' rest and then, in the hottest weather, marched by stages, passing the Commander-in-Chief on the way, to billets and bivouacs at Meteren, near Bailleul, which brought it, of course, into the immediate vicinity of the two regular battalions.

VI.　7TH BATTALION

As has already been shown, the 6th Battalion was much over strength within a very short time of its raising, and from the surplus of this unit arose the 7th Battalion. By the 17th September this consisted of two thousand men, all in plain clothes. There was a common expectation at this time that khaki uniform was all ready for the recruits who came up voluntarily to serve and that the men would be turned out soldiers, as far as clothes were concerned, with the utmost promptitude. This was unfortunately not the case, and as, naturally,

72

the recruit under the circumstances joined in his very worst garments, the battalion, like others, was soon ridiculously ragged. It was some days before uniform of any sort was handed out, and then it was but a temporary makeshift. A few D.P. (drill purpose) rifles were available for each company.

The birthplace of the 7th Buffs was Purfleet, Essex, and the first officers belonging to it were Captain B. E. Furley (temporarily), Lieut. E. H. Allen and 2nd Lieut. A. G. Kenchington, who were transferred from the 6th Battalion with 1,600 recruits, 600 of whom passed on again to start the 8th Battalion. The first regularly appointed commanding officer was Lt.-Colonel Gilbert Johnson, who assumed command at the end of September, and his second-in-command was Major A. F. Campbell Johnston, very well known a few years back in the 2nd Battalion and who did good work as regards instilling the ancient regimental spirit into new soldiers' minds. Both the new officers and the new men showed the greatest keenness and anxiety to learn, and with such a state of things the manufacture of a new fighting unit becomes comparatively easy. As in the case of other units, the senior officers and warrant officers were, generally speaking, men who had retired from the service, and though in some cases their knowledge and methods were somewhat antiquated, their experience was invaluable and their zeal indubitable. There were also a considerable number of veteran privates, and so it was that the new armies at first consisted of old soldiers time-expired, who felt bound to present themselves again, and spirited young fellows who did not wait for conscription. This was a great combination, for the former, though for the most part somewhat obsolete, were zealous and could, at any rate, teach the rudiments, and the latter were so eager to learn that teaching became a pleasure. Being young and business-like, they soon passed the old men as com-

73

petent soldiers because they assimilated what the others had to teach and added practical go-ahead methods. The respectful love and sympathy of the new soldier for his white-headed instructor was quite touching, and the old man, loving to come back to his ancient trade, appreciated fully the fine type of recruit he had now to deal with. Thus a quaint spirit of friendship and a curious comradeship arose, which did much to make Kitchener's armies what they were and to instil a spirit of *esprit de corps* and honour. It was a pity that later on recruits were posted to any corps that required reinforcements at the time, but, after all, these were for the most part conscripts. Amongst the new hands were men from various parts of England, though the majority came from Kent. The junior officers were of almost every profession and business and were wonderfully eager and full of *esprit de corps*.

The remainder of the year of 1914 was spent in hard and steady drill and training and short temporary moves of quarters. There were two changes of commanders by February, 1915, Colonel Johnson leaving on the 14th November and Lt.-Colonel Young, of the Indian Army, relieving him, being himself replaced by Lt.-Colonel W. F. Elmslie, of the Lancashire Fusiliers, a little later. On the 3rd March, 1915, Major Campbell Johnston was transferred elsewhere. He was relieved by Major C. Parmiter, of the King's Liverpool Regiment, who ten years before had been adjutant of the 1st V.B. The Buffs. By March the battalion had advanced as far as brigade training, and in April the route came for Colchester, where the rest of the 18th Division was assembled. Manœuvres in Suffolk under General F. J. Maxse, commencing at the end of April, were a preliminary to a series of pretty strenuous brigade and divisional field days in Wiltshire directly afterwards. On the 9th June General Poett left the 55th Brigade, which was taken over by Br.-General Martyn, late of the Royal West

74

Kent. H.M. The King inspected the division at Stonehenge on the 24th June and expressed himself well pleased. July saw the end of the preliminary work. Final leave was commenced on the 7th.

The Colonel of the Buffs, General Sir Arthur Paget, inspected the battalion on the 13th, and on the 27th July the brigade left its camp at Codford for Folkestone *en route* for Boulogne, to be merged into the valiant army of Britain and her Colonies, an army destined to prove, and which indeed had already proved, that the modern Englishman was bred true to type and was a worthy descendant of his heroic sires.

VII.   8TH BATTALION

In September, 1914, when all the real manhood of England not already soldiers were crowding to the Colours, and when elderly men and young boys were so strangely forgetful as to the years of their birth, and when all birth certificates of gallant Englishmen at either end of what is called military age were so universally mislaid and lost, Colonel F. C. Romer, C.B., C.M.G., then in his sixty-fourth year, was offered his choice of raising any one of three specified Service Battalions, and he chose to raise the 8th Battalion of the Buffs. He was a member of Boodles and at the time honorary secretary of the club. He was a believer in mature men and wished, at any rate, to have a certain leaven of the middle-aged amongst his officers, so his first step was to turn to a few of his club friends, and Major Dansy, Major A. Crawley, Captain Hare, Captain W. Howard, Lieut. Sir William Cooke and Captain W. D. Johnson immediately followed their leader, as did two of the club waiters. All of them were over forty years of age except, perhaps, the two privates. The considerable detachment from Boodles Club above referred to proceeded to camp at Shoreham, where

75

they found awaiting them Captain E. C. Norman (adjutant), Regimental Sergt.-Major A. Barton, four N.C.O.'s and a draft of five hundred odd from Canterbury. By the end of September the full complement of officers had arrived and training was going on in earnest and continued very strenuously all October, in spite of a complete lack of every necessity: clothing, arms, boots, equipment, camp furniture and even army forms. In the first week the battalion was inspected by the divisional commander, everybody but the officers and one or two N.C.O.'s being in mufti, and some in rags. This state of things, however, was common enough in our island at this period and nobody minded and all went well, because the old soldiers were keen to pass on all they knew and the young ones to absorb every kind of military knowledge.

The month of November brought a change for the worse in the way of weather, and things were not so pleasant. The parade ground was a sea of mud, tents leaked and men were seldom dry and never very clean. On more than one occasion rows of tents were flooded out and whole companies marched out at night to find what shelter they could. The officers' mess, the board-schools and even the station waiting-room were, at different times, used as billets for the soaked and shivering battalion. Hopes of moving shortly into new huts did something to cheer the somewhat drooping spirits, but, owing to shortage of labour, these were not completed till months after the specific date, and on the 1st December the brigade moved into billets at Worthing, a very welcome change. The winter passed comfortably in billets, but there were renewed delays as regards equipment.

On the 1st April, 1915, the battalion proceeded to Reigate for a hard fortnight of trench digging. The system of entrenching which now obtained in the army in France differed widely from that to which the instructors still in England were accustomed to, and the works turned out by the zealous new armies at this time differed considerably from those with which they later on became familiar. The next move was back to the old camp, where the hutments were at last ready for occupation. It is always easier to train during the summer season than at other times, and the long days at battalion and brigade field days brought the unit more forward than all the previous months. There were, about June, upwards of forty officers in the 8th Battalion, and even this figure was small when compared with other corps. In June there was another journey, this time to the Aisne Barracks at Blackdown near Aldershot. The object now was divisional training during July and August, culminating in a review by Lord Kitchener and a week's trench digging at Chobham. The battalion provided the King's Guard during His Majesty's visit to Aldershot in August. During the third week in August rumours of going abroad grew stronger, and the last week or so was spent in feverish preparation. The battalion eventually sailed on the night of the 31st August/1st September as part of the 72nd Infantry Brigade and 24th Division. And now five battalions of the Buffs were warring in France and two serving their country in India. The officers of the 8th Battalion who embarked for the war were Colonel F. C. Romer, C.B., C.M.G., in command, Major D. F. Robinson, 2nd in command, Captain F. W. Watson, adjutant, Lieut. A. Barton, recently promoted Qr.-Master, 2nd Lieut. E. T. Smith, M.G. Officer, Lieut. J. R. Spensley, R.A.M.C.

A Company.	*B Company.*
Major Guy Warden.	Capt. W. Howard.
Capt. A. M. C. Hollist.	„ A. G. Hamilton.
Lieut. F. D. Mont-	Lieut. P. J. F. Brine.
gomerie.	2nd Lieut. G. L. Thorp.

77

Lieut. T. H. Taylor.	2nd Lieut. Hon. H. E. J.
2nd Lieut. E. F. Corner.	Robinson.
„ E. C. Wanstall.	2nd Lieut. R. B. Carrow.

C Company.	*D Company.*
Capt. T. R. M. Shervinton.	Capt. J. Kekewich.
„ C. H. Cardozo.	„ W. D. Johnson.
Lieut. G. A. P. Jones.	Lieut. J. L. Samuelson.
„ C. H. Herepath.	„ V. S. Daniell.
2nd Lieut. J. Vaughan.	„ S. Vaughan.
„ G. Lindley.	„ B. H. Pickering.

VIII.   2ND AND 3RD LINE TERRITORIALS

In addition to the troops sent from our country to the various war theatres, there was a very considerable army kept up at home during the whole four years of war. The main duty of this force was, of course, to find reinforcements for the units abroad, but the safety of our own shores had all the while also to be considered.

Invasion, properly so called, may have been an impossibility, at any rate, till the British Fleet had been sunk, because an invasion takes time: armies and enormous quantities of munitions, stores and horses must be landed and arrangements made to keep up connection between the invading troops and the country they come from. But this is not the case with raids: comparatively small forces can sometimes be landed in an enemy's country, do an infinity of damage and destruction for a day or two and then re-embark. To guard against a possibility of anything of this sort happening was another and very important duty of the home army, and there were other reasons for its maintenance. When the bulk of the 4th and 5th (Territorial) Battalions of the Buffs volunteered for foreign service, those who did not do so were still willing enough to fulfil their original undertaking to aid in guarding their native shores, and these men formed the nucleus of new battalions for home service only, called the 2/4th and 2/5th.

The 2/4th was formed at Ashford, Kent, under Lt.-Colonel Skey, and the following month proceeded to Sunninghill and Ascot, but its station during the first portion of 1915 was Rochester, and its vicinity and later on it went to Sevenoaks. The intensive training which had necessarily obtained in the case of the battalions required for immediate war service was not in the nature of things pressed so persistently on units of the home army, and their training was of a steadier and slower description. Regular garrison duties were carried out, which included a considerable amount of guard work when at Strood and Rochester. In May, 1915, the 2/4th and the 2/5th Buffs each furnished one company complete for a Kent composite battalion to serve in the Gallipoli Peninsula, which unit will be referred to later. Lt.-Colonel Atkinson was in command about the middle of 1915, and a year later the 2/4th went back into the Ashford district. There were very numerous drafts found and sent overseas by the 2/4th. These generally went to the 1/4th in India, but there were notable exceptions; for instance, in August, 1916, nearly four hundred men went to France to the 18th and 19th London Regiment and to the King's Royal Rifles. The battalion was disbanded in August, 1917.

Colonel C. Hawley Williams, V.D., Honorary Colonel of the 4th Battalion of The Queen's Own (Royal West Kent) Regiment was appointed, when the 5th Buffs went to India, to command the home-keeping remnant which made the 2/5th. He had Major (Hon. Colonel) the Viscount Goschen, V.D., as his second-in-command. The battalion belonged to the Second-line Kent Infantry Brigade, and like its neighbour the

2/4th, it underwent several moves, and was at Ashford, Ascot and Bracknell successively. Recruiting was carried on, but as the Weald of Kent is not very thickly populated, the number did not increase as rapidly as in the case of some other units, though very considerable efforts were made. The progress of training was retarded by lack of instructors, lack of equipment and lack of rifles, but the officers and men neglected no effort to become efficient and difficulties were gradually overcome. The history of the 2/5th was much the same as that of the 2/4th. It, too, went through a period of service near Chatham and was worked heavily at the guard duties, and it, too, as has been stated above, sent a company to Gallipoli.

The 3/4th Battalion of the Buffs was raised by Major L. C. R. Messel, T.D., at Canterbury in July, 1915, and Lieut. G. C. Bateman from the 2/4th was appointed adjutant with the temporary rank of captain. The establishment was originally only one company, commanded by a major, but this was shortly increased to two and an excess of strength up to fifty per cent permitted. Lieut. R. Smith, late of the Buffs and Army Pay Department, became Quarter-Master, and that well-known and greatly respected veteran, J. Bennell, Regtl. Sergt.-Major, up till February, 1916, when he was relieved by C.S.M. C. Brown. On the 31st December, 1915, the battalion moved to Cambridge, together with other units of the third-line groups (as they were called) of the Home Counties Division. Later on the whole went to Crowborough.

The 3/5th was raised by Major Charles P. Kingsland of the 2/5th. The original description was Third-line Depot 5th Battalion The Buffs, but this was soon altered to 3/5th The Buffs, and in 1916 to 5th Reserve Battalion The Buffs. The establishment was the same as that of the last-mentioned unit, but in 1916 it was

increased to 750 men in consequence of the 1/5th being
in Mesopotamia. At this time also the commanding
officer was given the temporary rank of lieutenant-
colonel. Major A. Stuart Elmslie was at first the adjutant, but later became second-in-command. R.S.M.
Bolton, 1st Battalion The Buffs, was regimental sergeant-major. This unit also joined their third-line
group at Cambridge at the very end of 1915, and
it was accommodated in Trinity College, and it also
went to Crowborough in 1916, having sent a large
draft from Cambridge to Mesopotamia. On the 1st
September, 1916, the battalion was amalgamated with
the 3/4th, and with it became the 4th Reserve Battalion of The Buffs, under the command of Lt.-Colonel
L. C. R. Messel, T.D. It was part of the Home
Counties Reserve Brigade, and had a strength now of
no less than 1,560 men. A little later it became the
reserve unit for the 10th Buffs, of whom we shall hear
later. In October, 1917, Lt.-Colonel Messel was succeeded by Major W. D. Sword from the North Staffordshire Regiment.

IX. VOLUNTEERS

On the 6th August, 1914, a letter appeared in *The
Times* signed by Mr. Percy A. Harris, advocating the
formation and training of Volunteer Corps. At the end
of the month the War Office vetoed the raising of
volunteer units, but gave sanction to organize *Training*
Corps, and these sprang up all over the country and
began to recruit for the oversea armies. The county was
the unit of organization, and County Commandants
were appointed. At the end of 1915 the revival of
the Volunteer Act passed Parliament, which awarded
military rank and status, and from this time on the
Training Corps were termed Volunteer Corps, and if
called up to repel invasion the officers and men were to
become subject to military law. Only those men who

G   81

were too old to serve abroad or whose indispensable business or employment absolutely prevented them doing so were enrolled.

So far as Kent was concerned Lord Harris, the County Commandant, took charge of the county force and called it " Kent Volunteer Fencibles," but in August, 1916, the War Office, taking the matter more decidedly in hand, the several units were made into Volunteer Battalions of the county regiments.

In East Kent there were four of these :—

1st Volunteer Battalion was commanded by Br.-General W. Tylden; 2nd by Major J. C. Tattersall; 3rd Volunteer Battalion by Major-General C. F. Browne, C.B., D.S.O.; 4th Volunteer Battalion by Major H. E. T. W. Fiennes. General Brown retiring on the 16th December, the 3rd Battalion was taken over by Major H. T. Gullick, who had lost one son in the Buffs and had another still fighting with the regiment.

X. 9TH BATTALION

Mention has not been made yet of the very useful and important unit the 9th Battalion, because this held rather a unique position. It was not in August, when war broke out, in existence at all, and so could hardly be described as Special Reserve, though its duties were exactly similar to those of the 3rd Battalion from which it was, in fact, an off-shoot. Its history is briefly as follows: it was first of all raised as a Service Battalion, just as were the 6th, 7th and 8th, but being the junior unit its organization was delayed simply because there was so much work to do in connection with those battalions which were first for war. Early in October, 1914, instructions were issued to carry out the work of starting the new battalion, and as the number on the books of the 3rd, which was at the Citadel, Dover, was at this time far in excess of what is manageable as a single unit, some eleven officers and seven hundred men were struck off its strength, placed under the command of Major Layborn and sent into the old South Front Barracks close by, as the 9th Buffs. A few old members of the regiment had been detailed as instructors. Captain Hickman was sent to aid in starting the battalion and, until things got into good working order, Lieut. G. Dunster was quartermaster, Captain Courtney-Hood was the permanent adjutant, Reville Sgt.-Major, Edwards, Q.M.S. and Winstanley the O.R. sergeant. Very few of the company officers had any previous military experience, but energy and zeal are valuable assets, and the 9th was rapidly preparing to take its place in war; Lt.-Colonel R. A. Reith, a former commanding officer of the 3rd Battalion, was appointed to the command, and the 95th Brigade was formed from the 9th Buffs, 10th East Surrey, 14th and 15th Royal Fusiliers. Higher divisional training was expected to take place in the spring, and there seemed to be every prospect of a move across the Channel in the summer of 1915 when, in March, all hopes and ambitions were dashed to the ground by the receipt of news that the battalion's destination was after all to be Purfleet in Essex, and that it was to be a home-keeping and draft-finding unit, exactly like the 3rd Battalion. In July the first draft went to war. Three hundred men entrained at Purfleet for London and marched from Fenchurch Street to London Bridge Station by a circuitous route to show themselves and exercise the Buffs' old and long-established privilege of passing along the City of London streets with bayonets fixed and all honours of war. The party on this occasion was headed by the band and drums and the Lord Mayor showed himself at the Mansion House to take the salute. The London crowd gave the men a proper and, indeed, an enthusiastic

83

send-off, and there was much cheering and waving of handkerchiefs. In September came a move to Shoreham, Sussex, whence many drafts departed, mostly to the old regular battalions; but the enormous one of forty officers and five hundred men went to the 8th Battalion to replace the terrible losses that unit suffered at Loos. There is no space to record more. The 9th did its duty like the others, the headquarters moving sometimes, once again to Dover and later to Southend, but the men, as in the case of the 3rd Battalion, constantly proceeding overseas in batches. The only marked change that came was in January, 1917, when the battalion was selected for the training of a large number of "A4 Boys"[1] called out at that time, with the result that the numbers rose to nearly three thousand, and four new companies had to be organized.

Six months afterwards most of the original officers and permanent N.C.O.'s went back to the 3rd Battalion, and the 9th Buffs became the 52nd Queen's, in which capacity it went to France, when the dangerous days of March, 1918, had come; it ended its career as part of the army of occupation in Germany after the armistice.

The story of the 10th Battalion and of the Queen's Own Rifles of Canada will be told later in the book.

---

[1] "A4 Boys" were lads of eighteen passed fit, but retained at home for a year on account of age.

CHAPTER IV

THE WESTERN FRONT—LOOS

I. 1st Battalion

THE history of the 1st Battalion for June and July, 1915, is without any very striking incident, though abounding in what only a year before would have been considered as such. On the 10th June, for instance, the huts near Poperinghe, in which the men were resting, were heavily shelled and Lieut. W. F. Taylor and 10 men killed and 5 more wounded; whilst on the 19th of the same month, when in trenches in the salient east of Ypres, the battalion was badly bombarded with gas shells, while more gas was pumped from the enemy's lines, necessitating the wearing of gas helmets for four hours and causing the death of 5 and injury of 19 men. Then 2 more were killed on the following day and 4 wounded and 5 gassed. Between this date and the end of the month 10 more died and 39 were wounded. On the 2nd July Corpl. John Dormer of A Company, who had covered himself with glory as a scout, paid the last penalty. And so the weary business went on.

Sir John French's despatches contain the following remarks:—

" Since my last despatch a new device has been
" adopted by the enemy for driving burning liquid
" into our trenches with a strong jet. Thus supported,
" an attack was made on the trenches of the 2nd Army
" at Hooge, on the Menin road, early on 30th July.
" Most of the infantry occupying these trenches were
" driven back, but their retirement was due far more to

" the surprise and temporary confusion caused by the
" burning liquid than by the actual damage inflicted.

" Gallant endeavours were made by repeated
" counter-attacks to recapture the lost section of
" trenches. These, however, proving unsuccessful and
" costly, a new line of trenches was consolidated a
" short distance further back.

" Attacks made by the enemy at the same time west
" of Bellewaarde Lake were repulsed.

" On the 9th August these losses were brilliantly re-
" gained, owing to a successful attack carried out by
" the 6th Division. This attack was very well executed
" and resulted in the recapture, with small casualties,
" not only of the whole of the lost trenches, but an
" addition of four hundred yards of German trench
" north of the Menin road."

In connection with this incident mentioned by the
Commander-in-Chief, Major-General Congreve, V.C.,
commanding the 6th Division, addressed the 1st Buffs
on the 5th August: it was necessary, he pointed out, to
retake the trenches previously lost at Hooge. It was a
case either of going forward or going backward, owing
to the nature of the ground. The commander of the
2nd Army had selected the 6th Division for the task
because it was the best one in his command. He would
not minimize the difficulties of the job, but the battalion would remember their past record and the fact
that the eyes of Kent were upon them. He concluded
by wishing the battalion a successful issue and a safe
return.

Consequent on this a brigade order was issued on
the 8th August, of which the following are extracts,
and it may be as well to explain here that all over the
fighting front the soldiers had given names to the
different trenches in order to distinguish them, and
that these names, which were often those of London

ROAD NEAR HOOGE

streets, but sometimes of a comic nature, became officially recognized and used.

" The brigade will attack the enemy's position at " Hooge from the crater to Q.20 inclusive.

" The York and Lancaster will attack on the left and " the K.S.L.I. on the right.

" 1st Buffs' 2 machine guns in southern branch of " Oxford Street at end east. D Company and 2 " machine guns in F.2.

" A Company and 1 machine gun to dig themselves " in in line eighty yards in rear of Headquarters' " trench.

" B Company and Headquarters to occupy position " end of Oxford Street by 1.15 B and D.

" All companies to be in position 12.30 a.m., 9th.

" The 1st Leicesters will be in support in the ram-" parts of Menin Gate, Ypres.

" The right attack is allotted to the 18th Brigade, " and the 17th Brigade will be in divisional reserve.

" The K.S.L.I. can call on C Company The Buffs " for support, if necessary, and the Y. and L. on D " Company.

" Should the enemy drive us back and follow on, " these two companies must counter-attack at once " without hesitation."

The battalion took its places at 6.30 p.m. on the 8th. A Company, so as to be ready to occupy the positions vacated by C and D should they be called upon to move up, and B Company remaining as battalion reserve. At 2.45 a.m. on the 9th the British bombardment opened and a terrific fire was brought to bear on the hostile lines. The infantry attack followed about 3.10, the assailants having already crept up close to the enemy's lines, and the brave men from Yorkshire and Shropshire suffered pretty heavily, but were completely successful. D Company of the Buffs was called

87

up to help by the York and Lancaster Regiment. The
K.S.L.I. had rushed into the crater with great
rapidity and found much hand-to-hand fighting to do
when they got there. The telephone lines were soon
useless, being cut to pieces by the incessant fire. In the
small hours of the 10th August the Buffs were ordered
to relieve both the York and Lancasters and the Shropshires. D Company, therefore, advanced obliquely to
its right flank and took over the crater and half the
recaptured line which belonged to its brigade, the
remainder being occupied by A Company, under
Captain Gould, who placed one platoon in support of
both these advanced companies at H.12. C Company
remained where it was and B, with Battalion Headquarters, came up to a ruined farm, a tactical point in
the neighbourhood. Heavy shelling occurred during
the night, but the expected German counter-attack did
not eventuate. A and D Companies found great difficulty in getting into touch with friends on either flank.
It is true that some troops of the neighbouring 18th
Brigade had, during the previous day, got into the
crater and stables, but these were themselves now
adrift from their units.

Four machine guns had been placed at intervals
along the whole front, and these, to judge by German
prisoners' letters, had a discouraging effect on the pro-
jected enemy counter-attack, but nevertheless the
position occupied by the two forward Buff companies
was very far from being a satisfactory or pleasant one:
the trenches and crater were full of dead and wounded,
chiefly German, but with many English, too, and this
fact impeded free movement; shell fire was heavy
and continuous, and the Heavy artillery enfilade fire
from the direction of Hill 60 was in particular very
annoying and dangerous; while the supply of bombs,
food and water was precarious and difficult owing to
the lack of proper communication trenches to the rear.

The want of water was particularly felt, and made worse by the fact that the men were within easy sight and distance of the Bellewaarde Lake.

The night of the 10th/11th was a very busy one. Every kind of work was urgent and of great importance. The removal of the wounded was no easy task, and great praise was due to Captain Jones, the Buffs' Medical Officer, who did wonders. Indeed, this officer was remarkable for his coolness and gallantry, and continued his business, though wounded twice himself, in a manner which has become a sort of tradition amongst our army doctors. He was admirably backed by the regimental stretcher-bearers. There were dead to be buried everywhere; there was no doubt in anyone's mind of the urgency of this. Communications in rear were organized, the trenches were improved, and many other matters made this night a busy one. The night was, moreover, by no means peaceful. The German bombers were persistent and dangerous on the left of A Company, but a somewhat serious bomb attack just before midnight in this quarter was repelled by Captain Gould, though not without loss. D Company was also being heavily bombarded by high explosive and shrapnel, and Captain R. W. Homan was struck on the head and fatally wounded. He had exposed himself with great gallantry in organizing the defence, and his death was much felt. The 11th August passed like the previous day and was a strenuous one. There was abnormally heavy shelling. The parapets were destroyed both in A and D Companies' portions of the line, and one shell, landing where the supporting platoon lay, demolished the telephone dug-out and destroyed the operators, but not the instrument. Pte. Wilson came forward and continued to work this, the nearest telephone to the firing line, and as from here all messages had to be carried, Corpl. Foote of A Company greatly distinguished himself at this task. D Company was under a most accurate fire this day, but was materially aided by the French artillery.

About 10 p.m. a violent bomb attack took place on the left of A Company, both from a small side trench on the left of ours, which was still in the enemy's hands, and from Germans who had crawled out from their retained line in rear. These latter were made to suffer somewhat severely. 2nd Lieut. Ferguson led a counter-attack under somewhat critical circumstances and was twice wounded. However, the enemy's attempt was repulsed, and at 11.30 a relief of the battalion was successfully accomplished under company arrangements, superintended by the commanding officer, Lt.-Colonel Finch Hatton, aided by Captain Lucas (second-in-command) and Lieut. Birrell (adjutant). The battalion retired to the ramparts of Ypres by the Menin Gate, having lost since the 5th of the month 25 killed, 162 wounded and 5 missing.

At this period not only the Buffs, but the 16th Brigade generally, were suffering badly from the lack of senior and experienced officers. A considerable period of routine work was now the fate of the battalion. As a rule, billets in or about Poperinghe alternated with trench duty, generally at La Brique. This trench duty continued to take its toll of casualties and was not without its deeds of daring, notably the rescue and bringing in of the body of Captain Colville of the Shropshire Light Infantry, who was killed in front of Forward Cottage near La Brique on the 21st September, 1915, for which act Lieut. Clouting and C.S.M. Baker received the M.C. and D.C.M. respectively.

II. Loos

In order to understand the parts taken in the battle of Loos by the 2nd, 6th and 8th Battalions of the Buffs, it would be well to have a general idea of why the battle was fought. Turning, therefore, to Sir John

French's despatches we find that after a serious consultation with General Joffre and a full discussion of the military situation it was arranged that the Allies should make a combined attack from certain points of their line during the last week in September.

Very many brave soldiers died in the prolonged and desperate struggle which followed, and which is known as the battle of Loos, though it was in reality a series of bloody combats. It still remains a question whether the British sacrifices there made were worth the results obtained.

The reinforcements the British had recently received enabled our Commander-in-Chief to comply with several requests that the French had made as to taking over additional portions of their line.

" In fulfilment of the rôle assigned to it in these " operations, our army attacked the enemy on the " morning of the 25th September. The main attack " was delivered by the 1st and 4th Corps between the " La Bassee Canal on the north and the village of " Grenay on the south; at the same time the 5th Corps " making a subsidiary attack on Bellewaarde Farm to " the east of Ypres in order to hold the enemy to his " ground; other attacks with a similar object were " made by the 3rd and Indian Corps north of the " canal and along the whole front of the second army.

" In co-operation with the French 10th Army on the " right, the 1st and 4th Corps went up to the attack. " A strong reserve was kept in hand owing to the great " length of front to be assailed, and the general com- " manding the Second Army was directed to draw back " the 28th Division to Bailleul and hold it in readiness " to meet unexpected eventualities.

" Opposite the front of the main line of attack the " distance between the enemy's trenches and our own " varied from about one hundred to five hundred " yards. The country over which the advance took

" place is open and overgrown with long grass and self-
" sown crops. From the canal southwards our trenches
" and those of the enemy ran roughly parallel upon an
" almost imperceptible rise to the south-west. From
" the Vermelles–Hulluch road southward the ad-
" vantage of height is on the enemy's side as far as the
" Bethune–Lens road. There the two lines of trenches
" cross a spur in which the rise culminates, and thence
" the command lies on the side of the British trenches.

" To the east of the intersection of spur and
" trenches and a short mile away stands Loos (which is
" about twenty-eight miles south of Ypres). Less than
" a mile further south-east is Hill 70, which is the
" summit of the gentle rise in the ground.

" Other notable tactical points on our front were:—

" *Fosse* 8 (a thousand yards south of Auchy) which
" is a coal mine with a high and strongly defended
" slag heap.

" *The Hohenzollern redoubt.* A strong work thrust
" out nearly five hundred yards in front of the German
" lines, and close to our own. It is connected with their
" front line by three communication trenches abutting
" into the defences of Fosse 8.

" *Cite St. Elie.* A strongly defended mining village
" lying fifteen hundred yards south of Haisnes.

" *The Quarries* lying half-way to the German
" trenches west of the Cite St. Elie.

" *Hulluch.* A village strung out along a small stream
" lying less than half a mile south-east of Cite St.
" Elie and three thousand yards north-east of Loos.

" *Puits* 14 *Bis.* Half a mile north of Hill 70; another
" coal mine possessing great possibilities for defence
" when taken in conjunction with a strong redoubt
" situated on the north-east side of Hill 70."

The attack was admirably delivered, and it is noteworthy that a complete division of the new armies took

a distinguished part in it. This was the 47th, a Scottish unit. Loos and Hill 70 were gained, and altogether the first day was a success and caused Field-Marshal French's apprehension that a dangerous gap might occur between ourselves and the French to be considerably modified. He now ordered the Guards Division up from Nœux les Mines and the 28th to move south from Bailleul. At nightfall, after a heavy day's fighting and numerous German counter-attacks, the line ran from the Double Crassier south of Loos by the western part of Hill 70 to the western exit of Hulluch, thence by the quarries and western end of Cite St. Elie, east of Fosse 8, back to the original line.

Our hold on Fosse 8, backed as it was by the strong defences and guns of Auchy, was distinctly precarious.

In the course of the night of 25th/26th September the enemy delivered a series of heavy counter-attacks along our new front, and near the Quarries they were more or less successful, though repulsed elsewhere.

On the 26th the 7th Division retook the Quarries, but attacks on Hulluch and on the redoubt on the east side of Hill 70 were anticipated by the enemy, who organized a very strong offensive from that direction. These attacks drove on the advanced troops of the 21st and 24th Divisions (in the latter of which the 8th Buffs were serving) which were then moving forward to attack. Sir John French adds these words: " Reports regarding this portion of the action are very " conflicting, and it is not possible to form an entirely " just appreciation of what occurred on this part of " the field."

During the 29th and 30th September and the early days of October, fighting was almost continuous along the northern part of the new line, particularly about the Hohenzollern Redoubt and neighbouring trenches, to which the enemy evidently attached great value.

His attacks, however, almost invariably broke down with very heavy loss under the accurate fire of our infantry and artillery. Nevertheless, the enemy re-captured part of the Hohenzollern Redoubt on the 3rd October. There was particularly severe fighting in this direction on the 8th and 9th, the hostile attack being repulsed with enormous loss. The Commander-in-Chief reports in his despatches that we attacked about noon on the 13th October, with troops of the 11th and 4th Corps, against Fosse No. 8, the Quarries and the German trenches on the Lens–La Bassee road. The objective of the 12th Division (in which were serving the 6th Buffs) was the Quarries.

The day began with an artillery bombardment of the objectives in which the French assisted. Shortly before the attack was launched at 2 p.m. smoke was turned on all along our front, and under cover of this smoke the attack was started. At the same time the heavy artillery lifted to further objectives, while the enemy's front trench system was subjected to shrapnel fire. At 2.45 the 4th Corps reported having captured 1,200 yards of trenches on the Lens–La Bassee road, but as the left battalion of the corps had failed, the Corps Commander did not consider it practicable to under-take any further offensive towards Hulluch. The in-formation received during the remainder of the day was very conflicting, though it was known that one battalion of the 12th Division had gained the south-west edge of the Quarries. In the course of the next two days the whole attack died down without attaining the objective aimed at, and the situation on that part of the line remained much the same for some considerable time.

III. 8TH BATTALION

The 8th Battalion of the Buffs, under Colonel Romer, C.B., C.M.G., landed in France, as we have seen, on the 1st September, or twenty-four days only before the battle of Loos. After two days at Boulogne it went into billets at Maninghem, near Etaples, and there remained a fortnight, completing divisional training, and marching on the 21st to take part in the concentration prior to the battle of Loos with the rest of the 72nd Brigade, which was commanded by Br.-General B. M. Mitford, C.B., D.S.O., himself an old Buff. The march to Bethune, which was reached in the very early morning of the 25th September, was a trying one done by night, mostly over bad roads. On the second night no less than twenty-two miles were covered and the Buffs recorded only one man as falling out. Other battalions had many more—even as many as two hundred.

At 11 a.m. on the day of arrival at Bethune the battalion formed up and Colonel Romer addressed his men. " I am not going to make a speech to you," he said, " but only to ask you to remember that you are ' The " Buffs.' " The battalion then moved forward towards the fighting line, gradually approaching Vermelles. That very night it had orders for a night attack on Hulluch, which was, however, stopped in order to allow of artillery preparation. The first casualty occurred at this time: 2nd Lieut. Hon. H. E. J. Robinson was so badly hit that he died next day in hospital. The attack being thus postponed, the battalion got into what were the original German second-line trenches and remained there till 11 a.m. on the 26th.

At 10.30 a.m. orders came for the division to attack at 11, and then this unit of the regiment went " over the top " to take its part in a severe action only three weeks after arrival in France and without having gone through the apprenticeship and instruction under fire in the trenches, which was the rule in all cases of fresh troops arriving in the country.

The brigade, in which our battalion was a unit, advanced from the approach-trenches, which had been German and which it was then holding, to the objective, which was the third line of the German fortification running north from a point about a thousand yards east of Hulluch, which place the 1st Division was to attack simultaneously, while on the right the 21st Division had another portion of the enemy's third line assigned to it.

The 8th Buffs were in the second line, following the 9th East Surrey, who were on the brigade right in touch with the above-named division. On the left of the Surreys were the 8th Royal West Kent, with the 8th Queen's behind them.

There was a steady and persistent shelling on all these battalions as they advanced, and when our men got down to the depression running south of Hulluch they came under enfilade fire from several guns and machine guns, and the further they advanced up the eastern slope the more severe became the fire. All the battalions of the 72nd Brigade reached the trenches which were their objective. There they found the wire entanglement still quite intact, the wire being abnormally thick and difficult to cut. Endeavours were made to get over or under this obstacle, but to no purpose. Meanwhile the division on the right retired, leaving our people to be heavily enfiladed, with the result that the latter also had to fall back, which they did to some trenches five or six hundred yards to the west and southwest of Hulluch, and there, for four and a half hours, they were heavily bombarded.

When night came on parties were sent out to remove the killed and wounded, but the Germans after dark reoccupied their old trenches along the Hulluch-Lens road and the rescue parties therefore failed to get at the eastern slope of the shallow valley, in which Hulluch lies: the fatal slope on which the greater number of our casualties occurred. Only a dozen or so of the more lightly wounded of the Buffs managed to crawl back after nightfall.

This assault was made in daylight and over open country, and the German third-line trench which was the objective was nearly a mile away.

The men had started in what is termed artillery formation, but the lines, owing to the intensity of the fire encountered, had to be extended almost at once. The advance was carried forward very rapidly, and in half an hour the Buffs had arrived within twenty-five yards of the enemy's wire.

No gaps could be observed, and for twenty minutes the attempts to cut it were continued without avail.

It was at 11.55 that an order came to withdraw, and from that moment the hostile fire, especially from the left flank, became hotter than ever and, of course, the casualties heavier. The Buffs—what was left of them—were relieved during the night of the 26th/27th and rested in a field close by Sailly la Bourse, remaining till 7 p.m. on the latter date, when they marched to Nœux les Mines and bivouacked in very wet weather.

The casualties in the awful fight briefly described above were tremendous. That gallant old soldier Colonel Romer was early shot in the shoulder, but continued in his place, showing an example to all, till he was killed by a bullet through his heart. What a death for a hero of sixty-four! Though he was not originally a Buff, he was one indeed when he died, and his name will ever be remembered with those of Lathom, Moyse and so many others, from Sir Philip Sidney downwards, who have covered our regiment with glory in all quarters of the globe. With their colonel were killed, or soon after died of wounds, Captains Curtiss, A. M. C. Hollist, W. Howard, J. Kekewich and T. R. M. Shervinton; Lieuts. E. F. Corner, B. H. Pickering, Hon. H. E. J. Robinson and J. R. S. Pensley (R.A.M.C.), together with too many of the gallant men who followed them so well. Lieut. E. T. Smith was also killed in the trenches near Ypres on the 19th October. Altogether, counting killed, wounded and missing, the casualties amounted to the astounding figure of 24 officers and 610 other ranks.

Would any man a few years ago have believed that a time was close at hand when a battalion of the regiment was to suffer more casualties than fell to the lot of the Buffs at Albuera? Only one officer, Lieut. J. Vaughan, came out of the hell untouched, and he was given a right well-earned M.C. for bringing his unit out of action. Four of the men's names were sent in for distinguished bravery, but were not accepted by the War Office because they were prisoners of war; but the D.C.M.'s recorded later as bestowed on Sergt.-Major Brooker and Pte. Peet were bravely earned upon this day.

The remnants of the battalion were somewhat cheered by being informed, as they were on the morning of the 27th, that their attack drew off sixteen battalions of the enemy who were reinforcing the German line opposite the French, thus considerably helping the latter to capture Souchey and 14,000 prisoners.

The battalion was removed by train to Mollinghem, thence to Houtkerque, and later to Reninghelst. On the 4th October it was inspected by the G.O.C. of the division, who spoke of the way in which the regimental traditions had been maintained.

The usual instruction in trench warfare began on the 5th October, and Major Trueman took over command on the 7th.

On the 18th of this month the battalion passed to the 17th Infantry Brigade and two days afterwards took over the usual trench duty on its own account, and began its long acquaintance with the filthy life such duty meant: a life of danger, stinks, rats, lice, discomfort and misery such as no Englishman had ever conceived

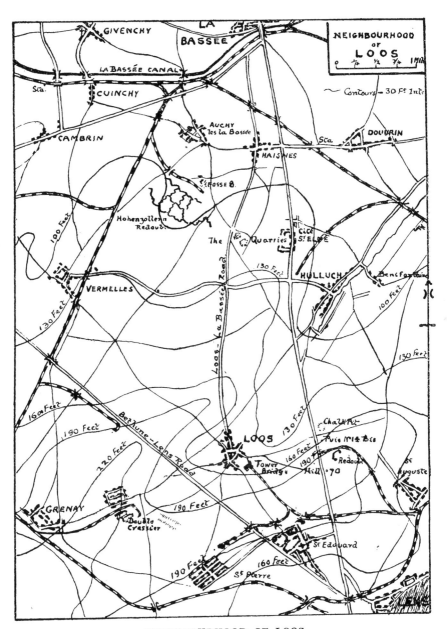

NEIGHBOURHOOD OF LOOS

it possible that he should one day be called on to endure.

IV. 2ND BATTALION

In connection with this great battle of Loos, the 28th Division, with which, it will be remembered, was the 2nd Battalion, had come, as has been seen, from Bailleul and was, on the 27th September, placed at the disposal of the First Army, arriving at Vermelles at 1 p.m.

The following description of the part the battalion played in the struggle would be somewhat difficult to follow without the accompanying sketch of the ground about the Hohenzollern Redoubt and the Dump.

At 2 o'clock A and D Companies, under Major Beevor, were ordered to relieve certain parties just north of Fosse 8, the situation at which point, it may be remembered, was described by the Commander-in-Chief as being " distinctly precarious."

Finding that the position in question had been abandoned, these companies were ordered by their brigadier, who accompanied them, to establish themselves in the Hohenzollern Redoubt.

Finding that the normal approach to this, that is, the communication trench, was too congested with troops to use, the Buffs quitted it and reached their appointed place across country, being very heavily shelled *en route.* In fact, both Br.-General Pereira and his brigade major, Captain Flower, were wounded, as was Lieut. Cory-Wright, who commanded D Company. On arrival, a platoon of this company charged the enemy vigorously and accounted for a score.

The companies remained in situation all night, during which our bombers had to be very active, while the wounded—and there were very many of different units —were being removed, a matter of great difficulty on account of heavy rain and the distance they had to be

99

carried. During this night the rest of the 85th Brigade came up and B and C Companies took up a position behind A and D.

After a contradictory order or two, an assault on the dump of Fosse 8 was arranged for 9.30 a.m. on the 28th, to be preceded by fifteen minutes' artillery fire.

The Buffs began at the hour named to file up the trenches, A Company leading, with D just behind.

The congested state of these avenues, due to dead, wounded and troops waiting to be relieved, rendered progress very slow, and many casualties were suffered from shell fire. The place from which one of the companies was to start the attack was still in the hands of the enemy, and all these circumstances prevented the men from getting into their approximate positions till after 10 a.m. The Middlesex Regiment was in support of the Buffs.

When the time came B and C Companies, followed by A, charged across the open and were greeted with the fire from machine guns massed on either flank, also shell and rifle fire. At least eleven machine guns were afterwards counted firing from the Miners' Cottages and Slag Alley. B and C Companies, every man cheering, gained the edge of the Dump and, clambering up the crumbling slopes of that 30-foot-high mound, gained the summit. On the way Captain W. R. Davis (commanding B Company) was killed and Lieut. S. C. Swayne and 2nd Lieut. M. Selby mortally wounded. Lieut. H. Mantle, 2nd Lieuts. C. H. B. Budd, G. E. Boon, Captain M. M. Brice (commanding C Company) and 2nd Lieut. G. E. A. Steggall were all wounded and the latter taken prisoner.

The Dump was then plastered with shells of all descriptions both from our own guns and those of the enemy and the attack was broken. The companies crossed the large expanse of the Dump summit and

100

attempted to reach the enemy in the trenches at the foot. It was a hopeless task, and those who attempted it were shot or grenaded. The companies re-formed and returned to the original trenches, leaving over one hundred men killed or wounded on the Dump.

The guns ceased fire and the bomb fighting commenced. Making use of all their trenches leading into their old lines, the Germans advanced swiftly under cover of showers of bombs and their machine guns. The enemy effected a gap (see sketch) between the Middlesex and Buffs and from it bombed both ways. Thus the Buffs found themselves to the south-east of the point where the enemy had penetrated and separated from their supporting battalion, the Middlesex, who were to the north-west of the gap. Here the struggle was fought out for a long period chiefly by the use of bombs, which were obtained with difficulty, having to be passed up the shallow trench from troops in rear. Barricades had to be built at certain points to keep the enemy in check.

Slag Alley was almost in complete possession of the Germans when A Company, charging repeatedly and with the greatest vigour, drove them back and accounted for about fifty. At this time 2nd Lieut. F. A. Booth was shot dead while accepting the surrender of a German officer. The enemy's supply of bombs was so superior to our own that the whole of A Company's gains could not be retained, but the men built a barricade across Slag Alley to secure the portion they could hold.

The fiercest fighting now took place at the gap in Dump trench. 2nd Lieut. W. T. Williams took charge of the bombers at this point and for 17½ hours kept the enemy in check. The greatest difficulty was experienced in obtaining a sufficient supply of bombs. The enemy's machine guns and snipers were particularly active and the advanced trenches were very shallow.

Lt.-Colonel C. A. Worthington,[1] commanding the battalion, and 2nd Lieut. T. Penington were killed by the same bullet.

The command devolved on the adjutant, Captain J. V. R. Jackson, in the absence of Major M. Beevor. The latter officer had been ordered to remain at Point 35 until the two rear companies of the Middlesex had filed past. As, however, the Germans had established themselves so strongly in the gap, Major Beevor had perforce to remain with the Middlesex. On the death of Colonel Neale of the latter regiment, he conducted operations on the other side of the gap and along South Face. As night fell the rain commenced again and never ceased. Shell and rifle fire slackened, but the bomb throwing was stronger than ever. Our bomb throwers were nearly all killed or wounded, and others were borrowed from neighbouring units. Owing to the rain, the fuses were damp, matches gave out, and the only way to light the fuses was by means of keeping cigarettes alight. The organization of the enemy as regards this weapon was astounding. He threw at least five to our one and of a much more powerful description. During the night every endeavour was made to get in the wounded. Neither rations nor water were obtainable. Attempts were made to dig in, but the mud rendered it a slow and laborious task. Dawn showed no cessation in the bomb throwing. Captain Jackson had sent messages for bombs and assistance: two messengers were killed, and finally an answer came that two companies of the York and Lancs were coming in relief and the Buffs were to make their way to Big Willie. At

---

[1] Claude Arthur Worthington, son of Captain Arthur Worthington of the Buffs, who carried the Colour into Sevastopol, was born on the 25th May, 1874, and joined the Buffs in 1898. He served with the 2nd Battalion in the South African War, acting as adjutant from February to May, 1900. He was later adjutant of the 2nd Battalion from 1905–8.

8.30 a.m. the relief was just entering the Dump trenches at Point 50 when the supply of bombs gave out altogether while the enemy kept up an incessant shower. The Buffs were forced back to the fork and filed down the advanced trench, whilst their relief filed in, leaped out of the trenches and held the enemy. During this critical period a little ground was lost owing to lack of bombs. Captain Jackson could not emerge from a deep dug-out near the gap from which he was conducting operations, and he was taken prisoner.

The balance of the regiment made its way back by Big Willie trench to near its junction with the South Face. Here Major Beevor took command. The Middlesex was being pressed back, and there being no room between them and the 3rd Royal Fusiliers, the Buffs filed back into the old front-line British trench, where they were able to materially assist the units in front by means of rifle fire. The night was spent in reorganizing and at midnight the battalion left the trenches and marched to Annequin.

Casualties. Officers, killed:—Lt.-Colonel C. A. Worthington, Captain W. R. Davis, 2nd Lieuts. F. A. Booth, T. Penington and N. E. Wood. Died of wounds: Lieut. S. C. Swayne and 2nd Lieut. M. Selby. Wounded: Captain M. M. Brice, Lieuts. G. Cory-Wright, H. Mantle; 2nd Lieuts. G. E. Boon, C. H. B. Budd and W. T. Williams. Taken prisoner: Captain J. V. R. Jackson and 2nd Lieut. G. E. A. Steggall (wounded).

Other ranks: killed, 57; wounded, 168; missing, 133. The majority of the latter are believed to have been killed or wounded on the Dump.

On the 1st October the battalion marched back to billets and began to reorganize after its terrific experience. Drafts from England arrived on the 2nd, 3rd, 9th and 15th of October, and a period of training and instructional parades of all sorts commenced. A turn at trench work, but a very short one, came on the 17th, but on the 21st startling orders arrived: no less than instructions to entrain on the following day for Marseilles for conveyance to the East.

No time was lost. On the 22nd the battalion marched to Fouquereuil, near Bethune, entrained there, arrived at the great port at 1.30 p.m. on Sunday 24th, and at 4 p.m. embarked, complete with transport, animals, vehicles and all, on the troopship *Transylvania* for conveyance to Egypt. Twenty-seven officers and 907 other ranks reached Alexandria on the 30th and marched to Sidi Bishr Camp.

During the European tour of this battalion, which lasted only nine months, 101 officers and 3,738 men had served in its ranks. Of these, 22 officers and 298 other ranks had been killed; 34 officers and 1,011 other ranks had been wounded; 5 officers and 199 other ranks had been taken prisoners; and 2 officers and 297 other ranks had been missing.

The stay in the land of Egypt was a very short one and was mostly devoted to training and marching. The whole of the 28th Division had moved and were to move again, for, on the 22nd November, came the orders for Salonica, the new base for operations against the Bulgarian forces. Salonica is a Greek port, but the monarch of that country was in secret a friend of the Germans, and the inhabitants proved none too friendly to the French and English forces which were making so free with Salonica.

The move of the division was a somewhat slow and gradual business, but at last the infantry got into camp at Lembet, about four and a half miles from the port. The weather was awful: heavy snow and gales of wind, as well as a most persistent fog, which hung about for days and which greatly interfered with reconnaissance. Early in December the authorities were apparently very undecided as to whether to remain at Salonica at all,

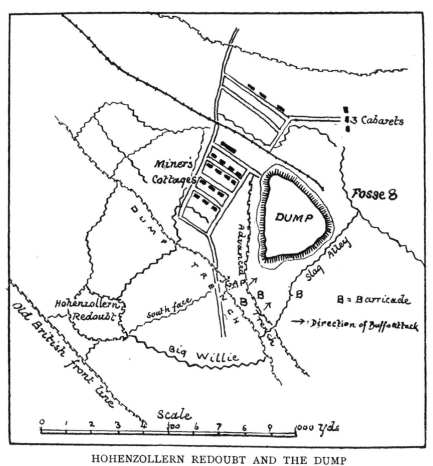

HOHENZOLLERN REDOUBT AND THE DUMP

and at one time all arrangements were made for re-embarkation. The attitude of the Greek officials was one of passive resistance and formal protest, but they were civil enough. Road-making was the first job and a most necessary one, for nothing but tracks were found inland. This work was, however, varied by the building of long defence lines, which were afterwards known as the bird-cage. The Buffs' section of these lines was near the village of Baldza, and the most important of the works was called Beevor's Redoubt, in honour of the commanding officer who had succeeded the gallant Worthington.

So ended the most tremendous year in the history of the 2nd Battalion of the Buffs, which had been raised in 1857 by Colonel F. F. Maude, V.C., the father of the great general of whom we shall shortly read.

V. 6TH BATTALION

We left the 6th Battalion at Meteren, near Bailleul, which place it reached early in June, 1915.

On the 12th of that month it moved up to Armentieres to undergo the usual instruction in trench warfare under a more experienced unit, and here occurred the first casualty. The remainder of the summer was passed in trench fighting, and many incidents might be recorded in connection with mining operations and small but boldly executed patrol adventures, particularly one by Corpl. Craven. Mines were sprung by the enemy and the craters occupied, and these had to be reconnoitred to ascertain for what further offensive work they were to be used. It would be impossible, however, without publishing long and somewhat monotonous journals, to describe fully the daily trench work of the several battalions. This important service was done, practically speaking, by half the troops engaged, the other half resting, as it was called, in billets in rear.

105

These billets were mostly leaky barns with many of the tiles off the roofs, furnished with closely packed tiers of beds one above the other, like bunks in a ship's cabin, each bunk being floored with fine wire-netting. There was not quite such a dearth of munitions by this time, and on the last day of July there was a very heavy and important burst of artillery fire on our part, the battalion being then in the Ploegsteert Wood.

Life was fairly monotonous, however, until the 23rd September, on which day careful instructions were given in the art of the production of heavy smoke, from the which it was hoped that an attacking party would be able to emerge unseen. After much conference, detailed instructions were issued on this same day regarding the proposed occupation of the German salient at Le Touquet, and it seemed as if the battalion, and indeed the whole brigade, was to take part in a great battle immediately. The 12th Divisional operation orders received at 9.30 a.m. on the 24th gave colour to this idea, and at 2 p.m. a trench-mortar bombardment of Le Touquet commenced, but the result proved disappointing and, no damage being done to the enemy's wire, an attack in force proved impracticable. The 26th brought an artillery bombardment on both sides and our people raised a smoke curtain which appeared to be more or less satisfactory, but the following night the whole brigade was relieved by other troops and billeted in Armentieres, and, on the last day of the month, the battalion was in Vermelles relieving the Coldstream Guards, and it then moved into what had been the German line just south of the Hulluch road.

On the 11th October the Germans recovered part of the Hohenzollern Redoubt, an object they had been struggling for for some days, and they made a resolute attack near Loos which was repulsed with enormous loss.

Two days after this operation, orders were issued by

the 12th Division for an attack on Hulluch. These orders were very complete and abounded in map references of the most detailed description. They point to a well-organized advance to secure an advanced line and put it in a state of defence.

The 37th Brigade, in which, it will be remembered, the 6th Buffs were serving, was to be strengthened by one company of the Northamptonshire Regiment and the 69th Field Company of the Engineers, was awarded a distinct task and was to join up with the 35th Brigade.

The divisional and attached artillery to cover the whole operation.

The start to be made from the trenches.

Orders were given for creating a smoke screen for about 1,200 yards.

This was to be most intense ten minutes before the start for the assault.

Although the men's packs were left behind, they had much to carry, as it was intended to occupy what the assault had secured. The artillery was to open fire, and did so, at 12 noon, and at 1 p.m. gas and smoke commenced, the former till 1.50 and the latter till 2 p.m., at which hour the assault was launched.

The 7th East Surrey were ordered to detail a party to carry up tools, sandbags and wire, wherewith to consolidate the position when won. This battalion, together with the Buffs, was to hold what was captured.

The Buffs were, by map reference, given a separate and distinct part of the enemy's trenches to assail and to make good; one end of their appointed portion was the east end of the Quarries, and the battalion was to join up with the East Surreys on their right and with the 35th Brigade on their left. Prior to the attack all troops were to wear smoke helmets with the fronts raised ready to be adjusted at a moment's notice.

On these elaborate and clear instructions Colonel Eaton based his battalion orders, giving each company

107

its place of assembly and all detail. The fifth paragraph of these orders reads: " The assault led by A Company will take place immediately the 35th Brigade reaches the line ' 54 to 82.' " Two hundred and fifty bombs were carried by each company.

The account of the actual fighting is necessarily meagre, for it was all over in a very short time, and during the struggle it was very difficult to get any information at headquarters as all the wires were soon broken. In fact, the Headquarter telephone dug-out was blown in before the advance had even commenced. The smoke, so carefully arranged, soon blew off and by 2 o'clock the air was clear again. Exactly at the hour, however, the battalion dashed forward, A, C and D Companies leading, with B a little way in rear in support. The keenness to attack and the precision and order with which the companies went over the top were wonderful to see. But, alas! the enemy's protecting wire was found to be uncut, and a withering fire was opened from front and both flanks as our men tried to hack their way through with the wire-cutters carried by the leading troops. The greatest gallantry was shown and the attack was renewed again and again by ever-diminishing numbers, but it was of no avail, and of the three leading companies but very few men returned. The enemy's machine guns were the cause of most of our casualties in this fight, as they so often were in later engagements.

Thirteen officers led the 6th Battalion into its first battle, and of these ten died in their duty, namely, Majors B. E. Furley and A. Soames, D.S.O.; Captains C. E. G. Davidson and H. W. Brodie; Lieuts. J. P. Phillimore and C. W. B. Marsh; 2nd Lieuts. C. G. Jelf, D. Lambert and C. Bainbridge. 2nd Lieut. Birkett was severely wounded. There were no less than four hundred casualties amongst the brave men of Kent who had volunteered so blithely to serve Old England at her need, and among these were the company sergeant-majors of A and C Companies, Burnett and Glover. On the 20th October the G.O.C. Division (Major-General Scott) congratulated the battalion on the gallant work it had done, and three days later the corps commander pointed out that it was because of the glorious effort made that it became possible for the regiments on the right and left to capture the enemy's trenches. To the end of the month the battalion, very weak in numbers, was mostly employed on fatigue work, such as carrying packs for the R.E.; but in November it saw some fighting in and around the Hohenzollern Redoubt, and it suffered a particularly wet and cold tour in the trenches at Givenchy and Festubert in December, where the water was waist-deep. Colonel Eaton was invalided home in November and replaced by Major H. R. H. Pratt, Northamptonshire Regiment. Eaton departed to the great regret of all and with the enthusiastic cheers of those who recognized his worth. As in the cases of all the other battalions of the regiment, a period of monotony set in in the winter of 1915–16 with the gallant 6th. It was a weary time indeed and took its toll of human life.

VI. 7TH BATTALION

During the earlier portion of their history at the seat of war the experiences of the 7th Battalion were not quite as exciting as were those of their comrades in the others. Unlike the 6th and 8th, there was no violent action to record during the first few months. The story is, in fact, the usual one of trench warfare. The regular instruction in this branch of warfare commenced on the 11th August, 1915, and company by company went up in the firing line at Carnoy from that date until all had had the experience, and, of course, the battalion very soon had trenches of its own to be responsible for. It

was, as the 2nd Battalion so often was, so unfortunate
at first as to take over from French troops. This is not
pleasant, as these have not the same ideas on the subject
of sanitation as we have, and they do not bury their
dead in a satisfactory manner when the burial is of
necessity an informal ceremony. In addition, they were
frequently not bullet-proof and very badly loopholed.

On the 1st September a German mine was exploded
under the Buffs' front-line trench, followed by an outburst of fire and a small attack, with the idea of capturing the crater. D Company had 4 killed, 5 wounded
and 6 missing that day. The men behaved in the most
gallant and satisfactory manner under this their first
experience. The position of the line occupied by the
55th Brigade was opposite the village of Fricourt and as
far as La Boisselle, and in this sector the enemy seemed
to have made something of a speciality of mining, which
is a mode of warfare very trying to the nerves of the
adversary, as it is not pleasant to live in momentary expectation of being blown up. The brigade kept two
battalions always in the line, while the other remained
at Dernancourt and Ville sur Ancre; eight days being
the average length of each tour of trench duty. The
portion occupied by the 7th Buffs was therefore miles
away from the other battalions of the regiment at this
time. Dernancourt is about three miles south of the
town of Albert.

VII. LIFE IN AND BEHIND THE TRENCHES

Viscount French in his last despatch remarks that
the exhaustion of men and materials which results after
a great battle necessarily leads to a time of comparative
inactivity. From August, 1914, till October in the following year the fighting, as we have seen, had been tremendous in France and Flanders, and both the Germans
and ourselves had suffered casualties till then unheard

of in history. It is not therefore surprising that after the comparatively unsuccessful efforts at Loos and its neighbourhood, warfare on the Western front subsided into dogged defence of the trenches occupied, into a sort of stalemate, as many people believed. It was a wearying and very trying time. The looked-for peace seemed as far off as ever. Each side appeared to be absolutely resolute to hold its own, but no progress towards a settlement could be observed. It is true that there was a good deal of fighting between the enemy and the French south of the British lines, that the Canadians made a raid south-west of Messines on the 18th November, and that another was made by British troops near Neuve Chapelle on the 12th December. It is true also that the artillery on both sides woke now and again to abnormal activity, particularly on the 30th November, and that the Germans fired, it is estimated, three thousand shells on our Ypres positions on the 10th December; but there is no first-class action to report for the remainder of the year 1915, though hundreds of interesting episodes occurred during the latter part of it, which are impossible to record here, and casualties were of daily occurrence.

People in England, both officially and by private arrangement, took care that the horrors of war should be mitigated as far as possible and that every indulgence that could be granted to our fighting men should be theirs. The greatest privilege of all and the most appreciated was a regular system of leave to England: every officer and man took his turn to go home, visit his friends and enjoy the most striking and tremendous change that can come to be the lot of man; change from the awful trenches and daily and hourly peril of life to a smiling, happy welcome in the Old Country; decent, cleanly existence for a few days; the delights of bed, baths, theatres, dinner-parties and other social delights; together perhaps with a little of the old sports and pastimes of a previous existence. Yes, leave to England was a glorious thing to live for and look forward to.

The rationing of the soldier when in France was truly marvellous. Never before had the old soldiers known the like. The food was excellent and more than sufficient and of very considerable variety. Except in cases of real emergency, too, it was punctually delivered. The Army Service Corps brought up the food, tobacco and rum to certain dumps behind the trenches; from these they were carried up by regimental transport to advanced dumps, where the stuff was packed into sandbags, eight complete rations to a bag, and carried by hand to the consumer. Half a gill of rum per man was issued in the presence of an officer two or three times a week and was naturally very much appreciated, and the Quartermaster always had a little reserve of this precious commodity in hand for emergency days.

For troops resting—that is, taking their regular turn behind the lines in billets—all sorts of sports were organized. There were divisional inter-battalion football cups to be competed for. There were long-distance cross-country races arranged and, in fact, all sorts of manly games, as well as dramatic entertainments, "sing-songs," and even divisional cinemas. During any war the arrival of the English mail is a tremendous event, and on the Western front it was immense. Ships and shiploads of letters and parcels were constantly crossing the narrow seas and bringing loving messages and welcome presents to the fighting men.

Mrs. Hickson, whose husband, Br.-General R. A. Hickson, C.B., commanded the 2nd Battalion in the South African War, had at that time organized a fund to provide soldiers with comforts at the front, and this organization had been a marked success; so that lady, being in 1914 settled in Kent, wrote to the colonels of both the 1st and 2nd Battalions and offered to undertake the very onerous task of doing the same again. Needless to say the proposal was eagerly accepted, and Mrs. Hickson promptly sent round the necessary notices throughout East Kent and elsewhere and commenced the kindly work. The immediate response to the appeal was splendid and help was offered by very many, including Lord Harris, Sir Arthur Paget, the officers of the regiment then in England and the regimental institutes at Dover and Canterbury. Mrs. Hickson, however, had all the real work to do unaided, except by her maid; yet bales of comforts were despatched weekly and work was placed in various organized centres —notably Hawkhurst, Canterbury, Cranbrook, Benenden and Chartham.

Yes, the fighting soldiers were well looked after; but it was soon made clear that the really needy were the unfortunate prisoners of war, and, when this fact was appreciated, a Prisoners of War Fund was promptly added to the one in existence, and this brought comfort and some resignation to many a wretched captive wearing out his heart in longing for the end. This good work was kept up till the Kent Prisoners County Fund was centred at Rochester.

Nor were Mrs. Hickson and her friends the only women to give practical expression to their sympathy: Lady George Hamilton and Mrs. W. D. Johnson soon started a small fund for the prisoners of the 8th Battalion and, indeed, sent many a parcel out themselves. Mrs. Eaton followed suit, taking her husband's 6th Battalion under her special care; and Viscountess Goschen interested herself in the 5th. The 7th was added to Mrs. Hickson's task, she being ultimately president of a committee to administer the funds collected by very many friends for the 1st, 2nd and 7th Battalions. Mrs. Geddes worked on this committee, as did the officers of the depot. As a mark of common gratitude it would be decent to publish here the list of

I   113 contributors, more especially as there appears to be no record of any formal thanks either to subscribers or those who worked so strenuously, but space forbids the publication of the names here. They appeared at intervals in the regimental newspaper.

VIII. Summary

In addition to the continuous fighting in France and Flanders many tremendous and stirring events of world importance took place during the latter portion of 1915, to a few of which it may be advisable to refer briefly.

On the 3rd June a Bill was introduced in Parliament for the formation of a Ministry of Munitions, and after this event our people at war were much better fitted to compete with the enemy in weight and number of projectiles, in the number of aeroplanes, observation balloons and in other important items.

South-West Africa was finally conquered by Botha in July, and a great German offensive against Russia commenced.

There was fierce fighting in Gallipoli early in August and, on the 15th September, Kitchener was able to make the statement that eleven divisions of the new armies had now proceeded to the wars.

On the 28th a British victory was scored at Kut in Mesopotamia.

The 11th October saw Lord Derby's new scheme of recruiting.

On the 15th of the same month Great Britain and Bulgaria were at war.

On the 11th November Lord Derby warned unmarried men of the likelihood of conscription becoming the law of the land should further recruiting prove unsatisfactory.

The Battle of Ctesiphon, twenty-five miles south-west of Baghdad, was fought on the 22nd. This was another victory for us, but our loss equalled one-third of our force. It resulted in the German Marshal, Von der Goltz, being placed in command in Mesopotamia.

The British retired to Kut on the 25th November, and the same day Salonica was selected as a base for a new theatre of war, some troops and much war material being landed at that port on the 4th December.

On the 5th the siege of Kut began, and on the 8th our troops were obliged to commence the evacuation of the Gallipoli Peninsula.

On the 15th December, 1915, General Sir John French, the Commander-in-Chief of our armies in France and Flanders, resigned his appointment and returned to England to receive the plaudits of his fellow-countrymen and the well-earned promotion to the rank of Viscount. He took over the duties of Commander-in-Chief of the troops at home, and was succeeded abroad by the most illustrious of his glorious lieutenants, Sir Douglas Haig, a man in whom the whole army believed.

The 20th December saw the successful and skilfully arranged evacuation of Anzac and Suvla, the details for which were worked out by an old officer of the Buffs, Major-General Sir A. L. Lynden-Bell. Our Gallipoli army had fought most nobly. Whether the Peninsula ought ever to have been invaded at all or, being invaded, should have been abandoned, is not a question which can be discussed in this place. We all know, however, that the final collapse of the Turks was very greatly due to the preliminary handling they had experienced here before they finally met their masters in Palestine and Mesopotamia.

On the 27th January, 1916, conscription was introduced in England, and with the exception of brave lads who between the 4th August, 1914, and this date had sufficiently grown to be capable of bearing arms,

and of other young men who, still in England, had had
no opportunity yet of reaching a seat of war, the future
drafts were to be composed of men who originally
shirked the bloody work their brothers were engaged
in and who now had no longer any option in the
matter.

Roughly, very roughly, speaking, the bronze star
marks the volunteer. Anyhow, a man with that decoration must have been one, though it does not follow
that a soldier without it was necessarily a conscript. It
is not fair to hint, nor is it a fact that the pressed man
proved inferior in fighting value to the volunteer, notwithstanding the old proverb anent the matter, but
the possession of the star carries with it and must carry
in the minds of all, the admiration due to the civilian
who, being untrained to the fighting trade, offered to
face all dangers and a dreadful life, or probably painful
death, for the safety and honour of Old England, as
well as to the regular or Territorial soldier who was
always prepared to do so when called upon.

CHAPTER V

THE TURKISH ENEMY

I. Aden

SINCE the 29th October, 1914, England had been at war with Turkey. Now both our own country and the Ottoman Empire were much interested in the East, and both had, of course, very extended Eastern possessions; consequently, we were always knocking up against the Turk, and in many parts of the world, such as the Gallipoli Peninsula, Egypt, Palestine, Mesopotamia and Arabia.

It was on the 2nd July, 1915, that, as it was discovered that the Turks had had the audacity to enter the Aden Protectorate, permission was obtained from the Indian Government (Aden being officially a part of India) to send out from the town a mobile column, with the result that a very small one, but the best the little garrison could do, proceeded on the 3rd to Shekh Othman, which is a point from which the isthmus which connects the town with the mainland, and which is only about a mile across, can best be defended against aggression from the land side. The sea power of our country was, of course, sufficient to prevent any hostile attempt from the water.

A Turkish advance into the Protectorate by about 900 men, nearly half of them Arabs, with 8 guns, was confirmed; but it was found that our own force, consisting as it did of only a little over 1,000 men, 10 guns and 10 maxims, was far too small to attempt operations in the hilly country, and it was compelled to remain on the defensive and hope for a chance of catching the enemy in the act of debouching from the mountains.

Another and very excellent reason for remaining quiet was that our native transport men were deserting in crowds. It was all very well for the canny Aden native to draw English pay in peace time as a transport servant, but he was not going to be shot at. On the 8th July, in fact, the mobile force had to withdraw into Aden and ask for reinforcements. The heat was tremendous; the roads mere sand tracks—quite unfit for mechanical transport, and along which it was reckoned that eight camels would be required to drag one gun.

There are a few brackish wells at Shekh Othman and good water for one brigade, but this supply was cut off by the enemy on the 10th July, and condensed water was all that was obtainable. On this day it was found that the Turks were being reinforced, and General Younghusband with his brigade was ordered to Aden from Egypt, with directions to take Lahej.

It was, however, later taken into consideration that Aden itself was safe enough, because, as we had the mastery of the sea, the enemy could only attack it along a narrow isthmus commanded on both sides by the fire of the ships; and therefore it came to pass that in this region active service for a long period degenerated into two forces remaining more or less passively facing each other: the English at Aden, and their enemies at Lahej. But Shekh Osman was reoccupied on the 21st July. The English infantry consisted only of the Brecknockshire Battalion of the South Wales Borderers.

Aden is not a white man's garrison, and in normal times a British battalion only remains there one year on its completion of an Indian tour and on its way home to England. The summer proved extremely trying to the Brecknockshires, and they suffered so much from sickness that they eventually had to be relieved from India by the 4th Battalion of The Buffs, which sailed on the *Varsova* on the 26th.

118

The battalion disembarked at Aden on the 4th August, 1915. By the 18th the Turkish force at Lahej was reckoned at 2,500 Turks, 1,500 Arabs and 20 guns, and it was supposed that only the absence of water between them and Shekh Othman prevented their advance.

On the 28th a reconnoitring force of ours reported that 2,000 Turks with 14 guns were at Waht. They assumed the offensive when approached and our party fell back on Shekh Othman with 20 wounded, and after this a passive defence of that place, covering Aden, was resolved on; General Younghusband and his men, therefore, returned to Egypt and the command devolved on Br.-General Price.

On the 25th September a column went out on a reconnoitring expedition and entered Waht after slight opposition. There was one Buff casualty, No. 2073 Pte. L. H. Fuller, being the first of the battalion to be slain in the great cause of England. The roads by this time were improved, but the heat was indescribable and proved a more serious enemy than the Turk. No less than fourteen men died of sunstroke, including Sgt. Brazier and Ptes. Bromley, Brown, De la Mare, Dyer, Martin and Steadman of the Buffs.

On the 26th November 80 men of the regiment were reported unfit for further service at Aden, and reference to sick reports shows that on the 1st of that month there were no less than 93 of the battalion in hospital and 121 attending daily. The determination not to attack the enemy and his disinclination to come on resulted in comparative peace till the end of the year.

On the 8th January, 1916, however, the Turks appeared to be contemplating a movement against the Fadli country, and it was considered that British prestige seemed likely to suffer from our inaction. It was reckoned that about 700 of the enemy with 4 guns were at Subar, 1,000 with 8 guns at Waht and a small body at Lahej; so another reconnoitring column was arranged and sent out from Shekh Othman to threaten the enemy's line Waht–Subar. The men carried two days' supplies of all sorts, and were afterwards to be rationed from Shekh Othman. Our force took up a position at 5.30 a.m. and a covering line advanced, but hostile artillery opened upon it from the Subar direction, and at 10.30 compelled a rearward movement, and the party was finally withdrawn at 2.30 a.m. Later, the Turks themselves advanced about 1,000 strong with 2 machine guns, but this advance on their part was checked at about 500 yards from our position. Attempts were made by our small body of cavalry to take this hostile movement in flank and rear, but the close country impeded movement and the enemy's artillery soon checked the horsemen. At 4.30 the Turks withdrew towards Subar. Their artillery had been well handled and had kept up a very persistent fire. The officer in command determined to return to Shekh Othman, being unable to carry out the programme and recognizing the impossibility of getting the upper hand of his enemy's artillery. The retirement was faultlessly carried out.

A telegram from India arrived early in February ordering the battalion to proceed to Bareilly on relief by the 4th Duke of Cornwall's Light Infantry from that place. The movement was duly carried out a few days later, and only some few men, who had been trained as gunners, remained behind until their places could be taken by newly made acting gunners from the new regiment. The 4th Battalion remained at Bareilly till July, 1918, and though as a complete unit it saw no more fighting, most of its men did so, for while at Bareilly it sent up detachments to the North-West Frontier, and several large drafts, about five hundred men in all, to the 5th Battalion in Mesopotamia.

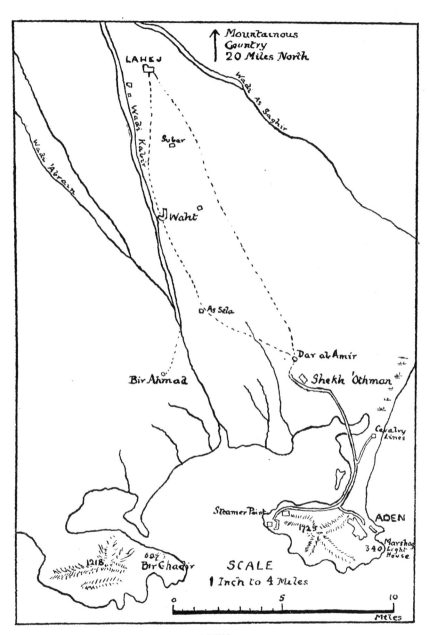

Mountainous
Country
20 Miles North

LAHEJ

Wadi As Saghir

Wadi Kebir

Wadi 'Abrain

Suber

Waht

As Sela

Bir Ahmad

Dar al Amir

Shekh 'Othman

Cavalry
Lines

Steamer Point

1925

ADEN

Marshag
Light
House

340

1218

607

Bir Ghadir

SCALE
1 Inch to 4 Miles

0   5   10

Miles

ADEN

II. MESOPOTAMIA

The war in Mesopotamia was quite a different one to any of the others, and perhaps resembled the operations of Lord Wolseley on the Nile in the early eighties more than any other in which England has been engaged. In fact, it was a river war and, until the siege of Kut-el-Amarah began, early in December, 1915, it had been a successful one.

A very brief sketch of the campaign, which ended in the surrounding of General Townsend's force in Kut, is perhaps necessary in order properly to understand what followed: Sir John Nixon commanded an Anglo-Indian army in the land of Mesopotamia, which was, of course, a Turkish province. His headquarters were at the port of Basrah on the River Tigris, about sixty miles from the real mouth of the river. In the spring of 1915 the forces were much scattered: one brigade being at Ahwaz, eighty miles away on the right (to the eastward), and another brigade was at Qurnah (or Kurna), forty miles further up the river than Basrah. The enemy, which had been driven from Basrah because the English wanted the place, had collected mostly about Nasiriyah, one hundred miles away to the westward. This was a most important place from the Turkish point of view. It is on the Euphrates river, and from it runs a watercourse into the Tigris. It was from there that any attempt the enemy might make to recover what he had lost must start. About one hundred miles, as the crow flies, above Basrah and on the same river, stands Amarah, a place which, in 1915, was in Turkish hands; from the garrison of this town, early in 1915, had been detached a party of six battalions and ten guns down-stream as far as Qurnah, and this force was, of course, in contact with our brigade there.

Early in May General Gorringe, with the 12th

Indian Division and a cavalry brigade, operated about
Arwaz and, crossing the Kharkeh river with some
difficulty, drove all the enemy in the eastern regions of
the province in upon the garrison of Amarah. Meanwhile General Townsend with the 6th Indian Division
advanced up the Tigris supported by the Naval
flotilla, and, pursuing the Turkish detachment before
him, entered Amarah practically unopposed, because
General Gorringe's operations had prevented the
enemy from reinforcing his garrison. Amarah was
entered on the 4th June, 1915. Immediately after the
taking of this place arrangements were made for the
capture of Nasiriyah, which was after serious opposition effected by General Gorringe on the 25th July.
The defeat of Nur-ed-Din and the occupation of Kut-
el-Amarah became the next objective as soon as
Nasiriyah was secured, and the transfer of troops towards Amarah was begun the following day.

Kut is another one hundred miles higher up the
Tigris than Amarah, without counting the bends, and
in the summer the river is the only approach to it.

The British force referred to, reached Sanna-i-Yat,
about eight miles below the enemy's Kut position, by
the 15th September, and halted there for ten days,
being reinforced during that period. General Townsend then advanced and, with the aid of the Naval
forces on the stream, drove the Turk back, who by the
5th October was at Ctesiphon, covering Baghdad; but
here the enemy received very important reinforcements and, moreover, his position was daily being
strengthened. Townsend, too, was concentrating at
Aziziyah, but he found he could not proceed till the
21st November, and on the next day his force attacked
the enemy and won the battle of Ctesiphon, though
his heavy losses in killed and wounded rendered it impossible for him to renew his progress to Baghdad. As
a matter of fact, the British Army was neither strong

enough in numbers nor equipment for the task on which it had been sent.

General Townsend at last found it absolutely necessary to withdraw, and this was done very gradually and with much fighting; on the morning of the 3rd December his force reached Kut-el-Amarah where it was decided his retirement should end. The force, considerably reduced in numbers, was now regularly besieged by the Turks, and a resolute attempt to relieve him by an army under Lt.-General Aylmer was organized and arranged.

This relieving force got under way in December. It consisted of the 7th Lahore Division from France, 3rd Meerut Division and the 35th Indian Brigade, lately brought to Mesopotamia; this brigade included the 5th Battalion of the Buffs. The job was immense, because of the difficulties of transport. The only possible way of carrying the impedimenta of an army and of feeding and supplying it was by means of the River Tigris, and this stream was a most unsatisfactory one in every way: it winds about like a cork-screw, and is provided with endless shifting shallows; when the rains come it is a raging torrent; and after that the whole country, which is quite flat, is covered with impassable marshes, which connect with the river by treacherous channels. All this, of course, meant that the rations were bad and more or less precarious. In fact, at this period of the war, the feeding of the troops in Mesopotamia could not be compared with the system obtaining in France. The sick, too, suffered extremely from the difficulties of transport as well as a reprehensible paucity of medical officers and medical equipment. In fact, the conditions of soldiering on the Western Front and in this cradle of the human race were as different as they well could be. In France nothing that could alleviate the sufferings of the sick and wounded was left undone, whereas under the Indian Government the contrary was the case, and it was only after many lives had been needlessly sacrificed that adequate arrangements were made.

Townsend's cavalry had left him on the 6th December, and retired down the Tigris till it reached Ali-el-Gharbi, at which spot it was reinforced by infantry and guns from Basrah.

The siege of Kut was full of incident and the defence was a very fine one, starvation being the only enemy that could not be defied, but it is only with the attempted relief of the place that the Buffs were concerned.

General Aylmer's leading troops, under Major-General Younghusband, who had moved up from Basrah by river steamers with open barges lashed on either side, started from the Ali-el-Gharbi on the 4th January, 1916, and moved up the river, using both banks and marching on Sheikh Saad. The Buffs were on the left bank and furthest from the stream. All surplus stores were carried by water. The length of the first day's march was about eight miles, the weather being very wet and the nights cold.

The second day took the force another journey up the course of the Tigris in the same formation. There was a considerable amount of sniping when night fell. Indeed, it was obvious from this and other signs that there was a strong force in front.

On the next day (6th January) the march was resumed and the outposts of the enemy were reached. The firing commenced about noon and lasted till 4.30 p.m., but our casualties were inconsiderable; 2nd Lieut. Holyman and three men being wounded. There was very heavy sniping that night.

The next day was fought the action of Sheikh Saad. Our force began to advance and came under fire almost at once, and the artillery opened at 8 o'clock. The firing increased hourly in intensity as the day wore on, from rifles and shrapnel and later on from machine guns, too, and casualties began to grow to an unpleasant extent. The adjutant, Lieut. H. S. Marchant, was killed, and Lt.-Colonel J. Munn-Mace, Major E. Clarke and many others were wounded. The advance was over open country and the available cover was so meagre as to be almost non-existent. There was a mirage, too, which interfered considerably with observation, but by the middle of the afternoon a much thinned-out firing line of Buffs, Black Watch and Seaforth Highlanders had got within about four hundred yards of the position. There were not enough men to keep up the pressure, however, and as there was every appearance of a counter-attack being contemplated, these British troops prepared a line about two hundred yards behind the place they had advanced to, and digging themselves in for the night prepared to resist any offensive on the part of the enemy. Beyond very heavy firing, which rendered the bringing in of the wounded a matter of great difficulty, however, nothing of that nature occurred, though the situation was anything but a pleasant one, for the firing was kept up all night, the weather was bitterly cold and showery, and the food consisted of a few biscuits with some bully beef for breakfast.

Saturday the 8th January was a day of rifle fire. The Turks attempted an advance, but were repulsed and all our men could do was to strengthen and improve their defences, which work was carried out at dusk. On the following morning the enemy had disappeared and nothing was found to be in front but a few snipers. The reason of this proved to be that, though our advance was checked, as has been seen, on the left bank of the river, our troops on the other side had captured the trenches in front of them. So, after burying the dead and clearing up the battle-field, Aylmer's force marched another six miles or so over what had been the Turkish position, which was found to be a very elaborate one, and camped at Sheikh Saad.

The part taken by the Buffs in this fight earned the very warmest praise from those in authority. The casualty list was heavy, 3 officers and 38 men were killed outright and 14 officers and 196 other ranks were wounded, some of whom succumbed to their injuries.

The list of officer casualties was as follows:—

Killed: Lieuts. H. S. Marchant and G. T. Baker, and 2nd Lieut. E. Rothwell.

Wounded: Lt.-Colonel J. Munn-Mace, Major E. Clarke; Captains B. Buss (afterwards died of wounds), F. O. Marchant, T. H. O. Collings; Lieuts. A. E. L. Hardcastle, G. Jessel, the Hon. G. J. Goschen (died of wounds), W. H. Winch (died of wounds), F. S. Fleuret, S. W. Weldon, L. E. Holyman, A. Goode (attached) and T. Bridgens (attached).

On the 11th January in the evening came sudden orders to get on the move again, and at 7 o'clock the force marched off in a north-easterly direction, but after proceeding three miles halted again and dug in. This procedure was repeated on the 12th, but the march (in the same direction) was this time about eight miles, and every preparation was made for an attack at dawn. The enemy had, however, gone when morning arrived, and our people moved after him and marched steadily from 7 o'clock in the morning till 2 p.m., when the foe was located and promptly attacked. His position was known as the Wadi, which is a stream running into the Tigris river on its left bank. The 35th Brigade, in which the Buffs were serving, being on the right flank of the relieving force, carried out a flanking movement and only really came into action about 4 p.m. Then it advanced under fire and closed with the bayonet, but the Turk thought it unwise to measure himself at close quarters with the men of Kent, though he is a brave and hardy fighter, so he made off and another battle was lost and won.

The Buffs' own principal loss was the new commanding officer of the battalion, Major J. S. Fraser, who was killed. Captain J. Body assumed command.

The weather was now very bad indeed, the rains were terrible and the wind very high. This state of things interfered sadly with military operations, and delay was the only thing that really disheartened the men. British comrades were being besieged in Kut, only some twenty-five miles away, and discomforts and inferior feeding could be easily borne if only progress could be made.

It is necessary to understand something of the nature of the country and of the Turkish lines of defence between Kut and the relieving forces and to remember that the only practical avenue of approach was by the river, because sustained operations in the desert which bordered the stream were impossible without adequate land transport, which did not exist. Within a mile or two of the stream on both sides were extensive and impassable marshes, and the enemy had constructed several lines of entrenchments, one behind the other, and each stretching across the water from the marshes on the left bank to those on the right. The first of these, and nearest to Aylmer's forces, were the lines of Umm-el-Hanna. Then came those of Falahiyeh and then Sanna-i-Yat. Behind all these, only about seven miles east of Kut itself, was the long entrenchment of Es Sinn. The main line of this, as it did not rest on marshes on the right side of the river, was thrown back at an angle till it rested on the Shatt-el-Hai, the watercourse which joined the Tigris at Kut to the great River Euphrates. At the salient angle of this long line of works stood the Dujailah Redoubt.

On the 21st January Aylmer attacked the Umm-el-Hanna lines, but alas! the attack proved a failure and the English army had to entrench itself and await reinforcements, it being that day fairly conclusively proved that our people were not in sufficient force for the work undertaken. The Buffs had, amongst others, Captain A. G. A. Adam and Lieut. J. Thorp Waite killed and Lieut. Goodland wounded. The weather of the 21st was terribly wet: by evening the trenches were full of water; it became difficult to carry away the wounded, and many of the stretcher-bearers fell with their burdens.

About this time several pairs of battalions, who had been depleted of men, were coupled up into one. This was of more or less frequent occurrence. Thus two companies of the Hampshires, whose other half battalion was in Kut, were sent to the Buffs, and together, until the following June, the Buffs and these two companies formed the " composite Territorial battalion," better known as the " Huffs," which was commanded by Major F. N. Thorne, of the 1st Royal Sussex Regiment.

Notwithstanding everybody's anxiety to get on, February proved a comparatively idle month. As has been stated, Aylmer had an insufficient force for his task. Reinforcements, however, were coming up and every effort to reorganize for a fresh attempt was being made. Soldiers, like sailors, will never leave a stone unturned to rescue comrades in distress, and a relief column may always be depended on to strive to the very end. The last day of the month brought a draft from the 3/5th Battalion of 6 officers and 302 men, and sadly was the draft needed. Very few indeed of the 627 men who left Basrah were now able to perform a day's duty.

On the 7th March a very resolute attempt to relieve the beleaguered garrison commenced. It being impossible to force the several lines in front, it was determined to try and turn them. This meant that our people must leave the river and their water supply and march out across the desert. The only possible chance of success was rapidity and a decisive victory. The desert column could not be fed, watered, relieved of its sick or reinforced until its work was ended and touch again obtained with the Tigris in rear of the formidable Turkish lines. A night march on the Dujailah Redoubt, in three columns, over the desert, started on the evening of the 7th March and marched in pitch darkness and in strict silence all night. At dawn the redoubt was reached and Kut was in sight. Intense eagerness and excitement reigned in every breast, but the result was the most bitter disappointment it is hoped that will ever fall to the lot of gallant rescuers. The attack was too late and failed to surprise, and the enthusiastic columns had to fall back again upon their old camp at Hanna. During the March the brigade in which the Buffs were acted as escort to the second-line transport, but moved up into the fight at Dujailah, which lasted all day. The enemy's guns followed up the British retreat and our men were under their fire during the greater part of the 9th. At 11.30 p.m. on that date a dispirited and terribly fatigued column reached the old camping ground again. They had suffered severely from want of water.

It was sad to have to remain inactive so near to Kut, but it was essential that more troops should arrive. These came at last in the shape of the 13th Division from Gallipoli, which had been evacuated early in January. General Aylmer, V.C., was replaced by General Sir G. P. Gorringe, and on the 5th April this commander attacked, frontally and with the utmost vigour, the Hanna trenches, before which the relief force had been held up so long. The attack took place early in the morning and was chiefly entrusted to the newly arrived division, which gloriously carried the obstacle in a couple of hours, though it consisted of no less than five lines of trenches. It was soon noticed by

K   129 our aircraft that the Falahiyeh and Sanna-i-Yat lines were being strongly reinforced. Absence of cover militated greatly against a successful further advance, but this was made as soon as night fell, and the Falahiyeh fortifications were soon also in our possession on both banks of the river.

Hopes rose again after this victory that Kut would, after all, be saved, and every man was prepared for any necessary effort, but unhappily the floods now rose with great rapidity. The river became a roaring torrent and the marshes more formidable than ever, not only in impassability but, what was worse, in extent as well. Nevertheless, attempts were made to pass the lines still intervening between Gorringe's men and their goal, but it was not to be. The last attempt was made on the 23rd April: on the evening of the 21st the Buffs, with the remainder of the brigade, crossed the river from the right to the left bank, marched three or four miles up stream and took up a position in reserve preparatory to an attack. Here the night was passed in the open air in artillery formation, and a move up into the reserve trenches was made the following morning. The attack was more or less successful at first, but the Turks were reinforced and drove those of our men who had penetrated their defences out again. Nothing but a frontal attack could possibly be attempted owing to the presence of and utter impassability of the marshes. The Buffs were sent back into the trenches from whence they had emerged so full of anticipation, and on the 29th April the garrison of Kut surrendered to the enemy.

During the end of April the Buffs had had to fight another enemy besides the Turk. There were a few cases of cholera reported on the 27th. On the 28th there were four deaths and for a few days things looked serious, but a bad epidemic was avoided.

The following is the list of casualties suffered by the 5th Battalion during these operations:—

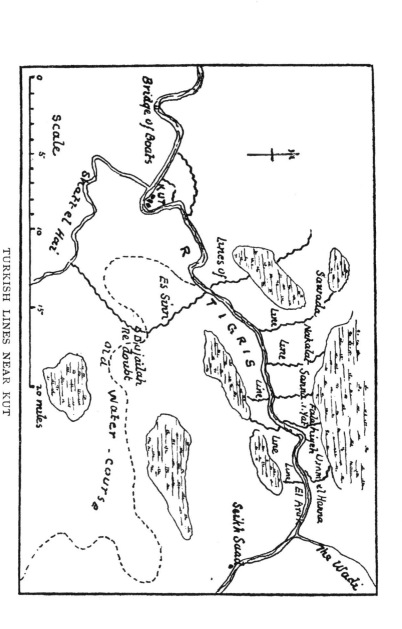

TURKISH LINES NEAR KUT

Officers killed, 8: Major J. S. Fraser; Captain A. G. A. Adam; Lieuts. G. T. Baker, Hon. G. J. Goschen, H. S. Marchant, E. Rothwell, J. T. Waite and W. H. Winch.

Twelve were wounded: Colonel J. Munn-Mace; Major E. Clarke; Captains B. Buss (afterwards died of wounds), T. H. O. Collings, F. O. Marchant and D. S. Wilkinson; Lieuts. F. S. Fleuret, A. E. L. Hardcastle, L. E. Holyman, G. Jessel, J. H. J. Peters and S. W. Weldon.

Eighty-four other ranks were killed up to the 29th April, and 259 wounded.

III. GALLIPOLI

Although no battalion of the Buffs served in Gallipoli, the regiment was not unrepresented on that sanguinary Peninsula, and John Turk was given a chance there also of confronting the Dragon badge. The story of how Buffs came to be in this region is a somewhat curious one and is briefly as follows: early in 1915 the Monmouthshire Brigade, which was a portion of the 53rd (Welsh) Division, was suddenly sent off to France, leaving the division one brigade short. In the month of April, therefore, a new brigade was made up from the home counties to swell the Welshmen's ranks and make their division complete. It consisted of the 2/4th Battalion of the Queens, the 1/4th Sussex, the 2/10th Middlesex and a composite Kentish battalion which contained one company from the 2/4th Buffs, one from the 2/5th Buffs and one company each from the 4th and 5th Royal West Kent Regiment. The Buffs were A and B Companies and the West Kents were C and D, but the latter regiment found the Battalion Headquarter staff.

For this reason the unit was generally known as the 2/4th Royal West Kent, though its proper designation

131

was the Kent Composite Battalion. At first it was suggested that a new badge should be found or invented for this composite battalion, but this was vetoed, as Kent is not a sufficiently populous county to maintain a new infantry regiment. The War Office therefore gave authority for the wearing of the Buffs' badge by A and B Companies, and the West Kent badge by the others. The two halves of the battalion had also different record offices at Hounslow, different regimental numbers and so on. It was trained with the rest of the division at Cambridge and afterwards at Bedford under the command of Colonel Simpson. The officers of A Company were Captains Jude and Taunton, Lieuts. Dixon and Filmer, and 2nd Lieuts. Morgan and Larkin. B Company was commanded by Captain Greatorex, with Captain Lamarque and Lieuts. Keble, Wood, Willows and Griffin, all of whom belonged to the 4th or 5th Battalion of the Buffs.

The division was ordered to the East instead of to France, so the Kentish men and men of Kent entrained together on the 17th July at Devonport and next day embarked on the s.s. *Northland*. They landed at Suvla Bay, Gallipoli Peninsula, on the 9th August, three days after the great surprise landing there and the attack on Achi Baba. During their stay in this theatre of war the men were mostly employed in making trenches and on fatigue work, and the movements from one part to another were unimportant. First they were at " C " Beach, where the commanding officer got wounded, then at West Beach and later on at Lala Baba, but fatigue work was still the occupation of the unit. December, 1915, brought the skilful and successful evacuation of Gallipoli and Suvla. Our battalion withdrew to Mudros, on the island of Lemnos, where it embarked for Egypt on board the *Haverford* and landed at Alexandria on the 19th December.

The Egyptian history of the Kent Composite Battalion is not of very great interest, although, after changing its name and organization, it took its full share in the Palestine campaign which came later on. Under its old constitution it proceeded to Wardan and afterwards to Fayoum in Central Egypt, but, towards the middle of 1916, Colonel Money, who was then in command, represented the great inconvenience of having his men administered by two record offices and a double lot of paymasters, with the result that an order came transferring all N.C.O.'s and men of the Buffs compulsorily to the 2/4th Royal West Kent Regiment, under which honourable title the men saw much service on their new front, but as they were no longer Buffs their doings must remain unchronicled in this regimental history.

CHAPTER VI

THE SOMME

I. Summary of Events

IN so far as the principal or Western theatre of war is concerned the chief events of 1916—and they were events of stupendous magnitude—were the resolute attack on the French troops around Verdun and the most magnificent and successful defence by our allies. In all their warlike and heroic past the gallant French never fought such a fight, and even the greatest of their historic victories, such as Jena, Austerlitz and the like, pale in renown when compared to Verdun. After many German offensives west of Soissons and about Ypres, the enemy appears to have definitely made up his mind to relinquish the idea of seizing Calais and the Channel ports as hopeless, and by forcing the French lines at Verdun to revert to his original plan of reaching Paris—this time by another route. It was on the 21st February that this great battle commenced, and the hostile lines swayed to and fro for days and weeks as the tremendous struggle continued. Men died by thousands and thousands, but never were our allies broken; " on ne passe pas " was the war cry, and the enemy never got through the Frenchman's line.

The battle of Verdun may have said to have lasted till the end of June, and there were not wanting many who murmured that we English were deserting our comrades and that some great attempt on our part should be made to bring aid to our exhausted allies in their desperate straits. We had, however, our work cut out to defend our own line, for our armies were not yet at full strength nor all our new soldiers fully trained for

war. What could be done was done. The British line
was extended, on the 23rd March, to include Souchez,
and, as Sir Douglas Haig, the new Commander-in-
Chief, pointed out, the principle of an offensive campaign during the summer was early decided on.

Preparations of a very extensive nature, however, had
to be made: Haig was in close consultation and agreement with Joffre, but the date was dependent on many
doubtful factors; the British armies were growing in
numbers and the supply of munitions steadily increas-
ing; also training was daily improving the new levies.
On the other hand, the Germans were continuing to
press their attacks at Verdun, and both there and on the
Italian front, where the Austrian offensive was gaining
ground, it was evident that the strain might become
too great to be borne unless timely action was taken to
relieve it. It was in June no secret throughout France
or England that an attack by us on a great scale was in
contemplation. The different units, brigades, divisions
and so on were all preparing for a very big event, and
were moving to the several points from which action
was to take place. It was on the 1st July that the Battle
of the Somme actually took place or rather began, and
it started by a grand combined Anglo-French offensive
on a twenty-five mile front, north and south of the
river of that name. The Somme operations lasted many
weeks and are divided in Haig's description into three
phases: firstly, the successes gained between the 1st of
July and the 17th, during which the southern crest of
the main plateau between Delville Wood and Bazentin
le Petit was gained; secondly, a long and severe struggle
for the mastery between the contending armies, which
may be said to have resulted in our favour by the first
week in September; and thirdly, the advance, which
was pushed down the forward slope and extended so
that the whole plateau was in our possession.

There are many works now available, as well as the

despatches themselves, which will give a military student a good and clear description of all this fighting; but the short sketch given above must serve one who reads merely to understand what the Buffs were doing in France during this momentous period.

II. 6TH BATTALION—1916

The 6th and 7th Battalions were the first of those engaged on the Western front to take their parts upon the Somme, and we will now note their story since the conclusion of 1915, when the 6th was in trenches at Givenchy—very cold, and waist deep in water. The New Year opened with a bombardment, and there were eighteen casualties on the 2nd January. After a short spell out of the line, the battalion returned to the trenches and for the next three months went through a time that was probably the severest of the whole war: the trenches were almost filled with mud—indeed, in some cases men were actually drowned in it; the cold was intense; fighting was continuous and the wastage by casualties appalling. The enemy had a preponderance of artillery and an unbelievable number of that most nerve-shattering of all engines of war—the heavy minenwerfer (mine-thrower). Mines were blown, all and every day and night, by both sides alike, and the orders then in force were to occupy at once any craters made, if within sixty yards of our line.

There was a somewhat notable attack on one of these craters made by the Buffs on the 6th March, 1916, which unfortunately, however, proved a failure owing, as the brigadier reported, firstly to the heavy condition of the ground, and secondly because the enemy had assembled in some force, presumably with the object of driving us out of our craters; consequently very much more opposition was met with than was anticipated. A short narrative of this minor operation may give an idea of certain incidents that are liable to occur in trench warfare. A scheme had been drawn up and the necessary orders issued for an attempt to seize what was known as the " triangle " crater, as well as certain portions of the trenches in the immediate neighbourhood of the Hohenzollern Redoubt, which were on the 6th March, 1916, in the hands of the enemy. C Company The Buffs was detailed for this minor enterprise and it was divided into three distinct parties, which were to emerge from craters in our own possession. The attempt was commenced at 6 p.m., but in ten minutes two of the attacking parties were held up by a barrage of bombs and the third by heavy ground—the mud being found to be knee deep. The party on the left managed, indeed, to reach their objective, but the fact that the others were not up necessitated their retirement, and at five minutes to seven the company had to report that its advance was absolutely stopped. Half an hour later another attempt was made, notwithstanding the fact that in the interim the enemy had attacked in his turn. At 8.5 and again at 8.35 p.m. the Buffs called urgently for more ammunition and grenades. They also requested reinforcements, and a company of the 6th Royal West Kent was ordered up to their support. Meanwhile the 7th East Surrey Regiment, which was on the left, was attacked, and, though the assailants were driven off, much damage was done to their trenches. There were two more attacks on this regiment before eleven o'clock, but they were unsuccessful. By midnight the situation on the Buffs' front was exactly similar to what it had been previous to the attack; the enemy had made several bombing attacks against our own craters, but they were successfully repulsed and during the remainder of the night the enemy was quiet.

Later in the month on two separate occasions the battalion was brought into the line from a hurriedly snatched two or three days' rest at Bethune, in order to resist German assaults or make a hurried counter-attack.

Amongst the many individual acts of heroism was that of Corpl. Cotter who, though himself at the time severely and, later on in the same engagement, fatally wounded, directed a bombing attack, throwing bombs himself after both his legs had been shattered, and thus saving a trench from being rushed by the enemy. Another regimental hero to be remembered for all time. It was sad that this glorious corporal died in hospital at Lillers, but very gratifying to know that he lived long enough to learn that his gallantry had been recognized by the award of the V.C.

The following official announcement was published on the 31st March, 1916, in the list of winners of the Victoria Cross:—

" No. 6707 Lance-Corpl. (Acting Corporal) William " R. Cotter, East Kent.—For most conspicuous bravery " and devotion to duty. When his right leg had been " blown off at the knee, and he had also been wounded " in both arms, he made his way unaided for fifty yards " to a crater, steadied the men who were holding it, " controlled their fire, issued orders, and altered the " dispositions of his men to meet a fresh counter-attack " by the enemy. For two hours he held his position, " and only allowed his wounds to be roughly dressed " when the attack had quieted down. He could not be " moved back for fourteen hours, and during all this " time had a cheery word for all who passed him. There " is no doubt that his magnificent courage helped " greatly to save a critical situation." His wonderful performance is still more remarkable on account of the fact that he had a glass eye. Unfortunately, he did not survive long to enjoy the great honour. At first he made good progress, but he died on the 14th of March.

For the following details of the hero's life we are indebted to the *Folkestone Herald* :—

CORPORAL W. R. COTTER, V.C.

" Corporal Cotter was born at Folkestone thirty-four
" years ago, being the eldest of six sons, all of whom
" entered the Navy or Army. He joined the Buffs when
" he was about twenty years old, and was on the Re-
" serve at the outbreak of the War. Being called up,
" he went to Canterbury, and was sent to France, not-
" withstanding that he had a glass eye, having lost the
" sight of his right eye through an accident some years
" ago. Excepting two intervals, he had been at the
" front ever since, and right up to March 6th he re-
" mained unwounded, although he had several narrow
" escapes from being shot. His letters home were
" always of a cheery type, and in the trenches he was
" one of the happiest and best of men. He kept his
" comrades in good spirits, and he was always ready to
" help the wounded or dying. Corporal Cotter distin-
" guished himself on several occasions in bayonet fight-
" ing, and in December last he was recommended by
" his officers for conspicuous bravery. He was then, it
" appeared, recommended for the D.C.M."

The 6th Battalion remained in the same sector until
Easter, when it went back for a well-deserved rest near
Lillers. Here it was refitted and reorganized and given
plenty of hard work and hard training with a view to
what was to come. It benefited much from the complete change; football and sports were indulged in, and
at last there came some decent spring weather.

On the 19th July six officers were mentioned in
despatches, but only two of them, Lea-Smith and
Smeltzer, were alive. The names were Major Soames,
D.S.O., Captains Furley and Smeltzer, and 2nd Lieuts.
Brodie, Lea-Smith and Jelf.

During this month the battalion moved south to
Amiens, and everybody knew where the ultimate destination would be. On the 28th the real warlike move
took place. All surplus kit was left behind and a posi-

tion finally taken up behind Albert, as the brigade was not to come into action just at first, but to form part of a reserve force. On the 30th three thousand Mills grenades were issued out and a move made to Bresle, from which place during the night tremendously heavy shelling from our guns was heard.

The 1st July was the opening day of the great Somme struggle and the Battle of Albert, 1916. Zero hour found the 6th just outside Lavieville, and when the moment came it marched through Millencourt and halted in a field north-west of that village—being, of course, in reserve. A great deal of firing was heard and some rumours caused a good deal of excitement: at first " all objectives had been gained," and then " the assault on Ovillers had failed "—which latter was unfortunately fairly true, as the attack on this sector did not achieve much success on the first day. At 5 p.m. orders came to be ready to move at a moment's notice into the intermediate line and the brigade actually moved off at 7 o'clock, finding the greatest difficulty in getting through the congested streets of the village of Millencourt, but at 8.15 orders were changed again and the 12th Division was now to relieve the 8th, which had suffered many casualties. This move was accomplished at night time, the Buffs, with the rest of the division, being all in the trenches by about 2.45 a.m. The 2nd of the month did not bring another important effort by our troops at this part of the line, though Ovillers was heavily bombarded.

At 1.15 a.m. on the 3rd, however, orders came that this village would be attacked by the 35th and 37th Brigades at 3.15 a.m., after an hour's intense bombardment. The order of battle for the 37th Brigade was 6th Battalion The Queen's on the right, supported by two companies of the Buffs; 6th Battalion Royal West Kent on the left, supported by two companies of the Buffs; the 7th East Surrey Regiment in support. After

a few casualties, sustained by reason of the usual re-
taliation to our bombardment, the Queen's and West
Kents attacked. Very heavy machine-gun flanking fire
met the Kentish men from the left and the Queen's
from the right. A Company of the Buffs " went over "
by platoons about 3.30 a.m., and the first wave suffered
few casualties until the German wire was reached; but
the succeeding waves of this company, and those of
C Company also, suffered heavily in their advance. The
few men that succeeded in getting into the German
trenches, under 2nd Lieut. Farmer, at once commenced
to bomb the dug-outs. Eyewitnesses report that the
accuracy and regularity of this advance was remarkable, and reminded them of field-day work. Two communication trenches were found to be blocked. Owing
to casualties amongst bomb-carriers the supply of these
necessities was soon exhausted, and casualties were inflicted by German bombs. Finding at length that it
was impossible to remain any longer in the trench, 2nd
Lieut. Farmer collected all the men around him and
brought them back to the English lines. The intense
enemy machine-gun fire held up also the attack on the
right, and B and D Companies did not go into the
struggle. The German artillery maintained a heavy fire
on our trenches with great accuracy and weight.

About 7.30 a.m. a message was received that the 10th
Corps was making another attack, preceded by artillery
preparation, at 8.15 a.m. If successful, the 35th Infantry Brigade would co-operate. A message was also
received that if the 37th should again attack, the 6th
Buffs were to lead it with the two companies that had
not suffered, and that they would be supported by the
Queen's. However, it was decided that no further
efforts should be made on this sector for that day; the
East Surrey took over the front-line trenches and the
brigade settled down to be shelled. During the night a
number of wounded were brought in. The casualties

of the 3rd July were, for the 6th Battalion The Buffs:
killed, Captain J. C. T. Leigh and 2nd Lieuts. H. G.
Cox and S. T. Hinkley; wounded, Captain Child,
Lieut. W. W. Chapman, 2nd Lieuts. Free, Carter and
Madden; missing, Lieut. G. W. M. Burton and 2nd
Lieut. L. H. Batson, both of whom it was afterwards
ascertained had been killed. Total casualties, 11 officers
and 263 other ranks.

It sometimes most unfortunately occurs that in war
all casualties cannot be discovered and collected. A
man may be killed outright or he may be wounded,
perhaps in such a way as to prevent his crawling or
staggering away. Every effort is always made to re-
trieve and bring away the sufferers, and it is most dis-
tressing to think this cannot always be done. After the
fight on the 3rd, the Buffs, together with the rest of
the brigade, had a comparatively quiet time, but on
the 7th 2nd Lieut. Bond left the trenches with a patrol.
He reported on the German wire as being in bad condition, and he brought in five wounded men who had
been lying out, poor fellows, ever since the early morning of the 3rd. Lieut. Lea-Smith was killed by a chance
shell during the morning of the 7th. The battalion did
not go into the trenches again till the 27th July, when
the whole brigade took its place in the Ovillers section
once more after being hastily refitted and brought up
to strength.

What is described by Sir Douglas Haig as the first
phase of the great fight was now over, and the discovery
had been made that the enemy was in an immensely
strong position, fortified, line behind line, to an extent
perhaps never before known in war, unless it be compared with Wellington's lines at Torres-Vedras, which
Massena never dared to assault. On the 3rd August,
the Battle of Pozieres Ridge being then in full swing,
orders were issued for an attack to be delivered by the
6th Battalion The Buffs on a certain German strong

142

point and for it to be carried out in conjunction with the 36th Brigade on the right; this brigade was to assail what was known as the Ration Trench, which communicated with the strong point in question. The attack was to be launched at 11.15 p.m. B Company was on the left, D Company on the right and A and C Companies in reserve. About 9 o'clock the enemy shelled our trenches heavily, but some French ·75 guns were turned on the German batteries with gas shells and completely stopped their fire. Had it not been for this timely action, due to the initiative of Lt.-Colonel Cope, commanding the Buffs, the casualties would probably have been very severe. At 11 p.m. 2nd Lieut. Hanmer and a party of bombers crept out under the barrage to be ready to bomb an enemy's machine gun should it open upon our men when they advanced.

Punctually to the hour ordered B Company went over the parapet and was immediately joined by D, the barrage lifting at the same moment. D Company then went through B to take the trench on the left of the strong point, but during its advance eased off a bit too much to its right; so A Company was brought up from the reserve and soon after C Company also, and these two took and consolidated the objective and, together with a company of Royal Engineers, pushed on a bit further; but when dawn came B Company found itself in the Ration Trench. However, touch was secured with the 36th Brigade, and the Buffs had done their job. Lieut. A. J. Hanmer did most gallant work during this action. He won the M.C., but was so severely wounded that he died of his injuries on the 7th October.

2nd Lieut. Routley and a Sussex officer made a reconnaissance as far as Mouquet Farm. The enemy tried a counter-attack from this place, but it melted away before our Lewis guns. Two German officers and 87 other ranks, mostly Prussian infantry, were unearthed from the dug-outs of the captured works. The

143

battalion was relieved, about 11 a.m. on the 4th, by the 6th West Kent, and went back to huts in Martinsart Wood, having lost 4 officers wounded and 114 casualties of other ranks.

On the 10th August a somewhat curious accident occurred. In the early morning our 60-pounder trench mortars bombarded a German sap with good effect. 2nd Lieut. McDermott crossed over to it when the bombardment lifted. After he had dropped a Stokes Mortar bomb down a dug-out the Germans all fled. It was therefore arranged to take this sap after some bombs had been got up. These were duly carried up and stacked ready for use, and Captain Ward and Lieut. Sir R. Onslow were ready to conduct operations. About 2.30 our trench mortars opened fire again by way of preparation, but unfortunately one shot fell short, right into the middle of our stack of bombs, exploding about 1,500 of them and wounding both the officers named and an orderly. As the bombs were lost the affair had to be given up.

On the 12th August the brigadier was informed that the attack on this portion of our line was to be in future of the nature of a holding one, and was not to be pushed home if much opposition was encountered. On this day news from England came that Captain Farmer and 2nd Lieut. Bond had been awarded the M.C., Corpl. Tamblin the D.C.M., and that there were Military Medals for Sgt. Fox and Ptes. Anderson, Blackshaw, Browning, Hughes, Luchford and Setterfield.

On the 14th August the brigade marched away from the Somme area to the northward and did not return to this district till the 29th September. It relieved the 34th Brigade in the neighbourhood of Beaumetz and Betrencourt, which are villages some seven miles or so south-west of Arras. Except for some trench-mortar activity this sector was fairly quiet. The battalion was here for about six weeks and then returned to the

Somme, where by this time the British line had been very considerably advanced. The 1st October found the 37th Brigade about Lonqueval, whence it passed into a reserve line south of Guedecourt.

The ground was now so bad and the roads north of this part of the Somme so inferior that transport became a great difficulty, and troops had to rely almost entirely on pack animals for the supply of the necessary food and warlike stores. Indeed, an attack arranged for the 4th October had to be postponed for forty-eight hours on account of rain and bad weather. On the 6th of the month the Buffs were in the front line of their brigade.

Then an operation order was issued commencing with the words: " The general advance of the Allies will be resumed." This order was, as usual, clear and minute as to detail, and it gave both a first and a second objective. The Buffs were on the right of their brigade and the Royal West Kent on the left. Of the Buffs themselves, A Company was on the right, B in the centre and C on the left, and each of these companies was given its own individual objective. D Company sent three platoons as carrying party to the other three companies, while its fourth was directed to construct a strong point. The attack was ordered to be carried out in four waves at fifty yards interval; each platoon extended to two yards interval, bayonets to be fixed and magazines charged. Each man carried 220 rounds of small-arm ammunition, and the carrying parties had a further supply. The artillery was to lift every minute and fifty yards at a time. Arrangements were made to signal to the contact aeroplanes. The zero hour was fixed at 1.45 p.m. on the 7th October, but the enemy must have known what was coming, for an hour before that the Buffs were heavily shelled, and at 1.30 the Germans opened a tremendous machine-gun fire and shrapnel barrage on the front trenches. However, at the correct moment the attack opened, and it was met

L   145 with an excessively heavy machine-gun and rifle fire which came from an unexpected quarter. This held up C Company, but A and B reached the first objective, suffering, however, somewhat severely. On trying to advance further they were completely stopped by the German machine guns, as were the West Kent on their left. About twenty men of A Company succeeded in joining the 61st Brigade on the right and they advanced with it; this brigade attained its objective. The first objective gained by our men was bravely held all the day until relieved at midnight by the 6th Battalion The Queen's. Throughout the afternoon the lines had been subjected to a great deal of bombing from the high ground above them and to enfilade fire from the flanks. Lt.-Colonel Cope was severely wounded, and Captain T. Pagen, R.A.M.C., was killed in attempting to go to his assistance. The battalion, forty strong, was taken out of action by the adjutant, Captain Page, the only officer who was not either killed or wounded. It was for no slight reasons that the 6th Buffs were stopped in their advance. Eight officers were killed: Lieut. P. R. Hatch, 2nd Lieuts. A. E. S. Ommanney, G. S. M. Norrie, E. G. Routley, Loft, D. A. Harnett and R. B. N. Moss, and Captain Pagen, R.A.M.C.; and twelve wounded: Lt.-Colonel Cope, D.S.O., Lieuts. Cumberbatch, Bond and Chapman, 2nd Lieuts. Kidd, Woolbridge, Taylor, Springay-Mason, Turk, Taylor and Jacobs. There were 347 casualties amongst the rank and file—killed, wounded and missing. Yes, the 7th October, 1916, was another dreadful day in the long history of the regiment, as well as in the short one of its 6th Battalion, but the ancient honour showed no sign of deterioration at this Battle of the Transloy Ridges.

Now reduced to a mere skeleton of a battalion, though drafts began to arrive almost daily after the 16th of the month, it was necessary after a few days' rest near Lonqueval to remove it, on the 21st October, to the quieter sector of Reviere, in the district from which it had come to the Somme at the end of September.

There was a certain amount of official correspondence about this great fight, as there always is when full success is not gained by British efforts; it seems clear that the artillery barrage was not strong enough to keep down the hostile fire, that our front line was not continuous, but had gaps in it, and that the ground was not suitable for forming for attack.

Major Dawson assumed the acting command of the battalion, rendered vacant by Lt.-Colonel Cope becoming a casualty.

III. 7TH BATTALION—1916

The commencement of the year 1916 found the 7th Battalion in billets at Dernancourt. Early in January Lt.-Colonel Elmslie was invalided, and Major Birch took his job until the arrival of the new commander, Lt.-Colonel A. L. Ransome, of the Dorsetshire Regiment. In February the battalion moved to St. Gratien, where it remained for fifteen days, being employed in making the Daours–Contay railway; and then, in March, it took over a position south of Maricourt about Corbie and Suzanne, where it remained till the end of the month.

The incidents worthy of note at this time were not very numerous, and the important move of the spring was to Picquigny, where strenuous preparation for the coming great battle was continuously and methodically engaged in: dummy trenches were laid out on a replica of the ground over which the men were to attack, and one full-dress rehearsal for the brigade took place with contact aeroplanes and flares, the Commander-in-Chief being present. This special preparation went on till the 10th June, when the battalion started for the line itself, and it is not too much to say that the soldiers were remarkable for keenness and zeal. There is always more of excitement and dash in an offensive than in the somewhat tame and monotonous business of a passive defence, though quite as much heroism can be exhibited in the one as in the other. " Let us get at them " is, at any rate, a more popular sentiment than " Stand fast, here they come."

From the 11th June onward all work was concentrated in preparing assembly trenches, communication trenches and dumps for the forthcoming attack. The battalion was at Bray sur Somme on the 17th June and remained there till the last day of the month, when it marched into its assembly trench in Lapree Wood ready for the assault. It may be remembered that on this day, the 30th June, 1916, the 6th Battalion was at Bresle, about nine miles away.

On the great 1st of July the 55th Brigade, a unit of which was the 7th Battalion The Buffs, to whose part in the struggle we will now refer, held the line in front of Carnoy, and its objective was a trench about two hundred yards north of the Montauban–Fricourt road. Zero hour was 7.30 a.m., and the following was the order of battle for the attack: the 7th Queen's were on the left, the 8th East Surrey on the right, the 7th Buffs in support, with the special task of clearing the Carnoy craters, and the 7th Royal West Kent were in reserve. At 7 a.m. our barrage became intense and remained so till 7.22, at which time all guns of the Trench Mortar battery opened for eight minutes, and at the zero hour the whole brigade went forward to the assault. Local conditions necessitated the breaking up of the Buffs for several and separate duties: two platoons of B Company, under 2nd Lieut. Tatam, were to clear the Carnoy mine craters; two platoons of the same company to assist the assaulting battalions by clearing up captured trenches or ground;[1] C Company

[1] This operation was known as "mopping up" and really meant finishing and completing work that the leading troops had to leave undone, such as the capture of men remaining in the dug-outs and so on.

148

to consolidate and garrison a certain trench called the Pommiers Trench. Two platoons of D Company to act as carrying parties. Two platoons of A Company to garrison two selected localities in rear of the Pommiers Trench.

The Carnoy mine craters took six hours to clear, and six hours' very heavy fighting it was, carried out under 2nd Lieut. Tatam, whose excellent work was rewarded by a M.C. C Company was soon called away to aid the East Surreys, as were later on two platoons of A Company. In fact, these two platoons of A, together with one of C Company, under Lieuts. Dyson and Budds respectively, reached the final objective and held that part of it allotted to the East Surrey Regiment until relieved by other troops. Again it became necessary about noon to send up half D Company to make good part of the final objective of the 7th Queen's. This was done successfully, but the company lost its commander, Captain G. T. Neame, during the operation.

There is no doubt that during the whole operation, which was carried out more or less as planned, our troops encountered far more opposition than was anticipated; particularly was this the case at the craters, to attack which only two platoons were originally assigned, a number of men quite inadequate. The whole position, indeed, proved to be a very strong one, consisting of four lines.

The battalion lost the following casualties on this day:—

Killed : Captain G. T. Neame; Lieuts. P. G. Norbury and E. H. A. Goss; and 2nd Lieut. J. F. Baddeley and 48 other ranks.

Wounded : Captain C. K. Black; 2nd Lieut. H. Owen and 144 other ranks; and 7 missing.

The Buffs remained in the front-line trenches till the night of the 4th/5th July and were heavily shelled, the

149

enemy relaxing nothing of his activity and energy in this respect. The Pommiers line had been consolidated and it was now the special mark of the German gunners. The battalion reached Bronfay Farm about 3.30 a.m. on the 5th after a very strenuous four days. The 5th was spent in resting, and the 6th in necessary reorganization.

The time allowed in the back area was not a long one, however, and, on the 12th July, the Buffs moved by companies via Maricourt to relieve a battalion of the Liverpool Regiment about Maltz Horn Farm, which is in the immediate vicinity of Trones Wood and marked the extreme right of the English line. Here the French were on the right of the battalion, and as the enemy still held Trones Wood and, as an old German communication trench running at right angles to the front was now held by us, it was necessary to have sentries facing both ways. On the 13th July orders came that the 55th Infantry Brigade was to attack this wood, and the following order was arranged for the Battle of Bazentin Ridge in so far as the brigade was concerned: the 7th West Kent to attack the southern half of the wood from the south; the 7th Queen's to attack the northern half from the west; the 7th Buffs, less B Company, to remain in Maltz Horn Trench, mentioned above as running at right angles to this line—one platoon to attack a certain strong point.

B Company was lent to the 7th Queen's, attacked with them and suffered very severe losses. 8th East Surrey to be in reserve.

At 7 p.m. one platoon of D Company, under 2nd Lieut. Scott, attacked the strong point mentioned above. A bombing party moved along the trench and entered it by a tunnel, but, on its entry, the enemy was encountered in strength and its force appeared to increase, reinforcements apparently coming in from the direction of the wood. The consequence was that Scott withdrew his party and reorganized it. He then proceeded to attack his objective over the open by parties from the flanks, but he was met by heavy rifle and machine-gun fire and was compelled to withdraw with loss. Verbal messages came over the telephone about 10 p.m. that the holding of Maltz Horn Trench, the defensive flank, was of the first importance and the line was not to be thinned in order to attack the strong point again. Nevertheless, attacks were continued on the morning of the 14th, and about 9 a.m. the point was evacuated by the enemy, and patrols were sent forward down the trench which led to Guillemont. No opposition was met with, as the enemy was retiring towards that place. Touch was then established with the 54th Brigade, and in the evening of the 14th the battalion (less the company attached to the Queen's) was lent to this brigade and remained with it in the front line, after their own had been relieved, until the early morning of the 18th, when it was withdrawn to Grovetown Camp; there it stayed till the 21st, on which date it was withdrawn temporarily from the Somme fighting and entrained at Mericourt for Longpré and later to St. Omer. From there it marched to Recquinghem, and finally to Hondeghem, about half-way between St. Omer and Ypres. A fairly quiet life was now the portion of this battalion for a few weeks, spent at first in the line near Bois Grenier, and afterwards resting at Monchy Breton, near the little town of St. Pol, reorganizing and training, always training, and absorbing fresh drafts from England.

At the end of September the battalion moved south again for the great struggle at Thiepval. This village is about a mile from the River Ancre, on the eastern bank, which is here very high and steep. Indeed, the place is quite four hundred feet above the stream. It had been taken from the Germans on the 26th September, and on that same date the Royal West Kent Regiment (of the 55th Brigade) had reached Crucifix Corner, though the Buffs were only at Hedauville but were still on the march, so that the battalion bivouacked that night somewhat nearer the scene of action. On the morning of the 27th, starting at 5.30, it moved by platoons to Crucifix Corner, where the men got into dug-outs and there remained till the afternoon of the 29th, when it relieved the 8th Suffolk Regiment, A and C Companies proceeding to Wood Post, and B and D to the old German line. One platoon of A Company acted as carrying party to Thiepval for the 8th East Surrey Regiment. At 7 a.m. on the following day came the S.O.S. signal from the northern edge of the Schwaben Redoubt and the Buffs were ordered to stand by in readiness. The Schwaben Redoubt was in shape roughly an oval and certainly not a square, though the terms north face, west face, etc., are used for convenience in the following narrative of the fight there. It was somewhere about five hundred yards long and two hundred broad, and the original parapets were so knocked about by the 1st October that they were mere mounds and ditches with shelving sides. For defence they had to be roughly and rapidly improved and adapted as occasion required, but on account of the constant bombardment it was impossible to shape them up properly.

What had happened in this place was that the enemy, making a somewhat sudden and resolute attack, had driven the defenders back from the southern face of the work, considerably weakened one of the East Surrey companies and captured the whole of the western face. Counter-attacks were immediately organized and, in connection with this, D Company of the Buffs was, at 9.35 a.m., sent up to occupy the northern defences of the village of Thiepval, and at 1.25 this company got orders to send two platoons to act in conjunction with the East Surrey in attacking and capturing the Schwaben Redoubt. These two platoons were given definite objectives and the zero hour was fixed at 4 p.m.

A Company moved up to Thiepval and reported to the O.C. 8th East Surrey. At 9.15 in the evening, the attack on the west face having failed, and that on the north one having succeeded, it was found that the Surrey battalion had suffered too much loss to be of much further use, and the rest of the Buffs went forward to take over the redoubt, together with the western defences of the village.

Soon after midnight came a short message from 2nd Lieut. Carman, who commanded the two platoons of D Company that had gone forward to attack with the Surrey men. It was to the effect that his men were almost entirely wiped out directly the starting-point was left.

One of the most difficult periods the battalion ever had to face during the war commenced with the month of October. The commanding officer held a consultation with the chief of the East Surrey and they decided that B Company of the Buffs (Captain Brice) should take over the whole of the front line occupied by the Surrey men, and this relief was completed by 5.45 a.m. on the 1st October. At 12.50 B Company was able to report that Point R.19.d.45 was taken and touch got with the Royal West Kent, so now the Buffs held part of the northern and part of the southern face of the redoubt, and the West Kent held the country down to the River Ancre.

It may be remarked that the contending forces were a good deal mixed in the Schwaben Redoubt on the 1st October. In fact, about half-past eight o'clock a German officer and twenty-six men emerged from a dug-out and gave themselves up to Captain Brice's men. The curious situation led to very extensive use of bombs on both sides. B Company was ordered to work the northern face with bombing parties, and great

153

attempts were made to clear the Redoubt by these means throughout the day, but no substantial improvement was made. C Company relieved B on the 2nd and was itself relieved next day, and still an indecisive bombing fight went on, alternating with rather heavy shelling. At noon on the 4th October it was decided that the only way to clear the redoubt of the enemy was by bombing, and bombing alone, and in still greater intensity and continuity. Orders came that this mode of fighting was to go on day and night with the greatest vigour, and that bomb-stops were to be made down all communication trenches which led northward.

The companies were by this time terribly depleted, and the brigade gave orders that all positions were to be held, but no further advance made. This was at 3.45 p.m., and it was not till 11.40 p.m. that the welcome news came that at 6 o'clock in the morning the 8th Norfolks would attack with bombing parties along the western face of the redoubt, Stokes and Vickers guns co-operating. At 3.30 a.m. on the 5th October, therefore, Norfolk bombing parties arrived at Thiepval in search of guides, and, these being supplied, they went on. The Buffs had received the simple orders to hold their own and nobly was that order obeyed: the conditions were terrible; heavy rain had reduced the shell-pitted ground to a sea of mud and it was thick with dead; German heavy artillery was concentrated on the position and bombing attacks were constant; but not an inch of ground was given up. The brothers A. S. and C. D. Hayfield and the regimental doctor, Captain McCullum Orme, particularly distinguished themselves. A. S. Hayfield was unhappily mortally wounded, another very fine officer being lost to the army. News came in the morning that the battalion was to be relieved in the afternoon and, by 5.15, this relief was effected. At 2.30 next morning (the 6th October) the battalion arrived by motor buses at

154

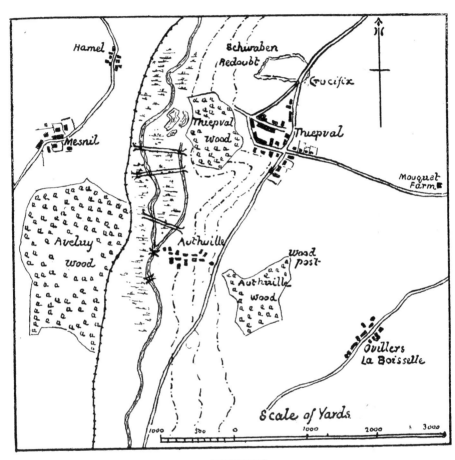

THIEPVAL

Hedauville and the next day to Candas, which is not far from Doullens. The 1st–6th October was a terrible time and not to be forgotten by the survivors. The estimated casualty list being: one officer killed, 2nd Lieut. D. M. Taylor; one died of wounds, 2nd Lieut. A. S. Hayfield; and nine others wounded. 26 men killed, 152 wounded and 23 missing.

Up to the 14th there came a rest, with training and the usual football and amusements, and then a three days' march back to Albert and into the Fabeck and High Trenches from the 22nd to the 26th. This proved a very strenuous tour and involved some casualties, a few being from shell-shock. We will leave the history of the 7th Battalion here. The great Somme struggle was considered at an end on the 18th November, and up to this date trench work and rest at Albert came each in their turn. It is pleasant to note, however, that the 7th November brought the M.C. to Captain Brice, 2nd Lieut. C. D. Hayfield and Captain Orme, R.A.M.C., and the D.C.M. to Sgts. Stewart and Steel.

IV. 8TH BATTALION—1916

The story of the 8th Battalion for the first half of the year 1916 is that of practically all the infantry units on the Western front. Tours of trench work alternated as a rule with periods of so-called rest. The misery of the former depended, as regards intensity, on the period of the year. When the weather was fine, rats and lice were the chief enemies in addition to the recognized foe; when the weather was bad, then wet and frozen extremities were added. There were always a few casualties in killed and wounded, and even the cheeriest-hearted were bound to find a turn of trench work a bit depressing. When it was the turn for rest, men crowded into leaky barns, 80 to 100 in each, sleeping one above another in tiers. Training and instruc-

155

tion of new drafts from England gave plenty of occupation, but in addition there were amusements, football, running and other sports by day, and entertainments by night in many cases. There were also baths.

At the beginning of January the battalion was at La Panne. On the 6th the Buffs were transferred to the 17th Infantry Brigade, still in the 24th Division, and on that day they entrained for their new divisional area about Poperinghe. The 14th of the month saw them in trenches near Ypres, where plenty of work in the way of digging, draining and revetting awaited the men. The 26th of January brought a welcome visit from the 1st Battalion which was still in the Ypres area. Lt.-Colonel Lucas, at the commencement of the war adjutant of the 1st Battalion, took over command of the 8th on the 16th March from Major Cunningham, a staff officer, who had relieved Lt.-Colonel Trueman a month earlier, Trueman having been taken into hospital.

The 4th June brought the birthday honour list; Lieut. C. Lindsay received the M.C., R.S.M. Brooker and Pte. Peet the D.C.M., Ptes. Buzzard and Hall the M.M., whilst 2nd Lieut. Shafto heard a week later that he also had the M.C.

On the 17th June, about midnight, there arose a cry of " gas," and the S.O.S. signal went up from the Royal Fusiliers who were on the left of the Buffs and, almost at once, a brisk bombardment broke on our front line. The gas itself arrived three or four minutes after the warning and lasted half an hour. However, it missed our companies in the front line, but spread somewhat over the reserves and headquarters.

On the 22nd June, after some rehearsal work at Bulford Camp, the battalion marched, via Bailleul, to St. Jans Capelle, where it was billeted in farms and continued its rehearsals. About this time Corpl. C.

156

Batchelor was awarded the M.M. for his conduct during the recent gas attack.

Although they may not very greatly or directly influence the winning of the war, raids were found to be of great use in fostering a manly and martial spirit amongst our soldiers. There is something about perfectly passive defence which makes for despondency and depression, but a raid on the enemy evokes a spirit of enterprise. These are perhaps very minor military enterprises in many cases and no description of them will be found in the military despatches, but they are naturally of intense interest to all concerned and show the enemy that the spirit of those opposite them is quite undismayed.

On the 28th June, then, a detachment of the Buffs under 2nd Lieuts. Anderson and Temple, to prove the value of the rehearsals, carried out a raid on the German trenches at a point known as Ash Road Barrier, which is near Ploegsteert. The men moved out in two parties so as to be in position outside our wire at 11.31 p.m., at which moment an intense bombardment commenced, directed on the points to be assaulted. Under cover of this the men crept forward, the guns lifting fifty yards at a time. Unfortunately the thing failed as a surprise, but Anderson's party succeeded in entering the enemy's front-line trench and then, after a bomb engagement, the raiding party withdrew successfully, bringing back with them all their wounded and some much-treasured trophies for the folks at home. The left party found the enemy's wire in front of them still uncut and it withdrew when the recall signal sounded, leaving one dead man. Lieut. Hall commanded the covering party, and Captain C. D. Gullick the whole operation. Three officers and a hundred men went over the top. Four men were killed and twenty wounded, and it is probable that the German loss was about the same.

157

THE SOMME

After a few days' careful training in the area north of Meteren this battalion left Bailleul by train for Longueau, which is two miles east of Amiens, and then fifteen miles back along the line to Le Mesge. This journey was memorable not only because it took our people into the vicinity of the great battle which was then raging, but also because of the tremendous reception given to the soldiers by the good folk of Amiens. This city is, of course, on the Somme river and was within sound of the guns. Had the enemy succeeded in some of their counter-attacks during the long and continuous struggle which was going on, Amiens would have been the first important city to feel his cruelty: the people were first of all Frenchmen, but they were Amiens citizens as well. They were hearing daily of the gallant deeds of their English friends almost at their doors, and they received those soldiers, who were on their way to join in the struggle, as perhaps only the French know how. After a week spent in training at the business of the attack, the brigade proceeded by train to Mericourt and marched to Morlancourt, some four miles south of Albert.

On the 6th of August the brigade got orders to take over the line between Guillemont and Delville Wood and elaborate arrangements were made accordingly, but they were altered at the last moment, and on the 9th the battalion found itself in reserve on the Carnoy–Montaubin road where, on the following day, an unfortunate accident occurred: something went wrong with the working of one of our own artillery guns which began firing short, so that our Battalion Headquarters found itself being shelled by our own gunners and a few casualties occurred before the matter was reported by a pigeon message. The 12th August brought an unusually severe hostile shelling. On this day two poor wounded fellows who had been lying out for three days were brought in by B Company, and, in

158

an attempt to bring in a third, Ptes. Jordan and Stevenson were themselves wounded by a machine gun from Guillemont. On the night of the 17th troops moved into the assembly trenches ready for the morrow.

On both the 30th July and on the 7th August, before the arrival of the 17th Brigade, the village of Guillemont had been entered by British troops, but in each case they had ultimately to withdraw again because of the failure of simultaneous attacks on the flanks of the place. It being obvious to the higher command that this position could not be taken as an isolated operation, arrangements had been made by both French and English commanders for a series of combined attacks in progressive stages on Maurepas, Falfemont Farm, Guillemont, Leuze Wood and Ginchy; and, with this in view, each unit had been given its particular objective which it was to endeavour to gain on the 18th August, starting at 2.45 p.m.

As far as the Buffs were concerned their orders were clear, and, with the elaborate and carefully prepared trench maps, easy to understand: two platoons of A Company under 2nd Lieut. D. Grant were to seize what was known as the Machine Gun House and convert it into a strong point, wherewith to assist the advance of the Rifle Brigade; the battalion bombers were to bomb out from the posts they had occupied to fill in the gap between the Machine Gun House and the left flank of the Rifle Brigade, which was attacking on the right of the Buffs. A third platoon of A Company was to be at the disposal of Grant as supports. C Company (Captain C. D. Gullick), with half B in close support, was to attack what was then known as the " Z.Z." trench and to form a strong point. Remainder of B to be at the disposal of Captain Gullick. The battalion reserve to consist of D Company, the remaining platoon of A and one company of the Royal

Fusiliers. These were in what was called Trones Trench.

At 2.45 the attack commenced and the 8th Battalion plunged into the Battle of Delville Wood. C Company, with half B, rushed out of their trenches and, keeping close under the barrage, successfully reached their objective with very few casualties, although 2nd Lieut. W. J. L. Peacock was killed about half-way across. On reaching the hostile trench, our men found the enemy completely unprepared. One man indeed was stark naked, and the greater part of the garrison surrendered at once. One officer with a machine gun and crew certainly made a fight of it, but the gun was captured and turned on the Germans. Captain Hodgson brought up the remainder of his company to reinforce and actually suffered more casualties than the assaulting party. He found himself in command, for Gullick had been hit several times and was very badly wounded. Two platoons of the Royal Fusiliers followed our men and consolidation at once commenced, a good deep trench being quickly made. A few dug-outs were found, but they were choked with German dead. 2nd Lieut. Grant and his party got safely across, and Machine Gun House was occupied, but the trench thereby was found to be strongly held. Lieut. Harrington, who had the right bombing party, was attacked by some Germans who had hidden in some shell holes with their bombs, but he succeeded in killing or driving them away and soon joined up with Grant. The left bombing party met with considerable resistance as they worked up the trench to where C Company's right flank should have rested. However, the men managed to capture the machine gun which was causing most of the annoyance. Machine Gun House was quickly consolidated and the communication and other trenches greatly improved. During this action communications were kept up with remarkable completeness by runners.

It may be well to note here that the Medical Officer, Captain Rankin, had been wounded in the face and part of his dressing station had been blown in, but he continued to work for several hours until ordered by the commanding officer to report himself wounded.

The casualties on this occasion were: 1 officer and 38 other ranks killed; 6 officers and 297 other ranks wounded and 16 other ranks missing; and the list included all the officers of C Company and all the company sergeant-majors, Dumbleton being among the slain.

On the 19th August the wounded officers were relieved and Captain Pearce assumed charge of the front line. 2nd Lieut. T. W. Underhill and four men were killed by shell fire during the evening and ten men wounded. On the 21st another attack was made by the Rifle Brigade, and the Buffs did what they could to help, particularly by sending up a bomb-carrying party under 2nd Lieut. Rainey over the open, which drew a tremendous fire on the Buffs' trenches. Our friends did not reach their objective.

The battalion spent the last week of August in comparative quiet near Bray, but on the last day of the month news came that the 73rd Brigade had been heavily counter-attacked between the Delville and High Woods, and the 17th Brigade went back into the line to their support. The Buffs took, however, no part in the successful attack which ensued on the 1st September. On this day D Company was placed at the disposal of the 72nd Brigade and moved off on the 2nd to join it.

On the 3rd September the Buffs were entrusted with an attack to start from the Worcester Trench, but, owing to the fact that all the runners sent to synchronize the time with the brigade on the left were killed, the battalion started too late and so met the enemy's barrage actually on their parapet as they

M   161 started and also heavy machine-gun fire. Within one minute all the officers and the C.S.M. of B Company were casualties and the attack was held up. The attempt had been made at noon, and in half an hour's time news of the failure reached Battalion Headquarters and the commanding officer, after personal reconnaissance, ordered Major Hamilton, who was in command of the front line, to organize a fresh attack. This was arranged for 4 p.m. and an artillery programme drawn up, Lt.-Colonel Stewart, commanding the group of guns that was helping our infantry, being fortunately met with exactly at the right moment. At 4 p.m. the second attack took place, but, owing to the artillery not lifting and to heavy machine-gun fire from a strong point, it was stopped. The bombers managed to work their way up the trench towards the strong point, but all the supporting infantry were hit. The following day the three companies were withdrawn and went into the reserve brigade camp, having suffered the following casualties: 2nd Lieut. T. Firminger killed; six officers wounded: 2nd Lieuts. Grant, Hamilton, Twyman, Eyre, Rainey and Varge; other ranks, 16 killed, 81 wounded and 9 missing.

Meanwhile D Company, temporarily attached to the 72nd Brigade, as has been noticed, had gone up to support the 9th East Surrey Regiment in Delville Wood, and these had suffered very severely from shell fire. About 4 p.m. on the 3rd September Pte. Crick, one of D Company's stretcher-bearers, arrived at Battalion Headquarters, having made his way for about a mile along the trenches, and informed the commanding officer that all his company officers had been killed and most of the remainder wiped out also. 2nd Lieut. Morrell was sent to take charge of this company, but was only able to discover a few stragglers; Captain D. G. Pearce and 2nd Lieuts. B. G. Bowles and B. B. Blackwell were all dead. The assault delivered on the

BRINGING UP WIRE

3rd September had been a tremendous and most important one. It was delivered along the whole line: Guillemont was stormed; Leuze Wood and the Falfemont Farm were taken; and this meant a great deal more than the mere advancing of our line a few hundred yards or so. It meant that the quadruple and, as it was thought by our enemies, the impregnable positions, which had resisted all assault for seven weeks, had at last been broken and the fact established that no elaborate series of earthworks could be reckoned on as a safe preventative to the progress of the Allies.

The 5th of September took the 8th Battalion back to the reserve camp by Fricourt, and thence it proceeded to the rest area near Abbeville, where it got into excellent billets at Yaucourt and received drafts and, of course, trained. The 27th of the month brought welcome news of honours: to Lt.-Colonel Lucas a D.S.O.; Captains Gullick and Rankin (R.A.M.C.) and 2nd Lieut. Grant the M.C.; the D.C.M. for C.S.M. Carpenter, Sgt. Butler and Pte. Sheward; whilst a day or two later came news of M.M.'s for L.-Corpl. Tinmouth and Ptes. Baker and Hart.

From the end of September to the 16th November, which date being taken as the end of the Somme fighting, must be that from which the reader will be asked to switch off his attention from France to other regions, the 8th Battalion led the life so usual during the Great War and so well known to all men: that is to say one week, or other short period, found it in the trenches and the next in billets a bit in rear. Gouy Servins was the usual resting-place, but there were other places, notably Mazingarbe, where the men were in proper huts fitted with electric light. The turns at the trenches were taken at Carency and at Loos, and as the year wore towards its close the old trouble of the wet came on again. The trenches got out of repair and began to fall in, involving work for everybody and much discomfort.

163

At the end of October Sgts. Batchelor and F. Elson; L.-Corpls. Stevens and Wynne; Ptes. Abbott, Barge, Bignell and Kerman found themselves entitled to mount the M.M. ribband, and Corpl. Norrington got the D.C.M. On the 1st November Lt.-Colonel Green and some of the officers of the 1st Battalion came over from Bethune for a short visit.

V. 1st Battalion

The opening of the year 1916 found the 1st Battalion with its headquarters at Forward Cottage, which is only a mile north of the village of St. Jean and, of course, quite close to Ypres. On the 6th January the battalion was cheered by finding that Captain Cattley, 2nd Lieuts. Clouting, Dangerfield, Davies and Ferguson, Corpls. Wren and Duff, Pte. Gunn and the late Captain Homan, together with the good regimental doctor, Captain K. W. Jones, R.A.M.C., had been mentioned in despatches. On the 17th, too, came a welcome message from Admiral Jellicoe telling all and sundry of the high appreciation and esteem of the various bodies of the sailors, who had by arrangement visited the trenches in parties, and their admiration of the spirit of the troops. On the 25th of this month several officers and sergeants of the 8th Battalion dined with the 1st, and the opportunity of fraternizing was naturally made the most of. The two units were under the command of majors, namely Gould and Hamilton, Colonels Finch Hatton and Trueman being both on leave.

A curious incident seems worth recording as showing a fighting spirit a little out of the common, perhaps. On the 13th of February Pte. A. Ralph reported himself at the headquarters as a deserter—of all things. He had escaped from the home-keeping 3rd Battalion at Dover, made his way over to the port of Havre, presumably as a stowaway, and walked from that place to

Poperinghe, where the fighting battalion was at the moment. His trial by Court Martial was dispensed with.

On the 16th March the battalion entrained at Poperinghe and proceeded to Calais for a rest and for fresh training, for training and instruction was never allowed to drop during the war. New inventions, modes and methods were constantly taken into use, and any relaxation from manning the trenches was taken advantage of to bring a unit up to date and to teach the new drafts what could only be taught in France and Flanders. This rest lasted ten days, and then a three days' march brought the men back to Wormhoudt and into the Ypres area once more, and it was not long before the old trenches round La Brique and St. Jean were occupied by them again.

On the 19th April, while in the La Briques trenches, at 5.30 p.m., after a considerable amount of shelling all day, a heavy bombardment was opened on the 2nd Scots Guards on the Buffs' right, and on the 8th Bedfordshire on their left. No. 15 platoon of our battalion suffered a good deal, but the attack which followed the bombardment came chiefly on the right and left of the regiment. Soon after eight o'clock Captain Causton was able to get in touch with the Guards and learnt that on their side the enemy's attack had failed, but this was not so on our left, where the Germans had succeeded in penetrating several of the front-line trenches in the Morteldje sector; but two days afterwards all the ground so taken was recaptured by the King's Shropshire Light Infantry, who suffered several casualties, including the gallant Colonel Luard, D.S.O., who died of his wounds. The Buffs lost 21 killed and 36 wounded during these few days.

On the 4th May Captain Cattley took a staff appointment. He was the only officer who had never left the 1st Battalion since it arrived in France. On the 4th

June Colonel Finch Hatton, who had just rejoined and taken over command again, was awarded the C.M.G. Captain Cattley the M.C., Sgts. Trigg and Viggers, who had been killed, Corpl. Cullen and L.-Corpl. Jenrick got the M.M., and on the 12th July Colonel Finch Hatton went away again—this time to command a brigade. On the 16th July C.S.M. Ralph was awarded the M.C.

A very important move commenced on the 2nd August. By this time the fighting on the Somme had been raging for a month. It now fell to the lot of the 1st Battalion to emulate in that district the deeds of the 6th and 7th, so on that day came a start from Poperinghe by train, followed by marching and camping, till the 9th August found it in the trenches south of Beaumont Hamel with the 2nd Durham Light Infantry on its right and the 2nd Sherwood Foresters on the left. The Buffs were now under the command of Major H. W. Green, who was made a temporary lt.-colonel on the 12th August. A period of strict and hard training now ensued. It was a preparation for the fighting that was to come. As has been explained, the constant arrival of fresh drafts from England necessitated much teaching in France and teaching by men who were very up to date indeed. During the time devoted to this work the battalion, and indeed the whole brigade, was gradually approaching the fighting line, having been at Villers Bocage on the 6th September, Corbie on the 7th and so on. It marched to Carnoy on the 11th September and relieved the 167th Infantry Brigade in the line behind Guillemont and Combles.

By this time the fighting on the Somme was two months old. There had occurred, as has been seen, a great deal of heavy fighting on the 3rd September and following days, and this had on the whole been successful. The Allies had from the first been slowly but steadily pushing forward and gaining one position after another. The enemy had made a most determined resistance, but he had gone back. One line of elaborate defence after another was falling into our hands, and Sir Douglas Haig determined to keep up the pressure as long as the weather and consequent state of the country permitted it. A general attack then was opened on the 15th September, the objective being the rearmost of the enemy's original lines of defence, between Morval and Le Sars; and when the advance on this front had gained the Morval line the Commander-in-Chief arranged to bring forward the left of the British troops across the Thiepval ridge.

There is a road running from Ginchy to Morval, and as it approaches the ridge, on which the latter village stands, it is sunken and of course conceals anything in it, and just about half-way between the two villages a railway to the south of the sunken road almost touches it. Where the road and railway most closely approach, the Germans had constructed a very strong work which was known as the Quadrilateral and which was but a very little way from the edge of Bouteaux Wood. On the 13th of the month the 71st Infantry Brigade had attacked this Quadrilateral, but the attack had failed. The 15th was the first occasion on which tanks were used. Three of these new weapons had been told off to assist at the attack of the Quadrilateral, and consequently a gap in our barrage had been arranged so that these could advance before the infantry started. However successful the tanks were afterwards, these three proved worse than useless, because two of them broke down, and the third was so knocked about that it could do nothing, having amongst other injuries lost its periscope, so that it could not see. The unfortunate thing was, that there remained the gap in the barrage, exactly opposite the main face of the work to be assaulted. At 6.20 a.m. the 8th Bedfordshire advanced gallantly over the open, a bombing party attacking up a trench from

167

the south-east. The enemy's machine guns caught the Bedfordshire men on the top of the ridge and, though they tried in the most manly way, they could make no progress.

The Buffs supported the Bedfords with the finest courage, but could not stand against the very heavy machine-gun fire opposed to them. They suffered more casualties than any other unit in the brigade. A great number of men found cover in shell holes and managed later to get back into the lines. Captain Causton assembled as many of the battalion as he could in the trench originally occupied by the 8th Bedfords. The 2nd York and Lancaster Regiment had advanced behind the Buffs and had also assembled in the Bedfords' trench. On reorganizing there were found in this trench about forty Buffs, two to three hundred York and Lancaster and forty Bedfords.

About 12.30 p.m. a number of the battalion was still lying in shell holes in the open, and at that hour a message was received from 2nd Lieut. Hills: " Am in " a series of shell holes about two hundred yards from " German line. German line was apparently untouched " till midday bombardment. We got to present posi- " tion and were unable to proceed owing to machine " guns. No sign of Bedfords ahead. Baly killed, Kesby " and Miller wounded. Have about twelve men with " me and can't get in touch with anybody. Our shells " fell first right beyond German line, second just short, " third very short. People in valley on left have just " retired on account of our shell fire. Machine guns " are not touched, as all opened on retiring line. We " have fire from left and right and just off central " sweeping us occasionally." During the night of the 15th/16th the Buffs were withdrawn to a trench running south-east of Guillemont after losing the following in casualties: Lieut. C. J. P. Baly, 2nd Lieuts. G. W. P. Wyatt and G. R. Reid, and fifty-three men killed; 2nd Lieut. Hills wounded; Captain T. H. Kesby, 2nd Lieut. Miller and seven others wounded and missing; 2nd Lieut. Smith, Captain Jones, R.A.M.C., Lieut. Tuke and 2nd Lieut. Goodheart wounded. It was afterwards ascertained that Kesby was amongst the slain. One hundred and eighty-three other ranks wounded.

During the night the mass of wounded was cleared up with the greatest energy. At 7 a.m. on the 16th strong German reinforcements were seen to enter the Quadrilateral. On the evening of that day the K.S.L.I. made what proved to be an important move. That battalion got round to the south-west and dug themselves an assembly trench, the left of which rested on the railway.

On the 18th September at 5.30 a.m. the gallant Salopians advanced. The guns started to time and a party of the York and Lancaster bombed up the trench on the right flank of the Quadrilateral, the Stokes mortars bombarding as fast as possible. At 6.28 a wounded man, passing Brigade Headquarters, reported that the objective was taken. This was confirmed by Lieut. Marsh, K.S.L.I., half an hour later, and at 2.20 Germans were seen massing on Morval Hill. It is a pity that the Buffs were not amongst the troops that took the great obstacle. The battalion was too knocked about to be so, as were the Bedfordshire, but there was much rejoicing at the success of their good comrades.

On the 19th September the battalion, being relieved, marched sixteen miles back to billets at Morlancourt, expecting a good long rest and very, very weary. It got one day's rest only and, on the 21st, it moved up again to relieve a Guards brigade which occupied a sector of our line with a frontage of only about two hundred and fifty yards. This frontage, which was in the vicinity of and about one and a half miles to the west of the Quadrilateral, was occupied by the Buffs with the 8th

Bedfordshire in support, the remainder of the brigade remaining back in the Braquelerie area. A new attack had been arranged for the 23rd, but the dreadful weather caused a two days' postponement.

In the interval a very useful piece of work was done by a Buff patrol under Sgt. Dowman (afterwards recommended for V.C.): this patrol was very nearly cut off, but got back safely with valuable information. The following is the wording of the recommendation referred to:—

" 1st The Buffs. 5032 Acting Sergeant Edward
" Dowman. For most conspicuous bravery and devo-
" tion to duty on the 23rd, 24th and 25th September
" in front of Morval. He several times reconnoitred
" in daylight a trench held by the enemy and threw
" bombs on them, inflicting casualties; when an attack
" was made on our trench on the 24th, he organized
" the defence and himself led a counter-attack in the
" open, which drove back the enemy and ascertained
" the exact position they were holding.

" On the 25th he was killed whilst leading, with con-
" spicuous gallantry, a bombing party which took the
" German trench, capturing a machine gun, and about
" 50 prisoners. His excellent reconnaissance before the
" attack and his gallantry and determination in carrying
" it out were undoubtedly mainly responsible for the
" success of the attack on this most important trench.

" He gave his life in his supreme devotion to duty."

The enemy seemed to know what was coming, for on the 23rd, the day our attack should have taken place, they assaulted the whole of the front occupied by the 6th Division in which the 1st Battalion served, but they were driven back. During the night of the 24th/25th the Buffs cut all the opposing wire before them and, as far as possible, that in front of the 15th Infantry Brigade. The operations of the next few days were a

170

glorious success, and the following short extracts from the official despatches on the subject may serve to make clear the parts taken by the Buffs, both the 1st and the 7th Battalions, in the good work:—

" At 12.35 p.m. on the 25th September, after a bom-
" bardment commencing early in the morning of the
" 24th, a general attack of the Allies was launched on
" the whole front between the Somme and Martin-
" puich. The objectives on the British front included
" the villages of Morval, Les Bœufs and Gueudecourt
" and a belt of country about one thousand yards deep,
" coming round the north of Flers to a point midway
" between that village and Martinpuich. By nightfall
" the whole of these objectives were in our hands with
" the exception of the village of Gueudecourt. . . .
" In the early morning of the 26th September the vil-
" lage (Combles) was occupied simultaneously by the
" Allies. The British to the north and the French to
" the south of the railway. . . . On the same day
" Gueudecourt was carried. . . . Accordingly at
" 12.25 p.m. on the 26th September, before the enemy
" had been given time to recover from the blow struck
" by the Fourth Army, a general attack was launched
" against Thiepval and the Thiepval Ridge, the objec-
" tive consisting of the whole of the high ground still
" remaining in the enemy's hands extending over a
" front of some three thousand yards north and east of
" Thiepval and including, in addition to that fortress,
" the Zollern Redoubt, the Stuff Redoubt and the
" Schwaben Redoubt with the connecting line of
" trenches. . . . The attack was a brilliant success.
" . . . Schwaben Redoubt was assaulted during the
" afternoon (of the 27th September) and, in spite of
" counter-attacks delivered by strong enemy reinforce-
" ments, we captured the whole of the southern face of
" the redoubt and pushed out patrols to the northern
" face and towards St. Pierre Divion."

As far as the 16th Brigade was concerned the attack commenced with the Buffs knocking out with trench mortars two German strong points and capturing two machine guns. At 12.50 the infantry had their first objective. This was seized by the Buffs, and the second objective was the spoil of the K.S.L.I. and York and Lancaster. At 3.10 the whole objective was reached and the infantry was digging in. At 4.30 enemy's guns opened from Le Transloy and our side sent out advanced posts, Les Bœufs and Morval being in our hands. At 5.45 came a telegram from the Corps commander: "Hearty thanks. Sincere congratulations to you all. A very fine achievement splendidly executed. Cavan." The brigadier recorded his opinion in the following words: "A most successful day and casualties "slight. Success due to fine artillery work, 1st Buffs "excellent surprise attack on strong posts, and the "parade-like steady advance of the 1st K.S.L.I. and "2nd Y. and L."

On the 26th September the brigade was relieved and retired to Briqueterie for a day or two and thence to billets at Meaulte, seven miles away. The battalion was now sadly depleted, but the men had borne their hardships well and were still full of fight. On a special parade at Meaulte on the 1st October the battalion could only turn out 341 strong, with seventeen officers.[1]

Another short spell in the trenches near Givenchy with casualties every day, but amounting in all to eight

---

[1] The following is an extract from a letter to Sir Courtenay Vyvyan (late the Buffs) from the A.A.G. 6th Division :—

"Your old battalion is going very strong. It is commanded by "Green, and Gould is second in command. Otherwise I don't suppose "you know anyone. They did splendidly on the Somme and never lost "their discipline for a moment. I saw them on parade after the fight "of the 13th/18th September, when they only had 314 men left, and "they might have been parading for the King's birthday. It really was "a magnificent sight."

MORVAL

killed and thirty-two wounded, and then a complete change of scene.

On the 21st October the move came to Daours and a week later to Bethune, where we may leave the unit for the present, only mentioning that October brought some welcome honours to the 1st Battalion, namely: on the 4th, Military Cross for Captain Causton and 2nd Lieut. Brown; and Military Medals for Sgts. Randall and Langton and Ptes. Smith and Baines; a few days afterwards the Military Cross for Captain Corrall and Lieut. Jacobs, and Military Medals for Corpl. Twelftree and Ptes. Boseley, Ashdown and Gambell. While on the last day of the month came notification of no less than twenty-two Military Medals viz., to—

C.Q.M.S. Vincer.	Pte. Ellen.
Sgt. Denny.	,, Heathfield.
Corpl. Earl.	,, Jamieson.
,, Mutton.	,, Page.
,, Rose.	,, Minns.
L.-Corpl. Bevan.	,, Roberts.
,, Sheen.	,, Scrivener.
,, Taylor.	,, Spencely.
,, Wood.	,, Todd.
Pte. Baker.	,, Watkins.
,, Black.	,, Wren.

CHAPTER VII

A YEAR AT SALONICA

I. The 2nd Battalion

IT is advisable now to consider the doings of the 2nd Battalion in the immediate neighbourhood of Salonica. The life in this theatre of war was far less full of exciting incident than in France and Flanders, and, after their thrilling experiences in the latter theatre, those men of the Buffs that were still serving in the 2nd Battalion must have looked upon their new work in the light almost of a rest from war, though not from the labour and hardships incidental to it.

Early in the year 1916 the army was contracted into a small line just north of Salonica and was merely a defensive force guarding that base port, but Lt.-General Sir G. F. Milne arranged in May with the French General, Sarrail, that there should be an advance northwards and a greater area occupied, the British army taking the ground to the north and east, and the French the western area. On the 8th of June, therefore, the troops commenced to occupy advanced positions along the right bank of the River Struma and its tributary the Butkova river. In connection with this movement the 85th Brigade, and of course the Buffs with it, brought to an end what was becoming a somewhat monotonous life and, on the 10th June, was ordered to hold forward positions along the right bank of the Struma, with its right on Orljak.

Therefore, on the 17th of the month, the Buffs found themselves at a point three kilometres (say two and a half miles) west of Kopriva, with orders to take up an outpost line to cover the crossings of the Struma.

The line taken up by the regiment was about six kilometres long, and as the hills come practically down to
the stream, these formed natural positions to take up
and indeed had already been used by the French, who
had sited and just started a certain number of trenches,
which it was decided to complete. The river was found
to be fordable almost everywhere. Opposite the battalion front and some seven or eight miles away was the
town of Demirhissar, which was occupied by the
enemy. The battalion remained in this position till
the 15th July and, though there was no actual fighting
to do, another enemy soon became very troublesome
indeed: the heat down near the river was intense and
the local fever soon made itself apparent. This took
the form of very high temperatures, very suddenly developed, and was of such common occurrence that the
Field Ambulance became congested and the evacuation
of the sick a matter of great difficulty. Further, the
Buffs were without their Medical Officer for about a
week.

The welcome order to move to higher ground came
on the 9th July, but it was not till the 15th that the
Buffs were relieved by the K.O.Y.L.I., who belonged
to the 83rd Brigade. Then they marched to Paprat, a
two days' journey, where an excellent bivouac ground
was found and where the weather conditions were very
much better. Yet malaria has a nasty way of getting
into a man's system at malarial places and only showing
itself later on, probably in a healthy country, and the
sickness for the first few days at Paprat only increased
instead of diminishing; four officers and many men
going sick in the first ten days. On the 30th the battalion moved to Hamzali for work on the roads and to
take up a section of outpost line. This place is situated
on the same range of hills as Paprat, but is nearer the
river. The battalion still continued to lose officers and
men from fever. Two companies worked at head-

quarters and two were in the outpost line employed on the defences there.

Away off to the left and near the Doiran lake the British and French commenced a successful offensive on the 10th August, and this lasted for a week, resulting in the capture of some important positions. While these events were still in progress, the Bulgarians in the Struma valley began to advance, to be accurate on the 17th August. They did so apparently in seven columns, three of them moving southward from Demirhissar towards the Struma river. On the 18th an observation post in the outpost line reported seeing a battalion occupy the village of Barakli Dzuma and a considerable force with guns and transport moving in the direction of Seres. As these movements of enemy troops continued on the following day, and as on the 20th considerable activity of small bodies of mounted men were noticed, apparently reconnoitring the river about Ormanli, and as there was a considerable amount of shelling on this date, Elishan, a village on the further bank of the Struma, was occupied by a company of English infantry.

It appeared at this time to be probable that the Bulgarians might be bold enough to assault the British lines, and every effort was being made to strengthen the defences of the outpost line. The Buffs were terribly weak in numbers. Available men for drafts were, of course, just now required in every part of the world. The Somme offensive was in full swing and men were being killed and maimed there daily. Sickness had thinned the ranks of the 2nd Battalion to a terrible extent, and at the moment when a Bulgarian attack appeared imminent it could only place 185 men in the outpost line with 45 in reserve, though a welcome reinforcement of 123 arrived on the 30th of the month. However, two machine guns from the M.G. Company were attached to the battalion and the

SALONICA: ROAD MADE BY BRITISH

defence works were kept in repair and ready for emergency.

The line held by our troops was an exceedingly good one for defence, for the hills on our side approached very closely to the river and there was a broad, level plain on the other, so that it was difficult for the enemy to manœuvre unwatched and unnoted. The last day of August brought the welcome news that at last Roumania had made up her mind and had declared war on Austria. In announcing this important event to his troops the G.O.C. stated a hope that all ranks would realize that one of the most important aims in the military policy adopted in this region had been attained and he congratulated all ranks on the part they had played in achieving this object.

Passive defence by an enterprising army is only resorted to on very rare occasions, in the presence at some particular point of an overwhelming force, and the 10th September showed a renewal of activity on the English part. On this day detachments crossed the river at five several points. The villages of Oraoman and Kato Gudeli were occupied and Nevoljen gallantly stormed by the Northumberland Fusiliers. On the 15th six small columns crossed between Lake Tahinos and Orljak and burnt the riparian villages, the enemy's counter-attacks being defeated by our artillery on the hither side, but the Buffs appear to have been too weak to take part in these minor operations.

II. Action of Karajakoi

But when October came, General Milne determined on a continuous offensive on the Struma front, with a view to preventing the enemy from withdrawing any of his troops from this direction to oppose the advance of our French allies towards Monastir. Therefore matters became more active along the river banks and operations commenced by our seizing and holding cer-

N   177

tain villages on the left side of the river in the neighbourhood of the bridgehead opposite Orljak, so that a further movement on Seres or Demirhissar could be facilitated. The high ground on our side of the stream again came in very useful, for it enabled the artillery very materially to assist in these operations. Bridges were constructed by the engineers, and during the night of the 29th/30th September the attacking infantry crossed and formed up on the left bank. Strong counter-attacks were made by the enemy, but, by the evening of the 2nd October, our positions were consolidated and preparations made to extend them by capturing Jenikoj on the road to Seres. This was done on the morning of the 3rd, but the troops that took the village were three times resolutely counter-attacked and very heavily bombarded, and there ensued some very strenuous fighting. On the 5th October Nevoljen was occupied, and on the 8th our troops had reached a still further extended line with mounted men between Kispeki and Kalendra.

In connection with all this business the Buffs on the 2nd October were attached to the 84th Brigade as divisional reserve and proceeded to a camp in the vicinity of Orljak, and on the next day B and C Companies under Captain Vertue moved off and reported to the officer commanding the Welch Regiment, who directed B Company, less fifty men, to line the right bank of the river from the new pontoon bridge to the left of the 23rd Welch Pioneers. The remaining fifty, under 2nd Lieut. Steven, carried R.E. stores to the Suffolk Regiment in Mazirko village. C Company crossed Orljak bridge and took up a position in the bridgehead works under the Suffolk Regiment and were employed in carrying up rations and stores. These two companies came under both shell and rifle fire.

On the 4th October C Company took over part of the front-line trench from A Company of the Suffolks, and it was soon after joined by B, and later in the day the whole battalion was collected in the forward trenches in relief of the Suffolks and occupied a position along the Seres road on the south side of it. On the Buffs' left was the 1st Welch Regiment, and on its right the 10th Division, which held Jenikoj.

The 5th was a fairly quiet day, and on the 6th, as it appeared that the Bulgars had withdrawn their position some distance, the Buffs sent out three patrols under 2nd Lieut. Abbot-Smith, 2nd Lieut. Asprey and Lieut. Bremner in the directions of Nevoljen, Papolova and Kalendra respectively. These patrols did their work well, and indeed Bremner and Asprey's reports were both commended by the brigadier: they all succeeded in locating the enemy, and after that they retired correctly, having first exchanged a few shots. It was now clear that the enemy's forward line was still about Nevoljen and Kalendra.

The next few days were quiet enough; much reconnaissance work was carried out, and on the 10th the Buffs recrossed the river to their old camp, on being relieved by Northumberland Fusiliers. After some days' training, the battalion commenced, on the 24th, to furnish large parties, each under an officer, in connection with the making and defending the several bridges which now spanned the Struma. The river was at this time considerably swollen, and the bridges, which were a necessary adjunct to the commander's contemplated further offensive, were consequently difficult to construct; indeed, the work reflected the greatest credit on the Royal Engineers.

III. BARAKLI DZUMA

Constant reconnaissance, chiefly by aeroplane and armoured cars, had revealed the fact that the enemy had constructed a defensive line along the foot-hills on the left side of the river as far as Savjak and from there across the low ground to Lake Butkova. This line passed through the large village of Barakli Dzuma, and this village it was determined to capture.

The attack, which was a complete success, was carried out on the 31st October; Lieut. Sebastian with two platoons of D Company taking over Kopriva bridgehead trenches, whilst A Company and the other half of D were in reserve in camp; B and C Companies had proceeded to Ormanli the previous day to act as carrying parties for the 83rd Brigade. It commenced at 7.15 in the morning with an artillery bombardment which lengthened its range at 7.45, at which hour the infantry advanced. B and C Companies of the Buffs followed immediately behind the firing line carrying barbed wire, stakes, etc., and for the remainder of the day these two companies continued to carry up stores into the front line. C Company had one man killed and two wounded. B also had had two men wounded during the previous night. At 8 p.m. the battalion collected at Ormanli and reported to the 84th Brigade, and as there were no special orders the men proceeded to find billets for the night. On the 1st November the Buffs moved over the river again, and the next day an interesting official summary of the operations against Barakli Dzuma was issued, by which it appeared that the success was scored with comparatively little loss. In fact, the casualty list, when compared with those in France and Flanders, was a very short one. In the whole force 5 officers and 50 men had been wounded and only 15 killed outright. About 300 prisoners had been taken. This summary put on record that the work parties supplied by the 85th Brigade worked and carried splendidly.

For the winter months a new defensive line was now arranged. This was on the left or further bank of the Struma and stretching from Lake Tahinos to the Struma beyond the bend where the Butkova joins it;

it included in its course the villages of Jenikoj, Nevoljen and Barakli Dzuma.

On the 3rd November the 85th Brigade took over the defences of Barakli Dzuma, the Buffs being in the front-line trenches, D Company supporting the other three. A certain amount of the usual reconnaissance work incidental to all trench warfare formed the only excitement the battalion had during the first half of November, but on the 16th the enemy demonstrated against our part of the line with considerable shell and rifle fire, and at one time it seemed as if he were about to attack in earnest.

Some of our reconnoitring parties had, early in the month, discovered the existence of a small enemy's trench on the western side of a nullah known as "Sandy Brook," and about one thousand five hundred yards from our line. One or two unsuccessful attempts by small parties had been made to capture this, but without success, and the place became famous in its way under the name of "Little Ferdy" trench. On the 17th November A Company was told off to attack "Little Ferdy" in earnest: two platoons went out in front line and two in close support; there were also two platoons of C Company in reserve. On being attacked, however, the Bulgars withdrew to another trench about three hundred yards back, leaving six dead behind them. Patrols went on to examine this new position, which was found to be too strong to be assaulted with the men available, and as the objective had been gained no further advance was made; the Buffs' losses were one killed and three wounded.

On the 19th November news arrived of the capture of Monastir. The battalion remained at Barakli Dzuma till the end of the year 1916 and passed Christmas there. The time was spent mainly in making and perfecting the line of defence, digging communication trenches and placing barbed wire. The only event which is worthy of record occurred on the 16th December: an extensive and carefully planned-out raid was organized on " Little Ferdy " trench. B Company was selected to form the main raiding party and was supported by flank guards and, of course, by artillery, as well as by the usual supports in rear. The 3rd Middlesex operated on the Buffs' right and the 2nd East Surrey on the left. At 2 a.m. the front line advanced, lay down and opened fire, while the flanking party went to cut wire and attack the enemy right flank. This detachment, however, met with considerable opposition from a strong bombing post, and the result was a quarter of an hour's bombing competition which ended in our favour; for the enemy withdrew, leaving twenty to thirty dead; but Captain Lancaster, who commanded the main attack, was all the while expecting a signal from 2nd Lieut. Keasley of the flank guard that he was through, and not getting it, he reported the fact to Battalion Headquarters. The commanding officer (Lt.-Colonel H. A. Thewles) accordingly gave orders to Lancaster to advance, which was done, and the barbed wire in front proving to be only a single fence of no great proportions, both " Little Ferdy " and what was known as " Dry " trench were taken. As ordered, the company proceeded another fifty yards and lay down while the supporting platoon broke up the barbed wire and damaged the trenches as much as possible. Captain Lancaster then withdrew his men, and the flank guards were also brought in. The work done by the other flank guard under Lieut. Williams had been most useful and, of course, the assistance of the good gunners, the 75th Battery, invaluable. Lieut. Sebastian, Sgt. Spiller and L.-Corpl. Geohegan did very excellent service, and were awarded the D.S.O., M.M. and D.C.M. respectively. Our casualties were five men killed, and 2nd Lieut. Airey, C.S.M. Standford and eight other ranks wounded.

182

VALLEY OF THE STRUMA

CHAPTER VIII

WITH MAUDE IN MESOPOTAMIA

I. THE POSITION IN 1916

THE summer of the year 1916 was more or less an uneventful one for the Mesopotamia Force. The situation is very plainly set forth in the despatches of Sir Percy Lake, General Officer Commanding-in-Chief. He says: " No operations on a large scale have " been undertaken since the fall of Kut. On the Tigris " line the troops immediately facing the enemy were, " with the exception of those actually on duty in the " trenches, resting and recuperating and, at the same " time, consolidating their position. Fatigues were " very heavy, the heat of the summer came on rapidly " and a good deal of sickness prevailed."

A Russian advance from Persia began to make itself felt on the Turks, however, and on the 20th May the right bank of the Tigris as far as the Hai, with the exception of bridge guards on the latter water, was clear of the enemy. This, and the fact that the Turks still held the Sanna i Yat lines on the other side of the Tigris, materially influenced the plan of campaign which came later.

As far as the Buffs were concerned their summer work consisted mostly in harvesting barley early in the hot weather, and in road making. There was also a great deal of work in connection with the necessary supply of water. The battalion was between four and five miles from the river—the only supply, and consequently water had to be carried, Indian fashion, on mules in " packals," which held about eight gallons each. These, made of zinc and covered with felt, soon

183

got knocked about and, as they began to leak, much water was lost in transit. The so-called friendly Arabs were consistent and determined thieves, and if the water-carrying mules had been left under the sole care of their Indian drivers, they would soon have disappeared. Consequently water convoy work became a very heavy and regular duty amongst the many others our soldiers had to perform. The local Arabs were very enterprising marauders and gave considerable trouble sneaking about the camp. On one occasion some of them actually entered the orderly room tent, but they found nothing which they considered worthy of removal.

Sir Stanley Maude took over supreme command on the 28th August, 1916, a time of the year when active operations might soon be possible and when the improvement in communications, inaugurated by Sir Percy Lake, had begun to bear fruit. When early in the year every man's mind was eagerly bent on the relief of Kut he could, as soldiers in former campaigns always had to, digest his bully beef and biscuit somehow and sustain life on it; moreover, when sick, he contrived to do without luxuries and to bear discomforts. But now all this was rapidly changing for the better, and with improved communications came greatly superior comfort. The Turks seemed very full of enterprise and to be planning various ambitious campaigns, and Maude very rightly considered that the best way to stop all that sort of thing was to aim at the heart of the beast and to make Baghdad the object of resolute and determined attack.

First of all, however, there was still a good deal to do in the way of preparation, and August was too early a date, in any case, for active work. The men were, of course, still suffering from heat and were not by any means fit for a strenuous campaign. Then the communications still wanted perfecting, and large reserves of ammunition and stores of all kinds must be brought up to the fighting area. " By the end of November," he says, "preliminary arrangements were well advanced, " a steady stream of reinforcements had been moving " up stream and drafts joining. The health of the " soldiers was improving and the training for war was " advancing." The general concentration was at Sheikh Saad. The River Tigris was by no means a straight line, but still it flowed from Baghdad to Sheikh Saad, and, in order to defend himself against an advance up it, it is plain that the Turk should continue to hold positions astride the river; for these positions could be selected to rest with their flanks on marshes so that they could not be turned, and so would necessitate one frontal attack after another.

II. BATTLE OF KUT, 1917

As has already been seen, however, the enemy had withdrawn the bulk of his troops from the main river's right bank, though as a matter of fact he held a strong line of trenches across the Hai covering a bridge over that water just south of Kut and bending back to the Tigris at each end. His main line, however, was along the left bank of that river, his right flank, of course, being almost in the direction of Baghdad, while his left was thrown back along the Sanna i Yat lines, which he still held strongly. Seeing this, Maude determined to attack him up stream and so make him bolt back to his only road to his base or else cut him off from Baghdad altogether. One party of ours, under Lt.-General Cobbe, V.C., faced the Sanna i Yat lines on the left bank of the Tigris, and another, under Lt.-General Marshall, in which were serving the Buffs, were as much as eleven miles up stream of them and on the other side of the river. The first thing to do was to seize the Hai stream, and this was done by Marshall by surprise on the night of the 13th/14th December, 1916, while Cobbe demonstrated in front of the Sanna i Yat lines as if about to attack furiously. After getting possession of the Hai, which he crossed at Bessouia and Atab, Marshall extended towards the north and at the same time wheeled up the bulk of his command to attack the bridge-head. He broke through on the night of the 18th opposite Kut and reached the main river, thus securing command of the Tigris up stream of the Khadaira Bend. This was important because, after he advanced, his food and stores had to go up by land for some miles.

In connection with all this manœuvring the Buffs had on the 13th December struck their camp and marched out to reserve trenches, in support of the movement of that date, and had followed up and formed a backing to the troops in advance. At 7 a.m. on the 16th the battalion appeared to be going into a serious action and B Company was sent out to take a certain ridge in front, with C in support. Everything appeared to be working satisfactorily, but at 12.30 orders came for withdrawal to another position, where the men dug in as far as possible and connection was obtained with the 13th Division on the left of the Buffs. B Company had three men wounded in this advance and D had one during the retirement to the new position. On the 17th a concentration on Bessouia was ordered and carried out, and the next day a demonstration was made without much result, Captain Harrison receiving a shrapnel wound and the little expedition returning to Bessouia in the evening.

In connection with Maude's plan of getting up stream of his enemy, Major-General Crocker with his command attempted on the 20th to throw a bridge over the Tigris at the Shrumran Bend and the 35th Brigade marched up to that place to assist, the Buffs being in reserve; but somehow the enemy had got wind of this attempt, the enterprise proved a failure and the men returned to their old bivouac. The remainder of the old year and up to the 10th January was spent working west of the Hai and exercising in drill and musketry in the neighbourhood of Bessouia, the work being interrupted only on the 9th, when the cavalry attempted a raid supported by the Buffs; but the horsemen lost their way in a dense fog and the force returned to camp early, having effected nothing, on account of the weather.

During these early days of January, Cobbe's party, which, in addition to demonstrating in front of the Sanna i Yat lines, had the task of manning the right bank of the Tigris up to the point where Marshall was working, got orders to clear the Khadaira Bend, which occasioned some heavy fighting by the 3rd Indian Division and necessitated a diversion on the Hai bridgehead by Marshall and his men; so on the 11th of the month the Buffs went into the trenches and had four men killed and as many wounded on the first day. The clearing of the bend by Cobbe proceeded satisfactorily after this and by the 18th all was ready for the final assault, which was arranged for the following day. When dawn broke, however, it was found that during the night the whole of the Turks who had occupied this portion of their defences had cleared out and crossed the Tigris.

The next job the British forces had to take in hand was to reduce the very extensive trench system that the enemy still held across the Hai stream in the immediate vicinity of Kut. This was a slow and somewhat tedious business, but by the 24th January, after steady and persistent pushing, our troops got to within four hundred yards of the enemy, and an assault was arranged for the following day. This slow approach consisted of a series of small advances at various points and subsequent consolidation of what was gained. Thus

187

a new line was occupied by the Buffs on the 12th, and the next day, while this was made strong, 2nd Lieut. Hook made a reconnaissance to the front, which resulted in establishing an advanced post, which was occupied by a platoon under 2nd Lieut. Filmer. On the 15th two endeavours were made by 2nd Lieut. Angus to reach another point, but without success. Captain V. Arnold was killed on this date.

A still more important little action of the same nature took place on the 16th: a party of about sixty of all ranks went out from the trench in the morning and attempted the occupation of a point about 450 yards in advance of the line. This enterprise was successfully accomplished and, in the words of Sir Stanley Maude, " with great gallantry," but with severe loss considering the number engaged, and it was hard that, after the sacrifice made, the party was by superior authority ordered back again after dark. Lieut. Jeffreys and four men were killed, and Lieut. MacFadyen, 2nd Lieut. Gibson and twenty-seven men wounded—more than fifty per cent of the two platoons becoming casualties.

On the 18th another advanced point was reached by 2nd Lieut. Tustin and his platoon, and this time the place was consolidated and a communication trench dug. Later in the day the battalion was relieved from the trenches, but it was back again in four days' time, suffering the loss of three men killed on the 22nd and Captain Usher, 2nd Lieut. Western and nine men wounded on the 24th. On the next day an attack was made in conjunction with the 3rd Indian and 13th British Divisions, with a view to clearing up the corner of the east bank of the Hai. This operation, however, was not successful and the Buffs lost some casualties to no great purpose, one officer and eighty other ranks being wounded in the business. The next day, however, the 36th Brigade attacked with great success and the 35th was able to come into line: Lieut. Sergeant and four men of the Buffs being wounded. The first blow of a hammer will often not drive in a nail, but it prepares the way for a successful second or third blow. The next two or three days were spent in consolidating and improving the new line.

The 31st of the month brought a fresh attack, and the brigade was progressing with its work when orders came that it was to move no further till the 37th Brigade came up on its left. This move, however, never materialized and, in consequence, the advance came to a standstill. Two men were killed and eleven wounded on the 1st February, but 2nd Lieut. Tustin and a party of bombers established themselves in a forward position. A further attack was prepared and was to be executed on the 2nd, but the dense fog, rendering all work impossible, made postponement necessary on the part of the 35th Brigade. The Turk was making fairly resolute counter-attacks, but they were broken by our artillery or met resolutely by our advanced troops.

On the 3rd the Devons and Ghurkas carried the enemy's first and second lines, and in the evening there were signs that he contemplated withdrawal. In fact, it seemed a little later as if this retreat had actually taken place, for everything was very quiet, so much so that things looked like a withdrawal, partial at any rate, from the other bank as well; and the Buffs, Ghurkas and Dogras all sent forward strong patrols, while the whole brigade stood ready to move forward at a moment's notice. On the 4th February the whole of the left bank of Hai had passed into our hands and the enemy was found to have fallen back to the Liquorice Factory and a line east and west across the Dahra Bend. On this day the Buffs took up a line of picquets facing the enemy in the bend, being relieved at nightfall.

It was not Maude's intention to let any of the enemy remain on the south side of the Tigris, in case such could resist his contemplated march on Baghdad by

saving the communications with that city, and so
enabling the Turkish army to keep the field. Obviously,
therefore, the next task was to clear the Dahra Bend
and drive its occupants across the main river. With this
object in view, the King's Own Regiment effected a
lodgment in the centre of the enemy's line on the 9th
February, and the same day the Worcestershire, capturing some advanced posts, established a line 2,500
yards or so south of the river at the southern end of the
Shumran Bend, and on the 10th our infantry, lying
west of the Liquorice Factory, after being attacked all
night by bombing parties, began early to assail the
Turkish position. In this connection the Buffs moved
from their line against that of the enemy with the
2/4th Ghurkas on their right. The move was successful
because the Turks would not abide the issue but vacated
their trenches, and, after occupying them, the Buffs
pushed forward patrols and bombing parties who, on
the 11th, in pouring rain, took up a line well forward,
from whence a communication trench was started towards the north. Four men were killed during these
two days, and 2nd Lieuts. Tustin and Sergeant and
fourteen men were wounded. On the 12th there was
severe fighting over the job of driving in the enemy's
picquets and covering troops, and the 102nd Grenadiers of the 35th Brigade greatly distinguished themselves by gallantly capturing a redoubt and holding it
against all counter-attacks.

But the principal day of battle in the Dahra Bend
was the 15th February, and it was the date of a complete and glorious success. Quite early the Loyal North
Lancashires carried a strong point opposite our left;
then the South Wales Borderers and Welch Fusiliers
captured the enemy's right centre, taking many prisoners; and later, about 1.30 p.m., the Buffs and the
Dogras, of their brigade, took up the work. On the
occasion of occupying the forward position referred to

above, A Company of the Buffs had been detached a little distance from the rest of the battalion and on the morning of the 15th patrols, sent out from this company, reported that the enemy's line in front was strongly held. Nevertheless when the hour came, the remaining three companies, with the good and faithful Dogras, rushed forward and nothing could stay their onslaught. It was most successful and together they reached the river line, isolating the Turkish extreme left and taking one thousand prisoners, of which six hundred, together with five machine guns, surrendered to the Buffs. Tactically this success was of the greatest importance, for the Dahra Bend was cleared and nothing was left but to cross and try conclusions on the left bank of the Tigris. Our casualties were twelve men killed and 2nd Lieut. Brooke and sixty-seven men wounded. As Sir Stanley Maude pointed out in his despatches: " To eject the enemy from his horse-shoe " bend, bristling with trenches, and commanded from " across the river on three sides by hostile batteries and " machine guns, called for offensive qualities of a high " standard on the part of the troops." To take the army across the river it would be necessary to keep the Turk fully occupied at Sanna i Yat and all along the bank from there to Kut, while preparations were made to pass the great obstacle as far to the westward as possible; so orders were issued to Lt.-General Cobbe to attack the lines at Sanna i Yat on the 17th.

An abnormally heavy rain fell on the 16th which flooded everything. The river rose—the trenches in the picquet line along the river bank, which were the temporary home of the Buffs, were swamped—the country was half under water and it was impossible to clean up the battlefield. Our battalion being relieved from picquet on the 18th returned to camp at a place called Kala Haji Fahan and remained there till the 22nd, all this time being utilized by Marshall and his

191

men in methodical preparations for the great crossing which was to be about the Shumran Bend whilst Cobbe, fifteen miles away, was assaulting the lines, in front of which he had been so long, and inducing the enemy to believe that there was the point of danger. On the 17th he gained some trenches, but had to withdraw, only to attack again on the 22nd, on which date the two first trenches were taken and made secure.

Meanwhile Marshall made several feints as if to cross the stream, particularly one opposite Kut, but the real point selected was the south end of the Shumran Bend and there three ferries were arranged, while the bridge was being made. The first ferry trip was a success, but subsequent journeys were pretty strongly opposed; nevertheless by 3 p.m. on the 22nd February three battalions were established across the river about a mile north of the site selected for the bridge, and at 4.30 the work was ready for use. The enemy had tried more than one counter-attack which failed, on account of the quickness and accuracy of our artillery. The Buffs crossed about 7 p.m. on the 23rd and bivouacked three hundred yards or so from the bank.

The enemy on the 24th made a very good fight to retain possession of, at any rate, some portion of the Shumran peninsula, in the northern corners of which exist quite a network of nullahs which, giving good cover and excellent concealment for machine guns, were utilized to their fullest extent. It took four or five hours to clear the peninsula and push back the Turk, but it was done. The Buffs were in support of the 67th Punjabis who were held up on the left. Together these battalions at last made some progress, but were stopped some three hundred yards in front of a nullah which was strongly held; the Gurkhas attacked on the Buffs' right, but were also stopped, and an attempted flanking movement was of no avail. However, about 9 p.m. patrols which had gone out as soon as it was dark reported that the enemy had evacuated the place and the nullah was at once occupied. The Buffs' casualties on this day were twelve men killed and Lieut. Howell and thirty-four wounded. Meanwhile cavalry, artillery and another division crossed the river, and Cobbe finished his task by capturing Sanna i Yat and clearing the bank of the main stream as far as Kut.

III. Pursuit to Baghdad

On the evening of the 24th February there were clear indications that the enemy was in full retreat and that Marshall had been fighting a strong and well-posted rear guard. The next few days were strenuous and energetic ones, but they were triumphant to an extraordinary degree. Since March, 1915, the Turkish enemy in Mesopotamia had proved a stubborn and a dogged foe. Till now he had never been badly beaten and he had scored, to his credit, the capture of a British Field Force at Kut. At last, however, he was on the run; and Baghdad, after Constantinople, the principal city of his empire, as well as the main centre of his Asiatic operations, had lost its defensive positions—so patiently perfected and prepared, and now lay open to the advance of the British army. But for hundreds of years there have been few better fighting men than the Turkish soldier, and even now he proved ready to see the thing out to a finish. He took up a strong position in some nullahs eight miles from Shumran, and it took us severe fighting on the 25th, in which, however, the Buffs did not take part, to gain a footing in his line; but after that his retreat was rapid. On the 26th one column followed the river while another, in which our battalion was, made a forced march over the arid plain of from eighteen to twenty miles to intercept him while the naval flotilla pushed up stream; the Turkish vessels struggling to escape, by no means wholly with success.

o   193

All movements to intercept the retreat were too late, however: the enemy had gone, leaving guns and all sorts of impedimenta behind him; and he streamed through Aziziya in confusion, shelled by gunboats and harassed by cavalry. Our pursuit was almost too rapid, the reason being that there was at one time hope of huge captures of fugitives. These, however, proved too quick for us, and about the 1st March it was found necessary to halt at Aziziya because the Field Force had outstripped their supplies. On that day the Buffs had no rations and had to obtain leave to consume the emergency one which everybody carries, but which is never opened except by high permission and in extreme cases.

On the 2nd March the regiment obtained some Turkish flour and a few sheep, late in the evening, but the first supply ship arrived late that night. Cobbe and his force had been following in Marshall's footsteps and found on their way immense quantities of rifles, vehicles, stores, equipment and so on, which the enemy had abandoned in his flight.

On the 5th March, things being now a little more in order, Marshall marched to Zeur and the Buffs marched with him, in a terrible dust storm and over a network of nullahs. On the 6th, the dust still continuing, a position was found to have been carefully prepared by the enemy at Ctesiphon, but it was unoccupied and the men pushed on to Bustan: a terrible day's march, particularly when the weather was taken into consideration; but fatigue and exhaustion were treated with the light-hearted contempt of triumphant conquerors, who knew that the object striven for so long was now within their grasp.

On the 8th March our advance guard came in contact with the enemy on Dialah river, eight miles below Baghdad, where the country was as flat and afforded as little cover as a billiard table. At first it was thought

ARCH AT CTESIPHON

that the river bank had been abandoned, but the first pontoon that was launched was riddled with bullets from rifle and machine guns, and it was found that the crossing must be made with skill and care. A small party ferried across the Tigris to bring the Turks under enfilade fire, and a lodgment was made on the far bank of the Dialah by about seventy men of the Loyal North Lancashires, who formed a post there and held it alone for twenty-two hours, when they were followed up, after the river had been bridged. It was now ascertained that on the other bank of the Tigris the enemy had taken up a position at a place called Shawa Khan to cover Baghdad from the south and south-west; so, on the 8th March, a bridge was made near Bawi and a portion of Cobbe's force (the 7th Indian Division) crossed to drive him away from it. Prior to the building of the bridge, however, and on the night of the 7th/8th March, the 35th Brigade, which had marched to Bawi and reached that place about noon, crossed the river by river-boat and barges. This proved a very difficult job as a landing-place could only be found a mile downstream; the barges were very difficult to load, and the first-line transport carts had to be left behind to follow on the first opportunity. After getting across in two trips the brigade marched for the remainder of the night, with frequent and tiresome halts, for it was necessary to ramp the banks of the various nullahs which crossed the path. At length, on the 8th, however, more open ground was reached and the troops deployed and proceeded in two lines of platoons, the Dogras with their right on the Tigris directing the movement; then came the Buffs, with the Ghurkas in reserve. The march was kept up till 2 p.m., when a high-walled and extensive garden was reached and utilized for bivouacs.

At 11 a.m. next day the journey was continued in company with the 7th Division, which had also crossed

195

the Tigris, and at noon our brigade was directed to fit
in between this division and the river and advance with
it and under the command of its general, the Buffs,
nearest the stream, to act as directing unit; and the
battalion commander directed A Company to hug the
river and direct the whole movement. The enemy was
found and he was strongly enough entrenched, but his
resistance was somewhat feeble. His left was driven
back and an attempted counter-attack defeated by
A Company. The Turks vacated their position after
dark and it was occupied by our patrols. Lieuts. Johnson and Holyman and four men were killed and thirty-
nine men wounded on this day.

On the 10th March patrols, pushing forward, gained
touch with the Turks once more, about a mile and a
half further back than their original position. They
were apparently in force, and so heavily shelled the
28th Brigade on the left of the 35th that it had to withdraw. The patrols of the latter brigade also met with
strong opposition. Orders were issued for the Buffs to
attack in the middle of the night, but these were can-
celled, as the enemy was found to have vacated his
position.

There was a good deal of jealous anxiety in the Meso-
potamian Army at this time as to which unit was to
first enter the city of Baghdad, and it seemed now that
the honour must fall to some portion of Cobbe's force
on the right bank of the Tigris. It will be remembered
that the 35th Brigade, of which the Buffs was the
British or white unit, was only temporarily attached to
the 7th Division of Cobbe's Force. The divisional
general on the morning of the 10th sent round a cir-
cular note to his units directing that the 7th Division
should make sure that they should be first into the city.
By some error on the part of the messenger (presumably) this note was also taken round to the Buffs, and
Colonel Body promptly reminded his men that they,

by their position closest to the river, were actually the nearest soldiers to Baghdad.

During the coming night the brigadier, being really much fatigued after a strenuous day or two, was urged to take his rest, and the Buffs, with their Indian comrades, pushing out patrols and following them up, somehow by daylight found themselves a couple of miles further up stream at the bend of the river opposite Garabah Island and only three miles from the city.

That day, the 11th March, the brigade advanced to the Iron Bridge in two lines of platoons in fours, the Buffs on the right, the 102nd Grenadiers on the left, with the 2/4th Ghurkas and 37th Dogras in rear. They met with no opposition, but just as the bridge was approached the 21st Brigade of the 7th Division appeared, coming up rapidly from the westward with a view to entering the place. Now " Let all things be done decently and in order," as St. Paul says, and the whole party or whole of the parties were halted at the site of the Iron Bridge at 8.35 a.m. Then the welcome order came that the 35th Brigade was to enter the city first, the Buffs to lead the column. The crossing was no easy matter and was carried out by means of *goofahs*, which each contained about twenty men. The Turkish flag was hauled down from the citadel and the Union Jack[1] hoisted in its place by Captain G. K. Harrison of the Buffs at 9.40 a.m.

The city of Baghdad was found to be in a most extraordinary state, and fires were bursting out everywhere. There are no more determined and persistent

---

[1] This Union Jack now hangs in Canterbury Cathedral, it having been later on presented to the battalion as a trophy; later on still it was handed over for safe custody to the Dean and Chapter and accepted by them at a grand ceremony held in the Cathedral at which were present many of the Buffs, particularly of the 5th Battalion, amongst whom was Captain G. K. Harrison, the man who had hoisted it on the 11th March.

looters in the world than Arabs, and these and the Kurds had seized the opportunity of their lives with avidity. The Turk for the moment was too busy to protect his property, and until the English entered the city anarchy prevailed and the thieves were in paradise, and so it came about that our reception approached the cordial by the regular inhabitants. Guards, prepared beforehand, were quickly mounted and a few looters shot. The flotilla anchored opposite the British residency. The Buffs marched through the city and bivouacked in the compound opposite the American consulate and things soon began to quiet down generally.

An immense amount of booty was found in Baghdad, though the enemy had been removing stores and so on for over a fortnight; still many guns, machine guns, rifles, ammunition, machinery and other things were left behind, and in the arsenal were found Townsend's guns which had been taken at Kut, after having been rendered useless before the surrender.

The hoisting of the flag on the citadel would seem a natural point at which to leave for a while the history of the 5th Battalion and turn our attention to the doings of others, but Sir Stanley Maude ends his despatch on the campaign, which included the fall of the great Turkish city, three weeks later, on the 31st March, and, though the Buffs had no very stirring adventures during this period, it may be as well to finish the record for the present at the end of the month.

A junction with our Russian allies, who appeared to be advancing from the direction of Persia, caused Maude to stretch out a hand, so to speak, in that direction: that is, up the River Dialah. Another matter that required arranging was that the Tigris is protected from overflowing by means of banks (or "bunds," as they are called), and if the enemy cut these up stream of the city disastrous floods would result. Another river, the Shatt el Adhaim, flows into the Tigris above Baghdad

and runs roughly parallel to the Dialah, which enters
the Tigris below the city, and on this river the enemy
made attempts at a stand. Altogether during March
there was fighting on these rivers and some gallant work
was done, notably by the Manchesters on the 25th.
Taking it all round, however, further opposition on the
enemy's part was but feeble. The most notable event
of this period was perhaps the occupation of Feluja on
the Euphrates river on the 19th March, giving the
English, as it did, the control of both the great rivers
of Mesopotamia. The Buffs spent most of the latter
end of March in camp at Hinaidi, just south of Baghdad, and in the careful preparation and excavations for
a permanent camp to be occupied during the rapidly
approaching hot season.

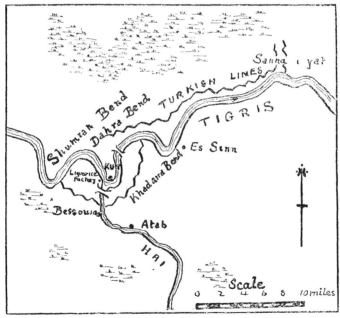

VICINITY OF KUT

199

CHAPTER IX

PALESTINE

I. Formation of 10th Battalion

AT the commencement of the year 1917 another battalion was added to the Buffs and from that time onward took a very interesting and important part in the fighting done by the regiment. The first deeds of arms accomplished by this, the 10th Battalion, were in Egypt and Palestine, and it may be as well to state baldly what had been happening in this region from the commencement of the war till the end of the year 1916 and to explain then how the 10th Buffs suddenly came into existence, as they did, on Egyptian soil on the 1st February, 1917.

As early as November, 1914, the Turk, who claimed to be the suzerain of the Land of Egypt and had always been jealous of the practical governorship exercised by the English, had advanced in considerable force on the Suez Canal; and perhaps it was only the arrival in the country, soon afterwards, of strong Australian and New Zealand contingents which had enabled the somewhat meagre garrison to hold its own. Even as it was the enemy had made a determined attempt to cross the Canal in February, 1915, and only retired from its neighbourhood in the following April.

Sir Archibald Murray was appointed to the supreme command in December, 1915, and Sollum, on the sea coast, something over two hundred miles west of Alexandria, was occupied in March, 1916, because of a troublesome tribe in those parts called the Senussi, who had been egged on by our enemies to make themselves a nuisance and who had to be dealt with. In August,

1916, the Turks had attacked at Romani, near the sea
and a few miles east of the Suez Canal, but they had
been badly beaten, and in September had withdrawn
further along the coast to El Arish. On the 21st December the British occupied El Arish and two days
later Magdhabar. They also carried the Turkish position at Rafa, near the coast and on the frontier of
Egypt and Palestine, on the 9th January, 1917. To
follow up these successes and advance on Gaza was now
Sir Archibald Murray's plan of campaign, and the army
under his command was carefully prepared and reorganized for the adventure.

There was at this time in Egypt a considerable quantity of dismounted Yeomanry, dismounted simply because of the paucity of horses, and it was determined to
form of them the 74th Infantry Division, consisting of
the usual number of infantry brigades and infantry
battalions, and working entirely on infantry lines, excepting for certain slight matters such as the use of
trumpets instead of bugles and the like.

Every decent soldier is proud of the arm to which he
belongs and which he deliberately joined of his own
free will on enlistment or enrolment, and it is hard on
him to ask him to serve in any other, but it has sometimes to be done, and it has been proved once and
again that an Englishman of pluck, spirit and average
intelligence can serve his country and serve it well
under any circumstances. In the Boer War, for instance, thousands of foot soldiers had to take over
horses and act as mounted men. In the same campaign,
after the Boers had lost their artillery, many of our
gunners were formed into battalions of infantry. In
the Great War hundreds of all arms took to fighting in
the air, and, if the navy wanted them, soldiers would
man submarines to-morrow. As a matter of fact, soldiers have in the old days served on the fleet in the
capacity of marines. It being recognized, then, that if

at any time there be a surplus of one kind of soldier and a deficit of another, that surplus will easily be taught to fight in other guise than he has been trained to do, the bulk of the Yeomanry in Egypt changed on the 1st February, 1917, into infantry soldiers. The county ideas and associations were respected as much as possible, and so it came about that the Royal East Kent Yeomanry then at Sollum was amalgamated with the West Kent (Q.O.) Yeomanry quartered at Matruh, a coast town about 125 miles west of Alexandria; they became the 10th Battalion of the Buffs, under the command of Major A. O'B. ffrench Blake, who was appointed Lt.-Colonel in the absence, due to sickness, of Lt.-Colonel Lord Sackville. The strength of the battalion was 46 officers and 875 other ranks; A and B Companies were men of the East Kent, and C and D West Kent Yeomanry. A period of intensive infantry training now commenced. The 10th Battalion formed part of the 230th Brigade and 74th Division. The other battalions of the brigade were made from the Sussex, Suffolk and Norfolk Yeomanry and became battalions of the same county regiments.

Early in March the battalion moved to Sidi Bishr, near Alexandria, the move taking no less than thirteen days to accomplish, and here the battalion was equipped. Drafts of 2 officers and 140 men joined on the 16th March and these were nearly all Buffs, no fewer than 64 with previous war service. Thus came into being the 10th Battalion of the "Old Buffs."

Its earlier history is as follows: at this time the Eastern Force under Lt.-General Sir Charles Dobell was concentrated about El Arish, through which the railway ran, on the northern coast of the Sinai Peninsula; whilst the Desert Column, under Lt.-General Sir P. Chetwode, was at Sheikh Zowaid about twenty miles further up the coast towards Palestine. This column was very strong in mounted men, and some of them were in advance of Sheikh Zowaid covering the further construction of the coast railway line, which was being pushed on towards Rafa, the frontier town of Egypt and Palestine. Murray's plan was to advance slowly and steadily up the coast, moving troops forward just as fast as the railway could be made to supply them. The railhead, by the 16th March, was at Rafa, and now it became necessary to hold the great Wadi[1] Ghuzze in order to protect what had been constructed. The enemy occupied the ground from Gaza through Sheria to Beersheba. Though the Buffs did not arrive on the scene of conflict at Deir el Belah till the 11th April, it is as well to state here that in March an attempt was made on the town of Gaza, and on the 26th of that month it was actually enveloped; but our mounted troops could not keep the field for want of water and had to retire across the Wadi Ghuzze while the enemy was pouring in reinforcements from the north and north-east, so that a second attempt met with such strong opposition that the whole force retired over the Wadi and took up a strong defensive position.

II. SECOND BATTLE OF GAZA

The next attempt was arranged to commence on the 15th April and was to consist of two stages: the first object being the occupation of Sheikh Abbas and the ridge south of Gaza; then, these points being held, careful arrangements in every detail were to be made and a supply of water organized. Meanwhile, however, the enemy was getting stronger every day, not only in numbers but in the development of his fortified line. Gaza itself became a very important fortress. On the 15th April the Buffs were ordered on outpost duty to take a line just north of the Wadi Ghuzze, and the next

---

[1] Wadi is the Arabic for water-course or river-bed ; as a rule innocent of water, but occasionally, during the rains, rushing torrents.

day came battle orders and company commanders went out to reconnoitre the position for the Second Battle of Gaza.

From Sheria to Gaza is sixteen miles and the enemy was in force the whole distance. The 52nd and 54th Divisions were told off to seize what was known as the Abbas Ridge and the 74th (Yeomanry) Division was detailed as General Reserve; therefore at 1.15 a.m. on the 17th our brigade left its bivouac and reached its battle position at 4 a.m. The ridge was taken shortly after with very little opposition, and the remainder of the day and the whole of the 18th were devoted to consolidating what was won and preparing for further advance by the 52nd Division on the left and the 54th on its right, which was to be aided by a containing attack by cavalry. The work was carried out according to plan, and the task set the troops was found to be a very difficult one. The casualties were heavy, particularly in the case of the 54th Division. The cavalry attacked at dawn and achieved success, but only one brigade of the reserve (74th Division) was utilized this day and our battalion, bivouacked in a barley field, had merely to watch the cavalry action in progress.

As a net result of the fighting the 54th Division had advanced as far as possible without exposing the flank which rested on the 52nd, but the latter had found such extremely broken ground, which was occupied by so many nests of machine guns, that its progress had been stayed and another day's fighting seemed to be a necessity. Orders were therefore circulated that all ground was to be maintained with a view to the renewal of the attack the following morning, namely, the 20th April, but it appeared that Sir Archibald Murray changed his mind, on the strong representation of General Dobell that the prospect of success was not sufficient to justify the great number of casualties bound to occur. So slow, deliberate trench warfare was decided on until more reinforcements should arrive, and, on the 23rd, the Buffs occupied a line in Wadi Ghuzze in the neighbourhood of Tel el Jemmi, and then commenced a long period of trench digging saddened by the inevitable conclusion that the great victory, which had been confidently expected and greatly looked forward to, had failed to eventuate.

The heat was now becoming intense; that scourge of the country, the hot Khamseen wind, was blowing, work was hard and, what was worse than anything else, water was scarce. However, after a few days, a move was made to Shellal and Hisea, still in the Wadi, and here more water was found and men could indulge in a wash. For a considerable period the digging of trenches was proceeded with, amidst all sorts of trials and troubles: the heat grew fiercer and fiercer as the season advanced; and, with the heat, animal life in the shape of scorpions, lice, flies, mosquitoes and spiders flourished and multiplied exceedingly. Wadi Nukahbir runs from near Sheikh Abbas into the great Ghuzze Wadi at Sheikh Nebhan, and there are many tributary Wadis to Nukahbir. These smaller nullahs received from our army the names of the tribes of Israel in order to distinguish them, and the next move of the Buffs, which took place on the night of the 27th May, was to the Wadi Levi, which is close to Sheikh Abbas, and from this centre working parties were sent out day and night to improve the front-line trenches or make elaborate redoubts in the second line of defence. During the stay in this Wadi the battalion suffered a good deal from sickness, there being many cases of scarlet fever and diphtheria; also nearly everybody developed boils and blains. It was discovered later that the dug-outs occupied had been previously inhabited by men suffering from the more serious complaints, but the sores were directly attributable to the want of vegetables owing to the difficulties of transport. It has nearly always happened in war time that septic sores have broken out amongst the soldiers and it has always been from the same cause. Lack of transport meant amongst many other things lack of vegetable food, and this in its turn means corruption of the human blood.

On the 28th June, 1917, General Sir Edmund Allenby, G.C.M.G., K.C.B., took over from Sir Archibald Murray the supreme command of the Egyptian Expeditionary Force, and the principal result of this was, to the Buffs, that their long period of hard digging work was very soon changed to one of strenuous training. On the 9th July the battalion left Wadi Levi and marched to a reserve area, and there, after a few days' refitting and rest, commenced the practice by day and night of attacks over open country together with some musketry. On the night of the 7th August the battalion marched to the sand dunes two miles south-west of Belah for field firing, and, after another move to the hills above Belah, the 5th of September found the Buffs commencing to dig again, the work being done at night at a point near where the Wadi Ghuzze joins the sea and where sea bathing made a very welcome change in the mode of life. Signs and tokens were at this time becoming more and more noticeable that, as the hot summer was nearing its limit, the new Commander-in-Chief had been arranging for some active and energetic war business against the enemy and that a fighting period was coming with the autumn. As a matter of fact, Allenby had early determined to postpone his great operations till the cooler season. The Turkish front extended from what was now the fortress of Gaza as far as Beersheba. There were well-fortified localities all along this line, which was thirty miles in length. This was a considerable extent to hold, but the lateral communications were good, and help and reinforcements could be comparatively easily brought to any particular point on the front which might be threatened by the English.

Water was Allenby's trouble. He could not keep the field without it and it affected his whole plan of campaign. No stroke at all could be effected without long and careful preparations for the necessary supply of water, and no preparation, however careful, could make that supply anything but a meagre one. A pipe-line 147 miles long brought up what was actually necessary from the Land of Egypt as far as the Wadi, whence it was camel-borne to the troops. There was, however, water at Beersheba and the general determined that it should be his. He would make a tremendous demonstration, in which the fleet would co-operate, opposite Gaza and cause the enemy to believe that he was determined to take that place. Then, while this great feint held the Turks' attention, he would strike resolutely at Beersheba on his other flank. There were great difficulties in the way. There were no roads, which meant that pack animals must carry all necessary stores, and the country was so cut up by Wadis that even to move these camels and mules became a very considerable difficulty. The railways were improved: the coastal line was pushed on to Khan Yunos; another was made from Dera Belah to a point on the Wadi Ghuzze, and a new one as far towards Beersheba as was safe. The men were carefully trained to exist on as little water as possible and to march with empty water-bottles. Operations were to commence on the 31st October, and cavalry was to make a wide turning movement and come down on Beersheba from the north and north-east.

III. Third Battle of Gaza

On the 25th October the march south-eastward commenced. It was carried out by moonlight, and the fourth night brought the Buffs, together with the bulk

of the division, to El Khasif and on the night of the
30th into their battle position. The march was a
memorable one. The ground varied but was always
open, so that movement in line was easy, and the moon
was always shining. The operation seems to have been
a triumph of staff work, and all the units slipped into
their allotted positions for the attack that was to follow
without a hitch of any kind. Khasif was some six miles
from the Turkish lines, and, after a quiet day there, the
230th Brigade moved off at night and got into the
places from which it was to attack at dawn.

The following description of what followed is given
by one who was there: " We reached our jumping-off
" point about midnight, and at 4 a.m. on the 31st the
" advance began with B and C Companies, the unit on
" our right being the 25th Royal Welch Fusiliers and
" on the left the 12th Norfolks. Our objective being
" Z.6 Z.7 works. This position consisted of a line of
" trenches cut in white lime-stone rock, cleverly sited
" on the forward slope of a steep gully. A communica-
" tion trench ran back into sloping ground in the rear
" and the wire was about seventy to one hundred yards
" down the sloping front. The leading waves of B and
" C Companies came under heavy shrapnel fire almost
" directly they started and the battalion suffered about
" sixty casualties, but, by continuing their advance and
" making use of the dead ground, they reached Hill 960,
" which was about one thousand two hundred yards
" from their objective. It became necessary to bring
" D Company into the line to fill a gap caused by the
" brigade on the right being drawn away. About
" 10 a.m. the 60th Division, who were on the right of
" the 74th, took Point 1070, and at 12.30 the final
" attack on Z.6 works was begun and, after a fierce
" fight, the position was captured. An intensive bom-
" bardment had previously been concentrated on the
" wire, but it was found to have been very ineffectual.

208

" By 1.30 the outpost line had been thrown out east of
" the captured positions and there the men remained
" for the night. It had been a very long and trying
" day's fighting in the hot sun and wearing heavy packs
" and winter serges, which had been issued two days
" before the advance."

In this Third Battle of Gaza 9 men were killed and
Lieuts. Garle, Haughton, Hollom and Stockdale, 2nd.
Lieuts. Aylward and Maddick, with 98 men, were
wounded, 4 missing, 2 got shell-shock and 2 received
injuries owing to the rough nature of the ground; 122
casualties in all. On the evening after the fight, news
came that Beersheba had fallen.

On the 1st November the battalion bivouacked in
Wadi Saba and were busied with salvage work, and on
the next day at a public parade for the presentation of
medal ribbands, Corpl. Webb of D Company got the
Military Medal. In the afternoon a march northward
commenced, and on the 3rd November the battalion
relieved the left unit of the 229th Brigade on outpost
line in the vicinity of El Muweileh, which it held for a
day, during which a half-hearted Turkish attack was
easily repulsed and large bodies of troops were observed
moving north and north-east.

During this period the scarcity of water was very
severely felt and men and animals were suffering badly,
as the Khamseen was blowing and all water had to be
carried fifteen miles by camel. The available supply of
the necessary fluid at Beersheba had been found to have
been exaggerated by report and to be inadequate to
sustain for long a large force in the field. This fact
greatly influenced the Commander-in-Chief in his
plans and determined him to attack Sheria on the 4th
or 5th of November, and Gaza forty-eight hours earlier
—this latter operation being in the nature of a feint
rather than a determined attempt at capture.

P   209

At 5.30 p.m. on the 5th November, therefore, the battalion received orders to go forward, take up an outpost line previously held by another unit and then advance one thousand yards before dawn. There were no landmarks in the region and no points on the map which could be identified, and the greatest difficulty was found in complying with instructions. A guide was supposed to be provided, but when, after some trouble, he was found he said he only knew his way to his own brigade headquarters and from these to the outpost line. Notwithstanding these troubles the battalion got into position ready for the coming advance by 3 a.m. on the 6th, but this was not the case with the units on either flank. Finally, the Buffs started their advance, the objective being a Turkish trench reported very lightly held, but after proceeding about five hundred yards, they came under a tremendous fire from a somewhat unexpected quarter. A fierce fight ensued and the Suffolk and Sussex men were pushed up into our line to reinforce it, with satisfactory results, and that portion of the Sheria defences was captured, after which, while the others pushed on, the Buffs were withdrawn into reserve in Wadi Union only to be ordered out again at 3 p.m. to fill a gap between two brigades away to the left. The pace of the attack throughout the day had been abnormally fast and the men suffered considerably from thirst. That evening the battalion took up an outpost line on the Wadi Sheria, and, just before dawn, a tremendous bombardment and explosion was heard from the town which announced that the capture of the place was complete. The casualties to the Buffs on the 6th November were fortunately very slight, but Lieut. R. W. Mitchell was severely wounded and subsequently died of his injuries. The same day the Turks evacuated Gaza.

On the 10th November the Buffs moved back to Kharm and on the 17th to Shellal on the Wadi Ghuzze, the reason being that the transport of the 74th and another division had to be taken away to keep the cavalry and the 53rd Division in contact with the defeated enemy; so the remainder of the force had to be near the railway. Lists of decorations for Beersheba and Sheria were made public on various dates, and the following were awarded to the Buffs: Military Crosses to Captain D. S. Campbell and Lieuts. J. A. S. Aylward and M. G. Haughton; the Distinguished Conduct Medal to Sgt. D. G. Turner; and Military Medals to Sgt. L. G. Betts, L.-Corpl. W. Timmins, Ptes. C. Hughes, D. O. Melrose, H. Scott, H. Tidcombe and G. A. Wiles. Another move on the 18th took the battalion to the neighbourhood of Gaza for salvage work, and on the 23rd came orders for a march to the north.

The general situation, while the Buffs had been without transport at Kharm and Gaza, had developed considerably. Although the enemy made attempts to stand, it was necessary for his right flank to retire rapidly from Gaza, so much so that as early as the 9th November we had troops at Beit[1] Duras with supports at Mejdel, and as the enemy's left flank was retreating towards Hebron, it became a case of direct pursuit by as many troops as could be fed and watered away from the railhead. There existed water, but in deep wells, and it takes much time to draw water from such. This is easily understood if one considers the actual number of seconds or minutes it takes to draw a bucket up two hundred feet. If that bucket is drunk by a cavalry horse it will be found that by the time the five hundredth animal or so of a cavalry unit is watered, the first is thirsty again. The Turkish forces were mostly supplied by the railway that comes from the north to the junction for the Jerusalem line, which is about nine miles south of El Ramle, and Allenby's object now was the capture of this junction.

[1] Beit is the Arabic for house, and so comes to mean village.

PALESTINE

About the 11th November the Turks appeared to be making a final effort to save Jerusalem, which is a sacred city to them. The resistance about the Wadi Sukerier was considerable and the Hebron wing of the enemy's forces moved towards Beit Jibrin to get more into touch with their brethren, so that by the 13th the enemy was facing west along the twenty-mile space between El Kubeibe and Beit Jibrin. Here they were resolutely attacked on the 13th November and the junction was occupied the following day, the enemy's army being cut in two, one part retreating north and the other east through the hills towards Jerusalem, in which direction the Turk was energetically followed up, all going very well until the 23rd of the month, on which date came a check. By this time our troops, namely, those of the British forces which could be provided for in the field, were very close to Jerusalem, the main objective being the road to Nablus. Beit ur el Tahta was in our hands as well as Kuryet el Enab to the south of it. Some Yeomanry had got within four miles of the Nablus road, but were stopped by strong opposition about Beitunia. On the 21st November a body of infantry was on the ridge where stands Nebi Samwil, about five miles north-west of the city. On the 23rd and 24th the Turks held a position west of the Nablus road which was gallantly attacked by the British, but without success. The road itself proved the deciding factor in the struggle, because the enemy not only brought up his guns and machine guns by it, but used it as an artillery position, whereas our people were on very rough ground and had no road at all. And so it came to pass that a pause in our hitherto triumphant progress became apparently necessary. The army must be organized and preparations made and completed for further efforts. Also reliefs must be brought up, and thus, as has been said, the Buffs, who were as far back as the Wadi Ghuzze, got orders to move to the north.

212

The journey was done by Mejdel, Nahr Sukerier, Junction Station and Latrun to Beit Nuba, which was reached on the 29th November. The sixty-miles' march was accomplished in six days.

It is between the two latter places that the mountainous region commences and marching becomes climbing, for Jerusalem stands very high and the approaches to it are by no means a gradual ascent. At Beit Nuba the battalion was employed on road-making to enable the guns to move, the result of the Buffs' labour being known as the New Kent Road. By the 4th December Allenby had completed his final preparations and a line was held from Kustol by Nebi Samwil Ridge, Beit Izza and Beit Dukka to Beit ur el Tahta, the Buffs moving to Kubeibeh on the 6th December. On this day the rains broke and fell consistently and determinedly for three days and three nights, rendering roads almost impassable for camel transport, so that the battalion was put on one-third rations. Observation was most difficult; the bivouacs were soaked and comfort for the time being abolished. The morning of the 8th December was fixed upon for the grand attack, and during the previous night the troops moved into their positions of assembly to take their share in the Battle of Nebi Samwil.

IV. BATTLE OF NEBI SAMWIL

The 230th Brigade was at dawn to attack some high mountains close to Nebi Samwil: the Buffs and the Norfolks in the first line, with the 229th Brigade on the right of the Buffs. To reach the position it was found necessary to move in single file down the slippery slopes of a great Wadi, and this made the keeping of touch extremely difficult and the subsequent proper deployment no simple matter. A battalion in single file in a difficult country will tail out to almost any length.

213

However, all was well, the job was done and the men deployed along the lower slopes of the great hill, C Company on the right and A Company on the left—the ground in their front being almost precipitous. However, the first wave of troops got half-way up the slope before the dawn broke and the Turk took in the situation. Then he opened heavily with machine guns and snipers, both very well concealed. C Company being a good deal exposed, suffered somewhat severely; but A Company was fairly well covered by a spur, and the 229th Brigade on the Buffs' right was still more fortunate and was able to push on more rapidly, so that the enemy, fearful for his flank, withdrew and our people successfully occupied his trenches. No further advance was now possible for some hours, as a tremendous fire was brought to bear against the assailants. An attempt was made before dark, as it was incorrectly reported that the left flank of the brigade was secured by a successful advance of the 231st Brigade, but this force had in reality failed to clear the whole of the hill, and consequently the renewed attack of the 230th was held up till dusk by a sweeping machine-gun fire. A miserable night was the sequel of this fight: practically no rations, and pouring rain. In the morning the Sussex Regiment moved through the Buffs and continued the advance, only to find that the enemy had abandoned the place during the night. This manœuvre seems to have been a favourite one of the Turkish forces both in Palestine and Mesopotamia and one at which they were adepts. At the top of the hill the British troops got their first view of Jerusalem. By this time the London troops and the Yeomanry had got across the Nablus road four miles north of the city, and Welshmen were across the Jericho road to the east of the town. Jerusalem was isolated; and about noon on the 9th December the Holy City surrendered. Two days later Sir Edmund Allenby officially entered the place. The casualties of

GENERAL ALLENBY ENTERS JERUSALEM

the Buffs at Jerusalem were 14 men killed and 1 officer and 42 other ranks wounded. Directly after the fall of Jerusalem, while at Beit Iksa, the 230th Brigade lost its commander, General McNeill, who was taken to hospital with malaria.

On the 13th December the Buffs took over the outpost line between Nebi Samwil and Beit Hannina, and this period will be difficult to obliterate from the memories of those who were serving, because the advance of the armies had now far outstripped that of the railway line and by this time the winter rains had set in in earnest. The Wadis, which were practically the only means of communication, were streaming with mud and water, making the country in the vicinity impossible for camel transport, with the immediate result that food grew very scarce and the soldier had to exist on half rations, while tobacco, cigarettes and matches ran out altogether. The state of things is thus described by a member of the regiment: " Only those " who have been through it could realize the awful " days and nights which the transport men and camels " spent trying to get up ammunition and supplies. The " camels falling down at every turn and preferring to " die rather than get up again, while the natives in " charge of them wrapped themselves in their blankets " and howled through the night like a pack of dogs, and " many of these too died." Donkeys were tried, but without much success. The donkey is a very hardy beast, but the majority of these came from the warmer parts of Egypt and they did not thrive.

The military situation in Palestine after Jerusalem became ours was simply that the portion of the Turkish army, which had retreated northwards after our capture of the junction railway station, was now halted on the hills north of Jaffa and Ramle, faced by our 21st Corps, while the 20th Corps held a position covering the Nablus and Jericho roads about four miles to the northward and eastward of the city. To provide for the security of Jerusalem and of Jaffa it was necessary for these two army corps to advance, and, to enable such an advance to be successfully carried out, it was necessary first to undertake an abnormal amount of road-making as well as to make important arrangements for the organization of the supply of food, ammunition and all the various military requisites. The 21st Corps moved north and, supported by the fleet, crossed the Nahr el Auja north of Jaffa—a difficult job, well carried out. The 20th Corps was employed meanwhile in minor operations. Thus on the 18th December the 60th Division, on the right of the 230th Brigade of the 74th, attempted an advance, and at 6.15 a.m. A Company of the Buffs went out in support of the movement; but the thing was a failure, the Turk having evidently been quite aware of what was going forward and having made all due preparations; in fact, A Company had some difficulty in withdrawing, but happily the casualties were light. But road-making was the usual fate of the Buffs at this time and the men had long since become experts at the business. There was no work done on Christmas Day, but up till then the roads claimed much labour. The 25th itself was one of the wettest days yet experienced and there were only half rations; but singing seems to have kept the soldier from feeling his hardships too acutely, and Boxing Day saw the Buffs in the outpost line again.

V. Defence of Jerusalem

Now at this time the enemy had conceived it possible that on account of our supposed despair at the shortage of rations and difficulty of transport it would be possible by a resolute attack to recover possession of Jerusalem, which is a place as sacred to Mahommedans as it is to Jews or Christians, and so, on the night of the

216

26th/27th December, John Turk marched resolutely southwards, astride the Nablus road, until he came up against the 60th Division, who refused to make way, and the enemy soon found himself resolutely counter-attacked by the 10th Irish Division, which was on the left of the 20th Corps. The struggle lasted three days, for the enemy also attacked the 53rd Division to the east of Jerusalem, and it was quite evident that the operation was not a minor affair by any means, but had been carefully prepared and planned out and was being determinedly attempted. By noon on the 27th, however, the great counter-attack made by the 74th and 10th Divisions, which was launched at 6.30 a.m., had made itself felt, and on the following day, this counter-offensive continuing, the 230th Brigade, Buffs included, of course, was pushed up the centre of the line towards Ram Allah. Fortunately the day was fine and dry. At first this forward movement took the Buffs up the valley and the battalion was in artillery formation, but, later on, broken and rocky ground was experienced again until there came a rest as darkness fell, and the men sat down and made preparations for some food. Very soon, however, came orders to advance in line on Ram Allah, taking direction from the 60th Division on the right. The companies were somewhat scattered, and in the stony country with a night as black as pitch it was a terrible job for the runners to discover the several companies and for them to come back into touch with battalion headquarters. There were no paths or tracks and the map was useless. As one who was out that night remarked, " If you take a line to march on and then bark your shin on a rock, next have to circumvent a boulder and immediately afterwards fall into a bog, you are apt to lose your direction." The Buffs stumbled about till they reached a large marshy valley, where they came across the Royal Sussex and learnt that the division was resting close by with no intention

217

of going on to Ram Allah that night; so an outpost line was thrown out and the men lay down till dawn. About 8 o'clock next morning an advance was made straight across a most tremendous country of vine terraces and walls, and, with but little opposition, A and D Companies got into the town, a filthy place on the brink of another precipice. On the top of the hill opposite to it the Turks had several machine guns and snipers posted and they now began to show some activity, the Sussex Regiment coming under a fairly heavy fire, so that B Company was held in readiness to go to their aid, while C and A Companies took post along the front of the village overlooking the precipice. That night was as black as the former, and a line of advance allotted to the Buffs was so precipitous that the battalion formation was bound to get into some sort of confusion, though every effort was made to keep touch with the companies and with other units. Opposition had died away, however, and so ultimately a new outpost line was taken up with the Suffolk Regiment on the Buffs' left, and here the regiment remained for several days. The weather was terribly wet at this time and the ground so saturated as to be almost impassable for mules.

The Jerusalem–Jaffa road was now in our hands and was the principal lateral communication. General Allenby now decided that no further advance was possible or necessary for the present and that his next task was to drive the enemy over the Jordan. The outpost line referred to above was relieved on the 3rd January, 1918, and the Buffs went back to Beit Izza and Beit Likia, the rain still continuing with fury and the shortage of rations proving still a considerable hardship. The 10th Irish Division had commenced making a new road to supply the front line and save to some degree the permanent Latrun–Jerusalem one. This engineering work was called, out of compliment to that division, the Irish Road, and it now became the scene for some weeks of the Buffs' activities. The battalion began work on it on the 9th January near Beit Sirra, and it was not till the 7th March that it took over an outpost line, this time in front of Lake Balua. This period of labour was lightened on the 18th January by a parade for the distribution of medal ribbands, on which occasion Sgt. Turner got the D.C.M., and Ptes. Kite, C. W. Scott and Betts the Military Medal.

The above-mentioned move was in reality a very complete change from two months' heavy work to real soldiering again, even if it were only infantry soldiering, as the gallant Yeoman of Kent may possibly have put it. A patrol of B Company advancing from this outpost line found Yebrud occupied by Turkish snipers and the battalion got orders to occupy the village by midnight, but it was found to be so strongly held that the reserve companies had to be absorbed into the line to support the attack, and it was not till 8 a.m. on the 9th that the place was occupied and a new outpost line on Burj Bardawile taken up. 2nd Lieut. F. W. H. Cooper was killed in this affair and Captain Ponsonby and seven other ranks wounded. Next day the advance continued, the country getting worse and worse, but more positions were taken in the evening, A and B Companies having a climb of three and a half hours before the Turkish trenches and sangars, perched on the forward slope of a precipice, were theirs. Eight other ranks were wounded. The Buffs were now three thousand feet up, and it was bitterly cold and wet. Moreover, the old ration and supply difficulty became once more acute; the stuff could only be got to the foot of the precipice on which the men were, and then the tired soldiers, after a heavy day's work, had to scramble down to fetch it. On the 11th March El Tel was occupied, which meant another very stiff climb. After this road-making south-east of El Tel and on the Nablus road was resumed, and outpost work near Turmus Aya. A very good piece of patrol work is recorded during this period. It was carried out by Lieut. Barnard of the Buffs and a few of his men on the 1st April. These men met an enemy's patrol and promptly charged them with the bayonet, though the enemy were backed by machine guns. The Buff party killed three Turks and had one of their number slightly wounded.

On the 21st March, 1918, the Germans, who had now been freed from all anxiety as regards Russia, commenced in France their last stupendous effort for victory and were so far successful that all troops that could possibly be spared from other theatres of war were hurried to the rescue of our Western front. For this reason it came to pass that early in April it was decided that the 74th Division must be taken from the Egyptian Force, in which it had served one year, and be shipped off to Europe, where it was grievously needed. On the 8th of this month, therefore, the march to the railhead at Ludd commenced, the Buffs moving by Beitunia and Beit Sirra. On the 13th they entrained for Kantara, and on the 28th left that place for Alexandria and for France.

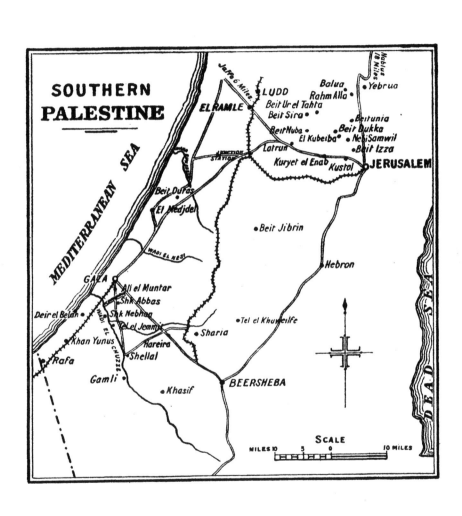

CHAPTER X

THE WESTERN FRONT

(*November*, 1916, *to July*, 1917)

I. SUMMARY OF EVENTS

AS has been seen, both Baghdad and Jerusalem fell to British arms during the year 1917, but other mighty events of war were happening on the various fronts, and, while England was knocking out the Turk with her left hand, so to speak, she was still engaged in a furious fight against Germany on the Western front with her right, in conjunction, of course, with her faithful allies. Moreover, other things happened in 1917 which very materially influenced the course of the great struggle. The two most important events were the coming in of the United States of America and the dropping out of the Russians.

On the 1st February, 1917, Germany very foolishly declared unrestricted submarine warfare: that is, she issued a notice that, within what she was pleased to lay down as a War Zone, she intended to sink both combatant and neutral shipping at sight. This directly brought her into a state of war, which was declared on the 6th April, with America, and the first American contingent landed in France on the 25th June, and on the 27th October infantry and artillery belonging to that nation were actually in action. Of course, the armies from across the Atlantic were at first very small, like our own had been in 1914, but, like the British forces, they swelled with rapidity.

On the 12th March of this year of 1917 a revolution started in Russia and three days later the Czar abdi-

221

cated. Notwithstanding this, however, the Russians, under General Brusilov, commenced a determined offensive in Galicia, which was at first successful, but which soon died away. On the 21st October the new government practically determined on peace, though there was a mutual agreement between the three countries of England, France and Russia that no one of them would make peace without the other two. These kinds of arrangements, however, did not affect the new rulers very much, and, on the 22nd November, Lenin authorized the troops at the front to negotiate for cessation of hostilities, and next day he started to work to disband the army. Preliminaries being signed with the enemy at Brest Litovsk on the 5th December, it became actually necessary for Rumania to follow suit. On the 21st June the Order of the British Empire was established.

At the end of October our friends the Italians were suffering disaster at the hands of the Austrians, and early in November a British force had to be sent to their assistance.

II. The 7th Battalion—The Ancre

Meanwhile war went on steadily in France and Belgium, and the 1st, 6th, 7th and 8th Battalions of the Buffs were all there and taking part; so we must now take up their history from the 18th November, 1916, which is the date Sir Douglas Haig assigns as marking the close of that lengthy struggle called the Battle of the Somme. Of the units mentioned above, the 7th was the first to participate in a general action, for it must be understood that fighting in the neighbourhood of the Somme and the Ancre rivers by no means ended on the fixed date mentioned; in fact, our 7th found itself in the thick of a fierce battle on the 18th November itself. Sir Douglas Haig, in describing his plans for the winter, makes it clear that it was desirable to allow the enemy no respite during the cold season, and he tells us why he resolved to keep up as much offensive work in the neighbourhood of the River Ancre as the weather and the state of the ground would allow. In fact, the German was to have no rest until the new spring offensive was brought into being, and further operations on the Ancre, as well as many minor enterprises and raids, were organized to annoy him while, at the same time, all troops that could be spared from actual touch with the enemy were to undergo a period of training and refitting as well as the rest they so much required; for after all rest is only a change of occupation, just as in civil life a man who daily fatigues his body rests in a long chair under a tree; so an office man, sedentarily employed, rests himself on a holiday by a game of cricket or football.

To get back to the history of the 7th Battalion, then, it was on the 16th November that it received a message from its brigadier that operations might recommence on the following day, and, together with the 7th Queen's, it went into trenches in relief of the Cheshire and Welch Regiments, and on that date 2nd Lieut. I. H. Hess and two men were killed and six wounded. Near Mouquet Farm and stretching eastwards from the village of Grandcourt was a trench of the same name, and about five hundred yards south of it, also stretching east from the southern edge of Grandcourt, and covering the village of Miraumont, lay a long trench line called Desiré; both these were occupied by Germans. Facing Desiré trench, about six hundred yards from it and nearly parallel, ran the English line called Regina, and in it had been for some few days the East Surrey and West Kent Regiments. The line was prolonged to the left by the Queen's and Buffs on the 17th November, so it came about that on the morning of the 18th, on which day Desiré was to be assaulted, the

223

ground was new to these two regiments. Behind Regina was Hessian trench, and Zollern trench was behind that again. The ground was very difficult to move over and it was snowing when the attack began at 6.10 a.m. The enemy opened fire almost at once, and at 6.45 his barrage was intense. No news from the assaulting companies could be got at the Buffs' headquarters and several runners were killed in trying to obtain information; but at last the officer commanding the Queen's sent news that the Buffs and Queen's were in touch and that they were consolidating. It was, however, only at 6.30 p.m. on the 19th that the whole of the original objective of the Buffs was secured by the help of D Company (Captain Wood). The ground over which the original attack had passed was now examined and the secret of the heavy casualties discovered: it was found that in front of A Company, particularly opposite its right flank, a number of shell holes about thirty yards the English side of Desiré had been improved by the enemy into most excellent cover and connected backwards to their trenches by well-constructed narrow slits or passages. The Germans had remained covered in this place till our barrage lifted over it and then come to life again, so to speak, and opened quite unexpected and very deadly fire on every living man who approached. Captain Dyson was killed, and there remained but one unwounded soldier of A Company. The 7th Buffs' casualty list for this Battle of the Ancre amounted to 3 officers killed, 4 wounded and 1 missing, and 23 other ranks killed, 76 wounded and 124 missing.

A discovery was made by Captain Wood on the evening of the 19th which, to the disgrace of our enemies be it written, was practically unique in the history of the war. He found an officer, several men of A Company and two of the West Kent all severely wounded in a dug-out in Desiré trench; they had been carried in

SCENE ON THE ANCRE

by the enemy and had been bound up and treated well by them.

III.   7TH BATTALION—*continued*

The next important general action in which the regiment was engaged was the Battle of Arras, which commenced on the 9th April, 1917, and in which it was represented by its 6th Battalion. The story of the 1st, 6th, 7th and 8th up to that date is consequently not so full of incident as some other periods, though casualties continued to occur. For the purposes of continuity, however, it will be as well to consider a brief account of the doings of each, remembering that Haig had decreed that the enemy was to have no rest prior to our spring offensive, which offensive commenced with the said Battle of Arras. Regular and continuous training for this offensive was, however, to be the key-note for the winter work of our people. As regards the 7th Battalion a rest was imperative; it was weak in numbers and much war worn, and so it, with its brigade, moved away westwards, at first by bus to Hartonville and then by march route to Candas Beaumetz and Marcheville, which latter village it reached on the 27th December and where it remained till the 14th January, 1917, receiving seven new 2nd lieutenants and a draft of no less than 315 men. On the latter date the unit moved to Hautevillers. About six weeks were very well spent in training and refitting in this, the Abbeville district, and the good work done at this time, together with the arrival of excellent drafts and several capable officers, resulted in the reproduction of a very fine battalion. It was on the 11th January that the brigade began moving towards Albert again, billeting in the wayside villages each night, reaching Hedauville, which is about three miles north-west of Albert, on the 16th and remaining there for nearly a month, which was mostly employed in road-making.

Q

On the night of the 11th February the 55th Brigade relieved the 54th in the trenches near Martinsart and for a few days were near Mouquet Farm and the Zollern trench again. 2nd Lieut. Butler was wounded on the 22nd February.

Although the winter was supposed to be mainly a preparation for a spring campaign, both the enemy and our people had been fairly busy ever since the close of the Somme fighting. The Germans, who still held three lines of defence about the Ancre river, had been busy establishing a strong fortified position called the Hindenburg Line, which, starting from the old lines near Arras, ran south-eastward for twelve miles to Queant and from there west of Cambrai towards St. Quentin; and this line was connected up with various switches. By means of continuous offensive work our armies had gradually gained certain positions about Grandcourt, and the spur which runs northward from Courcelette towards Miraumont, which gave complete command over the enemy's artillery in the upper valley of the Ancre and his defences about Pys and Miraumont.

On the 23rd February the 7th Buffs took over the advanced line from the 7th Royal West Kent, C Company being on the right front with D on the left; A right support, B left support; headquarters in Boom ravine. This relief was carried out by daylight and in full view of the enemy from the neighbourhood of Loupart Wood, the consequence being that our men were shelled as they went up and twenty casualties resulted.

It was thought probable about this time that the enemy was withdrawing, and when the West Kent were relieved they reported signs of a retirement, so, when night fell, the Buffs were ordered to send out patrols along the road leading north-east towards South Miraumont Trench until touch was gained with the enemy, to find out whether that work had been evacuated and,

226

if so, to occupy it. The darkness was intense and movement most difficult, but D Company found the South Miraumont Trench deserted and, in conjunction with a company of the Queen's, established posts there. When daylight came C Company, assisted by A, commenced a complete reconnaissance which was most admirably carried out under Captain Clapperton of C Company, who, with Lieut. Hayfield, 2nd Lieuts. Mathias and Church and Captain Row, did some skilful and useful work. They found Petit Miraumont abandoned by the enemy, and by evening it was ascertained that Pys and Miraumont had also been evacuated. When night had again fallen (on the 24th February) a line was established running along the East Miraumont road as far as the railway where it passes the village, and this was held by A Company (Captain Allen) on the right, and C (Captain Clapperton) on the left.

On the 25th news came that the 2nd and 63rd Divisions were about to advance, one on either side of the 35th Brigade, who prepared to go forward in their company with the Buffs in front. There was a very thick fog, and the task of collecting the scattered companies was thus rendered a most difficult one, but the work was well and comparatively quickly accomplished and the advance successfully carried out. A Company covered the advance with patrols while D moved on Pys with the near edge of Irles as an objective. C Company moved with its left on the railway, B being held in reserve on the East Miraumont road. The fog was so dense that compasses had to be used, but, notwithstanding all difficulties, the several parties all reached their objectives and gained touch inwards. D had to throw back its right flank to join with the 2nd Division, which came up much slower. This company was admirably handled by Captain Wood, but this is also true of all the company and platoon leaders. In the course of the afternoon the positions gained were consolidated under a certain amount of shelling and machine-gun fire from Irles and a position east of Pys. That evening the battalion was relieved by the 7th Queen's and went back to the Zollern Redoubt, after placing to its credit a very fine piece of work.

The early part of March was spent in the same area, that is between the Zollern Redoubt and Miraumont, but no event of great importance to the Buffs occurred, though indications were at this time being observed by the staff of a coming German withdrawal, and on the 14th March any doubts as to the truth of this conjecture were dissolved and three days later a general advance of our whole line from Roye in the south to just south of Arras took place. The enemy had retreated to his Hindenburg Line. Unfortunately he could not be properly pursued: our people were travelling over devastated country and smashed and broken roads, bridges and communications, while the German had of course kept everything of that sort in his rear in perfect order.

The 55th Brigade, with the Buffs, moved away from the district altogether, commencing the journey on the 21st March by marching ten miles to the south-west and billeting at Harponville. On the 25th they entrained at Saleux for the First Army area, detraining next day at Steenbecque, south-west of Hazebrouck, and thence marching to billets at Boeseghem, in which vicinity the battalion remained for a considerable time, undergoing the usual course of training.

On the 8th April the brigade paraded for the presentation of medal ribbons, on which occasion Lieut. Hayfield received a bar to his M.C., and Captain Wood, 2nd Lieuts. Church, Mathias and Cotching the ribbon of that decoration. The special training period continued at Boeseghem until the 20th of the month, on which day the brigade moved by route march through Bethune to La Bourse; back to Bethune on the 26th, and finally reached Neuville Vitasse and went into re-serve trenches on the 28th. Neuville Vitasse is between four and five miles to the south of Arras and nearly the same distance from the village of Cherisy.

On the 1st May the battalion took its place in the front-line and support trenches: A and B Companies relieving the Queen's, and the other two companies the Royal West Kent.

IV. 1st Battalion

We left the 1st Battalion at Bethune and the trenches in that vicinity. Though casualties were not uncommon, the 1st December, 1916, was rather a worse day than most: on that date L.-Corpl. Willey was killed and ten men wounded, while Pte. Tattersall and 2nd Lieut. Kingham went down with shell-shock. On the 20th of the month the Buffs got back to Bethune with a casualty list for the first twenty days of the month of no less than 12 killed (including C.S.M. Freemen), 31 wounded and 2 shell-shock cases. On the 24th pleasant Christmas gifts in the shape of decoration ribbons were handed at Bethune to Captain Brown, C.S.M. Randall, L.-Corpls. Ashdown and Baines and Pte. Higgins.

The beginning of 1917 brought no change except slight ones in the way of locality, such as a move into huts at Noyelles on the 9th January and change of trenches. There came a list of mentions in despatches near the middle of this month, and the names of Lt.-Colonel Green, Captain Stone, 2nd Lieut. Ford, R.S.M. Harrington and C.Q.M.S. Poole were included. On the 3rd February C.S.M. Brown, D.C.M., was appointed Actg. R.S.M. vice Harrington, who went to a cadet school.[1] On the 12th February the battalion

[1] These cadet schools were started after the war had been some time in progress, and when they were established commissions were no longer given except to graduates.

was inspected by Sir Douglas Haig. On the 15th it retired into billets at Robecq, some seven miles further back than Bethune. The fortnight spent there was passed in strict professional training for four hours from 8.30 a.m., and equally strict recreation in the form of cross-country running, boxing and football in the afternoon.

March brought no relief from the almost daily tale of casualties. On the 1st of the month headquarters were in the village of Loos, with the men in the trenches; and by the 17th 2nd Lieut. S. Major and 10 others had been killed and 35 wounded. On the 18th the enemy carried out a raid on our trenches and succeeded in getting a footing in them, but after a short time was ejected leaving 7 dead; but we lost 2nd Lieut. H. M. Norsworthy and 10 men killed, 2nd Lieut. Hughes and 24 wounded, besides 8 missing. This raid seemed to have had the effect of raising and fostering a very firm determination on the part of the Buffs to get " a bit of their own back," and on the last day but one of March a party consisting of Captain Strauss, 2nd Lieuts. Brown, Davis and Griffiths and a hundred rank and file carried out a successful raid on the German front and support works, blowing up several dug-outs and bringing back a prisoner and many trophies. Four of our fellows, however, were killed and four more died of wounds. 2nd Lieut. Griffith and 29 men were wounded, and 2nd Lieut. P. W. T. Davis and 7 others originally reported missing, were afterwards found to have been killed in the action. It was estimated that about 200 of the enemy were slain during this little expedition.

On the 1st April the battalion was in support in Loos village, remaining there seven days, when a return to the trenches was made, and here the 1st Battalion was still serving when the Battle of Arras opened on the 9th.

V. 8TH BATTALION

For the most of this period our 8th Battalion were near neighbours of the 1st, and indeed there were at times meetings between them. On the 18th November it was at Mazingarbe, only three miles west of Loos, taking its usual trench tours in the " Bis " section. On the 21st Captain Vaughan was evacuated sick after serving continuously since the unit arrived in France, and leaving only Lieut. Herapath with this record.

It is interesting to note that, on the 24th and again on the 20th December, the 1st and 8th Battalions met in combat on the football ground, the former proving on each occasion too strong. As they were due in the trenches again on the 22nd December the men kept Christmas at Mazingarbe on the 20th of the month with great festivity, some of the 1st Battalion officers dining with those of the 8th. The trenches were much knocked about by the enemy during the Christmas tour of work, so much so that the front line almost ceased to exist.

The new year found the 8th in what was called the Village Line, and the German started the New Year with a heavy dose of gas and lachrimatory shells, and on the 5th January an extensive raid. Fine work was done by 2nd Lieut. Darling, who organized and led bombing squads with great success; by Captain Morley, who, with three men, held a bombing post although completely surrounded and cut off; and by Pte. Setterfield, who, being company runner, killed three of the enemy and rescued one of our own people, while carrying messages. Two days after this fight the unit moved back to billets in Mazingarbe for training work, the monotony of which was lightened by regular football.

After another turn at trench warfare a raiding party of 4 officers and 120 other ranks on the 26th January, all clad in white smocks on account of the snow, and

231

acting in conjunction with the 12th Battalion Royal Fusiliers, started at 6.30 a.m. for the German trenches. The result of this expedition was very satisfactory and was the cause of great elation to the men. Heavy casualties were inflicted and several dug-outs were blown in. The wire had been well cut by the gunners and the enemy's resistance did not prove very considerable, but 2nd Lieut. R. G. Phillips was killed and fourteen men were wounded. Unfortunately most of the Germans were in dug-outs and could not be extracted.

The battalion was in the front-line trenches from the 30th till the 6th February. It was what might be termed a normal tour, but very cold. In fact, the winter of 1916–1917 was almost a record for bitter and continuous frosts. The next turn in the rest areas was from the 7th February to the 2nd March, first at Mazingarbe and then at Nœux les Mines, a little further west. The time was, of course, devoted to training, and in addition to that work, done under divisional auspices, special practice was given to 125 picked men as a preliminary to another raiding expedition. On the 14th February 2nd Lieuts. Sankey and Darling were awarded M.C.'s for the recent successful little operation.

The battalion came up to the strength of 1056 about this time owing to the arrival of a draft on the 21st and the fact that a number of instructors who had been lent to a training battalion, recently organized, returned now to their own unit. By the end of the month everybody was well prepared and equipped and very ready for whatever might befall.

The 2nd March saw the brigade in a new trench line called " Angres," taken over from Canadian troops; and a week later it was at Bully Grenay, three miles west of Loos; but the inhabitants were still in the place —children and all. It was wonderful how bravely the French peasants throughout the war stuck to their homes near the firing line, regardless of roofs broken by shells and the constant danger of being blown to atoms.

Bully Grenay was, on the 5th April, so heavily shelled that three companies had to leave the place and the fourth go into the cellars. 2nd Lieut. W. L. Donelan was killed in his billet. Gas shells also came over and one or two N.C.O.'s were badly gassed. Concerts, however, which had been arranged for certain dates early in the month, were not interfered with or postponed. The alternating process of trench work and so-called rest in billets, roughly week and week about, had been going on for a considerable time and, in fact, described the life of the unit during the early part of 1917.

On the 27th March a special party of 125 men of A Company got into position at 3.30 a.m. Captain Morrell took post in the front line, and 2nd Lieut. Young and party moved across No Man's Land opposite the place known as " The Pope's Nose." The men moved forward under a perfect barrage, just as dawn was breaking; but owing to the imperfect light the two parties converged on entering the enemy's lines and a certain amount of confusion ensued. However, no enemy was encountered, though the left party proceeded some way down the communication trench. A dug-out was blown in. The Germans retaliated in a half-hearted sort of way and we had a man killed and two wounded.

On the 8th April our artillery bombardment on Vimy Ridge was very active and continuous, and reached its maximum about 5.30 a.m. the following day, which was to the battalion a more exciting one than can well be imagined by those who have never seen the like; for it falls to the lot of few soldiers to observe any fighting— that is to say, fighting not in their very immediate vicinity: the Canadians were attacking, and our men could tell by the way our barrage was creeping steadily forward that they were gaining their objective. The

233

Battle of Vimy Ridge was in progress and the Buffs were watching, as if at a theatre, while the men of Canada gave a display.

VI. 6TH BATTALION—ARRAS AND THE SCARPE

On the date chosen by Haig to define the end of the Battle of the Somme the 6th Battalion of the Buffs were at Beaumetz in the Arras district, and the rest of 1916 was spent in that vicinity and passed without incident. Roughly speaking, one week the battalion was in trenches and the next week out; but on the 17th December a move was made to Sombrin, a few miles west of Beaumetz, for a quiet period of rest, if arduous work at parades for a new method of attack, bombing, the use of rifle grenades, musketry, bayonet fighting and physical training can be called quiet rest. These military exercises were, however, interspersed with the usual football and other manly relaxations, and, as usual, Christmas occurred on the 25th December.

On the 9th January, 1917, the battalion being still at Sombrin, the New Year honours list was read, and the following found themselves mentioned in despatches: Captains Hunter, Page, M.C., and Ward and Sgt. Brown. Lieut. and Qr.-Master Linwood was granted the higher rate of pay. Two days afterwards came a most gratifying inspection by the G.O.C. 12th Division, who highly complimented the battalion on its smart and soldierly appearance. This was the occasion of the presentation of the following awards: bar to Military Medal, Sgt. Setterfield; Military Crosses to C.S.M.'s Harrison and Maxted; Military Medals to Sgts. Callaghan, Knight and Ross, Corpls. Alexander and Richards, L.-Corpls. Ielden and Millington and Pte. Miller. On the 13th January the battalion left for Arras in buses and went into the trenches in the bitter cold weather which prevailed at this time in France.

WINTER ON THE WESTERN FRONT

Up till the end of March the normal routine obtained. The billets were at different times in Montenescourt, Noyellette, Givenchy le Noble, Agnez Duisans and Lattre St. Quentin, all of which places are close to the westward of Arras except Givency le Noble, which is about fifteen miles away and where some special instruction in practice trenches was given.

On the 10th March 20 officers and 650 men, under Lt.-Colonel Cope, left Agnez Duisans for Arras for work under the orders of the 35th Brigade, the remainder of the battalion remaining at Agnez Duisans under Major Smeltzer. Arras was very considerably shelled at this time and a great deal of work was being done in the town constructing new caves and greatly enlarging existing ones. These were to be the assembly places for thousands of troops prior to the great contemplated attack, as well as a refuge for those inhabitants who had not left the city. Electric light was installed in these caves and cellars, which were linked together by tunnels and the whole connected by long subways with our trench system east of the town. On the 5th April, our 6th Battalion being then in Arras, a heavy bombardment of the German trenches commenced, as well as other preparations for Sir Douglas Haig's spring offensive. This was the most prolonged and most furious artillery that had as yet been possible during the war.

On the 9th of the month the Battle of Arras commenced. The brigade was all formed up in the reserve trenches by 3.30 a.m. The 6th Queen's were in first line on the right and the 7th East Surrey on the left. The 13th Liverpool Regiment of the division was on the right of the Queen's, who had the Buffs in support; while the 6th Royal West Kent supported the East Surreys. At 5.30, the zero hour, the guns opened an intensive fire on the German lines and at the same time the whole moved forward to the attack in artillery formation. The Buffs had C Company on the right and D on the left, with A, plus one and a half platoons of B, as right support, and the remainder of B left support. After passing through the Queen's the first objective (Black Line) was reached and quickly captured by the Buffs, without much loss. A two hours' bombardment of the enemy's second system of trenches (Blue Line) followed, and then the barrage lifted and the advance was resumed. More opposition was now encountered, snipers and machine guns being active on both flanks. After some stiff hand-to-hand fighting D Company was able to get round to the flank and, by overcoming concealed machine guns, which the enemy had pushed forward into shell holes, reached and captured the point on the Blue Line which was its objective. C Company on the right was troubled by enfilade machine-gun fire operating on its right flank from the ruins of Estaminet Corner. By means of Lewis-gun fire and rifle grenading, however, these were eventually silenced and the company enabled to proceed. Then the Blue Line was consolidated, Lewis guns pushed forward and strong points dug. At 2.18 p.m. the 35th Brigade came up, passed through the 37th and pushed on to the final objective. The whole attack made on this day was entirely successful, even more so than was expected. Great numbers of prisoners, machine guns, field guns and material fell to the Buffs. All objectives were seized and consolidated and advance parties sent forward. By the afternoon no enemy was to be found except dead or prisoners in the "cages" or wired-in enclosures erected for the captured. On the 10th the cavalry went through and reached Monchy le Preux, where the battalion followed that night, having lost during the whole first Battle of the Scarpe 2nd Lieuts. R. G. K. Money and T. W. Buss and 23 men killed; Captain Gordon, 2nd Lieuts. Wilks, Good, Figgis, Thornley, Squire and Baldwin, and 149 men wounded, with 18 missing.

The Buffs were relieved on the 11th and went back into the old German lines, spending the day in clearing up the battlefield, burying the dead, forming dumps of tools and wire; after moving forward to the Brown Line they were informed that the brigade would have to relieve the 37th Division and part of the cavalry brigade before Monchy. Owing to perfectly blinding snow and as no guides were available for the Buffs or East Surrey, these two battalions had, however, to remain where they were while the Queen's and West Kent, who got guides given them, went up into the new line. The next day the Buffs were standing by in readiness to proceed to Monchy, a German counter-attack being expected, but they were relieved at nightfall by the 29th Division and marched back by the Cambrai road to the caves in Arras. On the 14th they left that ruined city and marched for billets at Montenescourt with the band playing the regimental march, which is an exhilarating piece of music, especially on triumphant occasions.

The battalion was out of the line only a fortnight at Noyellette, Duisan and so on, and was on the last day of April in the front at Monchy once again, all four companies being under the command of subalterns, though one of them held the acting rank of captain. The village of Fresnoy is roughly eight miles north-east of Arras, and Bullecourt, on the Hindenburg Line, is about the same distance south-east of the city. Between these two villages, on a fairly straight line and commencing from the north, are Rœux, Monchy le Preux, Cherisy and Fontaine lez Croisilles. Monchy and Cherisy are a little over three miles apart.

On the 3rd May, 1917, Haig attacked the enemy with the Third and First Armies from Fresnoy to Fontaine lez Croisilles, while the Fifth Army assaulted the Hindenburg Line about Bullecourt, and together these forces fought what is known as the Third Battle of the Scarpe. To quote the Commander-in-Chief's de-

spatches: " Along practically the whole of this front
" our troops broke into the enemy's position. Austra-
" lian troops carried the Hindenburg Line east of
" Bullecourt. Eastern County battalions took Cherisy.
" Other English troops entered Rœux and captured the
" German trenches south of Fresnoy. Canadian bat-
" talions found Fresnoy full of German troops assembled
" for a hostile attack, which was to have been delivered
" at a later hour. After hard fighting, in which the
" enemy lost heavily, the Canadians carried the village,
" thereby completing an unbroken series of successes."
It is necessary to remember that the 6th Battalion the
Buffs was on this date at Monchy, and the 7th opposite
Cherisy.

In this battle our 6th Battalion was very far from
being fortunate, and it is not easy to obtain a correct
description of its doings, owing to abnormal casualties
and great difficulty, if not impossibility, of those in the
foremost fighting line communicating with their commanding officer in the rear. The chief cause of this
difficulty was the darkness, for the zero hour was fixed
at 3.45 a.m. The battalion was, during the preceding
night, in shell holes, A being on the right, B on the left,
C supporting A, and D being behind B. Punctually on
time our guns opened, and an intense barrage was timed
to lift and advance one hundred yards every three minutes, and as the guns fired our men went off into the
darkness, too many of them never to see the sun rise
again. Every effort was made to keep communication
with them, and 2nd Lieut. McAuley, the Signalling
Officer, with two signallers and two orderlies, went forward to establish an advanced headquarters in what was
known as Devil's Trench, but returned at 4.30, no communication being possible. Two prisoners were sent
down and apparently the battalion was advancing satisfactorily, but nothing definite could be ascertained.
Even later on, when daylight came, gunfire and snipers

made it hard to get any news of how matters were proceeding; but at dusk it was discovered that the Buffs had suffered much and that the line in their front was practically as before. It would seem a pity that the ground was quite unknown to the battalion which had not held the same position previously and that the orders to attack came so late that there was no time available for systematic reconnaissance.

The continuous loss of officers at this time was so serious that 2nd Lieuts. Seago and Sowter were sent for from the detail camp and, arriving about 10 p.m., were sent forward to reorganize what was left of the battalion. A bright episode occurred to lighten what must otherwise be considered as a gloomy day for the regiment, although it was a costly act of gallantry. Part of the objective allotted to the Buffs in the morning had been a spot called Keeling Copse, and it was found, after the battalion had taken stock of its losses, that 2nd Lieuts. Cockeram and Gunther with about forty men and a Lewis gun had actually got there, only to discover that they were completely isolated, the enemy having reformed his line behind them, and both sides being in their original trenches. Thus three lines of Germans intervened between this handful of men and their comrades. Nothing daunted, however, they held their own all day, accounted for many of the enemy and then, when night fell and they had expended every cartridge and bomb they possessed, they gallantly fought their way back again, breaking through one line after another, until at last the two subalterns and thirteen of their stout lads were enabled to report themselves to battalion headquarters. Cockeram and Gunther both received the M.C. for their gallant conduct on this occasion. It is sad to have to add that Gunther was killed shortly afterwards within half a mile of Keeling Copse gallantly defending a trench the German was attacking. Cockeram lived to do good and gallant work later on in the Flying Corps. The casualties in this terrible action were 2nd Lieuts. J. H. Dinsmore and H. V. Hardey-Mason killed, and Captain J. B. Kitchin died of wounds; Captain McDermott and 2nd Lieuts. Williams and Nesbitt wounded; 2nd Lieuts. C. Warnington, A. Kirkpatrick, H. W. Evans and R. L. F. Forster, Lieuts. K. L. James, Grant, King and Willis missing, of whom the first five were found to have been killed; 25 other ranks killed, 128 wounded and 207 missing.

About 2 a.m. on the 4th the remnant was relieved and got back and, next day, was reorganized into two companies each of only two platoons, No. 1 Company, 2nd Lieut. Stevens in command, with Sowter, Seago and Sankey under him; and No. 2 Company, under Captain Carter, with 2nd Lieuts. Gunther and Cockeram. It was only rested in Arras for forty-eight hours and then underwent another ten days in the trenches before being relieved on the 17th, on which day it went to Duisans.

VII. 7TH BATTALION

While the 6th Battalion of the Buffs was suffering as briefly described above, their brethren of the 7th, on the night of the 2nd/3rd May, were opposite the village of Cherisy preparing for the attack: A and B were the assaulting companies, C the supporting company, and D was in reserve, in shell holes, in rear of the support trench. The Buffs were on the right of their brigade with the 54th Infantry Brigade on their right and the 8th East Surrey on the left. The Royal West Kent supported both Buffs and East Surreys, and the 7th Queen's were brigade reserve. The orders given to our battalion were to advance in conjunction with the 54th Brigade and to capture Keeling Copse.

It must be admitted at once that the attack was a

failure, due, in the opinion of all, to the intense darkness at 3.45. The attack of the Buffs and East Surreys was successful in itself, however, and both units showed great dash, but failure on the flanks led to a subsequent retirement, and it is sad to think that, taking part in what Sir Douglas Haig describes as a successful battle, both the brigades in which battalions of the Buffs were serving failed in the part allotted to them. There seems to be no doubt that the front waves reached their objectives, but the 12th Middlesex and 11th Royal Fusiliers, both of the 54th Brigade, failed to get past the wire covering the German front line. Little opposition was experienced at first, but the second and subsequent waves came under very heavy fire, causing their progress to be slow, so that the men who started first were more or less cut off for a time. The Germans, being unable to reinforce in masses owing to our guns, dribbled up men from their rear in very small parties. As regards details of the Buffs' advance: all companies of the battalion got clear of the front trench before the enemy's barrage commenced, but, owing to the darkness, sections, platoons and companies soon got mingled up together and at one time part of the Middlesex belonging to the 54th Brigade came across the Buffs' front in the dark, but the error was skilfully rectified.

At the first glimpse of dawn the village of Cherisy was reached and passed through. As it was entered the right company had touch with the Middlesex, but on reaching the bed of the Sensée river, which is just beyond, its officer, Captain Black, discovered that this touch was lost and that the flank was in the air, though the other was in proper prolongation of its left-hand neighbouring company. He therefore determined to halt and form a defensive flank along the road which runs south-east from the village across the stream. Before this could be done he was heavily attacked, and the message he sent back to that effect failed to get through.

R

Meanwhile the left assaulting company, reinforced by portions of C and in touch with the East Surreys, gained the first objective, or Blue Line. D Company had halted, according to order, in what was called the " Cable " trench, which was perfectly straight and which was found to be occupied at its right extremity by a considerable number of the enemy, some of whom the company destroyed or captured, together with a machine gun. However, the Germans still held one end and a bomb-stop had to be constructed and an attempt made to progress down the trench; but it was not until a Stokes gun was brought up that any progress was made, the work being deep, narrow and difficult to bomb. Thus the situation at 9 a.m. was that Captain Black's company (A) on the right was still open to assault and unable to move, thus causing the left, which had gained certain advantages, to lose ground for want of the support expected from the Middlesex battalion, while the reserve company was still struggling for possession of " Cable " trench, and B and C Companies had both fought their way to the Sensée river.

A little afterwards came an order that the Buffs and East Surreys were to advance to the Red Line, the West Kents to consolidate the Blue Line. About 11 o'clock reports came that a general retirement was taking place, and the enemy established an intense bombardment of our front line and back area. " Cable " trench was now full of men in addition to D Company, who had not yet been able to emerge from the trench; but our own rescuing people were hopelessly intermingled with the enemy, so that it was impossible to open fire. The Englishmen, however, who passed over and beyond the trench in their retirement, were soon rallied and brought back to the original lines, so that in half an hour or so the situation was well in hand, though " Cable " trench had been evacuated. An attempt was made at 7.15 p.m. to retake this, the assaulting battalion being the Queen's supported by the Buffs, but the hostile machine-gun and rifle fire was too much and the attack failed. The Queen's fell back and the Buffs occupied the original front-line trenches for the night, having suffered a casualty list of 2 officers killed, 6 wounded and 4 missing; 25 other ranks killed, 169 wounded and 174 missing.

VIII. 1st Battalion

As this chapter is intended to record the doings of the four battalions on the Western front for the first half of the year 1917, the record will now take each in turn from the Battle of Arras up till the 30th June or thereabouts.

The great war storm that was raging south of that place caused ripples and splashes to be noticed about Loos and its neighbourhood, and the 1st Battalion was in that village at the opening of the great spring offensive, having taken its place in the front-line trenches on the 7th April. On the 9th the battalion on the left attempted a raid which brought on a fierce hostile barrage on all trenches and back areas, causing the death of four men of the regiment and the wounding of 2nd Lieut. Harman and six others, and casualties continued at odd times for several days, the enemy appearing very alert and naturally nervous owing to the progress of our people to the southward. At 4 p.m. on the 13th the 2nd York and Lancaster Regiment, on the Buffs' right, advanced and found that the Germans had abandoned their front-line system. B Company joined in this movement and occupied German trenches south of the Loos Crassier, and although the enemy's rear guard offered good resistance the British advance was persisted in, and during the night a new line running south from Harts Craters was established, though it came under very considerable fire on the 14th. During the

243

following night strong patrols found no resistance west of the Loos Crassier railway, and in the morning the York and Lancaster, aided by our B Company, attacking again, gained the railway and, being then reinforced by A Company, consolidated the new ground which had been gained and which included Fosse 12. This was done in spite of two vigorous counter-attacks.

On the 16th, commencing at noon, the right group artillery bombarded the area in front, and at 2 o'clock the 8th Bedfords on the right and the Buffs on the left commenced an advance and gained a sunken road which was resolutely held by two companies which became involved in very heavy fighting, so much so, indeed, that at last a short retirement to the Double Crassier railway line had to be made, a redistribution of the brigade being arranged after dark; by this arrangement A and B Companies, which had held the sunken road, went back into support at the enclosure and at B Keep, at the head of the Loos Crassier, where they were later on joined by C Company, D remaining in the front line. On the morning of the 17th, therefore, the front line was held by the Bedfords on the right, Shropshires on the left, York and Lancasters right support, Buffs left support. It became evident now that the Germans had managed to get up more guns, and the shelling became very severe. A strong reconnaissance towards the sunken road, made by the Shropshire Light Infantry, met with powerful resistance, and it was not until the 18th that that regiment, aided by the Bedfords, were able to make that objective good. The following casualties were suffered during this combat: Captains A. K. Harvey James and T. A. Brown, 2nd Lieut. G. B. Saunder and 10 men killed; 2nd Lieuts. Griffiths, Groom, Walters, Witty and 65 other ranks wounded, one of whom died of his injuries.

On the 20th the Buffs retired to billets at Les Brebis for a couple of days and when there received a complimentary letter from the Commander-in-Chief which was addressed particularly to the 6th and 24th Divisions, the latter having joined in the advance on the right of the 6th Division. Many honours came to the battalion during this month, the list being: the Military Cross to 2nd Lieuts. Brown, Griffiths and Hughes; the Distinguished Conduct Medal to C.S.M. Field; and Military Medals to Sgts. Edwards, France and MacWalter, Corpls. Brownrigg, Port, Richards and Stuart, L.-Corpls. Admans and Platts, and Ptes. Carey, Downes, Eldridge, Martin and Moss.

On the 22nd April the Buffs went back into the front line of the Loos trenches and there, in three days, lost 2nd Lieuts. L. E. A. S. Bilton and T. E. G. Bullock and 3 men killed and 28 other ranks wounded.

The month of May was spent partly in huts at Mazingarbe, partly at La Bourse and partly in the trenches, a toll of casualties being still exacted by the fate of war. This month brought the M.C. to 2nd Lieuts. Waters and Worster; the D.C.M. to C.S.M. Vincer; and a mention in despatches for the Quartermaster, Lieut. Corney, as well as to Sgt. Chatfield and L.-Corpl. Ayres.

The first eight days of June passed in the trenches at Hulluch and brought casualties as usual, 2 being killed, 4 died of wounds and 22 getting wounded in that short period. On the 11th a turn came for the comparative quiet of a week on divisional reserve at Fouguieres, but C and D Companies went off to Allouagne to train for a raid; so that when A and B returned to trench work on the 20th these two only followed three days later. On the 24th a party composed of Captain Jacob, Lieuts. Buss, Chester, Dyer, Harrington, Marshall, Moss, and Wyatt, with C and D Companies, made a raid on the German trenches in the Hulluch sector to obtain identification and inflict casualties, to capture prisoners, to destroy dug-outs and emplacements, and to draw the enemy's attention from other parts of the

245

divisional front. The companies attacked in three waves. The first wave, under Lieut. Marshall, crossed over and went straight for its objective, the enemy's third line. The second, under Lieut. Moss, followed twenty-five paces behind the first; and then came the third, under Lieut. Buss, thirty paces in rear again, accompanied by the Lewis guns. This party remained in the enemy's trenches for three and a half hours, doing very considerable damage and collecting fifteen prisoners and two trench mortars. Some trouble was experienced in getting the German out of his dug-outs, but this was effected by means of tear-bombs and mobile charges. The enemy during this raid was very unsettled. His barrage was weak and quite general. In fact, he did not seem to know from what point he was being attacked. Our barrage was excellent. Lieuts. P. C. Buss and Harrington behaved with the greatest gallantry; the former was most unfortunately killed and Harrington was wounded twice, but still continued to lead his men. Besides Lieut. Buss, 8 men were killed; Lieut. Harrington and 1 man were wounded and missing; Lieuts. Chester and Wyatt and 62 other ranks wounded; Lieut. Moss and 2 men wounded, but remained at duty; 17 other ranks missing, and 2 more missing, believed killed.

The battalion as a whole remained in the trenches till the 29th, suffering occasional casualties. After that date it returned to Mazingarbe, but left A Company with the K.S.L.I. and B with the York and Lancasters.

IX. 6TH BATTALION

After its terrible experiences up to the first week in May there is but little to relate regarding the 6th Battalion for the remainder of the first half of 1917. It remained in the trenches for ten days, during which time careful reconnaissance work was carried out; and it was relieved on the 17th/18th, withdrawing to Duisans for baths, refitting and reorganization into four companies again. On the 19th it went further back to Montenescourt, from which place, on the 24th, it was removed by bus to Ivergny, twelve miles to the south-west, for a term of drill, exercises and musketry training. On the 27th 2nd Lieut. Morley and C.S.M. Pritchard got the M.C., and Sgt. Real, Corpl. Scott, L.-Corpl. Cooling, Ptes. Middleton and Skinner were mentioned in despatches. On the 8th June Lt.-Colonel Cope,[1] who had been so long in command of the battalion, was promoted to command the 115th Brigade, and a day or two later was awarded the Legion of Honour. On the 16th June there was a parade to receive medals, when the Military Medal was handed to Ptes. Atkinson, Brooks, Hardie, Mack, McDonald and Philpott; to Sgts. Brunger and Wood and to L.-Corpl. Hook. The 19th of the month found the battalion back in Arras, where it remained for the rest of the time now under consideration.

X.   7TH BATTALION

The day after its great fight at Cherisy the 7th Buffs, or what was left of it, was relieved from its place in the trenches and moved to Beaurains, close to Arras; it remained there and at Boisleux, to the south of it, for sixteen days, reorganizing and training; it was in the trenches again on the 21st May and in such close proximity to the enemy that the Germans could be heard talking. There was a good deal of patrolling work to do and this was most successfully accomplished, the line being considerably advanced; but on the 27th 2nd Lieut. S. B. Johnston and one man went forward from their post to reconnoitre and were not heard of again.

---

[1] This officer belongs to the Royal Fusiliers and went to France as adjutant to the 8th Battalion of that regiment, being promoted to command the 6th Buffs in March, 1916. He twice won the D.S.O.

247

Up till the 15th June the routine was much as usual; a turn in the trenches and a turn in reserve; but on this day the brigade retired some miles into the back area and took up its headquarters at Couin, the Buffs being at Coigneux.

On the 20th Captain Black was awarded the M.C. for Cherisy, and the Corps Commander handed M.M. ribbands to C.S.M. Nevard; Sgt. Nash; Corpl. Hyde; L.-Corpls. Berry and Castleton; Ptes. Davis, Purkiss, Reynolds, Thirkettle, White and Wise.

The only other point of interest worth mentioning in the history of the 7th up to the end of June is that it won the ten-mile cross-country relay race for the 26th Division and that its old friends, the Queen's, were second.

XI. 8TH BATTALION—BATTLE OF MESSINES

As the 8th Battalion of the Buffs was not in action on the 3rd May its story must now be taken up from the 9th April, on which date the men were spectators, from the trenches at Angres, of the victorious advance of the Canadians, punctuated, as it was, by the steady lifting of the barrage.

There was much aerial activity at this time on both sides and some ground fighting in the vicinity, and, on the 14th April, it was found that the enemy had left his trenches, so at 4 p.m. the brigade moved forward unopposed and a new position was taken up and patrols pushed forward. On the following day, the Rifle Brigade pushing through, the Buffs followed and bivouacked that night at Lievin, which is on the road to Lens.

The Germans, however, had not retired very far and an attack on their position was arranged for the 17th. It appears to have been a poor business, but this was not the fault of the 17th Brigade. The artillery preparation was a feeble one, because sufficient guns could not be brought up in time. The enemy at once opened heavy machine-gun fire from strong points in his line and from Hill 65 outside Lens. He also shelled the advancing troops heavily, with the result that both the brigades on the right and on the left were stayed by 10.30, and, this being the case, it was obvious that the 17th would only be courting disaster if it advanced alone exposing both its flanks, so there was nothing to do but to hold the position in which our troops stood and consolidate as far as possible during the night. The Buffs had one officer and thirty other ranks put out of action. The relief came during the night, and the battalion marched away to the westward into a quieter area. Indeed, this marching, being a more or less new experience, caused a good deal of inconvenience in the way of sore feet and fatigue. However, the 21st of the month found the brigade at Bourecq and a few days later at Erny St. Julien, and at both these places serious training was undertaken; but the stern business of war gave place each evening to football, very much to the astonishment of the Portuguese troops in the district.

On the 28th the men were back in La Bourse and from there to Robecq, Hazebrouck and Steenvoorde, all in turn. Steenvoorde was a special training area and most corps took a turn of work there when they could be spared. This visit of the Buffs lasted a fortnight, and on the 26th May they were close to Poperinghe. On this day 2nd Lieut. Lilley was awarded the Military Cross. On the 4th June the wandering troops were at Heksken, south of Poperinghe, and at midnight on the 5th/6th they moved from there to a camp situated in a wood where special stores and ammunition were issued.

The Battle of Messines commenced on the morning of the 7th June and was fought by General Plumer's army to capture a ridge from which the Germans over-looked our lines and much of the area behind them. The preparations for this offensive action on Plumer's

249

part had been going on for a very long time and were thought out with the greatest care and trouble. The most remarkable point in connection with the battle was the fact that it opened by a tremendous explosion of nineteen deep mines, the noise of which was distinctly heard in parts of England. As far as the Buffs were concerned, the 8th Battalion paraded in fighting kit at 11.30 p.m. on the 6th June, proceeded to assembly positions via Dickebusch and spent the middle portion of the night in two great dug-outs, one of which held four hundred men. At 3.10 a.m. the soldiers were awakened by the most tremendous explosion they had ever heard in their lives, and this was immediately followed by the opening of the barrage. The 17th Brigade was in support near St. Eloi, and at 11.30 a.m. it moved forward to occupy the line already taken up by the 41st Division, from whence, at 3 p.m., a further attack was launched, during which the battalion reached its objective, known as the Green Line, with but few casualties.

The whole of the two following days were spent in the newly taken positions, being shelled and suffering a few casualties: mostly men of A Company, which with C was in the front line; Lieut. Sherwill was hit on the 8th. On the 10th the Buffs were relieved by the 9th Warwicks with great difficulty: the hostile gunfire being very heavy and causing several casualties, including Captain A. F. Gulland and Lieut. H. C. Arnold, who both died of their injuries, and also Lieuts. Curtis and Hilary, who were wounded but not quite so severely. After a day's much needed rest, which was mostly spent in sleep, the battalion at nightfall relieved the 18th London Regiment at the " triangular dump " and the 3rd Rifle Brigade in Battle Wood.

An attack on the enemy's position was arranged for and carried out on the 14th. The Buffs were told off to take one side of the railway while the Royal Fusiliers took the other. Battalion Headquarters were in Larch Wood. 7.30 p.m. was chosen as the zero hour; before this hour a certain amount of sniping was experienced in getting to the assembly position, but luckily the enemy's artillery did not discover our moving companies. A and C Companies led the advance, each having two platoons in front line. Our barrage was good though perhaps a little short at first, and our men kept well up under it, casualties being small; the guns lifted their range a hundred yards every four minutes. Six minutes after our opening shot the enemy began his heavy fire on our assembly positions, but by then our men were clear, or indeed they would have suffered severely. A Company had for its objective Spoil Bank, which was about thirty feet high and three hundred yards long and running parallel to the Ypres–Comines Canal. The bank had been the object of an attack by some of the 47th Division a week earlier, but was still in German hands. There was a fine view of the country beyond the canal from its summit. It was afterwards officially known as The Buffs' Bank, out of compliment to the 6th Battalion. A good deal of savage hand-to-hand fighting took place here, and the success of the company was very largely due to the extraordinary courage and initiative of two private soldiers, Dunning and Cornell, who together rushed a German machine gun in a concrete emplacement, killed the team, captured the gun, and thus saved the lives and limbs of many of their comrades of A Company; they were both awarded the M.M. for this exploit. The other leading company, C, was directed on the tramline and suffered considerably on the way. The company commander (Captain E. F. Hall) and all the rest of the officers were hit before the objective was reached, but 2nd Lieut. Wilkinson was able to remain with his men until it was taken and consolidated; and it was not till all work was done and midnight had come that this gallant officer

251

withdrew to have his wounds dressed, when he had to leave his company under the command of Sgt. Pells. As soon as C Company had reached its objective, Sgt. Shute took his platoon about sixty yards ahead of the newly won line and there cleared a system of dug-outs, killed a great number of the enemy and brought back four prisoners. Touch was soon obtained with the battalion on the Buffs' left, but the other flank was not so easy, and it was not until morning that the troops on the right were discovered. While the two leading companies had thus been busy their comrades had not been idle. D Company had come up behind the Spoil Bank and at the zero hour two platoons, less one bombing section, had advanced towards its western edge and cleared up the southern side in conjunction with A Company, while the bombing squad attended to the dug-outs on top of the bank, most of which were occupied, there being ten to twelve men in each. Several of the enemy attempted to escape across the canal at Lock 6, but these were dealt with by men of C Company and no one escaped that way. Further down Spoil Bank the enemy made a more considerable resistance, and 2nd Lieut. Paige was killed leading an attack at this point—in fact he was chasing a platoon of Germans across the canal all by himself. Many of the enemy then tried to get away round the eastern edge of Spoil Bank, but these were also shot and a German feldwebel[1] captured after a really heroic resistance. D Company then dug itself in on the southern slope of the Spoil Bank, with A Company in support on the northern slope. Digging in was no very easy matter on account of the continuous shelling, which the enemy kept up all night; however, morning found the job satisfactorily completed and the work cleverly camouflaged from aerial observation, which was a very necessary precaution, for the hostile aeroplanes showed in the morning

---

[1] Regimental sergeant-major.

very considerable interest in the exact position of our people. Many times they swooped right down and fired their machine guns into our trenches.

About 5 p.m. on the 15th the enemy started a heavy barrage and were seen to be massing on our right, but our guns were at once turned on these and dispersed the assembly. The Buffs were relieved the same night by the 2nd Leinsters, and three days later moved to Burgomaster's Farm at Dickebusch under Major Vaughan, the commanding officer, Lt.-Colonel F. C. R. Studd, D.S.O., having been wounded the previous day. The casualties from the 7th to the 10th inclusive were Captain A. F. Gulland, who died on the 16th, 2nd Lieuts. Sherwill, H. C. Arnold (died on the 12th), Hilary and Curtis and 28 men wounded and 4 killed; but during the 14th, 15th and 16th the loss was more considerable, 2nd Lieuts. Paige, Carlos and Edwards, with 14 men, were killed; Captain Hall and 2nd Lieuts. Darling, Wilkinson, Young, Lilley, Greig and Lt.-Colonel Studd, with 89 other ranks, were wounded, though the commanding officer remained at duty for some time. There were also 4 men missing.

Times in this neighbourhood and at this period were, however, too strenuous to allow of much rest to anyone, and when the 23rd June came round again it found the Buffs once more in the trenches and, forty-eight hours afterwards, under an abnormally heavy fire, which did little damage to the front line, but found several victims amongst working parties in rear. 2nd Lieut. J. B. Millard was killed and Major Vaughan and Lieut. Hancock narrowly escaped from the same shell, and it is curious that both these officers were slightly hurt by another one only a few minutes later. 2nd Lieut. A. H. Webb was also killed. It was decided to push forward certain posts during the night of the 26th/27th, and B Company on the left actually did so and got to the edge of a wood which was on its front and there consolidated, but A Company, on the right, found that any advance would be impossible without heavy artillery assistance. The 23rd of the month brought a Military Cross for 2nd Lieut. Sherwill. On the 28th relief came in the shape of the 8th Battalion York and Lancaster Regiment, but the change over was a nasty job. The enemy appeared to have got wind of what was going forward and opened a heavy fire, wounding Lieut. Newcomb and three other men. The 29th took the battalion away. It travelled by train to Reninghelst for the training area round Lumbres, and on the last day of the month it marched fourteen kilometres to Escocuilles.

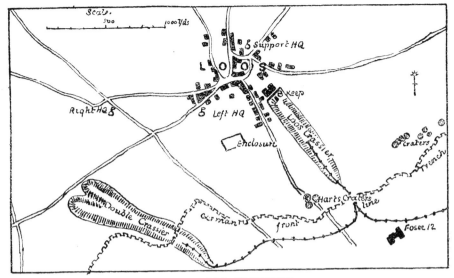

THE LOOS CRASSIERS

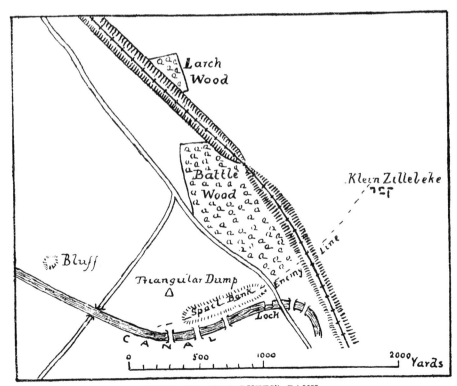

SPOIL (OR THE BUFFS') BANK

CHAPTER XI

THE WESTERN FRONT

(*Continuation till March,* 1918)

I. 1ST BATTALION

AT the commencement of the last chapter the readers were reminded that the Russians made a separate peace with the enemy towards the end of 1917, and that the Americans having declared war against Germany in April the vanguard of her troops began to come into action on the 27th October, so that the defection of the one nation was in the end counteracted by the determination of the other. As has been said, America at first possessed but a tiny army, and though a few troops were fighting in Europe at the end of 1917, still her real force could not make itself felt for months afterwards. Consequently there was an interval between the collapse of Russia and Rumania and the arrival of a capable American army. During this space the French and English must bear the whole brunt of the struggle, and the Germans, whose railways were planned strategically, with the idea of being able to rapidly transfer armies from her eastern to her western frontier or vice versa, were not the people to fail to take full advantage of such an opportunity.

These facts must be borne in mind in studying what follows. As a matter of fact, our enemies started on the 21st March, 1918, a mighty effort to sweep us into the sea and overwhelm the French. This chapter will therefore continue the story of the doings of the Buffs on the Western front up to this date. Like the previous chapter, it is a record of trench warfare varied by fight-

255

ing and the necessary rest and reorganization which followed each battle.

The most important action was perhaps that of Cambrai, in which both the 1st and 6th Battalions took part, and it may therefore be as well first to continue the narrative of these two units: the village of Mazingarbe is, roughly speaking, four miles from Loos in the direction of comparative safety, and this place may be considered as the chief station of the 1st Battalion up to the 15th November—that is to say, that it was the resting-place when trenches were not occupied somewhere near Loos or Hulluch. Of course, there were certain alterations, for troops took turn to go into the reserve of the division or some higher formation, and the more important that portion of the army was, the further back from the front line were stationed its reserves; for instance, on the 13th July the Buffs went into divisional reserve for a week at Fouquieres, near Bethune, and for a time in October they were in G.H.Q. reserve at Flechin.

The most important and the pleasantest change of programme, however, was a long period of rest at Monchy Breton (about twelve miles west of Mazingarbe), which is an area set apart for giving a change of scene to tired troops. The battalion was allowed a month here which, in addition to training, was devoted to sport and health-giving recreation; a composite company, under the command of Captain Strauss, it secured the highest number of marks in the brigade sports and won the divisional challenge cup for the smartest turn-out and work in an attack scheme.

During the period between the 1st July and the 15th November officers and men of the 1st Battalion received a considerable number of decorations and honours: on the 3rd July the Corps Commander inspected C and D Companies, which had furnished the raiding party on the 23rd June; after offering his con-

256

gratulations he presented Military Medals to Sgts. Cross, Goodall and Poole, Corpl. Sindon and L.-Corpl. Spenceley, and to Privates Halliday and Searle, all of C Company. In D Company Military Medals were given to Sgts. Barker, Buss, Evans and Moorcock, Corpl. Duff, and to L.-Corpls. Curd, Green and Page. During this period Lieuts. Marshall, Moss and Wyatt were awarded the M.C., and Captain Jacobs and Lieut. Worster the clasp to the M.C.; C.S.M.'s McDonough and Randall received the D.C.M., the latter also being given a commission and posted to C Company; Pte. Sage received the M.M., and Corpl. Duff the *Decoration Militaire* (Belgian).

On the 30th August B Company, having gone to relieve one of the K.S.L.I., A and D Companies being already in front-line trenches with C in support, the enemy at 8 p.m. ventured an attack on our three-company front, which was quickly dealt with by the Canadian gunners and our Lewis guns. Notwithstanding this repulse another hostile attack was launched at 2 o'clock next morning, but this again was stayed by our Lewis guns and we did not suffer much.

Another incident worthy of note was the departure from France of Captain Birrell, the adjutant, who left the battalion on the 10th October after no less than two years and ten months' service on the Western front and was succeeded by Lieut. Davies. This length of war service, other than at the base or on the staff, was very exceptional indeed. On the 1st November the 1st Battalion marched to meet their comrades of the 6th at Grand Bouret. Early in the month the question of combined infantry and tank work in the field became an extra tactical study that all must learn.

As to casualties, they of course continued. There is a horrible regularity in recording these. Men were always being killed or wounded. A battle removed a lot of good fellows in a few hours, trench warfare corroded

S

the battalion strength little by little, and this had to be patched up either by raw hands from England or men who had already done their share but, after being invalided, had to come out again. Ten men were wounded on the 26th August, one killed and five wounded on the 30th. 2nd Lieut. G. E. Sewell died of wounds on the 2nd September and two men were killed and two wounded on the same day, five more getting hit on the morrow. Eighteen men of the pioneer company were gassed on the 5th September. A little bit of joyful news reached the regiment in the middle of September, namely, that the gallant Harrington, who had done so well on the 24th June and who had been missing since that date, was still alive, though a prisoner in Germany. A Company on the 16th October lost eight men killed and three wounded, the enemy opening a barrage on our front line at 8 p.m. On the 15th November, Sir Douglas Haig having planned a further attack on the German lines, the 16th Brigade, in which the 1st Battalion still served, was attached to the Third Corps to take part in the same, and the battalion entrained for Peronne and moved to the forward area on the 17th.

II. 6TH BATTALION

There is a great high road running dead straight from Arras east-south-east for four-and-twenty miles to Cambrai. Two miles and a half from Arras along this road lies the village of Tilloy, and three miles further on Monchy is to the north and Wancourt to the south of it. Two miles south-east of the latter place and about two miles to the south of the great road is the scene of the 7th Battalion's fight on the 3rd May, 1917—the village of Cherisy. It was round these places that the 6th Battalion fought and endured up till the 23rd October, when it retired away west to a more

258

peaceful region for a few days and there saw a good deal of the 1st Battalion.

On the 1st July the 6th moved from Arras to the Wancourt line, and on that date it mustered 33 officers, but only 483 other ranks. While in this sector it was sometimes in front, sometimes in support and sometimes further back.

Amongst the various excavations of this region is what is known as " The Long Trench," which, commencing about 1,200 yards south of Keeling Copse, runs southward and is continued in that direction by Tool Trench. In this long work was the 6th Battalion on the 10th July, when it received orders to raid the enemy's shell holes east of Tool Trench at 7.30 a.m. the next day. The enemy, however, had made his own plans and, taking the initiative himself, attacked at 5 a.m. after an exceptionally heavy bombardment of guns of all sorts and sizes, smoke and liquid fire being also used. This heavy rain of projectiles was directed not only on Long and Tool Trenches, but on the supports. The infantry attack was directed chiefly on Long Trench, and the Germans managed to penetrate at one point after feinting or making a holding attack along the whole front of it. Having effected his penetration he rapidly deployed and occupied shell holes in rear or on our side. 2nd Lieut. Stevens, who was holding a post near by, at once realized the situation and organized and carried out a counter-attack along Long Trench, and almost at the same time L.-Corpl. Edgington and two men, who were all on duty with the 37th Brigade Sniping Company, seeing that the attack was serious, at once dashed up to ascertain the true situation. These three went up Long Trench for three or four hundred yards till they reached the point where the break through had occurred. Here, of course, they came across a lot of Germans who hurled bombs at them. The corporal, however, was a good and resolute

259

Buff soldier, and he, posting one of his men in an advantageous position in the trench, with the other commenced to erect a block or stop in the work. He was soon joined by 2nd Lieut. Stevens and another man, and between them they consolidated the block and opened fire at close range on a number of the enemy. About two hours and a half later on the Buffs tried a counter-attack which was duly preceded by artillery preparation, but it failed owing to the heavy machine-gun fire it was subjected to. The enemy's aeroplanes were very noticeable during this affair, flying low over our lines all day, particularly during the attack. 2nd Lieut. Gunther was killed, as were 9 men; another officer and 26 men were wounded, and there were 30 missing. Long Trench was recovered a week later by the 35th Brigade and the Royal West Kent Regiment.

On the 3rd August, at 6 p.m., the Buffs being then in rear in what was called the Brown Line, the enemy opened a heavy barrage and later attacked Hook Trench. Two officers and one hundred men of the Buffs were sent up about 8.30 to aid the Queen's and West Kent in the front line. The attack was beaten off and heavy casualties were inflicted on the enemy, who withdrew, leaving several prisoners. On the 6th August the whole brigade was relieved and went into Beaurains Camp, near Arras. 2nd Lieuts. Hunt, Mason-Springgay, Russell and Sowter, with eighty-six men, who had been training for a raid, proceeded from here to take their part in an organized minor adventure which took place on the 9th of the month and which was most successful: the moral of the enemy had every appearance of being severely shaken and he suffered heavy casualties; his trenches were entered, many dug-outs destroyed and eighty prisoners brought back, and it was just a regimental misfortune that the men of Kent were in the flank which became subject to the enfilade fire and consequently suffered the following casualties and failed to get on as far as was hoped.

2nd Lieuts. J. Russell and F. I. Sowter missing, Mason-Springgay wounded and thirty-five men either killed, wounded or missing. It was afterwards ascertained that both Russell and Sowter had been killed. The raid party returned to camp about 3 a.m., played in by the Drums.

On the 24th August, while in the Levis Barracks at Arras, Corpl. Horton, L.-Corpl. Parker and Ptes. Hoare, Lane and Scott heard they had been awarded the M.M., and about the same time, while in the trenches again, news came of a M.C. for 2nd Lieut. Mason-Springgay.

On the 1st September the Royal Fusiliers, aided by the Buffs' covering fire, made a neat little raid, sustaining only one casualty and bringing in twenty-six prisoners; and the next day a telegram came saying that 2nd Lieut. Stevens had the M.C. and Pte. Barham the M.M. An attempt was made by the enemy on the 24th to raid the brigade front, but it was repulsed with loss.

The 3rd October brought the battalion thirty-three casualties, including 2nd Lieut. Needman killed. This was because the Sussex Regiment, on the Buffs' left, made a raid and the German heavily barraged the latter corps' lines. Two days afterwards 2nd Lieut. N. E. FitzRoy Cole and one man were killed in the front line. The 24th of October took the 6th Battalion off westward, and the 29th found it billeted at Vacquerie le Bourg.

November opened with more than one pleasant meeting with the 1st Battalion. The 6th marched to Frevent with this object on the 1st November, and two drawn matches at football were played between the units, first at Beaudricourt and afterwards at Vacquerie, but the real business of life at this time was training and

261

preparation for a coming attack. On the 16th the battalion entrained for Peronne, and by the 19th it was in position of assembly behind the village of Gonnelieu, which is about four miles south of Ribecourt, in the vicinity of which the 1st Battalion stood. Before describing the parts taken by the Buffs in the action before Cambrai it may be well to explain shortly why the battle came to be fought.

It was now past the middle of November and the collapse of the Russians had already become so apparent that large bodies of Germans had been withdrawn from their Eastern front to swell the armies in France, and it was quite clear that more and more would be arriving shortly. Under these adverse circumstances Haig determined on a surprise attack on a considerable scale before more reinforcements could arrive, and so he directed General Byng to attack in front of Cambrai, reckoning that that portion of the German line was not quite so strongly held as some others and that it would take the enemy forty-eight hours to draw troops from other portions of his front to the rescue. Secrecy and despatch, therefore, were the main points to be considered, and it was for these reasons that the fight under notice differed from almost all others in so far that no artillery preparation was to take place, but the overcoming of wire and other obstacles was to be entrusted to the action of tanks, and careful arrangements were made for their initial employment and close co-operation with the infantry. It would occupy too much space to describe this battle in detail, but it must be understood that, though the British attack achieved considerable success at first, the enemy was able ultimately to increase his force about Cambrai, particularly in guns, and so he managed at last such a mighty counter-attack that about the last day of the month our original offensive was perforce changed into a somewhat anxious defensive operation.

A NEW TRENCH

III. CAMBRAI

Now, on the 20th November and following days the Third Army Corps consisted of the 6th Division, which included the 1st Battalion of the Buffs, the 12th Division, with the 6th Battalion, and the 20th Division. This Corps attacked with the 12th Division on the right, the 20th in the centre and the 6th on the left, and the zero hour was 6.20 a.m. Thus it came about that the 1st Battalion moved out preceded by B Battalion of tanks and in artillery formation from the vicinity of Villers Plouich.

The first objective, the village of Ribecourt and the spur to the south-east of it, was soon taken, D Company, which formed the first wave, securing that portion which was entrusted to the 1st Battalion. The ground won was known as the Blue Line and was part of the main Hindenburg entrenchment.

The rest of the 1st Battalion co-operated with the divisional sniping section and then passed through and secured the second objective, the Brown or Hindenburg support line, one thousand yards further on.

These positions were taken with small loss, the Buffs only having eight men killed and thirty-three wounded. This was satisfactory enough, as the two points which had caused anxiety to the divisional commander were Couillet Wood and Ribecourt, whereas the first fell to the Buffs and the latter to the 71st Brigade. The formations adopted were suitable; the hostile artillery was weak; the enemy was late in opening fire and it was scattered and inaccurate when opened; the tanks had no difficulty in crossing the trenches; the enemy appeared to be surprised and demoralized; the positions were quickly consolidated because there was no hostile fire, and in fact all was very well. The 6th Division had a most successful day: the bridge at Marcoing had fallen, and everything had gone like clockwork; the

263

artillery pushed forward to advanced positions, as did the machine guns which were brought up by pack animals. The next morning the Buffs, with the assistance of the tanks, completed the clearing of Noyelles. This was a creditable bit of initiative on the part of Captain Moss, who, finding the place but lightly held, collected a few men and with two tanks captured the village there and then.

Meanwhile a little further south the 12th Division was equally successful. During the whole of the 19th, battalion after battalion of tanks, R.E. equipment, ambulances and so on had been coming up to the front and, in accordance with Operation Orders, had been doing so in absolute silence. The scheme for the 20th had included five objectives. The 37th Brigade was assembled on the right of the 36th and it was to go forward on a two-company frontage only. The two companies of the 7th East Surrey were given the task of seizing the first objective, and the remainder of this battalion was to take the second. The third and fourth objectives were allotted to two companies each of the 6th Buffs and the Royal West Kents had the fifth.

The Surreys were quite successful; then the Buffs moved forward in artillery formation and, crossing the first lines of defence, moved on with marked success, sending back numerous prisoners and attacking the Hindenburg Line. There took place some fierce hand-to-hand fighting and a systematic " mopping up " of dug-outs, but everything went like clockwork and by the afternoon the battalion headquarters was in Pam-Pam Farm with three companies holding Lateau Wood and B Company at Bonavis, though the progress had been delayed somewhat by machine-gun fire from the two named farms, and the enemy had been difficult to drive from Lateau Wood. At 3.45 p.m. the West Kent reported to brigade headquarters that they were in touch with the Buffs and that no enemy was in sight.

264

The battalion casualties for the 20th were 5 officers wounded and 105 other ranks killed, wounded or missing, mostly only wounded.

On the 21st the positions occupied were consolidated. Much movement of lorries was noticed on this day behind the enemy's lines. Strong patrols, however, from the regiment covered the bridges over the canal. It became apparent on the 23rd that the German artillery had been considerably reinforced, as the hostile shelling very perceptibly increased in volume. On this date Captain A. F. Worster of the 1st Battalion died of wounds. He had been twelve months with the battalion and was greatly respected and universally loved. He had twice won the M.C.

On the 26th both battalions were relieved and withdrawn, the 1st into the Hindenburg Line as divisional reserve, and the 6th into support, though it sent up strong working parties to labour on the communication and front trenches for the West Kent Regiment, as a counter-attack on the part of the enemy now seemed imminent, he having evidently been greatly reinforced. On this date Lt.-Colonel Green left the 1st Battalion to assume command of a brigade.

On the 30th November a great German counter-attack was launched. Being in divisional reserve, the 1st Battalion did not on the first day suffer much from the shock, though six men were wounded; but the following morning it reinforced the troops who were now holding the line round Gonnelieu and La Vacquerie, where the enemy had broken through the previous day. Here Major B. L. Strauss, who was commanding, was killed, as were seven of his men, another dying of his wounds. Captain Allen, the adjutant, was wounded but continued for a while to command the battalion which duty had devolved on him. Captain Tibbles, R.A.M.C., Lieut. Blake, 2nd Lieuts. Clark, Fisher and Owen, C.S.M. Vincer and forty-five others were also injured.

In the evening Captain Pill, R.A.M.C., attached to the Bedfords, took over medical charge, Allen retired to the dressing station, Major Hardy, of the York and Lancasters, assumed temporary command and the Buffs were withdrawn again into divisional reserve to go up once more in the night of the 3rd to take up a defensive flank on Highland Ridge, as the enemy had broken through near Marcoing that morning. One company of R.E. and the Brigade Pioneer Company were attached for aid on Highland Ridge.

On the 5th December five men were killed and sixteen wounded, one of whom died the following day, on which date a new doctor, Lieut. McVey, relieved Captain Pill. Three were killed on the 7th and Lieut. L. F. Clark died of his hurts; two of the men were lost in the same way on the 8th. On this latter date the Buffs were relieved from the Ridge and moved back into trenches in rear of the main Hindenburg system. On the night of the 9th they moved further back still and on the 11th were taken twenty miles westward to Courcelles to refit, and Lt.-Colonel Power, who had commanded the 2nd Battalion at Ypres when Colonel Geddes was killed, was appointed commanding officer.

The 6th Battalion suffered severely on the 30th November, but showed that the men were made of magnificent fighting material. The enemy's offensive was most successful on the sector which was on the right flank of the battalion. Here he penetrated right through to the rear, and the first news the men in the line had of this success was that their own brigade headquarters was being attacked behind them. This attempt, however, was beaten off by the staff, the orderlies and the signallers, though the transport, which was bringing up water and supplies, was captured. This hostile movement of course exposed the Buffs' flank. Dense German masses were successful on the other flank also, but a ray of light in the gloom was occa-

266

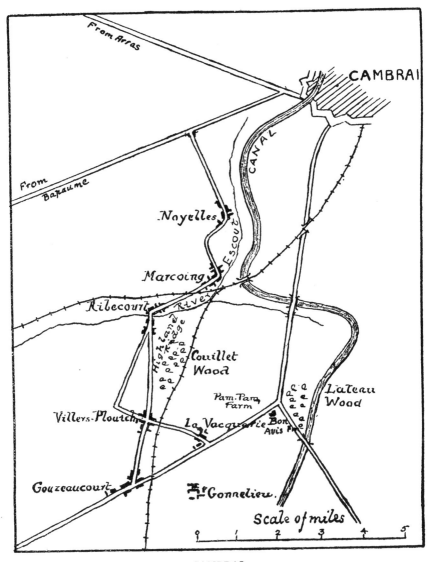

CAMBRAI

sioned by a very successful counter-attack made by the Buffs on Pam-Pam Farm, which had fallen. This place was recaptured and the enemy's advance in this region held up for three hours. Overwhelming masses, however, at last proved impossible to withstand and the small garrison withdrew fighting from shell hole to shell hole. The enemy was now on front, flanks and even in rear, and the struggle was hand-to-hand, obstinate and desperate. It was a case of the remnants of a fighting unit cutting its way back through all obstacles to regain a line that was forming in rear. This was finally effected and the line straightened out, but, as may be supposed, it was a bloody affair and our casualties numbered 14 officers and 317 other ranks, Major C. F. Cattley, M.C., being amongst the killed. The new position taken up was successfully held against all attacks, though it formed a very acute angle, as the divisions on the right and left had fallen back, leaving, of course, a greatly exposed salient. The line was held, however, until relief came next day, when the battalion moved back to the old British front, which was heavily gassed by means of shells.

On the 2nd December this battalion moved back into billets in Heudicourt, thence, on the 5th, to Dernancourt and on to Albert, where train was taken to Thiennes, in the peaceful country some seven or eight miles south by west of Hazebrouck, for the necessary rest and refit and to receive and train fresh men from England to fill the terrible gaps.

IV. 1ST BATTALION

After Cambrai the 1st Battalion, except for a short time near Moreuil, was kept out of the trenches till the 25th January, 1918, on which date it relieved the 9th Battalion of the Norfolks at Demicourt, about half-way between Bapaume and Cambrai. During this interval it had been lent to the 3rd Division and posted at Ervillers, Noreuil and Courcelles, all of which places are fairly close together. Christmas was spent at Courcelles in a quiet and restful manner, and a slight change of scene occurred soon afterwards by a move to Bellacourt, near Riviere, which is somewhat nearer Arras. The arrival in this place was marked by the rejoining of Captain Jones, D.S.O., of the R.A.M.C., who, an old, much respected and greatly beloved medical officer to the battalion, had been over fifteen months absent from his friends.

The New Year brought some honours with it. The late Major Strauss was gazetted to a M.C.; Sgt. Pass got the D.C.M.; and the M.M. came to Ptes. Alexander, Elliott, Wilson and Wright; and Lt.-Colonels Green, D.S.O., and Power, Major Blackall, Lieut. Whitlock, Corpl. Troy and Pte. May were all mentioned in despatches. The 21st January took this unit to Fremicourt, near Bapaume, and into divisional reserve, and the 25th, as has been said, back into the dreary trench work again. Captain Marshall on this date, who had already the M.C., was awarded the D.S.O. The trench tour was quiet enough, for the enemy was nearly a mile away, and the battalion was back at Fremicourt on the 3rd February.

Here, or rather at Le Bucquiere close by, on the 8th, a somewhat startling and apparently an unexpected change of organization took place which affected nearly everybody in the army. It had been decided that infantry brigades would be of more use, or at any rate that certain saving of power would be effected, if, instead of four, they should consist in future of only three battalions. This resulted in the disbanding of many brave and tried units which had repeatedly proved their value. Thus the 16th Brigade lost the 8th Battalion of the Bedfordshire Regiment which had been comrades of the Buffs, York and Lancaster and

268

Shropshire Light Infantry since March, 1915, when they came into the brigade in place of the Leicester Regiment. Of course, the disbanding of these units did not mean that the soldiers composing them went home to their mothers. They merely were transferred to other battalions in the form of huge drafts. Thus our own 8th Battalion of the Buffs, which had so nobly up-held the ancient honour of the regiment on many a stricken field, now ceased to exist in the same way as did the 8th Bedfords, and in consequence the 1st and 6th Buffs became the richer for strong reinforcements of fighting men. Five officers and 250 other ranks arrived at Le Bucquiere from the 8th for the 1st Buffs.

On the 12th February the battalion went into trenches at Lagnicourt, near Queant, and it was at this place when it received the shock of the German great offensive in March. It was in February a quiet and fairly comfortable place, though on the 14th an un-lucky shell killed three N.C.O.'s of D Company in a dug-out and blew a fourth clean through the roof. Beugnatre was the rearmost resting-place for Lagni-court, and each battalion of the brigade of course took its turn there.

Now that the Russians had finally collapsed and so set free the enormous hostile armies which, up till now, they had, at any rate in part, kept occupied, the whole of Central Europe had for some time been crowded with troop trains bringing division after division from east to west; these divisions had been specially trained for open as opposed to trench fighting, and the Kaiser and his staff fondly hoped they would suffice to drive the French to Paris and the English into the sea, more particularly as thousands of Russian guns were now available for German gunners to use on their western foes. It was clear to everybody, from the Commander-in-Chief to the last recruit from England, that a great offensive might commence on any day and we were

269

busily engaged in preparations. Battlefields were made ready for defence, strong points heavily wired and mine fields laid as protection against tanks. This attack was expected in the early morning of the 13th March and the whole British front was covered with a series of listening patrols, special precautions were taken and all ranks exhorted to quit themselves like men. On the 19th the rainless spring weather, which had lasted a fortnight, gave place to mist, with cold showers. On the 20th before midnight orders came to withdraw all working parties, to man all battle and alarm posts before dawn, and to be in readiness for the enemy's onslaught.

V. 6TH BATTALION

The 6th Battalion did not come into the front line again till the 22nd January, 1918, on which date it was at Fleurbaix, in the direction of Armentieres. The interval had been passed round Merville and Estaires. Some well-deserved decorations came to the unit in January and some medal ribbons were presented by the Army Commander. Captain Ferrie and 2nd Lieut. Gray got the M.C., L.-Corpl. Parker a bar to his M.M., and the decoration itself came to L.-Corpl. Clements and Pte. Woodcock. A little later 2nd Lieuts. Kidd, Stevens and Turk were gladdened with the news that each had the M.C.; Lt.-Colonel Smeltzer, M.C., was given the D.S.O., and R.S.M. Jeffrey the M.C.

Though Fleurbaix itself was reached on the 13th January, the battalion did not move into the front line in that region till the 22nd, and then it was quiet enough till relief came and a move back some five miles or so to Sailly, except that there was a certain amount of bombardment on the 28th, and just before relief was due the next day an enemy's party of about twenty attempted a raid on a post known as " Richard." They worked round behind this point with a view to cutting off the retreat of its little garrison, but at the exact moment the relieving party of Fusiliers arrived on the scene and the raiders, caught between two fires, were surprised and dispersed.

There was a good deal of work to be done in February in the way of preparation for the coming assault, and the 6th of the month saw the battalion in the front-line trenches, after C.S.M. Woodhams had heard on the 4th that he had got his D.C.M. The 9th of the month brought the big draft from the now defunct 8th Battalion of the Buffs. This consisted of 5 officers and 200 men.

Remaining in the same vicinity for many days, now in brigade reserve at Rouge-de-Bout, then in divisional at Nouveau Monde, and again in the trenches, all the men's energies were directed to work at defensive positions; for the British army and its allies were now for a time definitely on the defensive and experiencing what may be described as a lull before the storm. Of course, there still were some few signs of activity on both sides, for it is not nowadays customary in war to remain many days in total inactivity. Thus the enemy attempted " Robert " Post on the 7th March, and next day, after a preliminary artillery bombardment, the West Kent carried out a successful little raid; but things at this time were, generally speaking, quiet enough. On the 9th came a shower of gas shells, but there were no casualties that day, though on the morrow 2nd Lieut. T. A. Brown was killed and 2nd Lieut. Barnes wounded.

The British in this region appear to have expected the attack about the 11th. The enemy was believed to be forming in vast masses on the immediate front, and the Buffs remained during the night of the 10th/11th in battle formation with patrols going out in front at frequent intervals. In fact, these night patrols were now in pretty constant use. On the 16th transport was noticed to be very active behind the German lines. On the 17th at 10.10 p.m., after a quiet day, the enemy opened a very heavy artillery fire on the front and support lines. Two of his patrols, of about thirty men each, attempted to approach " Richard " and " Reggie " posts, but were driven off by Lewis guns and rifle fire. 2nd Lieut. C. F. Peters, however, met his death that night and ten men were wounded. On the 19th March the battalion was relieved and went into billets at Pont de Nieppe, which is a mile or two outside Armentieres on the Bailleul road, and there it was on the morning of the 21st.

VI. 7TH BATTALION

The story of the 7th Battalion from the 1st July, 1917, to the 21st March, 1918, must now come under consideration. The chief area of its operations was Dickebusch and its neighbourhood, and the chief event a great and grim combat at Poelcappelle on the 12th October. It was on the 3rd July that the 55th Brigade, with the Buffs, railed from Doullens to join the Fifth Army and went to the Second Corps area, detraining at Hupoutre and marching to Ottawa Camp at Ouderdom, a couple of miles west of Dickebusch; and on the 7th it was in the line again, where things were comparatively lively, especially as regards gas-shelling, and where much patrolling work was done. A raid was arranged for the 14th, but had to be abandoned, as the guns could not come into action on account of the gas, and two days afterwards the battalion was relieved for a while and went into camp at Chateau Segard. Very many men were wounded about this period, namely, sixty-one in seventeen days, which is a high average for trench warfare.

At the commencement of August at Dickebusch the enemy was fairly active and Captain A. O. Sherren, commanding C Company, was killed on the 3rd and Captain Clapperton wounded the next night. These casualties occurred in relieving a portion of the line but little known to the battalion and which had been held by the 30th Division. The Buffs were back again at Chateau Segard on the 8th and into divisional reserve on the 10th, on which date an attack was made by the brigade, the 7th Battalion The Queen's being in the forefront of the fight and the Buffs going up in reserve to a place known as Railway Dug-outs, which was south-east of Ypres. At 6 a.m. orders came to send one company to support the 8th East Surrey in what was called Crab Crawl Tunnel. Therefore A Company was despatched, and it was joined in the evening by B. These two companies, under Major Wood, were in support to the 17th Brigade of the 24th Division, in which the 8th Buffs were serving.

Directly after this the Buffs were entrained and moved off for a period of training at Eringhem, nine miles north-west of Steenvoorde, Wood's two companies rejoining headquarters at Arbeele on the 13th. On the 15th August Pte. Roberts (since killed in action) and Sgt. Baldry were awarded the M.M.

Of course, there was a great deal of training at this time, but, even if the numerous drafts which required teaching and the ever-changing conditions of warfare had not made this a necessity, still it does not improve the health nor the spirits of men so often exposed to the danger of death to encourage or allow periods of utter indolence and the consequent loafing and brooding. The work at this time was mostly practising the assault of positions. On the 12th September Captain Nicholson got the M.C. and L.-Corpl. Streat the D.C.M., and about the same time eight soldiers got the M.M. and one a bar to the same. On the 23rd September the Buffs moved by train to St. Jan Ter Biezen, where, five days afterwards, hostile aircraft dropped bombs into the camp, doing a very great deal of damage. The men were in huts and tents and the area

T   273

a very congested one, which fact probably tempted the enemy to his enterprise. It was dark when the aeroplane flew over and it dropped six bombs (two of which were blind) right into the camp, resulting in the death of 2nd Lieut. R. E. C. Mead and twenty-six men and the wounding of Lieut. and Qr.-Master Rye, 2nd Lieuts. Malton and Tyler and sixty-three others. This misfortune had the effect of disorganizing the arrangement of platoons and sections just at a time when the regiment was being braced up and perfected in the new method of attack called "Leap-frog."[1] However, the training still went on and, moving by stages, the battalion, with the rest of the brigade, was on the 11th October opposite the village of Poelcappelle, because for various reasons, one of which was a desire to assist the French, our Commander-in-Chief was arranging a considerable offensive movement before the weather, which had been much against movement, got absolutely too wet and wintry for any kind of manœuvre.

This offensive operation was made over a six-mile front northwards from a point east of the village of Zonnebeke and so brought the 55th Brigade to the position indicated. As far as the 55th Brigade was concerned no circumstances could have been less in favour of a successful attack, for several reasons: no shelter was to be had for the assaulting troops, who had to be out in the open, in mud and rain, close up to the front line and in full view of hostile aircraft, thus advertising the coming movement, so to speak; much detail in the way of attack orders was altered and amended at the last moment, and these details consequently could not be made known to everyone in time, for the night of the 11th was pitch dark and the various platoons and sections were scattered about wherever cover could be got —in shell holes and the like, and so had no chance of receiving detailed orders.

[1] For an example of the "leap-frog" method, see pp. 385–7.

274

The Buffs' line was from Gloster House, or Farm, to Poelcappelle Church; C Company was on the right and D on the left, A supporting C and B behind D. The objective, together with the battalion area of activity, is shown on the accompanying sketch map. A and B Companies were to act as what was known as "leap-frog" companies—that is, they were to pass the others and go on to the second objective. All companies were in position by 4 a.m. on the 12th October; outposts were withdrawn at 5.15; the barrage opened at 5.25, and C and D moved forward.

All reports agree in stating that our barrage was not a success; it was erratic and not heavy enough, and when the infantry attack was getting into difficulties it passed too far ahead. The officer commanding C Company (Captain Nicholson) reported that the guns opened thirty seconds too late on his front, that the barrage commenced very thinly and thickened right on top of the leading troops. D Company got caught by the enemy's gun fire as it was waiting for ours to lift and the whole front line came immediately under very heavy fire, particularly C, which suffered much from machine guns from the neighbourhood of Gloster House and from point " 37." D Company got through the houses and enclosures which were on its front, but, on emerging, met heavy cross machine-gun fire from Meunier House and the Brewery, and thus our attack was checked throughout our line. A and B, moving up in rear so as to keep close, came in their turn under intense machine-gun fire, B Company especially suffering very severely. These supports were eventually merged into the leading line and every effort was made to struggle forward, but the heavy ground prevented anything but laborious movement which was ill suited to a rain of bullets, and at last things came to a standstill.

C Company managed to rush one hostile post, where the men captured a machine gun and turned it very

275

effectually on its late owners. Captain Nicholson, M.C., who commanded C Company, tried to dig in where he was, but the ground was terribly swampy for this; however, he was, about noon, able to report a perceptible slackening of the enemy's fire. About this time he noticed 2nd Lieut. Knight with the elements of A Company about four hundred yards to his right, and he sent off 2nd Lieut. H. M. Spencer to get touch with him with a view to together making an attempt to gain ground; Spencer, on his way, fell, mortally wounded, and Nicholson went out to help him. As he was doing so he heard a shout and saw that Knight and about thirty men had been overwhelmed and made prisoners. He could not get back to his men in time to order them to open fire. This affair caused a gap on Nicholson's left and he directed his remaining officer, 2nd Lieut. Tupper, to form three posts to protect that flank while he himself established five others on his front. He then attempted to consolidate these, but the state of the ground prohibited digging. About 2 p.m. a party of Germans was observed near the Brewery advancing down the main street of Poelcappelle which had every appearance of a counter-attack and preparations were made accordingly, but the enemy was successfully stopped by parties of the West Kent and of the Suffolk Regiment which were in the village. About 5.30 the enemy shelled our lines and the village, but defensive posts were established and all was well, though the bombardment continued during the next day, the 13th, and at dusk the remnant of the Buffs withdrew to Counter Farm on relief by the 7th Battalion of the Queen's.

It is worthy of note that on the 12th and 13th both the Germans and ourselves were able to attend the wounded by flying a white or Red Cross flag, white handkerchief or rag. The enemy never fired on a wounded man. It is eloquent of the state of things

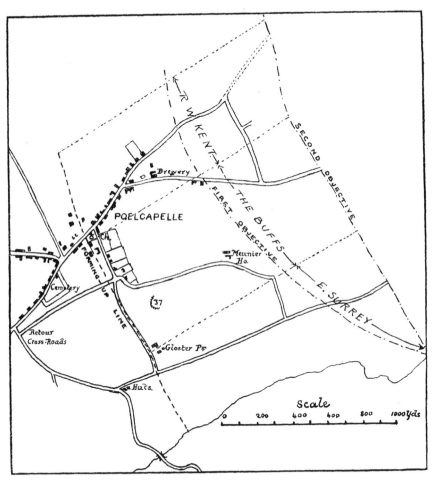

POELCAPELLE

during a war between so-called civilized nations that such should be considered as exceptional.

The Buffs' casualties in this action were: killed, Captain E. B. C. Burnside, 2nd Lieuts. R. W. Bone, H. M. Spencer and H. Thomas and 52 other ranks; wounded, Captains Blood-Smyth and West, Lieut. Boner, 2nd Lieuts. Amos and Bull, and 178 men; missing, 2nd Lieut. Knight and 145 men. A Company had left at duty one sergeant and one corporal; B, one corporal; C, two sergeants and four corporals; and D, one sergeant and one corporal—no less than 62 N.C.O.'s being amongst the casualties. As has been seen, several circumstances contributed to prevent this action from being an entire success, but the chief was the deplorable state of the ground, which prevented movement and consolidation and which, worst of all, prevented fire, by clogging up the men's rifles with mud.

On the 24th of the month the battalion went into billets at Poperinghe, where nine men got M.M.'s. On the 1st November it moved, by means of lorries, to Parroy Camp, where it worked on the roads. On that day a second bar to Captain C. D. Hayfield's M.C. was announced, as well as one to Captain A. C. L. Nicholson's. The M.C. was awarded to 2nd Lieut. Tupper, the D.C.M. to C.Q.M.S. Burt and Sgt. Pellandine, and the M.M. to ten more of the men.

A long spell of quiet at Emile Camp now ensued, the battalion being very weak as regards numbers. It moved up into the forward area, however, on the 9th December, occupying small posts till the 17th, when it entrained at Boesinghe for Bayenghem and went into billets. There the battalion remained till over Christmas, after which it led a somewhat nomadic life—that is, it wandered a good deal about the region west and north of Ypres. Proven perhaps might be taken as a centre of the country visited, but early January found the men in the trenches again near Boesinghe for a few days. There was always a New Year list of honours during the war, and the commencement of 1918 gave Lt.-Colonel Ransome, already an M.C., the coveted D.S.O. as well. Captain Clapperton got the M.C., and Captains Fine and Hallinan (the battalion doctor), together with Sgt. L. G. Moon,[1] who had died of wounds, were mentioned in despatches. Further, C.Q.M.S. Wickington got the D.C.M., he having already received the M.M.

The last day of January the battalion went into billets at Herzeele, some ten miles west of Poperinghe; and the 11th of February found it in billets in the back area at Viry Noureuil, where it worked hard on defensive preparations in the area of the expected battle, for ten days or so. Then came a very long journey and complete change of scene.

Sir Douglas Haig foresaw that the enemy was likely to throw his principal weight south of Arras, and most likely about the point of juncture of the French and English forces, which at this time was about the River Oise. He therefore very greatly strengthened this threatened area, and so it came about that the 7th Battalion with its comrades were carried off in haste to the Liez area on the 26th February, and set energetically to work in what was termed the battle zone, in contradistinction to the forward zone, in which the first shock of the oncoming Teuton armies was to be received.

Liez is about three miles north of the River Oise, and two from the St. Quentin Canal, which practically here defined the forward line of defence into which the Buffs moved up on the 13th March and continued their preparations to receive the enemy. On the night of the 15th a single platoon, under Lieut. C. W. Jemmett,

[1] No. 4181 Sgt. Moon had been recommended for the V.C. the previous August for gallant conduct at Zillebeke, where he received his death wounds.

278

made a reconnaissance in force on the canal bridge on the Vendeuil–Chaugny road, in which Jemmett unfortunately lost his life. The bridge was found to be held in force. The records of this period are somewhat meagre, as nearly all the papers referring to it had later on to be destroyed in a hurry to prevent them falling into the enemy's hands, but it seems clear that some casualties resulted from the attack on this canal bridge. On the 20th March came the order "Prepare for Action," and next morning the fight commenced.

VII.   8TH BATTALION—BATTLE OF PILCKEM RIDGE

The 8th Battalion after its fight at the Buffs' Bank enjoyed a good long rest and pleasant change. It was at Escoeuilles in the Lumbres area for over a fortnight, and from there went on to the seaside at Ecault, about four miles south of Boulogne, for two or three days. This was really an enjoyable holiday; passes were granted into Boulogne, and the camp authorities were most kind; but all good things come to an end, and the 16th July found the men on the march again for Mic Mac Camp and the trenches. It took nearly a week to cover this distance, as no forced marches were called for, and so, on the 22nd July, the battalion started on the monotonous old trench work once more. Headquarters, with C Company, were quartered in a tunnel, some of these having been constructed of late by regular tunnelling companies of specially selected troops. This trench tour of the 8th Buffs, which lasted only six days, was a very strenuous one and occasioned no less than 160 casualties.

On the 25th one of our own heavy guns dropped a shell on our left front post and buried it. The post had been held by one N.C.O. and eight men, and four of these were wounded and the remainder badly shaken. Gas alarms were very numerous on this date. The fol-

279

lowing day was marked by minor enterprises undertaken by units on the Buffs' left, our artillery opening
at 5.5 p.m. The result was satisfactory, but unfortunately the regiment was unable to take part. On the
27th, a little before noon, a large shell pierced a tunnel
occupied by our men, killing four, gassing about thirty
and causing considerable delay to the carrying parties
by blocking the gangway. On the 28th the Buffs were
back for a day or two at Mic Mac Camp, and on the
31st the Battle of Pilckem Ridge commenced.

This was a carefully organized attack on our part
with a view to gaining the crest of the high ground east
of Ypres, and though troops were to be engaged all the
way from Deulemont to Steenstraat—a fifteen-mile
front—the brunt of the work was apportioned to the
5th Army under Sir Hubert Gough, acting between
Boesinghe and the road which runs from Zillebeke to
Zandvoorde. Thus it came about that on the 30th
July the Buffs moved up to assembly positions in Ecluse
Trench, passing Dickebusch *en route*. Barrage rations
were issued and the men awaited the break of day and
zero hour, which was fixed for 3.50 a.m. on the 31st.
They were not in the front line, and one hour after zero
moved up to the position vacated by the 12th Royal
Fusiliers in Canada Tunnel, reaching it without casualties, after meeting several wounded men from different
units of the division, from whom only garbled accounts
of what was going forward could be gleaned. For the
whole of this first day our men lay in the stifling tunnels,
where the heat was tremendous and the odour most
offensive. It was not till 8.30 the next night that
the Buffs emerged from their unpleasant surroundings
and pushed forward to relieve the 3rd Rifle Brigade in
our new front line, which was, however, not as far off
as had been planned; for the British advance had been
halted by very heavy opposition from shells, machine
guns and rifle fire. The Rifle Brigade proved very diffi-

cult to discover, owing to the darkness and inefficient guides and, when found, their portion of the new line was far from comfortable, especially on the left, where D Company was. It proved a chain of posts in shell holes which were mostly half full of water; the rain was falling, too, and the hostile shelling was heavy.

However, a welcome relief came on the evening of the following day, and in the dark, over very heavy and unknown ground, the battalion stumbled through the night, suffering a few casualties, including Captain Morrell slightly wounded, until at daylight the men made the camp again and rested at Dickebusch for some two or three days before going up into line once more on the 7th, on which occasion battalion headquarters was established in Canada Tunnel as before.

At 4.35 a.m. on the 10th August, in accordance with orders received, an attempt was made to capture Lower Starpost, 2nd Lieut. Lowles and forty-seven men of B Company being detailed for the job. This little party formed up at 3.45 and was subjected to very heavy shelling while waiting for the zero hour. Then our barrage opened and three minutes later the majority of the guns lifted, but one of the batteries failed to do so for another minute and a half, which mistake cost twelve casualties and greatly disorganized the party. However, the men advanced, only to find that, owing to the delay in the lifting of some of the guns, the enemy was all ready and, having left the dug-outs, was awaiting what was to come. By this time Lowles and all his N.C.O.'s except L.-Corpl. Simson were wounded, but the stout lance-corporal immediately opened fire with his Lewis gun and ordered his men to charge. The gun jammed almost immediately, and the enemy defended himself briskly with stick bombs. The remaining one-third of the party—two-thirds of the original number having dropped—could make no headway against the strong opposition encountered and returned to the lines, having had 5 killed, 23 wounded and 3 missing, and having shown great courage and determination.

From this date until the 21st September life was somewhat monotonous and consisted, as usual, of work in the trenches and rest in camp in alternate periods, Larch Wood tunnels being the scene of the one and Mic Mac Camp and Dickebusch of the other. Clear weather and a bright harvest moon the first week in September caused the enemy to try bombing a good many British camps at night from aeroplanes, and the Buffs experienced this form of annoyance together with other units. On the 11th September, while moving up into the trenches, two men were killed and another wounded, and 2nd Lieut. Cooper and R.S.M. Dare were so badly shaken up that they had to be sent away for a while. The next day the enemy shelled the ration dump, causing some minor casualties. L.-Corpl. Bussell and Pte. Gasking later on got M.M.'s for coolness and bravery on this occasion.

On the 16th September the battalion was put into buses and removed to Oultersteen, which is three miles beyond Bailleul, and five days later it entrained for Bapaume and marched to Ypres. On the 27th it marched to Haut Allaines, on the 29th to Hervilly, and on the 30th took its place in the line with French on their right, the battalion being thus at the extreme right of the British line.

The first week in October, in this portion of the line, was devoted mostly to patrol work, and a few casualties occurred, two men being killed and another wounded on the 3rd, but the work was the same as usual. Bernes and Vadencourt were the resting-places, and Ascencion Wood the chief object of the patrols.

On the 4th November an American officer was attached to the regiment—one swallow does not make a summer, but this was a welcome sign of what was to be expected later on. On the 6th one of our patrols at night, being south of Ascencion Wood, came across a similar party of the enemy, and both immediately opened fire, the Buffs losing two killed and five wounded in the little affair. Life towards the end of the year was uneventful. On the 23rd November a post under Sgt. Smith was attacked by thirty or forty Germans, but they were driven off without casualties to us, and one dead officer and a N.C.O., badly wounded, were found on our wire afterwards. The average company strength during the month of November was only eighty-four.

The 3rd December found the battalion in the line again and expecting a hostile attack, but on the 7th it was back in Hancourt. About Christmas a good deal of movement on the enemy's part appeared to be going on around Bellicourt. The Buffs being then opposite, at Montigny, Christmas was kept on the 31st of the month at Montigny.

On the 1st January, 1918, the brigade moved back a few miles to Vraignes, but only for a short time. On the 21st, whilst at Hancourt, orders arrived that the 8th Battalion of the Buffs and the 12th Battalion of the Royal Fusiliers were to be disbanded, so, on the 30th, all employed men of these units rejoined, and on the 6th February the drafts of men already noted [1] started for the 1st and 6th Battalions. Thus ended the only 8th Battalion the regiment ever had. Ever since the 26th September, 1915, when it suffered so severely near Loos, and when it lost the gallant Romer, this unit had borne a brave share in the great struggle. Very few, if any, of the men raised by the gallant Colonel Romer in 1914 were passed on in February, 1918 (Major J. Vaughan, M.C., being one of the exceptions), but the regimental spirit was still a living thing, and it was a right and happy order that the men should remain Buffs and no new badge should replace the ancient dragon.

[1] See page 269.

CHAPTER XII

THE QUEEN'S OWN RIFLES OF CANADA

AS members of the Queen's Own Rifles of Canada were fighting from early in 1915 till the end of hostilities, perhaps the centre of the war history between the more or less evenly contested portion of the struggle and the beginning of the end would be a suitable place to insert a short chapter describing who and what this regiment was and is, for no war history of the Buffs would be complete without reference to their allied regiment of Canadian Militia.

This was an existing corps long before August, 1914, and so could hardly be referred to in our third chapter, which dealt chiefly with the raising of new units. On reference to the official Army List it will be seen that, under the headings of certain of our regiments, such for example as the Somerset Light Infantry, the Suffolk Regiment, the Black Watch and our own, are entered the words :—

Allied regiment of Dominion of New Zealand.
Allied regiment of Australian Commonwealth, or
Allied regiment of Canadian Militia.

The idea is a very pretty one, naturally induces the very best of cordial good feeling, and emphasises in a pleasant and soldierly way the idea of blood brotherhood which exists between warrior Englishmen and their soldier cousins over the seas.

The regiment is an old one and belongs to Toronto, Ontario. The foundation of the Canadian Militia was practically laid by the gallant band of loyalists who, in spite of ill-treatment on the part of old England to her colonists, stuck manfully to their King during the

American upheaval of the year 1776. This militia turned out again in the war between England and the United States in 1812, in which struggle the Canadians saw some great fighting and succeeded in keeping their country safe and intact in spite of their powerful neighbour.

The actual formation of the Toronto regiment was in 1860, and it first paraded on Queen Victoria's birth-day of that year. More active service was experienced during the Fenian raids of 1864, 65 and 66, and in the Red River rebellion of 1870 ; but it is not of course possible, nor even desirable in this place, to give the regimental history as a whole, and reference is merely made to these campaigns in order to show the reader that our allied regiment is of no new growth.

As regards recent history, however, it is interesting to note that when a military contingent was sent to represent Canada at Queen Victoria's Diamond Jubilee, one of the units was made up of the Rifle Regiments of Canada and commanded by Major H. M. Pellatt, for this is a well-known regimental name. The regiment was also represented in the Boer War.

In 1902 Pellatt, now Lieutenant-Colonel command-ing the regiment, headed the Canadian contingent which attended the coronation of King Edward VII, and on the occasion took with him, at his own expense, the regiment's famous bugle band.

In the summer of 1910 a provisional battalion of six hundred and fifty men, drawn from the regiment, sailed for England to take part in the army manœuvres. This was made possible by the generosity and patriotism of Colonel Sir Henry Pellatt, who bore the entire ex-pense. It is almost superfluous to add that a hearty welcome awaited these soldiers both on landing in England and on arrival at Aldershot.

On September 3rd the Canadians performed a thir-teen-mile route march with the Buffs, and in connection with this exercise the following words were written by a distinguished officer of the Corps: "There had " been a friendly feeling existing between all ranks of " these two regiments since the arrival of the Queen's " Own in England, due to the fact that they both used " the same regimental march. Permission for the " Queen's Own to use this march had been given by " the Buffs over forty years ago. The friendly feeling " between the two units was greatly strengthened that " day, and during the whole of the stay in England the " Queen's Own were indebted to the Buffs for many " acts of kindness and thoughtfulness."

Immediately after the return of the battalion to Toronto steps were taken to bring about an affiliation with the Buffs, but it was not until 1914 that this was finally accomplished, when the following appeared in Militia orders: "His Majesty has been graciously " pleased to approve of the 2nd Regiment, Queen's Own " Rifles of Canada, being made an allied regiment of the " Buffs (East Kent Regiment)." The annual mess dinner of the Queen's Own was held on the 23rd April, 1914, at the Military Institute, Toronto, and the 1st Battalion dining at the same time at Fermoy, an all-British cable communication between the two places was arranged to permit an exchange of messages; the first time direct cables were sent between Toronto and Ireland. This was made possible at the request of Sir Henry Pellatt. Cordial interchange of greetings resulted.

As regards the Great War, which, after all, is what the readers of this book are primarily interested in: immediately upon the news of the declaration of war reaching Canada, Lt.-Colonel M. S. Mercer,[1] Commandant of the Queen's Own Rifles, offered to his government a battalion of his regiment for immediate

[1] This officer was killed in action at Sanctuary Wood on the 3rd June, 1918, as major-general commanding the 3rd Canadian Division.

286

service abroad. Upon the acceptance by the British Government of one complete division from Canada with reinforcements for the same, Lt.-Colonel Mercer was notified that the battalion offered by the Queen's Own could not be accepted and that the regiment, with the others, could only be allowed to furnish 250 volunteers per battalion in accordance with instructions already issued to all infantry units of the Canadian Militia. At this time few, if any, in the country foresaw the extent of Canada's ultimate effort, and many believed that one division, which represented the first contingent, would probably be all that would ever sail for the war. This being the case, and the authorities desiring that all units of the militia, of which there were 110 battalions of infantry, should be represented and have an opportunity of furnishing their quota, it came about that battalions were not raised upon the regimental system, as was done in Great Britain, but composite battalions, as forming part of the Canadian Expeditionary Force, were made up from drafts contributed from the various militia corps throughout the whole country.

From this it may be seen that the Queen's Own Rifles did not serve in the war as a single unit, but as parts of many, and so it may be easily conceived that portions of the regiment fought in each and all of the many great battles in which Canada so gloriously distinguished itself. This fact makes it impossible in this short history to follow their doings in the detailed manner which is attempted in the cases of the English battalions. Nevertheless we are able to trace the Queen's Own to a certain extent, and we know that about eight hundred of the regiment were formed at once on the declaration of war into a service battalion and that very strong representations were made to the Canadian government to allow this unit to proceed overseas in its entirety, but that permission was refused.

THE QUEEN'S OWN RIFLES OF CANADA

On the 31st August, 1914, orders were issued that the infantry of the first contingent would consist of seventeen battalions numbering from one onward, that twelve of these would be selected for the fighting division and that the remaining five would form a Canadian reserve in England. The 1st, 2nd, 3rd and 4th Battalions were brigaded together, with Colonel M. S. Mercer as brigadier. The service battalion of the Queen's Own was assigned to the 3rd Battalion, together with detachments from other corps. The contingent spent five months on Salisbury Plain, was inspected by H.M. The King, accompanied by Lord Kitchener, on the 5th February, 1915, and embarked for France three days later, landing at St. Nazaire.

The 3rd battalion soon afterwards was at Armentieres and in the trenches, to learn the life and duties under the tuition of the Sherwood Foresters. It was this 1st Canadian Division which fought so gallantly at the Second Battle of Ypres in April, 1915, only two months after landing in France, and these were the men that Geddes' detachment were so intimately associated with and to whose assistance Captain Tomlinson's ill-fated company was sent on the 24th April. The 3rd Battalion, which included, as we have seen, in its ranks the Queen's Own, were very much in the thick of this terrible fight, and two of its companies, A and B, were fighting actually alongside Tomlinson's company, engaged in the same and identical enterprise.

How many of those men who route-marched with the Buffs at Aldershot in 1910 ever dreamed that in less than four years they would be fighting desperately alongside the old regiment (though, of course, a different battalion of it) in one of the greatest battles ever contested?

Sixty-one officers and nearly four thousand N.C.O.'s and men of the Queen's Own served with this 3rd Battalion during the war, and it was always commanded by one of the regiment's own officers.

In October, 1914, it was decided that Canada should furnish a second division, and one complete company of the 19th Battalion, serving with this, was furnished by the Buffs' Allied Corps. This division reached France in September, 1915.

On the 14th November twelve extra mounted rifle battalions were authorized for war, and one of them was raised in Toronto and subsequently fed with drafts from our regiment. These were originally intended for mounted troops, but were transformed into ordinary infantry when it was found that that arm was the one most in request.

The men generally went to France as drafts for existing units, but the 4th and 5th Canadian Mounted Rifles became two battalions of the 3rd Canadian Division which was formed in France in the spring of 1916 and placed under the command of Major-General M. S. Mercer, C.B.

The 35th Battalion of the Canadian Expeditionary Force was raised in 1915 and it also contained a company of the Queen's Own Rifles, and indeed in course of time 17 officers and 650 men of the regiment passed through this particular unit.

Then, again, it was strongly represented in the 58th, 74th, 75th, 83rd, 95th, 166th and 255th Battalions, some of which were draft-finding units, and others served complete in the war.

In fact, officers and men of the Queen's Own Rifles found their way into all units and services of the Canadian Expeditionary Force, which fought in nearly all the considerable battles on the Western front from the Second Battle of Ypres up to the armistice; and wherever it fought it is safe to affirm that some, at any rate, of the Queen's Own fought too.

It seems, therefore, almost as impossible to give a list

of engagements the men were present at as it always has been in the case of the Royal Artillery, which corps, it is well known, is obliged to fall back on the single word " Ubique " instead of a battle-roll.

The following is a summary of the work done by our Canadian Allied Regiment and the honours its members won:—

Total enlistments for service overseas .	9,104
Killed or died of wounds or disease .	1,324
Wounded	3,198
Prisoners of war	117
Granted commissions in the field .	257 [1]
Number of officers who served in theatre of war	205 [2]
Number of officers killed or died of wounds	47

DECORATIONS

Victoria Cross	I
Commander of the Bath . . .	2
Companion St. Michael and St. George	2
Distinguished Service Order . .	12
Bar to D.S.O.	5
Military Cross	51
Bar to M.C.	11
Commander British Empire . .	I
Order British Empire . . .	6
Member British Empire . . .	2
Croix de Guerre (French) . .	10
Croix de Guerre (Belgium) . .	5
Legion of Honour	2
Médaille Militaire	I
Distinguished Conduct Medal . .	29

[1] B.E.F., 42 ; C.E.F., 215.
[2] These were actually officers of Q.O.R. before leaving Canada, and are separate to above.

DECORATIONS—(*continued*)

Bar to D.C.M.	6
Military Medal	175
Bar to M.M.	14
2nd Bar to M.M.	3
Meritorious Service Medal . .	13
Distinguished Flying Cross . .	2

Besides the battalions alluded to above there was another in which we are interested, though not connected with the Queen's Own Rifles of Canada, except that several of the latter's officers assisted in the raising and organization of it: the 198th Battalion of the Canadian Expeditionary Force was raised in Toronto by men of Kent.

We in England are inclined affectionately to term the Queen's Own " The Canadian Buffs," but this is not its name.

The 198th War Battalion was, like our 6th, 7th, 8th, 9th and 10th, a war unit only, but during its existence it was called by the name of " Canadian Buffs," though never formally or officially allied to the old regiment.

It was commanded by Lt.-Colonel J. A. Cooper and had colours presented to it on the 1st November, 1916, by Sir John Hendrie, the Lieutenant-Governor of the Province of Ontario, who in his speech on the occasion laid stress on the honour granted to the battalion by His Majesty The King, in allowing it to be called by the name of such an historic regiment.

The Canadian Buffs lost seven officers and ninety-nine other ranks killed.

CHAPTER XIII

THE END OF THE SALONICA AND MESOPOTAMIA CAMPAIGNS

I. 4TH BATTALION

BEFORE studying the final phases and great events of 1918 in France and Flanders, and the conclusion of the war in that area, it may be as well to see how matters ended further afield and in other regions where the Buffs were engaged. It may be remembered that the 10th left Palestine in March, when the initial successes of the German offensive rendered it necessary to reinforce the Western Armies with every available man. Therefore the continuation of the history of that battalion is similar, as regards locality, to that of the 1st, 6th and 7th. The 4th remained in India till some time after the end of the struggle. The 5th endured a weary time in Mesopotamia, and the 2nd was in the neighbourhood of Salonica. As far as the 4th Battalion is concerned, with the exception of the tour of work at Aden, already described, it saw no war as a unit, though nearly all its individual members at some time or another were seriously engaged. For instance, when this battalion returned from the Aden campaign and was stationed at Bareilly, it sent, as well as detachments to the north-west frontier of India, about five hundred officers and men to the 5th in Mesopotamia.

In July, 1918, the 4th Battalion proceeded to Multan, in the Punjaub, and was in this place when news of the armistice reached India. Now, the great cessation of hostilities brought the blessings of peace to all the rest of the Buffs, even if it brought no immediate change of surroundings, but this was not the case as regards the

292

garrison of India; all sorts of internal troubles were fomented in the great eastern dependency, particularly in the Punjaub, chiefly because certain ignorant and foolish folk at home are too full of the sense of their own importance to leave the ruling of foreign lands to those of our nation who really know all about it and have made their adopted country their life study. Troublous times there were, and in May, 1919, six months after war was supposed to have ended, martial law having been proclaimed, the Buffs were employed on different important points on the railway line and at Amballa, Lahore and other places. Another Afghan war, too, broke out and about half the battalion was employed upon it, both officers and men being called upon to perform various duties at the front. Head-quarters, under Lt.-Colonel Dunstan, who had suc-ceeded Lt.-Colonel Gosling, remained at Lahore during the hot weather of 1919. At last, at the end of October, a year after the European peace, the men were col-lected, embarked on the s.s. *Nevasa* and landed at Devonport in November, after five years' foreign ser-vice, which must be a record, or nearly so, for a strictly home service unit.

The good work of this battalion is recorded in the following letter written, just before its departure from India, by the Commander-in-Chief, General Sir C. C. Munro:—

" Officers, Warrant Officers, Non-Commissioned " Officers and Men of the 4th Battalion the Buffs, " East Kent Regiment. On your departure from India " I desire to place on record my high appreciation of " your services to the Empire during the period of the " Great War.

" Many of you, previous to the outbreak of War, had " by joining the Territorial Force already given proof " of that patriotism and public spirit for which the " Force has rendered itself so conspicuous.

" On the declaration of War, your ranks were filled
" by eager volunteers animated by the same spirit of
" self-sacrifice. When called upon to undertake the
" further obligation of service overseas your response
" was immediate and unanimous. By so doing you set
" free a large number of regular units for service in the
" main theatres of war, at a time when every trained
" soldier was of the greatest value. Many of you have
" seen service, and by your conduct and bearing have
" added to the reputation of the famous regiment
" whose name you bear.

" Since the termination of active fighting in all the
" theatres of war you have been subjected to the fur-
" ther stress of waiting for your relief. That you appre-
" ciated the difficulties which the authorities have had
" to face in this respect is clear from the patience with
" which you have borne this trying period.

" You are returning to your homes in Kent, and I
" bid you God Speed and a Happy Homecoming.

" As an old Commander of a Territorial Division at
" home I am proud to have again been associated with
" you in India."

The government of India, in a long resolution at
Delhi (dated 31.12.19), recorded that:—

" The Governors-General in Council desire to ex-
" press to all ranks of the 4th Battalion the Buffs, East
" Kent Regiment, the thanks of the Government of
" India for their patriotic services, which will long be
" remembered and will serve as a noble and enduring
" example of good citizenship to future generations."

II.   5TH BATTALION

On the 1st April, 1917, the defeated Turkish 14th
Corps was broken into fragments and driven up the two
great rivers and the Diala, while their 13th Corps was

falling back before the Russians, who were coming down from the hills to the north-east of Baghdad. Our own people were covering the city from any possible attempt that the enemy might make down the rivers. On the 2nd April touch was established with the Russians, so our people from the Diala were withdrawn, a further advance up both banks of the Tigris considered and, as a preliminary, about the 8th of the month portions of the enemy were driven over the Shatt el Adhaim river. The Buffs at this time were at Hinaidi, which is about two miles below Baghdad, but in view of the contemplated operations the battalion started for the north on the 3rd April, doing no less than twenty-six miles the first day, the distance being divided into two considerable marches. This journey was continued during the following two or three days, and on the 8th April the battalion was at Dugamia. It was discovered, however, on this date that over six thousand of the enemy, with thirty-two guns, had issued from the Jebel Hamrin and were moving down the right bank of the Nahr Khalis Canal towards Deltawa. Indeed, by the evening of the 9th they had reached a point seven miles or so south-west of Deli Abbas. The Buffs, with the rest of the brigade, were ordered at short notice to Deltawa, in support of a force under Lt.-Colonel Champain, and a picquet line was thrown out to the north of the place, Dogras being on the left and Buffs on the right. The following day it was found impossible to reach the position which it was intended to occupy, owing to the presence of several very steep nullahs deep with water, and the brigade counter-marched and moved through Deltawa.

On the 10th it proceeded to a point opposite Abdullah Effendi and found the country partially inundated, the banks or " bunds " having been broken. All this day and part of the next, the enemy continued his advance down the canal, lured on by our cavalry which retreated before him; but on the 11th he met with failure, for on that day British troops, including the Buffs, had been sent up the right bank of the Nahr Khalis towards Deli Abbas to meet him, while another column, after a night march from Dogamia, fell upon his right flank. This latter movement proved a complete surprise, was entirely successful and resulted in a Turkish retreat, hurried somewhat at first, but soon covered by an efficient and properly worked rear guard, which caused the pursuit to be a slow one, though quite continuous. On the 12th the Buffs reached the junction of the Nahr Khalis, with the Nahr Tahwila, where they bivouacked with B Company, and the Dogras in front on picquet. The next day the cavalry tried a turning movement, with a view to reaching the Kifri road at a point behind the retreating army, but lack of water caused this adventure to fail. The Buffs, leaving B Company and the Dogras behind, continued the advance with the 13th Brigade R.F.A. and took up, in conjunction with the 102nd Grenadiers, a fresh picquet line for the night. The regiment lost two men killed and nineteen wounded on this date. On the 14th this new picquet line was sniped all day by a few men supported by a rear guard with machine guns, and Captain Dolamore of the Middlesex, who was attached to the Buffs, was killed, thirteen men being wounded. After marching forward a few miles on the 15th, it was determined to stop the pursuit, as it was not advisable to enter the hilly country of the Jebel Hamrin, where the defence would have great advantages; so the original idea of crossing the Shatt el Adhaim was resumed, those who had interfered with the scheme having been now driven away. So the marching of the next two days was in an opposite direction, and on the 18th at 4 a.m. the Buffs started, in support of the 38th Brigade, for the point where the smaller stream joined the Tigris, at which place a bridge was thrown and the crossing at once commenced. The Buffs got over about noon without opposition, proceeded to Deluiya and at dusk went out on picquet along the Nahrwan Canal. The Turkish opposition on the left bank of the Tigris had collapsed and many prisoners were taken. The following day all available lorries and ambulances spread away over the country behind the cavalry, with a view to collecting booty, but this enterprise was of no avail at all: the local Arab had seen to all that business. The enemy still had some fight left in him on the other side of the great river, however, and on the 20th April the Buffs marched up the left bank as escort to the R.F.A. The next day the Turks stood to fight on the other side of the water, and, their aeroplane having been destroyed, they were unaware of anything likely to interfere with their plans on the bank opposite to them; but our guns enfiladed their position with very marked success and, after this participation in the action, the troops marched back seven miles to Deluiya. Of course, the main avenue of communication between the army of Mesopotamia and the base had always been the river, and the spot up to which the boats could come with safety was constantly being changed as the armies advanced up stream. This river-head, as it was called, was the advanced depot for supplies, and when troops wandered far from river-head they were badly fed. Consequently, the 22nd April was a red-letter day because a better and fuller supply of rations was issued, as the boats now came up to Samjali, where a bridge over the Tigris had been made on the 19th.

While operations had been going on on the right bank of the main river it became clear that the other Turkish corps was again issuing from the Jebel Hamrin, this time down the Shatt el Adhaim, and that it was advancing against our troops on the left bank. On the 23rd his leading units had reached Dahuba with the remainder seventeen miles in rear, and it was determined to endeavour to crush this leading force before it could be reinforced, so a night march and attack at dawn was arranged. The enemy's position ran north-west from the Shatt el Adhaim, and his right flank was bent back in a northerly direction in front of Dahuba. Specially detailed parties of a hundred Buffs and a hundred Dogras, under Captain Jones of the latter regiment, proceeded in motor-cars to surprise and attack the Turks' extreme right at 6 a.m., but our guns had already so cleverly made use of the surprise element, and with such great effect, that the position had already been abandoned. The Buffs took up a picquet line, but, being relieved by the 102nd Grenadiers, they marched back to bivouac on the river. The next day the pursuit commenced. The enemy was retiring up both banks of the Shatt el Adhaim, and the British force followed for three sultry days, reaching Satha on the evening of the 27th. Here the Turk was close to his Jebel Hamrin, from which hilly region he had so recently issued, and here, amongst the foothills, he elected to stand while a strong rear guard covered the withdrawal to his selected position. Opposite to this the Buffs bivouacked for the night, being in reserve to the rest of Thomson's force, which was holding a portion of our picquet line, about two miles separating our main line from that of the enemy. Reconnaissance was rendered almost impossible by reason of the heat and low visibility, besides during the night there came on one of those dreadful dust-storms so common in these regions, and this one lasted for about forty-eight hours. The last day of the month saw a very successful attack made on the position, in spite of the dust-storm, which, however, greatly assisted the enemy to secure his line of retreat after he had been defeated. During this fight the Buffs were in reserve; the 35th Brigade, however, bore their full share of the victory, which resulted in the capture of numerous prisoners and trophies. In describing the events recorded above, Sir Stanley Maude in his official despatches uses the following words: " During this period of hard marching and heavy fighting the Buffs specially distinguished themselves on several occasions." On the 1st May our aeroplanes reported the enemy seven miles away in full retreat.

Sir Stanley Maude now determined that a redistribution of the troops for the hot weather was a necessity, and as the resistance of the enemy was thoroughly broken the chief matter to consider now was the well-being of our men during the trying portion of the year which was before them. On the 5th May the Buffs marched to Satha, thence on to Dahuba, and on the 10th crossed the pontoon bridge over the Adhaim, escorting transport and guns. A certain amount of time was spent at Bakuba and more at Abu Kamed, on Diala river. At the latter place the battalion remained all the early summer and was employed chiefly in digging and wiring. Hot weather in the plains of India, with all the appliances and inventions of long experience to mitigate the discomforts of existence, is trying enough, but month after month of lassitude and exhaustion caused by summer in a burning country without any such mitigation is a terrible trial to the strongest; the experience was just one that had to be lived through, and that is all about it.

Early in August a little break came, bringing with it, at any rate, a change of scene: our aeroplanes reported that the Turks were entrenching a position south-west of Shahroban, and it was determined to occupy that place at once. Therefore on the 13th August the Buffs with the remainder of their brigade crossed the Diala river to Bakuba, and then moved towards the north-east and on the 19th reached Misdad from Abu Jisra without opposition. The next day the brigade moved out at 4.30 a.m. to march on Shahroban with orders to skirt the town, the Buffs to go round the south side and the Dogras the north. The great objective was a certain nullah, and this was occupied without opposition at 6.35 a.m. Then another period of monotony set in and until the 18th October the battalion was at Shahroban in Mesopotamia, and that was all its history.

The Jebel Hamrin, though not a lofty range of mountains, is a very broken set of hills, and it is from this region that the waters which feed the canals is obtained. So long as the Turks remained in possession of these hills, so long had they control of the canals. Early in October, therefore, it was decided to take over this Jebel Hamrin, but first to clear the left bank of the Diala from the enemy. This was done by attacking a position he held near Deli Abbas, on which occasion all objectives were gained, and the British were enabled to take up a line astride of the Diala river where it issues from the gorge of the Jebel, and so gain control of the head waters of the canals. In connection with these operations the Buffs, who had a series of canals on their front, began their work on the 18th October by sending A Company out to seize two bridges—Lieut. Bonner's platoon to attack, while that under Sgt. Turnbull occupied a mound close by. Certain opposition was encountered, but we held the bridges by 10 a.m., at which hour no enemy was in sight. Two Buffs were killed and one wounded. During the evening B Company advanced and took up a picquet line along the Haruniyah Canal without opposition, C Company took over the mounds and D was in reserve three hundred yards to the south-west. The next day picquets were pushed out early and occupied the line of the Ruz Canal. Meanwhile Egerton's force had secured the Jebel Hamrin, and at 3 p.m. the battalion was ordered through the hills. The next day Kizil Robat was occupied by cavalry and the Norfolk Regiment. The Buffs had four men wounded while digging, the working party being shelled by a camel gun from across the Diala. On the 30th October the battalion, with many others, was issued with winter clothing and settled down to road-making in the Jebel, for the General Commanding-in-Chief had decreed that all the communications in this district were to be made good, the canals bridged in many places and the wild hills penetrated everywhere by roads fit for wheeled traffic. The enemy tried a counter-demonstration on the other side of the Tigris, and what was still a war rolled away to the westward of the troops in which we are interested.

On the 19th November the army received the sad news of the death by cholera of their Commander-in-Chief, Sir Stanley Maude—a soldier much beloved and highly respected by officers and men. He had won the war in Mesopotamia, and all had gone well there from the moment of his taking over. He was the son of General Sir F. F. Maude, V.C., G.C.B., the first commanding officer of the 2nd Battalion The Buffs, which unit was added to the regiment in 1857.

Towards the end of November the enemy had retired so far both up the Tigris and the Euphrates that Sir W. R. Marshall, who had succeeded Maude, considered that the only way to strike him was to attack that portion of his forces which were holding certain passes in the Jebel Hamrin and Kara Tepe. There is a stream called the Nahrin which, flowing from the north, joins the Diala to the east of the Jebel, and the Turks had flooded the low land east of the junction of the two streams, so creating a considerable obstacle in connection with any attack from the southward on Kara Tepe. At midnight on the 2nd/3rd December the brigade held the left bank of the Diala from Tawila to Sawaya, with the Buffs in the centre, and the orders were to engage the enemy's picquets on the far bank at dawn, while the 37th Brigade attacked due west from the north of Kizil Robat, but the scheme was found

301

unworkable in its entirety, simply because the 35th Brigade had no means of crossing. The fords had disappeared and it was two o'clock in the afternoon before the Buffs got over, after which the brigade concentrated again and bivouacked for the night. During the day the enemy was reported to be retiring on Kara Tepe, having been driven from the Jebel passes by the 13th Division. On the 4th December the advance on Kara Tepe continued, the 35th Brigade halting about five miles short of it. The Buffs were the brigade advance guard during this day. It was a trying march, for two reasons: water was very scarce—and it is an undoubted hardship to have to work and march, even in December, without an adequate supply of water, and also the progress was terribly slow because the ground was intercepted by nullahs, many of which had to be filled in and prepared for crossing. At daybreak on the 5th the march was continued and, after moving about four miles, water was found in some small nullahs. Here the brigade deployed for attack, the 37th Dogras leading, with the 2/4th Ghurkas in support, the Buffs soon coming up in echelon on the right of the Ghurkas. The attack of the brigade was materially assisted by a flank advance by the 40th (British) Brigade and the whole work proved extremely easy, the previous marching being the worst feature of the operation. The whole position was taken and the enemy soon in full retreat on Kifri. The pursuit was not pushed far, and the Buffs, after passing through a dust storm on its way to Kizil Robat on the 7th, and after a long and dusty march the next day, found themselves back in their old camping ground north of Shahroban.

January, 1918, proved a very wet month, but work of all sorts was carried on during the early part of the year, and this work included extensive gardening and farming operations. There is but little to record for the year 1918; as far as the 5th Battalion is concerned, their enemy was broken, but the final surrender was not till the end of October, and in the meantime the men remained for the most part in the same camp and worked at gardening and also at a new railway which was in progress. The news of a few honours was received during the hot weather. On the 21st May Pte. A. W. King was mentioned in despatches; as were Captain W. A. Harrison, attached from the 4th Battalion, and Lieut. Weldon on the 11th June. R.Q.M.S. Middleditch, C.Q.M.S. Woodruff and Pte. Friend all got the Meritorious Service Medal in August.

The news of the armistice with Turkey was received on the 1st November, 1918, and of the armistice with Germany on the 11th. There is nothing to show that the story about the latter news being received by the men in silence, and that later on wild cheering was heard but ascertained to be only because a belated consignment of ration rum had at last turned up, relates to the 5th Battalion of the Buffs. As after every war, when peace or its equivalent is proclaimed, the exiled soldier's thoughts immediately and naturally turn to home; of course they do. However that may be, orders came that the Buffs were to be one of the regiments to remain in Mesopotamia for another hot season.

The cadre of the battalion, a very tiny remnant of those who embarked in 1914, reached home in January, 1920, under command of Lt.-Colonel J. Body, D.S.O., O.B.E. This battalion was therefore actually a few days longer abroad than the 4th. Casualties during the war were 12 officers and 118 other ranks killed; 26 officers and 533 other ranks wounded. Honours: two D.S.O.'s, one bar to D.S.O., one Albert Medal, two O.B.E.'s, one M.B.E., six M.C.'s, sixteen D.C.M.'s, one M.M., eight M.S.M.'s, five foreign decorations and fifty-two mentions in despatches.

III. 2ND BATTALION

New Year's Day, 1917, found the 2nd Battalion at Barakli Dzuma, on the eastern side of the River Struma, on the flat ground and under the hills which were occupied by the Bulgarian troops. A more or less quiet time ensued after the raid on " Little Ferdy " trench previously described, though the Buffs made a demonstration on the 8th January in aid of the Middlesex, which regiment carried out on that day a somewhat similar attempt on two trenches on their front. There was, too, at this time a good deal of patrol work done, mostly in the direction of the railway. On the 23rd the battalion, changing places with the 3rd Royal Fusiliers, moved to Ormanli, and a few days later to Lozista, where it remained working very regularly all February. News had arrived on the 9th January of a D.S.O. for Captain Sebastian, and D.C.M.'s for L.-Sgt. Spiller and L.-Corpl. Geohegan. Some little excitement about this time was caused by a rumour that numerous Turks were slipping through our lines and sailing over the lake to join the Bulgarians, but, in spite of several efforts, none were ever caught.

There came a distinct change of scene early in June, and the chief incidents immediately before that date were as follows: on the 4th March the Bulgarians tried to burn the village of Butkova; on the 13th C.S.M. Andrews was awarded the (Italian) Bronze Medal for Military Valour; on the 17th there was heavy shelling on the right of the battalion and the Bulgarians made a demonstration, their infantry advancing to within six hundred yards of our trenches, but we suffered no casualties; and on the 19th the battalion moved to Haznatar, B and C Companies going on three days later to Ormanli to find the guard on Koprivi Bridge. L.-Corpl. Arnold, of D Company, died on the 24th of wounds received when out patrolling. On the 28th and 29th

Haznatar was flooded owing to the rising of the river. From the 4th to 14th April the Buffs were at Orljak and then returned to Haznatar. There was always a good deal of patrolling work to be done at this latter place, which was in the advanced British lines, so that casualties from the enemy's shell fire were not altogether infrequent. For instance, five occurred on the 21st April, one of the men dying of his wounds. On the 2nd May Captain Vertue had a narrow escape and indeed owed his life or his liberty to C.S.M. Andrews. The captain and the sergeant-major were out together, and seeing a Bulgar they fired on him. A minute or two later several of the enemy appeared and then returned the fire; Vertue was wounded, but Andrews immediately picked him up and carried him back. 2nd Lieut. Goodheart was wounded on the 12th.

In the middle of May a minor action was arranged and carried out by the Buffs and 3rd Royal Fusiliers. The latter were on the Buffs' right and opposite the " Ferdy " group of enemy trenches. During the afternoon of the 15th troops began to get into assembly positions and were ready at 6 p.m. Half an hour later our artillery opened and C and D Companies deployed and advanced, each with one platoon in front extended to five paces; another fifty yards in rear, and the remaining two a hundred yards behind again. These went through the enemy's line and took what was known as the " Essex " group of trenches, while the Royal Fusiliers on the right took the " Ferdy " group. The Buffs' casualty list was but six wounded, and several thousand rounds of ammunition and some rifles were found in the captured trenches. Patrols were immediately sent out to front and flanks and the place consolidated, in case of counter-attack, which was, in fact, attempted but without result. On the 27th May the brigade was relieved by the 84th and marched to Orljak.

During the month of May, as has been seen, the

x

casualty list from the action of the enemy was a very small one, but this flat valley of the Struma appears to have been a very unhealthy and malarious place in the summer time and not fitted for even the temporary home of Englishmen. During the month ninety-three Buffs were admitted to hospital, and 63 per cent of the cases were diagnosed as malaria. What was worse, during the following month, though the regiment left the valley, it took the malarial germs with it in the men's blood, and no less than 240 were admitted to hospital. On the 7th June the battalion left Orljak and marched away, making for the healthy hills. The final object was Paprat, which was reached on the 29th June by a circuitous route, and after a stay of ten days at a place called Vaisili. Here the battalion remained for the whole of the month of July, the men's health wonderfully improving by the change.

August took the battalion into what was to them an entirely new region. The Allied Army covered Salonica by means of a line north of the town, and roughly some forty miles away from it, the right of this line being thrown back about Butkova, Barakli Dzuma and the River Struma. Up to now this flank had been the scene of the Buffs' adventures and activities, but August was to be spent in the main part of the line and in the vicinity of Lake Doiran. A deep valley or pass runs up a gentle slope from Lake Doiran towards the east to Dova Tepe, and thence downward again to Butkova lake and the vale of the Struma. On either side of this pass are lofty ranges of mountains. That on the south was in our hands and is the same range on which Paprat stands. The mountains to the north were occupied by the enemy. The railway, which passes over the flat land on the eastern side of the Struma, crosses that stream above Demirhissar, makes a sharp turn westward and penetrates the valley in question, going on to Doiran. The British line was just south of this railway and on

306

the foothills of the southern range of hills which are called the Krusha Balkans. The positions taken up by the companies were as follows: D Company was on Hairy Hill, B Company on Lucky Hill, C on Bermondsey Ridge, with A Company in reserve on a small spur behind it. The enemy at this part of the line was at some distance away, but he had posts of varying strength in all the villages north of the railway line. The first work undertaken was the strengthening of all our defences, which, with the making of the Buffs' redoubt, was no light labour on account of the hard and rocky ground. A great deal of reconnaissance was also undertaken mostly in the direction of Chalki or Cakli Station and village. There is a great deal of wood, shrub and vegetation about this portion of the country, which rendered patrolling a matter of some difficulty and danger.

However, on the 25th August a raiding expedition was carried out by C Company, under Captain Sebastian, having D Company in support; the plan being that the first-named was to be just south of the Cakli railway station by 3.30 and that two Lewis guns were to be on Lonely Hill. The raiders were then to rush the station, turn south-west and clear Cakli village, push on to Erdzili and Karlu Ovacu and ultimately to withdraw as soon as the villages were clear, covered by a rear guard. A party of the enemy was seen by 2nd Lieut. W. G. Neve's platoon when close to the railway line and fire was opened through the dense scrub, the Bulgars at once retiring. Seeing this retreat, Neve at once dashed on ahead of his men and reached the railway embankment, where he was shot in the head; he died on reaching the aid post. Our scouts now discovered that the enemy had retired to a trench four hundred yards north-north-west of the station, but from there he continued his retreat up a nullah to Garbali, so the trench was occupied by our people, and from there

307

C Company turned left for Cakli village; but two platoons had to be left behind at the station while
Sebastian advanced, having scouts out on his right flank,
that is to the north of him. However, he entered the
village unopposed. Here, finding that one platoon
would not suffice to guard it even temporarily, he put
two in position and asked for more men, with the result
that Lieut. Marden came up from the reserve with half
the company, one platoon going to the village and the
other to the station. After scouts had been out to reconnoitre north of Stevens Wood, Sebastian went on
and entered the two villages of Erdzeli and Karlu
Ovacu and, after reporting his success, got orders to
withdraw. Before these orders came to hand, however,
2nd Lieut. Manning with one platoon had been sent to
take up a position north and north-west of the villages,
and he was told to find 2nd Lieut. Renton, who was in
charge of the scouts. This was the commencement of a
hunt for the scouts in the dense bush. The order to
withdraw had come through, but the scattered men
could not be found, though Sebastian sent patrol after
patrol in search. This, of course, had the effect of
greatly delaying the withdrawal, but Renton and his
men were found at last and all was well and a lesson in
bush warfare learnt.

The battalion was relieved from this part of the
country on the 27th and for a good many days was on
the march again, mostly on the high ground till Turbes
was reached; here work was commenced on the main-
line defences on the right bank of the Struma about
Orljak bridge. The battalion remained at Turbes till
the 14th October. Towards the end of August Lt.-
Colonel Thewles, D.S.O., Captain Vertue, M.C., Lieut.
Beswick and L.-Corpl. Boswell were mentioned in despatches.

In the middle of October a move was made to
Nevolyen and a winter scheme of work and arrange-

308

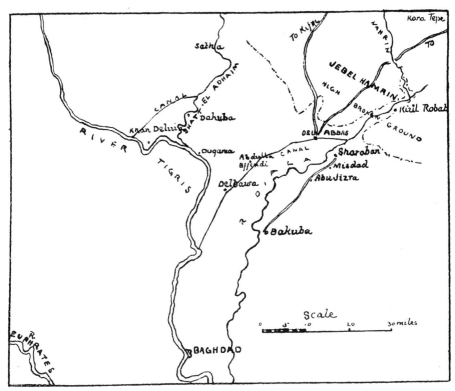

COUNTRY NORTH OF BAGHDAD

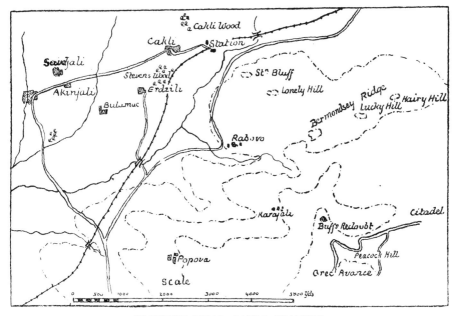

COUNTRY NEAR CAKLI STATION

ments commenced. The orders were to hold a line on the left bank from Nevolyen to Jenikoj, so on the 13th two platoons of C Company proceeded to the former to clear the village and hold it, while a similar party of the 3rd Royal Fusiliers occupied Jenikoj and some of another brigade Cuculuk. No opposition was encountered.

About this time there was established what was called an enterprise company: that is, one at a time, the companies were struck off all digging and other work, of which there was a good deal, and was kept apart solely for patrolling and minor enterprises. On the 25th October C Company, which had the first turn of this work, sent two patrols to Papalova to look out upon the enemy. About 7.15 a.m. some fifty Bulgars approached from Prosenik, but these were driven off.

The battalion remained at Nevolyen till the 14th November, and those few days were remarkable only for certain actions of minor enterprise and for scouting. For instance, on the 27th October Lieut. Renton, who was in charge of the scouts, found signs of the enemy about Prosenik and fired on one or two of them. Two days later about fifty Bulgar cavalry and thirty infantry were seen to enter Prosenik by our scouts who were well handled by Sgt. Rand but eventually had to withdraw, losing one killed, one wounded and one missing. On the last day of the month Captain Vertue took C Company out at 3 a.m. to take position round Papalova and lie in wait for hostile scouts. About 6.15 a.m. some thirty infantry with a few horsemen appeared and opened rapid but wild fire. They advanced a little and the company hoped they were coming right on, but they halted; our platoon, which had observed them, immediately opened fire with rifle, Lewis gun and grenade. Other parties, each about the same strength, appeared opposite our other platoons and similarly fired wildly, but all shortly withdrew and soon afterwards

309

the enemy opened a small barrage between Papalova and Prosenik which apparently caught their own people, for shouting was heard and men were seen to fall. At 9.45 the company was ordered to withdraw and in doing so was heavily shelled, 2nd Lieut. Young and one man being wounded.

The 14th November took the Buffs back to billets at Orljak, where labour and training took place on alternate days for some time. On the 14th January, 1918, the regiment relieved the 3rd Middlesex in what was known as the West Line and occupied six redoubts there, on the improvement of which a good deal of labour was expended and which was the battalion home till the middle of February, when A, B and C Companies retired to Orljak on relief, and D Company, under Lieut. Bremner, became enterprise company in lieu of one of the East Surrey Regiment. This company soon got busy laying ambushes and so on and, as usual, watching Prosenik and, for a change, Kalandra as well; but on the 5th March it got rather into trouble attempting a more extensive raid with the aid of B Company and one platoon of A. Bremner left Nevolyen at 8.30 p.m. and, moving by Kalandra and dropping B Company as supports upon the way, arrived within one hundred yards of the Bulgar trenches, when a heavy fire was suddenly opened with rifle and bomb. Lieut. Asprey with four or five men got up to the wire round one of the posts and were engaged in cutting it when a bomb fell amongst them, wounding them all but one. Finding that the posts were strongly wired and the enemy alert, and being hampered by the darkness, Bremner withdrew, having Lieut. Asprey and six men wounded. The next day B Company relieved D as raiding company.

On the 27th March the Buffs moved away again, but an incident which occurred on the 13th to the enterprise company is worthy of record. Two platoons, under Captain Howgrave-Graham and Lieut. Wilson, lay up as day ambushes in the vicinity of Prosenik, and they were visited by small parties of the enemy at 9 o'clock and again at 3.30. Every effort was made to capture some of these. Wilson with five or six of his men made a sortie for the purpose, and one of the party was hit by a Bulgar who had ensconced himself in a cunning spot from which he could enfilade Wilson's communication trench. Two stretcher-bearers went out to fetch in the wounded man, but the wily Bulgarian hit them both. This seems to have annoyed L.-Corpl. Wykes, who went out to see about matters. Of course, he too was fired on, but he managed to kill the troublesome fellow, and then, picking up the wounded Corpl. Stanley, carried him away. The enemy seeing this, opened heavy fire, but Wykes was one of those men who like to carry through any job they may undertake, so he staggered along with his comrade for a thousand yards till he reached the support sections, the shells screaming and bursting around him the whole time. Wilson, being now heavily shelled, withdrew. He was wounded in doing so, but gamely stuck to his job of commanding his men. Captain Howgrave-Graham, noticing Wilson's withdrawal, conformed and the whole party returned to Nevolyen; the supporting platoon, however, remained at Papalova till evening. The advanced platoons had, besides Wilson, seven men wounded and Pte. Harrold, one of the stretcher-bearers, killed. L.-Corpl. Wykes was given the M.M. for his gallantry and Wilson got the M.C.

The move alluded to above was ultimately to the same neighbourhood as before, near Lake Doiran, headquarters being at a place called Grec Avance, but the march took ten days, round by Mirova, Kirkul and Alexia, and on arrival the old work of patrolling toward Cakli and its neighbourhood was undertaken anew. The men were in a number of posts, wired all round, but on the 1st June they were withdrawn a little to a second line in rear, the wire of the old position being demolished and the works destroyed. The enemy at this period were observed to be mostly about the village of Akinjali, near Lake Doiran. A great number of the Bulgarians were deserting about this time to our lines. No masses of them came over, but there was a pretty constant dribble. The old line was reoccupied and the works repaired in August.

The Greek King Constantine having been deposed, the people, under his son Alexander, had by this time definitely thrown in their lot with the allies and their armies had now been in the field against the Bulgarians since the beginning of March. The enemy was obviously losing heart, as the desertions proved. Victory was crowning the allied arms at last on the Western front, and a grand general offensive in the neighbourhood of Salonica was consequently planned to commence in the middle of September. The part allotted to the British contingent was the attack and capture of the heights to the west and to the north-east of Lake Doiran, and in this it was to be assisted by two divisions and other troops of the Greek army.

On the morning of the 15th September the English General, Sir George Milne, got orders from the French General-in-Chief of the allies that the troops were to take the offensive on the morning of the 18th. On that date the Greeks attacked and pierced the Akinjali outpost line while the British conformed; with the result that the Buffs took up position along the railway line on their front, remaining there all day, but concentrating at 10 p.m. ready for a move. The next day orders came to take up a line from Akinjali Wood to Lake Doiran, to cover the retirement of the Greeks and to dig trenches and erect barbed-wire defences. In this way four days passed, hostile cavalry being seen in Akinjali on the evening of the 21st. Our line was along the

Koja Suju and at Brest. On the 23rd the regiment, being relieved, marched to Surlovo and in the evening to Doiran town. On the 25th the battalion moved to Obasi, but owing to the great congestion of the roads only reached that place at 8.30 p.m. The next two or three days were spent in more or less strenuous marching, and on the 26th the advance guard was held up by machine guns, but these were silenced and the march resumed. On the 28th the Buffs were back at Obasi and, on account of the paucity of their numbers, had to be reorganized into two companies each of two platoons. There had been recently an epidemic of what was called Spanish influenza, and both the Buffs and the Middlesex Regiment had suffered considerably.

On the 30th September at high noon hostilities ceased with Bulgaria, and four days later Sir George Milne's order of the day read as follows:—

" Thanks to your gallantry, determination and devo-
" tion to duty the Bulgarian army is now defeated and
" the Bulgarian nation has sued for peace. This result
" has been obtained only by your extraordinary exer-
" tions after three summers spent in a malarious coun-
" try and against obstacles of great natural and arti-
" ficial strength.

" What appeared almost impossible has been accom-
" plished. I gratefully thank you all, of every arm and
" of every rank, for your steadfast loyalty, your perfect
" discipline and for the magnificent manner you have
" answered to every call made on you. No one knows
" better the odds against which you have had to con-
" tend, and I am proud to have had the honour of
" commanding you."

Thus the war history of the 2nd Battalion of the Buffs concludes.

The unit was not kept long in the neighbourhood of Salonica: after a stay of a few days at Organdzili, doing salvage work, it moved by stages down to Summerhill, which was reached on the 5th November, for re-equipment prior to leaving the country. On the 11th it marched through Salonica to the quay, where it embarked on the s.s. *Katoomba* for Constantinople. At 10 o'clock on that date, Salonica time being, of course, in advance of Greenwich, a telegram came from the brigade that an armistice with Germany had been declared, so the journey on the *Katoomba* was a joyous one. On the 14th Constantinople was reached and anchor dropped at Stamboul. Next day the men disembarked and were conveyed by ferry boats to Bryukdere, where they went into billets and there remained for some little time. On the 28th November the battalion, 13 officers and 286 men strong, was inspected by Sir George Milne.

CHAPTER XIV

HOLDING ON

I. Preparations

IT has been noticed that the great German offensive had been foreseen by our commanders long before the storm actually broke. The transfer of German divisions from their Eastern to their Western front began as early as November, 1917, and it was known that the Russian guns and munitions were at our enemy's disposal. In fact, it became a question of the French and English holding their own till the Americans could make their weight felt, and thus the war was for the present to be a defensive one and all preparations were made to this end. The defensive area or belt was divided into the forward, the battle and the rear zones, and each of these was carefully chosen; but there was a tremendous amount of work to be done in the way of preparing the ground to be defended, as well as the construction of roads, railway lines and so on. The men, too, required much training in defensive tactics. The whole military art is not taught in a few months, nor is a man an educated soldier when he can take his part in a route march or a field day. Most training had to be imparted during intervals of fighting, and until now the chief subject of study had been the preparation for the offensive.

Very early in 1918 the British had taken over from the French another considerable extension of front, one, in fact, of over twenty-eight miles, and this brought our line down to the River Oise and gave no less than 125 miles of country to our care. At the same time the indications of an imminent attack became

315

more marked than ever, particularly in front of the
3rd and 5th Armies. Now at this time the 1st Battalion the Buffs was with the former of these and the
7th Battalion with the latter. The enemy's immediate
objective would seem to have been to separate the
French and English armies, which joined where the 7th
Battalion was, and to capture Amiens, a very important
centre of communications.

The 3rd Army was under General the Hon. J. H. G.
Byng, K.C.B., and held a front of twenty-seven miles
with four Corps; and the 5th Army, under General
Sir H. de la P. Gough, K.C.B., occupied forty-two
miles, also with four Corps. The weakest part of our
line perhaps was that portion so recently taken over
from the French, where the defences were not quite so
good as elsewhere.

Sir Douglas Haig reckoned that sixty-four German
divisions took part in the operations on the first day of
the battle; " the majority of these divisions had spent
many weeks and even months in concentrated training
for offensive operations and had reached a high pitch of
technical excellence in the attack." To meet the
enemy's assault the 3rd Army had eight divisions in
line with seven in reserve. The 5th had eleven divisions
in line with six divisions (three being cavalry divisions)
in reserve. Later on, when it was found the enemy was
using his whole strength in the battle, Haig was able to
bring eight more divisions from north to south, and by
the end of March the supreme German effort was
broken. This, however, did not result until after a
terrible period of danger had been passed through.

On the 21st March the attack opened after a short
but very violent bombardment and, owing to dense
fog, the Germans were able to penetrate the British
front and force the 5th Army to retreat precipitately.
On the 25th of the month the enemy reached Albert,
and this day was perhaps one of the most important in

history because Marshal Foch, by agreement between the Allies, was appointed to the supreme command of the armies of the West; and from that time onward final victory was secure, whatever troubles might intervene. On the 27th March the Germans took Montdidier.

To meet the crisis all the available reserves, totalling 350,000 men, were hurried to France from England, Palestine and the East, and this brought the 10th Battalion The Buffs on the scene. The despatch of American troops was greatly accelerated, so that between 200,000 and 300,000 men a month were embarked for France. The Germans were stopped before they could reach Amiens by the united efforts of English, French and American troops, yet another offensive south of Ypres developed on the 9th April which was only really stayed three weeks later. During these offensives the German casualties were enormous, but so were ours; and our loss in guns, aerodromes, ammunition, machine guns, trench mortars, tanks and rolling stock was stupendous.

It will be convenient now to trace the history of the 1st, 6th, 10th and 7th Battalions of the Buffs one by one from the 21st March till the 8th August, the date usually ascribed to the commencement of the Allies' great counter-offensive, which, once started, was maintained without intermission till the end of the war. It may be as well to take the 7th Battalion last, for it was heavily engaged on the 6th August, and the 8th of the month found it practically in the midst of a great battle.

II.   1st BATTALION

The 6th Division, in the middle of March, held the ground opposite the villages of Queant and Pronville. The country consists of alternate long spurs and narrow valleys of down-like country, stretching from the high

317

land on the west of our forces down to the valley in which Cambrai stands, and our position was at right angles to or astride these spurs and re-entrants. There were trenches in a state of readiness, but the entire scheme of fortification had not been completed, chiefly owing to a month's hard frost in January. Still, the front and reserve trenches were in good order, and there was an excellent Corps trench called the Vaulx–Morchies line, a little over a mile in rear of the reserve system. There were, however, hardly any support trenches and no dug-outs. The 16th Brigade was on the left of the division. The distance from the front or outpost zone to the battle line was about two thousand yards on the day of the battle, the York and Lancaster, on the right, and the King's Shropshire Light Infantry, on the left, were in front line, and it happened to be the turn of the Buffs to be in reserve, where the men were hard at work as usual.

At 2 a.m. on the 21st the latter got the order to take up their battle positions and to be in the Vaulx–Morchies work by 5.30 o'clock, so off the battalion marched, leaving no one behind at Favreuil except the company quartermaster-sergeants and spare drummers and bandsmen, who were detailed as extra runners and stretcher-bearers. While still on the march, at 5 a.m., the battle opened by a tremendous bombardment directed on the front system and Lagnicourt trench, and also on the village of Vaulx. The Buffs were, of course, in ignorance of what was occurring on their front, but they recognized from the continuous and tremendous roar that the bombardment was terribly severe, and themselves suffered casualties. Indeed, the operation of getting into place was attended with great difficulty, as it was dark and gas masks had to be worn on the march. By 5.45 all the forward wires were cut and there was no more telephonic communication. Gas shells were intermingled with the others, and as the

Buffs approached the scene they found it more and more difficult to get into position, particularly as it was still dark. However, by 6 o'clock D Company had got to its place on the Noreuil–Morchies road, A Company to posts 21 to 24 in the Vaulx–Morchies lines, B Company to Macauley Avenue, while C, the reserve company, filled gaps between post 22 (battalion headquarters) and the Vaulx–Lagnicourt road. All kits, drums, documents and such-like possessions had been left behind in camp, and subsequent efforts to regain possession of these were almost entirely unavailing.

A most anxious and depressing morning followed the battalion's arrival in position. Casualties were mounting up from distant shelling: Lieut. P. W. Newington and six men were killed by a shell which struck battalion headquarters, but no definite news was received till 10 o'clock. Then the enemy was seen slowly but steadily advancing under a creeping barrage: now they were moving up the Lagnicourt valley upon the village; then news came that they had broken through the right of the 71st Brigade and were approaching " Skipton Reserve "; again they were in the villages of Noreuil and Lagnicourt; and soon it became plain that the forward part of the battle zone was in the hands of the Germans. Moreover, it was equally certain that the troops of the 6th Division that had defended it had all been killed or captured, for none returned.

The Buffs, to avoid casualties, had moved into the Vraucourt Switch (as it was called), about post 7, and had been joined by D Company, who having got no call from the battalion it was out to support, and being quite exposed, withdrew when the position seemed hopeless. Two platoons of B Company were sent up, however, to the aid of the K.S.L.I., and these were absorbed into the general ruin of the forward troops. They were under the command of Lieut. T. L. V. Moody and 2nd Lieut. Wotton, and they never rejoined. A wounded man stated that he had seen Buffs in " Leeds Reserve," and that a strong point there was still holding out. Colonel Smith, who commanded the K.S.L.I. and two platoons of the Buffs, showed the greatest gallantry and fought his battalion to the last: not one of his officers who were in the front line ever came back. Later on it was ascertained that Moody had been killed trying to lead a break-through instead of surrendering. With reference to this day's work in the forward positions, Sir Douglas Haig writes: " The prolonged defence of these different localities, under conditions which left little hope of any relief, deserve to rank among the most heroic actions in the history of the British Army."

At noon a message came from the brigadier that the enemy was in force east of Lagnicourt. In fact, he was advancing up both valleys and endeavouring to cut off those troops which were still holding the battle zone. The message directed the reserve company (C) to move to the Vaulx–Morchies line to garrison that part near the Bois de Vaulx. The move was successfully accomplished, and C Company's place was taken by the York and Lancaster headquarters, which had withdrawn, by machine gunners, sappers and a mixed lot of men from various parts of the field. C Company patrolled to its right, but failed to find any friendly troops on its flank. There now came a lull, and it was not till later that the enemy's advance recommenced. The orders from the brigadier were plain and simple: the flanks were to be watched and every foot of ground was to be disputed. From now onward the position, as far as the Buffs were concerned, became obscure, but the enemy, working up the valleys, was gradually outflanking position after position, causing the defenders to form defensive flanks whenever any line became threatened. Thus the reserve company of the K.S.L.I., leaving Lagnicourt trench, manned Macauley Avenue, and later in the day a message came from Lieut. Collison-Morley, of the Buffs, that the enemy was getting round his No. 24 post, and a defensive flank was formed there. However, the Germans got into the main trench at No. 24 post and for about five hundred yards to the north of it. It appeared later that the little garrison of No. 24 was safe, having withdrawn to a position in some shell holes across the valley, and having got touch of a battalion of Scots Fusiliers on their left. An attempt to eject the enemy from the Vaulx–Morchies line was made by Lieut. Spence, but he was wounded in the foot while reconnoitring. A counter-attack was, however, organized by 2nd Lieut. Rogers of the K.S.L.I., who, with thirty men belonging to the Brigade Grenade School, had come up as a reinforcement. Some progress down the trench was made, but it was found to be occupied for a long extent and so a block was established, for Rogers could get no further. Lieut. E. Foster Hall was holding the post on the extreme left and rendered distinguished service throughout.

Meanwhile there had been developments on our right. At 3.30 p.m. Captain Hamilton reported that the enemy was attacking him there and that he was not in touch with anybody on that flank; that he had a very mixed lot of men and no officers, and was short of ammunition. Now, this particular advance by the enemy failed, notwithstanding very great courage displayed by the German troops. It could be seen from most parts of the field, and so came under fire at all sorts of ranges. Also a counter-attack, by a strong collection of British, got into and occupied the trench into which a few of the enemy had penetrated. There were no further determined attacks, and at dusk the fury of the struggle died away. The Buffs during the day, being in reserve, had suffered far less than the rest of the brigade and had been called upon to resist no frontal attack, though towards noon and afterwards their flanks

Y

had always been in danger from the steady hostile advance up both the L'Hirondelle and the Lagnicourt valleys.

At dusk rations, water, ball ammunition and bombs were sent up. The remnants of the York and Lancasters and the K.S.L.I., reinforced from the transport, were reorganized into one unit and were withdrawn and held in reserve, and at 9 p.m. the brigade front was readjusted. The remains of the Border Regiment, which had reinforced the 16th Brigade soon after noon, and a company of the Leicesters held from the right boundary of the Bois de Vaulx to the Lagnicourt–Vaulx road, and the Buffs from there to No. 24 post. The night passed quietly and during it touch was regained with the 71st Brigade on the right, but with no friends on the other flank because of the gap in our line which was held by the enemy. A fresh line of defence some one thousand yards in rear of the Vaulx-Morchies line had been hastily constructed by the engineers and partially manned by men from the Corps Reinforcement Camp, and the 40th Division had been pushed forward on the left of the 16th Brigade, but there was a large gap between it and the Buffs, so that the left flank of the regiment was still unsupported.

The morning of the 22nd was heralded by steady and violent hostile shelling, but no news reached the Buffs till about nine o'clock. It was evident, however, that the enemy were upon both flanks in force and therefore that these were in danger of being turned at any moment.[1] Defensive flanks were therefore arranged down the communication trench and the lower Noreuil road. At 10 a.m. the enemy attacked on the immediate

---

[1] This was the first practical illustration of the German method of infiltration which had lately been introduced and which now influences our own tactics. Blobs of Germans with light guns could be seen advancing wherever they could make progress—wherever they saw a " soft spot."

right of the Bois de Vaulx and broke through the front of the brigade on our right, so a defensive flank had to be made by swinging the right round to the road just outside the village of Vaulx to the eastward. A counter-attack made away off to the right gave some hope for a moment, but it was too far away to relieve the pressure on what was left of the 16th Brigade, and the enemy quickly reorganized and pushed forward resolutely and with great vigour to improve his advantage, causing the right of the new defensive flank to close in. At 2 p.m. a determined attack was made on the Vaulx line where it crossed the road to Lagnicourt, and a wedge was driven in between the Borderers and the Buffs. This caused the former regiment to withdraw, and now the Buffs were left with both their flanks exposed and resting on nothing. The old simple order was then given out again: " contest every foot of ground, conform as far as possible with the movement of other troops and only retire fighting." Hand-to-hand fighting resulted, in which Captain Hamilton greatly distinguished himself as a leader.

During the afternoon the regiment formed fresh defensive flanks, one near the place where the Lagnicourt road leaves Vaulx, and the other facing west across the spur, because the posts hitherto held in the valley had been driven in. These movements, as well as others, were immensely assisted by a machine-gun battalion which showed great pluck and ingenuity in selecting positions. The Buffs held on till 4.15, when the enemy launched a very heavy attack on Vraucourt and the ridge immediately north-east of Vaulx from the L'Hirondelle valley, and this was attended by low-flying aeroplanes which were very audacious. It was in and around Vraucourt that the Buffs concluded their two days' combat. A very lively battle ensued here; as the Germans advanced up the valley they were met with rapid fire and the fighting was ultimately at point-blank range. The men were heartened by knowing that they inflicted many casualties, but at last the Buffs, together with the rest of the brigade, were forced to commence a withdrawal. Other troops had all gone, and it became obvious to those on the spot that to remain longer merely meant to be surrounded by sheer numbers, so a general retirement to the new army line was ordered. This was successfully carried out, and the battalion was then reorganized and placed in support to the 41st Division, which was now holding the line. The enemy did not attempt any further advance at this time, though he directed a lively machine-gun fire on men of many units who were holding various shell holes which existed between the Vaulx–Morchies and the "Army" lines. At nightfall the 6th Division was withdrawn from the fighting area and, after marching to Favreuil, was embussed there for Achiet le Grand, where it arrived about 3 a.m. on the 23rd.

To sum up the Buffs' experience during the two momentous days, the 21st and 22nd March, the fighting for them meant a process of being continually outflanked, for that reason forming defensive flanks, and of their straightening out the line again in conformity with the movements of other troops whenever such straightening out became a possibility. These manœuvres were twice carried out at most critical moments, and on each occasion the enemy suffered severely while the battalion experienced but little loss. Great credit is due to the officers and men who rendered this possible by their coolness and quick grasp of each situation as it arose. The net result perhaps was that the battalion delayed the enemy on this front for many hours and withdrew from the fight with less than two hundred casualties, a large percentage of which were lost with Moody's party. It was the last unit to leave Vaulx, as it had been the last to leave the Morchies line, and it was never disorganized nor out of hand for a moment.

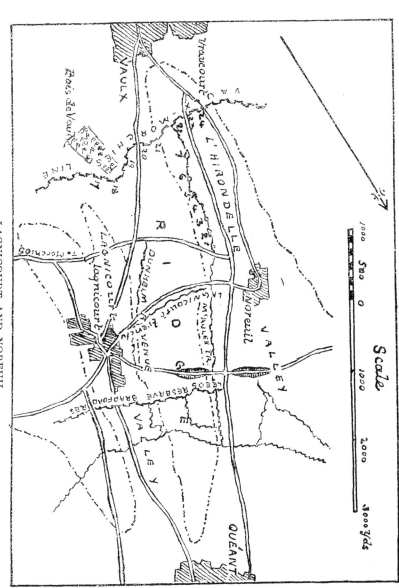

LAGNICOURT AND NOREUIL.

" Steady, the Buffs " is an expression often heard in the army and even outside it; it has been used in reference to this old battalion through the ages.

Casualty list:—Officers: killed, Lieuts. T. L. V. Moody and P. W. Newington; missing, 2nd Lieuts. Davison and Wotton; wounded, Lieuts. Buss and Spence and 2nd Lieut. Froome.

Other ranks: killed, 24; wounded, 112; wounded but remaining on duty, 2; died of wounds, 5; missing, 65, of whom 40 were with Moody; wounded and missing, 3; missing, believed killed, 1.

For his able handling of the battalion (in the absence of Lt.-Colonel Power, who had been called to Brigade H.Q.) on the 21st and 22nd March, Captain H. de R. Morgan was awarded the D.S.O.

The 23rd March was a fairly peaceful day, but in the morning the men had to get into position and the battalion to push forward patrols towards Courcelles because the enemy was vaguely reported to be within three miles of that place. Gun fire was heavy, but no enemy was discovered in the immediate vicinity. An attempt was made to recover kits, drums and band instruments from Favreuil, but the searchers were promptly turned back by the military police. Two sporting drummers, however, managed to slip through these guardians of law and order and they rescued the big drum and three side drums. On the 24th the 6th Division was transferred to the 2nd Army and at 2.30 p.m. the Buffs entrained for Doullens and next day for Rousbrugge in Belgium, where they arrived at six o'clock on the 26th and from whence they marched six kilometres to Crombeke, going into scattered billets near Watow (some five miles west of Poperinghe).

On the 28th of the month H.M. The King visited Steenvoorde, close by, and the commanding officer, Lt.-Colonel Power, Captain Hamilton and one N.C.O., who had done well in the recent fighting from each company, attended his parade there.

At the very end of the month the battalion moved into the trenches again at Zonnebeke. A second German offensive, which commenced south of Ypres on the 9th April, was referred to at the commencement of this chapter. The 1st Battalion of the Buffs was engaged in no severe fighting in connection with this phase of the war, though it naturally joined in the general gradual withdrawal which was rendered necessary. This withdrawal, as far as it concerned the battalion, commenced on the 15th April, when after a few days of the usual trench warfare, losing eight casualties, one of which was Lieut. S. W. Taylor killed, and receiving a couple of drafts amounting to 230 men, it moved to Westhoek and the neighbourhood, being, in fact, somewhat scattered about to man several posts which were occupied up till the 23rd. The posts were heavily shelled on the 17th, with the result that C.S.M. Field and eleven men were wounded. The situation at this time was that the second German offensive had developed south of Ypres and that Messines Ridge and Kemmel Hill had been taken from us, these two positions being of the greatest importance for the defence of Ypres. Consequently the troops all round this area were in a somewhat desperate position and, as Sir Douglas Haig expressed it, " with their backs to the wall." The gradual withdrawal of our forces west of Ypres into or immediately around the ruins themselves resulted; and so it came about that on the 23rd April the Buffs moved by detachments into the ramparts of Ypres. On that day the place was heavily gassed and twenty-two of our men were caught in the fumes. On the 26th the K.S.L.I. withdrew from the front line, leaving the York and Lancasters on outpost duty. After this withdrawal the enemy advanced very quickly, but they stopped at the York and Lancaster picquets. There were daily casualties now; men

326

died by twos and threes and some were wounded more or less severely, and there was a continuous toll of gas casualties. A big attack was expected on the 28th, but it did not materialize, for now French reserves were hurrying up to the threatened portion of our line, and the second great German effort to wrest a victory before the Americans were in strength had proved a failure.

The month of May was a remarkable one to the 1st Battalion for the terrible list of casualties from gas. This mode of warfare began, as we have seen, at Ypres, and now, after three years of warfare, it seemed almost as formidable a weapon as ever, notwithstanding the mask, respirators and so on which had been invented to cope with it. During this month alone the 1st Battalion counted 119 casualties from this cause, and the unit was all the month (and up till the 12th June) either in Ypres or its vicinity. There was, however, a bright side to life this merry month of May. There was a gracious and fairly liberal distribution of honours to gladden the hearts of both the recipients and their friends. These were nearly all awarded for the fighting at Vaulx, and it is somewhat curious to note how well the number of awards compares with those given to our 2nd Battalion in 1915 and in connection with their terrible struggle north and east of Ypres. This remark is not for an instant to be misconstrued into an opinion that the 1st Battalion medals were not most magnificently won; it is only by way of a sigh of regret for the brave 2nd Battalion's bad luck. Military Medals were given to Sgt. Morgan, Corpls. Andrews and Thomas, Ptes. Croft, Highton, Johnson, Kear (attached T.M.B.), Knight, Rainsbury and Stevenson. A bar to his M.M. to L.-Corpl. Wilson; to C.S.M. Peters a D.C.M.; to Major Morgan the D.S.O.; to Lieut. Spence the M.C.; and to Sgt. MacWalter, who had the M.M. already, the D.C.M. Corpl. Brookman also got the M.M. on the

29th. In addition to the gas casualties twelve men were killed during May and twenty-three wounded, as this part of the line, never a quiet one, was the scene at this period of unusual activity.

At 12.45 a.m. on the 27th May the whole of the back area of the brigade was very heavily shelled with gas and high explosive for three hours while the forward area was untouched. A number of direct hits was obtained on brigade headquarters without damage, and the Buffs (in reserve) were obliged to wear their respirators for more than four hours. Meanwhile the enemy attacked the French on our right and penetrated their line to a depth of about seven hundred yards, but did not reach his objective. No attack took place on the 6th Divisional front, but the 71st Infantry Brigade was constrained to form a strong defensive flank. During the day the French partially re-established their position and artillery activity continued on both sides, particularly by the enemy on our back area. During the night the 71st Brigade relieved the French regiment on their right and, in order to supply the number of men required by its brigadier, the Buffs were placed under his tactical orders a˙ his reserve battalion. After this the enemy became for some days comparatively inactive except for the shelling of back areas and the use of aircraft, and on the 8th the brigade retired temporarily to Corps Reserve, moving by train to St. Omer for a few days' musketry near that city, and afterwards returning to Poperinghe. On the 26th the Buffs relieved a French battalion in the Dickebusch area, taking over a bad line almost unprovided with wire and with no communication trench, so that movement by daytime was impossible. Then casualties recommenced and in four days 2nd Lieut. Thompson (attached from the Queen's) and three men died, 2nd Lieut. Collett and seventeen were wounded, and this kind of thing went on steadily all July, the battalion losing 2nd Lieut. P.V.

Drake-Brockman killed, Captain W. A. C. Hedley, who died of wounds, and eight men killed, one of whom was buried by a shell. 2nd Lieut. Balding and fifty men were wounded, fourteen of whom were, however, able to remain at duty. During June the following were mentioned in despatches for good work during the German offensive: Lt.-Colonel Power, D.S.O.; Major Blackall; Captains E. H. Allen, Marshall, D.S.O., M.C., and Stone; Lieuts. Corney and Froome; Sgt. French; and Ptes. Dewhurst and Keyes.

Towards the end of July two companies of Americans, numbering 4 officers and 340 men, arrived and were distributed amongst our people to learn the hang of things and prepare themselves for the early advance which was now every day becoming more clearly a certainty.

On the 2nd August C Company and No. 7 platoon of B carried out a raid which was arranged and organized by Captain Moss, M.C., the battalion being then on the left sector of the brigade front. The 18th and the 100th Brigades on either flank co-operated with demonstrations and so on, and great help was given by the 6th Divisional Artillery. The object of the expedition was the capture of prisoners and consequent obtaining of identification, and this object was very successfully gained, but at a terrible loss. The story is briefly as follows: two platoons, commanded by Lieut. Hollis, M.C., had for their objective the Brasserie, and another, under Lieut. Harper, a certain cabaret; while No. 7 Platoon, under 2nd Lieut. Lister, was directed on the Brasserie Farm. The raiders left our trenches at 7.5 a.m., and at the same time our barrage opened; a trench mortar of ours engaged the objectives and did great service; the divisional artillery engaged the enemy's positions and also put up a smoke screen on the right of the raiders, and all neighbouring troops rendered assistance. The affair was most successful and all objectives were gained. The main opposition came from the hostile machine guns. The enemy lost heavily, several prisoners were taken and the fact was established that it was the 153rd regiment of infantry in front of our force. After this success, however, came trouble. It was while returning that the centre and left parties came under the heaviest machine-gun fire and casualties became very numerous. Besides, as there were no communication trenches and our lines were much exposed, the raiders had to scatter into any available cover there was behind our trench. Owing to the hostile sniping, which became very active after the barrage had ceased, it was impossible to remove several badly wounded men, and a machine gun which had been captured could not be brought in. The casualties resulting from this minor affair were, in fact, far too high. Captain R. W. Jones, D.S.O. (R.A.M.C.), Lieut. C. F. G. Hollis and thirteen men were killed; twenty-seven were wounded, of whom two died, and five men were missing. The death of Captain Jones was a very sad blow to the Buffs. With his usual utter disregard for personal safety whenever there was fighting or his assistance needed, this officer had gone over with the raiding party and though himself hit in the arm continued to move about bandaging the wounded until he was again hit, this time fatally. Except for a period following a wound which he had received on the Somme, Captain Jones had, at his own wish, remained always with the battalion since the early days of the war, and no British unit loved or reverenced their Medical Officer more than the Buffs their dear old " Doc." In Lieut. Hollis, too, another very good officer fell. He had distinguished himself at Cambrai and, poor fellow, was almost back in safety when he received the bullet that killed him.

On the 5th August the battalion was relieved at night and withdrew to the Malin House area, and next day

330

H.M. The King visited the Corps, and two hundred of all ranks, from each unit of the 6th Division, under Lt.-Colonel R. E. Power, D.S.O., went to greet him.

On the 8th August the Buffs became reserve battalion, but did not change their position.

III. 6TH BATTALION

On the day that the 6th Division, with the 1st Battalion The Buffs, were taken from the 3rd Army, namely, on the 24th March, 1918, the 12th Division, which included the 6th Buffs, was posted to it, and so the regimental history, as far as the 3rd Army is concerned, becomes more or less continuous. The 1st Battalion left from Favreuil in the neighbourhood of Bapaume, and the 6th Battalion reached Contalmaison, ten miles to the south-west of it, on the same day, having moved rapidly by march and by bus from the neighbourhood of Armentieres. Of course the rest of the 37th Brigade was with them, and in the evening the Queen's and West Kent sent reconnoitring patrols into Pozieres, which was found to be unoccupied; so at 11 o'clock a line was taken up in front of Ovillers. On the 25th the Buffs were on the left of the brigade, joining up with the 63rd Division, the 6th Battalion West Kents being on the right. Battalion headquarters were at Crucifix Corner, Aveluy. In the early morning of the 26th it was reported that the enemy had entered Thiepval and it became necessary to withdraw across the River Ancre. The Buffs were detailed as rear guard while the 47th Division and the rest of the 12th effected the crossing, and, at 7.30 a.m., the 37th Brigade took up a fresh position opposite Hamel, the Buffs being in support in front of Mesnil.

On the following day the most extraordinary mistake was made, due to a false and erroneous report made to brigade headquarters by some unit or other. The Buffs,

331

as has been seen, were at Mesnil, and there were some of the 188th Brigade details, including sailors, at the village of Martinsart, a little over a mile to the southward. An enemy's patrol was reported on the road which connects these two, and as this seemed to imply considerable danger, the men at Martinsart were placed at the disposal of the brigadier of the 37th Brigade. Then came the report that Mesnil had fallen to the Germans, and the Anson Battalion of the Naval Division was ordered to counter-attack the village from Martinsart, advancing astride the road and engaging the enemy wherever met. Now, as a matter of fact, a strong reconnoitring thrust had been made on the line at Mesnil held by the Buffs, but the attack was completely repulsed by Lewis gun and rifle fire, numbers of the enemy being killed and fourteen taken prisoner. When the naval battalion therefore arrived on the scene, eager for blood, it attacked the Buffs' headquarters, who defended the post with their usual resolution, so that for a while quite a lively fight between the two raged, each under the impression that the other force was German, until the error was discovered. The Queen's had also been attacked (about 1 p.m.) and a few Germans entered our lines on the extreme left after a heavy bombardment, but these were driven off by a counter-attack delivered by D Company. The enemy having entered Hamel, the Queen's had to throw back their flank, but all the dispositions of the Buffs remained intact at nightfall. A large hostile division had been seen during the afternoon about Pierre Divion and our lines had been heavily shelled, this continuing all next day. The Buffs' casualties on the 27th were Lieuts. E. F. Henderson and W. T. Score killed, Captain Dixson, 2nd Lieut. Caney and about twelve other ranks wounded. And next day, the 28th, 2nd Lieut. E. M. S. Hoare and two men were killed by a shell at the foremost Lewis gun post.

The battalion was relieved late at night by the Oxfordshire Light Infantry in order to enable it to move further south. Indeed, the whole division took up position next to the 2nd Division, because a message had warned everybody that a strong attack was pending, but, after being in support in Martinsart Wood all the 29th, the Buffs were relieved and marched back to billets in Warloy, where they remained for three days of very wet weather, marching to Henencourt on the 2nd April, the rumour of an attack being still very persistent. In fact, the period spent at Warloy had mostly been used for work, particularly at night.

On the 5th April Henencourt was very heavily shelled and the divisional authorities were informed at the same time that it was considered by the Higher Command that it was intended to attack Amiens on that day. There was a very thick mist when the firing commenced and this rendered observation impossible, so the Buffs were ordered to go forward, occupy the reverse slope of the ridge in front and send patrols on from there. The battalion started at 7.5 p.m. and moved through an intense barrage in artillery formation to what was known as the Old Corps Line, which was west of Albert, and did as it was bid. This day's fighting is known as the Battle of the Ancre. At 7.45 the situation being still obscure, the Queen's were sent up to support the Buffs, partly, it would seem, because Henencourt was now no place to rest in, as the shelling was terrific up to about a quarter-past ten, when it died down somewhat. The hostile artillery kept both Buffs and Queen's under very heavy fire, but no infantry attack eventuated; an hour later, however, news came that Dernancourt, which is a couple of miles or so away and down in the Ancre valley, was being very hardly pressed. At 2.30 the Buffs moved forward over the ridge and occupied some old trenches there. Here a bitterly cold night was spent; rations were brought up by Lewis gunners and signal-

333

lers who had been left behind because they had been out at training when the sudden order to move came. The morning march cost the regiment 2nd Lieut. L. J. G. Davis killed, Lieuts. G. C. Allen and C. S. Newcomb severely wounded (died of wounds), 2nd Lieut. Dorman slightly wounded, twelve men killed and thirty-three wounded. The enemy had put down a barrage on the old Corps trenches directly they were occupied, and fifteen more casualties occurred there. Another fourteen were killed or wounded on the morning of the 6th, and in the afternoon the battalion relieved the Queen's, which regiment had been sent off to support the 36th Brigade south of Bouzincourt. 2nd Lieuts. Cooper and Dalton were wounded during the relief.

All this time and for several days the weather had been very wet, and about now that old and persistent enemy called trench feet began to raise his head again and there were several cases of this disease in the battalion about this time. After a day in the front line in relief of the West Kent, the battalion marched on the 11th to Herissart, which is some miles to the westward, and there went into billets. The latter half of April was spent in the regions lying west of Albert. Nothing of any great regimental importance is to be noted. There were some changes of scene in so far that Harponville, Mirveux and Acheux were all visited before the next tour of duty in the line, which commenced on May Day, when the brigade relieved elements of the 35th and 36th Brigades in the centre of the divisional front.

This tour lasted only a week and the incidents were not of an uncommon nature. The enemy tried a little modest raid which was easily repulsed, but, on the 3rd, Puchevillers was heavily shelled and one projectile hit battalion headquarters, killing one man and wounding nine others. After this ensued a week at Acheux, and

334

then the trenches again on the 13th May. On the 16th D Company carried out a successful little raid on the enemy with four officers and ninety-six men, who started at 9.20 in the evening. They advanced in good order and with great *élan*. All ranks speak very highly of the evenness and accuracy of the barrage under which they advanced. The first of the enemy encountered were two listening posts. Their occupants offered no opposition, but refused to leave them. These posts were unexpected and only fifteen minutes had been allowed for the work in hand, so they had to be left. On proceeding, D Company found that it had come up just when an inter-company relief was in progress, with the result that the Germans were in greater strength than was anticipated and considerable opposition was encountered. However, when our right attack had penetrated the wire the enemy vacated his line, suffering many casualties as he retired over the open. The left attack was equally successful or nearly so. Altogether some dug-outs were bombed; a good deal of damage was done to the trenches by our artillery; and three unwounded prisoners were brought back, in addition to considerable casualties as noticed above. We lost four men killed, 2nd Lieut. Davis and eleven wounded and one missing.

On the 25th the whole division was relieved by the 17th. The battalion went away west to Puchevillers, where it remained till the 16th June in G.H.Q. reserve, undergoing special training which included a course of musketry on the ranges. On the 16th the battalion marched to the front line, relieving a battalion of the 35th Division on the left of our divisional front. Next day 2nd Lieut. E. A. M. Stevens, M.C., and Pte. Beadle of C Company were unfortunately killed by a shell at the entrance of C Company's dug-out. On the 20th of the month, identification of the hostile units in front being desirable, our artillery fired on the enemy's position in the southern portion of Aveluy Wood, and then the Buffs sent out four strong patrols to obtain the required information. These, however, met with considerable opposition, because the Germans occupied certain small posts forward of their general line and these little places had been overlooked by the artillery bombardment, so our patrols were fired upon by machine guns and rifles and, owing to casualties, were unable to complete their task. 2nd Lieut. E. F. Robinson was killed, 2nd Lieut. Towers and nine men were wounded and four killed; and at 8.15, in shelling the support company (D), the hostile artillery obtained a direct hit, killing one man and wounding four.

On the 22nd the battalion moved to brigade reserve at Senlis, where working parties, four hundred strong, were found each day, till the next trench tour, which commenced on the 29th and which was undertaken under certain difficulties: during the relief, the back areas were kept under heavy gas-shell fire which affected the movement of the troops; moreover, when the battalion headquarters of the Buffs were closeted with the headquarters of the Royal Berkshire Regiment, which it was relieving, a shell made a direct hit on the spot, and it was only with difficulty that the double party emerged from the wreckage. The Medical Officer of the Royal Berkshire was the only one wounded, and he but slightly.

At 9.35 p.m. on the 30th June the Queen's and West Kent, with the Buffs in support, under cover of heavy artillery, trench mortar and machine-gun barrage, attacked the front-line system of the enemy 1,000 yards north-west of Albert on a frontage of about 1,100 yards with a view to destroying or capturing the garrisons of the first three lines of trenches and holding the front line. Practically the Buffs this day had only to stand to all the time of and after the operation, because it was completely successful with very little help from them, though five men were killed and 2nd Lieut. Symonds and thirty men wounded. The Queen's, who were on the right, met with a stubborn resistance and suffered many casualties, and C Company the Buffs went forward to their immediate support. Notwithstanding these casualties, both the forward battalions were able at 11.40 to report to the brigadier that they were consolidating; but at 1.23 on the morning of the 1st July the Queen's, who had sent the message earlier that the Bedfords on their right had been repulsed, reported that they could not hold on without support, and at 2.10 a.m. the S.O.S. signal was up along the line and the Royal Engineers acknowledged that they could not do the wiring satisfactorily on account of casualties. However, the day proved fairly quiet and the Queen's and West Kents were reinforced by C Company The Buffs, while the remainder were in readiness to move forward, and very early in the morning of the 2nd the battalion relieved the Queen's in the right half of the brigade front line. The Germans were now taking the offensive and towards nightfall very notably so, though they had been fairly quiet during daylight. At 9.35 p.m. a very intense barrage was put down along the whole brigade front, followed by a counter-attack which caused the West Kent on our left to withdraw to the old British line. Soon afterwards a report was received that the 18th Division on the right had also withdrawn to the old British line, leaving A, B and D Companies of the Buffs still occupying the German front line. The battalion's casualties this day were 2nd Lieut. Harvey slightly wounded, two men killed and forty-one wounded.

At 6 o'clock on the morning of the 3rd, whilst the Buffs were still holding on and defending, in particular, two blocks which they had made during the night, orders came to withdraw and join the others. This movement was rendered very difficult owing to the clear visibility

z

of that particular morning, which caused our men to be observed when about two-thirds of them had got back into the new or rather into the old position. Thus the Germans sent up a strong bombing party to destroy 2nd Lieut. Hobbs and the small party with him that had been left behind to cover the retreat, but the stubborn resistance of this detachment resulted in there being only two more casualties on account of this move. In fact, the bravery and devotion of Hobbs was beyond all praise: entirely regardless of his personal safety, he not only handled his men to perfection, but himself carried a wounded soldier to safety under heavy fire and persistent bombing. Lieut. Dudeney also showed his manhood by his defence of one of the posts against overwhelming odds. The whole of the battalion's front was in order by 7.45 a.m., though the condition of the line was now, it is true, far from satisfactory owing to the intense bombardment and other causes. That day the 37th Brigade was relieved by the 36th and the Buffs went into divisional reserve at Senlis and so remained till the 10th July without any further incident.

The brigade was now in G.H.Q. reserve in tents south-east of Harponville and under orders to join the 22nd Corps of the 4th Army. In consequence of this order it marched to Rubempre on the 13th, and next day proceeded by bus to Quevanvillers and marched to Rumatsnil and afterwards to Plachy Buyon, remaining in this district, about ten miles south-west of Amiens, up to the end of July, or rather until the 30th, on which date a movement was made by train to Canaples and thence by route march to Berleaucourt (about twelve miles north-west of Amiens). On the 2nd August the 12th Division relieved the 58th in the centre section of the 3rd Corps front, the 37th Brigade being in divisional reserve. The Buffs, going by bus to a wood on the Behencourt–Franvillers road, thus came into the neighbourhood of Warloy once more; but the next day they proceeded to Dernancourt on the Ancre, and on the 4th relieved a battalion of the United States Army in the front line. There they remained for three days, when, on relief by another American unit, they became part of the Corps Reserve at Franvillers. On the 8th August the battalion moved into trenches south of Morlancourt with orders to attack at 3 a.m., but this was postponed. When the second order came the companies told off for the job were already in No Man's Land and had to be recalled. The withdrawal was a very difficult business, and one platoon of D Company, under 2nd Lieut. Hearson, could not be got back and had to remain where it was till dusk. Unfortunately the enemy was quite aware of this and opened machine-gun fire on the party, wounding Lieut. Le May, 2nd Lieuts. Gray, M.C., and Thornley, and twenty-four men and killing two. Next day came our British attack.

IV. 10TH BATTALION

In comparison with the other battalions of the Buffs in France the doings of the 10th during the momentous period between the 21st March and the 8th August, 1918, were uneventful as, naturally, units which came from overseas were chiefly used as reliefs and not pushed at once into the fighting line.

The 10th landed at Marseilles from Palestine on the 7th May and entrained two days later for Noyelles, near Abbeville, where it went into billets and instantly began training to fit itself for the methods of warfare in vogue in the western theatre of war. On the 22nd it proceeded to Buneville and on the 25th to Izel lez Hameau, in the Arras district, where it was billeted for a month and where it lost its commanding officer, Lt.-Colonel Lord Sackville, who was sent to do special work at French G.H.Q. On the 25th June the next move came, this time to Enguin les Mines, which is about ten miles south of St. Omer; but on the 10th July the General Headquarters were left behind and the 10th moved by motor bus into divisional reserve at Ham en Artois, then into brigade reserve at La Perriere. Here the first losses in France occurred, two men being killed and seven wounded when on a working party. Finally, till the 4th August, Miquellerie was the home of the unit. All these above-mentioned places are fairly close together, being south of the town of Hazebrouck, southwest of Merville and not far from the River Lys. On the 4th August the right sub-section of the left sector of the Adjusovres–Averskerque line near St. Floris was taken over, and now the time was rapidly approaching for the Allies to assume their turn for offensive work, work which was only to cease with the complete subjection of all our enemies.

On the 5th August the division on the right of the 230th Brigade had advanced its line and the Buffs were warned to be ready to do the same should the trenches in front be found to be evacuated as they had been on the right. There was no doubt at all at this time that the enemy was showing every sign of nervousness, but what follows belongs to the story of the final victorious advance and must be reserved for another chapter.

V. 7TH BATTALION

Without a doubt the most smashing blow that was dealt during the great German offensive fell upon the British 5th Army, in the very forefront of which stood the 7th Battalion of the Buffs. On the night of the 20th/21st March the 55th Brigade was at Liez holding, as its forward zone, from the village of Travecy, exclusive, up to a point about a mile north of Vendeuil, which sector was garrisoned by the 7th Buffs, eleven machine guns, four Stokes mortars, two six-inch trench mortars, one section of a field company of Royal

340

Engineers, with two infantry platoons attached. Fort Vendeuil held as a garrison one platoon of the Buffs' support company, the section of Royal Engineers, the two attached platoons and the two trench mortars. These attached platoons were a divisional idea and were No. 17 or extra platoons of the Buffs and the Queen's. They were composed of men who were bad marchers and were usually employed with the Engineers as unskilled labourers. The Buffs' headquarters were at a quarry called " Clarence Keep," though it was only protected by a very light trench. It was close to the Vendeuil–Remigny road and about three-quarters of a mile from the fort. The two forward companies were: B to the northward, holding the main St. Quentin road, about half-way to Le Vert Chasseur, down to the railway station at Vendeuil, with headquarters in the middle of the village; A carrying on towards the south, holding part of Vendeuil, the quarry, which overlooked the river, and a post some nine hundred yards to the south-west of it, which was the company headquarters. C Company was immediately behind A and B, from near Vendeuil Fort to a post some fourteen hundred yards behind A's headquarters. D Company was further west again and just in front of Poplar and Rouquenet Woods. Thus the battalion front was enormously extended, there being about four thousand yards between the right and the left platoons, and the nearest West Kent post (Le Vert Chasseur) being another twelve hundred yards away. The fighting strength of the Buffs was only 550, many of the men being recently taken over from the late 8th Battalion. The chief unit in the battle zone behind was the 7th Queen's, and there was no brigade reserve because the 8th East Surrey happened to be in divisional reserve. The 4th Dismounted Brigade was attached to the 55th for the day.

At 4.45 a.m. on the 21st March the enemy's artillery

fire commenced, and almost immediately afterwards the order to man battle positions was sent out, but the Buffs were, of course, already in their places. The hostile shelling was intense and at first many of the shells were gas-laden. When day dawned it was found that the country was wrapped in so dense a fog that a man could not see twenty yards in front of him. It was a misty morning everywhere along our lines on this fateful 21st March, but perhaps in no part lay a thicker blanket of fog than in the valley of the Oise with its neighbouring canals. It was not long before the shelling began to cut, as was often the case, the telephone wires which connected the various distant posts, the first to go being that which connected "Clarence Keep" with B Company (Captain Chant), and soon afterwards Captain Fine, who commanded in Fort Vendeuil, failed to answer calls. Therefore in the morning the situation was very far from pleasant. Little isolated parties of Buffs were scattered about the countryside, blinded by fog, deprived of communication with their neighbours and with the suspicion, which amounted almost to a certainty, that silently closing in upon them were unknown numbers of the enemy intent on their destruction. The mist began to clear about noon, and it was only then that the defenders were able to gain some notion of the hostile movements which up till then had been screened. In the meantime the battalion signal sergeant, Browne, with three men[1] were working desperately to repair the line between "Clarence" and the Fort, and after four hours' hard labour communication was re-established and Captain Fine reported "all correct."

The first intimation of any hostile infantry on the sector held by the Buffs came from A Company (Captain Grant) reporting about 10 a.m. that thirty Ger-

[1] One of these, Pte. A. C. Coleman, won the D.C.M., the M.M. and the M.S.M.

mans were about Canal Post, near the quarry. After this headquarters lost communication with Captain Grant. At 11 o'clock C Company made out about two hundred of the enemy going north along the main St. Quentin road. At 11.45 A Company got communication with C and informed the latter first that there seemed to be much movement in their rear, and then that they were surrounded; after this the line "went." D Company then observed a party of Germans between them and the Fort, and it was found that some, covered by the fog, had actually visited the company headquarters and broken the signalling lamp. The Buffs' Headquarters now directed D Company to be ready to make a counter-attack, and at " Clarence Keep " itself the meagre defences were manned with spare runners, cooks, sanitary men, pioneers, police and servants, and these prepared to see the matter out. Then the chaplain and doctor arrived from Vendeuil, where they had been billeted, and told how B Company had been surrounded, but that Captain Chant had escaped into the fort. Strong bodies of Germans had come down the road from the north and surprised the defenders, though some had escaped in the fog and joined C Company; the enemy had got the two machine guns which on the left flank of the company had been stationed on the road and had surrounded the platoon that was there. There was no news of a party which had been at the railway station.

About this time a bugle sound, evidently German, was heard from the direction of Ronquenet Wood and a party, seen north of " Clarence Keep," was fired on and dispersed. The second in command, too, trying to get back to report the state of the case to brigade headquarters, was wounded crossing the open ground near Ronquenet Farm, probably by the party that sounded the bugle. All this, of course, meant that the defences had been penetrated during the fog. The length of line held by the Buffs was roughly a couple of miles, and the posts or platoon garrisons had on an average about eight hundred yards between them, and so it came to pass that they were, one by one, isolated and surrounded. In fact, the Germans tried about 1.30 to assail the Fort itself from the south and south-west, but by this time the weather was clearer and, rifles and guns being turned upon them from several points and our artillery firing at very close range or " over the sights," this attempt was abandoned; nevertheless they began to close on " Clarence Keep," and later brought up a machine gun which began to fire into the backs of the men, the garrison being disposed now for an all-round defence. Several attacks on this headquarters post were beaten off by rifle fire, greatly due to the gallant behaviour of L.-Corpls. Berry and Harris.[1]

During the afternoon many hostile aeroplanes appeared on the scene. These, flying very low, were directing the shell fire by means of signal, one consequence being the shelling of our guns just east of " Clarence," under cover of which shelling hostile infantry worked up very close and at last caused our gun detachment to surrender. In fact, the enemy had complete air command in this region. During the whole afternoon " Clarence Keep " kept up communication with D Company by flag, and headquarters had seen the Fort signalling to Liez, where the brigade staff was. The constant message was " counter-attack essential," and this was because Captain Fine had been led to believe that the divisional reserve had arranged to carry one out, in the case of its being necessary in order to save the Fort. From 6 to 6.30 p.m. an intense hostile bombardment was directed on Captain Fine's command, after which all was silent and it seemed as if the

[1] These two young men served right through the war from the landing of the battalion till the armistice, and always with distinction. They both got bars to their M.M.'s for this day's work.

344

place had fallen, but it was afterwards ascertained that the little garrison had held out for another twenty-four hours. A Company was despaired of. The best that could be hoped was that the men were prisoners; but firing from their direction was heard up till midnight, and it was supposed that they were then still refusing to surrender. As a matter of fact, it was afterwards ascertained that Lieut. Kennett's platoon fired on the German transport on the 22nd and held out till the evening of that day. B and C Companies had lost posts and garrisons and were now but fragments of the units they had been, but the enemy had not passed and what they had gained had been won in the morning, when they were so greatly aided by the fog.

C Company had been especially well handled by Captain Tupper and had defeated all hostile attempts during the day, and D Company, under Lieut. Morell, with 2nd Lieut. Halliday to aid him, had made a fine local counter-attack and driven the Germans back at a critical time. A project was entertained by the 55th Brigade, when reinforced by the 4th Dismounted Brigade, for relieving the pressure at Fort Vendeuil, but this was vetoed by the Divisional General, who issued very emphatic orders that touch was to be maintained with the brigade on the right about Quessy, and it was clear that the battle zone of this latter force was in the hands of the enemy. This order therefore meant a withdrawal and that those troops in the forward zone of the 55th Brigade which could not be extricated must just surrender or die. Before withdrawal orders reached the Buffs, they had been busy, under cover of night, reorganizing, serving out food and ammunition and digging in.

The first hint of retreat came at half an hour after midnight, when an officer of the Machine Gun Corps arrived at " Clarence " with orders to take away the two Vickers guns which were there and with the information that a general withdrawal had been ordered to a position west of the canal. This was confirmed shortly afterwards by patrols of the 7th Queen's. These patrols had been sent up from the battle zone by the brigadier to deliver the orders to all the scattered parties of the Buffs and others which could be reached. Even now Colonel Ransome would not go back unless the order was confirmed, and his adjutant bicycled into Remigny to telephone for instructions. He, however, got a clear and distinct order that the Buffs were to retreat. So at 1.10 a.m. on the 22nd March the battalion headquarters retired by small parties to the brigade at Liez, after destroying all papers and leaving behind many useful and pleasant stores. C Company had already arrived here with fragments of B, and soon after D Company came in, and before daylight in the morning the battalion had concentrated about La Faisanderie, but it now consisted of only three companies. The 55th Brigade Headquarters moved from Liez to Rouez.

It was later ascertained that the 7th Battalion The Buffs was the only unit of the 3rd Corps that was, on the afternoon of the 21st March, still holding out in the forward zone, and that its doing so resulted in other units being enabled to reorganize behind the Crozat Canal. At 2 o'clock in the afternoon the Buffs withdrew into a wood a little to the south and started to dig in on very empty stomachs. It was not, however, till 3.30 a.m. on the 23rd March that the battalion occupied its new position, as it had been called away to the support of the Queen's, and indeed very early on this date, too, C and D Companies had to be again placed at the disposal of the C.O. of that regiment, in order to fill a dangerous gap that existed between the left of the Queen's and the right of the East Surrey.

Everybody prepared himself for a new day's fighting, the 55th Brigade being now in support of the forward troops. At 6 o'clock a French regiment, which had

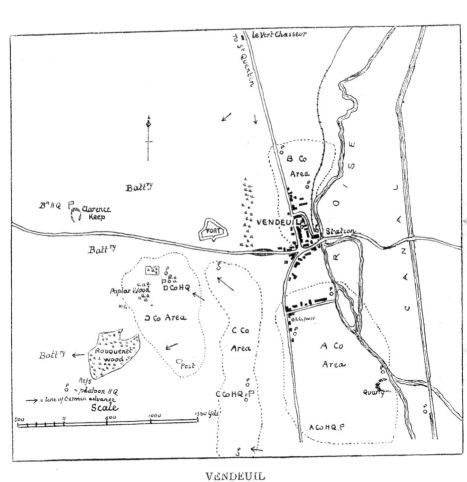

VENDEUIL

been expected, duly arrived. This unit had been detailed to make a counter-attack on the town of Tergnier and was to be supported by the Queen's, who fought that day under the command of Lt.-Colonel Bushell. This counter-attack was duly attempted, but the Frenchmen were very shortly back amongst the Buffs again. They seemed a fine, resolute lot, and they said they had gone up with only thirty-five rounds of ammunition per man and had expended it all. Moreover, they had lost their way in the mist. The story of this counter-attack is not the history of the Buffs, but it may be here mentioned that Lt.-Colonel Bushell of the Queen's was the hero of the attempt. He appears to have led his own fellows and Frenchmen too with the greatest gallantry, and he was rewarded with a V.C.

From 8 o'clock in the morning there was confused fighting in the wood, where nothing beyond a range of fifty yards or so could be observed. Wounded men kept coming back to where Colonel Ransome's little party was, and all brought with them the same tale of the enemy's steady advance. Both Captain Morrell and 2nd Lieut. Halliday of the Buffs were badly wounded. Both were very gallant officers and a great loss at such a time. It appeared to Colonel Ransome, who commanded the Buffs, that it was not much use stopping in the wood: nothing could be seen, and it was thought that its northern edge was being passed by the enemy; so it was decided to take up two old lines of trenches and pits which existed in an orchard two hundred yards in rear, and the headquarters of both Buffs and Queen's, with all sorts of fragments of companies and other small units, fell back to this place and there remained all day fighting a grim battle with the advancing foe. There were nine machine guns with the party, but only just enough personnel to work them. It was principally a machine-gun fight and for a long time our weapons did very well, but the enemy kept bringing up more and

347

more, while our supply of ammunition began to fail as the afternoon drew on. Every effort was made to get up more from the rear, but the difficulties were too great to overcome, and the enemy gradually began to gain fire superiority. During the afternoon those companies of the Buffs which had gone forward by direction of the O.C. the Queen's, as well as other advanced parties of British troops, had rallied on Ransome's position, which proved an invaluable post for the purpose. The opinion of the brigadier of the 55th Brigade on this point is as follows: " In the light of subsequent " knowledge it is clear that the stand made here by " Lt.-Colonel Ransome's force was of the greatest value " not only to the rest of the brigade, but to the whole " line in this vicinity. . . . This stand was due in the " first place to the skill and foresight of Lt.-Colonel " Ransome in establishing a line outside the wood on " which the withdrawing troops, scattered and dis- " organized by the confused fighting in the wood, " could be rallied and reorganized. In the latter part " of the work Lt.-Colonel Ransome was assisted princi- " pally by Major Tortise and Captain Snell of the 7th " Queen's, and by Captain Black and Lieut. Howcroft " of his own battalion. All these officers behaved with " the utmost gallantry."

About 6 o'clock a French battalion which had come up behind the English party during the afternoon essayed a frontal counter-attack. There was no artillery preparation. The attempt was beyond praise as regards the gallantry of the soldiers who made it, but the brave Frenchmen were met with a perfect storm of machine-gun bullets and they could not go on. After lying down for a few moments they got up and retired, and the retirement took the whole of the English first-line troops with it. This was by no means a misfortune. Anxiety had been felt already about the possibility of holding the position till nightfall, but it seemed to be suicidal to attempt to retire before the German machine guns by daylight. However, fortunately these ceased fire as the hostile infantry came forward to pursue, and so our retirement was far less costly than could have been expected. It was a very mixed lot of men that went back through Rouez Wood. Frenchmen and all sorts of English units mixed up in great confusion as regards their ranks. A fresh line was formed inside the wood and Captain Black actually led a small party forward to check the pursuit, which prevented any great pressure before darkness set in, and the fugitives were able to collect, reorganize and march back to Villiguier Aumont. During this final phase Sgt. Browne and Pte. Coleman, two signallers who had greatly distinguished themselves on the 21st by mending the line from "Clarence" to the Fort under quite extraordinary difficulties and heavy shell fire, were wounded.

The march to Villeguier was without incident, though it was thought by some that the party was surrounded. On arrival, the details belonging to the 55th Brigade were directed on to Bethancourt, where Br.-General Wood, commanding, already was, as was also the 8th East Surrey Regiment. About 10 a.m. on the 24th March the 55th Brigade was ordered to withdraw to a line approximately east of Caillouel; here it had the 53rd on its right flank and the 54th Brigade on the left. The Buffs, who were the supporting battalion of their brigade at first that night, withdrew later into divisional support, and at 7 a.m. on the 25th the whole division fell back to the line Grandru–Mondescourt–Appilly and later to a position covering Babœuf, these retrograde movements being carried out in good and soldier-like order by platoons in artillery formation. At 2 p.m. on this day the Buffs were sent back to a position west of Babœuf, to cover the canal bridge at Varesnes, and later to Varesnes itself, which was reached at 10 p.m. On the 26th March the whole of the 55th

Brigade marched to Caisnes. The casualties suffered by the 7th Buffs between the 21st and 26th March amounted to:—Officers: killed, 1; wounded, 5; missing, 11. Other ranks: killed, 17; wounded, 108; missing, 410. When a force has to retire after fighting, it is generally quite unknown whether a man who fails to answer his name afterwards is dead or a prisoner of war. He is simply described as missing.

By the 28th March the brigade had got to Audignicourt and was in billets and caves there, but now the scene of its activities was changed. There was considerable enemy pressure on our defence works covering the important city of Amiens, and the whole of the 29th March was spent by the Buffs and their comrades in buses undergoing a weary journey to help to relieve the situation in that region. On the 30th the battalion debussed at St. Nicholas, east of Boves, and marched to Gentelles. In fact, the Buffs and Queen's had to march direct from the buses into a support line east of this village. That night the 55th Brigade took over the front line south-east of Villers Bretonneux, but for the present the Buffs remained where they were, but on the 31st moved to a large farm close to the monument which is on the road which runs south from Villers Bretonneux. This farm was the battalion headquarters and was in full view from the German position at Marcelcave, but had never been shelled. After two days the Buffs relieved the Queen's in front line and took the left of the brigade with D Company on right, B on the left and C, which was only two platoons strong, in reserve.

At 3.45 a.m. on the 4th April a German prisoner was captured by the battalion, and this man stated that our enemy was going to attack at dawn and that, in fact, they were at that moment " standing to." Notice, of course, was immediately sent round to everybody and thus an absolute surprise was avoided, though, of

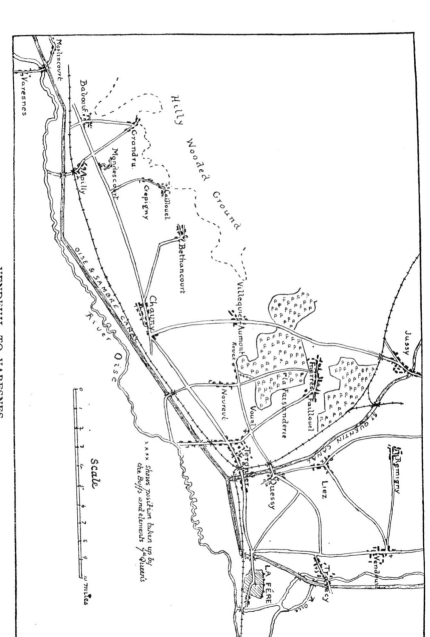

VENDEUIL TO VARESNES

course, the force was always kept ready for contingencies of the sort. At dawn there was a thick mist and, communication being otherwise impossible, the Queen's dropped a chain of connecting files between battalions and brigade headquarters. At 6 o'clock the hostile bombardment commenced. It was indiscriminate shelling followed by rifle and machine-gun fire, and at seven the attack developed on the Buffs' front and that of the 35th Australian Battalion on their left. At or about 9 o'clock the Australian troops further away to the left fell back, which caused the 35th Australians and the Buffs to conform, the latter getting back to the bridge over the railway. One company of the Queen's was at this juncture put under the Buffs' orders, and an hour later a company also of the 2/6th London Regiment, which had been temporarily placed at the disposal of the 55th Brigade. The Australians withdrew somewhat further, making it necessary for the left of the Buffs to conform, though the right of the regiment remained in position. At four in the afternoon the enemy was seen advancing from the line Marcelcave–Aubercourt, and at the same time his artillery shelled our people heavily with gas, and the Germans got round our right flank, causing our whole line to withdraw, but the Buffs rallied about Villers Bretonneux railway station to cover there a battery of our artillery.

The casualties of the first week in April were:—Officers: killed, 1; wounded, 5. Other ranks: killed, 3; wounded, 34; missing, 13.

Early in the morning of the 5th the battalion got orders to move to Gentelles and later in the day to billets at Boves; it had remained out by the station all night, because those who bore the orders for the retirement failed to discover it. The 55th Brigade Headquarters moved next day to St. Fuscien, and the Buffs and East Surrey were attached to the 53rd and the Queen's to the 54th Brigade; but the several battalions were by now so weak that a composite one had to be formed under the command of Lt.-Colonel Ransome, D.S.O., M.C., the Buffs finding two companies and the East Surrey and Royal Berkshire one company each. The English forward posts in this portion of the line were now about Gentelles and were manned by the troops in the neighbourhood till the 12th of April, when the 55th Brigade was withdrawn, moving by march to Dreuil les Molliens and Cavillon, about nine miles west of Amiens. The Buffs being close by at Le Mesge. Ten days' intensive training was now undergone and then the brigade returned to St. Fuscien, only to move four days later north-east to Baizieux to be attached to the 2nd Australian Division. The area west of Albert was occupied by the 18th Division up till the 12th July, when it went into G.H.Q. reserve.

The story of the battalion from May Day till this date is lacking in the tremendous incidents which have been recorded above: the Buffs was soon again a battalion of four companies—such a loss as even a whole company was very quickly replaced in these days. A short history such as this necessarily occupies its available space with the exciting record of valorous days and strenuous combat and must reluctantly pass over with only slight allusion the hard, faithful and continuous work of the draft-finding units in England.

The battalion was a good deal at Lavieville and Baisieux about this time and, of course, were alternately in front line, support and reserve. When in the former a good deal of patrolling work was done: for instance, strong fighting patrols went out on the 3rd June; they got into their objective, but failed to get identification. On the 6th 2nd Lieut. Richardson with fifteen of C Company's men had a small encounter with the enemy. On the 15th a raid was attempted, but, owing to the enemy's resistance and the thickness of his wire, the objective was not reached, though some im-

352

portant information was gained. Protective patrols also were out nightly early in the month of June and much digging and wiring work was undertaken, because there were strong and persistent rumours of a hostile attack, and, as a matter of fact, on the 16th, three trench mortars, together with some rifle grenades, played frequently upon B and C Companies, and during the night a barrage was put down on the battalion, consisting of trench-mortar and high-explosive fire, which lasted over an hour. On the 30th June and following two or three days there was some fighting in the neighbourhood of the 55th Brigade, and indeed their comrades of the 54th were engaged, but the Buffs were at the time in divisional reserve and did not come into action. On the 12th July the whole division was relieved and on the 13th marched to Warloy and there embussed for G.H.Q. reserve at Briquemesnil until the 30th, the time being much occupied by strict training, as was usual when in G.H.Q. reserve.

On the 30th this spell of peace was over and the Buffs went into line again on the last day of the month, this time near and a little south of Warloy, the fighting lines being now at this part of the front somewhere about thirty miles westward of their position after the Somme battles of the last year. But by now the great American army was in France and reinforcements were pouring in. The tremendous German efforts to snatch victory between the collapse of Russia and their arrival had failed and our enemy was, so to speak, anxiously looking over his shoulder towards the dear homeland. By the 1st August he had already withdrawn from one or two dangerous points in France and Flanders, and there was a general feeling amongst our people that it was time he was on the move. However that may be, the 7th Battalion patrols on the 4th discovered that the Germans were still on its immediate front, and next day considerable movement was observed in the hostile lines.

HOLDING ON

Then, on the 6th August, a most unexpected event took place. For the last three days the brigade had been warned to expect and to look out for an enemy's withdrawal, yet on this morning, before it was fairly light, the 27th German Division astride the Bray–Corbie road actually advanced to the attack at a time when we were relieving certain companies by others. Only a couple of hours or so earlier some of the Buffs had rushed an enemy's post and found it empty. The authorities, being so certain that the German was going, attributed the movement noticed above as merely a blind on his part to cover an imminent retrograde movement. The battle that followed, though it commenced with a German attack on the 6th, lasted some days, and towards the finish the rôle of the two armies was reversed. It will therefore be convenient to relate what occurred in the following chapter, which will deal with the Grand Advance of the Allies.

CHAPTER XV

THE GRAND RESULT

I. 7TH BATTALION: BATTLE OF AMIENS

THE 7th Battalion of the Buffs on the morning of the 6th August, 1918, was holding the brigade frontage which was north of the Bray–Corbie road and was in a trench which had recently been taken from the enemy and occupied by an Australian force. South of the road at the time of dawn a relief of companies was in progress, and the East Surrey Regiment was experiencing certain difficulties in connection with the operation. The Germans, discovering this fact, seized the opportunity to launch a very sudden and resolute attack which succeeded in piercing the British line. This unfortunate event seems to have been due to a variety of causes, such as incomplete relief and extension of front, but the element of surprise figured largely. Our troops were holding the ground very thinly; the men were anything but fresh; the forward trenches were knee-deep in mud, and their occupants were expecting to leave them only for a forward and not a retrograde movement. The German barrage commenced at 4.20 a.m. No " S.O.S." signal was made for some time and the general idea seems to have been that the enterprise was merely a raid, but the bombardment lasted two hours and cut the telephone wires, which was the greater disaster because the shape of the ground forbade visual signalling. After about an hour it became clear enough that this was no raid, but a determined attempt to gain and hold on to our trenches and position. The hostile troops succeeded in penetrating along the road to a considerable distance, about

355

eight hundred yards, in fact. The south of it being
held but lightly, the 34th Brigade was requested to be
responsible for this portion of the line, and a counter-
attack by men of the East Surreys was attempted along

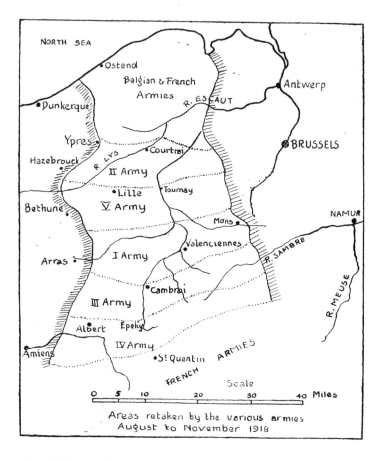

Areas retaken by the various armies
August to November 1918

the highway itself. At 8.36 it was clear to the headquarters in rear that part of our old first line was now
in the hands of the enemy; but at 9.45 the Buffs were
in the Burke line behind it, had established posts at all

the junctions of trenches, and had pushed patrols out to the front, after which there was a lengthy bombing fight for the various trench junctions. During the morning the 55th Brigade had consisted of two battalions only, because the Queen's had been sent back to rest and get fit, prior to our attack on the 8th. The enemy having anticipated our programme and date of fighting, this battalion was now ordered to the front again and arrived about noon. At 4.45 a conference was held, the principal point for consultation being the possibility of a counter-attack by the 54th Brigade. The leader of this force objected that he required another battalion to make such an attempt feasible, but this objection being overruled, the counter-attack was decided on and one company of the East Surreys placed at the disposal of the 54th Brigade. During the following night the lines were subjected to very heavy shelling, but at 4.40 a.m. the counter-attack was launched and proved a great success, the 54th Brigade gaining all their objectives, as did the detachment of the East Surreys; the latter at 5.47 reported themselves as being where they had been told to go and as having several prisoners and two of the enemy's machine guns.

The following day saw the commencement of the allied offensive, but the 55th Brigade was practically only represented by the 7th Queen's, which battalion had been nursed for the occasion. Extraordinary efforts had been made to keep the coming operations a dead secret. Only battalion commanders were supposed to know anything whatsoever about the matter, and they only the barest outline of the plan. The job the Queen's were given was to form the extreme left of the defensive flank of the 4th Army. The battalion was to be accompanied by certain tanks. The morning was almost as misty as on that dreadful day, the 21st March. The tanks failed to turn up and the Queen's were forced to start without them. In the fog the battalion appeared to have missed its way, and while endeavouring to get right again and into good order it suffered a terrible loss, in that its gallant colonel was mortally wounded. Christopher Bushell, V.C., D.S.O., was a very prominent hero in an army of good soldiers, and his regiment must deeply have felt his loss. Lt.-Colonel Ransome, of the Buffs, was, immediately the news came in, placed in command of all troops in the foremost zone, with directions to clear up the situation and to establish the flank with all speed. In the words of the official account, " He handled the situation most ably." He was well and worthily assisted by Captain Snell, adjutant of the Queen's, by Captain Hayfield, of the Buffs, now attached to brigade headquarters, and by Captain Heath, who commanded the 55th Trench Mortar Battery.

The following day, the 9th August, the 55th Brigade was squeezed out as the English armies advanced and so became reserve troops, the Buffs proceeding to Warloy, where they received two large drafts from home which were badly needed. Most of these men were miners and munition workers who all did good work later on. On the 13th August the Buffs moved into line beyond Senlis and with them went American soldiers, one platoon being attached to each Buff company, and the Buffs leaving four platoons of their own in the transport lines. On the 19th, the battalion having relieved the Royal Berkshire Regiment west of Albert, its patrols got touch with the enemy in and about that town, and on the night of the 21st/22nd assembly positions were taken up for battle almost on the western edge of Albert.

The great battle, or rather series of battles and pursuits, which now commenced in this area was fully shared in by other divisions besides the 18th in which the 7th Buffs were serving. Amongst these was the 12th, and in that division was the 6th Battalion of the regiment. These two Kitchener units, then, were during the latter part of August and early September serving shoulder to shoulder, or very nearly so. Therefore before the tale be told of how the enemy was driven from the Ancre river step by step over the Tortille and back to his Hindenburg Line, it would be as well to note how the 6th was spending the time from the 9th to the 21st August.

II. 6TH BATTALION

At 2 a.m. on the former date the battalion, with the rest of the 37th Brigade, which, it may be remembered, was near Morlancourt, began to move into its assembly position, but at 3 o'clock a message came postponing the attack. This message reached the Queen's and West Kent in time and these two units were stopped ere reaching their places, but the Buffs, having a longer approach to make subsequently, had to leave their assembly positions much earlier in order to get up to the artillery barrage. Thus it came to pass that the leading companies had already commenced operations when the important message came and it was impossible to stop them, so that the battalion had actually penetrated the enemy's position at one point when the order for postponement reached it. These forward troops therefore detailed one platoon to occupy a quarry, which was handy, and from there cover the retreat of its comrades. Under cover of this platoon, the remainder withdrew to their assembly positions, but the men took with them a prisoner and a machine gun just to show where they had been. The covering platoon maintained its position. This little error cost one officer and forty men wounded.

The new zero hour was fixed for 5.30 p.m., at which time the Buffs were already in assembly position on the right of the line. The Queen's and West Kent were to

be in position at the zero hour to commence the assault
fifty minutes later. The attack proceeded now according to plan, and at the correct moment the Queen's and
West Kent advanced co-operating with the Buffs. Considerable opposition was met with and a large number
of Germans killed and taken prisoner. A quantity of
machine guns and trench mortars and two 77-mm.
cannon were captured. In fact, the whole thing was
done in excellent order, and at eight in the evening all
objectives were gained and outposts put out. This
attack seems to have come as a surprise to the enemy,
yet, owing to their numerous machine guns, our casualties were by no means light. The night was quiet, but
at 3 o'clock next morning the Germans tried an attack
with a few troops, but these were repulsed. The
casualties of the Buffs consisted of Captain J. W.
Laurie, Lieuts. V. W. J. Hobbs and R. J. Pavitt and 12
other ranks killed; 11 officers and 145 men wounded
and 56 missing. With this loss the battalion alone was
responsible for the capture of 340 prisoners, a battery
of 4·2-in. howitzers, two minenwerfer, twelve machine
guns, two 77-mm. guns and seven light minenwerfer.

During the 10th the enemy snipers were very active,
and as our front consisted of a series of shell holes linked
up, observation on the enemy's part was fairly easy, and
consequently any movements on our side very difficult
and dangerous. Lieut. D. A. W. Hill (afterwards died
of wounds), 2nd Lieut. Harris and five men were
wounded on this day. The next few days were spent
in this same locality, either in front line or support, and
the shelling and sniping continued to be severe. There
was a report on the 15th that the enemy was withdrawing, but patrols sent out soon found the falsity of this
story. On the 20th the Buffs were in divisional reserve
at Treux, on the Ancre, and next day were attached
temporarily to the 35th Brigade, in order to take part
with it in the grand attack on Albert planned for the

22nd, in which the 18th Division, with the 7th Battalion of the regiment, was also to be engaged.

III. 6TH AND 7TH BATTALIONS: ALBERT, ETC.

The enemy was holding the line of the Ancre river, using Albert as a bridgehead. The stream here is only about fourteen feet wide, but it averages six feet in depth and has nasty marshy edges and approaches. Thus it is an obstacle requiring the carrying up of bridging material and so forth. The Germans were nearly all on the eastern bank of the river, but the cellars and ruins of the town of Albert, even on the western side, proved to be full of hidden parties cleverly availing themselves of what were in truth considerable facilities for defence. The rôle of the 18th Division was to cover the flank of the main attack of the 4th Army by taking Albert and the high ground beyond it. The 12th Division was on the right of the 18th and had the task of capturing the village of Meaulte, a little to the south, as well as other points. The 35th Brigade, however, was bound for Meaulte and was in immediate touch with the 18th Division.

The scheme of the 18th Division was as follows: the 55th Brigade was to capture Albert itself, and the 54th to operate south of that town and between it and Meaulte. Commencing at zero and for sixty minutes, all the houses of Albert which were to the east of the river were to be submitted to a heavy bombardment while the East Surrey Regiment worked through those to the west of the stream, " mopping up " the small hostile parties which were reported by our scouts to be there. Then our artillery was to lift and devote its attention to certain strong points on the east edge of Albert while the Surrey men crossed the Ancre and continued their work through the place. Finally, the guns were to lift again and allow the battalion to complete its job. Then the 7th Buffs were to come through the town, advance east-north-east till it got touch with the 54th Brigade, which would be attacking between Albert and Meaulte, and then to halt with its left flank on the floods. As it was quite impossible to reckon at what hour the East Surrey would have finished their work, the Buffs must make their advance without the help of a barrage.

As a matter of fact, the battalion debouched from the town at 10 a.m. and touch was got with the 54th Brigade, but then, heavy machine-gun fire being met with, progress astride the Albert–Pozieres road became impossible. All the country just outside Albert is dominated by Usna, Tara and Shamrock hills, which high ground was the especial objective of the 18th Division. When the Buffs emerged from the streets a false report was received that Tara Hill was occupied by the 54th Brigade, and our artillery got orders not to fire upon it. As a matter of fact, however, the enemy was still there and all their machine guns, which of course were not interfered with, were free to play on our battalion as it came on. This state of things caused a halt a little short of the Blue Line, for which the Buffs were bound, and the brigadier came to the conclusion that it would be impossible to push on further without the assistance of tanks and until it was dark. However, at 2.30 a.m. on the 23rd the Blue Line was made good. The Buffs had suffered about two hundred casualties, which were immediately made good by men originally left out of action.

Meanwhile the 35th Brigade, with which for a day or two the 6th Battalion served, was in position at 1.30 a.m. and endured heavy gas shelling during the night. 4.45 a.m. was the zero hour, and then the 6th moved forward, C Company being on the left and D on the right front, A left support and D right. The battalion moved behind the 7th Norfolk Regiment, to which unit

362

had been assigned the first objective. The 9th Essex was on the right of the Buffs. The whole operation this day was completely successful, all objectives being taken and consolidated. The second of these being secured by the 6th Buffs at 8.35 a.m., though unfortunately the Essex were held up by heavy machine-gun fire. There is no doubt that the work was done most creditably; eleven machine guns and fourteen prisoners fell to the share of the battalion we are interested in, and its own casualties were light: 2nd Lieuts. Gibbs and Green were wounded, five men killed, twenty-nine wounded, thirty missing and one gassed. Furthermore, when the second objective was gained the remainder of the day was quiet. The following day, the 23rd of the month, revealed the fact, however, that the situation on the right of the Buffs required much clearing up, so much so that tanks were sent up to investigate matters, and preparations were made for forming a defensive flank which necessitated some small rearrangement of the troops. It is interesting to note that during this day an aeroplane, in response to a call, managed to drop three thousand rounds of small-arm ammunition by means of a parachute.

On the 23rd the 18th Division had been busy. As has been seen, the original objective of the 7th Buffs had been gained at 2.30 a.m., but this move was chiefly made to enable other troops to get possession of the hills which up till then had dominated the British front. This was done, in spite of tremendous difficulties, by the 53rd Brigade with the 7th Queen's from the 55th, and it was greatly aided by seven tanks which had to approach from Meaulte along the east bank of the Ancre. The work was supported by a brigade of the 38th Division on the left of the 18th, which brigade had to get through Albert and then more to the north and pass the floods so close that many men were wading nearly breast high. Everything now going well, the

363

55th Brigade, less the Queen's, was temporarily withdrawn to divisional reserve west of Albert. The first stage of the attack had been a marked success, and all went so well during the time the 55th Brigade was away that when it returned to the front line in relief of the 53rd, which occurred on the night of the 24th/25th, it bore orders to push on the advance relentlessly. This relief was very different from those to which everyone was so well accustomed. It was a mobile business. No taking over of dug-outs and trenches, but the 7th Buffs simply walked into the place of the West Kent on the right of the brigade near the Becourt Wood and took up the running, so to speak.

As regards the 12th Division, the 6th Buffs, on the 24th, returned to their own 37th Brigade, which was ordered to carry on the advance, relieving the 35th, which had been ahead so far. At 1 a.m. the brigade, under an artillery barrage, attacked the enemy's position in front. At 1.30 the Buffs reported that all was going well but that they were facing heavy machine-gun fire, and they asked for the assistance of tanks to clear away certain pockets of the enemy which were giving trouble. Two hours later the Queen's reported that their right was held up, so, at 7 o'clock, three whippet tanks were placed at the disposal of the brigadier. At 1.30 these tanks, with the West Kent, attacked, but they were back again in an hour, having completely failed; one tank had its guns jammed, and one was badly damaged, for on crossing the ridge they had met with heavy machine-gun and trench-mortar fire. The enemy was still a force in being and knew exactly where to make a resolute stand. A consultation now took place as to the best mode of carrying on the advance on the morrow, and it was determined to leave the German strong place, which was giving so much trouble, and to pass on either side of it, so at 9.30 p.m. orders were issued for the task of the 25th: the Buffs were to

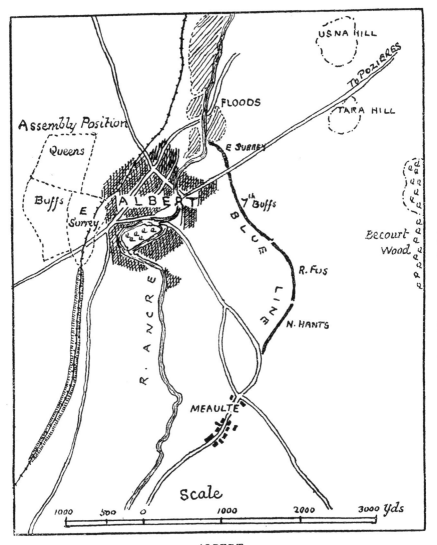

ALBERT

advance on the right, and Queen's on the left, with the West Kent in support. At midnight the Corps cavalry was placed at the disposal of the 37th Brigade. It was now found that the enemy had withdrawn, and it was pretty evident that he had gone back some considerable distance. On the 25th, therefore, the 36th and 37th Brigades, with the 35th in reserve, advanced, in order to maintain their touch with the retiring Germans. The move commenced in the middle of the night and was quite successful, so that by 5.15 the Buffs were holding a new line, once more in contact with the enemy, and with patrols pushed out in front. 2nd Lieuts. Barr and H. J. Hine, with eight other ranks, were wounded during the morning, Hine unhappily dying of his wounds. There was no doubt about the enemy's temporary stand—indeed, the British line was shelled all day; and at five in the evening the 55th Brigade came up from the reserve and went through as an advance guard, in conjunction with similar movements in the flanks. These troops drove the Germans back about two thousand yards and consolidated a new line, while the Buffs and Queen's, with the West Kent in reserve, held the old one. The tactics of the 25th were renewed on the 26th. On this day the 36th Brigade took up the advance guard duties, passed through the 35th and carried on the drive for about 3,500 yards. The 37th Brigade remained in position. On the 27th the fighting part of the programme was transferred to the 37th Brigade. Its units came through those of the 36th and at 4.45 a.m. attacked the enemy's position north of the Somme, captured the village of Carnoy and assisted the 58th Division to take Maricourt. It also took a valuable position north of Hardecourt. During these operations the brigade had been assisted by the cavalry, and after so prolonged a period of trench warfare it was strange to be working with so mobile an arm. The West Kents reporting themselves at 7.32 as being on their objective, and the Buffs doing the same at 7.45, the horsemen were sent forward to occupy the Maurepas ridge far ahead. At 9.20 a counter-attack appeared to be developing south of Bernafay Wood, and the 35th Brigade was ordered to send a battalion up to La Briqueterie to be at the disposal of the brigadier of the 37th, and at 10 o'clock a company of the Machine Gun Corps was added to his force. At 10.45 the Buffs found themselves being seriously enfiladed by machine-gun fire, so much so that their position became untenable and the battalion withdrew in good and correct order some two hundred yards. About this same time the cavalry, after reporting that Faviere Wood, between Hardecourt and Maricourt, was still occupied, had to be recalled as the ground was impossible to work over, owing to wire, shell holes and trenches. At 2 p.m. the brigade was directed to advance its line sufficiently to join up with the 18th Division east of Bernafay Wood, and later on a message came informing the brigadier that the 18th Division intended to attack at seven that evening, its objective being the east edge of Trones Wood, and directing that the battalions of his brigade should keep touch. The casualties to the 6th Battalion the Buffs on the 27th August were Captain L. P. Figgis and ten men killed, 2nd Lieuts. Findley, Hobbs, C. Hunt and H. M. Hunt and forty others wounded; twelve men were missing.

As regards the 7th Battalion, it too was moving forward at 2.30 a.m. On the 25th August the 54th and 55th Brigades, the latter on the left, pushed on without much opposition, the Buffs being on the right and East Surreys on the left of their own brigade. All went well until the neighbourhood of Montauban was reached, and here the opposition began to strengthen somewhat, the enemy showing that he thoroughly understood the scientific use of machine guns in rear-guard action.

Lieut. G. B. Mason, commanding A Company, was wounded crossing the crest north of Bottom Wood and progress became slow owing to very wet weather, but by nightfall the battalion had reached a line south of the western edge of Mametz Wood and were in touch with the troops on both flanks. The day's fighting had resulted in an advance of about a mile and a half. As soon as it was light on the 26th B Company, under Captain A. J. Whitmarsh, was sent forward to continue the advance, but now the enemy's resistance became more stubborn. The ground east of Montauban was very suitable for machine-gun rear guards, and each little position occupied by these had to be located before they could be first outflanked and then rushed in front. Captain Whitmarsh, with A Company on his left flank, which again kept pace with the East Surreys, took his own men on with great steadiness and skill, and at about 3.15 p.m. assaulted the village of Montauban, taking about sixty prisoners and killing the remainder of the garrison. He was greatly aided by flanking fire brought to bear by machine guns to the north of him. Whitmarsh was awarded the D.S.O. for his work on this day. At 6 p.m. the 7th Queen's was ordered up as vanguard to the division, the Buffs remaining east of Montauban, with Bernafay Wood full of Germans just in front of them. The next day B Company went back to Caterpillar Valley, where C already was, and these companies were joined by the other two on the 28th, the whole brigade being on that day withdrawn into divisional reserve.

The fighting described above was quite a revelation to most of the young officers and men of both the Buffs' battalions. Long experience of trench work, only varied by occasional raids or a battle, in the course of which one side or the other gained two or three hundred yards, made it difficult for most men to understand what open warfare really meant, and probably

367

many wondered why such stress is laid in England on the necessity of field days, with their extensive movements. Yet now they saw cavalry at work, infantry skirmishing and artillery galloping into action as if on Salisbury Plain, and behold it was very good.

On the morning of the 29th August the 54th Brigade advanced with very little opposition to the western edge of Combles, but was unable to get further because the enemy still held the ridge where the remains of Morval stood, and thus threatened the flank of any troops which tried to move further eastward.

Meanwhile the 6th Battalion, with the 6th West Kent on their left, had got as far as Maurepas, for that part of the enemy which was opposite them had withdrawn some distance during the night of the 27th/28th, so that in the morning these two battalions had pushed on, in artillery formation, and got into touch again at Maurepas. Here it was found that there was no sign of troops further to the south: the 58th Division, which should have been there, had apparently failed to come up. This meant, of course, that the Buffs had to form a defensive flank in this direction, but after a while the patrols managed to discover some Australians. During this day B Company completely outflanked a similar German unit, taking from it seventy-nine prisoners. Six of our men were wounded.

The several divisions and brigades relieved each other with great frequency during the grand allied advance we are describing. Of course, strong bodies of troops must always be behind those actually in touch with the enemy, and it was so arranged that everybody should have a turn at work nearest the foe and then be passed by some of those in rear, and so take on the business of reserve troops. On the 30th of August, therefore, the 12th Division was relieved by the 47th, the 24th London Regiment taking the place of the 6th Buffs, who retired to Faviere Wood and remained there till

368

the 4th September. On that date the 12th Division relieved the 18th in the left divisional sector of the 3rd Corps front, the Buffs going into trenches east of Fregicourt.

The 18th Division was now faced with the difficulty of passing the high ground about Morval. On the 30th an attempt to advance on Rancourt in conjunction with the 47th was met with very heavy machine-gun fire, particularly from Priez Farm, which was strongly held by the enemy. It was therefore found that for the present the pursuing tactics lately in use must be abandoned and a regular attack undertaken, for here was an obstinate stand. So on this date the 7th Buffs, with the rest of the 55th Brigade, were hurried up by bus to the neighbourhood of Montauban and Bernafay Wood, the Buffs being south of the latter place. It was decided that the 47th Division was to capture Rancourt and to the east of it as far as St Pierre Vaast Wood. The 38th Division was to take Morval and Sailly Saillisel, while the 18th Division was to assail the north-west corner of St Pierre Vaast Wood and form line facing north-east across the Sailly Saillisel–Rancourt road, the idea being to cut off the enemy holding the Fregicourt–Morval position. The 55th Brigade represented its division in this partition of work, and to the East Surreys was assigned the assault in the corner of the wood; the Buffs were to follow them, form to the left and attack northwards, and the Queen's to mop up the area north-east of Combles. Smoke barriers were arranged to cover the movements of the 55th Brigade. The day for the fight was at first fixed for the 31st August, but the position appeared so strong and the enemy's artillery so much more in evidence than had recently been the case, that it was resolved to first make exhaustive preparation with artillery and postpone infantry action for twenty-four hours. The operations necessitated for the Buffs a night march from their bivouac south of

2 B 369

Montauban. Little time was given for the issue of orders or reconnaissance, and the manœuvre contemplated was, if not intricate, at any rate somewhat out of the ordinary and the map issued the only guide to the ground. For these reasons, and in case of any accident, Colonel Ransome left B Company, under Captain Whitmarsh, in the assembly area of the East Surrey Regiment. The remainder were to advance in platoon columns for as long as possible in order to facilitate changes of direction. The move to the assembly area was a slow and tedious business; it was intensely dark, roads were scarce, landmarks few and country pitted with shell holes and strewn with wire; however, it was accomplished and in time. The next morning the attack developed according to plan. All accounts of it agree in according the highest possible praise to the 8th East Surrey Regiment, which unit bore the brunt of an action which was a complete success, all objectives being carried with comparatively few casualties. The principal opposition met with came from Priez Farm, which from the very start caused much trouble to the East Surreys, which was, however, not sufficient to stay that regiment's triumphant progress. The leading companies of the Buffs were also temporarily held by machine guns which had allowed the Surrey men to pass them; these guns necessitated a somewhat wider detour for those that followed than had been anticipated. However, with considerable management and able leadership, especially perhaps on the part of Captain Stronge, of D Company, the difficult advance and still more difficult wheel, during which seven thousand yards was covered, was accomplished. When near Rancourt C and D Companies wheeled to the north and occupied the high ground east-north-east of Fregicourt. The enemy was completely surprised and demoralized and began to stream away northward from Fregicourt, many being killed by C and D Companies while trying

370

to escape to Sailly Saillisel along the valley. The difficult task of seizing the high ground in rear of the enemy holding Fregicourt was successfully carried out and the division had done its part in the Second Battle of Bapaume.

The Buffs' casualties on this occasion were only two; Captain Stronge, Lieut. Wellman and 2nd Lieut. Lawrence were awarded the M.C. for their gallant conduct on this occasion.

A very large number of prisoners were taken. Receipts, for instance, were given to the Buffs for fourteen officers and nearly eight hundred men, though a good many of these were not actually captured by the battalion. Captain Whitmarsh, of B Company, was after the action ordered to send forward two platoons as patrols into St Pierre Vaast Wood and towards Sailly Saillisel, and as the enemy appeared to be greatly demoralised the 7th West Kent was ordered to attack the village at 7 p.m., which move necessitated a further advance on the Buffs' part to conform. During the operations between the 22nd August and the 1st September the 7th Buffs had 3 officers killed and 14 wounded; 26 men killed, 84 wounded and 55 missing.

On the 2nd the 53rd Brigade passed through to continue the pursuit. This day was a proud if a sad one for the 7th Battalion, for the commanding officer, Lt.-Colonel Ransome, D.S.O., M.C., who had so often led it to victory or stood in the gap during a necessary retreat, was removed on promotion to command the 170th Infantry Brigade of the 57th Division.[1] Next day Lt.-Colonel Curtis, D.S.O., joined on appointment

[1] Captain and Brevet Lt.-Colonel A. L. Ransome, D.S.O., M.C., went to France at the beginning of the war as adjutant of the 1st Battalion of the Dorsetshire Regiment, and after serving as Brigade Major of the 15th Infantry Brigade was appointed Commanding Officer of the 7th Buffs in February, 1916, with which he served without a break till September, 1918.

to the command. On the 4th September the battalion marched to Trones Wood, the division, as has been seen, being relieved by the 12th, and it remained there training till the 16th of the month.

Two days after this relief of divisions the 6th Buffs marched into Riverside Wood on the Tordille stream. While it had been in rear the other troops had, of course, driven the enemy considerably to the eastward, for the 53rd Brigade had taken up the pursuit after the turning of the Morval position. Therefore, when on the 7th the 37th Brigade advanced through the others to take up the duties of advance guard to its division, it became its duty to attack a line of trenches which ran from Heudicourt to Guyencourt, some eight miles east of St Pierre Vaast Wood. The 6th Buffs moved into its assembly position at 4.30 a.m., having C Company on the left, D on the right, A left support and B right support. The battalion had the West Kent on its left with the Queen's in support, and the objectives were: first, the east edge of Guyencourt; second, the high ground beyond; and third, the eastern outskirt of Epehy and the railway east of Peiziere. Both the Buffs and the West Kent had with them a section of Field Artillery, another of a Trench Mortar Battery and two sections of the Machine Gun Corps. The zero hour was 8 a.m., when an artillery barrage commenced. The enemy's machine guns were very active from the start, and his artillery fire, though somewhat feeble at first, gradually increased in density. At 9.30 the Buffs had to report that they were held up by numerous machine guns opposite their centre and they asked for artillery aid, which was at once arranged for, with the result that at 10.10 a.m. the battalion was in possession of Guyencourt. The second objective, the hill line east of the village, was taken at 11.15 and consolidation commenced. At 5.50 p.m. orders came to endeavour to make good Epehy and Peiziere. That evening, patrols

372

were pushing on, and at 8 o'clock both the leading battalions reported that they were moving forward; but a little later orders came that the 47th Division would continue the attack the next morning. The day had been a successful one, but the Buffs had Captain Tuke, 2nd Lieut. Thompson and twenty men wounded, four killed and six missing.

The 47th Division experienced some trouble the next day in gaining their objective, a line of trenches two thousand yards west of the Hindenburg Line, as the nearer the Germans were driven to their vaunted series of defences the stronger their opposition became, but at last the advance, which had been temporarily held up, was successfully renewed and a line of trenches gained and consolidated. The 12th Division again relieved the 47th on the evening of the 8th, but the Buffs were told off as divisional reserve and retired to St Pierre Vaast Wood, where they remained till the 17th, training, resting and playing football.

On the 16th of September the 7th Battalion embussed for Moislains and marched east to Longavesnes in a very heavy rainstorm, and next day the officers reconnoitred the approaches to Ronssoy from the high ground near Saulcourt; meanwhile the 6th Battalion was moving into assembly positions three hundred yards west of Guyencourt, cheered before going into action again by the news that Lt.-Colonel Smeltzer had a bar to his D.S.O., and that C.S.M. Coffin and Sgt. Ashby were each to wear the D.C.M. The enemy's opposition was now getting quite determined, and on the 18th it was arranged to assail him in force. For this purpose the 21st Division on the left, the 18th in the centre and the 12th on the right prepared to carry on the great eastward push, which had now gained some five-and-twenty miles from Albert. Put very briefly, the 35th and 36th Brigades captured the villages of Peiziere and Epehy, but owing to strong machine-gun resistance

were unable to make further headway; so the 37th
Brigade went forward at 3.30 p.m. to clear up the
situation. The objectives were then gained and everything settled by 6 p.m.

Also, a couple of miles or so to the south-east, the
7th Battalion co-operated in an attack by the 55th
Brigade on Ronssoy and the exploitation of the enemy's
position beyond the village. To amplify the stories of
these attacks a little: in both cases it was noticed that
the confidence of our soldiers was supreme; after years
of fighting what had seemed more or less a drawn battle,
victory was now daily crowning our arms, and success
was looked upon as a certainty. At 6.30 the 37th
Brigade, being then in reserve just north of Guyencourt, was informed that the Norfolk Regiment on its
front was being hardly pressed. At 8.25 it was reported
that our troops were seen retiring from Epehy pursued
by a tank which appeared to be an English one, manned
by a German crew. At 8.40 the brigadier of the 36th
Brigade reported that his troops had gained their first
objective, but had then been heavily enfiladed from
the north and by three tanks, one of them being
English; so the West Kent were sent off in this direction. There is no doubt that the German defence of
Epehy was a resolute one and of a different type to
what the British had now become accustomed to, and
the Queen's battalion, which of course belonged to the
37th (or reserve) Brigade, was ordered to keep touch
with the troops to the south and, if necessary, to move
round south of Epehy to do so; also a divisional order
came to the brigade soon after 9 o'clock that the Buffs
were to be kept in hand. By 10 o'clock the West Kent
were in Peiziere, with their forward company east of
the village, though the enemy's machine guns and
trench mortars were still holding out in the place. The
Queen's, with a battery, were in action two hundred
yards west of Epehy. It was now decided, as things

374

were not progressing too well, to attack formally at
3.50 p.m. with the Buffs and Queen's, so the barrage
started and these two battalions went forward, but
both were held up by machine guns before the objectives were gained. Captain S. S. Beall, Lieut. R. W.
Durdle, 2nd Lieut. A. Mount and eleven men were
killed, twenty-two wounded and two missing.

A considerable amount of dogged attack and equally
dogged defence on the part of the enemy formed the
story of the 6th Battalion up to the end of September.
On the 19th the Buffs and Queen's attacked the Germans in what were called Mule Trench, Bird Trench
and Braeton Post. The Buffs had been given the two
latter as objective. Very considerable machine-gun
opposition was met with, but a line a hundred yards
short of the objective was consolidated at 1.30 p.m. At
7.45 the " S.O.S." signal went up from part of the 18th
Division's front and there was heavy artillery fire on
our forward line, but no infantry action followed.
Lieut. Brooke was wounded, one man killed, twenty-
seven wounded and seven missing. The shelling continued next day, one projectile falling close to battalion
headquarters and wounding two servants and three
runners. At midnight on the 21st/22nd, under an
artillery barrage, the West Kent, with D Company of
the Buffs, made another assault which was at first unsuccessful—the opposition being most resolute. A
second attempt, at 3 p.m., had better fortune and a
new position was consolidated. Buffs' casualties: seven
killed and twelve wounded.

Then the 37th Brigade was relieved by the 35th and
the Buffs went into the sunken road south of Epehy,
where a comparatively quiet time was enjoyed till the
29th, the only time that action was called for being
that on the 27th of the month the Queen's, who were
temporarily attached to the 36th Brigade, carried out
another attack in conjunction with troops to the north

375

and south of them, and this battalion was supported by C Company The Buffs in the eastern outskirts of Epehy. Sgt. Alexander got a bar to his M.M. about this time, and C.S.M. Ashby and Pte. Bellchambers that medal itself.

Meanwhile the 7th Battalion had been far from idle. In conjunction with the rest of the 55th Brigade it attacked Ronssoy on the 18th. The work was at first extremely difficult owing to adverse weather conditions, which, however, fortunately improved during the day. The attack was led by the 54th Brigade, who were to capture and pass the village of Ronssoy. This force was to be followed by the 55th, which brigade was to emerge from the eastern edge and form up on the Green Line at 100 minutes after zero. This arrangement had the effect of so limiting the time available to the leading brigade for properly clearing or " mopping up " the village as it passed through, that it was necessary to warn the troops following to move to their places by a route south of the houses and to avoid street fighting as far as possible. The Germans, it was quite evident, expected an attack on this day and the assembly position was heavily bombarded, gas shells being so extensively used that respirators had to be worn for a considerable time. The East Surreys led its brigade, which was intended to leap-frog or pass through the 54th. The morning was wet and misty, which interfered sadly with visual signalling and caused some difficulty in keeping the proper direction. It was soon found that the ground was by no means clear, and machine guns and snipers gave a great deal of trouble. However, the men of Surrey pushed on and, emerging from the houses at the stipulated time, endeavoured to reach the Red Line, but were held up by machine guns from Lempire and Z Copse. Even the other battalions which followed met with much trouble in Ronssoy or on its borders, so many little parties remaining in

376

hiding. The general state of this place at 9 a.m. is exemplified by the fact that the brigadier, walking alone along the road, captured thirty-four Germans himself out of various dug-outs. General Wood threw lumps of chalk and old boots into these places and took the surrender of the men who came tumbling out. These men were fully armed, but dazed and cowed. By 11 a.m. the three battalions were concentrated in the objective trenches and sunken road, but Lempire and the Copses X, Y and Z still held out. Prisoners informed our people that the Red Line was only held by two German companies, so arrangements were made to advance upon it at 5 p.m. under a creeping barrage. On the right the assaulting troops reached this line in parts, but on the left progress was very slow, as machine guns in Lempire enfiladed the advance and the copses gave much trouble; moreover, it was clear that fresh German troops had come up during the afternoon. At 7 o'clock the attempt had to be abandoned for the time and, to prevent complete isolation, those parties which had succeeded in getting ahead were ordered back again. The struggle to get on proved a very protracted one. It is true that the 53rd Brigade captured Lempire post on the 19th, but it was not till 7 a.m. on the 20th that the Queen's got X Copse and the Buffs Y and Z. The progress of the East Surreys was stayed by opposition from Duncan's post. At 10 a.m. the enemy commenced a very heavy bombardment on our position, causing our advanced posts to be temporarily withdrawn to avoid casualties. The 53rd and 54th Brigades attacked the Red Line at 5.40 a.m. on the 21st, and when these were well up the 55th was brought back into divisional reserve in the village of Ronssoy. The two first-named found.very bitter resistance and, indeed, only captured parts of their objectives. However, on the night of the 22nd, the 55th Brigade, marching up again to relieve the front line, managed to place the Buffs from Cat's post to Duncan's post and the Queen's to the north of that, the Surreys being in brigade reserve. The 23rd of the month was a quiet day and devoted to reconnaissance, and at 6.45 on the 24th the Buffs tried Guillemont Farm, but failed owing to very strong opposition. During that night the brigade was relieved by American troops and retired to Combles. It was afterwards found that this action at Ronssoy had stayed a contemplated counter-attack on a large scale which had been planned by the enemy, the 231st German Division having been diverted to Ronssoy and rushed up to that post of danger by motor buses.

It was on the 28th that the 7th Battalion came up again into the area of active operations, moving on that day by bus to Guyencourt and bivouacking in a sunken road two thousand yards east of the village, ready for an attack next morning, their comrades of the 6th being close by just outside Epehy. On this Michaelmas Day the 12th Division, with an American one on the right and the 47th English on the left, attacked the Hindenburg defences in the neighbourhood of Vendhuille, while the rôle of the 7th Buffs was to assist in protecting the left flank of the Americans and to " mop up " Vendhuille village later on.

The 37th Brigade passed through the 35th with the 6th Buffs on the right and West Kent on the left. The 9th Battalion of the Essex were attached to the Buffs and the 6th Queen's to the 6th West Kent. The objective of the brigade was a line just west of the St Quentin Canal. The zero hour was 5 a.m. when, after a short artillery barrage, the forward move was commenced, the Buffs having A Company on the left, B on the right, C left support and D right support. Owing to the very strong resistance of the enemy, mostly by means of machine guns, the progress was rendered very slow, but at 8.45 the Buffs reported all going well, and

378

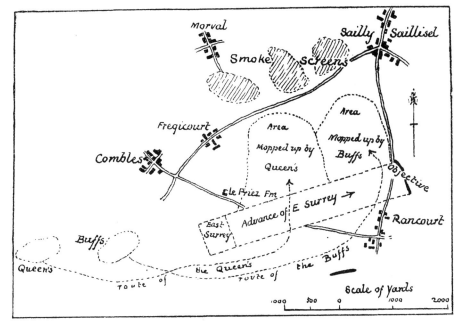

COMBLES AND MORVAL

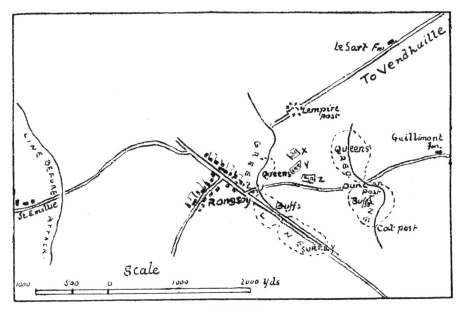

RONSSOY

at 9 o'clock the Americans were on all objectives. As the canal was approached the opposition became stronger, and this was particularly so at the Quarries, which fell to the lot of the Buffs to take. Indeed, at 10.30 the battalion had to report its left company as being held up here. However, delay was the worst misfortune that befell; gradual advance was made and the objectives were at length reached about 5 p.m. and consolidated after really stubborn fighting, which lasted all day without a break. The Buffs were, however, the only unit of the division that had attained the Blue Line. They captured 120 prisoners and about 40 machine guns, but lost Lieut. H. Thompson killed, Lieut. Dunkerley wounded, 2nd Lieut. Beard missing and about 40 killed or wounded.

The following day the battalion, working forward, reached the canal bank, having picked up four prisoners on the way, captured a 77-mm. gun and bombed many of the enemy's dug-outs.

The 12th Division was then relieved by the 18th, the 6th Battalion marching back to Guyencourt, while the 7th, who had marched off at 8.20 a.m. on the 29th and, moving south of Epehy, crossed the Epehy–Ronssoy road into St Patrick's Valley, where it halted about 10.10 a.m. Orders were then received to push on into the Macquincourt Valley to a position of deployment, but trouble came now and the further movements of the newly arrived battalion of the Buffs and others were altered more than once by varying circumstances, the end of the day coming without any marked episode, and evening finding the men in Sart Farm and the neighbouring trenches. The Buffs had moved forward according to order, following the 7th Queen's, and these were held up by enemy's machine guns near Guillemont Farm. Further movements not being possible, orders came to occupy an area of trenches in the neighbourhood. An abortive attempt at attack on the

Knoll was commenced soon after one o'clock, but the situation was found to be too obscure and the fire too hot to advance against, so the brigade settled into the trenches for the night. During the morning of the following day an officer's patrol from A Company pushed on and established a post in Macquenet trench, and orders came about 1 p.m. to make all progress possible in the direction of Vendhuille, so by 5 p.m. A Company was established in Macquenet trench, losing its leader, Lieut. A. N. Widdop, while moving there, and B and C well forward; but at night the battalion position was taken over by the East Surreys and the Buffs were placed in brigade reserve, and on the 2nd October were taken away to Contay, some ten miles west of Albert, for a fortnight's rest and recreation, which of course included training.

An endeavour has been made to trace the history of the 6th Battalion and the 7th together from the capture of Albert to that of the Hindenburg Line at Vendhuille, that is from the 22nd August till the end of September, because during that very strenuous and historic period the 12th and 18th Divisions, to which the Buff units respectively belonged, were working hand in hand, supporting and relieving each other and so on, but from the 1st October till the end of the war the 6th and 7th were far apart again; the former, together with the whole division in which it was serving, was transferred to the 1st Army very early in October, and therefore the area of their activities was no longer identical, and the 6th Buffs were at Rumegies, ten miles south of Tournai, when the war came to an end; while the 7th celebrated that event at the village of Pommereuil, not very far from Le Cateau. It will therefore be convenient now to complete the war story of the 6th Battalion and then consider that of their comrades of the 7th.

IV. 6TH BATTALION

On the 1st October, then, the 6th Buffs proceeded by bus and by march route into billets at Caucourt, which village may be about twelve miles or so north-west of Arras, but rest here was for an extremely short period and the 6th of the month found the battalion in buses again for Avion, from whence it marched into trenches at Mericourt, just south-east of Lens. This region was not yet clear of the enemy, who had been driven back since August considerably further in some directions than in others. The old and familiar machine gun was soon heard again, therefore, and they were very active the day after the battalion arrived, and the usual patrols which went out in front experienced also their fire on the 8th. However, these patrols established themselves at Molly Villers, a thousand yards in front of our own line, being relieved by the West Kent soon afterwards. On the 13th the 6th Royal West Kent advanced from Mericourt to the Drocourt–Queant trenches, and they had the Buffs in support during the move which brought both regiments into this line for the night, the Buffs' headquarters being at Floquieres. At this time there was a certain amount of movement occasioned by the readjustment of the larger commands preparatory to a grand processional march towards the east; the enemy was at his last gasp, so to speak, and there was no longer any very strenuous opposition. The 37th Brigade ultimately concentrated at Auby on the 18th October and the advance commenced the next day, the units taking turn to lead and encounter any opposition that might have been organized. Thus the West Kents led off and the Buffs followed, the first day taking the brigade to Flines. On the 20th the Buffs led and advanced as far as Beuvry, arranging the front line at Orchies–Beuvry. This was a very satisfactory day, because the Buffs were able to set free hundreds of un-

381

fortunate civilians who had been in the power of the beastly Germans, who, of course, had not actually evacuated the country which was now being passed over. There was always an attempt to sting during the great retreat, even if no regular resistance was made. Thus a soldier was killed on the way to Beuvry, and 2nd Lieut. Roper-Curzon and four men wounded.

On the 21st the Queen's led the way, and the West Kent, being in front on the 22nd, reached the banks of the River Scarpe, where it was found that all civilians had been released by the retreating German. On the 23rd, when the Buffs were in front, a little more opposition was met with, in so far that a fairly strong machine-gun fire was encountered at Cubray; but this was successfully dealt with, heavy casualties inflicted on the enemy and several prisoners taken. During the night the Buffs rushed what was in front of them and established themselves in Haute Rive. Captain H. Hunter, M.C., and nine men were wounded on this day, the success of which was marred by the death on the same day of the gallant captain from the result of his injuries.

The enemy were making a better stand now than had been the case during the last week, and on the 24th it was found that the villages of Bivridon and Bruille were strongly held. Nothing however at this time, when success had been ours for days, was at all likely to stop the British dash. The Buffs attacked at 9 a.m. and so rapidly and unexpectedly that the enemy was taken by surprise during his breakfast meal and utterly discomfited, so that our line was established upon the River Escaut, after capturing some prisoners, four machine guns and two trench mortars, the Buffs being the first on the whole Corps front to reach that stream; but they lost 2nd Lieut. J. D. Thornley, M.C., and one man killed, Captain Kidd, M.C., Lieuts. Fiske and Hoskyn, 2nd Lieut. Foreman and sixteen wounded.

The General Officer Commanding the Army Corps appreciated the work done on the 24th, for he sent a message to the 12th Division: " Please convey to the " officers, N.C.O.'s and men of the 6th Buffs my appre- " ciation of the well-thought-out plan and good organi- " zation and fine offensive spirit that led to the capture " of Bruille on the 24th of October. It is an operation " that reflects great credit not only on all who took part " in it, but also on the brigade and the fine division to " which they belong." Thus this good and glorious battalion finished up their war history, for it was its last action. Very few old officers of four years back, not even perhaps Colonel Eaton himself, could have thought it possible to manufacture and train a new fighting unit, even though that unit bore an ancient and honourable name, that could do the deeds that the 6th Buffs had done, not once or twice, but over and over again, and could earn at the last such an eulogy from an experienced general as is quoted above.

The battalion now moved back in support and ulti- mately found itself in billets at Coutiches, where it remained till the 10th November, on which date it marched to Rumegies, so that it was at this latter village that Armistice Day was spent. The great news came through at 10 a.m., and at 11 o'clock, the hour of cessa- tion of hostilities, a thanksgiving service was held in front of battalion headquarters, the commanding officer and the padre both addressing the battalion, which then marched through the village with its drums beating and the men singing at the top of their voices. On the 14th of November Captain Gullick, M.C., 2nd Lieut. Ayres and forty men formed part of a guard of honour for the Army Commander on the occasion of his entering Mons accompanied by H.R.H. The Prince of Wales. On the 25th the battalion moved south-west to Auberchicourt, there to be quartered, the time being taken up with salvage fatigues and the soldiers kept fit

by means of running drill. Christmas Day was properly
and religiously kept, and for once the stereotyped wish
of the season contained some sense in it. The interval
between the great peace day and the end of the year
brought some honours to the 6th Battalion which were
awarded at different dates. Thus Sgt. and Acting
C.S.M. J. Smith obtained a bar to his M.M., and Sgt.
Sparks and Corpls. Mount and Penfold were given that
decoration itself. Captain Gullick was awarded a clasp
to his M.C., Lieut. Fiske got the M.C. and Pte. Mitchell
the D.C.M. L.-Corpl. McDonald a little later headed
a batch by virtue of a clasp to his M.M., and the following got that coveted decoration for the first time:
Sgts. Fisher, Latter, Odell, Pennell, Shelley and
Smurthwaite; L.-Sgt. Knappett; Corpls. Allbright,
Buxton, Holman, Miller, O'Rourke and Williams;
L.-Corpls. Istead, Richardson, Soulsby and Stobart;
Ptes. Brazier, Jones, Setchfield, Smithers and Wise.
Also at the end of the year Lt.-Colonel Smeltzer,
D.S.O., M.C., was again mentioned in despatches, as
was Corpl. Pilcher.

V.   7TH BATTALION: THE SELLE, ETC.

The story of the 7th Battalion for October and afterwards is as follows: on the 16th October, when the
well-earned fortnight's rest was completed and the unit
fit and ready again, it was taken by train to Roisel and
marched to Templeux la Fosse, moving on again on the
18th by familiar Ronssoy to Beaurevoir, and after a
night in billets there to Élincourt, where the men were
interested to find civilians once again. It was really
wonderful how the brave French peasants, both men
and women, clung to their homes. On the 21st to
Maurois, four miles further on, where at last hostile
signs were met with once more, shells coming over and
bombs arriving per aeroplane at night time. The next

384

day took the brigade to Reumont and the concentration area west of Le Cateau.

The 3rd Army was now engaged in important operations in the strip of country to the immediate north of the region awarded to the 4th, of which the 18th Division now formed a unit, and on the 23rd October it fell to the lot of the latter army to attack for the purpose of protecting the major operations to be carried out by the former. The country now forming the theatre of operations was widely different to the Somme Valley and other parts to which the troops had become so accustomed. The numerous hedgerows and ditches affected the style of attack and defence. The arrangements for the attack by the 18th Division on the 23rd October, which formed part of the battle of the Selle, were made with most elaborate care. The area over which the advance was to take place was most exactly divided into portions with an objective at the further end of each portion and, of course, troops detailed to take each objective; moreover, each piece of ground was to be gained by a certain time and each halting place left for further adventure exactly so many minutes afterwards. (See diagram on next page.)

The 53rd Brigade on the right, with the 54th, less the Northamptonshire Regiment, on the left, were to make good the first and second objectives, and the 55th Brigade, with the Northamptonshire and certain details, were to capture the third, fourth and fifth. The 55th and Northamptonshires' attack was arranged to be carried out leap-frog fashion, so that the ground between the second and fourth objectives was to be made good by the Buffs and East Surreys, the latter being on the right. The advance was not to be covered by a creeping barrage, but was to be proceeded with at the regular rate of one hundred yards in four minutes, and no one unit, if instructions were carried out, could ever find itself unsupported by another through advancing

DIAGRAM OF ADVANCE OF 18TH DIVISION AT BATTLE OF THE SELLE [1]

Oct. 23rd, 1918

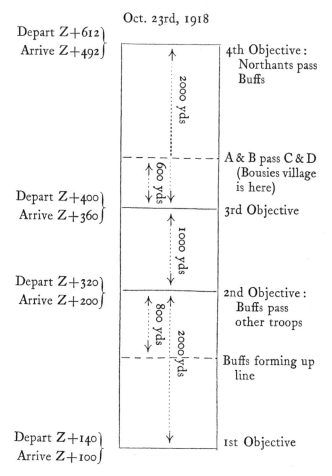

Depart Z+612
Arrive Z+492

2000 yds

4th Objective:
Northants pass
Buffs

A & B pass C & D
(Bousies village
is here)

600 yds

Depart Z+400
Arrive Z+360

3rd Objective

1000 yds

Depart Z+320
Arrive Z+200

2nd Objective:
Buffs pass
other troops

800 yds

2000 yds

Buffs forming up
line

Depart Z+140
Arrive Z+100

1st Objective

[1] Z + a number means that number of minutes after zero hour.

too fast. This leap-frog system of advance obtained even amongst battalions. At any rate, the Buffs arranged that C Company on the right and B on the left should be responsible for the ground from the second objective to a certain line, where A and B should pass through them bound for the fourth objective, at which the Northamptonshire would leap-frog the Buffs and go on to the end. A section of machine guns and one trench mortar was with the battalion reserve and a section of tanks in the immediate rear; the idea being that any company getting into trouble was to apply to the commanding officer, who would send tanks to its aid. Communication was carefully arranged with the accompanying aeroplanes. The zero hour was 2 a.m.

The Buffs arrived at their assembly position at 4.15, suffering fifteen casualties from shell fire on the way. At five they moved in artillery formation towards the forming-up line. Before reaching this the leading companies came under heavy machine-gun fire from the right flank, the brigade in front having only established the line of the first objective. This little trouble, however, was obviated by our aeroplanes dropping bombs on the machine guns. The second objective was passed at 8 o'clock, or forty minutes late. D Company (Captain E. V. Morse, M.C.), on the left, cleverly outmanœuvred and captured a battery of guns, but soon afterwards the captain was killed. He had ably led his company and dealt with many difficult positions. C Company also captured its battery, but, after passing the second objective, the enemy's opposition stiffened and a great deal of machine-gun fire came from the village of Bousies. However, at 10 o'clock the leading companies were close up to the third objective, which, by the way, should have been reached four hours earlier. At twenty minutes past ten a message was dropped from the air: " Huns still in Bousies. Our boys in eastern part ' mopping up.' Huns' transport just galloped from village." Ten minutes later Colonel Curtis ordered Captain Whitmarsh to take command of all troops in the battalion sector and endeavour to establish the Green Line, or third objective. At 12.30 the officer in charge of tanks reported that he had been in the village of Bousies with A Company (the right support) and that he had left that company there " mopping up " the village. At 2.40 p.m. all the Buffs' companies were on a road which is beyond the point where B and A Companies were to relieve the other two. The battalion was in touch on their right, but its left flank was exposed, though patrols were busy in this direction, and these soon reported that the 2nd Argyll and Sutherland Highlanders, though in rear of the Buffs' position, were pushing forward. A and B Companies were then directed to hold the road, with the others in close support. Heavy machine-gun fire was experienced from the high ground a little distance in front. At 6 o'clock A and B moved forward and made good their objective by 7.15, and an hour afterwards were relieved by the Northamptonshire Regiment, the Buffs going into brigade reserve. Great credit was given in connection with this day's work to the accompanying tanks under Lieut. Grey, who very fearlessly reconnoitred to the front and dealt with the machine-gun difficulty.

During the afternoon of the following day the Buffs moved into positions in Bousies and there formed a line of resistance. While still in this village on the 25th a report came in that the right sector of the brigade was withdrawing and C Company was pushed forward to deal with any possible German counter-attack, but found the battalion of the Queen's alert for that duty. The Buffs relieved the East Surreys on outpost duty. On the 26th the brigade on the left made a determined effort to gain ground, but without much success, owing to the usual machine-gun fire. The next day the Buffs became divisional reserve in billets in Bousies, but were back again in forty-eight hours.

There was a considerable pause in the proceedings after the fight just recorded, and no further advance was made until the 4th November, the brigade taking its turn with the others both in the front line and in the trenches, but never very far from the village of Bousies. For the above-mentioned date, however, another blow had been planned. The enemy was despairing and discouraged, but must not be given too much time in which to pull himself together. The task set was very similar to that of the 23rd October. The 53rd and 54th Brigades were first to capture Preux and Hecq and get into the western part of the Mormal Forest, which is a very extensive one, but easy to pass by reason both of the numerous roads and paths and by the absence of thick underwood. After this the Buffs and Queen's were to pass through at a certain fixed hour. For this purpose Bousies was left at 8.15, two hours after zero, and a sunken road west of Landrecies reached after a few shell casualties had been suffered by the way. Here the headquarters of a Bedfordshire battalion informed the Buffs that the attack on the left had developed satisfactorily; but the 54th Brigade on the right, having come up against strong nests or pockets of hostile machine guns just west of Preux, had made but poor progress through the orchards on its line. Owing to this the 10th Essex had been unable to reach their forming-up position, and as it was the Buffs' job to pass through this 10th Essex they were, of course, looking out for them. The officer commanding the Buffs therefore decided not to proceed till the Essex had got on a bit, but put his battalion for a while into the trenches with the Bedfords, and sent on patrols with a request to be kept informed of the movements of those they were to relieve. At last, at 12.50, orders came to advance gradually and an hour later to push on with speed to the third objective, and so, after passing Preux, the Red Line was reached at 3.40 without further incident. After the morning's first stubborn resistance the enemy had, as a matter of fact, retired hurriedly through the forest and put up no further fight. At 10.50 at night orders came to continue the advance at 6.30 in the morning, and at that hour the 8th East Surrey started as divisional vanguard, the Buffs following at the head of the main guard. Very little resistance was met with, and the final objective, the bank of the River Sambre at Sassegnies, was gained about noon.

At 7.50 a.m. on the 6th the 55th Brigade was by arrangement squeezed out, as it was termed, and so had finished its long fighting record. The Buffs marched back to Preux tired and very cold and wet, for the weather throughout these operations had been bad. The 8th of November took the battalion further back to Pommereuil, and there, as nothing must be left to chance, immediate reorganization and making up of deficiencies was commenced. Then came the armistice and with it the finish of the war record of the 7th Battalion of the Buffs, a record which is comparable with any battalion in the army and which includes the First Battle of Albert in 1916, the Battle of Bazentin Ridge, Thiepval Ridge, the Ancre heights, the Battle of the Ancre, the Battles of Arleux, of Poelcappelle, St Quentin, Amiens, Second Battle of Albert in 1918, the Second Battle of Bapaume, the Battle of Epehy, Battle of St Quentin Canal, the Battle of the Selle and the Battle of the Sambre.

There is not much to record for the remainder of the year. The 7th Buffs was not one of the units told off to move into Germany on the 13th November; it went into billets at Elincourt, and on the 17th there took place a brigade thanksgiving service. Then a great deal of salvage work was done, as was the case with

390

most corps. On the 4th December His Majesty The King came to Elincourt and passed on foot between the rows of his soldiers. On the 12th of this month the battalion moved to Mallincourt, and five days later came a most unfortunate occurrence, which strikes one as particularly bad luck after the armistice had been concluded only a month or so. During salvage operations a blind shell exploded, killing seven men and wounding twenty, as well as four more who, being only slightly injured, remained at work. There was a distribution of medals, etc., to the Buffs and East Surreys on the 23rd December.

VI. 10TH BATTALION

The great Allied advance to victory began with our 10th Battalion near St Floris, which is seven miles south of the town of Hazebrouck. This unit and the 74th Division, to which it belonged, was part of the 5th Army, whose area was considerably north of the country in which the 6th and 7th Battalions operated. During the very strenuous and important month of September, however, the division went south to the 4th Army where the others were, and there saw fighting at the Battle of Epehy before it returned to its regular area and wound up its military experiences at Tournai in November.

The advance, as far as the 10th was concerned, commenced on the 6th August, for on that date an attempt was made to push forward. The brigade on the right succeeded, but, owing to considerable opposition, the Buffs were unable to do the same except on their right, where B Company threw out three posts to keep in touch with the 16th Devons. The battalion had one man killed and three wounded. The next day, however, C and D Companies got ahead with but little trouble, and on the 8th a further advance was made. The companies in front were now B and C, and they went forward about one thousand yards and crossed the enemy's trenches. This progress might perhaps have been continued had other parts of the British line in the neighbourhood been equally successful. Next morning, the other two companies being in front, the advance started again, but A Company was somewhat heavily counterattacked on its right flank, which drew back to maintain touch with the 229th Brigade on its right, which was stationary. However, at 7 o'clock D and A Companies got on to the west bank of the River Lys and would have crossed had not all the bridges been destroyed. The crossing, in fact, had to be delayed till the Royal Engineers brought up three bridges, which were quickly in place, and then the infantry dug themselves in on the far bank. The Buffs had six killed and Lieut. Atkinson and thirteen wounded.

Patrols, working to the front, soon discovered that the Germans, armed with many machine guns, were prepared to dispute any further progress, so that an effort made at 9.30 p.m. on the 12th to get forward had to be a properly organized one. It was extremely dark and the ground all shell holes and irregularities, so that the attempt to advance was a failure, though it was the means of ascertaining that it was a considerable force to which our people were opposite and not merely a small rear guard, mostly consisting of machine guns. The battalion had three killed and seventeen wounded, one of whom died, and seven missing.

On the 14th the Buffs were relieved and became supports, and two days afterwards occupied a reserve line just outside St Venant and facing east-north-east. Here the men set to work on the reserve trenches and remained at this job for a week. Soon after this the 10th Buffs entrained at Lillers for Heilly, and by the end of the month the 74th Division was down with the 4th Army in the Somme Valley, the Buffs on the 31st

August being at Maurepas, near Combles. It will be remembered that this was the day first arranged for the fight round Fregicourt, which was, however, postponed for twenty-four hours; it was in this fight that the 7th Battalion took so prominent a part in cutting off the Germans who tried to defend the Morval position on the 1st September.

It was on the 2nd of the month that the 74th Division made their attack and the scene was just south of Moislains, some four miles from the other battlefield. The 229th Brigade, aided by one battalion of the 230th, made the attack. It failed to reach the objective, the machine-gun fire being too heavy. The Buffs were in reserve in a valley to the south-west of Moislains and were heavily shelled all day with high explosive and gas; two men were killed and Captain Vickery (the doctor) and twelve men wounded.

The enemy's rapid retreat did not commence till the 5th of the month; in the interval the 10th Buffs had, on the 3rd, moved into the front line, 2nd Lieut. Onions being on that day wounded by gas shell. The battalion had what was called the Midenette trench in front of it, and this was reported to be occupied by Germans; but on the morning of the 5th two platoons of C Company, pushing forward to keep touch with the 47th London Division on the left, captured the trench without much opposition, and at 6 p.m. the battalion advanced, captured another line and tried to get on still further; but the usual machine-gun opposition began to get heavy and the whole line remained for the present along the Peronne–Cambrai road. The next day the advance continued and with rapidity. The battalion started at 8 a.m. with D and A Companies, C in support and B in reserve. At 3.45 p.m., finding that the 47th Division on the left had dropped behind, and having passed through Templeux la Fosse and reached Longavesne, a halt was called, an outpost line arranged

393

and a defensive flank formed for security till the Londoners arrived. Three men were killed and twelve wounded this day.

On the 7th September the 230th Brigade was relieved in the front line and became reserve to the division, in which capacity it remained for a couple of days, taking a forward place again on the 10th of the month and passing, on its way to do so, the village of Villers Faucon. The ensuing little tour of four days before going into reserve again at Longavesnes was more or less uneventful, for heavy and consistent shelling can hardly be termed an event. During this short time Lieut. Mathews and 2nd Lieut. Jackson were wounded, two men killed and sixteen wounded, one of whom died.

On the 16th September the battalion moved into the Faustine Quarries, ready for a further advance. The rain was heavy, and gas and high-explosive shelling were heavier and aeroplane bombing very severe. Having taken its place in the front line on the 17th, the 10th Battalion next day took its share with the 1st, 6th and 7th Battalions of the Buffs in the Battle of Epehy. The 74th Division on the opening day of this fight was more immediately successful than the 12th or 18th, which units, it will be remembered, met with considerable opposition about Epehy and Ronssoy. The 15th Suffolk and 16th Sussex were to lead the way up to the first objective and the whole began to move up very early in the morning, which was an exceedingly wet one. A pitched battle on French soil was a novelty for the 10th Battalion, and the severity of the opening barrage impressed the men considerably. The German opposition in this part does not appear to have been quite as resolute as at most points in front of the Hindenburg Line. At Templeux le Guerard there are some quarries where pits, refuse heaps and holes and corners generally, offer an exceptionally good position for defence, but these were soon given up, as the Suffolk and Sussex, with the Buffs and Somerset in close support, came resolutely on; these quarries were passed and the Hargicourt trench, which was the first objective, taken without a check at 8 o'clock. Here half an hour's breathing time was given and then the advance resumed; this time with the Buffs in front, the next objective being what were called the Zogda trench and Rifle-pit trench another mile away. Success continued with the division. The artillery barrage was perfect and the infantryman's confidence in it supreme, which is exactly as it should be. The enemy's machine guns presented difficulties, and indeed held up the oncoming line for a little while, but at noon, or soon after, the Zogda trench was ours and a short further advance commenced. But now the trouble which was being experienced at Epehy and Ronssoy began to make itself felt; the stoppage of the 18th Division prevented the left brigade of the 74th getting on, so there was a check all along the line, which extended to the Australians on the right of the Yeomanry Division. About 5 p.m. Very lights were put up on the left of the division, which meant that a counter-attack was expected. This drew our own barrage which came down along the line of the second objective. The Buffs, with others, being by now about three hundred yards in front of this, were very much in the way, and an immediate withdrawal into the Zogda and Rifle-pit trenches was the result. An enormous number of prisoners and considerable booty had been taken. Indeed, many Germans seemed most anxious to come in and so end their fighting days. Captain H. L. Allfrey, 2nd Lieut. E. G. Porter and ten men were killed this day, forty-eight wounded and two missing. The Buffs remained in their captured trenches for a couple of days and were under a good deal of shell fire. In fact, eight men were wounded on the 19th.

395

The next advance was arranged for the 21st, the objective being about 1,200 yards in front of the Zogda trench and up-hill towards Quennemont Farm. At 5.40 a.m. D and C Companies formed in front line, with A in support, and advanced to take the Blue Line. The country to be crossed was like an old-fashioned glacis, very bare of cover and of a more or less regular slope, the summit of which was well protected by wire and full of machine guns. The Australians were on the right, then the 230th Brigade and on the left, but a little in rear, the 231st Brigade. The start was made behind a barrage, almost before it was light, and was successful enough in so far that regular progress was made until the day broke, when the assaulting troops got among thick belts of wire near Zoo trench, which, of course, checked the infantry while the barrage went on. A few men got through the wire, and then the enemy emerged from his dug-outs and commenced a tremendous fire of shells and machine-gun bullets. C and D Companies, which were in front, could do nothing but take cover in shell holes, wait and hope. The supporting A Company was just as badly off as C and D and could not move, and troops on the left fell back before a counter-attack, so that the Germans who made it were, in the nature of things and merely as a result of their success, now threatening the Buffs in rear and the battalion was in a tight place; the telephone was disconnected, no movement was possible, and, though two gallant runners got back with a report of the situation, both men being wounded over their job, no message could come up from behind to the forward companies. The troops on the left took up a new line parallel to the Zogda trench, and when darkness fell the Buffs managed to get back in small parties to this shelter, having lost Captain C. E. Hatfield, M.C., 2nd Lieut. H. A. Oxley and 12 men killed, Lieut. Turnpenny, 2nd Lieut. Hoare and 58 wounded, Lieut. Wilkinson and 6 other ranks " wounded and missing," also 20 more " missing."

After this action the battalion, being relieved by the 15th Suffolk on the following day, remained in reserve under intermittent shell fire till the 25th, during which period three more men were killed and four wounded, one of whom died. The authorities now decided that the 74th Division would again be required in its own army, so, after being relieved by American troops, the Buffs entrained at Peronne for Villers Bretonneux, and again on the 27th at Heilly for Lillers, from whence the battalion marched to billets at Allovagne and remained there refitting and so on till the end of the month. The total casualties during the fighting epoch of the month of September were very considerable, namely, 11 officers and 218 men killed, wounded and missing. Previous to his death Captain Hatfield was given the M.C. for his share in the business, and eleven men the M.M., namely, Sgts. Denton and English, Corpl. Dunn, and Ptes. Dennett, Dier (both of whom died), Forscott, Hibbs, Mather, Sidwell, Sutch (R.A.M.C.) and Willis; and Captain Haughton, M.C., was mentioned in despatches.

On the 1st October the Buffs relieved the 9th Royal Welch Fusiliers in the Richebourg sector, advancing to the front line just west of Lillers next day. This was the commencement of a slow but certain push eastward on the part of the 74th Division, and indeed of the army to which it belonged. There were many delays. The roads and bridges were destroyed by the retreating foe, and a delay caused to one unit on account of either these reasons or by a hostile rear guard meant a check to the whole movement, for the German resistance was not so wholly broken down as to render it wise or safe for the pursuers to break their line by pushing one body of troops in front of another. Sainghin was reached on the 3rd October and there ensued a halt for some days, chiefly because the 55th Division on the right was stayed by the La Bassee Canal. The enemy refused to allow this halt to be a quiet one, and the troops were shelled pertinaciously and thoroughly. The Buffs took their turn in front line and in support and, when in the former, sent out many patrols; in fact, patrolling at this time was kept up both by day and by night, as it was of the utmost importance to keep in touch with the enemy. These parties were able to discover some of the hostile machine-gun nests, and on the 9th of the month our artillery was able to deal with several of these which had been located.

On the 15th the forward move was resumed and the patrols pushed through Rosoir. On the 17th, the Suffolks leading and the Buffs following, Emmerin was reached at 12.10, and the Buffs, passing through, pushed onward in the afternoon towards the road east of Faches, for the division was to pass to the southward of the great town of Lille. Owing to the darkness, progress after leaving the Suffolk was slow and the road was not reached till 6.30 a.m., after which posts were established slightly to the east of the roadway. This country had been for four years in the possession of the Germans, and it is impossible to describe the joy manifested by the French inhabitants at their release at last from their horrible servitude. The Buffs never experienced, nor are they likely to again, such exuberant tokens of welcome and gratitude as they met with in the neighbourhood of Lille. The Frenchman feels very deeply indeed, and he is a demonstrative man. The march continued, every day adding a few miles to the completed journey, and on the 24th the Buffs were at Marquain, only three miles west of the city of Tournai. Here it became pretty evident that the enemy intended making a stand. The shelling, both gas and high explosive, became very severe; night patrols met with heavy machine-gun fire and in every detail resistance was stiffening on the line held by the Germans between our front and the city. Hertain, Marquain and Orcq are all villages just outside the western edge of Tournai, and all these were occupied by the English during the last few days of October, and up till the 7th November the Buffs were first in one and then in the other, according to the nature of their duty as front-line troops or reserve. The brigadier-general commanding inspected the 10th Battalion of the Buffs on the 4th November just as if they had all been at Aldershot, and he took that opportunity of presenting the M.M. ribband to Ptes. Mather and Sidwell. The battalion made a very smart appearance on parade, for the men were ready to enter Tournai and this was not to be done in a slovenly, untidy manner. On the 8th came news that the enemy had withdrawn, and the Buffs, moving up at 11.15 a.m., made a grand entry into the Faubourg de Lille well groomed and turned out and with the band playing triumphantly. All went very well up to a certain point, and then machine-gun fire from the town itself commenced. The German was not so far off, after all, so the march was stayed and all was war again in so far that street fighting continued during the night. The British intelligence might have been somewhat at fault when the Faubourg de Lille was entered in parade style, but it was only a little premature. The German rear guard quitted the place next day, but, of course, blew up all the bridges over the Scheldt. The Germans evacuated the city of Tournai only on the 9th November, and the very next day it was entered by the good King Albert of the Belgians, who was accompanied by his Queen. They came to congratulate their faithful people on their release from German thraldom which had oppressed them for so long.

The next day was the 11th November and at eleven o'clock in the morning there was no more war in France nor Flanders, and the Yeoman of Kent had done his work even if it was not done on horseback. The 10th Battalion was, on receipt of the great news, in the Faubourg de Lille. At 11.45 it marched through Tournai and moved away to the eastward, halting at Montreuil au Bois and Herquecies till, on the 14th of the month, it reached Barry, where it remained for nearly a month. During the operations which culminated in the capture of Tournai and which ended in the armistice, the Military Cross was awarded to Captain J. I. H. Friend and the Military Medal to Sgt. Rudman and to Pte. Hale. The casualties were 2 officers and 18 men killed, 2 officers and 71 men wounded.

On the 7th December a visit was received from His Majesty King George. It was, at his own request, a very informal affair. The men were drawn up on each side of the Tournai–Leuze road just outside Barry, and the King walked quietly down between them, but the welcome he received was one which it is pretty safe to believe was pleasing to our monarch.

The demobilization of such of the men as were miners commenced on the 10th December; but the total dispersal to their homes of an army the size of the British one at this period is a long and tedious job.

VII.   1st Battalion

We left the 1st Battalion in the Malin House area in the vicinity of Dickebusch. It did not immediately take part in the great triumphant and final push, and indeed its history up to the middle of September is not so exciting or full of incident either as that of the sister battalions or as certain periods of its own recent history. It remained in the neighbourhood of Dickebusch, taking its turn in trench work, till the 23rd August; during this period two American companies were attached for a few days, which not only gave our men the pleasure of making new and interesting friends, but

400

was a tangible proof that matters were going well and a successful end to a very awful and strenuous existence fairly in sight; during August, too, came the news of honours, which is always pleasant. First Sgt. Hills got the M.M.; then 2nd Lieut. Lister the M.C. The D.C.M. fell to Sgt. Ayres; and on the 19th there was news of the M.M. for Corpl. Swaine, L.-Corpl. Voyle, and Privates Cook, Dockerill, Lovesey, Stapley and Whiskin.

On the 23rd August the 16th Infantry Brigade was relieved by the 106th American Infantry Regiment and withdrew for training into the St Omer area, the training consisting of the practice of open warfare, and on the 1st September a long railway journey, which was completed next day, took the Buffs with the others all the way to Heilly (between Amiens and Albert). The 16th Brigade spent nearly a fortnight in this neighbourhood, first at Bonnay and then at Fouilloy and Aubigny; and so it was not till the 14th, or five weeks after the British offensive had begun, that the first brigade move was made to Montecourt, the Buffs going to Trefcon, a few miles west of St Quentin. On the 17th the battalion moved to St Quentin Wood and into the battle line after dark, Captain Morley being wounded.

The 1st Battalion, like all the other Buffs in France, was now in the 4th Army, which, as we have seen, was busily engaged in pushing on and fighting its way from Albert to the Hindenburg Line. On the 8th September and following days was fought the great and prolonged Battle of Epehy, the limits of which battle area is officially given as extending from St Quentin (exclusive) to Villers Plouich, a distance of nearly twenty miles as the crow flies. Sir Douglas Haig in his despatches makes use of the words: " Next day at 7 a.m. on the 18th " September the 4th and 3rd Armies attacked in heavy " rain on a front of about seventeen miles from Holnon

" to Gouzeaucourt, the 1st French Army co-operating
" south of Holnon "; and a little later on he writes:
" On the extreme right and in the left centre about
" Epehy the enemy's resistance was very determined,
" and in these sectors troops of the 6th, 12th, 18th and
" 58th Divisions had severe fighting."

The country over which the 16th Brigade and its
immediate neighbours were working during the battle
of September may briefly be described as follows:
Three miles or so west of St Quentin is a large wood
called the Holnon, but sometimes described as the St
Quentin Wood. St Quentin itself is commanded to the
west and south by high ground; the Hindenburg Line
ran just outside this town to the canal at Bellenglise.
Holnon village lies in a hollow commanded by Round
and Manchester Hills, which latter height lies in the
area that was allotted to the French. From the east
edge of the wood the ground is a bare slope rising to
the high ground overlooking St Quentin. At the highest
point and opposite where the centre of the 6th Division was to attack was a network of trenches called the
Quadrilateral, which could be reinforced unseen from
the enemy's side of the hill. It was expected that the
Germans would stand on the heights commanding St
Quentin, but they were reported as being much disorganized and that resistance might not be very obstinate.

The 1st and 6th Divisions, in co-operation with the
French, were to capture, on the 18th September, a
starting-place for the assault of the Hindenburg Line,
and to do this the 11th Essex had, on the 16th, after
tremendous effort, secured trenches clear of the Holnon
Wood for an assembly position, while with the same
object the West Yorkshire had endeavoured to secure
Holnon village, but had only gained a part, because the
French on the right had failed to take the hills. This
failure had its effect on the forming-up arrangements

of our troops, as had the fact that the Holnon Wood had become almost impassable from gas shells and wet weather, so much so that the 16th and 71st Brigades had to move round to the north and south of it to get to their places. This fatigued the troops and rendered communications difficult. There was not much time for reconnaissance, for the advance had to be timed in accordance with the movement of the troops to the northward. So on the afternoon of the 17th the 16th Brigade concentrated west of St Quentin Wood preparatory to forming up the next morning. The 18th Brigade had attacked at dawn on the 17th in order to capture the starting-place for the later date, but without success. It was at 6 p.m. that the brigadier of the 16th went out with the commanding officers of the Buffs and the York and Lancaster and chose assembly positions.

On the morrow, with the 71st Brigade on the right and the 16th on the left, the 6th Division attacked the Quadrilateral, being the point where the two joined, and the left of the 16th Brigade being on Fresnoy le Petit. Zero hour was at 5 a.m., the barrage started and the York and Lancaster Regiment moved to the attack. The Buffs were at the north edge of the wood and the objective was south of the village of Gricourt. The York and Lancaster were to capture a line east-south-east of Fresnoy le Petit, and then the Buffs and K.S.L.I. to pass through to their objective. Two tanks were taken to assist the attack, but one failed to start, and the other, after being seen going through Fresnoy le Petit, was never heard of again. At 6.40 the York and Lancaster were reported on their objective, and A, B and C Companies of the Buffs, who had already advanced some distance and suffered a little from shell fire, prepared to play their part. At first they lost direction somewhat owing to the darkness and rain, and then discovered that the satisfactory report about the York

403

and Lancaster Regiment was not quite accurate and that the whole of its objective had not been reached; so that the left company of the Buffs had been held up by machine guns from Fresnoy le Petit, and the support company, after reaching the outskirts of the village, had had to withdraw somewhat. All these causes prevented the remainder of the Buffs with the K.S.L.I. from advancing beyond the position gained by their comrades. Nothing could be heard or seen of the 71st Brigade, which should have been on the right, so this flank was exposed and D Company the Buffs had to be placed on guard there. By evening the different events of the day, together with the difficulty of maintaining direction in the early morning, had completely mixed up the units of the 16th Brigade so much so that the immediate unravelling seemed almost impossible, and the senior officers at various points had to collect all troops in their immediate vicinity and take command of them, thus forming temporarily three composite battalions wherewith to carry on. The 1st Buffs lost 6 officers and 150 men killed and wounded on the 18th.

On the 19th the two more forward of the composite battalions were ordered to attack again at dawn, but the Germans evidently anticipated this move, for they opened a very heavy artillery and machine-gun barrage before the attackers had even started. Fighting went on throughout the day, the Buffs having seventeen more casualties; but no success crowned the British effort, and it became evident enough that the Germans were making a real stand and not merely fighting a rearguard action. Indeed, it was very noticeable all along the line how the opposition to our advance increased the nearer to the Hindenburg Line we penetrated. Everybody had now experienced heavy fighting and some battalions had suffered heavy loss, and so it was determined to remain comparatively quiet for a day or two and to prepare the way for another regular attack by means of a proper artillery preliminary work. About this time the officer commanding received a petition, signed by thirty men, asking that the gallantry of their company commander might be recognized by the authorities. Captain W. T. Johnston was the officer concerned, and he was awarded the Military Cross.

The renewed attack was commenced on the 24th. The 18th Brigade was on the right and the 16th on the left. The 18th failed to take the Quadrilateral, which was its objective. The front of the fighting, as regards the 16th, was allotted this day to the York and Lancaster and K.S.L.I., the Buffs being in support. It was a very gallant affair and all objectives were taken, but the right of the brigade was exposed as it advanced, owing to the Quadrilateral still being in German hands; so bombing operations on that stronghold were commenced by the Buffs and K.S.L.I. and most of the northern face was taken. The 3rd Brigade, assisted by the York and Lancaster, took Gricourt in the afternoon, and at night the Buffs relieved the K.S.L.I. in first line. The battalion had a list of twenty casualties.

On the 25th the 18th Brigade made good the objectives before which they had at first failed. They took the Douai trench, and by midnight the 25th/26th the 16th and 18th, in co-operation, had completed the capture of the Quadrilateral, which the enemy had considered an impossibility. Two German counter-attacks on the 16th Brigade were repulsed, though the enemy managed to rush and to hold one of the forward posts; but the opposition was now obviously dying down and the German spirit sadly broken, and our patrols were able to gain further ground. On the 27th a prisoner was captured, who stated that he was the last patrol covering the withdrawal of the enemy, and this proved correct, for next day our people could by no means get touch of him.

405

The 6th Division was relieved during the 29th and 30th of September by the 4th French Division, and by this time our posts were round three sides of the village of Fayet, which was ultimately captured by a patrol under Lieut. Lushington, and Manchester Hill was in the hands of our allies. The Buffs went back to camp at Trefcon.

While the fighting recorded above had been in progress on the right of the British Army, the 47th Division, with the 1st protecting its right flank and an American force on its left, had by means of a magnificent attack on the 29th September broken the Hindenburg Line and crossed the canal, together with the 32nd Division, after which these units experienced very severe fighting about Ramicourt and Sequehart. It was therefore necessary that they should rest, and when the 6th Division had had four days in the back areas, which was largely utilized in absorbing reinforcements and generally reorganizing, it was ordered to relieve these others with a view to attacking, on the 8th October, in the direction of the little town of Bohain.

Therefore on the 4th October the Buffs marched, complete with transport and all else, to the Bellenglise area and billeted by the banks of the canal, and on the night of the 5th/6th the 16th Brigade relieved the 3rd Brigade about Preselles Farm, which is between Ramicourt and Sequehart and opposite the position to be attacked. This position was in a country of rolling downs, divided by a valley opening out towards the British and closed at the far end by a ridge on which stood the village of Mericourt. In the valley itself stood Mannikin Wood and other points suitable for hidden machine guns. The 6th Division was to attack up the left spur which bounded the valley, and the French up the right one; but our allies had been delayed in passing through St Quentin and by opposition on the way, and although the whole operation had been

406

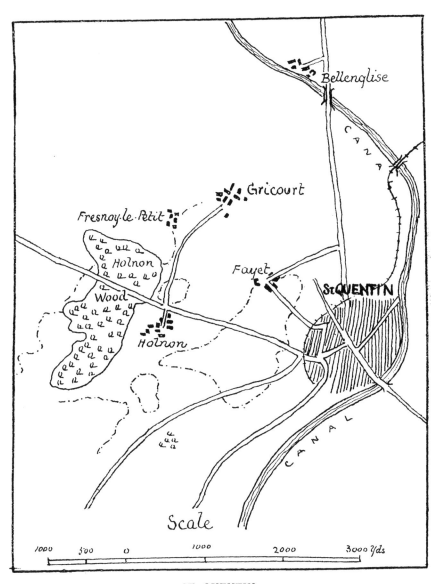

Scale

1000   500   0   1000   2000   3000 Yds

ST. QUENTIN

postponed for twenty-four hours, namely from the 7th to 8th October, it was pretty obvious that at first, at any rate, the British right flank would be exposed. A battalion of the West Yorkshire Regiment and three whippet tanks had the task of clearing the valley, but, as a matter of fact, the tanks were knocked out almost immediately. The 16th Brigade was on the right next the valley, and the 71st on the left next the Americans.

On the night of the 7th/8th the Buffs moved up to their forming-up line for the second time, for when the operation was postponed the battalion had gone back to Bellenglise for a day, and the marching and counter-marching had proved a strain on the men. The hour was 5.10 a.m., at which time the Shropshire Light Infantry were to move off and secure the first objective, after which the Buffs, passing through, were to go on to the second, which was in front of Beauregard Farm. The men were not in position till a quarter of an hour before zero, on account of the darkness and the difficulty of guiding, and Lieut. H. H. Carter and his batman were killed on the way; but the attack started in good order, the Buffs having B and D Companies in front line, C and half A in support and the remainder of A in reserve. The first objective was soon in the hands of the Salopians and the Buffs quickly on the move for the second. The shelling was now, however, very heavy both from the other side of the valley, which had not yet been reached by the French, and also from Mannikin Wood, in the valley itself, which kept up fire for some time, in spite of some magnificent work done by the West Yorkshire Regiment. A counter-attack appeared to be likely, and Lieut. Stainforth, with the two reserve platoons, was ordered up to get touch with the front line and reinforce it, if necessary. At 11.45 battalion headquarters, moving forward, found the situation well in hand on the battalion front, though no reorganization was possible, as the slightest movement was observed by the enemy from the right. In fact, A and C Companies were harassed by ·77 guns all day. However, a defensive flank was formed later on. By 3 p.m. the French, too, began to advance and completely changed the situation. The West Yorks pushed up the valley and got touch with them, and so towards evening the companies were reorganized and patrols pushed forward through Beauregard Farm and Copse and the line established east of these. By nightfall Mericourt was taken and the 6th Division had done all it had set out to do. Captains Hamilton and Moss were both wounded early in the day, but remained with their companies until the objective was reached. The latter was again seriously wounded whilst waiting for a stretcher at battalion headquarters.

The work of the day had hardly been accomplished when orders came for the 6th Division to take over part of the American front on the left and hand over some of their own to the 46th Division on the right; in fact, to side-step to the left, as it was called. As far as the Buffs were concerned, their reorganization during the night was barely complete when, about 3 a.m., the 4th Battalion of the Leicestershire Regiment arrived in relief with orders that they were at once to move off to a position two miles away to support a new attack, this time on Bohain, timed for 5.30 a.m., which was to be made by the K.S.L.I. and York and Lancaster Battalions of the 16th Brigade. This meant, of course, that a brigade of very tired troops had to move off two miles to a new position, issue all detailed orders, make elaborate arrangements and take up position all in less than three hours in pitch darkness and over unreconnoitred country. It was a most extraordinary performance, but it was done and the 16th Brigade duly advanced at the correct zero hour, though the Buffs themselves were not called upon to take part. Both the 16th and 71st

Brigades carried their first objectives successfully, and the whole operation ended during the following night by the capture of Bohain, the release of some four thousand French civilians and the acquisition of considerable war booty.

After returning to Doon Mill, from whence the start on the 9th had been made, coming back to the front line again and having Lieut. Lloyd wounded on the 15th, the Buffs on the 16th October were preparing for another battle. On that date A and C Companies were in billets and bivouacs east of Bohain, and B and D in the outskirts of Becquiguy, the battalion being under the temporary command of Major Lord Teynham. Orders were issued for an attack on the 17th from Vaux Audigny and the Buffs formed up to the north-west of that place. The objective, or Blue Line, was a trench system which included the Bois St Pierre and a level crossing on the railway and was in front of the village of Wassigny. Then the 1st Division was to pass through and take Wassigny. The Buffs attacked on a two-company frontage, A on the left, C with a platoon of B on the right, D in support, and B in reserve.

The morning proved to be one of the foggiest that had been experienced during the war. Nothing could be seen anywhere and direction was naturally extremely difficult to maintain. The Buffs had to pass the village of Vaux Audigny in fours and to deploy outside it. The advance was made by compass bearings, and more than one instance occurred of sergeants taking the compasses from their injured officers and leading their companies on, so that the battalion reached its objective correctly, which was more than all the troops contrived to do. The railway which runs from Vaux Audigny to Vaille Mulatre is not by any means a straight one, but it was of considerable assistance in keeping direction. With the exception of making it so difficult to keep the line, the fog was an advantage to the British advance, because parties of the enemy were come upon unseen and in one or two cases machine guns were outflanked unobserved. Both the leading companies reached their objective about 7.30 a.m. Lieut. Stainforth, who commanded C, found that his flank was exposed, so he at once established a post and pressed into the service of the defence certain stragglers of the 1st Division. He remained here himself for some hours and until a battalion of Cameron Highlanders arrived. Nothing could be found of the 11th Essex which should have been on the Buffs' right. They had utterly lost their way in the fog, though it was afterwards discovered that the men had resorted to the expedient of attempting to advance arm in arm. Our artillery barrage was excellent and the enemy's shelling somewhat light after leaving the railway station. The hostile machine guns were very active throughout the fight. At 11.45 a report came that the enemy had a division in reserve for a counter-attack and preparations were made to meet it, but nothing materialized; headquarters moved forward, and the battalion set to work to consolidate. The casualties, considering the nature of the operation, were slight, though four officers were killed and one wounded, five of the men killed and thirty-one were wounded.

On the 19th October battalion headquarters moved back to Vaux Audigny, and next day the whole battalion was billeted there, and the battle surplus, as small bodies kept back from action to reinforce in case of heavy casualties were called, as well as a draft of eighty-eight men, was sent up. On the 21st the complete unit marched to St Souplet and was billeted in that village. Two days later the 71st Brigade was in action again and the Buffs moved up to its support, starting at very short notice. They bivouacked round Baziel, and on the 25th took over the line in Bois L'Eveque from the K.S.L.I.; there were three men killed and fifteen wounded on this date.

CAMBRAI ON THE MORNING THE ENEMY WAS DRIVEN OUT

On the 26th the list of Military Medals awarded for gallant conduct at the Battle of St Quentin on the 18th was issued, and no less than twenty came to the Buffs, namely: C.S.M. Bones; Sgts. Carr and Jenkins; Corpl. Millen; L.-Corpls. Cain, Child, Ellis, Hobbs, Hook and Hutchison; Ptes. Blackford, Brown, Carpenter, Colley, Ericksen, Stapley, Walters, Whiddett, Wicken and Wright. On this day battalion headquarters went to Pommereuil.

The 30th of October was the last day of actual fighting that fell to the lot of the 1st Battalion, and its long record, which as far as the Great War is concerned began four years before, closed well and gloriously, for what is termed a minor enterprise was on that date carried out under the command of a subaltern officer, an enterprise which in the old days would have made a field officer's name for the rest of his service: orders had been received for the relief of the division, and in order to hand over to the relieving troops a satisfactory position for continuing the forward movement on the line of the canal, it was determined to capture on the 30th an important farm and spur which overlooked the waterway. The business was entrusted to Lieut. L. W. Barber, M.B.E., of the Buffs, who had at his disposal B and C Companies and, later on, a platoon of D, also a section of the Machine Gun Battalion and two light trench mortars. Zero was at six, at which hour a creeping barrage opened, heavy artillery bombarding the railway. The attack was made on a platoon frontage, with other platoons on either flank to protect the advance. The attempt on the farm was at first frustrated by our own barrage falling too short and causing casualties in the leading platoon. When it lifted, another was brought up, but at first could not get in by reason of the hostile machine guns, and it was not till 10 o'clock that the farm and another behind it was taken. Meanwhile a separate small body, which had advanced on the high ground, had also attained its object and had captured some machine guns, our barrage here being correct. The enemy now heavily bombarded the farm with medium and light trench mortars and with field artillery, after which a counter-attack was the cause of the withdrawal of Barber's men, but two sections of Lewis gunners and some riflemen succeeded in preventing the enemy from advancing beyond the buildings. The last reserves were now brought up and the line reorganized and reinforced by a platoon of D Company. Under a well-directed bombardment by our light trench mortars the farm was again attacked and captured at the point of the bayonet. Two heavy and three light machine guns were taken and heavy casualties inflicted, and by evening the village of Happegarbes was practically cleared. Casualties: 2nd Lieuts. Hart, Herrmann and Simpson and twenty-seven men wounded, eight killed and four missing. And so the last fight of the 1st Battalion ended in congratulations, the divisional commander expressing his great appreciation.

The first few days of November were spent at Fresnoy le Grand and at Bohain, to which small town the move was made on the 5th. This early period of the month was brightened by no less than three little batches of honours awarded, and joy, of course, culminated on the 11th November, when the officers dined together to celebrate the occasion, and four days afterwards the battalion commenced its march into Germany.

For their work at St Quentin the following were awarded bars to their M.M.: Sgts. Goodall, Holloway, Stuart and Swaine; Corpl. Dockerill; L.-Corpl. Rainsbury and Pte. Wright. The M.M. was awarded to Sgts. Harris, Lawrence, Morey and Waby; L.-Sgt. Caley; Corpl. Pragnell; L.-Corpls. Kibble and Elsey and Pte. Shackcloth. For Barber's fight on the 30th the M.M. was given to Corpls. Cotton and Oliver and L.-Corpl. Todman.

The oldest unit of the Buffs was thus the only one to represent the regiment in the enemy's country. It had been the first to take part in the war, though, of course, the battalion, so far as individual members were concerned, was an entirely different one to that of 1914. However, the unit was the same one that had fought in Flanders over three hundred years before, and, being the oldest representative of the Buffs, it was perhaps fitting that it should have the honour. Therefore Lieut. Milles was despatched to England to fetch the Colours. These have not been carried in war since the Zulu campaign of 1879, as the tactical use of such flags is obsolete; but the Colours were to be planted on German soil, all the same, so Milles went off on his mission. It is not necessary here to describe the march, which was a long one: first of all, the army destined for the Rhine had to be collected and reorganized into brigade groups with divisional troops; there were long halts upon the way until the 2nd December, owing chiefly to the difficulty of feeding the leading troops, because the railways had been destroyed and, as far as the frontier, roads had been cratered and bridges blown up.

This crossing of the frontier was made an impressive function by the Buffs. Colours were uncased, as afterwards they always were on entering a town, drums were beating, bayonets fixed and the men were beautifully groomed and turned out—equipment polished, the harness and saddlery of the mounted men shining, pomp and circumstance of glorious war once more in evidence. Once across the frontier, the roads were excellent and delay only caused by the necessity of closing up now and again, as there was only one road to each division.

It seems a pity that Christmas Day could not be

413

adequately kept by the Buffs in 1918, but the wherewithal, in the way of extra provisions and so on, failed to arrive from England in time. However, perhaps the general joy and triumph which reigned in every heart, even if the extraordinary reserve of Englishmen failed to show or advertise the same, compensated for the lack of extra cheer. It was a notable Christmas, in any case, and could be nothing else. On the 30th December the battalion was quartered in the little village of Vettweiss, strength 43 officers, 786 other ranks, and demobilization soon commenced. During the march into Germany notification of the following honours was received: M.C. for Captains Barber, M.B.E., Johnston and Stainforth; Lieuts. Milles and Piper; 2nd Lieuts. Chater and Hendin, and a bar to the same for Captain G. F. Hamilton; the D.C.M. for C.S.M. Poole, Sgt. France, M.M., L.-Sgt. Souster and L.-Corpl. J. Smith, M.M. (since killed in action); and the M.M. to L.-Sgt. Waby.

CHAPTER XVI

CONCLUSION

EXCEPT in certain remote places and in India, war ended on the 11th November, 1918, and, though the said remote spots still found work for a small number of our English warriors, the demobilization of the great majority was immediately put in hand. Of course, the old standing battalions of the Buffs were to remain in being, but most of the individuals forming them were entitled to discharge, while in the cases of the 6th, 7th and 10th Battalions, those units which had sprung into being at the call of duty and patriotism, had done their work and were now to disappear altogether from the Army List, as the 8th had already done.

Those men most required in England to carry on her civil business and trade went back to their accustomed life almost at once, and resumed old occupations much as if nothing had happened; but the men have been through experiences undreamt of by even the old regular soldier and which can never be effaced from memory. The men not belonging to what were called key industries had to remain with their war battalions for some months, for the returning to civil life of a vast army is by no means a light or easy matter to arrange. In the case of the 6th Battalion demobilization may be said to have commenced more or less seriously in January, 1919. On the 4th February the King's Colour was presented to the battalion, the ceremony being performed by no less a personage than H.R.H. The Prince of Wales. In March a move was made from Auberchicourt to Bruille, owing to the return of the civil population to the former place. The sending home

415

of batches of men continued pretty steadily all the time and, at the beginning of May, the battalion consisted of Captain Page, M.C., in command; Captain Turk, M.C., adjutant; Captain Linwood, quartermaster; Lieut. Hickmott in charge of the Colours, and thirty-two rank and file. This party returned in June to Sandling Camp, handed their Colours to the Dean of Canterbury at a parade which will be referred to later, and was finally disbanded at the Crystal Palace. The 6th had always been a fighting unit, and its total casualties numbered 4,864, of which 56 officers and 702 men had actually been killed in action.

The first stages of demobilization in the case of the 7th Buffs were carried out at Montigny. Somewhat slow at the start, the work took a turn for the better in January, 1919, and large bodies began to leave for their dispersal stations. The cadre strength, as laid down in Army Orders, was reached in April, and all similar parties of the 18th Division were billeted in Ligny en Cambresis. In early July orders were received for the sending home and dispersal of the slender relics of the 7th Queen's, 7th Buffs and 8th East Surrey; but there was a good deal of delay at the railhead at Caudry, at Dunkerque, where equipment was handed in to the Ordnance, and at Boulogne; but, on the last day of July, Folkestone was reached and the Colour party went on to Canterbury, where it was billeted till arrangements were made with the Dean and Chapter to deposit its charge in the great cathedral.

The following extract from the *Kentish Express* of the 9th August, 1919, describes the last act of the famous fighting 7th Battalion, which throughout its career had added so much to the reputation of the Buffs: " The King's Colour of the 7th Battalion the " Buffs was deposited at Canterbury Cathedral on " Thursday morning for safe custody by two officers " and three other ranks, representing the cadre of the

" battalion. Major Peake was in command and Lieut.
" C. H. Rowe bore the Colours, while a detachment
" from the Buffs' depot, under Major J. Crookenden,
" D.S.O. (commanding the depot), formed a guard of
" honour. The band of the 1st Battalion, under Mr.
" Elvin, took up its position on the nave steps, as did
" the Cathedral choir, while Dean Wace was accom-
" panied by Dr. Bickersteth and Canon Gardiner.
" Major Peake asked the Dean to receive the Colours
" into safe custody. Dean Wace, in accepting them,
" said he did so with pleasure on behalf of the Dean
" and Chapter, and they would be placed in the
" Warriors' Chapel, the chapel of the regiment."

Lt.-Colonel Charles Ponsonby in his book, *West Kent
(Q.O.) Yeomanry and 10th (Yeomanry) Battalion the
Buffs*, describes the last days of his unit, and with his
permission the following few extracts from his work are
reproduced in this place:—

" On the 15th December we marched to Fresnes, and
" from there, after a night at Deux Acren, arrived at
" Thollembeek and Vollezeel, two villages about thirty-
" five miles from Brussels.
" Though many of the railways and roads in the
" neighbourhood had been destroyed before the enemy
" retired, this part of the country had not been in the
" fighting area at any time during the war. But the
" population had suffered much from four years of
" occupation. They had had little food; they had re-
" ceived no money for troops billeted on them; they
" had had their men taken from them to work behind
" the line or in Germany. . . . The release from
" such an existence, combined with a very real desire to
" express their thanks to the English nation, not only
" for its great share in winning the war and rescuing
" their country from oppression, but also for having

CONCLUSION

" provided a haven of rest for so many of their fellow-
" countrymen in England, incited the inhabitants of
" Thollembeek and Vollezeel to stretch their hospi-
" tality to its utmost limits. They made every effort
" to make us comfortable in our billets during the long
" and rather tedious period of waiting for demobiliza-
" tion. . . . Towards the end of January the bat-
" talion was selected to represent the division, and inci-
" dentally the British Army, in a royal review at Brussels
" by the King of the Belgians. After a week of prepara-
" tion we went by motor bus to Anderlecht, a suburb
" of Brussels, where we were billeted for the night.
" The following day the review took place, and after
" two days' holiday we returned to our Belgian villages.
" . . . On the 27th February the battalion moved to
" Grammont, a town of about thirteen thousand in-
" habitants, and a few days later all the remaining men
" (about one hundred and twenty) who joined the
" Army after the 1st January, 1916, went off to the
" 1st Battalion The Queen's (Royal West Surrey
" Regiment). The battalion was now reduced practi-
" cally to cadre strength of four officers and forty-six
" men. During the month of March a cordial and
" appreciative Order was issued by Major-General E. S.
" Girdwood on relinquishing the command of the 74th
" Division. . . . On the termination of hostilities
" Captain G. H. Peckham received the M.C., and
" C.S.M.'s P. Faulkner and L. Salt and Sgts. H. J.
" Smith and S. F. Sparrow received the M.S.M. . . .
" The act of placing their colours in Canterbury
" Cathedral marked the end of the 10th (Yeomanry)
" Battalion the Buffs. In the short period of its exist-
" ence it had fully played its part in the war. Formed
" on the 1st February, 1917, it ceased to exist on the
" 21st June, 1919. It fought in Palestine and France.
" Its casualties numbered 8 officers and 134 men killed,
" and 24 officers and 486 men wounded."

418

The 4th and 5th Battalions had, of course, quite a different status to those alluded to above. They had been for some time and still are[1] permanent portions of the regiment, and so when war was over they could not be disbanded, but merely disembodied in the same way that they were each year after the annual training. As has already been noticed, circumstances postponed this desirable rest from soldiering for a very long time. The unrest and continued wars in India and her frontiers kept the 4th abroad, and the necessity of maintaining white troops in Mesopotamia had similar results in the case of the 5th. The former did not embark for home till November, 1919, a full year after the armistice, and the battalion was disembodied the same month. The cadre of the 5th Battalion, still under Lt.-Colonel Body, D.S.O., O.B.E., a very tiny remnant of those who embarked in 1914, reached home in January, 1920, and were also, of course, disembodied. The story of the 3rd or Special Reserve Battalion after the 11th November, 1918, is as follows: the unit was still quartered in the Citadel at Dover and was about 1,400 strong, many of the men awaiting demobilization, and of the officers orders to proceed to India, for which duty they had volunteered. Towards the end of the month several companies had to proceed to Folkestone for police duty owing to trouble with certain leave-expired soldiers, who could not see the necessity of returning to their units in France. In February, 1919, came orders to move to the south of Ireland in relief of the 3rd Argyll and Sutherland Highlanders, who had been in that country a considerable time. After a short period in Kinsale, the 3rd Buffs were quartered in Victoria Barracks, Cork, and there remained during the summer of 1919, except that, owing to certain troubles,

1 This was written before the 5th Battalion ceased to exist as such.

a tour of duty at Limerick for a fortnight or so had to be undertaken.

On the 7th September the whole of the men were handed over to Lt.-Colonel R. McDouall, C.B., C.M.G., D.S.O., who had just been appointed to command the 1st Battalion of the Buffs; and as there now hardly existed such a unit, as far as the necessary soldiers went, the members of the 3rd were simply handed altogether over to the 1st.

This 1st Battalion had been, in January, 1919, at Vettweiss, in Germany, about fifteen miles from Cologne, and demobilization was in progress till the 15th March, on which date eighteen officers and three hundred men, under Major Lord Teynham, the second in command, were transferred in one body to the 6th Battalion Royal West Kent Regiment. This left but a strength of forty-six men, but the regular officers, of course, still remained, as these had cast in their lot with the Buffs for the greater part of their professional lives, and not for emergency times only, so every two private soldiers had an officer to look after them. The ranks, however, were somewhat swollen by the arrival of the band from England. The cadre was now quartered at Sinzenich and remained there till the middle of May, occupied in amusements and recreation and generally having a happy time of relaxation after all that had been gone through.

On the 22nd May the 1st Battalion landed at Tilbury, having travelled by Antwerp, and, on the 26th of the month, it was received, welcomed and entertained by the mayor and officials of the good old city of Canterbury. It was at last in very truth home again, but the cadre now consisted of only about twenty men.

With these twenty Lt.-Colonel McDouall, accompanied by his own adjutant and quartermaster, proceeded in September to Cork and, as we have seen, took over there the 3rd Battalion in a body. In fact, only the Permanent Staff of the latter remained to return to Kent. Soon afterwards the 1st Battalion was again quartered at Fermoy, the garrison it had left for war five years before. Of the nine hundred soldiers or thereabouts who marched out of the little Irish town under Colonel Hill in 1914, five officers and thirty-five other ranks returned; but these, of course, had not been with their unit during the whole of the interval.

The names of these forty soldiers are appended:—

Lt.-Colonel R. McDouall, C.B., C.M.G., C.B.E., D.S.O.
Major R. G. D. Groves-Raines, D.S.O.
Major and Brevet Lt.-Colonel L. W. Lucas, D.S.O., M.C.
Captain H. C. C. Morley.
Captain and Quarter-Master T. Cook.

R.Q.M.S. W. K. Martin.
C.S.M. G. Barrell, D.C.M.
   ,, J. R. MacWalter, D.C.M., M.M.
   ,, F. G. Verlander.
C.Q.M.S. G. Bridgland.
   ,, S. Croucher.
Clr.-Sgt. (O.R.S.) E. J. Evans.
Sgt. A. Burville.
   ,, J. Cross, M.M.
   ,, G. Dennis, D.C.M.
   ,, W. Denny, M.M.
   ,, E. B. Hills.
   ,, W. Holmes.
   ,, J. Mullen.
   ,, J. Morgan, M.M.
   ,, J. Stuart, M.M.
L.-Sgt. A. Larkin.

L.-Sgt. G. Russell.
   ,, C. Truby.
Corpl. W. Adams.
   ,, A. R. Amos.
   ,, C. Collier.
   ,, E. Hall, D.C.M.
   ,, F. Harvey.
L.-Corpl. S. Clover.
   ,, A. Forster.
   ,, W. Phelan.
Pte. H. Barker.
   ,, W. Bone.
   ,, E. Downes.
   ,, H. Staples.
   ,, F. Stroud.
   ,, F. Wanstall.
   ,, E. Wood.
Bdsm. W. Gammon.

CONCLUSION

The 2nd Battalion came home to England from the Bosphorus in April, 1919, and was quartered in Connaught Barracks, Dover, where it remained till November of the same year, when, under the command of Lt.-Colonel Trevor, D.S.O., it embarked at Southampton for India, where it had been when the war commenced. Multan, in the Punjaub, was the new station into which the 2nd Battalion of the Buffs settled down to take up the threads again of routine garrison life in the East. The following are the names of officers and other ranks who left India in 1914 and returned there in 1919:—

Officers.

Captain Peareth.   Captain Howe.

Other Ranks.

R.S.M. Andrews.   Sgt. Potts.
Band-Master Hewett.   ,,   Webb.
R.Q.M.S. Edwards.   ,,   Wilkins.
O.R. Sgt. Ings.   Corpl. Cornwall.
C.S.M. Cook.   ,,   Farr.
C.Q.M.S. Austen.   ,,   Robinson.
   ,,   Blackman.   L.-Corpl. Stubbins.
   ,,   Slender.   Dr. Murdock.
Sgt. Ambrose.   ,,   Stevens.
 ,, Coaster.   Pte. Goldsmith.
 ,, Deeks.   ,,   Howland.
 ,, Freeman.   ,,   Levenson.
 ,, Hamblin.   ,,   McGann.
 ,, Manering.   ,,   Spooner.
 ,, McMahon.   ,,   Woodhams.

On the 21st June Canterbury Cathedral was once again, as it had been many times before, the scene of an impressive military ceremony in connection with the

422

Buffs. It was a great memorial service at which every battalion was represented, the grand old church being crowded with soldiers and their relatives. On this occasion the 2nd Battalion received back its Colours which had during the long war been in the safe keeping of the Dean and Chapter. The Colours of the 6th and 10th were solemnly placed in the custody of the same Church dignitaries, to be hung upon the walls together with those under which our sires and grandsires fought. Captain J. C. Page, M.C., who had served so long as its adjutant, was in charge of the party of the 6th, and Lt.-Colonel Ponsonby of the brave Yeomen. It was an occasion that those present will never forget.

The real conclusion of the Buffs' great war history, however, was another and still more solemn ceremony and service in the same church: this was the unveiling of the memorial to our glorious dead, whose names will be found not only in the Warriors' Chapel, but in an Appendix to this book, numbering nearly six thousand. Space will not permit of a description of this touching service. The unveiling was performed by Lord Horne, General Officer Commanding-in-Chief Eastern Command, and a full description is to be found in the regimental paper, *The Dragon*, for September, 1921.

We have merely to note that the celebrated general who unveiled the memorial, after giving a short account of the doings of the regiment in the war, made use of the words:—

" There is a record! one and all, Regulars, Terri-
" torials, and those who fought with the Service
" battalions, all serving, all nobly maintaining the
" discipline and traditions of their regiment, all in-
" spired by the spirit of the Buffs."

Veteri frondescit honore.

APPENDIX I[1]

Nominal roll of Officers who were killed in action, or died of wounds or disease in the Great War, 1914–1919:—

MAJOR-GENERAL
Edward Charles Ingouville Williams, C.B., D.S.O.

BRIGADIER-GENERAL
Julian Hasler.

COLONEL
Frederick Charles Romer, C.B., C.M.G.

LIEUTENANT-COLONELS

Donald Knox Anderson, M.C.

Charles Walter Blackall.

Harold Duke Collison-Morley.

Augustus David Geddes.
Herbert Walter Green, D.S.O.

Henry Denne Hirst. [D.S.O.
Harry Fearnley Kirkpatrick,

Nathaniel Newnham-Davis.

Francis Cyril Rupert Studd, D.S.O.

Arthur Philip Hamilton Trueman, O.B.E.

Claude Arthur Worthington.

1 The appendices have been compiled by Major F. W. Tomlinson, Hon. Sec. of the Buffs' History Committee, with the assistance of Miss Olive Tomlinson and Major E. F. Gould, to whom he offers his grateful thanks, as well as to the War Office and Officer in Charge of Records. The names of the dead have been taken from the official lists, but corrected and amplified as far as possible ; they correspond with the names in the Roll of Honour which is to be placed in Canterbury Cathedral, in the Warriors' Chapel.

APPENDIX I

MAJORS

Cyril Francis Cattley, M.C.

Charles Meredith Bouverie Chapman, M.C., Chevalier de l'ordre de Leopold, Croix de Guerre (with palms).

James Scholfield Fraser.

Bernard Edward Furley.

Roger Cecil Slacke.
Alfred Soames, D.S.O.
Bernard Lewis Strauss, M.C.

Robert Oscar Cyril Ward.

CAPTAINS

Alan Gordon Acheson Adam.
Hugh Lionel Allfrey.
Victor Arnold.
Maurice Asprey.

Wilfred Saxby Barham.
Stephen Spencer Beall.
Hugh William Brodie.
Theodore Anthony Brown, M.C.
Eustace Bruce Caldecott Burnside.
Benjamin Buss.

Arthur Edwin Cheesman.
Edmund Basil Chichester.
Alfred Sackville Cresswell.

Christopher Edmund Grant Davidson.
William Richard Davis.
Hubert Archibald Dyson.

Lenox Paton Figgis, M.C.
Lawrence Fort.
Edward William Lanchester Foxell.
George Burton Taddy Friend.

Percy Shene Bernard Hall.
Charles Eric Hatfield, M.C.
Anthony May Capron Hollist.
Ralph William Homan.
William Howard.
Herbert Hunter, M.C.

Arthur Keedwell Harvey James.
George Millais James.
George Alfred Prime Jones.

John Kekewich.
Pryce Atwood Clive Kelsey.
Thomas Herbert Kesby.
John Buchanan Kitchin.

John William Laurie.
John Charles Thomas Leigh.
John Herbert Lomax.
Alwyne Travers Loyd.

Harold Lisle Morley, M.C.

Gerald Tassel Neame.

Archibald Edward Osborne (Croix de guerre, with palm).

Dudley George Pearce.

APPENDIX I

CAPTAINS—*(continued)*

James McBain Ronald.

Kenneth Shelton.
Arthur Oswald Sherren.
Thomas Robert Munro Shervinton.
John Sutton Sill.
Sydney Skelton.

Charles Cecil Stanfield.
Bernard Puckle Steinman.

John Ogilvie Taylor.

Walter Neave Wells.

Alexander Frederick Worster, M.C. and clasp.

LIEUTENANTS

Geoffrey Charles Allen.
John William Butts Archer.
Guy Talbot Baker.
Cyril James Price Tyson Sugar Baly.
Reginald Aubrey Richard Bayard.
Percy Harold Budds.
Geoffrey Walter Melvin Burton.
Edward Henry Underwood Buttanshaw.

Hugh Harry Carter.
Angelo Lycestre Lyne Chamberlain.
William Wetherall Chapman.
Anthony Alfred Cheesman.
Geoffrey William Church, M.C.
Eric Foster Clark.
Nigel Edwin FitzRoy Cole.

Robert James Docking.
Reginald William Durdle.
Laurence Charles Dyer.

Noel Vansittart Earle.

Kenneth Rowley Forde.

Richard Spencer Glyn.
Edouard Herbert Allan Goss.
James Gordon Hamilton Greig.
Charles Herbert Gribble.
Alexander Falkland Gulland.
Arthur Louis Gullick.

Philip Randall Hatch.
William Alexander Cosgrave Hedley.
Edward Francis Henderson.
Howard Dudley Hewett.
Robert Myles Heywood.
Douglas Agar Worsley Hill.
Victor William John Hobbs.
Charles Frederick Griffith Hollis, M.C.

Wilfred George Jackson.
Charles William Jemmett.

George William Ambrose Kingham.

Percy Lambe.

427

APPENDIX I

LIEUTENANTS—(*continued*)

Leslie Arthur Lea-Smith.
Maurice Aden Ley.

Ronald McDougall.
Hugh Stephen Marchant.
Charles Walter Brockwell
Marsh.
Ronald Walter Mitchell.
Leonard Morgan.

Fred Naylor.
Roy Nettleton.
Charles Stuart Newcomb.
Percy Wilmott Newington.
Philip Giesler Norbury.
Douglas Horace Gilbert
Northcote.

Harry Alfred Oxley.

Reginald James Pavitt.
Joseph Douglas Philips.
Jasper Prescott Phillimore.

Arthur William Ramsey.
Thomas Ruddock.

Cecil Martin Sankey, M.C.
John Scrace.
Eric Sharp.
Lewis Victor Henry Shorter.
James Eliot Stephen.
Stephen Cormack Swayne.

Cedric Charles Okey Taylor.
Frederick George Taylor.
Stanley Waterman Taylor.
William Frederick Taylor.
John George Thorn-Drury.
George Robert Thornhill,
M.C.

Joseph Thorp Waite.
Frederick George Wallis.
Arthur Norman Widdop.
Jack Douglas Wild.
Frank Dudley Wilkinson, M.C.

2ND LIEUTENANTS

Harold Norman Adcock.
Charles St. Vincent Allen.
William Hope Amos.
Edward Norman Andrews.
Albert Erskine Carson Archer.
Hugo Cholmondeley Arnold.

John Frederick Baddeley.
Carlyle Bainbridge.
Frank Bernard Baker.
Bertram Stacpoole Bambridge.
Leonard Henry Batson.
Leonard Josiah Baxter.

Frederick Parkman Beagley,
M.C.
Robert Gerald Beer.
Lewis Edward Albert Samuel
Bilton.
Basil Bernard Blackwell.
Ronald Walter Bone.
Frederick Atkins Booth.
Bernard Geoffrey Bowles.
Guy Bracher.
Horace Leslie Brown.
Thomas Eben Grainger Bul-
lock.

428

APPENDIX I

Eric George Bungard.
Percy Charles Buss.
Thomas Weston Buss.
James William Butler.

Charles Caney, M.C.
Ernest Stafford Carlos.
Leslie Guy Carman.
John Metcalfe Chill.
Laurence Fraser Clark.
Stanley Harvey Coates.
Leslie Ernest Combridge.
Frederick William Harvey Cooper, M.M.
Edward Franklin Corner.
Donald Threlkeld Cousins.
Henry George Cox.
John Marr Craighead.
Edward Herbert Cramer-Roberts.
Reginald Crisp.
William Guy Cronk.

Wilfrid Stephen Dann.
Leslie James George Davis.
Percy Warren Theo Davis.
Leslie James Derrick.
John Hastings Dinsmore.
William Lawrence Donelan.
Paris Villiers Drake-Brockman.
Francis Herbert Dungey.

Arthur Edwards.
Spenser Ernest Edwards.
Hubert William Evans.

Thomas Firminger.
Ralph Louis Francis Forster.

Phineas Freedman.
Francis Conrade Shenstone Frost.

Horace John Gates.
George Joachim Goschen (the Hon.).
Norman Greiffenhagen.

Charles Hall.
Douglas William Hammond.
Alexander John Hanmer, M.C.
Harold Victor Hardey-Mason.
Donald Alfred Harnett.
Allan Sydney Hayfield.
Rycharde Mead Haythornthwaite.
Ivan Henry Hess.
Harold Sutton Hilder.
Malcolm Arthur Hills.
Herbert Josiah Hine, M.M.
Siegfried Thomas Hinkley.
Evelyn Melville Shovell Hoare.
Leslie Ebenezer Holyman.
Maurice Pinney Horrabin.
Adrian George Hubbard.
Harold Montague Hunt.
Ernest Stanley Patrick Hynes.

Douglas Peacock Jack.
Henry Croome Jackman.
Basil Lister James.
Kenneth Lister James.
Charles Gordon Jelf.
Howard Fife Johnson.
Sinclair Beatty Johnston.

Athol Kirkpatrick.

APPENDIX I

Charles William Laing.
Douglas Lambert.
John Elston Lane.
Henry James Little.

William Lawrence McColl.
Stanley Major.
Michael Innes Malton.
John William Mann.
Charles Arthur Stirling Mathias, M.C.
Ralph Edward Culverhouse Mead.
John Barnard Millard.
George Stuart Moke-Norrie.
Roy Granville Kyrle Money.
Thomas Lewis Vyvyan Moody
Vernon Leslie Morgan.
Frank William Morley.
Eyre Percival Morris.
Eric Victor Morse, M.C.
Reginald Barnes Newton Moss.
Allan Mount.

Henry George Nesbit.
Walter Gregory Neve.
William McDonald Noble.
Mervyn Noott.
Harold Milford Norsworthy.

Alfred Erasmus Stuart Ommanney.
Henry Douglas Osborne.

Jack Brian Paige.
George Alexander Palfreyman.
Leo Bernard Parsons.

William James Leonard Peacock.
Thomas Penington.
Charles Frederick Peters.
Charles Walter Peters.
Reginald Gurwen Phillips.
Basil Horace Pickering.
Edward Crewdson Pitt Pitt-Pitts.
Edgar George Porter.
Charles Ronald Prior.

Stanley Randall, D.C.M., M.M.
Walter Geoffrey Redshaw.
John Sleeman Reed.
George Robert Reid.
Arthur Gordon Richardson.
Frederick Ricketts.
Edgar Francis Robinson.
Hercules Edward Joseph Robinson (the Hon.)
Edward Henry Ronca.
Sidney Rothwell.
Ernest George Routley, M.C.
John Russell.
Cecil Harold Sowerby Ruston.

Edwin Richard Sansom.
George Bertram Saunder.
Harry Sayer.
William Thomas Score.
Millin Selby.
Geoffrey Edward Sewell.
John Stanley Horsfall Shafto.
Ernest Kennedy Smith.
Edward Thompson Smith.
Geoffrey Herbert Smith.
Francis Ingle Sowter.

430

APPENDIX I

Hugh Manning Spencer.
Filmer Blake Spicer.
Wallace Henry Squire.
Arthur Renolds Stallworthy.
Douglas Harcourt Stevens.
Edward Alfred Murtagh Stevens, M.C.
Edgcumbe Leopold Stiles.
Hubert Reginald Stock.

Douglas Mervyn Taylor.
Harold James Taylor.
Heber Thomas.
Harold Thompson.
John Dales Thornley.
Frederick Herbert Trowles.

Thomas William Underhill.
Charles Vincent.

Elton Cyril Wanstall.
Charles Warnington.
Arthur Henry Webb.
James Hoste Welldon.
John Leslie Wellesley-Miller.
Harry Lloyd Wheeler.
William Haffenden Winch.
Noel Ernest Wood.
Reginald Ewart Wood.
Geoffrey Wilfrid Penfold Wyatt.

Philip Harold Ziegler.

APPENDIX II

Nominal roll of Warrant Officers, Non-Commissioned Officers and Men who were killed in action, or died of wounds or disease in the Great War, 1914–1919:—

QUARTERMASTER-SERGEANT

T/200013 Hutchens, G.

COMPANY SERGEANT-MAJORS

G/870	Aldridge, E.		S/194	Glover, T.
L/8907	Alexander, D., M.M.		G/206	Holman, E.W., M.M.
L/8781	Baker, F., D.C.M.		G/8798	Kite, T. W.
L/7809	Banks, W. W.		G/2319	Knight, C. J., M.M.
T/242778	Blackburn, C. S.			
T/201	Brunger, T.		L/6271	Lond, J. T.
L/5726	Cooper, F. W.		L/7741	McLean, A.
S/562	Cornwell, F.			
			L/7621	Terrell, W.
L/8385	Davis, W. S., M.M.			
L/8112	Dumbleton, F.		L/4834	Walsh, J.
			L/7619	White, E.
S/410	Field, A. W.		T/240012	Wickens, A. F.
L/6005	Freeman, G.		T/240339	Wright, J.

COMPANY QUARTERMASTER-SERGEANTS

T/240440	Back, L.		T/3148	Screen, F.
T/200524	Barr, W. D.		T/156	Stone, H. O.
G/3635	Burt, W., D.C.M.		T/270505	Thorpe, C. H.
L/9098	Read, S.		L/8058	Wilson, G. T.
L/7817	Rosam, G. W.		T/270045	Wolsey, P.

432

APPENDIX II

SERGEANTS

T/722	Ades, J.	L/9439	Carrier, S. W.
T/201075	Allwater, E.	G/3605	Casey, W. J.
S/718	Andrews, W. A.	L/6875	Charleys, W.
T/242995	Arter, H.	G/1289	Clark, F. W.
S/9268	Asprey, W. S.	G/2659	Clarke, S. A.
G/2529	Austen, H. G.	S/8546	Clayson, J.
G/6884	Ayres, A. J., D.C.M., M.M.	G/15733	Clinch, J.
		L/8026	Cocks, S. C.
		L/8533	Cole, W. A.
G/12976	Barnes, R. J.	G/3164	Connah, H.
T/270898	Barnett, C. L.	L/10550	Cook, E. T.
G/340	Barrett, A. J., M.M.	G/1018	Cook, J.
T/200119	Batchelder, R. H.	T/241856	Corrigan, T. M.
G/1373	Batchelor, G., M.M.	G/13673	Couchman, F. W.
L/8158	Beeching, A. J.	T/242964	Cozens, E.
T/240242	Benfield, G. S.	G/3301	Crame, C. J., D.C.M.[1]
G/4275	Betts, F. E.		
G/707	Bing, L., M.M.	G/1959	Cranston, W. T.
L/7812	Bishop, G.	L/8014	Crouch, E.
L/8917	Bloomfield, J., M.M.	G/6591	Croucher, W. G.
G/12871	Booth, P.	G/212	Culmer, A. T.
S/32	Brand, B.		
T/337	Brazier, W. T.	T/200300	Dale, H. S.
G/1367	Briers, T.	G/628	Danton, W. F.
T/240883	Broadbridge, L. A.	G/304	Dennett, W. A. H.
G/2158	Bromley, A.	G/14710	Donohoe, R. F. P.
G/3743	Buddle, J.	L/5032	Dowman, E.
L/9747	Bulgin, W. A.	L/5204	Drummond, J. F. J.
L/6036	Burnett, J. E.	S/9467	Dunbar, E. T.
L/9663	Burns, W. P.	G/288	Dungey, G. A.
G/466	Burton, F. S. H.	L/9332	Dunk, P. W.
G/5148	Butler, W., D.C.M.	T/504	Dyer, E. G.
S/8696	Butler, W. E.		
L/4661	Butterworth, H.	G/2663	Eastmond, G. E.
		G/1752	Eldred, W. E.
L/6380	Cadman, A. G.	T/242828	Emery, F. J.
L/10559	Carlin, J., M.M.	G/2782	Everitt, C. F.

[1] Medal of St. George, 3rd Class.

SERGEANTS—*(continued)*

T/270843 Farroll, F.
L/9221 Featherstone, J. R.
L/9203 Fogg, A. F.
T/270587 Francis, A. E.
L/8129 Francis, T.

L/7690 Gard, G.
G/17371 Gardner, G.
T/270604 Garland, J. R.
G/1321 Garner, F. W.
L/9310 Glass, A. G.
G/944 Goad, W. T. F.
L/8361 Goddard, H.
T/270020 Godsiff, R. J.
T/2178 Goldsmith, B. H.
G/18668 Goldup, S. F. W.
G/22475 Gosden, A., M.M.

G/3258 Hammond, C., M.M.
L/9575 Harrington, G. J.
L/8406 Harris, J.
L/9275 Harrison, A. W.
L/8975 Hart, J.
G/13761 Hatcher, C.
G/13675 Heskett, F. T.
L/9402 Hills, H. W.
T/200029 Hinchcliffe, W. E.
G/13672 Hoare, F. G.
L/8475 Hoare, H. W.
L/8413 Hogben, W.
L/9041 Hollands, C. S.
L/5990 Holloway, A. J.
T/270196 Holmes, D.
L/8887 Holness, F. E.
G/20245 Honey, F.
T/201128 Hopkins, A.
G/5308 Howard, J.
L/8861 Howlett, E. A.

G/1865 Huggins, A. E.
G/1889 Hyde, A., M.M.

G/3591 Keal, A. C., D.C.M.
G/4227 Keen, J. T.
G/1983 Kelly, G.
G/8066 Kerman, F., M.M.
S/10881 Keywood, S. G.
T/240230 King, T. [M.M.
G/616 Kingsford, W.,

S/9435 Lakin, C. H.
G/18830 Lamb, E.
L/8011 Lancaster, P. G.
L/8610 Langdon, F. C. A.
G/2042 Langley, G. H.
G/501 Lawrence, E. G.
T/242998 Leman, G. E.
L/9453 Lemar, A. J.
G/1316 Lomax, C. W.
G/3452 Lord, F.
G/469 Luck, F.
G/1385 Lusted, F. A.

S/595 Marchant, A. J.
T/270035 Marchant, E. W.
S/9005 Margrie, M. T.
L/9603 Marsh, A., D.C.M.
G/3126 Matthews, J.
T/270065 May, W.
L/8829 Maycock, G.
L/10011 McNeir, G. A., M.M.
L/8149 Miles, W. J.
G/19120 Mitchell, P.
L/9751 Mitchell, S. M. J.
G/128 Monro, J.
G/4181 Moon, L. G.
G/3526 Morley, A. [M.M.
L/6174 Murdock, A. J.,

APPENDIX II

L/7098	Murphy, F.	G/4500	Smith, H. T.
		L/8019	Smith, W. T.
L/8238	Newing, C.	L/9157	Stevens, A. F.
S/582	North, A.	L/8046	Stroud, W. F.
		S/715	Styles, J.
G/1882	Oxley, J.	L/8529	Sutton, G.
G/4002	Page, L.	G/2786	Tapsell, A.
G/13570	Pain, A. T.	L/7206	Taylor, H. E.
G/1785	Paine, H. J.	L/10218	Taylor, W. J. S.
G/1221	Palmer, P.	G/589	Terry, H.
T/270585	Parker, H. W.	G/2236	Treversh, T. H.
S/515	Parsons, W. J.	G/994	Trigg, A. E.
L/9349	Pascall, P.	S/7746	Tulett, W. G.
T/200597	Payne, C., D.C.M.	G/1407	Turner, C.
G/6494	Pearce, H., M.M.	G/4665	Turner, W. A.
L/9396	Pennel, W. J.	G/851	Twelftree, A. T., M.M.
G/2026	Penny, C. W.		
L/8632	Petts, E. H.		
G/9154	Phipps, C.	G/2561	Upton, P. C., D.C.M.
G/6779	Platts, A., M.M.		
G/2226	Plowright, A.		
L/7851	Port, C. W., M.M.	G/13746	Vandepeer, S. L.
		G/9314	Vaughan, G. H.
L/8448	Rope, C.	L/6163	Viggers, J., M.M.
L/5640	Rumley, C. H.		
		T/2459	Walker, H. J. G.
G/7793	Saggers, A. A.	G/13680	Watson, H. B.
S/228	Saxby, S. C.	L/10044	Watts, A. H.
S/193	Sedgwick, G. A.	T/200014	Welch, F.
S/9609	Semark, W. R.	L/6992	Welsh, A. C.
T/1573	Shepherd, A. G.	G/1637	West, W. D.
L/7779	Shrubsole, W.	G/3569	Whipps, A., M.M.
T/201239	Simmons, A. J.	G/6046	White, E. G.
G/13685	Slocombe, C. G.	G/13557	Wickham, W. E.
G/1802	Smith, E. C.	G/3677	Wilbourne, A. H.
L/7142	Smith, E. E.	L/9673	Williams, E. A.
G/5705	Smith, F.W., M.M.	G/3576	Williams, R. C.
L/9285	Smith, H. J.	L/8664	Wills, J.

435

SERGEANTS—(*continued*)

G/447	Winter, A. E.	G/12521	Wright, G. F. E.,
L/9817	Wood, A., M.M.		M.M.
L/8906	Woolley, P.		
G/69	Woolston, C. F.	L/9289	Young, H. E.

LANCE-SERGEANTS

G/2635	Brewer, E.	G/1097	Mantell, B. G.
G/346	Bushell, S.	G/1655	Matthews, F.
		G/3644	McCluskey, H.
G/2258	Chapman, A. H. R., D.C.M.	L/9009	Meloy, G.
		G/15649	Morgan, J. H.
G/3345	Childs, E. O.	G/8900	Mount, G. H.
G/3555	Cleave, E.	L/8032	Mummery, W.
G/3254	Collier, G. W.		
G/2315	Copus, W. H.	G/3557	Neville, J. W.
G/3896	Craven, H. S.		
		G/4538	Oates, W. T.
L/5995	Duff, W. G., M.M.		
		G/15754	Quaife, T.
G/5521	Finnes, E.		
G/5774	Ford, F.	G/9259	Riley, J. H.
		G/15674	Rowland, C., M.M.
L/9049	Freemantle, E. L.		
		L/10272	Savage, E. J.
G/1233	Gillett, W. G.	G/1128	Scruby, J.
G/13036	Goodsall, G. B.	L/9852	Smith, H. J.
T/241291	Green, J. B.	G/8334	Spencer, H.
		L/8708	Spice, P. M.
L/4611	Hazelton, G. E.	S/8355	Spicer, W. F.
G/1682	Huntley, P. J.		
		L/5943	Taylor, J.
G/1074	Jenner, D. P., M.M.	G/8037	Tierney, M. P.
		G/1143	Tomlins, A. J.
G/2099	Langhelt, S.		
G/18771	Lee, W.	G/1892	Vyse, H. F.
L/8470	Lowe, F. S.		
		G/803	Weaver, H. W.
G/173	Manser, J.	G/3491	Wilby, A. C.

APPENDIX II

CORPORALS

G/18767	Aitchison, A. J.
T/203604	Andrews, W. V.
G/13807	Baillie, A. P.
T/6054	Baldwin, W. A.
S/24	Banks, J. E.
G/3041	Banwell, F. N.
G/17883	Barnes, G. F.
G/84	Bayley, T. W.
L/9902	Beale, C. L.
G/4236	Bennett, J. A.
T/270991	Betts, J. P.
G/14145	Bettles, L.
G/18823	Biggs, H. N.
T/2067	Binks, G.
G/13021	Blackett, J. T.
G/15553	Bones, W., M.M.
G/3500	Bowyer, W. T.
G/614	Bray, G. V.
G/13014	Bright, J. H.
G/21828	Brooks, L.
G/2122	Broom, J.
L/6014	Brown, P.
T/204454	Buckell, W. G.
T/203647	Bullinaira, G. W.
T/1367	Burchett, A. E.
G/8657	Carr, S.
G/4308	Cavey, A. E.
G/1721	Chapman, F. H.
G/3655	Charlesworth, J.
G/13452	Chatfield, A. W.
T/240552	Checksfield, F. H.
G/7509	Clark, E. E.
G/1156	Clarke, F. E.
L/9804	Cockerill, W. J.
L/6984	Colley, J. T., M.M.
L/7825	Collins, H.

S/10746	Cook, F. J.
G/6615	Cook, H. J.
G/3072	Cooper, J. H.
L/7738	Cooper, S.
L/6707	Cotter, W. R., V.C.
G/20111	Cox, E. A.
G/3282	Cox, H. E.
G/7783	Cox, T. H.
L/7185	Crayford, W.
L/9337	Cremer, W. J.
G/12818	Croucher, W. S.
S/9623	Curd, S. P., M.M.
G/11748	Cushion, A. J.
G/3300	Dale, J.
G/1756	Danks, C.
L/7237	Davey, T.
L/8722	Denton, A. L.
L/9208	Dobson, T. H.
T/265244	Dobson, W. T. F.
L/9765	Dorman, L.
L/8510	Dray, T.
G/3969	Drayson, W. C.
G/8135	Drury, W.
L/8367	Duckworth, A. P.
G/4338	Dyer, F. E.
G/17617	Eales, J. A.
G/300	Edmonds, J.
G/5503	Evans, R.
G/8976	Faulkner, A. E.
L/9320	Finnis, A. A.
G/8995	Flory, S. B.
G/11674	Floyd, C. W.
G/1850	Fowler, P.
G/19122	Freeland, P. A.
G/20886	Fuller, E. M.

437

CORPORALS—(*continued*)

G/1684	Garrett, C.
G/1875	Giles, O. R.
G/3504	Hammond, H. H.
L/8211	Hannaford, R.
L/9767	Harden, H. J.
G/5559	Harding, E. E.
L/9094	Hare, S.
G/7785	Hargreaves, T. W.
T/201920	Harlow, W. A.
G/60	Harris, F.
G/20108	Hastings, R. W.
G/2897	Heal, J.
T/204464	Heasman, A. A.
G/1958	Hoare, R. A.
T/240075	Hodge, F. S.
G/771	Hogben, A.
G/8367	Hogben, J.
G/8183	Holliday, W. T.
T/207404	Hoose, W. H.
G/460	Hopper, G.
G/1866	Hopper, J. H.
G/593	Howe, F.
G/26593	Hozier, R. [M.M.
G/2810	Huckstep, W. H.,
L/6553	Hurst, W. J.
L/8578	Jackson, G.
T/3224	James, R.
G/3430	Jarrett, W., M.M.
G/1403	Jeffery, C. J.
L/9845	Jeffreys, F. W.
G/1800	Jope, R.
T/270181	Keen, T. S.
T/1015	Kempton, C. E.
G/1317	Kendrick, H.
G/884	Kerslake, E. P.
G/5335	Kingsford, A. C.

G/12687	Langford, H. S.
G/954	Langston, A. G.
G/13580	Lashmar, H.
G/2464	Lawrence, E. F.
G/2270	Laws, R.
G/2578	Lee, W.
L/8976	Levenson, H.
L/8426	Limpus, C.
G/5564	Link, A. E.
G/18775	Lloyd, F. G.
G/24673	Loveday, A.
T/1638	Luckhurst, H.
G/434	Maloney, A., M.M.
L/9197	Mannings, C.
L/8939	Martin, H.
G/118	Martin, L. E.
G/18812	Martin, T. D.
G/402	Maxted, A. E.
G/9561	Maynard, A.
G/12975	Millgate, H. J.
G/564	Minter, P.
L/9166	Mitchell, M.
G/13669	Moore, P.
G/115	Moore, W.
G/3527	Morley, G.
S/9063	Morris, E. W.
T/270267	Mussared, S. H.
G/5059	Naylor, A. W. H.
G/4029	Neal, C. H.
L/4520	Neely, D.
T/240393	Nickalls, A. D.
G/677	Noakes, J. H.
L/9934	Page, F. T., M.M.
L/6660	Palmer, W. J.
L/9246	Pankhurst, H.
S/10373	Parker, E. E.

APPENDIX II

L/8549	Parsons, E. J.
L/5520	Peake, A.
G/9	Pellatt, W. G.
L/9728	Perkins, W.
L/10342	Pettman, A. T.
G/682	Plumbridge, E.
G/530	Preston, J. W.
T/200030	Purser, F. C.
L/9544	Ralph, F. E.
G/514	Rendell, R. F.
G/2024	Russell, J. L.
L/6109	Sales, T. W.
G/9430	Saunders, F.
G/581	Scott, E.
L/5118	Seager, W.
S/823	Sharp, B. H.
T/200148	Simmonds, T. G.
L/10442	Simpson, S.
G/495	Simpson, T. R.
L/9759	Smith, W.
L/8093	Smith, W. G.
G/3187	Snell, C. A.
S/260	Stone, W. H.
G/5803	Stonham, C. T.
L/8263	Stroud, L.
G/3329	Summers, E.

G/22390	Swan, E.
T/200593	Tanton, E. F.
G/14796	Taylor, G. T.
G/13497	Taylor, H.
G/590	Terry, S.
L/9737	Thompson, A. E.
G/20966	Thompson, G., M.M.
G/3554	Thompson, J.,M.M.
G/7754	Tillstone, C.
G/5338	Tuck. E. C.
T/1710	Tyrrell, F. W.
G/2603	Tutthill, W.
T/203979	Voller, F. J.
G/10206	Waldron, A. W.
G/13677	Warren, S. J. R.
L/9754	Weeks, F.
T/270838	Wells, A. W.
L/10424	Wells, W. D.
L/8832	Westacott, E.
G/1868	Wickens, H. H.
G/339	Williams, A.
G/11177	Williams, F. W.
T/270055	Woollett, W. A. R.
T/1621	Wordsworth, F.

LANCE-CORPORALS

L/10279	Abbott, E. W.
G/5053	Ackerman, L. L.
G/5490	Addley, J. H.
L/10028	Ahearn, H.
G/731	Aitken, W. W.
G/8532	Alborough, F.
G/3411	Allen, E. A.
G/13700	Allen, S.

G/2566	Amos, P. W.
G/1498	Anderson, O.
L/9826	Anderson, W.
G/3211	Ansell, F. O.
G/5553	Appleton, T. E.
G/15735	Apps, E. A.
G/124	Argrave, F. S.
G/539	Arman, C.

439

APPENDIX II

G/6688	Arnold, L.	G/8697	Blunden, P. C.
G/6798	Ashdown, G.	G/18720	Bolst, N. J.
G/946	Ashford, T. W.	L/7608	Bone, D.
G/23747	Axtell, R. P.	L/9198	Booth, W. H.
		G/6489	Borley, A. L.
G/3128	Babbage, H. A.	G/6490	Borley, S. J.
S/10707	Back, W. F.	L/9667	Boxall, L.
G/13145	Bagnall, H.	G/1060	Bradford, C.
L/9592	Bailey, A. E.	G/838	Brasher, W.
G/2051	Bailey, R. G.	T/206093	Breckon, T.
G/338	Baines, T.	G/2652	Brenchley,G.,M.M.
G/4744	Baker, G. E.	L/9450	Bridgland, H.
G/4210	Baker, W.	G/20957	Briggs, E. W.
L/8799	Baldock, J.	T/470	Bringlow, T.
G/17710	Baldwin, C. H.	G/2500	Brockman, G. P.
G/449	Baldwin, J. W.	L/10492	Brome, H.
G/18137	Barden, G.	L/8936	Brook, R. E.
G/2606	Barnard, A.	G/8385	Brooks,G. R., M.M.
G/4732	Barnard, W. J.	L/9225	Broughton, A.
G/2263	Barnes, E.	S/7033	Brown, C. D.
T/270631	Barratt, D. F.	G/2336	Brown, E. G.
G/12739	Barrett, C. A.	G/146	Brown, J.
L/8967	Batchelor, A.	S/886	Brown, R. J.
G/3596	Batt, A. H.	G/12746	Brown, W.
G/6365	Beach, H. A.	L/7716	Browning, J. W.
G/257	Beeching, A. O.	G/10270	Buckland, W. E.
G/1008	Bell, J. A.	G/18980	Bugg, J.W.,D.C.M.
L/9977	Bellamy, V. S.	T/2408	Burgess, C. D. W.
L/9185	Benge, W. C.	L/9719	Burgess, J. H.
G/20203	Beresford, T. M., M.M.	L/9089	Burrows, J.
		S/10621	Burton, W. C.
G/1831	Berry, D. W.	G/1000	Butcher, A. H.
G/5282	Best, C.	G/6547	Butler, H. H.
L/9364	Bevan, G., M.M.		
T/240411	Bevan, F. H.	G/18989	Caress, J. T.
L/8284	Bishop, F.	G/15855	Carey, A. V., M.M.
G/18689	Blackford, C. S.	G/1997	Carey, G. J.
G/138	Blown, J.	G/3663	Carr, C. T.
G/5535	Bloxam, F.	G/2309	Castle, E. H.

440

LANCE-CORPORALS—(*continued*)

G/11676	Castle, T. W.		G/2094	Cronin, W. E.
G/7583	Catling, F.		G/3908	Crook, H.
T/270364	Cavell, J. L.		G/6814	Crossley, J. W.
G/4673	Chandler, C.		L/8865	Crouch, W. J.
G/12947	Chantler, T. W.		L/8407	Cullen, A., M.M.
G/8975	Chapman, B. F.		G/12501	Cummings, P. J. D.
L/10075	Chapman, E.		G/11678	Curzon, R.
G/6681	Chapman, H. V.			
G/1059	Chapman, J.		G/18748	Dagg, C. C.
G/14154	Childs, J. A.		L/8536	Dale, G. W.
G/3565	Christmas, J. W.		G/864	Daniels, A. H.
G/12690	Clack, E.		G/2568	Darrell, G.
T/241341	Clappinson, J. G.		G/4315	Davies, R.
G/13329	Clark, W. H.		L/6861	Davis, R. F. L.
L/9192	Clarke, A. R.		G/14421	Davis, T. G.
T/241240	Clarkson, H. J.		G/4601	Day, A.
G/7332	Clifton, F.		G/12820	Deacon, F.
L/8334	Cole, H. W.		G/1883	Denney, F.
G/3062	Coleman, P. W.		L/9525	Dennis, T. A.
G/8753	Coles, H. W.		G/4265	Dennis, W.
G/4523	Collins, H. H.		S/9875	Deverson, L.
L/10118	Conrade, A. E.		L/8696	Doherty, A.
G/9042	Constant, J.		G/839	Dommett, J. S.
T/270936	Cook, W. J.		G/718	Dove, G.
G/14967	Coombes, T. J.		G/18958	Downham, W.
G/8989	Coombs, F.		L/8663	Drury, F.
L/6341	Cooper, E.		L/6842	Dunn, W. J.
L/8921	Cooper, H. W.		T/240455	Dunnett, F.
G/9756	Coppen, C. H.		L/9985	Dunnings, W.
L/10577	Cork, F.		G/902	Durbridge, A.
G/1049	Corsan, J.		L/9851	Dyer, F. J.
G/11553	Couldridge, H. A.			
G/293	Court, F. D.		G/1228	Eade, F. G.
L/9505	Cox, G. H.		G/7703	Eacott, H. V.
G/1119	Cox, T. H.		G/13194	Eddy, A.
T/240051	Cramp, C.		G/12821	Edwards, W. W.
T/241261	Creek, G.		L/8539	Elms, W. L.
G/1245	Crick, C. G.		G/5283	Eve, W. E. E.
G/7	Croft, J. F.			

LANCE-CORPORALS—*(continued)*

L/9861	Fagg, J. T.	T/200097	Goodall, G. H.
L/9843	Farrell, W.	G/18946	Grand, F.
S/649	Fayers, W. E.	T/203643	Green, A.
L/9919	Fedarb, R. A.	T/241232	Green, A.
S/268	Felton, H. W.	T/3281	Green, F.
S/820	Field, W. E.	G/792	Griggs, T. J.
G/3002	Finn, J. W.	T/1335	Grossman, L. H.
G/20207	Fleming, J.	L/9313	Gunn, A. E.
G/3510	Floyd, G. T.		
G/3155	Ford, E. G.	G/3130	Halfacre, S.
L/8690	Foord, W. H.	L/8484	Hall, G. A.
G/15783	Foote, S. A. L.	G/6363	Halliday, W.
L/9043	Forster, W. G.	G/2142	Halsey, C.
G/17605	Foulsham, J. H.	L/10040	Hamblin, C. C.
G/4802	Fox, G. E.	T/203572	Hammond, T.
G/12683	Franklin, T.	L/9449	Hankins, J. J. F.
L/10041	Fray, P. E.	T/270053	Hardaker, J. H.
G/3422	Fricker, H. A.	L/9732	Hare, F. W.
G/4730	Friend, H. C.	S/10810	Harris, H.
L/9894	Fruin, T. E.	G/2254	Harrison, R.
L/8163	Fuller, J. G.	G/470	Hatcher, E. S.
G/343	Fuller, R. J.	G/847	Hatter, C.
		L/9427	Hawkes, F.
G/3696	Gascoine, C. H. G.	L/8547	Higgs, F.
G/6959	Gaskell, J.	T/242936	Hill, F. J.
G/3907	Gaston, G. E.	S/8398	Hines, H. T.
L/9429	George, F. E.	L/9862	Hinkley, F. R.
G/3502	Giles, E. A.	T/270789	Hoare, F. D.
L/8972	Gilham, A.	L/9015	Hoare, W. R.
G/24273	Gilham, B. E.	G/22495	Hoath, R. L.
G/1510	Gilson, H. W.	G/2268	Hobbs, W.
G/1667	Gledhill, G.	G/17755	Hockley, C. H.
G/566	Glover, J.	T/241674	Hodges, H. E. G.
L/8558	Goatham, C.	G/13617	Hodgkins, P. W.
G/1727	Goddard, H. C.	G/8980	Hollands, F. T.
L/9036	Godden, A. E.	G/3990	Hollman, A. L.
S/10806	Godin, A. E.	G/6827	Holt, C. F.
G/4375	Goldfinch, N.	G/15808	Holtum, L. E.
G/20815	Goldsmith, V. A.	G/3668	Hooker, W. J.

LANCE-CORPORALS—*(continued)*

T/240382	Hopcraft, A.	G/15632	Keates, A., M.M.
G/622	Horne, G.	G/3137	Keefe, W.
G/5334	Horswell, F.	G/6277	Keen, L. R.
G/945	Hoskins, C.	G/4108	Keen, T. W.
G/4888	Hover, E. A.	G/6153	Kendall, J.
G/18874	Howard, H. J.	L/9485	Kennett, T.
G/386	Huggin, B.	L/7595	Kesby, W. W.
L/6814	Hughes, G.	G/1769	Kilby, W.
T/203948	Hunt, H. O.	G/13676	King, J.
G/18793	Hurry, J. D.	G/1538	King, P. J.
G/20816	Hurst, A. E.	L/7854	Kingdom, C.
G/2333	Hutchinson, F. F.	G/11792	Knight, A. E.
L/7546	Hutchinson, H. J.	G/9127	Knight, A.S., M.M.
		T/242678	Knight, A. E.
L/6719	Iddenden, E.	T/3589	Knight, G. A.
G/8905	Ide, L. G.	G/474	Knight, V. J.
L/7640	Ireland, W.	G/5133	Knight, W. J.
G/8499	Jackson, A. C.	G/4569	Lake, H. J.
T/240840	Jagelman, S. A.	L/9878	Lake, J. A.
G/13225	James, T. H.	G/18045	Lamb, H. C.
G/4067	Jannoti, L.	G/2996	Lambert, C.
G/2822	Jarman,W.T.,M.M.	L/7200	Lambkin, W.
G/13095	Jeffrey, R.	T/176	Lawford, P. J.
G/1389	Jenkins, A. C.	L/8520	Lawson, W. H.
L/7624	Jennings, C.	G/5224	Leach, C. W.
T/203570	Jode, E.	G/7015	Ledger, R.
L/9268	Johncock, R. M.	L/8154	Lee, C. S.
G/1301	Johnes, G. W.	G/26638	Lee, J. S.
L/8784	Johns, F. G.	G/2579	Lee, T.
G/8824	Johnson, H. R.	G/13892	Lishman, J.
T/243007	Johnson, W.	G/7148	Lloyd, A. F.
L/5959	Johnson, W.	G/4814	Lond, A. R.
G/246	Jones, N. A.	G/19145	Long, J. S.
G/9025	Jones, W. G.	G/9727	Lott, W.
G/2761	Jordan, A.	G/9048	Low, S. J.
T/1791	Jordan, G. H.	G/11928	Lucas, F. C.
L/9031	Judd, E.	G/452	Luck, G., D.C.M.
L/9706	Judge, F. T.	L/7772	Lusted, A. P.

LANCE-CORPORALS—*(continued)*

L/10154	Malnick, G.		G/1266	Newton, H. H.
G/1728	Mandale, J. T.		G/14460	Newell, F.G., M.M.
G/25	Mann, H.		G/1020	Nichols, A. V.
T/270592	Marsden, W. G.		G/1141	Nickes, E. E.
L/7653	Marsh, A.		T/6136	Norfolk, S.
L/9781	Martin, F. A.		L/9502	Nutley, F. E.
L/6523	Martin, J. B.			
G/2455	Martin, L. F.		G/4176	O'Connor, E. J.
G/14206	Mason, G. E.		G/2292	Orsler, H. J. E.
G/10081	Mason, W.		T/240752	Osborne, H.
G/3044	Mather, F.		L/9263	Osborne, T. E.
G/8459	Maxted, H. J.		S/349	Ovenden, H. J.
G/4123	May, A.			
G/8529	May, W. E.		L/8660	Page, S.
L/8871	McAlpine, A. W.		G/7881	Palmer, J. E.
L/8527	McDonald, W. G.		L/10204	Palmer, J.
L/6370	Mepham, H. F.		G/13148	Palmer, L. G.
G/15646	Mercer, P.		L/8548	Parker, L.
S/53	Merrick, W.		G/132	Parsons, H.
T/202957	Miller, G. T.		G/14466	Patching, W. M.
G/2524	Miller, J. T.		G/5577	Pearce, S. G.
G/12974	Millgate, W.		G/6316	Peerless, V., M.M.
L/7548	Mills, P. J.		L/8611	Penfold, H.
S/648	Mills, R.		S/10278	Perrem, S. W.
T/200642	Milton, H. T.		G/18973	Perry, J.
L/8868	Minter, E. W.		G/225	Petts, W. C.
L/8833	Mitchell, L.		G/3455	Petty, J.
L/8767	Morgan, F.		G/6812	Phelps, A. J.
G/25406	Morgan, T. Ll.		L/9713	Philpott, G.
S/10666	Moss, W.		L/8713	Phipps, F. E.
G/6229	Mott, J.		G/8273	Pike, A.
G/4107	Moyce, H. S.		G/5223	Pile, W. J.
L/10181	Moys, H. W.		L/9834	Poole, J.
G/4870	Mundy, W. V.		G/278	Poole, T.
G/749	Murch, H. W.		G/2551	Pooley, J. P.
L/9743	Murrell, A. J.		L/6477	Potter, J. T.
			G/6802	Povey, S. A.
G/527	Newble, E.		L/8552	Powell, P.
G/13566	Newman, P. C.		G/4322	Pyle, H. W.

APPENDIX II

LANCE-CORPORALS—(*continued*)

L/8916	Quinnell, O. J.		S/10430	Savage, R. S.
T/6137	Quinton, L. L.		L/9979	Sayer, H. G.
			G/1942	Scott, J. E. R.
G/1797	Randall, P. A.		S/637	Scriven, W. T.
G/4725	Raper, W.		G/15812	Scutt, V. A.
G/9320	Rayner, F. W.,		L/9783	Seath, T. W.
	M.M.		L/10373	Setterfield, W.
G/20113	Read, F. G.		G/1520	Sewell, L. D.
G/4392	Read, S. T.		L/9980	Shapcott, R. C.
G/3484	Reed, J.		G/4707	Shaxted, W. H.
G/5558	Reeves, W. F.		S/8999	Shea, O.
G/15669	Reid, G. H. S.		G/2546	Sherwood, C.
G/12959	Rich, G. E.		G/9735	Shillits, W. H.
G/5872	Richardson, E.		L/7648	Ship, F. A.
T/203977	Richardson, G. H.		G/4022	Shipp, D.
G/1262	Richardson, H.		G/20801	Shirley, C. H.
T/243012	Richardson, P.		T/243013	Shoveller, H. J.
T/265243	Ride, H. J.		L/8397	Shrubsole, J.
L/10001	Rigden, G.		G/17628	Sines, H.
T/270584	Roberts, K.		G/12932	Sizer, C. A.
G/2172	Robinson, C. W.		S/10813	Smallwood, A.
G/6921	Robson, C. M.		S/10400	Smith, A. E.
S/10613	Rogers, F. C.		L/10036	Smith, A. T. J.
L/9106	Roots, A.		G/3032	Smith, F.
G/6632	Rosendale, F. W.		T/1093	Smith, F. G.
G/89	Rowe, H.		G/24040	Smith, H. D., M.M.
S/9359	Ruane, B. T.		L/9656	Smith, J. G.
G/6543	Rudland, G.		G/3961	Smith, J. H.,
G/852	Ruffett, G. H.			D.C.M., M.M.
S/10969	Russell, A.		L/8029	Smith, T.
T/200204	Russell, F.		T/1790	Smith, V.
G/1140	Russell, J. A.		G/2667	Smith, W. E.
S/10560	Russell, J. H.		L/8823	Solley, W.
G/13314	Rutter, W.		G/3906	Solly, G. C. L.
			G/5389	Sonntag, F.
G/15805	Salame, J.		T/200817	Spain, A. C.
G/3399	Saunders, F. St. J.		G/9053	Spanner, C. E. A.
G/6067	Saunders, H. P.		T/1068	Spice, A. S.
L/10035	Savage, F.		L/7724	Spillett, V.

445

APPENDIX II

LANCE-CORPORALS—(continued)

L/7625	Squires, R.		S/153	Warren, M.
G/23604	Stace, G. W.		L/9338	Watson, E.
L/7740	Standen, F. E.		G/3412	Watts, R. H.
L/9808	Stanley, L. G.		L/5728	Webb, C.
L/9363	Startup, A.		G/13258	Webb, G.
G/13355	Stauffer, R.		L/9911	Webster, C.
L/8381	Stedman, G.		G/885	Weeden, H. E.
L/8819	Stevens, A. S.		L/4580	Weller, F.
G/13379	Stone, A.		L/6938	Wells, A. L.
S/158	Stone, W.		S/10416	Wells, G.
G/77	Storr, P. F.		T/206013	Welsh, W.
L/9091	Stratford, E. W.		G/1425	Weston, W.
L/6985	Street, F. D.		L/7766	Wheeler, F.
T/204442	Street, R. H.		G/19495	Wheeler, F.
L/6850	Streetley, A.		G/1308	Wheeler, J. A.
G/2912	Stribling, C. H.		G/67	White, A.
L/9098	Stuckey, A. J.		G/3361	White, F.
L/8359	Sutton, A. G. L.		S/8453	White, T.
G/10213	Swallow, T. H.		G/3475	Whitman, A. E.
G/23845	Swann, P. F.		G/8841	Whybourn, J.
			G/1676	Wilkinson, N.
L/8515	Tabrett, H. J.		G/584	Willey, A.
L/7988	Tabrett, S.		G/13747	Williams, A.
L/10226	Thomas, E. S.		G/9755	Williams, F.
G/4567	Thomas, W.		G/9815	Williams, F. C.
T/242822	Thompson, F.		G/12786	Williams, H. S.
G/510	Thompson, P.		G/20116	Williams, P. J.
G/4520	Tibbles, J.		G/2234	Williams, W.
T/203050	Timson, M. S.		G/18674	Wilson, B. [M.M.
G/6278	Tookey, A. H.		L/8827	Wilson, S., D.C.M.,
T/1358	Topham, G.		L/9936	Winfield, S. J.
G/15019	Tupper, J.		G/3710	Wise, D. W., M.M.
G/8829	Turner, F.		S/710	Wisking, G.
L/9132	Tutt, G.		G/1326	Wood, C. V.
			G/5870	Wood, E. F.
G/15700	Uden, R.		L/10462	Wood, T. J.
			G/13861	Woodley, W. J.
G/3078	Vickery, H. H.		G/12968	Woods, A. W.
L/9550	Veitch, G. A.		G/840	Woodward, L. C.

446

APPENDIX II

LANCE-CORPORALS—*(continued)*

G/12964	Worsfold, A.	G/543	Young, T.
L/8540	Wyatt, G.	S/10601	Youngs, A. B.
L/6570	Wynder, J.		

DRUMMERS

L/8113	Beer, W. E.	L/8569	Royes, E. G.
L/8199	Bingham, A. W. G.	L/9078	Rye, T. E.
L/9622	Dundas, R. S.	T/153	Saunders, W. C.
		L/7813	Sharp, T. A. F. J.
L/7785	Firks, E. H.	L/5753	Smith, W. A.
		L/9136	Summers, H. R.
G/6090	Gallow, A. E.		
T/1023	Joy, W.	G/10838	Tyler, F. W.
L/8309	Penn, A. G.	L/8965	White, W. J.

PRIVATES

G/9221	Abbott, A. L. V.	G/14752	Aikenhead, A.
G/3342	Abbott, E.	G/14140	Ainge, A. E.
G/15761	Abbott, J. S.	T/203482	Ainsworth, E.
G/14138	Abbott, V. F.	G/20185	Akehurst, W. H.
G/4189	Abbott, W.	G/5015	Akhurst, H. T.
G/22404	Abel, C. W.	G/13343	Akhurst, J. W.
G/8373	Abel, R.	L/10783	Aldgate, H. C.
G/10251	Abraham, W.	G/9845	Aldred, H. J.
G/22504	Abrahams, E. W.	G/9883	Aldridge, A. W.
G/22012	A'Court, L. P. F.	L/9720	Aldridge, E. S.
G/21768	Adams, A. C.	G/249	Alexander, A.
G/4851	Adams, E. C.	G/1056	Alexander, A. H.
G/15533	Adams, F.	G/8814	Allaway, W. T. W.
G/708	Adams, F. G.	G/17877	Allder, H. G.
L/6928	Adams, J.	G/21245	Allen, A. L.
T/240312	Addison, P. F.	G/9376	Allen, B. R.
T/1314	Addy, F.	G/4537	Allen, C. H.
G/8737	Agnew, C.	G/15534	Allen, G.

447

PRIVATES—(*continued*)

L/7633	Allen, G.
G/25933	Allen, H. J.
G/3408	Allen, H. J.
G/6767	Allen, H. P.
G/20216	Allen, T.
G/13622	Allen, T. H.
T/3209	Allibone, G.
G/20235	Allison, H. J.
T/200757	Allison, W. E.
G/29102	Allsebrook, J.H.R.E
G/6578	Almond, A. R.
G/23865	Ames, A.
G/703	Amies, N. G. R.
G/2298	Amos, E.
G/12979	Amos, F. H.
G/11459	Amos, P. J.
G/26607	Amos, W. J.
G/18837	Amps, C. G.
G/5770	Anderson, H.
G/20850	Anderson, P. O. R.
G/11884	Anderson, W.
T/1753	Anderson, W.
G/15535	Andrews, A. J.
G/5402	Andrews, C.
G/6670	Andrews, G. T.
G/15536	Andrews, H.
L/9350	Andrews, H.
G/408	Andrews, H. E. M.
G/21166	Andrews, J.
G/19016	Andrews, L. B.
G/20049	Andrews, S. J.
G/25896	Andrews, W.
G/22353	Andrews, W.
L/6680	Angell, J. G. H.
G/20833	Angus, N. M.
G/9850	Anthony, W. J.
G/12680	Appleford, I.
G/2696	Appleton, A. E.
G/5019	Appleton, A. E.
T/4590	Appleton, C. E.
G/4527	Appleton, E. W.
G/25904	Appleton, R. W.
G/4953	Appleton, W. W.
S/10477	Apps, A.
G/8166	Apps, E. T.
G/1967	Apps, W.
G/2411	Archer, H.
G/2318	Archer, W. J.
L/8566	Argent, J. W.
G/3993	Argrave, A. G.
G/14597	Armitage, W. E.
G/21037	Armstrong, A. C.
G/12803	Armstrong, B.
L/7007	Arnell, L. W.
G/5863	Arnold, C.
G/8585	Arnold, E. D.
G/20016	Arnold, E. F.
G/1844	Arnold, F.
G/4394	Arnold, H. J.
G/12981	Arnold, P.
G/13717	Arnott, H. W.
G/12983	Arscott, W. C.
L/6859	Ashby, A. H.
G/358	Ashby, E. J.
G/15538	Ashby, H. E.
G/5547	Ashby, S. J.
T/240581	Ashdown, A. J.
G/4209	Ashforth, D.
G/5072	Ashman, C. W.
G/426	Ashman, F. R.
G/25950	Ashpole, H. W.
S/441	Ashworth, R.
G/1210	Aslett, E.
G/1419	Aslett, F. J.
G/2351	Asplin, E. E. V.
L/9311	Assiter, W. J.
L/10572	Astbury, P. S.
G/5056	Atkins, G. C.

APPENDIX II

G/1238	Atkins, G. W.
L/8217	Atkins, R.
G/9807	Atkins, W.
G/3910	Attewell, R. F. W.
G/25687	Auburn, H. G.
L/9180	Austen, C. R.
G/17571	Austen, J.
L/8103	Austen, S.
S/9580	Austin, A.
T/201134	Austin, J.
G/7830	Austin, S.
T/270358	Avery, A. H. P.
T/270781	Avery, S.
T/1223	Avery, T. F.
T/202430	Ayres, C.
T/3321	Ayres, E. E.
G/20828	Back, C. H.
G/3614	Bacon, F. F.
S/10709	Baddeley, C.
G/2448	Baddock, F. H.
T/203928	Bailey, A. E.
G/9690	Bailey, B.
G/4965	Bailey, C. E.
G/13105	Bailey, E. E.
G/7889	Bailey, G. R.
G/1590	Bailey, P. T.
T/203929	Bailey, S.
G/18177	Bailey, W.
G/4350	Bailey, W. H.
G/4805	Bailey, W. H.
G/11431	Bailey, W. T.
G/20230	Bainbridge, J.
S/10714	Baines, A.
T/203972	Baker, A. E.
G/2974	Baker, A. D.
G/24742	Baker, A.
T/1660	Baker, A. L.
L/10531	Baker, C. W.

G/1370	Baker, E. W.
G/7858	Baker, F. C.
G/9745	Baker, F. B.
G/4743	Baker, G.
T/270166	Baker, G. F.
S/614	Baker, G. R.
T/2434	Baker, G. W.
S/10530	Baker, H.
G/8893	Baker, H. W.
G/12944	Baker, J.
S/156	Baker, J.
G/8690	Baker, J.
G/5787	Baker, J.
T/2435	Baker, P. J.
G/26551	Baker, W.
G/3947	Baker, W.
L/7059	Baker, W. H.
G/6411	Balcombe, H. G.
G/4916	Baldcock, W. C.
G/20127	Baldock. J. E.
L/7796	Baldwin, F.
G/4447	Balfour, A. H. L.
G/3671	Ball, H. C.
L/9465	Ball, W. W. M.
G/3708	Ballard, H. H.
T/204205	Ballard, J.
G/2842	Balls, F. L.
G/4239	Balls, G.
G/17489	Bancroft, A. W.
G/1904	Banks, F. J.
G/7927	Banks, G. H. C.
G/22702	Banting, H. H.
G/14400	Barber, E.
G/107	Barden, L. C.
T/1765	Barden, W.
G/20129	Barden, W. J.
L/6339	Bare, E. A.
G/21887	Barfield, A.
T/241584	Barham, A. C.

2 G

APPENDIX II

G/26419	Barham, G. E.	T/202812	Barton, D. W.
G/21289	Barker, A.	L/8444	Barton, E. E.
G/22991	Barker, A.	G/9029	Barton, H. F.
T/204450	Barker, F.	L/10388	Barton, J.
T/243158	Barker, H. G.	G/12580	Bartram, C.
G/13928	Barker, W.	L/8097	Basford, H. F.
S/10842	Barkham, W.	G/6305	Bass, C. W.
G/1231	Barkson, H.	G/10193	Bass, G.
G/18215	Barlow, J.	G/12641	Bassett, P.
G/21238	Barnard, A. E.	G/22245	Bassett, W.
G/1822	Barnard, C. W. E.	T/271012	Batchelor, W. L.
G/6795	Barnard, R. C.	G/8378	Bateman, G. H.
S/9217	Barnes, E. A.	G/5332	Bates, A.
S/10797	Barnes, F. L.	G/13116	Bates, W. C.
L/9548	Barnes, G. W.	G/3535	Batt, S.
G/14401	Barnes, L. H.	G/23771	Battle, A. K.
T/270289	Barnes, W.	G/2330	Baulson, R.
G/12588	Barnes, W. E.	G/1055	Baxter, H.
G/4903	Barnes, W. J.	G/24815	Baxter, H.
L/9830	Barnes, W. J.	G/20847	Bayley, C.
G/13870	Barnes, W. W.	S/68	Beach, A.
L/9598	Barnett, A. W.	L/8096	Beach, E.
G/4365	Barnett, B. L.	G/13761	Beach, F.
G/6679	Barnwell, H. J.	G/10207	Beach, H.
G/8468	Barr, H. J. S.	S/10891	Beacher, W.
G/8567	Barr, T.	G/12679	Beachey, W. J.
L/7149	Barranger, G.	L/9483	Beadel, A. S.
G/1541	Barrett, H. P.	L/9935	Beadle, A. T.
G/7579	Barrett, W.	G/22046	Beadle, L.
T/204123	Barrett, W.	L/6554	Beale, S.
G/13196	Barrett, W.	G/9311	Bean, A. J.
G/9137	Barrow, J.	G/8115	Bean, A.
G/6866	Barry, D.	G/2789	Bean, C.
G/1992	Barry, W.	S/180	Bean, J. T.
G/15547	Barsley, C. H. J.	G/4452	Bean, L.
G/477	Bartholomew, W.	G/4081	Bean, R.
G/14094	Bartle, B.	G/5120	Beaney, A.
G/19195	Bartle, F. H.	G/17709	Beaney, E. W.
L/8131	Bartley, A. J.	S/10696	Beaney, F.

APPENDIX II

G/644	Beard, G.	S/10898	Bennett, A. G.
G/13073	Beard, G. F.	G/18838	Bennett, F. C.
L/9960	Beard, W. E.	G/5734	Bennett, H. W.
T/3251	Beasley, B.	G/14302	Bennett, J.
G/22392	Beasley, F.	S/10448	Bennett, S.
G/22273	Beasley, H. F.	T/1227	Bennett, W.
G/21181	Beauchamp, P.	G/26251	Bennett, W. A.
G/21169	Beaumont, S. H.	G/7795	Benoy, H. H.
T/243272	Beaver, W. J.	G/4251	Benson, E. T.
G/1813	Beavis, G. B.	G/20056	Bentley, R. C.
G/1449	Beazley, H.	G/29122	Bentley, W. C.
L/8806	Beck, A.	G/14639	Bentzing, J.
L/8788	Becks, W. J.	G/13633	Berry, A. E.
G/24423	Bedford, R.	G/352	Berry, E. G.
G/13437	Bedwell, S.	G/24951	Berry, H. W.
G/14127	Beeching, S. F.	G/9362	Berry, J. H.
G/2230	Beecliff, R.	G/32	Berry, S.
L/7665	Beecroft, P.	G/18878	Berryman, G. H.
G/13367	Beeden, S. C.	G/19197	Best, H. W.
G/13344	Beedle, J. C.	G/2171	Beston, H.
L/8124	Beeken, T. H.	T/241218	Bevan, R. E.
G/3073	Beeling, W. I.	G/15552	Bew, F.
G/30	Beer, H. H.	G/17684	Bicker, A.
L/9933	Beer, L. W.	G/3599	Bigwood, V. L.
G/4259	Beer, W. R.	T/270405	Bills, P. W.
L/8018	Beerling, A.	G/5813	Bilsby, E.
G/13654	Beerling, F. W.	G/6826	Bilton, E. S.
G/5297	Beerling, G. A.	G/13814	Bing, H. J.
G/29120	Beighton, E.	L/9057	Bingham, C. H.
S/10871	Beken, G.	G/4710	Bingham, F. J.
G/35644	Bell, A.	G/8236	Birch, F. W.
G/73	Bell, D.	G/13020	Birch, R. T.
G/5052	Bell, G. W.	L/7699	Bircham, E.
G/64	Bell, R.	L/7920	Birchett, H.
G/2377	Bellamy, H. C.	G/18883	Bishop, C. H.
S/10443	Belsey, A. I.	G/22508	Bishop, F. E.
G/7560	Belsey, H. G.	G/35516	Bishop, H.
G/13277	Bending, F. W.	G/12895	Bishop, H. G.
G/11846	Benge, F.	T/202128	Bishop, H. J.

APPENDIX II

PRIVATES—(continued)

T/3080	Bithell, J.
G/15504	Blackaby, R. H.
G/15822	Blackburn, C. J.
L/10275	Blackhurst, W.
G/1371	Blacklock, A.
T/203078	Blackman, A.
G/6043	Blackman, A. J.
G/8902	Blackman, B. P.
T/202276	Blackman, J.
T/240257	Blackman, J. S.
L/6857	Blackmore, B. M.
G/894	Blacktin, F.
T/242785	Blake, C.
T/4315	Blake, J. H.
G/18839	Blake, P.
G/8731	Blakeman, J.
G/12713	Blanchard, W. H.
G/9033	Bland, J. H.
G/24058	Bland, W. H.
L/10283	Blandford, W. H.
G/3434	Blay, S. G.
G/18681	Blewitt, F.
L/9669	Blewitt, W. J.
G/8754	Blight, F. C.
T/270982	Bloomfield, F. G.
S/9212	Bloomfield, H. H.
G/10225	Blott, H. W.
G/2716	Blowers, G.
G/17387	Blowers, P. N.
G/14970	Blundell, W. C.
G/2648	Blunt, J.
T/201845	Boakes, J. S.
G/14032	Boakes, T.
G/12525	Boardman, F.
G/14836	Boardman, W. H.
G/21069	Boarer, W., M.M.
G/17711	Bobby, J.
L/7736	Bodman, W.
T/204310	Bohannan, W. G.

G/2220	Boiling, E.
T/270198	Bolton, A. J.
T/3513	Bolton, W.
L/7677	Bolton, W.
G/12807	Bomford, H.
G/4728	Bond, E. E. J.
G/5631	Bond, H.
G/11781	Bond, J. R.
G/18758	Bone, H. L.
G/4926	Bones, W. J.
G/18841	Bonwick, W. C.
G/1743	Booker, F. T.
G/14405	Boon, H. V.
T/203066	Boorer, E. T.
T/240284	Boorman, A. G.
G/20813	Boorman, H.
G/968	Booth, J.
G/8309	Borland, A.
G/3750	Borrer, E. G.
L/8229	Bosely, P., M.M.
G/21123	Bostock, J. F.
T/240280	Botten, C.
G/4983	Botting, D.
G/915	Botting, E. C.
G/17643	Botting, J.
G/15555	Bourne, A.
L/7875	Bowden, S. D.
G/22005	Bowden, V.
G/13628	Bowe, G. J.
L/10242	Bowen, J. E.
G/1519	Bowen, T.
G/638	Bowen, W. C.
L/7234	Bower, W.
G/20040	Bowkett, R. C.
G/8534	Bowles, E. J.
L/6582	Bowles, F.
G/8648	Bowles, L. F
G/7927	Bowley, E.
G/734	Box, F.

452

APPENDIX II

G/19044	Box, J. A.	G/22298	Brinkley, A. W.
G/5542	Boxall, L. A.	G/18808	Brinn, F. W. F.
T/206065	Boyes, J.	G/6870	Briscoe, J. H.
G/20227	Brackley, H.	G/13733	Briscoe, S.
G/943	Bradbury, S. H.	T/270780	Briselden, T. H.
G/3736	Bradbury, W.	T/204120	Britchford, C. C.
G/14300	Bradley, F. E.	L/7751	Broad, G. A.
L/9397	Bradley, G.	G/4268	Broad, W.
G/1418	Bradley, G. J.	G/4403	Broadhurst, J.
G/22467	Bradley, H. L.	G/2489	Brockman, A. T.
G/29110	Bradshaw, G.	G/8489	Brodie, W. H.
G/26656	Bradshaw, W. G.	G/25310	Brogden, J.
G/17396	Braisdell, G. H.	G/7643	Broker, F.
L/8166	Bramble, T. H.	S/10936	Bromley, A.
G/12984	Branchett, A. P.	G/4702	Bromley, J.
T/2443	Brann, R. J.	T/2330	Bromley, W. E.
T/1321	Brant, T.	G/24432	Brook, B.
L/7734	Brattle, E. W.	S/10267	Brooker, F.
G/456	Bray, J. W.	G/18924	Brooker, F. N.
L/6147	Bremmer, F.	G/19143	Brookes, H. G.
G/4948	Brenchley, J. E.	G/14499	Brooks, A.
S/10906	Brett, J. R.	G/14823	Brooks, A. W.
G/5452	Brett, R. B.	S/207	Brooks, C. E.
S/8278	Brewer, A.	G/11823	Brooks, C. F.
T/1807	Brewer, S. W.	G/1190	Brooks, E. W.
G/12619	Brewster, E. J.	G/8124	Brooks, H.
T/241907	Brice, A.	G/17828	Brooks, J. S.
G/2494	Brice, G. F.	G/1291	Broomfield, A.
T/265133	Brickstock, F.	G/15559	Brotherwood, H.
G/24791	Bridge, A. R.	L/9889	Brown, A.
T/957	Bridge, W. R. H.	G/14298	Brown, A. E.
G/17685	Bridger, A.	G/4939	Brown, A. H. G. P.
T/3714	Bridger, T.	G/13426	Brown, A. J.
G/19007	Bridges, L. A. F.	L/10229	Brown, C.
G/3523	Bridges, R.	G/9393	Brown, C. J.
L/9583	Bridgland, S.	G/11297	Brown, E.
G/1505	Briggenshaw, A.	G/5604	Brown, E. T.
G/1533	Briggs, C.	G/12990	Brown, F.
G/4037	Briggs, C.	G/505	Brown, F. A.

453

PRIVATES—(*continued*)

L/7824	Brown, G.
T/1940	Brown, C. R.
G/6820	Brown, H.
G/23311	Brown, H. H.
G/26166	Brown, H. J.
G/4640	Brown, J.
G/13201	Brown, J.
G/6081	Brown, J.
G/5983	Brown, J.
G/13100	Brown, J. H.
G/24748	Brown, J. L.
G/10238	Brown, J. T.
G/18285	Brown, O. A.
G/8758	Brown, P.
G/13076	Brown, P. E.
G/20038	Brown, R.
G/14574	Brown, S.
G/9879	Brown, S.
L/8964	Brown, W. R.
G/14964	Brown, W. T.
G/13771	Browne, A. G.
G/13786	Browne, A. V.
G/732	Browne, G. W.
T/270706	Browne, T. A. E.
T/241436	Browning, E. P.
T/240395	Browning, F. J.
G/18660	Browning, G. F.
G/11365	Bruce, R. H.
G/8376	Bruce, R. H.
T/240901	Brungar, E. F.
T/241817	Brunger, D.
L/8140	Brunger, E.
T/240374	Brunger, H.
G/12992	Brunger, H. T.
G/1404	Bruniges, R.
S/10920	Bryan, H. J.
G/8508	Bryant, A.
G/4644	Bryant, C.
S/883	Bryant, H. C.
T/242404	Bryant, J. T.
G/15756	Bubb, C.
G/3047	Bubb, E. J. W.
G/240845	Bubb, L. W.
L/11230	Buckman, E. W. J.
G/18963	Buckwell, C.
G/7715	Buddell, F. H.
L/9096	Bugden, F. C.
G/5794	Bugden, W. T.
G/842	Bull, A. J.
G/14947	Bull, A. S.
L/7919	Bull, L. F.
G/29272	Bunn, J.
G/22200	Bunting, C. H.
G/3625	Burbridge, G. T.
L/6937	Burcham, F.
G/4406	Burcham, H. E.
G/18956	Burchfell, W.
G/3261	Burden, F. J. C.
G/14098	Burdett, A.
G/10228	Burdock, C.
G/1944	Burfutt, J.
T/203452	Burge, J. A.
S/325	Burgess, F. S.
T/202522	Burgess, H. E.
G/15562	Burgess, H. J.
S/383	Burgess, H. W.
T/1939	Burgess, J. E.
S/684	Burgess, T.
L/10803	Burgoyne, J. W.
G/8103	Burke, G. S.
S/9160	Burke, J.
G/4575	Burnap, E.
G/20123	Burnap, R. J.
L/4672	Burns, C. J.
G/1438	Burrows, F.
G/2734	Burrows, H.
L/6175	Burt, R.
G/137	Burton, C. R.

APPENDIX II

PRIVATES—(*continued*)

G/19171	Burton, H. C.	G/3322	Calfe, E. C.
G/13010	Burton, W. E.	G/6048	Calver, B. J.
G/22496	Burton, W. J.	G/12776	Calvert, L.
G/15563	Busbridge, W. R.	G/2513	Cameron, F.
G/1688	Busby, J. A.	G/25263	Cameron, J. S.
G/24056	Bush, R.	G/14732	Cameron, I. C.
G/1443	Bushell, C. H.	G/26128	Cammack, A.
G/27	Bushell, J.	G/25745	Camp, F.
T/241864	Bushill, E. J.	G/22158	Camp, S. J.
G/9686	Buss, W. E.	G/14307	Campbell, C. S.
L/10254	Buss, W.	G/13709	Campbell, C. R. J.
G/21080	Buswell, E.	S/726	Campbell, J.
L/7583	Butcher, C. H.	T/1530	Campbell, W.
T/240707	Butcher, E. J.	L/9039	Candy, J. L.
G/4614	Butcher, H. M.	G/2921	Canham, A.
L/9326	Butcher, J.	G/11932	Canham, J. S.
L/8476	Butcher, W.	G/26592	Cansick, H. M.
G/100	Butcher, W.	G/11308	Capp, G. H.
G/24948	Butcher, W. A. S.	G/11378	Card, E. P.
T/241442	Butler, A. E.	T/242847	Card, T. W.
G/9607	Butler, A. E.	G/13346	Carden, E. T.
T/204211	Butler, G.	S/10584	Care, F. T.
G/9729	Butler, H.	G/14962	Carey, F.
G/8940	Butler, H. F.	L/6866	Carey, T. H.
G/14143	Butler, H. S.	S/10393	Carlton, F. P.
G/8910	Butler, J.	T/206104	Carlton, W.
G/13107	Butterfield, G.	S/7978	Carpenter, H.
S/9721	Butterfield, H. W.	L/9782	Carpenter, H. J.
G/26141	Butterworth, W.	G/14100	Carpenter, T. B.
T/2483	Button, A.	L/8306	Carr, C.
L/8602	Button, G. E.	G/2730	Carr, S.
G/9625	Button, J. G.	G/14656	Carrack, J.
S/10786	Buxton, A. J.	T/3518	Carter, A.
T/1661	Byford, C. V.	G/1548	Carter, C.
L/10553	Bysouth, A. W.	S/10973	Carter, H.
		G/12901	Carter, J.
G/3953	Cady, H. E.	G/15566	Carter, J. H.
G/9720	Cage, C.	G/6136	Carter, J. T.
G/19160	Calf, R. F.	G/2478	Carter, R. H.

455

PRIVATES—*(continued)*

L/7696	Carter, T. F.	G/11432	Chantley, A. H.
S/60	Carthew, J.	L/7647	Chapman, A. R.
G/14161	Cartwright, F. G.	G/19022	Chapman, C. F.
G/768	Carver, W.	G/4930	Chapman, E.
G/7706	Caselton, S.	G/4980	Chapman, F. J.
G/11131	Casey, H. T.	G/18846	Chapman, H.
T/242206	Casey, R. F.	G/10142	Chapman, J. P.
G/565	Cashman, J.	G/5682	Chapman, J.
G/10499	Cassidy, J.	L/10497	Chapman, R. W.
G/8455	Castle, F. H.	G/5397	Chapman, R. H.
G/4004	Castle, R.	T/240083	Chapman, V.
G/11317	Cath, H.	G/22423	Chapman, W.
T/3116	Catlin, E.	G/18844	Chappell, E. G.
T/20242	Catlow, W.	L/7227	Chapple, A. E.
G/5367	Catt, A. E.	L/6578	Charlton, F. J.
G/8894	Catt, A. H.	T/203521	Charlton, J. S.
G/11284	Catt, J. B.	G/3737	Charman, A. E.
G/544	Causer, E.	G/5646	Charman, H. J.
G/602	Causer, J.	G/1912	Chatterton, H. F.
G/8062	Cavalier, E. S.	G/13936	Cheadle, R. H.
T/271022	Cave, E. M.	G/22429	Cheeseman, C.
G/131	Cave, H. J.	G/18965	Cheeseman, C. A.
L/9330	Chaddock, W. E. V.	T/2164	Cheeseman, G.H.S.
G/11959	Chadwick, H.	G/6165	Cheeseman, H. J.
G/14158	Chaffer, A. T.	G/4911	Cheeseman, P. E.
G/9283	Chalk, H. G. W.	T/240214	Chenery, C.
G/21208	Chalkley, A.	G/18719	Cheney, C.
S/8730	Challis, C. J.	S/486	Cherrison, J.
G/14502	Chaloner, H. B.	G/9869	Cheshire, H.
G/12794	Chamberlain, H. F.	T/2338	Chesson, W.
G/1067	Chamberlin, H.	T/242075	Chester, E. J. P.
T/1620	Chambers, C. T.	G/26560	Chester, F. G.
G/21291	Champion, T. E.	L/10145	Chevous, S. G.
G/20132	Champkins, C.	G/325	Chidwick, F.
G/463	Champs, B.	G/17659	Chinnery, T.
G/22343	Chandler, A.	G/13077	Chittenden, G. A.
G/22426	Chandler, E. D.	S/860	Chittenden, T.
G/24355	Chandler, W. H.	T/1676	Chittenden, W.
L/8929	Chantler, J. H.	G/15762	Chown, W. H.

APPENDIX II

G/1792	Chubb, E. F.	L/9962	Clegg, R. H.
G/1057	Churchill, A. E.	G/3281	Clemence, J.
S/10954	Churchman, L. F.	G/13866	Clements, E.
G/17661	Churchward, W.	G/25499	Clements, G. C.
G/9876	Clack, A. C.	G/11182	Clements, H. E.
G/9511	Clackett, A. E.	G/7863	Clephane, D.
T/203581	Clackett, C.	G/26655	Clewley, J. H.
G/24192	Clampin, J. H.	G/12795	Clifford, E.
G/21209	Claridge, A. W. T.	G/6665	Clifford, J.
S/10428	Claringbold, F. W.	G/3632	Clifton, H. A.
G/21213	Clark, A.	L/10250	Clifton, J. E.
T/203583	Clark, A.	G/18210	Clinch, T. J.
L/8489	Clark, A. J.	G/6626	Close, W.
G/12596	Clark, C.	G/14153	Clough, T.
G/1535	Clark, C.	G/9712	Clout, H. W.
G/5934	Clark, J. E.	G/18993	Clubb, H. W.
S/10855	Clark, L. R.	T/206121	Cobain, H.
G/24258	Clark, R. H.	G/6286	Cock, E. J.
G/25322	Clark, S. H.	G/6731	Cockerill, E. A.
G/12902	Clark, W. E.	G/8631	Cockle, F.
T/270281	Clark, W. M.	G/12164	Coesheaell, L.
T/241334	Clarke, A.	G/18845	Coffield, E. C.
G/7908	Clarke, A.	G/4460	Cogger, H.
S/10231	Clarke, A.	G/22470	Cohen, O.
S/10981	Clarke, A. C.	S/10450	Cohsall, J.
G/2182	Clarke, A. W.	L/10260	Cole, A. G.
G/1576	Clarke, C.	G/5089	Cole, C.
L/10344	Clarke, C.	T/241451	Cole, F.
G/4364	Clarke, E. F.	L/9822	Cole, H.
G/2235	Clarke, H.	G/12113	Cole, J.
G/24264	Clarke, H. P.	G/25128	Cole, L.
L/9917	Clarke, R.	G/12597	Cole, S. M.
T/4440	Clarke, R. A.	G/730	Cole, W.
G/11874	Clay, E. W.	G/12016	Coleman, A. W.
G/18876	Claydon, T.	G/4098	Coleman, E. J.
G/986	Clayton, F.	G/8659	Coleman, G. B.
G/29265	Clayton, J. T. H.	G/12817	Coleman, H. J.
G/18248	Clayton, S. G.	G/751	Coleman, J.
G/13193	Cleaver, S.	L/9832	Coleman, J. M.

PRIVATES—(*continued*)

G/20133	Coleman, O.		G/18716	Cooke, F. W.
G/20236	Coleman, T.		G/13619	Coomber, H.
G/25877	Coles, R.		G/18728	Coomber, H.
T/240055	Coley, G.		G/1943	Coomber, R.
G/2481	Coley, H.		L/7848	Coombs, C.
G/1383	Collard, A. S.		G/12182	Coomer, C. A.
L/7164	Collard, P.		G/20954	Cooper, B. J.
G/5123	Collard, R.		G/1867	Cooper, F.
G/25210	Collier, F. C.		G/15574	Cooper, G. H.
L/9986	Collier, F. H.		G/15575	Cooper, G. L.
G/14102	Collin, R.		L/8968	Cooper, H. E.
G/13263	Collin, T.		L/8551	Cooper, J. H.
G/8946	Collins, E. A.		G/20853	Cooper, J.
T/203920	Collins, H. W.		G/9691	Cooper, P. B. A.
S/10547	Collins, J.		G/1705	Cooper, W. E.
L/10165	Collins, L. C.		G/18065	Coote, P. R.
G/7632	Collins, P. J. M.		T/204104	Cope, C.
G/1575	Collins, R. C.		G/3516	Cope, L. W.
G/22032	Collins, S.		G/38	Coppen, E. E.
G/1381	Collins, S. A.		G/5639	Coppin, W. R.
G/14416	Collins, T.		G/1582	Copping, T.
S/10704	Collins, T. G.		L/10127	Coppins, E. S.
G/15573	Collison, A. L. T.		T/240102	Coppins, G.
G/6535	Collison, W.		G/18691	Coppins, T.
G/4574	Colvin, D.		G/29291	Corah, A.
G/127	Comboy, D. P.		L/9084	Corby, W. J.
G/2479	Company, F.		G/14155	Cordarcy, S.
G/8517	Conley, A.		G/5333	Cordell, E.
G/7024	Connor, B.		G/21439	Cordell, F. C.
S/10327	Cook, A. E.		T/203939	Cordery, G.
S/10818	Cook, F. W.		L/10061	Cordier, A.
T/1887	Cook, G. F.		G/7271	Cordingly, W.
S/8883	Cook, H. J.		G/9765	Cork, A.
G/720	Cook, J.		G/4831	Cork, J.
G/7821	Cook, J. A.		G/9222	Cork, W. J.
G/1586	Cook, J. H.		G/1956	Corke, J.
G/20826	Cook, T. G.		G/21042	Corney, L. A.
G/2722	Cook, W.		G/10230	Cornhill, A. J.
S/9868	Cook, W. E.		L/6391	Cornish, A.

APPENDIX II

PRIVATES—(*continued*)

G/14315	Corrall, G. L.	G/13078	Craker, T. R.
G/20848	Corrie, E. G.	L/10249	Craker, W.
L/8242	Corry, E. A.	G/20254	Cramp, D. S.
G/19174	Cosens, W.	G/9467	Cramp, J.
T/242688	Costa, J.	G/4473	Crampton, P.
L/8881	Cotter, B.	G/15505	Crampton, W.
L/7996	Cotter, W.	G/6778	Crawford, W.
G/29285	Cotterill, F. A.	G/14974	Crawley, G. E.
G/8491	Cottingham, J. A.	G/13207	Crawley, J.
G/18804	Cotton, A.	G/9489	Crayden, H.
G/22238	Cotton, E. H.	G/15578	Crayford, S.
G/22445	Cottrell, A. E.	G/14931	Crean, H.
G/14733	Couch, J. W.	T/203567	Creed, S.
G/4606	Coughlan, J. J.	G/3297	Cresdel, T. F.
G/4478	Coulbeck, J. H.	G/29132	Creswell, G.
S/10338	Court, B. J.	G/10227	Crick, J. W.
T/20213	Court, E.	L/8657	Crickett, G. A.
T/240695	Court, J. S.	G/5241	Crippen, S. G.
G/25275	Courtman, F. A. L.	G/25314	Crisp, E. H. G.
T/202595	Courtney, A. G.	L/10217	Crispin, J.
G/1608	Courtney, W. G.	G/17906	Crockford, G. O.
L/6915	Cousins, F. W.	G/22440	Crofford, G. N.
G/26717	Cousins, T.	G/4677	Croft, J. S.
S/849	Couzens, T. J.	L/6179	Croft, W.
G/4237	Cowdrey, R.	S/9428	Croft, W. J., M.M.
G/139	Cowell, A. T.	G/8388	Crofts, E. L.
G/15577	Cowell, S.	L/9742	Crofts, F. W.
G/8778	Cowey, T. B.	G/7981	Cronin, D.
G/6353	Cowland, C. W.	G/12904	Crook, J.
G/4533	Cox, F. J.	G/1683	Crookes, F.
S/10743	Cox, H.	T/206185	Crooks, J.
G/1327	Cox, H.	G/14976	Crosby, E. H. S.
S/10249	Cox, W. T.	G/20071	Crosier, W.
G/2656	Cox, W. T.	T/202690	Cross, W. N.
T/206021	Crabb, F. C. G.	G/6072	Crouch, C. F.
G/3307	Crabb, W. H.	G/4838	Crouch, G.
G/6755	Crabtree, A.	G/12903	Crouch, H.
G/25157	Cracknell, E. P.	G/13282	Crouch, J. C.
G/8759	Craddock, W.	L/8763	Croucher, A. E.

APPENDIX II

L/10663	Croucher, C.
G/4856	Croucher, E.
G/39	Croucher, F. S.
L/5391	Croucher, J. R.
G/6151	Croud, F.
S/675	Crowhurst, P.
G/22428	Crowson, W. P.
G/24895	Crummey, D.
L/9214	Crump, E. H.
G/12993	Crumpton, E. H.
L/7845	Cudlip, H. D.
G/12815	Cuff, J. W.
T/1334	Cullen, J.
G/2840	Culling, W. G.
G/4023	Culver, A. E.
G/9894	Culver, T.
G/817	Culwich, W. J.
G/6876	Cummings, T. H.
G/9844	Curl, G.
G/4413	Curness, F. G.
L/7532	Curnow, G.
G/22159	Currall, E.
G/13874	Curry, T. W.
G/20449	Curtis, J.
G/20990	Curtis, P. J.
G/12584	Curtis, W.
G/7888	Curtis, W. G.
G/6100	Curtiss, H.
G/14018	Cuttress, H.
G/2055	Daborn, W.
G/13653	Dadds, T. W.
G/15581	Dadson, A.
T/923	Dadswell, T.
G/6697	Dainton, A. E.
G/9187	Daisey, W. H.
T/3417	Dale, A. B.
T/202600	Dale, F. A.
G/5974	Dale, F. R.

S/168	Dale, T. E.
T/202460	Dalton, A. F.
G/3900	Dalton, N.
G/23878	Dancer, G.
G/271	Danes, A. W.
G/12973	Daniel, R. M.
G/5711	Daniells, R.
G/13004	Daniels, D. B.
G/8803	Daniels, E. T.
G/9855	Daniels, G.
G/9774	Daniels, W. S.
L/7549	Dann, F.
L/8575	Danton, A.
G/14004	Darling, A. E.
G/14077	Dart, C. G.
G/7321	Darvill, C. H.
G/29137	Davey, H.
G/15759	Davey, P.
G/20941	Davidson, W. G.
T/242455	Davies, E. A.
G/6047	Davies, G.
G/825	Davies, S.
L/7883	Davies, W.
G/20933	Davis, A. A.
G/208	Davis, C.
G/21877	Davis, E. E.
S/10702	Davis, E. E.
G/14829	Davis, G. J.
S/303	Davis, H.
T/203632	Davis, S. E.
G/8661	Davis, W. R. V.
G/3899	Davitt, J.
T/270101	Davy, H.
G/2661	Daw, A. J.
G/23870	Dawes, A.
G/3911	Dawkins, W. G.
G/7041	Dawsey, G. H.
G/13316	Dawson, C.
S/10540	Dawson, E.

APPENDIX II

S/9182	Dawson, G.
G/2389	Dawson, H.
G/1782	Day, E. J.
G/563	Day, F. H.
G/25325	Day, H.
G/6874	Deacon, F. T.
L/10488	Deadman, E.
G/25264	Deal, H. E.
S/9857	Dearman, S.
G/2075	De Beger, A. L.
G/18889	Dedman, R. A.
G/3773	Deeprose, H. J.
T/203457	Degg, R.
T/2334	De la Mare, H. R.
G/12139	Dellaway, A.
G/13079	Deller, A. L.
G/25329	Dellison, J.
G/8959	Denham, W.
G/3195	Denley, F.
T/201627	Denmee, A. L.
G/20137	Denne, C. T.
G/20109	Denne, D. G.
L/9998	Denne, P.
T/271029	Dennett, G. C. C., M.M.
L/8254	Dennis, J. W.
S/9950	Denton, A.
G/24309	Derbyshire, J.
G/14503	Derrick, W. J.
T/271152	Derrick, W. W.
T/240659	Deverson, H.
S/10935	Dewhurst, W.
G/1711	Dews, E.
G/4376	Dicker, W. L.
G/14424	Dickerson, H.
G/385	Dickson, F. G.
G/5665	Dickson, W. C.
T/20040	Diddams, W.
T/270082	Dier, F. J., M.M.

G/2163	Dillingham, S. D.
T/265012	Dillon, H.
G/4968	Divers, A. W.
G/26186	Dives, W.
G/4913	Dixon, A. C.
G/15821	Dixon, MacD.
G/13300	Dobson, C.
G/18054	Dobson, J.
G/6815	Dodds, J. W.
G/24986	Dodge, A.
G/6544	Doe, A.
T/202561	Doe, A. E.
T/201289	Dolby, L.
G/17616	Dollin, C.
T/242735	Domoney, H.
G/14247	Donaldson, A.
T/3332	Dormer, A.
S/59	Dormer, J.
G/15738	Doubleday, S. C.
G/5822	Doubleday, W.
G/4836	Doubtfire, J.
G/22491	Dove, W. H. G.
G/18734	Dowling, C. J.
G/5100	Down, F. T.
T/202160	Down, G. A.
T/25507	Down, T. G.
G/25506	Downes, W. F.
G/5235	Downs, R. W.
T/20216	Dowsett, A.
G/2728	Dowsing, H.
L/10144	D'Oyley, E.
G/2029	Draper, S. J.
G/4862	Dray, A. J.
L/10383	Dray, C. C.
G/7618	Dray, H.
L/9638	Dray, H. W.
S/585	Dray, R.
G/26658	Drayson, T. H.
L/7787	Drew, E. J.

461

APPENDIX II

G/15004	Druce, W.
L/8015	Drury, A. E. L.
S/9810	Drury, J. P.
G/25983	Drury, W. R.
G/8909	Dryland, G.
G/5392	Dubbins, G. W.
L/5895	Duck, F. J.
G/4620	Duckers, A.
L/8662	Duff, G.
G/24312	Duff, W.
G/829	Duffell, A. V.
G/2655	Duffield, W. C. J.
G/6906	Duffy, P.
G/11890	Duke, E. J.
G/15583	Duly, P. W.
L/5659	Dumbleton, A. J.
G/21495	Dumbrell, A. G.
G/11836	Dumbrill, S. J.
L/9144	Dunbar, S.
L/9906	Duncan, A. H.
G/9743	Dungate, H. C.
G/21190	Dungey, A. E.
L/10109	Dunk, P. J.
G/3745	Dunkley, F.
S/10264	Dunn, E. A.
G/5743	Dunn, G. A.
G/3103	Dunn, L.
G/6560	Dunn, R.
G/9626	Dunster, G.
T/3726	Dunster, J.
G/14646	Duquemin, T. H.
G/4433	Durban, E.
T/242130	Durrant, G.
G/1297	Durrant, G. W.
G/11359	Durrant, H.
G/25176	Durrant, H. G.
G/3266	Dwyer, W.
L/9940	Dyer, A. S.
G/21045	Dyer, D.
G/916	Dyer, E. G.
G/25327	Dyer, F. H.
L/10013	Dyer, H. M. A.
L/8925	Dyke, A.
G/5595	Dynan, G.
S/9718	Dyson, H. C.
G/14739	Dyson, T. H.
G/12103	Eade, H.
G/14944	Eady, E. A.
G/24231	Eagles, G. S.
G/26616	Eales, E. W.
G/15585	Ealham, W. S.
G/5238	Eason, F. E.
G/6280	East, P. J.
L/10191	East, S.
G/8083	East, S. D.
G/13114	Eastaff, W.
S/445	Easterling, F.
G/8511	Eastland, F. W.
G/103	Eastland, G. E.
L/8986	Eastwood, E.
G/9849	Eaton, J.
G/10306	Ebbs, H. S.
T/203558	Ebsworth, G.
G/11653	Eddon, J. E.
G/14820	Ede, W. J.
G/26144	Edge, A.
G/5424	Edge, C. E.
G/1599	Edgeler, W. H.
G/13965	Edinburgh, F.
G/4233	Edmonds, A.
L/8002	Edmonds, A. J.
G/14168	Edmunds, H. R.
G/8008	Edwards, A.
G/41	Edwards, G.
G/14815	Edwards, G.
L/9876	Edwards, P. A.
G/1766	Edwards, T. F.

APPENDIX II

S/7768	Edwards, W.
S/310	Edwards, W.
G/20470	Edwards, W. I.
G/3989	Edwards, W. J.
G/24745	Edwicker, A. C.
G/4880	Eggledon, A. G.
G/3215	Eggleton, J. W.
L/9679	Eggleton, W. H.
L/7729	Egleton, H.
G/17712	Elder, J. R.
G/12760	Elderfield, F.
G/3918	Eldridge, F. H.
S/9617	Eldridge, H. B.
G/22645	Element, J. W.
G/5405	Eley, H. T.
T/2418	Elgar, E. W. E.
G/25101	Elkins, A. F.
L/8626	Ellen, W. F.
G/23871	Ellen, W. T.
T/201585	Ellender, E.
T/4055	Ellender, R.
G/18939	Elliman, T. J.
L/9888	Elliott, C.
T/270263	Elliott, F.
L/7593	Elliott, F.
G/25334	Elliott, J. T.
L/9819	Elliott, W. E.
L/8136	Ellis, A.
G/18907	Ellis, C. H.
G/3977	Ellis, F. T.
G/5325	Ellis, G. C.
G/13742	Ellis, H.
T/270917	Ellis, O.
G/18916	Elsegood, J.
G/26001	Elsworth, S. C.
G/20448	Emblem, F.
G/10864	Empson, W. E.
L/9174	Emptage, C.
G/1077	Endicott, E.

G/5655	England, A. E.
G/3582	English, J.
G/4605	Epps, A. A.
L/9418	Erridge, F.
G/18679	Escott, R. S.
G/4505	Etherington, P.
G/5828	Euden, A. T.
T/3186	Euden, H. F.
G/22447	Evans, A. E.
T/203458	Evans, A. V.
L/10356	Evans, C.
L/7922	Evans, E. R.
G/6650	Evans, F.
G/13522	Evans, G. C.
G/21016	Evans, H.
L/8889	Evans, I.
G/21013	Evans, J. H.
G/24067	Evans, J. R.
G/20855	Evans, R. B.
G/4942	Evans, S.
G/6324	Eve, G.
T/241666	Evenden, C.
T/241618	Evenden, V.
G/3991	Everest, E. A.
G/263	Everson, R. H.
T/202591	Ewers, C.
L/7072	Excell, G. F.
G/9132	Excell, G. H.
G/8921	Excell, S. E.
G/9082	Fagg, A. G.
L/10341	Fagg, C. F.
G/4977	Fagg, F.
G/13028	Fagg, W. J.
L/10387	Fairow, C. F.
T/206054	Fairweather, W. J.
S/10765	Fallowes, F. A.
G/14507	Falshaw, A.
G/17889	Fancy, H. W.

APPENDIX II

G/13213	Fannon, J.	G/13347	Filmer, H.
T/271032	Fantham, T.	G/25931	Filsell, A.
G/9634	Farmer, E. F.	G/17619	Finbow, J. T.
G/1466	Farmer, J.	G/23860	Finch, F.
G/8879	Farrance, R.	T/204441	Finch, H. G.
G/1598	Farrant, H.	G/6595	Finch, J.
G/11095	Farrant, W.	G/13410	Finch, V.
G/13214	Farrell, P.	L/8521	Finch, W.
G/8026	Farrell, W.	G/5807	Finn, E.
G/9687	Farrier, J. H.	S/357	Finn, J.
G/5883	Farrier, R. H.	T/2007	Finnis, R. M.
L/9659	Farrier, S. B.	G/15508	Finter, J. W.
L/7994	Farrow, E. A.	L/8707	Fishenden, J. T.
G/110	Fasham, W.	L/9444	Fisher, S.
G/2423	Faulkner, W. W.	G/2781	Fisher, R. G.
G/26312	Fearn, G. R.	G/12611	Fisher, W.
G/15721	Fedarb, W. L.	L/6265	Fisher, W. T.
G/757	Feist, A. G.	G/24828	Fisk, A. H.
G/25999	Fellows, P. J.	G/3697	Fisk, R. G. T.
G/22512	Felts, H. H.	L/6200	Fisken, J.
L/7529	Fendom, W. F.	G/2574	Fison, H.
G/36631	Fenn, G.	G/14757	Fitzgerald, E. P.
T/202536	Fenner, H.	T/3447	Fitzgerald, J. T.
G/18815	Fensome, L.	T/5107	Fitzgerald, W.
G/23774	Fentiman, C. J.	T/270274	Flack, G.
T/3467	Fentiman, T. H.	S/10674	Flanagan, J. W.
G/5773	Fenton, A. E.	G/12908	Flatt, E. V.
G/14433	Ferguson, W. J.	G/29145	Fletcher, H.
G/13698	Ferneley, E.	L/9231	Flick, J. E.
G/5903	Ferris, H. W.	G/5575	Flight, P. T., M.M.
G/6652	Ferry, T. H.	G/12825	Flin, D. J.
G/11395	Fewell, G. F.	G/10167	Flint, S.
S/6927	Fiddler, J.	G/650	Flisher, H. S.
S/846	Field, A. J.	T/242922	Flood, B. S.
G/3196	Field, C. H.	G/18213	Flowerday, H.W. G.
L/7997	Field, H.	G/1982	Flynn, F.
L/7888	Field, J.	G/20138	Foad, R.
G/12886	Field, R.	G/2081	Foglearde, R.
G/5824	Fielder, H. T.	G/676	Folley, R.

PRIVATES—*(continued)*

L/8627	Foord, T. H.	G/5568	Franks, A. J., M.M.
L/5158	Foord, W.	G/13291	Franks, G. E.
G/13337	Foot, G. F.	G/7338	Fraser, P. A.
T/270939	Ford, C. F.	G/23859	Freeman, A. W.
G/4763	Fordham, J. H.	G/9234	Freemantle, S.
S/10561	Foreman, F.	L/9651	Fremlin, J. H.
G/8956	Foreman, H.	S/10779	French, A.
G/4412	Forest, A. H.	G/15596	French, O. A.
G/692	Forster, P.	G/3269	French, W. E.
G/3333	Foster, A.	G/8943	Friend, H.
G/18717	Foster, A.	G/4966	Friend, J. R.
T/200835	Foster, A.	G/4967	Friend, J. T.
L/7991	Foster, F.	G/5664	Friend, T. A.
T/203944	Foster, G. H.	G/23861	Friend, V.
G/5138	Foster, H. E.	G/235	Friend, W. R.
G/715	Foster, H.	L/9142	Fright, A. W.
T/3560	Foster, H. L. H.	G/11067	Frost, G. M. R.
T/240550	Foster, W. H.	G/14612	Frost, W.
L/9287	Foster, W. J.	T/242741	Fryer, J. S.
L/9653	Fowler, F. W.	G/1546	Fulcher, A. G.
L/9612	Fowler, G. H.	G/14774	Fulker, J. H.
G/15594	Fowler, H. J.	G/8735	Fuller, H. R.
G/11262	Fowler, J.	T/2073	Fuller, L.
G/29144	Fowler, J. W.	G/5923	Fuller, S. W.
S/121	Fox, C.	G/18186	Fyson, G. P.
S/11082	Fox, F. J.		
L/10589	Fox, G.	G/2887	Gafford, P. G.
G/24187	Fox, L.	G/2387	Gage, E.
L/6148	Fox, W.	G/8884	Gage, W. J.
G/12509	Fox, W.	T/2356	Gage, W. R.
T/242923	Framingham, F. H.	G/18244	Gain, A. R.
G/14506	France, W. L.	G/22582	Gale, E. J.
G/3752	Francis, L.	G/11894	Gale, H.
L/8482	Francis, T.	G/1511	Gale, J. A.
L/6944	Francis, T.	G/25342	Gale, J. W. T.
L/7835	Francis, W. W.	G/972	Gallagher, A. E.
G/25338	Frankis, J. H.	G/13217	Gallagher, G.
G/10288	Franklin, E.	G/6706	Galloway, M.
G/2200	Franklin, G.	L/9112	Gambell, E.

2 H

PRIVATES—(*continued*)

G/15598	Gambell, R.
L/9617	Gambell, W.
G/20121	Gammon, H.
G/4721	Gannon, J.
T/1456	Gardiner, J.
G/1610	Gardiner, T.
L/7909	Gardiner, W. J.
S/123	Gardner, A. H.
G/4082	Gardner, D.
L/6918	Gardner, E.
G/8092	Gardner, W. A.
G/2713	Gardner, W. E.
G/18822	Garley, G. E.
G/12128	Garlick, H. W.
G/445	Garlinge, C. F.
G/9121	Garlinge, E. E.
T/270881	Garlinge, G. [M.M.
G/5196	Garlinge, W. J.,
L/10416	Garner, H.
G/18327	Gates, C.
G/2973	Gates, S.
T/3427	Gates, W. A.
G/2204	Gates, W. T.
G/13967	Gaughan, J.
L/10346	Gawler, F.
G/13937	Gee, E.
G/15602	Gee, L. F.
L/8051	Gee, W. B.
G/2180	Geere, W.
G/15509	Geering, A. R.
G/1557	Gentry, A. E.
L/9490	George, C.
G/1023	George, J.
G/746	George, T.
G/24764	Gibbard, E. J.
G/21210	Gibbons, T. W.
L/9383	Gibbs, A.
G/6552	Gibbs, C. H.
T/242005	Gibbs, D.

G/9111	Gibbs, E.
G/9559	Gibbs, E.
L/7617	Gibbs, E. A.
G/22590	Gibbs, P.
G/12887	Gibbs, R.
G/574	Gibbs, W.
G/6933	Gibson, R.
G/6508	Gibson, W. E. H.
G/4453	Giddings, S.
S/10789	Giggins, H. H.
G/2407	Gilbert, B. F.
G/19357	Gilbert, C.
G/4432	Gilbert, F. M.
G/8462	Gilbert, G.
G/5440	Gilbert, L.
G/18966	Gilbert, T.
G/5446	Gilbert, T. H.
T/4511	Gilbert, W.
G/14760	Gilbert, W.
G/22160	Gilbert, W. P.
T/2002	Gilbert, W. T.
G/3352	Gildersleeve, A.
G/1555	Giles, W.
L/9531	Giles, W. H.
L/10395	Gill, C. A.
G/9390	Gill, F. G.
G/18972	Gill, H. H.
G/1522	Gill, H.
L/6951	Gillard, J. E.
L/7580	Gillham, H.
G/7833	Gimber, S.
L/8659	Glass, W.
G/12536	Glassberg, A.
G/14982	Glaysher, F. L.
L/11072	Glayzer, F.
G/1241	Glover, A. E.
T/206051	Glover, E. H.
G/13119	Glover, J.
G/18976	Glover, S. G.

PRIVATES—(*continued*)

G/7820	Glover, T.	G/4400	Gordon, A.
L/6514	Goad, F. C.	G/9856	Gordon, G.
G/15604	Goatham, R.	G/9783	Gore, A. A.
G/8331	Goddard, P.	G/4700	Gore, D.
G/5099	Godden, A.	L/9092	Gouge, W. G. T.
G/5356	Godfrey, F.	G/8132	Gough, S.
G/35558	Godfrey, F.	G/24074	Goulborn, P. L.
T/270622	Godward, C. T.	G/1045	Gould, R.
G/20438	Godwin, A. H.	T/270896	Gower, R. G.
G/4087	Goggin, T.	L/8685	Gower, W.
T/241871	Golden, F. C.	S/389	Gower, W.
G/25211	Goldfarb, C.	G/9777	Gower, W.
L/7610	Goldfinch, G. J.	S/244	Gowler, J.
L/9625	Golding, J. H.	L/9594	Grace, P. J.
G/5230	Golding, T.	G/9060	Grainger, C. G.
G/5939	Golds, A. G.	S/10478	Grainger, H. G.
G/13384	Goldsack, E. C.	T/203530	Granger, J. A.
L/6559	Goldsack, F.	L/6855	Grant, A. J.
T/201157	Goldsack, H.	G/13961	Grant, G.
G/2710	Goldsack, W.	G/9595	Grant, G. T.
G/9369	Goldsmith, E.	T/240734	Granville, E. E.
T/3014	Goldsmith, F. C.	G/3627	Gratrex, W. J. C.
T/242570	Goldsmith, G. W.	G/13492	Gratton, W.
G/8469	Goldsmith, R.	G/934	Graves, A.
L/10045	Goldsmith, W. T.	T/204295	Graves, E. W.
G/14634	Goldstraw, B.	L/9925	Graves, S. L.
T/240366	Goldup, A. E.	L/8268	Gray, A. E. V.
T/204011	Goldup, H. G.	L/270531	Gray, C. D.
G/4638	Gollop, W. H.	G/14106	Gray, G. W.
G/6480	Goodayle, J. H.	G/5630	Gray, J.
G/22683	Goodchild, E.	G/1025	Graylen, W.
T/202713	Goodchild, S.	G/1069	Green, A. D.
T/203549	Goodger, P. G.	L/6177	Green, E.
G/24884	Goodsell, A. J.	G/1290	Green, F.
G/13121	Goodsell, W. C.	G/4347	Green, G.
G/21250	Goodship, D.	T/203718	Green, G. L.
G/9372	Goodwin, E. E.	L/8241	Green, H.
T/1663	Goodwin, T.	G/9996	Green, J.
G/20851	Goodwyn, A. W.	G/25878	Green, T.

PRIVATES—*(continued)*

G/4001	Green, W. E.	L/8030	Hadlow, J. J. W.
L/10120	Green, W. J.	L/7750	Hadlum, D. F.
G/11915	Greenaway, C. F.	T/240935	Haggar, W. G.
G/111	Greenbaum, B.	G/4281	Haines, R. G.
G/675	Greenhalgh, E.	T/3291	Haines, S.
G/11292	Greenland, W.	L/8069	Haines, W. R.
G/5290	Gregory, B.	T/3123	Hairpin, W.
G/321	Gregory, L.	G/22452	Hale, H. L.
G/2054	Gregory, W. E.	G/35640	Hales, S. A.
G/11969	Gregory, W. J.	L/6736	Haley, R. A.
G/1078	Gregory, W. J.	G/1517	Halford, F. C.
G/8228	Grenians, E.	G/6667	Hall, A.
G/7666	Grey, R. C.	G/22453	Hall, A. G.
L/8948	Griffiths, A.	G/8264	Hall, E. A.
G/10488	Griffiths, E. C.	G/9144	Hall, F.
G/1973	Griffiths, F. A. T.	G/22655	Hall, H.
T/128	Griffiths, F. W.	G/25980	Hall, R. E. M.
T/2477	Griffiths, J. H. C.	G/7314	Hall, W.
G/25351	Griffiths, S. W.	G/909	Hall, W.
T/3869	Grigg, A.	L/9140	Hall, W. A.
G/15	Grigg, C.	L/9365	Hall, W. G.
G/18505	Griggs, E. J.	G/1010	Hall, W. L.
G/4768	Griggs, J.	G/29161	Hallam, G.
G/209	Groombridge, A.W.	T/2986	Halliday, F. W.
G/9836	Groombridge, H.	G/22433	Hallock, H. J.
G/6111	Groombridge, J.	L/10480	Hallybone, W. T.
G/4245	Groombridge, S. D.	T/241476	Halse, A.
G/22580	Gross, A.	L/8037	Hambly, F. A.
G/25272	Grover, R. C.	G/18942	Hambrook, A. G.
G/14323	Guest, C.	S/307	Hambrose, J. E.
G/3131	Gunbie, L.	S/10551	Hamill, J. P.
G/21815	Gunstone, F. G.	G/18917	Hamilton, G. H.
S/491	Gurr, C.	S/10805	Hamilton, W. H.
G/14327	Gurr, G. E.	G/4882	Hamlin, J.
G/4518	Guy, H. S.	G/96	Hammerton, W.
		G/23517	Hammon, C. F.
G/20142	Hadaway, B. A.	G/1874	Hammond, A. W.
G/2909	Hadingham, S. E.	L/10535	Hammond, B. A.
G/9940	Hadlow, C. H.	L/8532	Hammond, E.

APPENDIX II

PRIVATES—*(continued)*

G/15608	Hammond, F.	G/2471	Harmden, H. J.
G/1873	Hammond, F. G.	G/3537	Harmer, A. J.
L/8087	Hammond, S.	G/5924	Harmer, H. H.
T/203573	Hammond, W. P.	G/24956	Harmer, W. H.
L/9915	Hampton, A.	G/12059	Harness, A.
G/3657	Hampton, J.	G/12249	Harper, A. E.
G/5107	Hance, G. W.	L/10043	Harper, F. W.
G/47	Hancock, F.	S/9725	Harrigan, J.
T/2010	Handcock, W. E.	G/1063	Harrington, H.F.A.
G/5276	Handley, W. E.	G/4223	Harris, A. V.
G/3264	Hands, W. T.	G/25364	Harris, C. W. H.
G/4624	Handy, G. H.	S/10539	Harris, C.
G/3938	Hanlon, P.	L/8160	Harris, G. H.
G/5449	Hannon, M. N.	G/24478	Harris, M.
G/21878	Hanton, E. I.	G/13122	Harris, P.
G/8736	Harban, H. W.	G/15510	Harris, R.
L/6681	Hard, C.	G/17821	Harris, R.
G/19178	Hardie, B.	G/9492	Harris, V.
G/8818	Harding, A. E.	G/186	Harris, W.
T/20210	Harding, J.	G/13123	Harris, W. H. J.
G/4393	Harding, J. R.	G/3277	Harris, W. J.
T/241556	Harding, P.	G/9739	Harrison, H. M.
G/4228	Harding, W. T.	G/701	Harrison, H.
G/12950	Hards, A. T.	G/7734	Harrison, J.
T/3202	Hardware, S. T.	G/14089	Harrison, J.
L/8636	Hardwick, F. W.	G/6850	Harrison, J.
G/12658	Hardy, C.	G/14983	Harrison, J. W.
G/22501	Hardy, J. W.	G/6638	Harrison, S.
L/8949	Hardy, P. R. M.	G/29158	Harrison, W. H.
G/967	Hardy, T.	G/5046	Harrison, W. H.
G/5431	Hare, C. L.	T/202541	Harrod, R. H.
G/4818	Harford, W.	G/1166	Harrold, H. C.
G/10351	Hargreaves, J. H.	G/25358	Harrold, H. G.
G/24487	Hargreaves, R.	T/3063	Hart, A. E.
L/9371	Harlow, A. W.	S/9151	Hart, A. C. R.
L/9238	Harlow, G. J.	G/23525	Hart, C.
G/4994	Harlow, G. W.	G/2228	Hart, E. F.
G/931	Harman, F. J.	G/8870	Hart, F. A.
G/11991	Harman, H. W.	G/21131	Hart, F. J.

469

PRIVATES—(*continued*)

G/24194	Hart, H.
G/12912	Hart, H. A.
T/2365	Hart, H. C.
G/18820	Hartga, H. C.
G/6735	Hartley, H.
G/15811	Hartley, R. P.
S/10650	Harvey, F. E.
G/4586	Harvey, F. G.
G/25282	Harvey, F. R.
L/10337	Harvey, W.
T/3125	Harvey, W. H.
G/14442	Harvey, W. J.
L/10235	Harvey, W. Q.
G/5757	Harwood, C. W.
S/782	Haselton, C.
S/133	Haslam, P. C.
G/4405	Hastings, W. C.
L/7046	Hatcher, F.
G/71	Hatcher, P.
G/6473	Hatcher, T. G.
T/206023	Hatchett, J.
G/9095	Hatton, D. J.
G/5897	Hatton, H. T.
L/9126	Hatton, J.
G/12080	Hatton, J. A.
L/9252	Hatton, W. P.
G/1521	Havard, A. T.
G/6828	Haw, T.
T/2947	Haward, R. C.
G/19052	Hawkesbee, W. H.
T/204075	Hawkins, A. E.
G/1972	Hawkins, A. H.
S/10274	Hawkins, B. T.
G/14720	Hawkins, C.
G/12647	Hawkins, E. H.
G/4815	Hawkins, W.
G/1105	Hawkins, W. H.
T/270398	Hawton, R. F.
G/12007	Hawtree, H. R.
G/411	Haxell, W.
T/203946	Hayden, W.
G/12916	Haydon, C.
G/18853	Hayes, H. P.
G/5053	Hayesmore, F. G.
G/5033	Hayesmore, H. H.
G/3034	Hayesmore, L. A.
G/5565	Hayles, A.
G/9324	Haynes, G.
G/11976	Haynes, L. G.
G/21134	Haynes, W. C. H.
G/4691	Hayward, A.
T/270160	Hayward, A.
G/932	Hayward, E.
S/9869	Hayward, F. G.
G/7922	Hayward, T. W.
L/8436	Hayward, W.
T/3670	Hayward, W. T.
G/13939	Haywood, A.
G/4754	Haywood, G. H.
G/561	Haywood, T. H.
G/15776	Hazel, C.
T/203047	Hazel, J.
G/18941	Hazelden, F.
S/52	Hazeldin, E. W.
G/22488	Hazlehurst, J. G.
G/1006	Head, E.
G/13671	Head, G.
T/203038	Head, W. G.
G/11282	Heading, W.
G/22575	Headlong, G. W.
S/10888	Hearn, W. J.
G/4486	Heasman, C.
G/4919	Heath, C. F.
G/5618	Heath, P. A.
G/5730	Heaton, H.
G/21821	Hebbs, A.
G/15618	Heckford, A.
G/10432	Hedgecock, E. J.

PRIVATES—*(continued)*

L/8403	Hedger, F. G.	G/19021	Hill, H.
G/12200	Hedges, H. G.	G/6596	Hill, J.
G/21751	Heine, L.	G/14188	Hill, J. C.
G/14444	Helmsley, D.	G/14131	Hill, J. E.
G/7025	Hemsley, J.	G/13275	Hillen, M.
G/20441	Heneron, J.	G/1507	Hillier, F.
G/12914	Herrick, E. J.	G/2979	Hillier, F. J.
G/7342	Heselwood, R. C.	G/1491	Hillier, J.
G/13041	Heuner, C.	G/5451	Hills, H. W.
G/19015	Hewes, H. O.	G/8466	Hills, H.
T/240437	Hewison, G.	G/9415	Hills, T. J.
T/3269	Hewitt, C. E.	L/5903	Hills, W.
G/1746	Hewitt, F. W.	G/13681	Hinchley, J.
G/624	Hewitt, T. H.	S/10948	Hinchon, J.
G/162	Hewitt, W. R.	G/13980	Hindson, D.
T/2010	Hewlett, J. H.	G/17664	Hine, A. W.
G/3956	Hewson, G.	G/8425	Hines, P. J.
L/10443	Heyman, A. W.	G/1309	Hinton, H.
G/20148	Hickman, P.	G/5815	Hird, G.
G/13770	Hickmott, C.	G/4876	Hisee, C.
G/7043	Hickmott, C. F.	G/13050	Hoad, E.
S/10770	Hickmott, E.	T/1326	Hoad, H. V.
G/1925	Hickmott, G.	L/9716	Hoare, G.
G/18753	Hickox, F.	G/9113	Hoare, H.
T/202941	Hicks, C.	L/9067	Hoare, T.
G/22454	Hicks, S.	G/22431	Hobbs, B.
G/4131	Hicks, W.	G/1678	Hobbs, F. G.
L/8326	Hickson, A. J.	G/4027	Hobbs, H.
L/8970	Hickson, S.	L/7968	Hobbs, W.
G/3043	Higgin, G. A.	G/22003	Hobbs, W.
G/773	Higgins, H.	L/6215	Hobbs, W. C.
L/9567	Higgins, W. J.	G/21193	Hobbs, W. H.
G/14907	Higginson, J.	G/13970	Hobson, J. D.
G/4778	Higgs, F.	G/20002	Hocking, L. V.
L/10412	Highgate, J.	L/8779	Hodge, F.
G/13906	Highton, H., M.M.	G/4727	Hodge, P. C. A.
G/9021	Hilder, F. C.	T/204430	Hodges, G. H.
G/29156	Hill, A.	L/9798	Hodges, H.
G/3405	Hill, A. J.	L/9630	Hodges, H. J. G.

PRIVATES—*(continued)*

T/270448	Hodges, H. S.	T/204251	Holmes, W. P.
G/13614	Hodges, J.	G/794	Holness, C. J.
G/3498	Hodges, W. E.	L/7870	Holness, T. G.
L/9590	Hodges, W. J.	G/5433	Holt, W. G.
G/8970	Hodgkin, W.	G/3018	Holton, H. C.
G/14714	Hodgson, F.	S/10501	Holtum, T. A.
G/22166	Hodnott, J.	G/18799	Homersham, A. D.
G/5350	Hogben, A.	G/24780	Hood, W. H.
G/9667	Hogben, F. C.	G/9128	Hook, C. W.
T/270308	Holbrook, J. H.	T/200839	Hook, E.
G/11656	Holbrook, T.	G/11839	Hook, F.
G/14334	Holbrow, J. R.	G/6710	Hook, F. G.
G/18852	Holden, E. W.	G/22411	Hooker, E. R.
G/9809	Holdstock, C. H.	G/21441	Hooker, G.
G/4774	Holdstock, E. S.	T/270955	Hop, B. T.
L/10448	Holdstock, L. S.	T/200695	Hope, F. W.
G/13042	Holdstock, S. J.	G/3541	Hope, G. W.
G/18009	Holdstock, W. A.	G/8983	Hope, T.
G/14621	Holich, J. C.	S/605	Hope, W. T.
T/204451	Holland, A. J.	S/9594	Hoper, A.
G/24795	Holland, E. F.	G/18947	Hopgood, A. R.
G/12539	Holland, G.	G/9957	Hopkins, A. F.
G/14658	Holland, J.	T/270291	Hopkins, G. T.
G/1641	Holland, R.	G/22704	Hopkins, J. G.
G/8413	Hollands, E.	G/232	Hopkins, R. T.
G/35491	Holliday, W. A.	T/203947	Hopkins, S.
G/2197	Hollingsworth, G.	G/541	Hopkins, S.
G/19050	Holloway, C. W.	T/20130	Hopson, E.
G/20997	Holloway, F. L.	G/4824	Horrex, A.
G/12743	Holloway, G. A.	L/10176	Horrigan, J.
G/10314	Hollox, G.	L/7587	Horsford, L.
G/22432	Hollway, A. J.	G/9613	Horton, G.
L/8753	Holmans, A.	T/203107	Horton, J. R.
G/142	Holmans, A. G.	T/270260	Hoskin, P. G.
G/13564	Holmans, F.	G/7629	Howard, H. G.
G/20229	Holmes, E. H.	G/7689	Howard, O. C.
G/4679	Holmes, G. W. V.	G/12631	Howard, W.
G/793	Holmes, H. H.	G/4502	Howarth, H. E.
G/8515	Holmes, P.	G/22435	Howe, E.

APPENDIX II

G/25982	Howe, G.	G/22434	Huson, W.
G/4681	Howell A.	T/242294	Hussey, G. E.
G/5666	Howell, H.	G/4324	Hussey, T.
T/1729	Howland, A. H.	L/9385	Hutchings, W. W.
G/22387	Howland, H.	G/3290	Hutson, A. V.
G/4301	Howland, W.	G/4229	Hutson, A.
G/24921	Howlett, J. D.	S/9463	Huxstep, G. A.
G/13925	Howlett, W.	G/1716	Hyam, T.
G/24492	Hoyle, J. M.	G/17400	Hyde, C. N.
G/20144	Hubbard, E.	L/6001	Hyland, E.
S/10697	Hubbard, G.	L/7130	Hyland, W.
G/4242	Hubbard, T.	G/210	Hylands, C.
G/291	Hubbard, W. G.	G/24964	Hynd, A.
L/10158	Hubbell, I. W.		
G/3067	Huckstep, A. F.	T/203587	Igglesden, H. W. E.
G/2759	Huckstepp, F. E.	G/8805	Igguldon, W.
G/15625	Huckstepp, T.	G/13388	Iles, W. H.
G/3915	Hudson, C. J. E.	G/24885	Illman, C.
G/13043	Huggett, E.	G/2871	Ing, A. G.
G/1976	Huggins, G.	G/11671	Ingham, R.
G/336	Hughes, A., M.M.	L/8005	Ingram, A.
G/24501	Hughes, A. S.	G/21194	Ingram, G. A.
L/10114	Hughes, E.	G/922	Ingram, J. H.
L/7248	Hughes, E.	L/9021	Ingram, L.
T/265137	Hughes, E. E.	G/7759	Ingrey, G. A.
S/106	Hughes, J.	G/1219	Inkpen, W.
G/12833	Hughes, J. J.	G/26293	Instein, J.
G/4119	Hukins, R. J.	G/20912	Inwood, G.
G/15793	Humphrey, G. S.	T/206070	Ipson, W.
G/11882	Humphries, T. A.	G/518	Ireland, E. C.
G/20974	Humphries, W. W.	G/5511	Ireland, G.
G/7197	Hunt, A. J.	T/3102	Ireland, G. H.
G/12510	Hunt, C. W.	G/6500	Iverson, F. C.
G/12104	Hunt, F.	G/9105	Iverson, H.
G/6076	Hunt, J. W., M.M.		
T/2383	Hunting, C. W.	G/19003	Jacklin, W. T.
G/7729	Hunwick, A. E.	G/4495	Jackson, A.
T/3583	Hurford, S. J.	G/20841	Jackson, D. E.
G/18725	Hurrell, W. J.	G/21171	Jackson, E. J. T.

473

PRIVATES—(*continued*)

G/6831	Jackson, J.
G/7345	Jackson, R. S.
G/24912	Jackson, T.
G/24352	Jacques, F. C.
G/25836	James, E. A.
G/7943	James, G. T.
T/1610	James, R. A.
G/14197	James, S.
L/10208	Jameson, H.
G/5280	Janaway, L. H.
G/3140	Jarlett, W.
G/6590	Jarman, A.
G/20476	Jarman, F. E.
T/3050	Jarman, S.
G/197	Jarrett, A.
G/5186	Jarvest, A. J.
G/22555	Jarvis, H. P. V.
G/11229	Jarvis, O. A.
T/20169	Jarvis, W. E.
L/6706	Jay, A.
T/240487	Jay, W. P.
L/5794	Jayes, T. H.
S/10904	Jeffcott, A.
G/14764	Jefferies, W. T.
T/203159	Jeffery, G.
G/21099	Jeffs, F.
T/241293	Jeffs, G.
G/3923	Jell, C.
T/201481	Jemmett, S. E.
G/9358	Jempson, C.
G/5685	Jenkins, F.
G/15628	Jennaway, R. E.
G/20440	Jenner, A.
T/1340	Jenner, G.
G/13651	Jenner, J.
G/2872	Jenner, R.
G/13131	Jenner, T. C.
G/5673	Jenner, T. W.
G/22456	Jenner, W. A. E.

G/4358	Jennings, A. H.
G/3921	Jennings, W.
G/26298	Jensen, L. E.
G/7346	Jermey, J. H.
T/204076	Jesshope, H. L.
G/4690	Jesshope, P. N.
G/4795	Jessop, H. A.
L/7053	Jeyes, E. A.
T/202379	John, C. D.
T/241210	Johncey, M.
L/8081	Johnings, W. H.
G/14384	Johns, J. W.
G/14845	Johnson, A. A.
G/25239	Johnson, A.
G/4258	Johnson, B. W.
T/1582	Johnson, B. A.
G/591	Johnson, D. C. A.
G/22631	Johnson, E.
T/270422	Johnson, E. W.
G/5298	Johnson, F.
G/572	Johnson, F.
G/12174	Johnson, F.
G/3081	Johnson, G.
G/2425	Johnson, H. G.
S/22	Johnson, H. H.
G/5560	Johnson, J.
L/10087	Johnson, P. H.
G/2125	Johnson, S. A.
G/21020	Johnson, W.
S/9367	Johnson, W. J.
G/12791	Johnston, H. M.
G/13393	Johnston, P.
L/9110	Johnston, R.
S/10892	Johnstone, T.
G/35569	Jones, A.
L/8391	Jones, A.
G/15629	Jones, A. H.
G/17419	Jones, A. H.
G/913	Jones, C.

APPENDIX II

PRIVATES—(*continued*)

S/151	Jones, C.	G/14200	Keen, F. A.
G/15630	Jones, C. F.	G/23781	Keen, W.
G/9590	Jones, C. H.	S/10952	Kellsey, G. J.
G/14133	Jones, C. P.	G/5764	Kelly, D.
T/202389	Jones, D. T.	G/14051	Kelly, M.
G/4657	Jones, E.	G/7878	Kelsey, C. A.
T/203590	Jones, E.	G/5364	Kelsey, H. G.
L/6552	Jones, F.	G/14582	Kemble, F. T.
G/24894	Jones, F.	T/203949	Kemish, G.
G/1377	Jones, F. C.	G/12463	Kemp, D.
L/9791	Jones, F. W. J.	L/8110	Kemp, F.
G/2036	Jones, J.	G/2850	Kemp, G.
G/6711	Jones, J. H.	G/516	Kemp, H. F.
T/1256	Jones, L.	G/21417	Kemp, J.
L/10171	Jones, S.	G/9420	Kemp, R. H.
G/4961	Jones, W.	G/14339	Kemp, W. W.
G/6403	Jones, W. L. R.	G/23940	Kempshall, A.
G/4934	Jordan, B. G.	L/9378	Kempster, W. H.
G/13312	Jordan, G. H.	S/802	Kendall, A. C.
G/11925	Jordan, J.	G/18666	Kennett, G. W.
G/8756	Jordan, R.	G/5201	Kennett, H.
G/172	Jordan, T. F.	G/5422	Kennington, A.
G/8447	Jordan, W.	L/8346	Kenton, W. J.
G/9716	Joy, H.	G/2732	Kerridge, J. J.
L/8502	Joy, W. B.	G/1064	Kerrison, R.
L/8159	Judd, W.	G/7199	Kerry, G.
G/1918	Judge, R.	G/6000	Ketley, H. N.
L/5101	Judges, S.	G/2499	Kettley, W.
G/18205	Jupp, J. H.	G/8429	Kibby, R.
		G/13228	Kidd, F. R.
G/19035	Kaby, J. T.	G/1775	Killick, J.
G/12951	Keates, A.	G/18243	Killick, S.
L/9470	Kechane, W.	G/2373	Kilsby, C.
T/2863	Keeler, A. M.	G/2412	Kilsby, J. H.
L/8629	Keeler, E. G.	G/2345	Kinch, W.
G/5448	Keeler, F. P.	L/10068	King, A. J.
L/7726	Keeley, C. W.	G/889	King, A. W.
G/412	Keeley, T. J.	G/14381	King, C. C.
G/13722	Keen, A. G.	T/1840	King, E. J.

PRIVATES—(*continued*)

G/26750	King, G.
T/271045	King, J. H.
G/14585	King, M.
L/9237	King, P.
G/35628	Kingham, A. E.
G/558	Kingsford, W. T.
T/2775	Kingsmill, L.
G/4548	Kirby, C. J.
G/13295	Kirby, H.
T/20053	Kirby, J.
G/3038	Kirby, J.
L/9506	Kirk, A. C.
G/12544	Kitchen, J. D.
G/5480	Kitney, L. W. H.
G/6747	Kitson, W.
G/14338	Kitteridge, H. H. A.
S/10630	Kitts, G.
G/25381	Knapman, R. R.
G/13135	Knapp, W. A.
S/48	Knibbs, W.
G/12121	Knight, A.
G/807	Knight, A. C.
G/13592	Knight, C. J. T.
G/13656	Knight, E.
G/13054	Knight, F.
G/13134	Knight, H.
G/8003	Knight, H. G.
T/202705	Knight, J. S.
G/12485	Knight, W. G.
G/22457	Knight, W.
L/9773	Knight, W.
L/9139	Knight, W. C.
T/203119	Knights, A. J. H.
G/4786	Knott, A. F.
G/546	Knott, W. C.
T/3422	Knott, W. J.
G/941	Ladd, F.
G/3116	Ladd, F. D. G.

G/13688	Ladd, J. R.
G/2005	Lake, G., M.M.
G/7684	Lake, H.
G/46	Laker, E.
T/1273	Laker, H.
T/270237	Laker, J. F.
G/9046	Laker, R. P.
G/21476	Laker, W.
T/3231	Laker, W.
G/9334	Laker, W. E.
G/13229	Lamb, M.
G/3020	Lambert, A. F.
G/5907	Lambert, G.
G/10158	Lambert, H. F.
L/8594	Lambert, R. T.
L/9810	Lambert, T. J.
G/5045	Lamberton, F. G.
G/14936	Lambeth, W. J.
G/2443	Laming, B. C.
G/2474	Laming, E.
G/12697	Lammas, A. V.
G/22249	Lancaster, A. G.
G/9630	Lancaster, J.
G/24849	Lander, E. F.
G/29178	Lander, W. H.
S/10688	Lane, H.
S/10867	Lane, R.
G/14728	Lane, W.
L/10590	Langham, H. A.
T/203992	Langley, A. V.
G/26000	Langrish, C.
G/13230	Langsharne, W. T.
G/21993	Langston, H.
S/92	Langston, S. C.
G/14605	Langton, J.
T/203786	Large, G. W.
G/3721	Larkin, J.
S/93	Larkins, T. H.
G/18255	Larkman, J.

APPENDIX II

G/9191	Laslett, W. S. B.
G/1164	Latham, A. E. C.
G/1016	Latham, F.
G/25385	Lattimore, J.
T/240331	Laurie, C. W.
G/21285	Lavender, W. H.
G/14205	Lavers, H.
G/3641	Lavis, G. D.
L/8164	Law, A. J.
G/7027	Lawless, M.
G/20019	Lawrence, G. C.
G/430	Lawrence, G. H.
G/6856	Lawrence, J. A.
G/4845	Lawrence, J. W.
G/2573	Lawrence, J. B.
G/20031	Lawrence, R.
T/202564	Lawrence, S.
G/22576	Lawrence, W. E.
G/8091	Lawrence, W. J.
G/1044	Lawrence, W. N.
G/18496	Lawson, A.
T/206140	Lawson, J.
G/13943	Lawton, B.
G/5766	Lea, A. W.
G/20442	Leason, F. W. J.
G/2787	Leaver, C.
G/6581	Ledger, M.
G/6455	Ledner, J.
L/7029	Ledsham, F.
G/21203	Lee, G.
L/7755	Lee, L.
G/11145	Lee, T.
G/21368	Lee, W. G.
T/241498	Leesley, J.
G/9134	Le Feaver, V. G.
T/1780	Leggat, A.
G/18744	Leigh, J.
T/242804	Lemar, W.
G/6479	Lent, G. L.

G/3429	Leslie, H. A.
G/25387	Lethbridge, R. A.
G/29179	Leverton, D.
G/2116	Levett, W.
G/25391	Levy, L.
G/19130	Lewin, H. F.
G/2777	Lewis, A. E.
G/14126	Lewis, A.
G/4715	Lewis, C.
G/9900	Lewis, E. C.
G/29177	Lewis, E. W.
G/3208	Lewis, J.
L/7776	Lewis, J. N.
G/7536	Lewis, J. R.
S/10662	Lewis, W. G.
G/3760	Lewis, W. P.
G/11995	Liddel, D.
G/29180	Lilley, S. T. J.
L/7963	Lindemann, H.
G/1202	Lindley, E. J.
G/6727	Lindon, G.
G/4020	Lindsay, W.
T/271157	Linkins, A. A.
G/20806	Linkins, C.
G/13752	Linklett, G.
G/5695	Linnett, E. G.
G/12836	Linnett, H. L. J.
G/9806	Linthwaite, W. H.
G/234	Little, E.
T/3127	Little, H.
G/12616	Littlewood, A.
G/2612	Littlewood, J.
G/35682	Littlewood, W. B.
T/270339	Lloyd, C. L.
G/18952	Lloyd, T.
G/9174	Loanes, J.
G/21022	Loasby, E. E.
G/21881	Lock, A. E.
G/5697	Lock, G. E.

477

PRIVATES—*(continued)*

G/767	Lock, L.		G/6909	Ludwig, S. F.
G/1452	Lockwood, J. W.		G/1029	Lunn, E.
G/9577	Lodge, W. T.		G/21138	Lunn, W. S.
G/9718	Lombardy, G.		T/242601	Lunniss, R.
G/13136	London, A.		G/914	Lupton, B.
G/6890	Long, A. E.		G/828	Lye, A.
G/4173	Long, A. J.		G/13413	Lyle, T. G.
G/763	Long, A. W.		G/22345	Lynch, A.
G/523	Long, C. H.		T/200926	Lynds, P.
G/17920	Long, F. C.		G/15513	Lyons, E.
G/5703	Long, G. F.		S/10735	Lyons, L. A.
G/202948	Longley, B.		L/11107	Lythe, D. S.
G/21762	Longley, F. E.			
G/12837	Longley, F. R.		S/10590	Macey, G. A. A.
T/6100	Longley, G. W.		G/18070	Machon, C.
T/2419	Longley, W. H.		G/8023	Mack, E. F.
G/13986	Lonsdale, J. R.		T/996	Mackelden, G.
T/203789	Loosley, R.		G/13907	Mackenzie, J.
G/9051	Lording, H. H.		G/1720	Mackessack, R.
L/9799	Lott, B. W. F.		L/7189	Mackrill, F.
G/66	Lound, T.		L/10530	Maddicks, F. W.
G/12801	Love, A.		G/4335	Madeley, J.
G/7538	Love, W.		G/18096	Madgwick, E.
T/1391	Lovell, A. W. L.		G/14788	Magee, F.
G/13689	Lovell, H. T.		G/17433	Maggs, W. H.
L/10032	Lovell, J.		T/241843	Mahoney, E.
G/4760	Lovell, T.		T/242304	Mahoney, P. W.
G/953	Lovesday, H. V.		G/5895	Maier, W. H.
G/397	Lowe, T.		G/8044	Maitland, W. T.
T/1397	Lower, J.		G/3968	Makin, F.
S/10418	Lucas, J.		G/16539	Makin, S. G.
G/15514	Lucas, R.		G/22462	Malin, H.
G/20562	Luck, A. E.		G/13156	Maloney, W.
G/160	Luck, E.		G/4595	Maloney, W. J.
G/6260	Luck, H.		G/7778	Maltby, A. H.
G/9810	Luck, J.		S/8727	Maltby, H. W.
T/200151	Luckhurst, G. H.		G/17432	Malton, A. F.
G/6446	Luckhurst, J. E.		G/9629	Manklow, R.
L/9920	Luckhurst, W. E.		G/5421	Mann, C.

APPENDIX II

G/14213	Mann, S. G.	S/57	Marsh, J.
G/17384	Mann, T. H.	G/13875	Marsh, J. E.
L/6519	Mannering, J. V.	G/603	Marsh, P.
G/8352	Mannering, J. W.	G/573	Marsh, P. T.
T/240650	Mannering, W.	G/9057	Marsh, S. C.
L/6838	Manning, E. T. H.	T/270477	Marsh, S. G.
G/22346	Manning, G. C. R.	G/63	Marsh, W.
S/10545	Manning, J.	G/9643	Marsh, W. J.
G/2452	Manning, J.	G/13401	Marshall, A. E. D.
G/3678	Manning, L. E.	G/8706	Marshall, F. J.
S/10899	Manning, R. P.	G/1323	Marshall, H.
G/13593	Manning, W.	L/6851	Marshall, H.
G/5731	Mannings, R.	G/23816	Marshall, R. A. O.
G/12700	Mansbridge, P. B.	G/5220	Marshall, S. V.
L/8430	Manser, F. C.	G/164	Marshall, W.
L/7208	Mantle, A.	G/6290	Marshall, W. H.
S/120	Maple, E.	G/332	Marskell, A.
G/419	Maple, G.	T/2013	Martin, C. A.
G/8866	March, A. W.	L/9147	Martin, F.
G/15801	Marchant, F.	T/203951	Martin, F.
G/3524	Marchant, W.	L/7119	Martin, G.
G/56	Maris, L. P.	G/223	Martin, H. J.
G/7581	Markham, A. W.	G/1170	Martin, J. C.
G/393	Marks, E.	T/3382	Martin, J.
L/7925	Marler, H. J.	L/7565	Martin, J. L.
G/22137	Marlow, T. E.	L/10484	Martin, R.
T/241500	Marnham, W. A.	G/515	Martin, R.
L/8674	Marriott, F. C.	G/22022	Martin, R. H.
G/35629	Marriott, W.	G/7879	Martin, S.
G/8168	Marsh, A.	G/1198	Martin, T. E.
G/14457	Marsh, A. F.	G/231	Martin, T. J.
G/429	Marsh, A. W.	G/4995	Martin, W.
S/373	Marsh, C.	G/21452	Martin, W.
G/5206	Marsh, C.	L/8782	Martin, W., M.M.
G/376	Marsh, C. H.	G/1118	Martindale, H.
G/1592	Marsh, F. A. E.	G/19024	Martinne, R.
G/13608	Marsh, F. J.	G/13152	Mascord, T. J.
G/5145	Marsh, H.	G/9420	Masey, H.
G/8281	Marsh, H. G.	G/25293	Masheder, J.

PRIVATES—*(continued)*

G/25407	Maskell, A.
T/2205	Maslin, W. R.
G/29189	Mason, C.
G/4867	Mason, H.
G/8022	Mason, J. W.
G/14896	Mason, J.
T/242576	Mason, R. L.
G/6968	Masters, A.
G/5213	Masters, A. S.
T/203238	Masters, C.
G/3980	Masters, F. C.
G/1793	Mather, E.
G/17428	Mather, H. S.
G/13635	Matthews, A. E.
G/20937	Matthews, G. W.
S/10764	Matthews, H.
G/873	Matthews, S. C.
G/20973	Matthews, W.
G/17624	Mattock, T. W.
G/24618	Matucha, J.
G/6566	Mawson, J.
G/441	Maxted, S. J.
G/240412	Maxted, W. C.
G/5742	May, C.
G/25405	May, H.
T/3598	May, T. W.
L/8315	Mayatt, W.
G/15	Maybourne, E. E.
G/22297	Mayes, F.
G/27388	Mayes, W. G.
G/22461	Mayes, W. I.
G/1420	Maygold, G. E.
G/19026	Mayled, W.
S/11	Maynard, A. E.
T/204219	Maynard, W.
T/240093	Maytum, W. G.
G/5060	McCarthy, D. J.
G/3162	McCarthy, J.
G/1092	McCarthy, P. M. V.

G/6702	McClatchie, J. E.
G/13234	McDonald, J.
G/13267	McDonnell, M.
G/15637	McEwen, J.
S/39	McGee, C.
G/23785	McGeorge, E. W. C.
G/15638	McGill, G. W.
L/6388	McGrath, D. J.
L/7035	McGregor, M.
G/3909	McLearie, J. T.
G/5393	McMahon, A.
G/2058	McMillan, H.
G/4404	McNamara, O.
G/5833	McQuillian, S.
G/8134	McWilliams, J.
G/14657	Mead, E.
G/10198	Mead, F.
L/8600	Mead, F. C.
G/12839	Mead, J.
G/3600	Meader, R. A.
G/14882	Mealing, S. J.
G/4042	Medcalf, W. H.
L/8362	Medgett, A. R.
S/10572	Medhurst, J. A.
L/5985	Medway, H.
G/2959	Meek, F.
G/13235	Mekins, L.
G/10826	Melhuish, R. M.
G/2104	Melville, E.
T/242044	Mercer, A. W. G.
G/13404	Mercer, H. J.
T/204083	Mercer, T.
G/4083	Mercer, T. F.
G/6841	Merifield, G.
G/3726	Merricks, G.
G/3604	Merriman, W. A.
G/9031	Metcalfe, J. W.
G/6842	Meyrick, J.
L/6211	Miles, A.

APPENDIX II

G/21139	Miles, H.	L/9482	Mitchell, F. T.
L/10020	Miles, S.	L/10327	Mitchell, H.
G/3368	Miles, W.	L/9076	Mitchell, L.
L/8971	Millard, P. W.	G/2975	Mitchell, R.
L/7571	Millen, C.	L/8991	Mitchell, W.
G/5013	Millen, C. V.	G/5200	Mitchell, W. S.
G/9600	Miller, A. G.	G/12718	Mizen, S. H.
G/685	Miller, A. J.	G/8820	Moat, A. G.
G/5342	Miller, C.	G/20934	Molyneux, N. W.
G/5684	Miller, C. B.	G/243	Monk, A. R.
T/270187	Miller, F. J.	S/10771	Monk, W. G.
G/4195	Miller, F. S.	G/13407	Monro, W. J.
L/6979	Miller, G.	T/242198	Montgomery, E. M.
G/1410	Miller, J. H.	G/7982	Moon, A.
G/4907	Miller, J. T.	T/6102	Moon, H.
L/9359	Miller, J. W.	G/745	Moor, W.
G/4577	Miller, L. A.	L/6829	Moore, A.
G/6184	Milling, R. A.	G/7644	Moore, A.
G/1554	Millington, H.	G/17697	Moore, A. E.
G/337	Mills, A.	T/270965	Moore, B. P.
T/241697	Mills, A.	L/9380	Moore, B.
G/262	Mills, C. H.	G/3167	Moore, C.
G/8864	Mills, E. W.	L/10441	Moore, C. W.
G/26654	Mills, L. C.	T/270258	Moore, F. J.
G/22529	Mills, R. A.	G/17601	Moore, H.
L/7770	Mills, S.	G/925	Moore, J.
L/8541	Mills, W. H.	T/265252	Moore, J.
G/5896	Mills, W. J.	L/9929	Moore, L. T.
G/17981	Millward, W. O.	T/265310	Moore, R.
T/1092	Milton, F. C.	G/22644	Moore, S.
G/23811	Milton, F.	S/10720	Moore, S. A.
T/241560	Milton, L.	G/22587	Moore, S. H.
G/5638	Milton, S. E.	G/29182	Moore, T. W.
G/15647	Minter, E.	G/1451	Moore, W. D.
G/4671	Missen, E. J.	G/26571	Moore, W. E.
L/8441	Mitchell, A.	G/18672	Moore, W. I.
T/242520	Mitchell, A. L.	L/8656	Moorman, F. G.
T/204280	Mitchell, C. H.	T/206090	Moran, J.
G/20205	Mitchell, C. T.	T/270709	Morecroft, J. C.

PRIVATES—*(continued)*

L/10329	Moren, H. A.
T/3130	Morgan, A.
G/3950	Morgan, B. L.
G/6829	Morgan, L. P.
G/14215	Morgan, R. A.
G/5519	Morgan, W.
G/3619	Morley, E. S.
G/2458	Morley, R. W.
G/1446	Morley, W.
G/11979	Morris, A.
L/10133	Morris, A. E.
G/739	Morris, C.
G/2132	Morris, C.
G/13948	Morris, E.
G/1428	Morris, G.
G/4303	Morris, H. W.
G/25399	Morris, T. E.
G/5425	Morris, W. T.
T/3435	Morrison, A. H.
G/21235	Morrison, D.
G/6167	Mortley, F. G.
G/5245	Morton, A.
G/14849	Morton, A. J.
G/23382	Morton, E. A.
G/25408	Moscovsky, H.
G/13155	Moss, A.
L/9193	Moss, B.
G/13947	Moss, S.
T/2757	Moss, W.
G/21140	Mosser, H.
L/6712	Mosto, R. W.
G/7206	Moulton, J. S.
G/14849	Mount, A. J.
G/15749	Mount, C.
T/241625	Mount, E.
T/270379	Mount, G.
G/4613	Mount, H.
L/9997	Mount, W. G.
L/9601	Mount, W. J.

T/3601	Mountford, R. J.
G/2737	Mower, E. J.
T/240673	Moy, G. W.
G/2327	Moyes, W.
T/204237	Mugeridge, R. H.
S/175	Muir, T. M.
S/250	Mullett, A. L.
L/7551	Mumford, H.
G/24728	Mumford, T. E.
G/3035	Mummery, A. E.
L/10012	Mummery, A. E.
G/417	Mummery, W. A.
T/2135	Munday, L. R.
S/10923	Munday, S. G.
G/9368	Munds, A. E.
L/6833	Munn, T. W.
S/716	Munton, A.
L/9394	Murdock, A. V.
T/242638	Murphy, J.
G/3563	Murphy, T. W.
L/8190	Murphy, W.
G/20843	Murray, P. S.
S/9429	Murrell, F. G.
G/2733	Myall, B. L.
G/3496	Nash, E. A.
G/9540	Nash, F.
G/2358	Nash, J.
T/241836	Naylor, M. E.
G/12842	Naylor, W. H.
G/10151	Naylor, W. J.
G/25758	Neal, W.
L/7832	Neame, J.
G/13240	Neave, A.
G/14699	Needham, H.
G/12954	Neeves, J. C.
S/10607	Neill, C.
G/2168	Nelson, B. A.
L/9892	Nevard, F. R.

APPENDIX II

S/62	Neve, A. W.	G/4374	Norrington, F.
G/8280	Neves, C. H.	T/270391	Norris, A. E.
G/12733	Neville, A.	L/7781	Norris, F.
G/1884	Newbold, C. F.	G/3454	Norris, S. L.
G/24726	Newby, W.	L/8705	Norris, W.
G/3616	Newcombe, H. V.	G/500	North, C. G. A.
L/6432	Newell, F.	G/3895	Norton, A. D.
G/821	Newell, F.	L/9324	Norton, A. E.
T/202566	Newell, W. J.	G/830	Norton, C. T.
L/9108	Newick, I. O.	G/20897	Notley, W. T.
G/2523	Newington, H.	G/17809	Nowell, H. H.
G/237	Newland, F. T.	T/3133	Nunn, A. W.
G/21934	Newman, C.	G/2600	Nunn, R. G.
G/17750	Newman, G. A.	G/7004	Nutley, G.
G/9733	Newman, J. W.	G/20827	Nutt, P. J.
G/25412	Newman, J. W.	T/203248	Nye, A.
G/2508	Newport, C.		
G/940	Newport, J. J.	G/20204	Oakley, E. W.
G/13086	Newson, G. A.	T/202494	Oakley, H.
L/7133	Newton, T. H.	G/3272	O'Brien, A. J.
G/5162	Nicholas, A.	G/3951	O'Brien, J.
G/5536	Nicholas, A.	G/634	O'Brien, T. E.
G/17997	Nicholas, R.	T/1737	O'Brien, W.
G/6707	Nicholas, T.	G/25994	Ockenden, F.
L/10343	Nicholls, A.	S/673	Oclee, C.
L/10252	Nicholls, A. E.	T/3033	Oclee, F. W.
G/17434	Nicholls, C.	G/20858	Odd, F. A.
G/12728	Nicholson, W. A.	G/13241	Oddy, C.
T/241973	Ninnis, A. E.	G/5571	O'Dell, J.
G/2639	Nixon, J.	G/2905	Offord, E. L.
G/1399	Nixon, S. C.	L/8570	Ogilvie, W.
G/2316	Nobbs, R. D.	G/3118	Ohlson, E. J.
G/7691	Noble, E.	G/12349	Old, J.
G/4470	Nolte, F. H. D.	G/14874	O'Leary, M. J.
T/243167	Norkett, W. T.	G/22995	Oleson, R. C. K.
T/203266	Norman, C. D.	G/12060	Oliff, E. G.
G/18207	Norman, F.	L/9186	Olive, C.
G/2199	Norman, O.	G/9713	Olive, R.
G/19025	Norman, W. H.	G/2908	Oliver, E.

PRIVATES—*(continued)*

G/3267	Oliver, H.
G/19133	Omerod, R. B.
T/240807	Onions, W. G.
T/270867	O'Regan, M.
T/242555	Orgar, G. E.
S/10481	Orpin, H.
G/6862	Orton, W. H.
G/13588	Osborn, T. A.
G/2527	Osborne, C.
G/21258	Osborne, H.
G/9286	Osborne, H.
G/25954	Osborne, J. S.
G/13648	Osborne, W. T.
L/6453	Ost, A. E.
G/14701	Oswald, W.
G/20161	Ottaway, A.
L/10196	Ottaway, F. H.
G/7548	Ottaway, J. W.
G/499	Ottaway, L. J.
G/21416	Ovenden, F. W.
G/2417	Ovenell, H.
G/20807	Overbury, H. H.
G/1364	Overton, T. W.
G/7727	Overy, T. J. D.
G/25415	Owen, E. H.
T/270284	Pack, J. H.
G/6274	Pack, S.
G/35535	Pack, S. R.
G/14803	Pack, W. W.
G/5677	Packard, W. H.
L/10453	Packer, G. A.
G/19038	Packer, H. E.
L/8875	Packman, B. E.
T/2817	Packman, S. A.
L/8262	Packman, W. J.
G/3770	Padgham, A.
T/270372	Pagden, S.
G/3788	Page, A. P.

G/571	Page, C. W.
G/15654	Page, F. H.
L/8700	Page, F. O.
G/6182	Page, H.
G/7885	Page, H. J.
L/7901	Page, J.
G/5237	Page, J.
G/6858	Page, J. W.
L/8590	Page, P.
G/17406	Page, W. J. F.
G/4190	Paget, A. E.
G/13378	Paice, A. S.
G/2875	Pain, E. S.
T/1418	Paine, A.
G/9136	Paine, A.
G/9183	Paine, F.
G/17445	Paine, J. H.
S/10921	Paine, R.
G/14069	Paine, S.
G/14875	Painter, A.
G/241	Painter, H. V.
G/1068	Palethorpe, R. E.
G/13630	Pallant, A. A.
G/12038	Palmer, A. E.
G/15518	Palmer, C.
T/202506	Palmer, C. W.
G/5181	Palmer, G. T.
G/5439	Palmer, J.
G/21232	Palmer, R. J.
G/6149	Palmer, T. J.
G/241742	Palmer, T. M.
G/2829	Palmer, W.
T/270492	Pankhurst, F.
G/26249	Parish, J. B.
L/9079	Parish, W.
S/330	Parker, A.
T/240678	Parker, A.
G/560	Parker, A.
G/4647	Parker, C. H.

APPENDIX II

G/567	Parker, F. R.	G/26586	Payne, W. T. H.
G/9297	Parker, G. W. G.	G/202773	Peacocke, G. F.
S/10453	Parker, J.	G/6790	Pearce, A.
L/8420	Parker, J. T.	G/19182	Pearce, A. J.
G/678	Parker, R. C. W.	G/8719	Pearce, E.
G/18762	Parker, S.	G/14467	Pearce, E. A.
G/2069	Parker, S.	G/6774	Pearce, P.
G/787	Parker, W.	G/24857	Pearce, R. W.
G/17440	Parkins, H. C.	G/13420	Pearce, T.
G/12800	Parks, E.	G/5413	Pearce, T.
G/8613	Parrish, E.	G/1019	Pearman, A. E.
G/5432	Parrott, G. F., M.M.	G/13405	Pearman, W. H.
		G/5791	Pearse, W. M.
L/8432	Parson, W. C.	L/8264	Pearson, A. C.
L/8300	Parsons, H.	T/1810	Pearson, A.
L/9255	Partridge, E. J.	G/6505	Pearson, J. F.
G/5546	Pashby, F.	S/10780	Pearson, J. G.
G/23829	Passingham, J. B.	G/21055	Pearson, T.
G/7594	Paterson, H. L.	S/9257	Pearson, W.
G/5366	Patrick, F.	G/3274	Peate, G.
G/13160	Patrick, G.	G/5876	Peck, W. B.
G/737	Patten, W.	G/3299	Peel, C.
G/18092	Pattenden, G. T.	G/5118	Peel, G.
T/20344	Pattenden, H.	G/14353	Peers, C. L.
G/15655	Patterson, G.	G/14832	Pegden, R. G. B.
G/24540	Paul, E. W.	S/9226	Pegg, J.
T/1361	Pavey, A. V.	T/3190	Peirce, A. E.
G/1490	Pavey, J. H.	G/5502	Peirce, C. H.
T/202530	Pavitt, C.	G/167	Pemble, F. W.
G/199	Pay, J. J.	G/24251	Pendry, W.
S/10271	Pay, J. W.	G/7657	Penfold, A.
L/9116	Pay, T. J.	L/8153	Penfold, A.
G/3461	Payne, E. J., M.M.	G/5489	Penfold, C. E.
G/20846	Payne, F.	G/8243	Penfold, T.
G/2988	Payne, G.	G/12515	Penman, R.
S/10934	Payne, H.	G/11916	Penny, E. D.
L/10230	Payne, J.	T/1628	Pentecost, F.
L/9784	Payne, J. F.	G/21056	Pepper, E. B.
G/26635	Payne, W.	G/15521	Pepper, S. M.

APPENDIX II

PRIVATES—(*continued*)

T/202275	Percival, G.	T/240268	Pierce, J.
G/12190	Perfect, A. J.	G/2958	Piesley, C. E.
L/6868	Perfitt, W.	G/5853	Piggott, H. W.
G/4249	Perkins, E. G.	G/21024	Piggott, H.
G/14912	Perkins, J. T.	G/12928	Piggott, J.
G/25822	Perkins, P.	L/7974	Pigott, R.
G/15797	Perriman, G.	G/22598	Pike, A.
G/5139	Perriman, H.	G/6730	Pike, B.
G/5659	Perrin, E. J. H.	L/7124	Pike, S.
L/10180	Perrins, D. S.	S/10975	Pike, S. S.
G/17448	Perrott, A. E.	T/1021	Pilbeam, A.
L/7791	Perry, W. J.	T/1141	Pilbeam, E.
G/11560	Petch, J.	G/5169	Pilcher, A.
G/15658	Petchey, W.	G/861	Pilcher, G.
G/13159	Peters, F.	G/18667	Pilcher, W.
G/1794	Petifer, F. A.	G/15517	Pilcher, W. H.
G/18995	Pettican, C. W.	T/1060	Pile, E. T.
G/6297	Pettifer, H.	T/240837	Pile, G.
G/15771	Pettman, A. L.	T/243066	Pinfold, G. H.
G/6386	Pettman, E. S. M.	G/15520	Pink, H. H.
G/1376	Petts, W.	G/17646	Pinnell, H.
G/5255	Petts, W. A.	G/12925	Pinnock, E.
G/22025	Philcox, W. A.	G/15659	Piper, E. G.
G/8395	Phillips, H.	L/10529	Pipier, W. J.
G/6585	Phillips, H. R.	G/4680	Pippard, S.
G/15519	Phillips, R. H.	G/15660	Piprell, S.
G/165	Phillpott, C. V.	G/140	Pitcher, E.
G/3395	Phillpott, E.	G/4979	Pitcher, R. C.
G/5166	Philpott, A. C.	G/23939	Pitt, S.
G/7944	Philpott, D.	G/9310	Pittock, G.
S/771	Philpott, F. J.	G/2853	Pitts, W.
G/7807	Philpott, R.	L/9445	Plant, A.
G/8226	Philpott, R. W.	G/24554	Platts, J. D.
G/5360	Phipps, C.	G/17950	Player, H. J.
G/5493	Phipps, C.	G/15661	Playford, G. T.
G/21458	Phipps, E. W.	G/13158	Pledge, A. E.
G/24348	Pickering, J. W.	G/21926	Plummer, R. J.
G/20919	Pickett, H. A.	G/3924	Pointer, A. E.
G/12032	Pierce, G.	L/9790	Pollard, J.

PRIVATES—(continued)

G/2718	Polley, B.	T/20081	Price, E. G.
G/5750	Poole, F. W.	T/2797	Price, F. A.
T/201668	Poole, J.	G/4895	Price, F. H. W.
L/8360	Poole, J.	G/4785	Price, G.
G/13692	Poole, H. E. W.	G/20004	Price, H. C.
G/14469	Poole, L. J.	G/8761	Price, J. W.
G/5104	Pope, J. G.	G/12927	Price, J. E. F.
G/10327	Popeley, H.	G/1962	Price, L.
G/203524	Pordage, S.	G/1920	Price, W.
G/9408	Port, J. A.	G/5345	Price, W. B.
L/5219	Port, W.	S/358	Price, W. T.
G/12557	Porter, P. S.	G/887	Pride, A. J. F.
G/18320	Portlock, H.	G/13615	Priest, C. W.
G/19123	Pott, E. H.	G/29202	Priest, J.
G/12604	Potter, B. L.	G/2089	Priest, S.
T/202484	Potter, C. A.	T/271000	Prince, P. O.
S/399	Potter, F. A.	G/14703	Pring, C. C.
L/9473	Potter, G.	G/18901	Prior, A.
G/1052	Potter, S. D.	G/25419	Pritchard, D.
G/13626	Potts, G.	G/6142	Proctor, J. B.
T/2997	Potts, R. V.	G/8662	Pryke, A.
G/25820	Poulter, H. W.	G/3704	Puckett, F.
G/1022	Poutney, G.	G/2053	Pugh, S.
G/892	Povey, H.	G/5619	Pull, O. C.
G/553	Powell, F.	G/5108	Pullee, W.
G/12612	Powell, L.	G/4013	Pullman, H.
G/11798	Powell, P. J.	G/3124	Purdey, J.
G/9344	Powell, T. G.	G/6463	Purdie, W. T.
L/9654	Poynter, W. R.	G/25881	Purkiss, H. E.
S/10485	Pratt, C.	L/10655	Pursglove, W. S.
G/6614	Pratt, H.	L/9413	Pye, F. R. C.
T/241155	Preece, A. J.	L/7861	Pyefinch, L. T.
S/489	Prendergast, D. E.	G/10330	Pyett, G. H.
G/8600	Prescott, E. G.		
L/7028	Prescott, W.	G/9198	Quaife, H.
G/8964	Prett, F. H.	G/9963	Quaife, R. W.
G/2914	Price, A.	T/270324	Quaife, T.
G/7614	Price, A.	G/18752	Quantrill, H.
G/1607	Price, A. W.	G/5095	Queen, F. W.

PRIVATES—*(continued)*

T/201898	Quinn, F. G.		G/661	Reader, H. W.
L/8750	Quittenden, L. F.		S/10156	Reader, J. H.
			G/13660	Reader, W.
G/12095	Racher, R.		L/10408	Real, F. W. G.
L/9785	Radford, S.		T/270512	Reardon, F.
G/18864	Rainbow, A.		G/3469	Reddick, C. A.
L/10366	Rainer, G. H.		G/8700	Redford, A.
L/10210	Raines, G.		G/5532	Redhead, T.
G/5240	Ralph, A.		G/19150	Redhouse, E.
L/9880	Ralph, A.		L/8453	Redman, L.
G/425	Ralph, E.		L/9251	Redman, W. S.
G/9088	Ralph, F.		L/9058	Redmond, R. L.
S/82	Ralph, J.		G/23841	Reed, C.
G/21188	Ramboux, A.		L/8278	Reed, G.
T/200871	Ramsden, C. A. L.		S/8313	Reed, J.
G/5981	Randall, A. E.		T/201799	Reed, T. G.
T/202924	Randall, C. R.		G/24030	Reeve, C. S.
G/4074	Randall, H. G.		G/3638	Reeve, G. A.
T/204236	Randle, H. G.		L/9201	Reeve, H. G.
G/3326	Ranger, C.		G/14227	Reeve, J.
G/25166	Ransom, E. J.		G/5117	Reeves, F. V.
G/13165	Ransome, F.		T/240098	Reeves, J. E.
G/14226	Rason, H. F.		G/1471	Reeves, R.
G/19572	Rastall, C.		G/7942	Reeves, W. J.
G/8745	Ratcliffe, H. F.		L/9668	Regan, P. H.
G/15522	Raven, A.		G/24776	Reid, M. C.
L/7689	Raven, F.		G/6255	Reid, W. J.
L/8760	Raven, I.		G/18794	Reilly, A.
G/3738	Raynor, E. G.		T/240764	Relf, F.
G/5315	Read, A. J.		G/557	Relf, F.
G/1530	Read, C. F.		S/152	Relf, R. G.
G/2645	Read, E.		G/6690	Rendle, W.
L/10033	Read, F. W.		G/36	Renouf, F. G.
T/270892	Read, H.		G/18996	Rew, E. J.
G/1928	Read, J. A.		G/25785	Reynolds, A. G.
G/3331	Read, P. W.		G/23836	Reynolds, B. E.
G/4391	Read, W.		G/9386	Reynolds, G.
G/2866	Read, W.		G/6720	Reynolds, G. C.
G/17634	Read, W. W. J.		T/202571	Reynolds, H.

APPENDIX II

G/552	Reynolds, J. T.	G/2396	Rist, G. R.
G/4622	Reynolds, J.	G/14538	Ritchie, E.
G/24859	Reynolds, L. W.	T/240769	Ritchie, J. L.
G/9819	Reynolds, W. F. H.	G/4024	Rivers, R. S.
G/568	Reynolds, W. C.	G/7208	Rivett, G.
G/10261	Reynolds, W. J.	G/3927	Rivoire, C.
G/5574	Rhee, P.	L/8738	Robbins, F. T.
S/124	Rhine, J.	G/976	Robbins, W. V.
T/1991	Rhodes, A. E.	G/12853	Roberts, A. P.
G/15777	Rhodes, E.	L/8935	Roberts, A.B., M.M.
G/3369	Rhodes, F.	G/14293	Roberts, A. W.
G/4419	Ribbons, F. C.	G/9398	Roberts, C.
G/21004	Rice, C. J.	G/9911	Roberts, E.
G/4873	Rice, E.	G/13708	Roberts, H. J.
G/13637	Rich, A.	T/241032	Roberts, J.
G/18584	Richards, C.	G/4025	Roberts, J. A.
G/6268	Richards, F.	G/1666	Roberts, R., M.M.
G/5116	Richards, F. W.	S/10843	Roberts, W. H.
G/4578	Richards, H. V.	G/4663	Robertson, J.
G/13430	Richards, J.	T/265247	Rohins, C. J.
G/4716	Richardson, A.	L/10552	Robinson, A. A.
G/13166	Richardson, E.	G/4278	Robinson, A. L.
G/6776	Richardson, J.	G/7029	Robinson, C. A.
G/13951	Richardson, J.	G/25152	Robinson, G. S.
G/21831	Richardson, J. A.	G/29289	Robinson, H. F.
T/2167	Richardson, R. J.	G/4993	Robinson, J.
L/8505	Richardson, V. D.	G/23875	Robinson, J. E.
L/9913	Richardson, W.	G/6849	Robinson, J. H.
G/3188	Ricketts, F.	G/10154	Robinson, R.
G/10006	Riddles, E. H.	G/14708	Robinson, S.
T/241081	Rider, A.	G/19185	Robinson, W. J.
G/17652	Ridgewell, W. A.	G/5598	Robinson, W.
L/6030	Ridlington, A.	G/3661	Robjant, A. J.
G/6164	Rigden, A. V.	G/22242	Roblett, F.
G/2927	Rigden, H.	T/206110	Robson, A. J.
T/3346	Riley, C. P.	T/242431	Roche, L. F.
G/18922	Riley, E.	G/9710	Rochester, W.
L/9947	Riley, G.	G/19928	Rodwell, C.
L/9205	Ring, G. T.	G/3238	Roe, A.

L/9910	Roff, W.	G/5466	Russell, A. G.
G/18866	Roffe, R.	T/240176	Russell, C.
G/24862	Rogers, A.	G/13149	Russell, E. A.
L/10358	Rogers, F. C.	L/9952	Russell, F.
S/418	Rogers, G.	G/10118	Russell, F. E.
G/15673	Rogers, J. C.	T/1431	Russell, J. G.
G/5912	Rogers, W. H.	S/10555	Russell, T.
G/1601	Roland, A. W. H.	G/4531	Russell, W. R.
L/8851	Rolfe, P. E.	G/18968	Ryan, J. B.
G/11873	Rollings, J. W.	G/18367	Ryan, M.
G/14011	Rollinson, J. G.	G/11484	Ryan, T.
G/596	Ronald, R.	L/8715	Rye, E.
G/21920	Rooke, B. A.	L/8027	Rye, H.
T/242631	Roome, C. H.		
G/1648	Rose, C.	L/9175	Sacree, S.
G/13573	Rose, G.	G/13641	Saddleton, S. F.
G/4073	Rose, T.	G/19126	Sadler, F.
G/13663	Rosier, S. M.	G/20167	Saffrey, J.
G/18819	Rosier, W. H.	G/7876	Sage, E. G.
G/6780	Rosser, A. D.	G/5968	Sage, J.
G/4282	Rossiter, A.	L/10567	Sage, V.
T/243294	Rowden, E. G.	G/26247	Sagon, W. S.
L/5668	Rowe, A.	T/6111	Sales, T.
G/18226	Rowe, E. C.	G/14547	Salisbury, W.
G/26614	Rowe, W. A.	C/14084	Sallese, J.
G/963	Rowkins, R.	T/204449	Salmon, E. G.
G/17453	Rowley, C. C.	T/1710	Salter, C. H.
G/14029	Roy, A.	G/3383	Salter, E.
G/23950	Royston, P. H.	G/13246	Sammon, M.
T/1234	Rudland, C. E. H.	G/1846	Sanders, B.
G/4550	Ruffle, A.	G/13715	Sanders, S. A. F.
L/9752	Ruler, H. J.	G/4724	Sandwell, S. J.
G/13271	Rumgay, R.	G/6661	Sandwick, J.
T/2451	Rumney, C. H.	G/21026	Sargeant, A. C.
G/5658	Rumney, J.	G/7932	Sargeant, J.
G/25175	Rump, E.	G/2547	Sargent, C. E.
G/24704	Rump, F. G.	G/24038	Sargent, H. W.
G/26968	Rush, R. E.	T/204108	Satchell, A.
G/4164	Russ, A. E.	G/394	Saunders, B.

APPENDIX II

T/242816	Saunders, C. S.	S/9988	Sedge, H. J.
G/3218	Saunders, E.	L/9970	Sedgwick, C. F.
G/7917	Saunders, G. W. W.	G/5202	Sedgwick, E. J.
T/203957	Saunders, P. R.	L/9885	Sedgwick, E. C.
G/5180	Saunders, W. C. R.	S/10525	Sedgwick, T.
G/14474	Saunders, W. F.	G/21061	Seekings, E.
G/23934	Savage, A.	G/631	Self, E.
G/7552	Savage, F.	G/7382	Self, J. E.
G/11740	Savill, A.	G/5141	Selling, C.
G/13160	Saward, C. E.	G/14711	Senior, S.
G/13877	Sawford, W.	T/202732	Seppings, H. S.
S/414	Saxby, A. C.	L/9833	Sergant, E.
G/4411	Sayer, A. E.	G/9734	Setterfield, E.
G/18936	Sayer, F. H.	G/5163	Setterfield, F.
G/1880	Sayer, H.	T/240127	Setterfield, J.
G/5675	Sayer, W. C.	G/2120	Sewell, E. A.
G/582	Sayer, W. G.	G/11689	Seymour, A.
G/15678	Sayers, R. C.	L/8461	Seymour, H. J.
S/690	Scales, W. H.	G/359	Shafford, M. P.
L/8117	Scamp, A.	G/13247	Shaill, A.
L/8607	Scarterfield, F. W.	G/6141	Shakespeare, R.
T/271011	Scherf, O. L.	G/19008	Sharman, W.
G/451	Scholes, J. A.	G/874	Sharp, T., M.M.
T/203762	Scillitoe, A. H.	G/219	Sharpe, A. J.
L/8416	Scotchbrook, G.	G/14259	Sharpe, E.
G/18867	Scotney, T. W.	G/241601	Sharples, J. E.
T/240474	Scott, E. M.	G/14542	Sharples, R.
L/9824	Scott, G. F.	L/10551	Sharpless, F.
T/201027	Scott, P.	G/25266	Sharrod, C.
G/10241	Scrivener, G.	G/6672	Shawyer, G. H.
G/15680	Scuddan, A.	G/444	Shaxted, G. W. T.
T/270935	Seal, H. P.	L/9348	Shaxted, H. C.
G/3974	Seaman, J.	G/6005	Shaxted, J.
G/22616	Sear, C. G.	G/18699	Shead, T.
G/21844	Searle, C. H.	G/9090	Sheaff, A. R.
G/3685	Searle, F. G.	T/271064	Sheen, C., M.M.
G/14389	Searle, J. C.	G/3543	Shelley, G.
L/8642	Sears, W.	G/6654	Shelton, S.
G/2860	Secret, T.	G/2673	Shelvey, S. J.

491

APPENDIX II

G/17481	Shepherd, H. T.	G/23516	Simpson, D.
S/10680	Sheppard, C.	L/10129	Simpson, G.
G/20471	Sherlock, A. H.	T/206112	Simpson, J. A.
G/2384	Sherwood, P.	G/2518	Simpson, S.
G/4334	Shilling, G.	L/8223	Simpson, T.
L/2747	Shilling, R. H.	G/2249	Simpson, W. E.
G/8903	Shilling, W. G.	G/1276	Sims, F. J.
G/3181	Shirley, J. H.	G/1214	Sims, G. R.
G/20949	Shoebridge, A.	L/10555	Sims, O. J.
T/1469	Shoebridge, C.	G/12589	Sinclair, D.
G/18868	Shoebridge, H.	T/202415	Sinnian, A. W.
G/10434	Shoebridge, J.	T/202909	Sitzler, G. F.
G/3930	Shoesmith, A.	L/9095	Sivyer, J.
G/1366	Shonk, S.	T/3138	Sizer, J.
G/29227	Shooter, H.	G/1223	Skelton, J.
G/14477	Short, G.	G/5854	Skinner, H. T.
S/745	Short, H. G.	G/559	Skinner, W. J. J.
L/9570	Shorter, E. G.	T/271163	Sladden, E.
L/7175	Shorter, P.	G/25098	Slade, F. G.
G/7216	Shreeve, C. F.	G/18938	Slade, G. H.
G/3415	Shrieve, H.	S/856	Slater, W. E.
G/25274	Shrimpton, W. O.	G/24039	Slater, W. J.
G/5605	Shrubsall, R.	S/10683	Slattery, H. W.
G/5175	Shrubsall, S.	T/1587	Slaughter, T. A.
G/797	Shrubshall, W. R.	S/497	Slender, C.
G/8144	Shrubsole, J.	L/8631	Slingsby, H. T.
G/17989	Shrubsole, W. H.	G/5135	Small, C.
T/202509	Shuter, C.	G/20007	Small, E. R.
T/203960	Siflett, T.	G/6185	Small, W.
G/3199	Sillett, L. A.	L/9523	Smallcombe, A.
G/18203	Silvester, C.	G/20006	Smalley, C.
G/3560	Simkin, J. E.	G/9863	Smalley, W. P.
L/9541	Simmonds, C. A.	T/202668	Smalls, C.
L/9795	Simmonds, W. E.	G/5179	Smith, A.
G/20047	Simmons, G.	G/6616	Smith, A.
T/240490	Simmons, P. C.	G/19152	Smith, A.
G/4839	Simmons, W.	S/10541	Smith, A.
G/25955	Simpkins, A.	G/6663	Smith, A.
G/29223	Simpson, A.	G/6013	Smith, A. B. G.

APPENDIX II

T/201856	Smith, A. C.		G/2009	Smith, L. S.
G/23926	Smith, A. G.		T/203081	Smith, L. W.
L/9660	Smith, A. R.		L/8612	Smith, P.
G/17455	Smith, A. S. A.		G/9702	Smith, P.
G/4110	Smith, C.		G/2071	Smith, R.
G/24943	Smith, C.		S/7	Smith, S. G.
T/202955	Smith, C. J.		G/5171	Smith, T.
G/18151	Smith, C. W.		G/4346	Smith, T.
G/18869	Smith, E.		G/4722	Smith, T. W.
G/6093	Smith, E.		G/3439	Smith, W.
L/7936	Smith, E.		G/6041	Smith, W.
S/26	Smith, E. F.		G/13302	Smith, W. A.
L/10423	Smith, F.		G/5941	Smith, W. C.
G/5203	Smith, F.		T/270833	Smith, W. E.
G/4912	Smith, F.		G/2459	Smith, W. G.
G/6799	Smith, F. G.		G/14543	Smith, W. H.
G/13296	Smith, F. R.		L/8132	Smith, W. H. T.
G/1724	Smith, F. S.		L/9391	Smith, W. T.
S/134	Smith, F. W.		G/21157	Smithers, E. W.
L/8712	Smith, G.		G/11889	Smithers, W.
L/11243	Smith, G. H.		G/3341	Snapes, J. T.
L/10108	Smith, G. T.		G/13643	Snashall, G. J.
G/6517	Smith, G. V.		G/10787	Snell, E.
G/5239	Smith, H.		G/13248	Snooks, C., M.M.
L/6303	Smith, H.		G/13610	Sole, W. H.
G/9133	Smith, H.		L/8867	Solly, A. G.
G/15685	Smith, H.		G/25201	Solly, W. E.
G/17795	Smith, H.		T/202549	Solomon, H. H. S.
G/8774	Smith, H.		S/609	South, W. H.
G/10287	Smith, H. A.		G/19991	Southard, R. C.
G/44	Smith, H. A.		S/10394	Southern, A. R.
G/13763	Smith, J.		G/10336	Spalding, W. P.
G/18745	Smith, J.		G/12133	Sparkes, E.
S/9424	Smith, J.		G/2114	Sparks, A.
G/15741	Smith, J.		L/9511	Sparks, W.
G/14603	Smith, J.		G/4371	Sparrowhawk, A.W.
G/6780	Smith, J. H.		G/7806	Spearpoint, W.
T/206155	Smith, J. H.		L/8783	Speller, W.
L/7574	Smith, L. J.		G/26664	Spells, E. E.

493

APPENDIX II

G/398	Spencer, F. W.	G/4549	Stevens, A. E.
G/17740	Spencer, J. H.	L/9469	Stevens, A. E.
G/22198	Spendiff, J. W.	G/20818	Stevens, C.
G/9161	Spice, A. E.	G/5755	Stevens, F. A.
G/9414	Spillett, E.	L/9899	Stevens, H.
G/583	Spillett, F. J.	G/4762	Stevens, P.
G/5252	Spillett, R. H.	G/1615	Stevens, P. J.
G/8560	Spinks, P.	L/9821	Stevens, T.
T/240825	Spooner, A. V.	G/7046	Stevens, W.
G/2160	Sprackland, W. L.	G/13872	Stevens, W. R.
G/11989	Spriggs, A. D.	G/4734	Stevenson, E. W.
G/23846	Springthorpe, R. A.	G/3774	Stevenson, L. P.
G/2147	Spry, W.	G/7738	Stevenson, S. W.
G/10347	Spurling, A. G.	G/14258	Steventon, H. T.
G/4957	Squire, E. M.	T/206123	Stewart, J.
G/15689	Squires, H. J.	G/9125	Stickells, H. W.
G/18873	Stanford, J. T.	G/8915	Stickells, T. G.
L/9566	Stanley, A. H.	G/2154	Stiles, E.
G/21682	Stanley, H. E.	G/19151	Stiles, H. R.
G/4122	Stannard, F. A.	L/8688	Still, J.
G/17459	Stannard, L. H.	G/6781	Stillwell, H.
G/19040	Stansell, R.	G/5651	Stinson, T. J.
G/22483	Stanton, A.	G/13724	Stitson, F.
L/6782	Staples, T.	T/240156	Stoakes, A.
G/998	Stapley, G.	L/10496	Stock, T.
G/1114	Starkey, W. E.	G/7969	Stocker, H.
G/22231	Starling, W. F.	G/9509	Stockley, E.
G/22210	Stather, A. E.	G/20856	Stockman, W. E.
T/2289	Steadman, A.	G/3457	Stockwell, W. H.
G/20201	Stear, F. C.	G/8223	Stokes, C.
L/6976	Steed, A.	G/14065	Stokes, E.
G/17716	Steeden, A.	G/1	Stokes, F.
L/9898	Steele, E.	S/722	Stokes, F. F.
G/13955	Steele, J.	S/10636	Stokes, G.
G/20206	Steer, F. W.	G/4800	Stokes, L. L.
G/2399	Stening, F. J.	G/8782	Stone, D.
G/23927	Stenson, C. E.	G/2890	Stone, G.
L/9379	Stephens, P. E.	G/3772	Stone, J.
G/6655	Stephenson, E.	G/4847	Stone, P.

APPENDIX II

G/10201	Stonebridge, H.
T/240011	Stoneham, R.
G/24126	Stonehouse, W.
L/5632	Stoner, S. J.
G/6762	Stonham, W. J.
G/29211	Stoppard, C. E.
G/10124	Stote, E.
G/4956	Strand, G. A.
G/12669	Stray, W. J.
L/10486	Streat, C.
G/639	Street, A.
L/7983	Street, J.
G/24867	Street, W. T.
G/14365	Streeter, G.
T/3388	Streeting, W.
G/26124	Stringer, A. A.
G/13250	Stringer, B.
G/25798	Stringer, J.
L/9504	Strong, G.
G/8677	Stroud, F. C.
G/9267	Strover, F.
G/11936	Stubbs, C. E.
G/1552	Stubbs, E.
G/6529	Stubbs, H.
G/20820	Stuckey, R. H.
L/9634	Stupple, G.
S/10883	Sturman, J. A.
L/5178	Sturmer, A.
S/10856	Styles, T. A. G.
G/18611	Styles, W. R.
G/12708	Suller, A. E.
T/242387	Sullivan, T. E.
S/11083	Sulsh, C. W.
G/14900	Summers, F.
G/1360	Summers, H.
G/4080	Summersby, A. L.
L/4621	Sunderland, W. W.
T/203445	Surplice, H.
G/1754	Sutch, J.
G/12564	Sutcliffe, A. G.
T/202546	Sutton, S. G.
G/12565	Swaffield, H. E.
G/13684	Swan, C.
G/21206	Swan, G. W.
G/21029	Swann, S.
T/3055	Sweeney, M.
S/10829	Sweetman, A.
G/7621	Sweetman, W.
G/13956	Swetman, A. V.
L/7545	Swift, B.
G/2765	Swinerd, R. J.
L/8686	Swinnard, A. D.
L/10658	Sydenham, A.
G/15695	Sykes, A. W.
G/17635	Symonds, F. J.
G/18761	Symonds, H. F.
G/13711	Symons, C. H.
G/23900	Syres, F.
L/9883	Tabrett, A.
S/10222	Tabrett, T.
G/2278	Taken, H. T.
G/17463	Talbot, H. H.
T/202828	Talbot, W.
L/7754	Tamsett, H.
G/23937	Tanner, F. R.
G/13177	Tanner, F. W.
G/14367	Tanner, S.
G/1268	Tanner, T.
G/21063	Tansley, G. W.
G/24106	Taplin, N.
L/6026	Tapping, H. A.
T/704	Tapsfield, C. R.
G/18242	Tasker, F. A. V.
T/270654	Tasker, W.
G/7824	Taylforth, C.
G/25870	Taylor, A. A.
G/19194	Taylor, A. C.

PRIVATES—*(continued)*

L/8236	Taylor, C.		T/1830	Theobald, G. W.
G/609	Taylor, E.		G/2839	Thirkettle, J., M.M.
L/8210	Taylor, E. J.		G/15697	Thirtle, H. G.
G/17475	Taylor, F. D.		G/9018	Thomas, C. B.
G/8878	Taylor, F. G.		T/201305	Thomas, E. R.
G/19190	Taylor, F. H.		L/8911	Thomas, F.
G/7906	Taylor, F. J.		G/4113	Thomas, F. G.
L/9989	Taylor, G.		G/35520	Thomas, G.
L/7213	Taylor, G. W.		G/7605	Thomas, H.
T/202521	Taylor, H.		S/10835	Thomas, J. T.
G/15803	Taylor, H. A.		G/20838	Thomas, J.
G/2537	Taylor, H. J.		T/241530	Thomas, J. B.
G/5537	Taylor, H. V.		G/18940	Thompsett, W.
G/9192	Taylor, J.		L/9932	Thompson, A. J.
G/8951	Taylor, J.		G/6708	Thompson, E.
T/271070	Taylor, J.		L/10688	Thompson, F.
G/6674	Taylor, J.		G/4134	Thompson, G. H.
G/17511	Taylor, J. P.		G/36715	Thompson, G. W.
G/12890	Taylor, J. S.		G/17718	Thompson, H. E.
G/4610	Taylor, J. T.		G/7665	Thompson, H. G.
G/14960	Taylor, J. W.		G/4224	Thompson, H. G.
G/25826	Taylor, P. W.		L/10265	Thompson, W.
G/5936	Taylor, R. D.		L/6700	Thompson, W.
G/21150	Taylor, S.		G/20220	Thorn, G.
G/3471	Taylor, W. J.		G/2512	Thornby, A. F.
G/25825	Tebbutt, T. W.		T/2100	Thornby, A.
G/14118	Teece, F. J. W.		T/202745	Thornby, H. G.
G/18870	Teeson, A.		G/13341	Thorne, E. H.
G/19043	Tegg, W.		G/19164	Thorns, H. C.
G/19029	Termeau, H.		G/15760	Thorpe, T. V.
L/8421	Terry, E.		G/25251	Thorrington, A. J.
L/10360	Terry, E. G.		L/8764	Thundow, E.
L/10361	Terry, F. A.		G/9886	Thurbon, W.
T/3060	Terry, F. G.		G/25898	Thurgood, A.
T/3424	Terry, G. E.		G/21879	Thurgood, B.
S/10519	Terry, G. H.		G/1529	Thurgood, F. W.
G/5246	Terry, H.		L/10622	Thurley, H. E.
L/8780	Terry, L.		G/1207	Thurston, F.
G/1330	Tew, A. J.		L/7165	Tibbles, F.

PRIVATES—*(continued)*

G/2207	Tibbles, T.
G/5484	Tickner, G.
G/5418	Tidmarsh, W. G.
G/576	Tilley, G. L.
G/12777	Tilley, G. W.
G/24274	Tillier, S. V., M.M.
G/26648	Timmins, V.
L/8424	Tindell, H. W.
G/19153	Tingcombe, G. C.
G/5763	Tingey, W.
L/9756	Tinsley, E. C.
S/766	Titterton, J.
G/5416	Toby, A. J.
G/4737	Todd, A.
G/29	Todd, A.
G/29234	Todd, C. H.
G/3898	Todd, J. R.
L/7881	Tolhurst, C. A.
G/926	Tolhurst, G.
T/3034	Tolhurst, G. F.
L/9104	Tomlin, E.
L/9419	Tomlin, G.
G/8192	Tomlin, H.
L/8139	Tomlin, H.
G/21947	Tomlinson, B. G.
G/15791	Tompkin, P. J. M.
G/13602	Tompkin, W. S.
G/4693	Tompsett, H. T.
G/6699	Toms, J. M.
G/10405	Tomsett, A.
G/9617	Tomsett, J.
G/24691	Tonge, T. H.
G/2538	Tooke, L.
S/10351	Toone, C. J.
G/23905	Tovey, E. H.
G/3298	Towler, B.
G/4559	Town, A. C.
G/4932	Town, J.
L/7944	Town, Y. T. E.

T/20369	Townsend, T.
G/22061	Toyer, E. C. J.
G/29238	Tranter, E.
G/25226	Treadgold, A.
T/203770	Tredwell, G. A.
G/1778	Tressidder, J. A.
T/242015	Trew, E. C., M.M.
G/26600	Trewin, F. S.
G/12938	Trewin, H. C.
G/20053	Trice, A. H.
T/242960	Trice, L.
G/139	Trice, W.
G/20174	Triggs, F.
G/7914	Triptree, A. G.
G/2302	Tritton, C. J.
G/409	Trott, H. J.
G/2511	Trowbridge, C. H.
G/12567	Trubody, P.
G/410	Trull, A. W. H.
T/3009	Trumpeter, A. J.
G/657	Tucker, A. H.
T/203479	Tucker, J. S.
L/6965	Tucker, J. W.
L/8090	Tucker, R. G.
T/204014	Tuffley, F.
T/202063	Tuffrey, H.
G/15699	Tugwell, W. T. B.
G/4731	Tully, F.
G/6741	Tunnicliffe, A.
S/429	Tunnicliffe, W.
T/241000	Tunstall, H. W.
G/577	Tupp, C. J.
G/23902	Tupper, A.
G/389	Tupper, C. E.
T/241532	Turner, D. J.
G/19042	Turner, E.
L/10406	Turner, G.
G/18930	Turner, G.
G/8377	Turner, G. S.

PRIVATES—*(continued)*

G/4585	Turner, H. W.	T/1580	Van Rooyen, G. J. C.
G/7959	Turner, J.	G/6662	Vaughan, F. C.
G/13071	Turner, J.	G/4962	Veitch, H. J.
G/10629	Turner, J.	T/4461	Velvick, C. E.
G/8249	Turner, M. J.	G/1380	Veness, J.
G/2516	Turner, R. H.	T/203965	Venn, M.
G/7219	Turner, R.	L/9181	Venton, F.
G/17717	Turner, S.	G/2128	Vernon, R. A. W.
G/5600	Turner, S. E.	L/10527	Vicary, L. J.
G/3864	Turner, W. A.	T/1746	Vidler, J. A.
G/21064	Turner, W. M.	G/15702	Vidler, S. C.
G/14086	Turney, M.	G/24588	Viggor, F.
L/9588	Turrell, J.	G/10426	Vinall, E. T.
G/29236	Turton, G.	L/8897	Vinall, G.
G/23904	Tutin, T. A.	G/831	Vincent, A. J.
G/5495	Tutt, F.	L/10303	Vincent, F. W.
S/10403	Tutt, T.	G/18880	Vincent, S. G.
G/19051	Twaite, G.	T/204552	Viner, A.
G/22099	Tween, W.	G/13089	Vining, C. H. E.
G/3973	Twigg, T. W.	G/14123	Virgin, F. T.
G/2313	Twin, C. F.	G/21009	Voller, G.
G/4878	Twinn, W. C.	T/240808	Vousden, C. R.
G/9329	Twyman, C. H.	G/5795	Vousden, H.
G/5140	Twyman, G. H.	G/645	Vousden, R. F.
G/5070	Twyman, P. C.	G/8550	Vousden, W. H.
G/4651	Twyman, T.		
G/21932	Tyler, A.	G/3503	Wade, G. T.
G/8682	Tyler, A. C.	G/1680	Wade, W.
G/13176	Tyler, A. H.	G/8200	Waghorn, F.
G/15525	Tyson, W.	L/7239	Waghorn, J. E.
		G/11443	Waghorn, T. E.
T/3380	Uden, A.	G/5967	Waight, J. H.
G/9893	Uden, E. G.	T/200855	Wakelin, F.
T/240388	Underdown, G.	G/14375	Waldie, J. D.
G/15807	Underhill, C.	G/3521	Walker, A. J.
T/24284	Upshall, C. E.	G/3397	Walker, B.
G/19004	Upson, H.	T/241300	Walker, J. H.
G/1760	Upton, A. G.	G/14868	Walker, J. H. A.
G/9118	Usherwood, H. C.	L/8766	Walker, R. J.

APPENDIX II

PRIVATES—*(continued)*

G/2870	Walker, R.	G/5792	Watches, P.
S/98	Walker, T.	G/29240	Waterall, T. W.
G/20967	Walker, T. G.	T/270967	Waterhouse, W. W.
L/7233	Walkom, G. A.	G/1192	Waters, H.
G/4144	Wallace, D.	G/18888	Waters, R. J.
L/7865	Wallace, W. J.	T/270439	Waters, T. J.
G/14651	Waller, J. R.	G/4317	Watkins, H.
G/20800	Wallis, A.	G/798	Watkins, H. J.
G/1296	Wallis, H. W.	S/229	Watson, B.
G/11693	Wallis, W. A.	G/190	Watson, F.
S/543	Walter, E.	G/171	Watson, G.
G/11667	Walter, R.	G/1702	Watson, H. E.
G/13284	Walton, J.	T/201021	Watson, J.
G/7626	Wanstall, T. F.	G/6429	Watson, J.
G/18902	Want, J.	G/7007	Watson, J.
G/10875	Warby, W. R.	G/6190	Watson, J. H.
G/24707	Ward, A. E.	G/18662	Watson, R. C.
L/10094	Ward, C.	G/2044	Watson, W.
T/206060	Ward, F.	G/1932	Watson, W. H. J.
G/8156	Ward, G.	G/13257	Watts, A.
G/17660	Ward, J. H.	G/22619	Watts, F. W.
T/241539	Ward, J. W.	L/7886	Watts, R. W.
T/203220	Ward, S. G.	G/6289	Watts, S. A.
L/7880	Ward, T. C. S.	G/5428	Watts, W. E. A.
L/8624	Ward, W. J. R.	T/2181	Wayte, J.
L/8571	Warden, C. H.	G/15753	Weare, L. T.
G/29253	Wardle, J. W.	G/9510	Weatherall, A. P.
G/11460	Ware, A.	T/242824	Weatherill, E.
G/35685	Ware, J. G.	G/18206	Weaver, A. G.
G/1611	Waring, S.	G/13599	Weaver, R.
G/13629	Warman, T.	G/12666	Weavers, T. J.
G/13431	Warman, W. R. H.	G/11957	Webb, A. A.
G/1007	Warne, R. G.	G/4723	Webb, E. C.
G/637	Warren, P.	G/4616	Webb, E. E.
G/1015	Warry, T. V.	G/14015	Webb, E. S.
G/20035	Warwick, F. H.	T/243088	Webb, F.
G/14922	Warwick, J. W.	G/2367	Webb, J. G.
G/1616	Washbrook, A.	S/10901	Webb, J. A.
G/11668	Wassell, H. J.	G/9076	Webb, L.

499

L/8856	Webb, P.	L/5748	Weston, F. J.
G/18821	Webb, P. J.	G/7068	Whale, R. F.
G/26568	Webb, S. C.	G/26642	Wheatley, A.
G/10344	Webb, T. W.	L/10276	Wheatley, A. J.
G/7070	Webb, W. H.	T/206156	Wheatley, H.
G/21207	Webber, H. G.	G/3334	Wheeler, C.
G/13181	Webster, J.	G/8574	Wheeler, F. G.
T/203970	Webster, W.	G/392	Wheeler, I. A.
G/13259	Weeding, J.	L/10209	Whenham, H. S.
T/203563	Weeks, G.	L/8620	Whiddett, G.
G/21288	Weeks, G.	G/6843	Whitby, G. E.
G/5207	Weeks, R. G.	G/8624	White, E. E.
L/8171	Weeks, T. E.	L/7918	White, G. T.
S/272	Welch, W.	G/20008	White, J. A.
T/243305	Welford, W. S.	G/13260	White, J.
G/15708	Wellband, N. K.	G/6889	White, J. F.
G/1354	Wellard, G. J.	G/17491	White, L. V.
L/7998	Weller, A. A.	G/21833	White, L. S.
T/203968	Weller, J. E.	G/20177	White, N. E.
L/9498	Wells, A.	G/2559	White, P.
G/5747	Wells, E. G.	G/17471	White, R. W.
S/889	Wells, F. H.	S/245	White, R. H.
G/9685	Wells, F.	G/1987	White, W. E.
L/9611	Wells, F. C.	G/5454	White, W.
G/188	Wells, G. F.	L/9440	White, W. D.
G/18977	Wells, J. W.	L/9522	White, W. J.
L/8074	Wells, S. J.	S/10367	White, W. T.
G/1395	Welsh, W. F.	T/1167	Whitehead, A.
G/356	Welton, F. C.	G/11100	Whitehead, J.
L/8122	Wenban, F. H.	G/19030	Whitehead, L.
G/6366	Wenham, J.	G/11669	Whiteley, G.
G/8118	Wenman, A. H.	G/22145	Whiteman, W.
G/4129	Wenman, H.	G/12940	Whiting, C. A.
T/3071	West, B. G.	L/8811	Whittingham, C. E.
G/29256	West, C. W.	G/404	Whittingham, G.H.
G/70	West, E. F.	G/14889	Whittington, G. W.
G/25652	West, F. W.	G/3962	Whittington, H.
G/5613	Westbrook, W.	L/9347	Whyatt, S. A.
G/17392	Westlake, H. G. S.	S/334	Whybrow, W. J.

APPENDIX II

PRIVATES—(*continued*)

T/2103	Wickens, F.
L/10039	Wicker, H.
T/1160	Wickham, T. H.
G/20183	Wiffen, E.
G/2286	Wiffen, T.
G/2900	Wigg, G. A.
G/14557	Wigg, W.
T/204112	Wilber, T.
G/13959	Wilbraham, W. J.
G/8005	Wilcox, A. H.
G/12863	Wiles, A.
G/5721	Wiles, H.
G/2841	Wiles, L. W.
G/18677	Wiles, P. H.
G/1774	Wilkins, H.
L/8100	Wilkins, J.
G/6523	Wilkinson, E. W.
G/1124	Wilkinson, W. J.
G/308	Willard, J.
G/9030	Willard, M. W.
G/1551	Willard, R.
G/2227	Willett, H.
L/9323	Willey, C. F.
G/25565	Williams, A. J.
T/1422	Williams, B. J.
L/10316	Williams, C.
G/1087	Williams, C. D.
G/4178	Williams, E.
G/12719	Williams, E. A.
L/8974	Williams, E. C.
G/405	Williams, E. H.
G/21199	Williams, F. A.
G/20054	Williams, G.
T/206029	Williams, G.
S/249	Williams, H. E.
G/14256	Williams, J.
L/9961	Williams, J.
L/6049	Williams, J. A.
G/6504	Williams, P.

G/1107	Williams, T.
L/9690	Williams, T. D.
G/6834	Williams, W.
G/17477	Williams, W. C.
S/8322	Williams, W. G.
G/26567	Williams, W. S.
G/1664	Williamson, H.
G/40	Willis, H.
L/10511	Willis, J.
G/4676	Willis, T.
G/23944	Willis, T.
G/3955	Willis, W.
G/8917	Willmore, G. H.
G/18871	Willmott, F.
G/17407	Willoughby, L. J.
G/9020	Wilshire, C. E.
G/17	Wilson, A.
G/3445	Wilson, A.
G/1084	Wilson, A. E.
G/23943	Wilson, F. W.
G/29262	Wilson, H.
G/303	Wilson, H.
G/9888	Wilson, H.
G/6660	Wilson, H.
L/10605	Wilson, H. P.
G/5506	Wilson, H. W.
S/10777	Wilson, J. C.
G/17385	Wilson, R.
G/5671	Wilson, R. H.
G/4820	Wilson, S. H.
G/14565	Wilson, T.
G/11866	Wilson, W.
S/10848	Wiltshire, H. W.
L/10070	Winch, J.
G/13289	Winch, O. E.
G/1355	Winchcombe, A. J.
G/5247	Winchester, W. S.
G/5867	Winder, C.
G/7565	Winkley, J. R.

PRIVATES—(*continued*)

G/9558	Winson, L.	G/6788	Woodward, A.
G/6372	Winter, A. E.	S/216	Woodward, A. J.
G/7505	Winter, W.	S/10736	Woodward, B. J.
G/12573	Winterbottom, F.	G/14952	Woodward, F. J.
G/6522	Winterbottom, R.	G/1921	Woodward, H.
G/17676	Winterflood, W.	G/5606	Woodward, H. H.
G/21187	Wisbey, L.	L/8516	Woodwards, F. J.
L/8345	Wisdom, W.	G/15719	Woolf, J. W.
L/8239	Wise, W.	L/10385	Woolgar, C. M.
G/13611	Witch, P. C.	L/9956	Woollett, H.
G/22700	Wollett, E. E.	T/1411	Woollett, T.
G/13307	Wood, A. E.	G/8044	Woolley, W. H.
L/9065	Wood, A. H.	L/10502	Woolven, S.
L/9869	Wood, C. E.	G/14494	Woplin, J.
G/585	Wood, D.	G/20033	Worley, B. E.
G/5064	Wood, F.	G/1701	Wormald, S. O.
G/9388	Wood, H.	G/17470	Worman, A. A.
G/729	Wood, H.	G/987	Wormley, H.
G/1957	Wood, H. J.	T/240190	Worsley, C.
G/20839	Wood, H. T.	G/4302	Worster, D. E.
G/3718	Wood, J.	L/9071	Wotherspoon, A.W.
G/26440	Wood, L. A. G.	G/13383	Wraight, A. B.
G/8581	Wood, R. G.	S/352	Wraight, G. A.
L/9182	Wood, R.	L/6991	Wraight, W. G.
G/5541	Wood, T.	L/10046	Wraith, J. A.
S/341	Wood, W. C.	T/203618	Wratten, A.
G/8852	Wood, W. F.	G/5178	Wrench, G.
G/3940	Wood, W. H.	G/1065	Wretham, A.
G/14135	Wood, W. H.	S/10637	Wright, A.
S/10588	Wood, W. J.	L/7568	Wright, A. E.
G/48	Woodcock, E.	G/14580	Wright, E.
T/1132	Woodcock, N.	G/20021	Wright, E. V.
G/18926	Woodfield, W. C.	S/379	Wright, F. G.
G/1086	Woodhouse, R. W.	G/4661	Wright, F. W.
G/10135	Woodland, E.	L/7680	Wright, G. T.
G/15718	Woodland, H.	G/20908	Wright, H. C.
G/4086	Woodley, F.	S/420	Wright, H. H.
G/13180	Woodman, W. T.	G/29257	Wright, J.
G/323	Woods, E.	G/3204	Wright, J. G.

PRIVATES—*(continued)*

L/9101	Wright, R. L.	T/241546	Yates, J.
T/20061	Wright, T.	G/10373	York, A.
S/10468	Wright, W. G.	G/6088	Young, C. T.
G/1790	Wright, W. H.	G/3056	Young, F.
G/3355	Wyatt, G. E.	S/87	Young, F. G.
G/2849	Wyatt, W.	T/2427	Young, F. G.
G/1435	Wyborn, C. G.	G/6635	Young, H.
G/8930	Wyeth, J. T.	G/8160	Young, J.
G/7223	Wyett, H.	T/201043	Young, S. W. T.
		G/14287	Youngman, G.
G/13354	Yates, A. A.		
G/14031	Yates, A.	G/24721	Zealey, G.

APPENDIX III

REWARDS

ALL RANKS

(The ranks shown are those held at the time of award)

V.C.
Cotter, W. R., L.-Corpl., 6707.

K.C.B.
Bainbridge, Major-General E. G. T., C.B.
Lynden-Bell, Major-General Sir A. L., K.C.M.G., C.B.

C.B.
Hill, Lt.-Colonel H. C. de la M.
Lynden-Bell, Major-General A. L., C.M.G.
McDouall, Br.-General R., C.M.G., D.S.O.

K.C.M.G.
Lynden-Bell, Major-General A. L., C.B., C.M.G.

C.M.G.
Finch Hatton, Lt.-Colonel E. H., D.S.O.
Hulke, Lt.-Colonel L. I. B.
McDouall, Colonel R., D.S.O.
Porter, Br.-General C. 'L., D.S.O.
Vyvyan, Colonel Sir C. B., Bart., C.B.

C.H.
Perrott, Colonel Sir H. C., Bart., C.B.

C.B.E.
Findlay, Colonel H.
McDouall, Lt.-Colonel R., C.B., C.M.G., D.S.O.

APPENDIX III

D.S.O.

Barnard, Major W. G. F.
Beevor, Lt.-Colonel M.
Body, Captain J.

Chapman, Major G. A. E.
Crookenden, Major J.

Friend, Lt.-Colonel R. S. I.

Green, Lt.-Colonel H. W.
Groves-Raines, Captain
  R. G. D.

Hayfield, Captain C. D., M.C.

Kirkpatrick, Lt.-Colonel H. F.

Lee, Major G., M.C.
Lucas, Major L. W., M.C.

Marshall, Captain F. A. J. E.,
  M.C.
Morgan, Major, H. de R.

Porter, Br.-General C. 'L.
Potter, Captain H. B.
Power, Lt.-Colonel R. E.

Sebastian, Captain E. G.

Smeltzer, Lt.-Colonel A. S.,
  M.C.

Stronge, Lt.-Colonel H. C. T.,
  M.C.

Studd, Lt.-Colonel F. C. R.

Thewles, Lt.-Colonel H. A.

Trevor, Major W. H.

Whitmarsh, Captain A. J.

CLASP TO D.S.O.

Body, Lt.-Colonel J., D.S.O.

Kirkpatrick, Lt.-Colonel H. F., D.S.O.

Ransome, Lt.-Colonel A. L., D.S.O. (Dorsetshire Regt.).[1]

Smeltzer, Lt.-Colonel A. S., D.S.O., M.C.

SECOND CLASP TO D.S.O.

Curtis, Lt.-Colonel H. M. C., D.S.O. (6/N. Staffordshire
  Regt.).[1]

O.B.E.

Body, Lt.-Colonel J., D.S.O.
Booth, Major W. H., D.S.O.

Dixon, Captain G. S.

Eaton, Lt.-Colonel W. A.

Forwood, Major H., D.C.M.

Gosling, Lt.-Colonel G., T.D.

Messel, Lt.-Colonel L. C. R.,
  T.D.

Raikes, Lieut. W. O.

Ternan, Major H. A. B.

Trueman, Lt.-Colonel A.P.H.

Ward, Captain H. E.

---

[1] Both these officers won clasps to their D.S.O. whilst commanding
battalions of the Buffs.

APPENDIX III

M.B.E.

Barber, Lieut. L. W.
Beale, Captain G. S.
Corney, Lieut. A.
Cree, Captain H. F.
Filmer, Captain W. G. H.
Hardy, Major H. S., M.C.
Marshall, Lieut. F. A. J. E.,
    D.S.O., M.C.

Mockett, Captain V.
Munday, Lieut. W. T.
Silverwood-Cope, Captain
    A. L.
Thomson, Captain A. B.
Watson, Captain F. W.
Wilkins, Captain D. A.
Wilson, Lieut. C. E.

M.C.

Allen, Captain J. F. W.
Anderson, Captain D. K.
Anderson, 2nd Lieut. L.
Asprey, 2nd Lieut. P. R.
Aylward, Lieut. J. A. S.

Baldry, No. G/1851 C.S.M.
    P. W., M.M.
Barber, Lieut. L. W.
Beagley, 2nd Lieut. F. P.
Beswick, Captain A. H.
Birrell, Captain W. R.
Black, Captain C. K.
Bond, 2nd Lieut. H. G.
Bremner, Lieut. C. J.
Brice, Captain M. M.
Brock, Lieut. A. G.
Brown, 2nd Lieut. G.
Brown, 2nd Lieut. T. A.

Campbell, Captain D. S.
Caney, 2nd Lieut. C.
Carles, Captain C. W.
Carter, Captain E. A.
Cattley, Captain C. F.
Causton, Captain L. P.

Chapman, Lieut. C. M. B.
Chapman, Lieut. E. R.
Chater, 2nd Lieut. E. C.
Chilvers, 2nd Lieut. J. E.
(Christopherson, Rev. N. C.)
Church, 2nd Lieut. G. W.
Clapperton, Captain T.
Clarke, Lieut. A. H.
Clouting, 2nd Lieut. C. E.
Cockeram, 2nd Lieut. P. A.
Connell, Lieut. W. C.
Corrall, Captain W. R.
Cotching, 2nd Lieut. E. G.

Dangerfield, 2nd Lieut. P.
Darling, 2nd Lieut. W. H. J.
Davies, Captain B. E.
Davis, 2nd Lieut. W. C.
D'Elboux, Lieut. R. H.

Emery, Major T. S.

Farmer, 2nd Lieut. T. C.
Ferguson, 2nd Lieut. D. G.
Figgis, Lieut. L. P.
Fine, Captain H.
Fiske, Lieut. C. W.

APPENDIX III

REWARDS—M.C.—*(continued)*

Fox, 2nd Lieut. P. R. H.
Friend, Captain J. I. H.

Gerard, 2nd Lieut. G. V.
Gold, Lieut. H. A.
Grant, 2nd Lieut. D.
Gray, 2nd Lieut. W. R.
Greig, Lieut. P. H.
Griffiths, 2nd Lieut. F. H.
Gullick, Captain C. D.
Gunther, 2nd Lieut. N. O. F.

Hale, Lieut. F. W.
Hall, 2nd Lieut. E. Foster.
Hamilton, Lieut. G. F.
Hanmer, 2nd Lieut. A. J.
Hardy, Captain H. S.
Harrison, No. 8798 C.S.M. A.
Hatfield, Captain C. E.
Haughton, Lieut. M. G.
Hawkins, No. 2948 R.S.M. A.
Hayfield, 2nd Lieut. C. D.
Hendin, 2nd Lieut. D. W.
Hicks, 2nd Lieut. P.
Holder, Lieut. F. D.
Hollis, 2nd Lieut. C. F. G.
Howcroft, Lieut. G. J.
Howgrave-Graham, Captain
   A. H.
Hudson, 2nd Lieut. F. N.
Hughes, 2nd Lieut. J. H.
Hunter, Captain H.

Jacobs, Lieut. B.
Jacobs, Lieut. I. A.
Jeffrey, No. S/191 S.-M. W.
Jessel, Lieut. G.
Johnston, Captain W. T.
Jones, 2nd Lieut. G. M.
Jones, 2nd Lieut. H. L.

Kenchington, Captain A. G.
Keown, Lieut. R. W.
Kidd, Lieut. L. G. M.

Laverton, Captain W. R. C.
Lawrence, 2nd Lieut. W. B.
Lee, Captain G.
Liles, 2nd Lieut. R. W.
Lilley, 2nd Lieut. A. A.
Lindley, Lieut. G.
Lister, 2nd Lieut. D. S.
Lucas, Captain L. W.

McCallum, Lieut. A.
Macfadyen, Lieut. W. A.
Marchant, Captain F. O.
Marchant, 2nd Lieut. S. H. S.
Marshall, Lieut. F. A. J. E.
Mason-Springgay, 2nd Lieut.
   W. H.
Mathias, 2nd Lieut. C. A. S.
Maxted, No. 141 C.S.M. G.W.
Milles, Lieut. H. L.
Mitchell, Lieut. H. V.
Morley, 2nd Lieut. H. L.
Morrell, Captain F. A.
Morse, 2nd Lieut. E. V.
Moss, Lieut. V. Newton

Nicholas, Captain W. L. J.
Nicholson, 2nd Lieut. A. C. L.

Page, Captain J. C.
Pannell, 2nd Lieut. H.
Parnis, Lieut. W. H.
Peake, Captain W.
Peckham, Lieut. G. H.
Piper, Lieut. J. D.
Pritchard, No. 635 C.S.M.
   W. J.
Prothero, Captain L. E. A.

APPENDIX III

Ralph, No. 6170 C.S.M. E.W.
Reader, 2nd Lieut. C. H. A.
Reid, Lieut. T. R.
Routley, 2nd Lieut. E. G.

Sandilands, Captain R. B.
Sankey, 2nd Lieut. C. M.
Scarlett, Captain Hon. P. G.
Shafto, 2nd Lieut. J. S. H.
Shaw-Lawrence, 2nd Lieut. L. E.
Sherwill, 2nd Lieut. A. J.
Smeltzer, 2nd Lieut. A. S.
Spence, Captain F. A.
Stainforth, Captain A. G. C.
Stevens, 2nd Lieut. E. A. M.
Stevens, 2nd Lieut. G. E. W.
Stevens, Lieut. H. F.
Stevens, 2nd Lieut. W. T.
Strauss, Captain B. L.
Stronge, Captain H. C. T.

Tatam, 2nd Lieut. V. G. H.
Temple, 2nd Lieut. W. H.

Thornhill, Lieut. G. R.
Thornley, 2nd Lieut. J. D.
Toynbee, Lieut. J. W. H.
Tupper, 2nd Lieut. H.
Turk, 2nd Lieut. J.
Tyrrell, Captain G. Y.

Vaughan, 2nd Lieut. J.
Vertue, Captain N. G.

Walters, 2nd Lieut. W. M.
Weare, Captain F. G. C.
Wellman, Lieut. R. S.
Whitaker, Captain F.
Whitmarsh, Captain A. J., D.S.O.
Wilkinson, 2nd Lieut. F. D.
Williams, 2nd Lieut. W. T.
Willis, Lieut. L. C.
Wood, Captain C. J.
Wood, Captain Ll.
Worster, 2nd Lieut. A. F.
Wort, Captain P. C.
Wray, 2nd Lieut. A. M.
Wyatt, 2nd Lieut. M. J.

CLASP TO M.C.

Black, Captain C. K., M.C.
Gullick, Captain C. D., M.C.
Hamilton, Captain G. F., M.C.
Hayfield, Lieut. C. D., M.C.
Jacobs, Captain B., M.C.
Kidd, Captain L. G. M., M.C.
McCallum, Captain A., M.C.

Morrell, Captain F. A., M.C.
Moss, Captain V. Newton, M.C.
Nicholson, Captain A. C. L., M.C.
Toynbee, Captain J. W. H., M.C.
Tupper, Lieut. H., M.C.
Worster, 2nd Lieut. A. F., M.C.

SECOND CLASP TO M.C.

Hayfield, Captain C. D., M.C.
Nicholson, Captain A. C. L., M.C.

APPENDIX III

D.C.M.

NAME.	RANK.	REGTL. NO.
Adams, J. T.	L.-Corpl.	135
Amos, E. T.	Pte.	9904
Andrews, A. W.	R.S.M.	L/7051
Ashby, F.	C.S.M.	G/15767
Atkinson, J.	Pte.	240261
Avis, H. J.	Corpl.	1519
Ayres, A. J.	Sgt.	G/6884
Bacon, F. N.	Sgt.	G/3494
Baker, F.	Sgt.	8781
Barrell, G., M.S.M.	C.S.M.	L/9036
Barton, L. R. W.	Pte.	200105
Batchelor, C. C., M.M.	Sgt.	G/3377
Bigg, W. J.	L.-Sergt.	L/8893
Bloomfield, F.	Pte.	10017
Bridges, F.	Pte.	1153
Brooker, J. G.	C.S.M.	511
Brown, A.	C.S.M.	8021
Bugg, J. W.	Pte.	18980
Burt, W.	C.Q.M.S.	3635
Butler, W.	Sgt.	5148
Carey, F. W., M.M.	L.-Corpl.	5800
Carpenter, J.	C.S.M.	6541
Caselton, T. G.	C.S.M.	G/1940
Chapman, A. H. R.	L.-Sergt.	2258
Coffin, W.	C.S.M.	G/1985
Coleman, A. C., M.M., M.S.M.	Pte.	1898
Cooper, H.	Pte.	7636
Court, E. J. T.	Sgt.	8999
Crame, C. J.	L.-Corpl.	G/3301
Dennis, G. W.	Corpl.	9038
Dines, D. W.	R.S.M.	5957

REWARDS—D.C.M.—(*continued*)

NAME.	RANK.	REGTL. NO.
Field, W. J.	C.S.M.	8213
Forwood, H.	Sgt.	8560
France, M., M.M.	Sgt.	G/12873
Geoghegan, J.	L.-Corpl.	4659
Gettins, F.	L.-Sergt.	1663
Goldfinch, A. H.	Sgt.	L/8205
Gurney, A.	Pte.	241138
Hall, E.	Pte.	9051
Hall, F.	L.-Corpl.	242905
Hamer, T.	Sgt.	4267
Hickson, H. C.	C.S.M.	242779
Hoddinott, H. H.	Pte.	243
Hodges, F.	Pte.	10464
Jagger, J. J.	L.-Corpl.	242907
Joy, H.	Sgt.	983
Keal, A. C.	Corpl.	3591
Lawrence, H. J.	C.S.M.	241496
Lever, H.	Sgt.	206086
Luck, G.	L.-Corpl.	452
Lucy, S.	L.-Corpl.	8077
McDonough, W. H.	C.S.M.	9074
McNeir, J. M.	Sgt.	8922
MacWalter, C. C.	L.-Sergt.	8669
MacWalter, J. R., M.M.	Sgt.	9682
Marsh, A.	Corpl.	9603
Mason, L., M.M.	Pte.	G/4269
Mitchell, A.	Pte.	206128
Mordey, P.	Corpl.	8777
Neve, G. S.	L.-Corpl.	8740
Newham, M. H.	C.S.M.	241481
Newman, H. J.	L.-Corpl.	L/8801
Norrington, V.	Corpl.	G/4202

REWARDS—D.C.M.—(*continued*)

NAME.	RANK.	REGTL. NO.
Ongley, A. V.	Corpl.	9905
Page, R. E.	C.S.M.	5777
Parsons, J.	Pte.	G/1295
Pass, W. W.	Sgt.	L/8270
Payne, C.	Sgt.	200597
Peet, S. T.	Pte.	3265
Pellandine, P. N. L.	Corpl.	1341
Pells, T. R.	Sgt.	1433
Peters, W.	C.S.M.	201277
Phillips, H. T.	Sgt.	1022
Poole, J. T., M.M.	C.S.M.	L/9405
Port, E. G.	C.S.M.	6605
Randall, S.	C.S.M.	9703
Reed, W., M.M.	C.S.M.	G/1147
Robinson, H. S.	L.-Corpl.	1542
St. John, F. R.	Sgt.	1111
Saunders, A. J.	C.S.M.	L/6243
Sheward, A.	Pte.	S/10800
Simkins, F. C.	L.-Corpl.	1723
Simmons, A. C.	Corpl.	9239
Smith, J., M.M.	L.-Corpl.	G/3961
Smith, V. R.	Sgt.	8926
Smith, W.	Pte.	5589
Souster, A.	L.-Sergt.	L/7613
Spiller, W. C., M.M.	L.-Sergt.	9872
Spurgeon, C.	Pte.	1402
Steel, G. J.	L.-Sergt.	3620
Stewart, T. G.	Sgt.	G/2542
Streat, W. J.	Pte.	5277
Swinyard, G. A.	Sgt.	240072
Tamblin, W. H.	Corpl.	957
Thorne, E. P.	Pte.	1667
Tritton, G. A.	Corpl.	4545
Turner, D. G.	Sgt.	27052

APPENDIX III

REWARDS—D.C.M.—(*continued*)

NAME.	RANK.	REGTL. NO.
Upton, P. C.	Sgt.	G/2561
Vincer, P. A., M.M.	C.S.M.	7967
Waby, R. W.	Sgt.	G/3424
Westwood, J.	Pte.	2432
Wickington, H. G., M.M.	C.Q.M.S.	G/1300
Wilson, S.	Pte.	L/8827
Woodhams, H.	Sgt.	G/9884
Wright, H. C.	C.S.M.	5781

CLASP TO D.C.M.

Wright, H. C.	C.S.M.	5781

MILITARY MEDAL

Abbott, B. E. J. C. P.	Pte.	G/22354
Abbott, J. T.	Pte.	2440
Admans, S. A.	L.-Corpl.	4217
Akers, B. J.	L.-Corpl.	6556
Alexander, D.	L.-Corpl.	8907
Alexander, F. P.	Pte.	G/15501
Allbright, T.	L.-Corpl.	G/26624
Allen, E.	Pte.	G/13261
Allen, G. E.	Pte.	799
Allen, R. T.	Corpl.	26591
Alsing, H.	L.-Sergt.	1088
Ambers, F. D.	L.-Corpl.	G/1419
Anderson, A. A.	L.-Corpl.	G/540
Anderson, G. H.	Pte.	883
Andrews, W.	Corpl.	12943
Arman, W.	Pte.	12980
Ashby, F., D.C.M.	C.S.M.	G/15767
Ashdown, C.	Pte.	5855
Ashton, O.	Sgt.	6003
Ashwell, W. E.	Sgt.	G/855
Atkinson, E. T.	Pte.	1513
Austin, C. J.	L.-Corpl.	12355
Ayres, A. J., D.C.M.	Sgt.	6884

512

APPENDIX III

REWARDS—M.M.—(continued)

NAME.	RANK.	REGTL. NO.
Baines, W.	Pte.	10950
Baker, F. G.	Pte.	8943
Baker, J. W.	Pte.	10932
Baldry, P. W.	Sgt.	1851
Barge, L.	Pte.	1780
Barham, A.	L.-Corpl.	20125
Barker, H. B.	Sgt.	9577
Barnes, A. E.	Pte.	G/14040
Barrett, A. J.	Sgt.	340
Barrett, F. R.	L.-Corpl.	8343
Bartlett, W.	L.-Sergt.	G/11422
Barton, C.	Pte.	1036
Batchelor, C. C.	Corpl.	3377
Batchelor, J. G. B.	Sgt.	1373
Beaumont, G.	Pte.	2531
Bedford, S. V.	Pte.	G/14671
Bellchambers, F. J.	Pte.	G/8018
Beresford, T. M.	L.-Corpl.	20203
Berry, G. E.	Pte.	3237
Beslee, L.	Corpl.	G/2649
Best, W.	Pte.	242088
Bethell, A.	Pte.	1677
Betts, J. P.	Pte.	270991
Betts, L. J.	Sgt.	270760
Bevan, G.	Pte.	9364
Bignell, F.	Pte.	5263
Bing, L.	Sgt.	707
Birchett, G. E.	Pte.	9650
Black, J.	Pte.	5936
Blackford, J. H.	Pte.	G/14241
Blackshaw, B.	Pte.	7564
Blake, E. W.	L.-Corpl.	L/8588
Bloomfield, J.	Sgt.	L/8917
Boarer, W.	Pte.	21069
Bolden, H.	L.-Sergt.	1650
Bones, J. R.	C.S.M.	L/8522
Bones, W.	Corpl.	15553
Bosely, P. H.	Pte.	8229

APPENDIX III

REWARDS—M.M.—(*continued*)

NAME.	RANK.	REGTL. NO.
Bourner, G.	L.-Corpl.	8973
Bradley, A.	Pte.	9399
Brazier, L. F.	Pte.	G/22060
Brenchley, G.	Pte.	2652
Bridger, A.	Pte.	17685
Brisley, A. T.	Pte.	270125
Broadhurst, J.	Pte.	G/14592
Brookman, A. T.	Cpl.	G/15503
Brooks, G. R.	Pte.	8385
Brown, H.	Pte.	G/22360
Brown, W.	Pte.	G/1411
Browne, G.	L.-Sergt.	3232
Browning, A.	Pte.	959
Brownrigg, P. D.	Corpl.	6593
Brunger, W. T.	Sgt.	781
Bullen, G. S.	Pte.	21227
Burden, C. C.	Sgt.	L/8220
Bushell, F. E. F.	Pte.	15564
Bushell, P. C.	Pte.	2130
Buss, F.	Sgt.	9981
Bussell, C. W.	L.-Corpl.	G/20197
Buxton, E.	L.-Sergt.	G/1243
Buzzard, J.	L.-Corpl.	1838
Cain, J. C.	L.-Corpl.	G/2137
Caldwell, K.	Pte.	G/6770
Caley, B.	L.-Sergt.	G/7949
Callaghan, A. V.	Sgt.	8181
Carey, A. V.	L.-Corpl.	G/15855
Carey, F. W.	L.-Corpl.	5800
Carlin, J.	Corpl.	L/10559
Carpenter, F.	L.-Corpl.	G/5501
Carr, J., M.S.M.	Sgt.	L/8908
Caselton, T. G., D.C.M.	C.S.M.	G/1490
Cheshire, C. E.	Sgt.	270743
Child, A. E.	L.-Corpl.	G/6696
Chivers, F.	Pte.	8551
Clark, A.	Pte.	G/1975

APPENDIX III

REWARDS—M.M.—(continued)

NAME.	RANK.	REGTL. NO.
Clements, C. W.	Corpl.	S/9983
Cochrane, G.	L.-Corpl.	6364
Coleman, A. C.	Pte.	1898
Colley, J.	Corpl.	6984
Colley, W.	Pte.	S/8555
Collins, H. H.	L.-Corpl.	G/17393
Condray, T. B.	Corpl.	6634
Cook, F. W.	Pte.	G/12814
Cook, W. F.	Pte.	G/8510
Cornell, W.	Pte.	10769
Cotton, G. S.	Corpl.	G/979
Cotton, W. R.	L.-Corpl.	G/2727
County, S. W.	Pte.	201544
Coxall, W. E.	Pte.	11937
Creasey, F. W. J.	Corpl.	G/1459
Cremer, A. H.	Corpl.	G/7649
Croft, W. J.	Pte.	S/9428
Cross, J.	Sgt.	9339
Cude, R.	Pte.	G/2192
Cullen, A.	L.-Corpl.	8407
Curd, S. P.	L.-Corpl.	9623
Curling, J.	Corpl.	G/13003
Daniel, N.	Pte.	2622
Daniells, F. W.	L.-Corpl.	G/1162
Davis, J. W.	Pte.	1886
Davis, W. S.	C.S.M.	8385
Dennett, G. C. C.	Pte.	271029
Denny, W.	Sgt.	6812
Denton, W. W.	Sgt.	270122
Dier, F. J.	Pte.	270082
Dockerill, L. T.	Pte.	G/21070
Doddington, T.	Pte.	G/11225
Downes, E.	Pte.	10019
Dowse, E.	Sgt.	11008
Draper, A.	Pte.	5299
Duff, W. G.	Corpl.	5995
Dunn, W. A. H.	Corpl.	270227

REWARDS—M.M.—*(continued)*

NAME.	RANK.	REGTL. NO.
Dunning, G.	Pte.	1626
Dykes, H.	L.-Corpl.	G/19175
Earl, F.	L.-Corpl.	9822
Edwards, W. A.	Sgt.	8512
Eldridge, E. G.	Pte.	9979
Ellen, A.	Pte.	8800
Elliott, E.	Pte.	L/6769
Ellis, T. F.	Pte.	G/25331
Elliss, F. H.	L.-Corpl.	573
Elsey, T.	L.-Corpl.	265246
Elson, A.	Pte.	1712
Elson, F.	Sgt.	4709
English, R. T.	Sgt.	L/9927
Ericksen, A. B.	Pte.	204252
Evans, F. C.	Sgt.	8155
Farmer, H. T.	Pte.	G/25191
Farrier, W. J.	Sgt.	G/13562
Feaver, S. S.	Corpl.	9609
Finnis, A. W. M.	Pte.	8500
Fisher, A. W.	Sgt.	G/2331
Flight, P. T.	Pte.	5575
Flowers, C.	L.-Corpl.	G/7339
Folley, C. A.	Pte.	G/11896
Forscott, H. A.	Pte.	21092
Fox, A. H.	Sgt.	35
France, W.	Sgt.	G/12873
Franks, A. J.	Pte.	5568
Friend, T. J.	Pte.	3681
Fuller, E.	Pte.	3214
Fullerton, A.	Pte.	G/1448
Gafney, A.	Sgt.	1298
Galloway, G. H.	Sgt.	G/11537
Gambell, H. D.	Pte.	6063
Gardiner, W.	Pte.	2723
Garlinge, W. J.	Pte.	5196

APPENDIX III

REWARDS—M.M.—(*continued*)

NAME.	RANK.	REGTL. NG.
Gasking, E. A.	Pte.	G/9461
Gavin, T. A.	Pte.	20
Gee, A. W.	Corpl.	G/14608
George, F. I.	Sgt.	G/1146
Gingell, A. H.	Pte.	G/14750
Goddard, H.	Pte.	2604
Godden, A.	Pte.	G/13650
Goldfarb, C.	Pte.	G/25211
Goodall, T. B.	Sgt.	L/8066
Gosden, A.	Sgt.	G/22475
Green, H.	L.-Corpl.	12740
Green, M. E.	L.-Corpl.	3529
Gundlach, R. T.	L.-Corpl.	G/639
Hale, B. G.	Pte.	24233
Hall, C. S.	Pte.	5272
Halliday, C. A.	Pte.	13898
Hammond, C.	Sgt.	3258
Hammond, H.	Pte.	13052
Hanlon, H.	Pte.	26625
Hann, A. J.	Pte.	206153
Hardie, F.	Pte.	7697
Hardiman, E. G.	Pte.	G/15610
Harman, G.	Pte.	G/13047
Harman, G. W.	L.-Sergt.	G/7855
Harrigan, J.	Pte.	S/8104
Harris, A. J.	Sgt.	L/9771
Harris, E.	Pte.	26632
Harris, W. O.	L.-Corpl.	3245
Harrison, J.	Pte.	G/14716
Hart, R. S.	Pte.	3111
Harwood, A.	Sgt.	277
Haskell, L. V.	Corpl.	8693
Hawkins, P.	Corpl.	5269
Hay, J. W.	Pte.	243155
Heathfield, S.	Pte.	8836
Hewett, W. C. H.	Corpl.	203636
Hibbs, H. G.	Pte.	270665

REWARDS—M.M.—(*continued*)

NAME.	RANK.	REGTL. NO.
Hierons, R. L.	Pte.	G/5696
Higgins, C.	Pte.	4206
Higgins, J.	Pte.	2825
Highton, H.	Pte.	13906
Hills, F.	Sgt.	L/9407
Hills, W. G.	Corpl.	7626
Hinkley, S. H.	Corpl.	L/8599
Hinton, P. H.	Pte.	271039
Histed, W. C.	Pte.	8498
Hoare, W. J.	Pte.	8293
Hobbs, W.	Pte.	G/13045
Holloway, G. R.	Sgt.	L/8120
Holman, E.	L.-Sergt.	G/3115
Holman, E. W.	Sgt.	206
Hook, J. T.	L.-Corpl.	G/9425
Hook, W.	Pte.	18754
Hope, H.	Pte.	12540
Horton, J.	Corpl.	9937
Howard, F.	Corpl.	5048
Howard, H.	Sgt.	9088
Hubberstey, R.	Sgt.	1659
Huckstepp, W. H.	L.-Corpl.	G/2810
Hudson, E. W.	Pte.	2598
Hughes, A.	Pte.	336
Hughes, C. G.	Pte.	271040
Hunt, J. W.	Pte.	6076
Hutchison, M. W.	L.-Corpl.	G/25367
Hyde, A.	L.-Corpl.	1889
Ielden, R. C.	L.-Corpl.	1767
Imber, R.	Pte.	1710
Impett, S. A.	Corpl.	G/420
Istead, E. J.	L.-Corpl.	G/6383
James, A. C.	L.-Corpl.	20014
Jamieson, G.	Pte.	9909
Jarman, W. T.	Pte.	2822
Jarrett, W.	L.-Corpl.	3430

APPENDIX III

REWARDS—M.M.—(*continued*)

NAME.	RANK.	REGTL. NO.
Jarvis, W.	Pte.	7969
Jenkins, F. J.	Sgt.	L/9928
Jenner, D. P.	Corpl.	1074
Jenrick, G. W.	Pte.	7655
Johnson, A.	Corpl.	G/18520
Johnson, S.	Pte.	13900
Jones, A. C.	Pte.	10277
Jones, C.	Pte.	58149
Jones, G.	Pte.	11303
Jordan, C.	Pte.	714
Justice, C.	Pte.	5266
Keats, A.	L.-Corpl.	15632
Keen, G. A.	Pte.	S/10420
Kempton, A. E.	L.-Corpl.	G/15633
Kennett, A. E.	Pte.	2152
Kerman, F.	Pte.	8066
Kibble, T. W.	L.-Corpl.	G/7707
Kingsford, W.	Pte.	616
Kingsnorth, W. F.	Corpl.	376702
Kitchingman, L. C.	L.-Corpl.	8947
Kite, W. R.	Pte.	270458
Knappett, C. H.	Sgt.	G/1480
Knight, A.	L.-Corpl.	9127
Knight, A. E.	Pte.	11792
Knight, C. J.	Sgt.	2319
Lake, G.	Pte.	2005
Landen, A.	Corpl.	204566
Lane, W. A.	Pte.	10885
Langley, C. E.	Pte.	5321
Langton, W.	Sgt.	9637
Latter, W. G.	Sgt.	G/4092
Lawrence, H. W.	Sgt.	265241
Lawrence, J. T.	Pte.	1872
Leech, W. H. B.	Pte.	G/13061
Lockwood, J.	Sgt.	3151
Loram, W. H.	Sgt.	8973

REWARDS—M.M.—*(continued)*

NAME.	RANK.	REGTL. NO.
Lovesey, C.	Pte.	21103
Luchford, A.	Pte.	1038
McDonald, A.	Pte.	3894
Macdonald, A. A.	Pte.	G/8208
McGregor, J. C.	Sgt.	206088
Mack, E. F.	Pte.	8023
McNeir, G. A.	Sgt.	L/10011
MacWalter, J. R.	Sgt.	9682
Malcolm, J. A.	L.-Corpl.	G/653
Maloney, A.	Corpl.	434
Marsh, C. A.	Pte.	1871
Marsh, J. W.	Pte.	6732
Martin, G.	Pte.	6600
Martin, W.	Pte.	8782
Mason, L.	Pte.	G/4269
Mather, A.	Pte.	270753
Matthews, F.	L.-Sergt.	G/1665
May, W.	Pte.	L/8219
Medgett, A.	Sgt.	220
Melrose, D. O.	Pte.	270630
Millen, E. F.	Corpl.	240941
Miller, H.	Pte.	555
Miller, J.	Corpl.	203589
Millington, H. J.	Pte.	7897
Minns, H. F.	Pte.	7846
Moorcock, F. C.	Sgt.	1349
Moore, N.	Sgt.	3673
Morey, E. L.	Sgt.	L/7083
Morgan, J. W. W.	Sgt.	L/9191
Morris, C. J.	Pte.	26650
Morrow, F.	Pte.	G/2169
Moss, A. J.	Pte.	8079
Mount, W. A.	Corpl.	L/10082
Murdoch, A. J.	Sgt.	6174
Mutton, C. J.	L.-Corpl.	6908
Myers, W. J.	Pte.	3652

REWARDS—M.M.—*(continued)*

NAME.	RANK.	REGTL. NO.
Nash, G. H.	Sgt.	19121
Nevard, A.	C.S.M.	3229
Neville, H. W.	Sgt.	269
Newell, F. G.	L.-Corpl.	G/14460
North, H.	Pte.	5886
Odell, E. F.	Sgt.	G/1232
Oliver, J.	Corpl.	G/6233
O'Rourke, J.	Corpl.	G/1478
Ottaway, C. J.	Pte.	2506
Ozenbrook, J. W.	Pte.	G/23606
Page, F. T.	Corpl.	9934
Page, G. A.	Sgt.	9801
Palmer, L. P.	Pte.	G/17438
Park, D.	Pte.	8422
Parker, F. W.	L.-Corpl.	G/498
Parrott, G. F.	Pte.	5432
Payne, E. J.	Pte.	G/3461
Peach, A. J.	L.-Corpl.	22412
Pearce, H.	Sgt.	6494
Peattie, F.	Sgt.	6470
Peerless, V.	L.-Corpl.	6316
Penfold, J.	Corpl.	G/12663
Pennell, R. H.	Sgt.	G/18563
Phillips, J.	Pte.	8116
Phillips, J. A.	L.-Corpl.	6486
Phillpott, D.	Pte.	7944
Pickering, H.	Pte.	G/19129
Pickford, R. E.	Pte.	G/17441
Platts, A.	L.-Corpl.	6779
Poole, J. T.	Sgt.	9405
Port, C. W.	Corpl.	7851
Potter, A. G.	Sgt.	1054
Powdrill, T. B.	Pte.	202928
Powell, E. A.	L.-Corpl.	G/1589
Pragnell, W. J.	Corpl.	G/13306
Prebble, F. R.	L.-Corpl.	G/659

APPENDIX III

REWARDS—M.M.—*(continued)*

NAME.	RANK.	REGTL. NO.
Price, W.	Pte.	G/9956
Purkiss, W.	Pte.	990
Rainford, J.	Pte.	G/375
Rainsbury, C.	L.-Corpl.	242321
Rand, F. C.	Sgt.	L/10038
Randall, T. E.	Sgt.	9703
Ratti, R. A. G.	Corpl.	20243
Ravenscroft, F.	Corpl.	1731
Rayner, F. W.	L.-Corpl.	G/9320
Reed, W. W.	Sgt.	G/1147
Reeves, J.	Corpl.	13068
Reynolds, A. W.	Pte.	2773
Richards, G. T.	Corpl.	6625
Richards, J. H.	Corpl.	10478
Richardson, W.	L.-Corpl.	G/23924
Ride, S. E.	Pte.	265245
Roady, T. J.	Pte.	8303
Roberts, A. B.	Pte.	8935
Roberts, B. R.	Pte.	1666
Rose, H.	L.-Corpl.	4329
Rose, W. C.	Corpl.	4741
Ross, A. G.	Sgt.	2260
Rowland, C.	Corpl.	15674
Rudman, J. B.	Sgt.	270221
Russell, E. M.	Sgt.	L/9075
Sage, W. C.	Pte.	12715
Saunders, G. E.	Pte.	10292
Saunders, H.	Pte.	G/17456
Schofield, F. B.	L.-Corpl.	G/23929
Scott, C. W.	Pte.	270928
Scott, H.	Pte.	270269
Scott, S.	Pte.	7767
Scrivener, F.	Pte.	10105
Seager, R.	Pte.	15681
Searle, J. V.	Pte.	12880
Seath, S.	Pte.	148

REWARDS—M.M.—(*continued*)

NAME.	RANK.	REGTL. NO.
Setchfield, E.	Pte.	G/23611
Setterfield, A. V.	L.-Corpl.	347
Setterfield, J. E.	Pte.	5456
Setterfield, W.	Pte.	10
Shackcloth, E.	Pte.	G/22266
Sharp, T.	Pte.	874
Sharp, W. J.	Pte.	G/26582
Shaw, T.	Pte.	5394
Sheen, C.	L.-Corpl.	6919
Shelley, W. J.	Sgt.	240668
Sidwell, F.	Pte.	L/10660
Sindon, G.	Corpl.	8891
Smith, F. W.	Sgt.	5705
Smith, H.	Pte.	7628
Smith, H. D.	Pte.	G/24040
Smith, J.	Sgt.	S/R11074
Smith, J. H.	Pte.	G/3961
Smithers, E. G.	Pte.	G/22478
Smurthwaite, J. T.	Sgt.	206148
Snook, C.	Pte.	13248
Soulsby, J. C.	Corpl.	G/14914
Spalding, R.	Pte.	2778
Spark, J. G.	Sgt.	G/13170
Spenceley, F. V.	Pte.	728
Spiller, W. C.	Sgt.	9872
Stapley, B. J.	Pte.	203963
Steed, A.	Pte.	G/597
Steeting, R.	L.-Corpl.	18687
Stevens, A. E.	L.-Corpl.	5268
Stevenson, G. E.	Pte.	1489
Stevenson, M.	Pte.	896
Stobart, T. W.	Pte.	265341
Stone, T. G.	Pte.	203492
Streat, C.	Pte.	10486
Stuart, J. F.	Corpl.	10026
Swain, F. G.	Pte.	17610
Swaine, H. F.	L.-Corpl.	20162

APPENDIX III

NAME.	RANK.	REGTL. NO.
Tamblin, W. H., D.C.M.	Corpl.	957
Tapley, E.	Pte.	G/26557
Taylor, B.	L.-Corpl.	5233
Thirkettle, J.	Pte.	2839
Thomas, M. L.	Corpl.	241641
Thompson, G.	Pte.	20966
Thompson, J.	Corpl.	G/3354
Tidcombe, H. J.	Pte.	265063
Tidey, J. S.	Pte.	G/8988
Tillier, S. V.	Pte.	G/24274
Timmins, W.	Corpl.	270040
Tinmouth, F.	L.-Corpl.	5429
Todd, F.	Sgt.	8277
Todman, J.	L.-Corpl.	G/23935
Towersey, J. T. H.	Pte.	G/13382
Treadaway, A. E.	Pte.	G/17401
Tress, W. G.	Sgt.	4455
Trew, E. C.	Pte.	42015
Trigg, W. J.	Sgt.	9435
Turner, J.	L.-Corpl.	S/R10695
Twelftree, A. T.	L.-Sergt.	851
Tyler, H. N.	Pte.	32566
Viggers, J.	Sgt.	6163
Vincer, P. A.	C.Q.M.S.	7967
Voyle, J. H.	L.-Corpl.	42440
Waby, R. W., D.C.M.	L.-Sergt.	G/3424
Wakeham, S. W.	L.-Corpl.	G/673
Walker, A. E.	L.-Corpl.	G/4076
Wall, W. J.	Corpl.	260
Wallace, R.	L.-Sergt.	25149
Walters, C.	Pte.	G/2269
Walters, H.	Pte.	G/14568
Warner, W. J.	L.-Corpl.	10482
Watkins, J.	Pte.	814
Watts, F. G.	Corpl.	L/8717
Webb, H. R.	Corpl.	270814

APPENDIX III

REWARDS—M.M.—(*continued*)

NAME.	RANK.	REGTL. NO.
Whall, R.	L.-Corpl.	2279
Whiddett, G.	Pte.	G/4929
Whipps, A.	Sgt.	G/3569
Whiskin, E. W.	Pte.	G/6031
White, W. A.	L.-Corpl.	2248
Wicken, P. C.	Pte.	G/12941
Wickett, S.	L.-Corpl.	G/13991
Wickington, H. G.	Corpl.	G/1300
Wiles, G. A.	Pte.	270212
Willcocks, P. R.	Pte.	421
Williams, F. J.	Corpl.	L/10246
Williams, J.	Pte.	G/21464
Willis, A. W.	Pte.	270872
Willis, C. W.	L.-Corpl.	5092
Wilson, S., D.C.M.	Pte.	L/8827
Wire, H.	L.-Corpl.	15714
Wise, D. W.	L.-Corpl.	3710
Wise, W.	Pte.	G/2504
Wood, A.	Sgt.	9817
Wood, E. C.	L.-Corpl.	10059
Wood, H. H.	L.-Corpl.	G/11670
Woodcock, J.	Pte.	G/42
Wraight, H.	Pte.	G/2509
Wren, W. H.	Corpl.	6635
Wright, G.	Pte.	G/20179
Wright, G. F. E.	Sgt.	12521
Wright, J.	Pte.	G/6329
Wykes, F. H.	L.-Corpl.	G/5587
Wynne, A.	Pte.	10760
Wynne, T. W.	Sgt.	10652

CLASP TO MILITARY MEDAL

Alexander, F. P., M.M.	Pte.	G/15501
Ashwell, W. E., M.M.	Sgt.	G/855
Barton, C., M.M.	L.-Corpl.	1036
Bellchambers, E. J., M.M.	Pte.	G/8018

APPENDIX III

REWARDS—CLASP TO M.M.—(*continued*)

NAME.	RANK.	REGTL. NO.
Berry, G. F., M.M.	L.-Corpl.	3237
Bloomfield, J., M.M.	Sgt.	L/8917
Browne, G., M.M.	Sgt.	3232
Cremer, A. H., M.M.	Corpl.	G/7649
Cude, R., M.M.	Pte.	G/2192
Dockerill, L. T., M.M.	Corpl.	G/21070
Farmer, H. T., M.M.	Pte.	G/25191
Galloway, G. H., M.M.	Sgt.	G/11537
Goodall, T. B., M.M.	Sgt.	L/8066
Hardiman, E. G., M.M.	Pte.	G/15610
Harris, W. O., M.M.	Corpl.	3245
Holloway, G. R., M.M.	Sgt.	L/8120
Impett, S. A., M.M.	Sgt.	G/420
Kingsford, W., M.M.	Sgt.	616
Macdonald, A. A., M.M.	L.-Corpl.	G/8208
Mason, L., D.C.M., M.M.	Pte.	G/4269
Parker, F. W., M.M.	Pte.	G/498
Pickering, H., M.M.	Pte.	G/19129
Purkiss, W., M.M.	Pte.	990
Rainsbury, C., M.M.	Corpl.	242321
Reeves, J., M.M.	Sgt.	13068
Reynolds, A. W., M.M.	Pte.	2773
Setterfield, W., M.M.	Sgt.	10
Smith, C., M.M.	L.-Corpl.	14635
Smith, J., M.M.	C.S.M.	S/R11074
Spenceley, F. V., M.M.	L.-Corpl.	728
Stapley, B. J., M.M.	Pte.	203963

526

APPENDIX III

REWARDS—CLASP TO M.M.—(continued)

NAME.	RANK.	REGTL. NO.
Stuart, J. F., M.M.	L.-Sergt.	10026
Swaine, H. F., M.M.	Sgt.	20162
Tapley, E., M.M.	Pte.	G/26557
Wilson, S., D.C.M., M.M.	L.-Corpl.	L/8827
Wood, H. H., M.M.	L.-Corpl.	G/11670
Wright, J., M.M.	L.-Corpl.	G/6329

SECOND CLASP TO MILITARY MEDAL

Kingsford, W., M.M.	Sgt.	616

MERITORIOUS SERVICE MEDAL

Ambrose, J. L.	Sgt.	8534
Austin, F. H.	Col.-Sergt.	L/8328
Back, A. E.	Q.M.S.	L/8910
Banks, E. R.	Pte.	10049
Barden, E. T.	Pte.	240073
Barrell, G.	C.S.M.	L/9036
Bennett, S. G.	Sgt.	G/1278
Benstead, C. S.	Pte.	240113
Bishop, C. U.	C.Q.M.S.	240525
Blackman, H. E.	C.Q.M.S.	L/8364
Bloxham, B. N.	C.S.M.	G/4865
Bolton, E. L.	R.S.M.	L/5504
Brooks, F. H.	C.Q.M.S.	G/3305
Brown, F. F.	Sgt.	7629
Bryant, G.	Pte.	240248
Campbell, H.	Corpl.	4848
Carr, J.	Sgt.	L/8908
Clem, F.	Q.M.S.	S/589
Clift, W. B.	Sgt.	243307
Coleman, A. C., M.M.	Pte.	G/1898
Constable, D. W.	Sgt.	243277
Cox, H. W. G.	Pte.	738

APPENDIX III

REWARDS—M.S.M.—(continued)

NAME.	RANK.	REGTL. NO.
Dann, F.	C.Q.M.S.	G/2633
Darby, J. R.	Pte.	S/600
Denness, S. W.	Pte.	240419
Dowse, E., M.M.	Sgt.	L/11008
Drew, A.	L.-Sergt.	G/21837
Dunn, G. W. H.	Sgt.	G/538
Edwards, W. S.	R.Q.M.S.	6397
Ephgrave, C. F.	Pte.	G/21598
Faulkner, P.	C.S.M.	270032
Fielding, A. W.	R.Q.M.S.	G/1765
Filby, A. F.	Sgt.	G/22333
Flannery, J. M.	Pte.	241095
Flynn, J. P.	Sgt.	L/7089
Follett, S. H.	C.S.M.	L/6942
Ford, H. G.	Sgt.	240364
Friend, E. A.	Pte.	200581
Gibson, A.	Sgt.	L/9484
Glover, F.	Sgt.	G/13686
Graves, F. R.	Sgt.	10264
Hamblin, I. C.	Corpl.	L/8825
Hayman, W. C.	L.-Corpl.	G/9312
Hearne, H. W.	Sgt.	200585
Hemens, W. G.	C.Q.M.S.	242934
Hill, E. B.	Sgt.	8373
Holloway, T.	R.S.M.	L/3589
Hutchison, T. E.	Pte.	6589
Ings, G. F.	Q.M.S.	L/7201
Jenkins, A. R.	C.Q.M.S.	G/1258
Johnson, A. W.	Pte.	G/824
Jones, H. A.	R.S.M.	L/2954
Julian, C.	C.Q.M.S.	G/3656
Lockyer, S.	Sgt.	G/15727

APPENDIX III

REWARDS—M.S.M.—*(continued)*

NAME.	RANK.	REGTL. NO.
Martin, W. K.	R.Q.M.S.	L/5886
Maulkin, A. G.	Sgt.	200712
Middleditch, F. J.	Q.M.S.	240048
Milnes, N.	C.Q.M.S.	241649
Mount, A. E.	Sgt.	4231
Munting, A.	C.Q.M.S.	200342
Ousley, F. W.	Sgt.	G/13631
Page, W. E.	R.Q.M.S.	20497
Pegrum, F. W.	Pte.	240472
Perry, E. R.	C.Q.S.M.	240456
Pursehouse, W. H.	Pte.	G/18750
Richardson, J. H. S.	Pte.	240421
Ronketti, P. A.	C.Q.M.S.	20491
Salt, L.	C.S.M.	270013
Slender, A. F.	C.Q.M.S.	L/8725
Smith, H. J.	Sgt.	270715
Smith, W. H.	—	6192
Sparrow, S. F.	Sgt.	270432
Talbot, W. E.	Sgt.	240372
Taylor, A. J.	Pte.	G/19355
Terry, B. N.	Sgt.	241016
Thomas, W.	R.S.M.	G/36901
Trafford, W. G.	Sgt.	G/1804
Turmaine, F. W.	C.Q.M.S.	L/6662
Usherwood, A. E.	Sgt.	203054
Webb, J. H.	C.Q.M.S.	3858
Wiggs, E.	S.M.	—
Williams, A.	Pte.	G/19585
Williams, T. E.	Sgt.	200497
Wood, F. C. S.	C.S.M.	200034
Woodruff, C. J.	C.Q.M.S.	200526
Wyles, H.	C.S.M.	200333

APPENDIX IV

FOREIGN DECORATIONS

ALL RANKS

(The ranks shown are those held at the time of award)

BELGIUM

ORDRE DE LEOPOLD

Chapman, Captain C. M. B., M.C.

Lee, Captain G., M.C.
Lynden-Bell, Major-General Sir A. L., K.C.M.G., C.B.

Trevor, Major W. H., D.S.O.

ORDRE DE LA COURONNE

Trevor, Lt.-Colonel W. H., D.S.O.

CROIX DE GUERRE

Blake, Lieut. H. E.

Chapman, Captain C. M. B., M.C.

Hadaway, No. L/7799 Pte. G. E.
Histed, No. L/8498 Pte. W. C., M.M.

Lee, Major G., D.S.O., M.C.
Lynden-Bell, Major-General A. L., C.B., C.M.G.

Taylor, No. G/3420 Sgt. R.
Toynbee, Lieut. J. W. H., M.C.
Trevor, Lt.-Colonel W. H., D.S.O.

DECORATION MILITAIRE

Diddams, No. G/3462 L.-Sergt. H. S.
Duff, No. 5995 Corpl. W. G., M.M.

Poole, No. L/6487 C.S.M. E.

530

APPENDIX IV

APPENDIX IV

FOREIGN DECORATIONS—*(continued)*

Kenchington, Captain A. G., M.C.

Knight, No. 3588 Pte. E. J.

Lynden-Bell, Major-General Sir A. L., K.C.B., K.C.M.G.

Neale, No. 5018 Pte. P. J.

Osborne, Captain A. E.

Ponsonby, Captain C. E.

Power, Lt.-Colonel R. E., D.S.O.

Rand, No. L/10038 Sgt. F. C.

Soames, Lt.-Colonel L. H.

Whitaker, Major F., M.C.

Wilson, Lieut. A. J.

Ordre du Merite Agricole

Scarlett, Lt.-Colonel the Hon. P. G., M.C.

Medaille d'Honneur avec glaives

Bushell, No. G/8588 L.-Corpl. C. W.

Chapman, No. L/9636 Corpl. F.

George, No. G/9303 Corpl. H.

Harrigan, No. S/8104 Pte. J.

Millen, No. 240161 C.Q.M.S. A. H.

Rainford, No. G/375 Pte. J.

GREECE

Greek Military Cross

Cook, No. L/7907 C.S.M. F. R.

Edwards, No. 6397 R.Q.M.S. W. S.

Thewles, Lt.-Colonel H. A., D.S.O.

Greek Medal for Military Merit

Barnard, Major W. G. F., D.S.O.

Manning, Lieut. W.

APPENDIX IV

ITALY
ORDER OF THE CROWN OF ITALY
Lynden-Bell, Major-General Sir A. L., K.C.M.G., C.B.
Trevor, Lt.-Colonel W. H., D.S.O.
Wilson, Lieut. C. E.

SILVER MEDAL FOR MILITARY VALOUR
Henriques, Captain B. L. Q.
Macdonnell, Lieut. R. G.
Peareth, Major A. J.

BRONZE MEDAL FOR MILITARY VALOUR
Andrews, No. 7051 C.S.M. A. W.

JAPAN
ORDER OF THE RISING SUN
Lynden-Bell, Major-General Sir A. L., K.C.M.G., C.B.

ROUMANIA
ORDER OF THE CROWN OF ROUMANIA
Jude, Captain P.

MEDAILLE BARBATIE SI CREDINTA
Butler, No. 22401 Pte. G. W.
Butler, No. 14975 Pte. R. L.
Piggott, No. G/17893 Pte. E. W.

RUSSIA
ORDER OF ST. ALEXANDER NEVSKY
Paget, General the Rt. Hon. Sir Arthur, P.C., G.C.B., K.C.V.O.

ORDER OF ST. VLADIMIR
Lynden-Bell, Major-General A. L., C.B., C.M.G.

533

APPENDIX IV

FOREIGN DECORATIONS—(*continued*)

ORDER OF ST. STANISLAS

Vyvyan, Colonel Sir C. B., Bart., C.B., C.M.G.

CROSS OF THE ORDER OF ST. GEORGE

Heasman, No. 9632 Pte. F.

St. John, No. 1111 C.S.M. F. H., D.C.M.

MEDAL OF ST. GEORGE

Crame, No. G/3301 L.-Corpl. C. J., D.C.M.

Hannaford, No. 8211 L.-Corpl. R.

Hills, No. 9402 Cpl. H. W.

Munday, No. 203 Pte. A.

Rose, No. 10223 Sgt. H.

Smith, No. 8926 Sgt. V. R., D.C.M.

Waghorn, No. 8796 Pte. G. J.

SERBIA

ORDER OF THE WHITE EAGLE

Barnard, Captain W. G. F., D.S.O.

Lynden-Bell, Major-General Sir A. L., K.C.B., K.C.M.G.

Paget, General the Hon. Sir Arthur, P.C., G.C.B., K.C.V.O.

CROSS OF KARAGEORGE

Lawson, No. 5691 Pte. W.

Twort, No. 2153 Pte. R. T.

SILVER MEDAL FOR VALOUR

Bebb, No. G/6676 Pte. J. E.

Hedger, No. 04888 Sgt. C. O.

GOLD MEDAL

Ransley, No. 1217 Pte. H.

534

APPENDIX V

MENTION IN DESPATCHES

OFFICERS

(The rank is given as stated in the *Gazette*; in the case of more than one mention the highest rank is given)

NAME.	RANK.
Adamson, G. R.	2nd Lieut.
Allen, C. V.	Captain
Allen, E. H.	Captain
Allen, J. F. W.	Captain
Anderson, D. K.	Major (2)
Archer Houblon, H. L.	Captain (2)
Bainbridge, E. G. T.	Major-General (4)
Barnard, W. G. F.	Lt.-Colonel (2)
Barris, J. A.	Captain
Beale, G. S.	Captain
Beevor, M.	Lt.-Colonel (3)
Beswick, A. H.	Lieut.
Blackall, C. W.	Lt.-Colonel (2)
Blake, N. G.	Lieut.
Blood-Smyth, H. B.	Captain
Body, J.	Lt.-Colonel (4)
Bowden, E. M.	Major
Brackenbury, E. A.	Captain
Brodie, H. W.	Captain
Carman, L. G.	Lieut.
Cattley, C. F.	Captain
Chamberlain, A. L. L.	2nd Lieut.
Chapman, G. A. E.	Major (2)
Clapperton, T.	Captain
Clouting, C. E.	2nd Lieut.

MENTION IN DESPATCHES—*(continued)*

NAME.	RANK.
Collison-Morley, H. D.	Lt.-Colonel
Corney, A.	Lieut. & Qr.-Mr. (2)
Corrall, W. R.	Lt.-Colonel (3)
Couchman, C. C.	Lieut.
Cree, H. F.	Captain
Crookenden, J.	Major
Dangerfield, P.	2nd Lieut.
Davidson, C. E. G.	Captain
Davies, B. E.	Captain (3)
Dawson, W. F.	Major
Digby, R. L.	Lieut.
Dixon, G. S.	Captain
Dolamore, A. W.	Captain
Dyson, H. A.	Captain
Elmslie, W. F.	Lt.-Colonel
Essell, F. K.	Lt.-Colonel
Fay, C. R.	Captain
Ferguson, D. G.	2nd Lieut.
Filmer, W. G. H.	Captain (2)
Finch Hatton, E. H.	Br.-General (2)
Findlay, H.	Lt.-Colonel (2)
Fine, H.	Captain
Fish, A. L.	Lieut.
Fisher, C. J.	Major
Ford, H. F. P.	2nd Lieut.
Fort, L.	Captain
Forwood, H.	Major
Foster, F. W.	Captain & Qr.-Mr. (3)
Fraser, J. S.	Major
Friend, R. S. I.	Lt.-Colonel
Froome, H. A. J.	2nd Lieut.
Furley, B. E.	Major
Geddes, A. D.	Colonel
Goss, E. H. A.	Lieut.

APPENDIX V

NAME.	RANK.
Grant, L. B.	Major (2)
Green, E. C.	Captain
Green, H. W.	Lt.-Colonel (2)
Greenway, C. D. K.	Captain (2)
Groves-Raines, R. G. D.	Captain
Hall, E. F.	Captain (2)
Hamilton, G. F.	Lieut.
Hammond, G. F.	Lieut.
Hardy, H. S.	Captain
Harper, N. A.	Lieut.
Harrison, W. A.	Captain
Hasler, J.	Br.-General (2)
Hatfield, C. E.	Captain
Hayfield, A. S.	2nd Lieut.
Hayfield, C. D.	Captain (2)
Hedley, W. A. C.	Captain
Henriques, B. L. Q.	Lieut. (2)
Hill, H. C. de la M.	Colonel
Hollebone, E. G.	Captain
Homan, R. W.	Captain
Hulke, L. I. B.	Lt.-Colonel
Hunter, H.	2nd Lieut.
Jackson, J. V. R.	Captain
James, A. K. H.	Captain
James, G. M.	Captain
Jelf, C. G.	2nd Lieut.
Jude, P.	Major
Keasley, W. E.	Lieut.
Keble, T. H.	Captain
Keown, R. W.	Captain
Kirkpatrick, H. F.	Lt.-Colonel (4)
Lamarque, W. C.	Captain
Laverton, W. R. C.	Captain
Lea-Smith, L. A.	Lieut.

MENTION IN DESPATCHES—*(continued)*

NAME.	RANK.
Lee, G.	Major (3)
Lilley, A. A.	2nd Lieut.
Linwood, N.	Captain & Qr.-Mr.
Lomax, J. H.	Captain
Lucas, L. W.	Lt.-Colonel (4)
Lynden-Bell, A. L.	Major-General (10)
McCallum, A.	Captain
McDermott, W. K.	Lieut.
McDonnell, R. G.	2nd Lieut.
McDouall, R.	Br.-General (6)
Macfadyen, W. A.	Captain
Marshall, F. A. J. E.	Captain
Marsh-Smith, C. W.	Captain
Mockett, V.	Captain (2)
Morgan, H. de R.	Major (2)
Morrell, F. A.	Captain
Nicholas, W. L. J.	Lieut.
Nicholson, A. C. L.	2nd Lieut.
Northcote, D. H. G.	Lieut.
O'Neale, G.	Captain
Overy, T. S.	Captain
Page, J. C.	Captain (2)
Peake, W.	Captain
Peareth, A. J.	Major (2)
Phillips, F.	Captain
Pinhey, R. A.	Captain
Pittock, J. A.	Lieut. (2)
Porter, C. 'L.	Br.-General (8)
Power, R. E.	Lt.-Colonel (4)
Prothero, L. E. A.	Captain (2)
Rawkins, R. A.	Lieut.
Reed, A. H.	Lieut.

APPENDIX V

MENTION IN DESPATCHES—*(continued)*

NAME.	RANK.
Sargent, L. C.	Major
Scarlett, P. G.	Captain the Hon. (2)
Smeltzer, A. S.	Lt.-Colonel (4)
Soames, A.	Major
Stone, W. T.	Captain (2)
Stronge, H. C. T.	Lt.-Colonel (2)
Strudd, F. C. R.	Lt.-Colonel
Taylor, C. C. O.	2nd Lieut.
Ternan, H. A. B.	Major (2)
Thewles, H. A.	Lt.-Colonel
Thomas, D. V.	Captain
Thomson, A. B.	Captain
Thornhill, G. R.	Lieut.
Toynbee, J. W. H.	Lieut.
Trevor, W. H.	Lt.-Colonel (4)
Trollope, A. G.	Lt.-Colonel
Vaughan, J.	Captain (2)
Vertue, N. G.	Captain
Ward, H. E.	Captain
Ward, R. O. C.	Captain
Weldon, S. W.	Captain (3)
Wilkinson, F. D.	Lieut.
Williams, W. T.	2nd Lieut. (2)
Whitaker, F.	Major
Whitlock, C. S.	2nd Lieut.
Whitmarsh, A. J.	Captain
Wilson, C. T. N. W.	Captain
Wort, P. C.	Lieut.
Worthington, C. A. V.	Lt.-Colonel

APPENDIX V

WARRANT AND N.C.O.'s AND MEN

NAME.	RANK.	REGTL. NO.
Akehurst, W.	C.Q.M.S.	270725
Anderson, H.	Pte.	9290
Andrews, A. W.	R.S.M.	L/7051 (2)
Appleton, C.	Pte.	G/2052
Arundell, S. R.	Pte.	242911
Atkinson, J.	Pte.	240261
Ayres, A. J.	L.-Corpl.	6884
Bacon, E.	Corpl.	G/13353
Barnes, H. J.	Pte.	L/10185
Barnes, J. S.	L/Sergt.	G/8537
Barton, L. R. W.	L.-Corpl.	200105
Bebb, J. E.	Pte.	G/6676
Beverley, H.	Pte.	L/8497
Bingham, C. F.	C.S.M.	265106
Bishop, C.	C.Q.M.S.	240525
Blacknell, E. J.	Dr.	240039
Blanch, W. E.	Pte.	G/8455
Borton, E.	Sgt.	241861
Boswell, A.	L.-Corpl.	10086
Boswell, T. A.	L.-Corpl.	L/9446
Boyes, G.	Pte.	206102
Bradley, E. J.	Pte.	241432
Bray, G. V.	L.-Corpl.	614
Brett, C. S.	R.S.M.	L/7906 (2)
Brown, F. F.	Pte.	7629
Brown, W.	Sgt.	6020
Burberry, D.	Sgt.	G/428
Buzzard, J.	L.-Corpl.	1838
Campbell, F.	Pte.	241014
Carpenter, H. F.	Sgt.	270618
Chapman, F.	L.-Corpl.	L/9636
Chatfield, G. E.	Sgt.	9710
Clancey, J.	Pte.	2183
Clarke, J. W.	L.-Corpl.	240422

MENTION IN DESPATCHES—(*continued*)

NAME.	RANK.	REGTL. NO.
Cleave, E.	L.-Corpl.	3555
Collings, B.	Pte.	G/22217
Constable, D. W.	Sgt.	243277
Cook, F. R.	C.S.M.	L/7907
Cooling, C.	L.-Corpl.	719
Cullen, A.	L.-Corpl.	8407
Dewhurst, W.	Pte.	S/10935
Dixon, E. F.	Pte.	484
Driscoll, F.	Corpl.	9066
Dunster, R. E.	Sgt.	201187
Duff, W. G.	Dr.	5995
Ferry, T. H.	Pte.	6652
Foley, P. G.	Sgt.	270049
Forrest, A. H.	Pte.	4412
Fraser, F. G.	Corpl.	9226
Freeman, H.	Sgt.	L/8192
French, F. W.	C.Q.M.S.	L/8071
Freshwater, T.	Pte.	L/10501
Friend, E. A.	Sgt.	200581
Garlinge, W. J.	Pte.	5196
Gibson, V. D.	C.S.M.	241021
Gilbert, B.	Corpl.	270746
Gilbert, F. T.	Sgt.	L/8546
Gittings, W. G.	Pte.	G/876
Goldfinch, A. H.	Sgt.	8205
Graves, F. R.	Corpl.	10264
Greenless, T.	L.-Corpl.	270275
Gundlach, R. T.	L.-Corpl.	G/639
Gunn, A. E.	Pte.	9313
Gurney, A.	Pte.	241138
Hackney, P.	Sgt.	200615
Hall, F.	Corpl.	242905
Hall, W. E.	Corpl.	G/12913
Harrington, T. F.	R.S.M.	8890

APPENDIX V

NAME.	RANK.	REGTL. NO.
Hart, E. G.	Pte.	G/3435
Harvey, J. W.	Pte.	242932
Harvey, O. F.	C.Q.M.S.	270024
Heaver, H. W.	Sgt.	200329 (2)
Hemens, W. G.	C.Q.M.S.	242934
Hickson, H. C.	C.S.M.	242779
Hill, H. W.	Corpl.	9402
Hills, J.	Pte.	8703
Horton, H. G.	Pte.	5091
Howard, H.	Sgt.	9088
Hull, F. V.	C.Q.M.S.	240047
Ings, G. F.	R.Q.M.S.	7201
Ivory, S.	Corpl.	13292
Jagger, J. J.	L.-Sergt.	242907
Jenrick, G. W.	Pte.	7655
Jordan, S.	Pte.	241875
Karop, A.	Sgt.	242980 (2)
Keyes, F. G.	Pte.	G/12834
King, A. W.	Pte.	24290
Kingsford, A.	R.Q.M.S.	27004
Kirkbright, W. S.	L.-Corpl.	290090
Lambeth, G.	Pte.	L/9648
Lawrence, H.	C.S.M.	241496
Lawson, W.	Pte.	G/5691
Linstead, W.	Pte.	364
Lockyer, H. J.	Sgt.	8055
McCann, J. E.	Pte.	S/145
Maloney, H. J.	Pte.	L/8152
Marshall, A. E.	Pte.	243290
Martin, H. J.	C.S.M.	8357
Matthews, T. F. H.	Pte.	G/882
May, W. A.	Pte.	8219
Meggett, W. A.	Sgt.	240381

APPENDIX V

NAME.	RANK.	REGTL. NO.
Middleton, J.	Pte.	8826
Monger, J. H.	R.S.M.	G/1460
Moon, L. G.	Sgt.	4181
Moore, S.	Sgt.	1379
Morgan, J. W. W.	Pte.	9191
Mosto, R. W.	Pte.	6712
Neville, H. W.	L.-Sergt.	269
Newham, H.	C.S.M.	241481
Page, F. H.	C.S.M.	7763
Page, W. E.	C.Q.M.S.	20497
Payne, E. J.	Pte.	G/3461
Peattie, F.	Sgt.	6470
Perry, E. R.	C.Q.M.S.	240456
Pilcher, A. C.	Corpl.	S/160
Poole, E.	C.Q.M.S.	6487
Potts, A. J.	Sgt.	L/8898
Prebble, S.	Sgt.	G/2549
Purser, L. J.	Sgt.	242947
Read, W. R.	Corpl.	8974
Real, W. A.	Sgt.	10382
Reardon, A.	Pte.	270478
Reed, W. N.	C.S.M.	G/1147
Ronketti, P. A.	C.Q.M.S.	20491
Rose, H.	Corpl.	20282
St. John, F. R.	R.S.M.	240118
Sanger, A. H. T.	R.S.M.	L/5692
Saunders, A. J.	C.S.M.	L/6243
Scott, F. F.	Sgt.	91
Seath, S.	Pte.	148
Setterfield, A. V.	Pte.	347
Sharpe, W. J.	Sgt.	241199
Sibun, J.	Sgt.	L/8337
Simmonds, F. T. J.	Corpl.	G/15862
Simmons, A. C.	Sgt.	L/9239

APPENDIX V

MENTION IN DESPATCHES—(*continued*)

NAME.	RANK.	REGTL. NO.
Skinner, W. J. J.	Pte.	559
Smith, C.	Pte.	242956
Spargo, H. T.	Pte.	202952
Stocks, J.	Corpl.	G/1829
Swinyard, G. A.	C.S.M.	240072
Thorpe, C. H.	C.Q.M.S.	270505
Trick, F. W.	Sgt.	243082
Turmaine, F. W.	C.Q.M.S.	L/6662
Turnbull, G.	Sgt.	242782
Vincer, P. A.	Sgt.	7967
Wall, W. J.	L.-Corpl.	260
Wanstall, F. N.	Pte.	G/7628
Ward, J.	Sgt.	8438
Wicken, P. C.	Pte.	G/12941
Wickington, H. G.	Sgt.	1300
Willis, F. E.	Col.-Sergt.	240043
Wren, W. H.	Corpl.	6635

APPENDIX VI

MENTION "B" (FOR RECORD)

NAME.	RANK.
Bayard, R.	Br.-General
Burge, M. R. K.	Lieut. (2)
Butler, E. M.	Lieut.
Cobbe, C. C.	Major
Cowell, A. V.	Lt.-Colonel
Dauglish, G. V.	Colonel
Dimmock, F. M.	Captain
Groves-Raines, R. G. D.	Major
Gullick, H. T.	Major
Hardy, H. S.	Major
Hart, N. S.	Captain
Hirst, H. D.	Lt.-Colonel
Hulke, L. I. B.	Lt.-Colonel (2)
Jackson, H. W.	Captain
Kingsland, C. P.	Major
Knight, L. C. E.	Major
Mantle, H.	Lieut.
Meakin, G. A.	Captain
Messel, L. C. R.	Lt.-Colonel
Moilliet, E. L.	Lieut.
Palmer, V. T. D.	Captain
Parry, E. C. M.	Captain
Pearson, R. F.	Colonel

APPENDIX VI

MENTION " B " (FOR RECORD)—*(continued)*

NAME.	RANK.
Phillips, W. A.	Captain
Pike, H. E.	Lieut.
Port, J.	Captain
Sparrow, H. F.	Lt.-Colonel
Tait, G. M.	Captain (2)
Tattersall, J. C.	Major
Twisleton-Wykeham-Fiennes, H. E.	Major
Tylden, W.	Major
Tylden-Pattenson, A. H.	Major
Ward, H. E.	Captain
Wilkins, D. A.	Captain
Williams, M. S.	Major
Williams, R. W.	Captain

WARRANT AND N.C.O.'s AND MEN

NAME.	RANK.	REGTL. NO.
Allen, W. G.	Pte.	6266
Ball, G. E.	Sergt.-Major	6127 (2)
Bosanquet, B.	R.S.M.	L/10853
Brown, C.	R.S.M.	L/8652
Buckley, J. W.	C.S.M.	200055
Butler, G. E.	Q.M.S.	6388
Carpenter, C. K.	S.M.	6124
Cavanagh, J. T.	Pte.	G/17555
Cooke, W. H.	R.S.M.	L/2531
Cooper, A. C.	Sgt.	8874
Coopey, T. G.	C.Q.M.S.	204472
Corke, W.	S.M.	6132 (2)
Cufflin, J.	Corpl.	L/10750
Cumbley, S. G.	—	6122
Dewey, H. J.	S.M.	6129 (2)

546

APPENDIX VI

MENTION "B" (FOR RECORD)—(*continued*)

NAME.	RANK.	REGTL. NO.
Early, J. H.	C.Q.M.S.	1461
Fisher, A. E.	S.M.	6227 (2)
Fox, F. W.	C.S.M.	200004
Gilmore, F.	Q.M.S.	6125 (2)
Glover, H.	Q.M.S.	6241
Gordon, C. J.	Q.M.S.	8307
Hanson, H. E.	Q.M.S.	6283
Hartridge, W. F.	Q.M.S.	8544
Hayes, S. H.	S.M.	6130 (2)
Hayhow, A.	Q.M.S.	7845
Johnson, H.	Pte.	19204
Jones, S. J.	Sgt.	53090
Kendall, S. C.	Q.M.S.	8117
Kinnear, G. V.	Q.M.S.	6119
Knott, R. H.	Q.M.S.	G/6370
Kottaun, W. F.	Corpl.	19318
Latham, G. F.	Q.M.S.	36902
Laver, G. H.	S.S.	G/5953
McKeen, J. J.	Sgt.	200062
McVey, J.	—	6195
Martin, R.	C.S.M.	5003
Masters, F. A. R.	Q.M.S.	8543
Milnes, N.	Sgt.	241649
Mousley, G. S.	Pte.	11103
Musty, W. J.	Q.M.S.	6010
Pearce, W. S.	Q.M.S.	8858
Potter, T.	S.M.	6131 (2)
Revell, D.	R.S.M.	TR.10/16001
Ritchie, F. J.	Q.M.S.	8810
Roberts, T.	Q.M.S.	6123 (2)

547

APPENDIX VI

NAME.	RANK.	REGTL. NO.
Robinson, J.	Q.M.S.	7924 (2)
Rowe, H. J.	—	8116
Rudge, T.	Pte.	19206
Scott, W. J.	C.Q.M.S.	265108
Scragg, F. C.	C.Q.M.S.	G/21586
Shoobridge, C. S.	L.-Sergt.	203601
Smith, H.	Pte.	G/17556
Smith, S.	Q.M.S.	6120
Stace, C.	Q.M.S.	5986
Streten, A. J.	Q.M.S.	6253
Thomas, W.	S.M.	36901
Waterfall, F.	Q.M.S.	8545
Watson, J. W.	L.-Sergt.	S/708
Weeks, E. O.	Sgt.	5458
Wellington, E. E.	Q.M.S.	5951
Whittard, R. H.	Q.M.S.	6182
Woodgate, H. B.	Sgt.	G/9185
Woodman, J. H.	C.S.M.	203428

APPENDIX VII

The following serving officers of the 1st and 2nd Battalions were awarded brevet rank for service in the field :—

Brevet Colonel :

Major and Bt. Lt.-Colonel C. 'L. Porter.

Brevet Lieutenant-Colonel :

Majors R. Bright, H. Findlay, H. W. Green, L. W. Lucas, R. McDouall, C. 'L. Porter, H. B. Potter, R. E. Power, L. H. Soames, H. A. Thewles and W. H. Trevor.

Brevet Major :

Captains W. R. Corrall, A. G. Kenchington and the Hon. P. G. Scarlett, and Lieut. A. S. Smeltzer (on promotion to captain).

LIST OF SUBSCRIBERS

LIST OF SUBSCRIBERS

Mrs. Adam
Sir Sidney Alexander, Kt.,
   M.D.
Captain H. E. Allen
J. E. Amos, Esq.
Rev. G. Archer, M.A.
Major H. L. Archer Houblon
P. R. Asprey, Esq., M.C.

Major-General Sir E. G. T.
   Bainbridge, K.C.B.
Captain H. H. C. Baird,
   D.S.O.
Mrs. Baly
Colonel A. S. Barham, C.M.G.,
   V.D.
Captain S. L. P. Barker
Lt.-Colonel W. G. F. Barnard,
   D.S.O.
J. J. Beall, Esq.
R. Beer, Esq.
Major M. Beevor, D.S.O.
J. P. Bell, Esq.
Mrs. Charles Blackall
Major H. Blackburn
Maurice L. Blaxall, Esq.
Colonel J. Body, D.S.O.,
   O.B.E., etc.
Major W. H. Booth, D.S.O.,
   O.B.E.
Colonel Sir Theodore Brinck-
   man, Bt., C.B.
Mrs. Anthony Brown
R. G. Bullock, Esq.
Major G. K. Burge

Major E. B. Burns
Edwin Buss, Esq.
A. G. Butler, Esq.

Marquess Camden
Major A. F. Campbell John
   ston
Captain L. P. Causton, M.C.
W. C. N. Chapman, Esq.
Borough of Chatham
W. E. Church, Esq.
C. J. Clark, Esq.
G. Foster Clark, Esq.
Major Eric Clarke
D. C. Coates, Esq.
Major C. C. Cobbe
Colonel A. H. Coles, C.M.G.,
   D.S.O.
Major A. E. Colley
Mrs. Collison-Morley
Captain C. L. Connellan
Colonel F. S. W. Cornwallis,
   C.B.E., D.L., etc.
Captain and Bt. Major W. R.
   Corrall, M.C.
W. H. Cronk, Esq.
Major J. Crookenden, D.S.O.
J. C. T. Crozier, Esq.

Major V. T. Dampier Palmer,
   O.B.E.
Colonel G. V. Dauglish
Mrs. C. L. Davis
G. T. Davis, Esq.
J. E. W. Dell, Esq.

551

LIST OF SUBSCRIBERS

Mrs. Docking
J. A. Druce, Esq., J.P.
Mrs. Dungey
Lt.-Colonel F. M. Dunstan, T.D.
Major F. Bradley Dyne

Lt.-Colonel W. A. Eaton, O.B.E.
Major R. P. S. Elderton
Colonel F. K. Essell, C.M.G.

Lt.-Colonel C. S. Fellows
Mrs. Figgis
Br.-General E. H. Finch Hatton, C.M.G., D.S.O.
Colonel H. Findlay, C.B.E.
W. R. Findlay, Esq.
Mrs. FitzRoy Cole
Borough of Folkestone
Mrs. Forde
J. Fort, Esq.
E. Foster Hall, Esq.
P. R. H. Fox, Esq., M.C.
Mrs. Fradgley
Lt.-Colonel R. S. I. Friend, D.S.O.
H. H. J. Froome, Esq.
Walter Furley, Esq.

Mrs. Glyn
Mrs. Goff
Colonel Viscount Goschen, C.B.E.
L. A. Goss, Esq.
Mrs. Gould
Mrs. Green
Mrs. Greig
Major A. C. Grigg

Lt.-Colonel R. G. D. Groves-Raines, D.S.O.
Major H. T. Gullick

D. H. Hamill-Stewart, Esq.
Captain G. F. Hamilton, M.C.
Captain J. Hamilton
Egerton Hammond, Esq.
Major H. S. Hardy, M.B.E., M.C.
Colonel the Rt. Hon. Baron Harris, G.C.S.I., G.C.I.E., etc.
Miss E. J. Harris
Captain N. S. Hart
Major G. T. D. Hickman
Br.-General R. A. Hickson, C.B.
George Hilder, Esq.
Br.-General H. C. de la M. Hill, C.B., C.M.G.
Mrs. W. Hinkley
Mrs. Hirst
Mrs. Hollis
Mrs. Hollist
Mrs. Homan
Colonel J. F. Honeyball
Captain G. R. Howe
T. Rowlatt Hubbard, Esq.
Lt.-Colonel L. I. B. Hulke, C.M.G.

Mrs. Ingouville-Williams

Major J. V. R. Jackson

Colonel W. E. R. Kelly
Mrs. Kelsey
G. F. Kingham, Esq.
Major C. P. Kingsland

552

LIST OF SUBSCRIBERS

A. Kitchin, Esq.
C. R. B. Knight, Esq.
Lt.-Colonel L. C. E. Knight

Mrs. Laing
Captain W. C. Lamarque
H. Lea-Smith, Esq.
Major G. Lee, D.S.O., M.C.
Mrs. Harry Lee
A. C. Leney, Esq.
Colonel D. F. Lewis, C.B.
D. S. Lister, Esq., M.C.
J. H. Loudon, Esq.
Major and Bt. Lt.-Colonel
   L. W. Lucas, D.S.O.,
   M.C.
G. L. Lushington, Esq.
Major-General Sir A. L.
   Lynden-Bell, K.C.B.,
   K.C.M.G.

Lt.-Colonel R. McDouall,
   C.B., C.M.G., etc.
W. A. Macfadyen, Esq., M.C.
S. W. Marchant, Esq.
Major R. G. A. Marriott,
   D.S.O.
Rev. W. Mathias, M.A.
Major G. A. Meakin
Lt.-Colonel L. C. R. Messel,
   O.B.E.
J. W. Millard, Esq.
Viscount Milner, K.G.,
   G.C.B., etc.
G. H. Mitchell, Esq.
Lady Mitchell
Mrs. Monins
Captain J. E. Monins
Mrs. G. Moke-Norrie, C.B.E.
Captain H. C. Morley

E. Morgan, Esq.
H. de R. Morgan, Esq.
Captain H. de R. Morgan,
   D.S.O.

G. J. Nettleton, Esq.
J. H. Newcomb, Esq.
J. Newton Moss, Esq.
Captain W. H. Nicholas
Mrs. Noott
Cecil Norman, Esq.
Lady Northcote

Captain C. H. P. O'Hagan
F. J. Oliver, Esq.
Rev. E. A. Ommanney, M.A.
H. D. Oxley, Esq.

General the Rt. Hon. Sir
   Arthur Paget, P.C.,
   G.C.B., etc.
Captain A. J. Peareth
T. N. Penlington, Esq.
Lt.-Colonel F. Phillips,
   D.S.O., M.C.
R. H. Plumb, Esq.
Major G. A. Porter
Lt.-Colonel R. E. Power,
   D.S.O.
Mrs. Prescott-Roberts
Captain R. K. Price
Captain T. R. Price
P.R.I. 1st Battalion The Buffs
P.R.I. 2nd Battalion The Buffs
P.R.I. 3rd Battalion The Buffs
P.R.I. Depot The Buffs

Lady Raines
Captain L. A. Ramsay

553

LIST OF SUBSCRIBERS

Lt.-Colonel A. L. Ransome, D.S.O., M.C.
A. H. Reed, Esq.
Major F. S. Reeves
Captain N. D. Rice
Mrs. Romer
Mrs. J. McB. Ronald
W. E. Rootes, Esq.
John Russell, Esq.
A. H. Ruston, Esq.

Mrs. Kennedy Sandilands
Borough of Sandwich
G. E. Sankey, Esq.
W. Sankey, Esq.
G. D. Saunders, Esq.
Captain W. Stewart Savile
Captain and Bt. Major the Hon. P. G. Scarlett, M.C.
J. Scrace, Esq.
Millin Selby, Esq.
A. R. Sewell, Esq.
E. B. Sewell, Esq.
Mrs. Sherren
Mrs. Shervinton
H. J. Skelton, Esq.
Major L. Howard Smith
Lt.-Colonel H. F. Sparrow
Mrs. Spicer
Mrs. Stallworthy
Lt.-Colonel G. N. Stephen

Miss Taylor
G. Hutton Taylor, Esq.
W. Taylor, Esq.

Major H. A. B. Ternan O.B.E.
Major and Bt. Lt.-Colonel H. A. Thewles, D.S.O.
Captain A. B. Thomson, M.B.E.
G. Thorn-Drury, Esq., K.C.
F. E. Thornhill, Esq.
Mrs. Tomlinson
Miss Tomlinson
Major F. W. Tomlinson
Lt.-Colonel W. H. Trevor, D.S.O.
Major H. J. Trueman

Colonel Sir Courtenay B. Vyvyan, Bt., C.B., C.M.G.

Mrs. J. T. Waite
F. N. Walker, Esq.
G. S. Wallis, Esq.
Mrs. Eldred Warde
Mrs. Warnington
R. M. Watson, Esq.
Mrs. Webb
R. M. Webster, Esq.
J. T. Welldon, Esq.
Captain T. Wheler
Captain F. Whitaker, M.C.
Captain D. A. Wilkins, M.B.E.
Miss Willats
Mrs. Williamson
J. R. Willows, Esq.
Mrs. Wolstenholme
R. G. Wood, Esq.

554